LANDLORDS, TENANTS, FAMINE

THE BUSINESS OF AN IRISH
LAND AGENCY IN THE 1840s

DESMOND NORTON

Published by the
UNIVERSITY COLLEGE DUBLIN PRESS
PREAS CHOLÁISTE OLLSCOILE BHAILE ÁTHA CLIATH

2006

First published 2006
by University College Dublin Press
Newman House
86 St Stephen's Green
Dublin 2, Ireland
www.ucdpress.ie

ISBN 978-1-904558-55-2 pb
978-1-904558-56-9 hb

CIP data available from the British Library

*The right of Desmond Norton to be identified
as the author of this work has been asserted by him*

Typeset in Ireland in Adobe Caslon and Bodoni Oldstyle
by Elaine Burberry, Bantry, County Cork
Text design by Lyn Davies
Printed in England on acid-free paper
by MPG Books Ltd, Bodmin, Cornwall

Contents

Preface

This book is based on perhaps the most extensive archive of its kind on the 1840s in private hands, the Stewart & Kincaid correspondence, which hitherto has not been researched. Most of it was acquired by postal history collectors in the 1980s and 1990s. Messrs Stewart & Kincaid was a firm of land agents based in Dublin, and most of the correspondence was addressed to its office there. Its successors ceased business in the 1980s. The letters pertain mainly to the estates managed by the firm during the 1840s.

By 1995 I had accumulated about 30,000 letters from the Stewart and Kincaid correspondence, the bulk of them dated in the 1840s. A majority of the letters obtained by me were original documents; others among them are photocopies of properties of four other collectors, three of them postal history enthusiasts. Those that remain in my possession (either as originals or as photocopies) from the above-mentioned sources I call, for brevity in what follows, the Stewart & Kincaid correspondence. In a relatively small number of cases I will refer to letters in my possession which have not come from the Stewart & Kincaid archive. The material which I possess is complemented by holdings in two other archives – the Broadlands Papers at the University of Southampton and the Pakenham archive at Tullynally Castle in County Westmeath. The book is intended mainly for professional historians and for students of Irish and British history, but it is hoped that it will also be of interest to more general readers in Ireland, in Britain, in North America and elsewhere.

Having collated the many thousands of pieces of paper and having conducted preliminary historical investigation, the first major problem which I encountered in drafting material on the various estates was that I had little or no real feeling for what those estates looked like in the 1840s. Rectification of such deficiency entailed visits to each of the former estates, thereby enabling me to study topographical details. The Smurfit Graduate School of Business at University College Dublin made such 'on-site' investigations feasible by providing me with research grants between 1998 and 2005. It was in fact while walking on one of the former estates – that of Sir Alexander Crichton in Roscommon – that I came to suspect that some historians had erred in regard to the location of perhaps the most famous landlord murder in nineteenth-century Ireland.

Some remarks in regard to editing are appropriate. In most cases I have not altered the spelling, punctuation, etc., in the reproduced extracts. In the interests of clarity, however, I have in some cases entered an upper case letter at the beginning of a sentence in place of a lower case letter in the original; similarly, in some cases I have added or deleted punctuation to/from the originals. In many cases I have replaced an upper case letter strictly within a sentence by a lower case letter. I have not corrected spelling errors in the originals. In regard to place names in my own text (as distinct from the text of the original letters), I have used either the current spelling, or the spelling in official publications such as the Griffith *Valuations*. It is likely that some of the letters cited, as written in the name of a particular tenant – say, Sean Doe – were not written by that tenant; rather, because Sean may have been lacking in literacy, some of them were written on his behalf by, say, a local schoolteacher. In such cases I have taken the only stance which is practical: I have attributed the letter to the person who has purported to add the signature, Sean Doe. On the matter of source-references, I have tried to avoid an inelegance of having endnote sections in any given chapter almost as lengthy as the main text of the chapter itself; I have therefore incorporated many references to correspondence within the main text itself.

Some of the material to be presented, as well as related details mainly of local interest, has already been published by me elsewhere, as follows: 'Viscount Frankfort, Sir Charles Burton and County Carlow in the 1840s, Part I', *Carloviana* 46 (1998), pp. 91–3; 'Viscount Frankfort, Sir Charles Burton and County Carlow in the 1840s, Part II', *Carloviana* 47 (1999), pp. 2–6 and 15; 'Progress and distress on the Stratford Estate in Clare during the Eighteen Forties', *The Other Clare* 26 (2002), pp. 50–7; 'On Viscount Frankfort's Kilkenny estates in the 1840s', *Old Kilkenny Review* 54 (2002), pp. 18–40; 'The Sherlocks of Sherlockstown, Jane Coleman and County Kildare in the 1840s', *Journal of the County Kildare Archaeological Society* XIX (2002), pp. 289–99; 'Distress and benevolence on Gertrude Fitzgerald's Limerick Estate in the 1840s', *North Munster Antiquarian Journal* 42 (2002), pp. 21–34; 'The Limerick estate of Sergeant Warren during the Great Famine', *North Munster Antiquarian Journal* 43 (2003), pp. 75–83; 'Lord Palmerston and the Irish famine emigration: a rejoinder', *Historical Journal* 46 (Mar. 2003), pp. 155–65; 'On the Dublin and Meath estates of the Earl of Howth in the 1840s', *Ríocht na Midhe* XIV (2003), pp. 177–93; 'Stratford's Robertstown estate during the 1840s', in Thomas J. Culhane, *The Barony of Shanid*, (n. p., 2003), pp. 120–37; 'Where was Major Denis Mahon shot?', *Co. Roscommon Historical and Archaeological Society Journal* 9 (2003), pp. 54–8; 'On the Kilglass lands of George Nugent in the 1840s', *The Bonfire, Newsletter of the Ballykilcline Society* (USA), 6: 1 (Spring 2004), pp. 1 and 4–9; 'Ballyfeeny in the 1840s', *The Bonfire* 6: 2 (Fall 2004), pp. 1 and 4–8; 'Life on a Kilmore property', *The Bonfire* 6: 2 (Fall 2004), pp. 1 and 8–10; 'On Lord Palmerston's Irish estates in the 1840s', *English Historical Review* CXIX, 484 (Nov. 2004), pp. 1254–74; 'On landlord-assisted emigration from some Irish estates in the 1840s', *Agricultural History Review* 53: 1 (2005), pp. 24–40.

I am indebted to many individuals. First, for her sustained advice and assistance I mention my wife Deirdre. The four private collectors who allowed me to photocopy Stewart & Kincaid letters in their possession, and to quote therefrom, are Anthony Hughes of County Westmeath, John Lennon of Dublin, Aiden Mannion of Sligo, and Uwe Netzsch of County Cork. For permission to consult and quote from materials in their possession or under their care I thank Thomas Pakenham of Tullynally Castle and the Trustees of the Broadlands Archive at the University of Southampton. For their assistance I also thank staff at the following repositories: the National Archives of Ireland; the National Library of Ireland; the Public Record Office of Northern Ireland; Roscommon County Library and Sligo County Library.

Two of my former academic colleagues at University College Dublin, James Heslin and the late Patrick Lynch, sacrificed weeks of their time in reading an early draft of the entire book and in preparing detailed written comments. Philip Bourke of University College Dublin, Martina Boland of Portarlington and my daughter Chantelle of New York also made helpful written comments. Two referees made excellent recommendations which I have tried to incorporate in the final revision. William Vaughan of Trinity College, Dublin indicated some useful secondary sources. The text also benefited from conversations with Cormac Ó Gráda, Tim O'Neill and Louis Smith of University College Dublin. Many others, most of whom have personal links with the former estates, assisted me on specific chapters. My indebtedness to those other people is expressed in endnotes.

When the final draft of this book was virtually ready for submission to the publisher, I became aware that an account book of the Roscommon estates of the Marquess of Westmeath in 1848 was being offered for sale by public auction. I then contacted Mary Lambkin, the then Dean of the Faculty of Commerce at University College Dublin, seeking funding for purchase of those accounts. On behalf of the Faculty, Professor Lambkin provided such (considerable) funding without hesitation. Some of the information therein has been drawn upon in chapter 8. I also thank the National University of Ireland for a grant in aid towards the costs of publishing this book. Finally, I wish to express my appreciation to Barbara Mennell, Executive Editor of UCD Press, who edited and generally administered my final typescript with great speed and professionalism.

DESMOND NORTON
Dublin, December 2005

Maps

Abbreviations

BR   Broadlands (Palmerston) Papers, Hartley Library, University of
      Southampton
FRS   Fellow of the Royal Society
JP   Justice of the Peace
PAK   Pakenham archive, Tullynally Castle, Castlepollard, County
      Westmeath
PP   Parish priest
SK   The Stewart & Kincaid correspondence archive in the possession
      of the author
UCD   University College Dublin

Maps

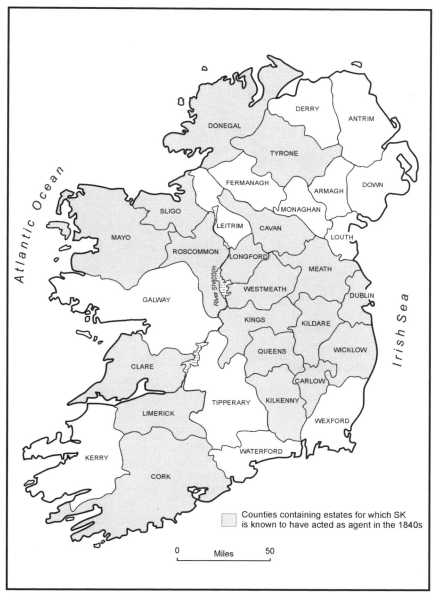

Counties containing estates for which SK
is known to have acted as agent in the 1840s

0   Miles   50

1 The 32 counties of Ireland

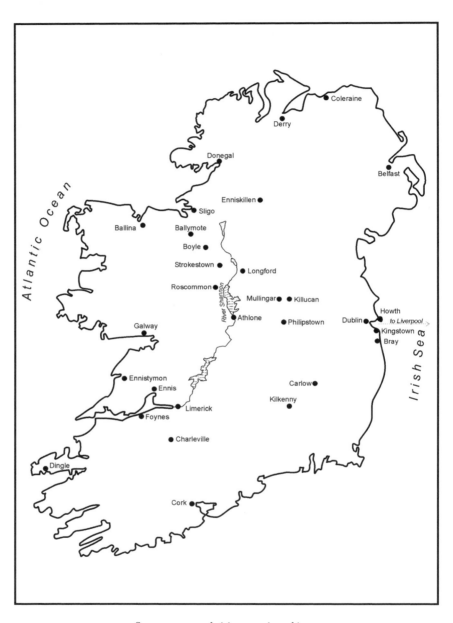

2 Some towns and cities mentioned in text

3 Places on or near the Palmerston properties in Sligo

4 Places on or near the Crichton and Wingfield lands

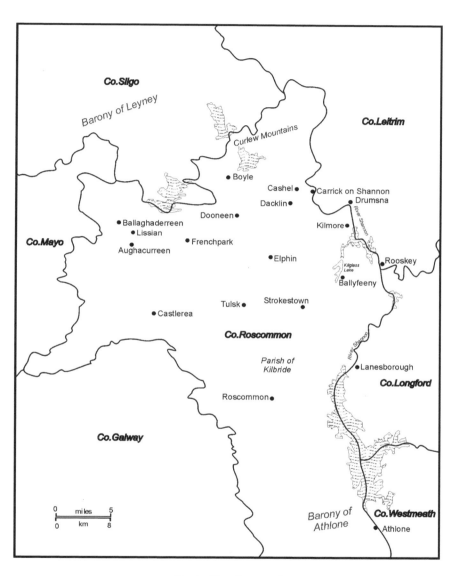

5 On the Ferrall properties

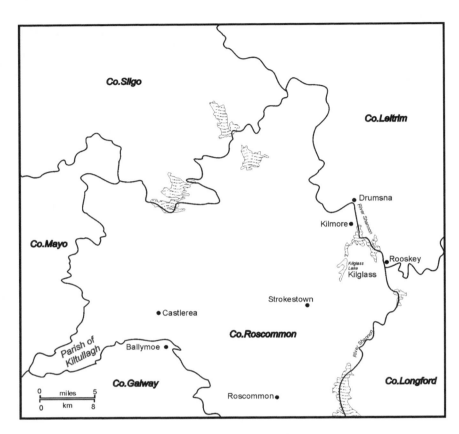

6 On the Nugent lands in County Roscommon

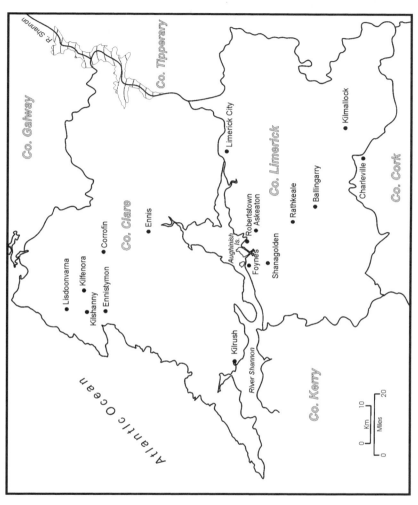

7 Places on or near the Stratford properties in Clare and Limerick

8 Places on or near the Frankfort and Charles Burton lands in Kilkenny and Carlow

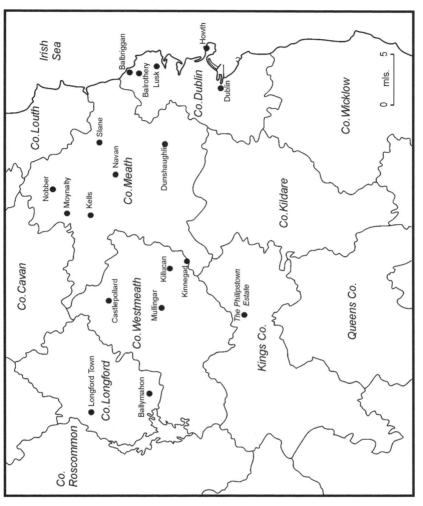

Irish
Sea

Balbriggan
Howth
Co. Louth
Balrothery
Lusk
Co. Dublin
Dublin
Co. Wicklow
Slane
Navan
Dunshaughlin
Co. Meath
Nobber
Moynalty
Kells
Co. Cavan
Co. Kildare
Castlepollard
Killucan
Kinnegad
Mullingar
The Phillipstown Estate
Co. Westmeath
Kings Co.
Longford Town
Ballymahon
Co. Longford
Queens Co.
Co. Roscommon

0   mls.   5

9 On Ponsonby, Pakenham and St Lawrence

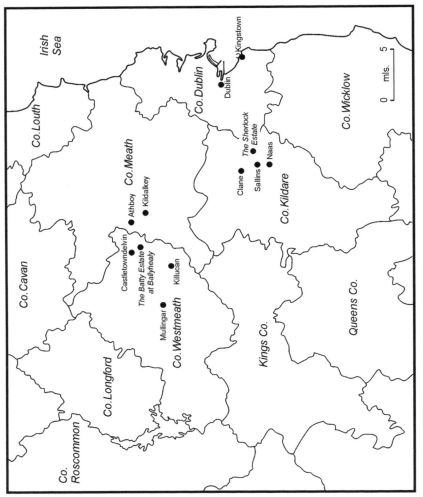

10   On the Sherlocks and the Battys

Introduction

The principal primary source material for this study is the 1840s correspondence archive of the land agency firm, Messrs Stewart & Kincaid. The letters consist mainly of communications to the firm from client proprietors, from the firm's local agents and from tenants on estates throughout Ireland which were managed by the firm. The primary objective in the chapters which follow is to record the core of the Stewart & Kincaid correspondence of the 1840s, to present research results which set the context of those letters, and to draw conclusions. Because the focus is on an archive which hitherto has not been researched, because of its extent, and conscious that I must not too often stray away from the central themes, I have constrained myself by not repeating a great deal of what is already known from existing printed sources. But some key facts should be recognised by the reader before proceeding.

The few decades immediately after the Napoleonic Wars saw the emergence of several land agencies. As Donnelly has noted: 'During the eighteenth century, the most common method of managing large estates in Ireland was to split them into considerable tracts of from 100 to 1,000 acres or more, and then to give them to middlemen on long leases'. But 'the two decades before the famine were marked by the expiration of a great number of old leases held by middlemen' and progressively more landlords replaced the middleman system by employing professional land agents to administer their estates.[1] By the 1840s the firm of Stewart & Kincaid was the largest of such agencies.

Much of the Stewart & Kincaid correspondence of the 1840s refers to the potato crop. Some observations on the importance of that vegetable in early nineteenth century Ireland are appropriate.

The Irish peasant became more dependent on the potato in the early nineteenth century. A letter to London, written on board HMS *Sapphs*, gives details of a voyage along the west coast in 1821 (see maps 1 and 2). It indicates that by the early 1820s it was not inappropriate to refer to the southwest of Ireland as 'the land of the potatoes': 'We are running along the Land of the Potatoes. . . . We arrived at a small harbour [Ventry] three miles from Dingle [in County Kerry]. . . . I went on shore and was much surprised to see the lower orders . . . in . . . wretched condition, both sexes almost in a state of nudity, more to be seen issuing from an aperture in a mud cabin that served . . . for a chimney and a door.'[2]

The Great Famine of the late 1840s was due to failures of the potato, upon which most of the population had survived. In the autumn of 1845 the failure was only partial. In 1846 it was complete. Partly because seed potatoes were exceptionally scarce, the potato acreage planted in 1847 was very small, but the yield per acre was high and the product was virtually blight-free. The total crop in that year was probably less than that of blight-ridden 1846. The potato again partially failed in 1848. The following year, 1849, 'might be deemed the first year of post-famine normality', though the pre-famine potato acreage was never to be regained.[3]

Note that 1845 and 1846 were not the first years in which the potato failed.[4] There were in fact several cases of localised failure in the first half of the 1840s. It was presumably following a poor potato harvest in the autumn of 1841 that Charles Gayer,[5] a Church of Ireland clergyman at Dingle, wrote to Stewart & Kincaid on 29 March 1842 confirming receipt of a gift of £50 – probably about £5,000 sterling in purchasing power at the beginning of the twenty-first century – from Miss Coleman, one of Stewart & Kincaid's clients.[6] Gayer again wrote to Stewart & Kincaid on 8 May, referring to 'the receipt of your favor containing nineteen pounds ten shillings from Miss Jane Coleman. . . . If you can collect anything for our *Starving* people *pray do*. . . . We are selling out meal, but it is only a *drop in the sea*. The people are really dying from want of food' (sk). Finally, on 3 August 1842 Gayer wrote to Kincaid 'to acknowledge the safe arrival of your note with the £20 from Miss Coleman. . . . The famine is nearly over' (sk). Several other examples of localised failures of the potato in the early 1840s will be provided later.

The text which follows makes many references to implementation of policy under the Irish poor laws and under related legislation. Brief explanation of those laws is desirable before proceeding.[7]

The Poor Relief Act of 1838 provided for the establishment of administrative districts called poor law unions for relief of the poor in Ireland. By 1845 the country was divided into 130 such unions, each administered by an elected board of 'guardians' and each with a workhouse. *All* relief under the Act was to be in the workhouse: outdoor assistance by local authorities was not then permitted.

The Act made provision for 'the due performance of religious service in the workhouse', and for appointment of 'chaplains for that purpose, one being of the established church [the Church of Ireland], another a protestant dissenter, and another of the Roman catholic church. . . . But no inmate of a workhouse is to be compelled to attend any religious service contrary to the religious principles of such inmate.'[8]

For defraying the expenses of providing poor relief in workhouses, the guardians were empowered to levy such *rates* (of taxation on estimated property valuations) as deemed necessary on every occupier of rateable property in the union. The Act indicated that 'the poor-rate is to be paid by the occupiers', but that in regard to smallholdings 'where the parties have agreed thereto, the lessor may be rated instead'.[9] All tenements (other than cemeteries, churches, schools, etc), whether rented or not, were usually included in the rate.

The fact that there was a huge number of small occupiers, from whom the amounts collected individually in rates was trivially small, imposed unnecessary work on the authorities. This led to administrative change: under the Poor Law Amendment Act of August 1843, 'where the property rated is not of greater value than £4 [annually] . . . the rate on such property shall be made on the immediate lessor', either a middleman or the head landlord.[10] Some modern historians have written that this legislation – on the question of who was *administratively* liable for payment of the rates on smallholdings – induced many landlords to clear their estates of small tenants. However, such a conclusion is invalid, or it is of much less significance than some historians have assumed.[11] (Following the Poor Law Amendment Act, the immediate lessor was administratively responsible for payment of the rates on small holdings, *whether or not* the land was rented to a tenant/undertenant.)

Purchase of £100,000 of American corn was the government's initial response to the partial failure of the potato in 1845. These supplies arrived during the spring of 1846, when depots were established in order to facilitate distribution. The corn was sold from the depots at a moderate price, to local relief committees and to others. Requisite funds of the relief committees were furnished by private subscriptions assisted by financial donations from government: they were not financed under the poor laws. Also during the summer of 1846, the government implemented schemes of public works to create employment and purchasing-power. At that time the mode of financing was: one half of the cost as a grant from central government, the other half as a loan to be repaid by the local authority out of grand jury (the precursors of county councils) cess (taxation); thus, these public works, which were terminated in August, were not financed under the poor laws.

Provision for schemes of public works was renewed a few weeks later, and the machinery of relief committees was reorganised. Under the Labour Rate Act of late August 1846, the entire expense of public works to be initiated under that Act was made a local charge, to be defrayed by a rate levied in a manner similar to the poor rate. However, in 1847 the financing of public works under the Labour Rate Act was retrospectively altered: central government agreed to make a grant of one half of such expenditures.[12]

Late in January 1847 the government announced that it intended to terminate the public works, and to substitute another mode of relief. At the end of February preparations were made for a change in the relief system by the passing of the Temporary Relief Act, which directed that a relief committee of specified composition be established in each electoral division to administer relief in the form of food, usually thick soup made mainly from meal, the expense incurred to be financed out of the poor rates; however, when private subscriptions were made, the government gave donations to an equal amount. Relief under this Act ended some months later.

The Poor Law Extension Act of June 1847 provided for relief of the destitute either in the workhouse or outside it 'as the guardians may deem expedient', the expenses incurred to be financed out of the poor rates. This legislation also directed that occupiers of more than one quarter of an acre of land were not to be deemed destitute, nor were they to be relieved out of the poor rates.[13] Two other relevant Acts followed in July. In 1856 it was observed that the three Acts of June–July 1847, 'taken conjointly with the original Relief Act of 1838, and the Amendment Act of 1843, may be considered as forming the entire code of Irish Poor Laws'.[14] The sanction of outdoor relief, other than on a temporary basis only, as under the Act of February 1847, was the most important departure from the principles of the statute of 1838. The key point to note is that by the end of the summer of 1847 virtually all government expenditures on relief of distress in Ireland had become charges on Irish property through finance of outlays under the poor laws.

Some of the poor law unions to be mentioned in the text had not been established in the early years of the famine. However, when a reference is made to any particular poor law union, the classification to be adopted is that of Griffith's printed *Valuations* of the 1850s.

The approach to be adopted is as follows: chapter 1 sets the background in regard to Stewart & Kincaid: those involved in the firm and how they operated in the 1840s. The chapters which follow investigate landlords, tenants and famine on the several estates which Stewart & Kincaid managed in various parts of Ireland. Maps which highlight essential geographic details are provided on pp. xi–xx above. The county boundaries in these maps are those of today (there have in fact been some changes in the boundaries between counties since the 1840s.) The conclusions in the final chapter suggest a need for revision and/or extension of some of the interpretations by modern historians who have written about the famine.

ONE

MESSRS STEWART, STEWART &
SWAN, STEWART & KINCAID

—

I EVOLUTION OF THE BUSINESS

The evolution of the land agency known in the 1830s to the 1880s as Stewart &
Kincaid can be traced from Dublin directories over a period of two centuries.
Those of the late eighteenth century indicate that Henry Stewart was called to
the Bar in 1773. That for 1788 describes him as 'army agent' in Chatham Street,[1]
a listing which was repeated up to 1792. The directory for 1793 describes him as
'agent', from which it might correctly be inferred that he had extended his
business beyond that related to the army. Although the Stewart & Kincaid
archive contains papers referring to rent collection on the Powerscourt estates
in Clare and Sligo from 1746 onwards, the first to mention Henry Stewart as
Dublin agent for those estates is dated 1791.[2] In 1788 Edward Pakenham, second
Baron Longford, wrote to the second Viscount Palmerston recommending
his 'friend' Henry Stewart 'as a proper person to be employ'd as an agent', and
in 1789, Henry Stewart indicated that he would shortly be going to London
with Palmerston rent rolls.[3] It is inferred that Stewart held the accounts of the
Palmerston estates (in both Dublin and Sligo) from about 1789 onwards.

Stewart moved his business to 6 Leinster Street in 1799. Until 1808 the
listing in directories was 'Henry Stewart, Agent'. The directory for 1809 listed
the firm as 'Stewart and Swan, Agents'.[4] Stewart's new business partner was a
barrister named Graves Swan. Stewart had entered partnership with him in
1805, when he wrote to the third Viscount Palmerston, then a student at
Cambridge, that 'we are desirous of extending our business'.[5] Directories[6] for
1809 to 1829 indicate that Swan was also Treasurer to the Irish Post Office,
which was then rife with abuse.[7] In an era of high postal rates, he used or
abused his position in the Post Office by sending and receiving letters free of
charge.[8] Swan died in 1829.[9]

Joseph Kincaid commenced employment at 6 Leinster Street around 1827
and in 1829 the name of the firm there was changed to Stewart & Kincaid.[10]

Kincaid first appears in the Dublin directory for 1831, which was the first to list '[Henry] Stewart and [Joseph] Kincaide'; also in the same year, the description was changed from 'Agents' to 'Land Agents'. The listing remained unchanged until 1838: for the next 44 years, directories referred to 'Stewart [or Stewarts] and Kincaid, Land Agents'.

Henry Stewart died in 1840. By the early 1840s the firm involved his son James Robert Stewart, and Joseph Kincaid. It was not merely by coincidence that in the mid-1840s J. R. Stewart resided in the newly built house at 11 Longford Terrace, Monkstown, County Dublin, beside the original suburban terminus of the Dublin and Kingstown Railway. Other considerations were also relevant.[11]

The directory for 1883 lists 'Stewarts and Kincaid, Land Agents'.[12] However, the partner named Kincaid (Joseph's son James) had left the firm at the end of 1882 to set up a rival business.[13] The directory for 1885 lists him as Land Agent at 7 Leinster Street. That for 1909 lists J. S. Kincaid, Land Agent, at 7 Leinster Street; however, the business was no longer there late in 1915: the directory for 1916 lists Kincaid & Matthews, land agents, at St Stephens Green. This firm closed down in 1919.

Following the departure of James Kincaid, the firm at 6 Leinster Street was known as J. R. Stewart & Sons. It remained at the same address until about 1968. However, the directory for 1969 lists the offices of the Pakenham estate at 6 Leinster Street, and J. R. Stewart & Son at Upper Mount Street. The location of the Pakenham offices in Leinster Street is interesting: the Pakenhams had been clients of Stewart & Kincaid in the 1840s and the J. R. Stewart of that era was related to them by blood. The directories continued to list J. R. Stewart & Son at Mount Street until 1984; however, the omission of any listing for the firm in *Thom's Directory* for 1986 indicates that the firm had ceased operations.

The foregoing has focused on the evolution of the firm in which Stewarts were owners or principal partners for about 200 years.

2 ON THE POWERS OF INFLUENCE

In the late 1840s Priscella Nugent spent much of her time in France and England. Poor performance of her agent in Ireland induced her to seek a replacement. In 1847 a clergyman wrote congratulating her 'on the selection you have made. . . . Stewart & Kincaid is . . . of . . . the highest character & I anticipate for you great satisfaction in *their* management of y'r affairs'.[14]

Some of Stewart & Kincaid's accounts originated from the firm's reputation. Others came through family connections. Links with the Pakenham family had far-reaching effects. In 1793 Henry Stewart married a daughter of his friend Lord Longford, whose family name was Pakenham. Such links may have been relevant to the fact that Henry Stewart was MP for the Borough of Longford from 1784 to 1799, which must have promoted his agency activities. It was presumably the same links which led to assignment of the Longford account to the firm which, in the 1840s, was known as Stewart & Kincaid. John Hamilton, an important landowner in Donegal, also married a daughter of the same Lord Longford. Hamilton's eldest son, who through the Pakenham link was a cousin to James Robert Stewart, inherited about 20,000 acres in Donegal upon coming of age in 1821. The firm of Stewart & Swan appears to have been Hamilton's agent in the 1820s.[15] Stewart & Kincaid represented him in the 1840s and beyond. In the early 1840s Thomas, another of Henry Stewart's sons, was friendly with Mrs Fitzgerald of Whitegate House in County Cork, who owned lands in Limerick. It seems that this brought to Stewart & Kincaid the Mount Blakeney, County Limerick, agency. J. R. Stewart married a daughter of R. B. Warren in 1835. A few years later Stewart & Kincaid obtained the account of Warren's estate in Limerick. As will be indicated in chapter 14, it seems that a sister of Joseph Kincaid married a Church of Ireland clergyman named Edward Batty, who was a brother of the owner of the Batty estate in Westmeath, and that it was this link which enabled Stewart & Kincaid to acquire the Batty account.

Kincaid had influence in the commercial life of Ireland. He was a director of the Dublin and Kingstown Railway which operated Ireland's first passenger line, opened in 1834. This meant that he could secure favours. For example, in 1841 Robert Corbet of the Royal Exchange Insurance Office in Dublin wrote to Kincaid 'recommending the bearer . . . to be appointed as one of the servants or attendants on your railway' (sk). Similarly, in 1843 John Vincent, a solicitor in Dublin and a brother of Stewart & Kincaid's principal agent in County Limerick, sent a note requesting Kincaid to 'use your influence to get [the bearer] employed on the railway' (sk). Other letters asking Kincaid to secure employment with the Dublin and Kingstown Railway could be cited. If Kincaid did agree to such requests, he was probably acting in Stewart & Kincaid's own interests: his co-operation may have brought business to the firm.

A letter dated 13 June 1842 to Kincaid provides curious details. The writer, a widow named Smith at Harold's Cross near Dublin City, explained that her father-in-law had arrived from Limerick (about 120 miles away) seeking financial aid, which she could not provide. She requested Kincaid to 'get him the *smallest* relief to help him to return *Home* to Limerick, as he is not able to walk it *Back*, as he walked coming up to Dublin' (sk).

It was not only with the Dublin and Kingstown Railway that Kincaid swayed influence. For example, on 14 September 1842 Henry Disney of

Portobello in Dublin wrote to him stating that 'as it was by your means I obtained my present situation, I . . . hope you will again grant me your influence with the Directors of the Grand Canal Co. in order that I may be promoted to the rank of *full Boatman*' (sk).

Kincaid was a director of the Midland Great Western Railway, incorporated in 1845 to connect Dublin to the midlands. He was also asked to use his influence to secure appointments with this company. For example, on 13 July 1846 H. K. Harmon, a midlands landlord, wrote to him seeking work with that company for a friend of his who was 'very well connected'. In 1848 an official at the Board of Works wrote to Kincaid on behalf of another job-seeker: 'The bearer . . . is a candidate for the Office of Station Keeper on the Midland Gr Western Railway. Any assistance you can render him in obtaining the appointment I shall esteem a personal favour.'[16] Kincaid himself sought favours at the Board of Works during the famine years. (In the 1840s the Board was responsible for public sector schemes of employment, and for administration of loans to the private sector for works of improvement.)

Stewart & Kincaid had influence within the Post Office administration. One of the estates which the firm managed was at Philipstown, King's County, where Catherine Ellis had been postmistress.[17] In 1846 her daughter Martha wrote that her mother had died. Martha begged Stewart & Kincaid to 'use your interest to have the Post Office continued to her children. A few days later Stewart & Kincaid received a letter written on behalf of Catherine's son: 'If you can in any way influence the powers that be with respect to the situation . . . you will never have cause . . . to regret it'.[18] A listing prepared in 1849 indicates that Thomas Ellis, a tenant on the local Ponsonby estate managed by Stewart & Kincaid, was then the postmaster at Philipstown.[19]

In one case a person who obtained an appointment, following Stewart & Kincaid's use of influence, declined the post. Thus, on 31 December 1841 an individual surnamed Spray wrote to Stewart & Kincaid:

Thanks for the kind interest you took in my behalf . . . respecting the situation of *Inspector of Collectors* of the Malahide Turnpike. . . . If the situation was . . . *only* that of what the title represents it to be . . . I should have had no hesitation in taking it, but as the Chairman said that I should not only be the Inspector *but also one of the Collectors* & have to *reside in the Gatehouse & receive the money taken at that Gate myself*, I at once declined it, as . . . my brother would not allow me to become a *common turnpike . . . keeper*. (sk)

It was above all during the famine that Stewart & Kincaid was asked to use influence to secure jobs. In 1846 the firm received many requests to use influence at the Board of Works in order to obtain employment on public works.

On a few occasions Stewart & Kincaid were asked to provide employment directly. In 1843 a barrister wrote to Stewart: 'Is there any likelihood of an opening in your office for a . . . good boy of 16 . . . ? He is a son of Edward Willson, who was Assistant Secretary to the Bible Society . . . who left a . . . family in great want.'[20] Edward Wingfield, whose estates were managed by Stewart & Kincaid, sought a similar favour. On 25 February 1848 he requested of Stewart & Kincaid: 'You will know what a sincere regard I had for . . . Robert Sandys & having been applied to get a situation for his son Henry in your house [i.e. firm] . . . I do not hesitate at once to ask this favor . . . as his mother [is] in great . . . distress' (sκ). Robert Sandys had acted on behalf of the Viscounts Powerscourt in the Enniskerry district of County Wicklow. Stewart & Kincaid managed some of the Powerscourt finances. The family name of the Powerscourts was Wingfield. Cork Abbey, near Bray, County Wicklow, but in County Dublin, was Edward Wingfield's main residence. When he was absent, Robert Sandys had attended to some of his interests at the Abbey. The amount of business which the firm obtained through the Wingfield family suggests that it may have been in Stewart & Kincaid's interests to accede to Wingfield's request.

3 SOCIETIES, CHARITABLE OBJECTIVES AND PROMOTION OF BUSINESS

Kincaid was a member of many societies. Some of them were charitable; others sought to promote agricultural knowledge. Links with some of these bodies were good for business at 6 Leinster Street; however, it is hard to see how Stewart & Kincaid could have made commercial gains through links with a few of the organisations with which Kincaid was connected.

In February 1841 the owner of a coach factory in Dublin sent Kincaid ten shillings for a 'Special Coal Fund'. He wrote that he 'considers Mr Kincade and the other gentlemen composing the committee of the "Special Coal Fund" are entitled to the thanks of the public . . . for their exertions in establishing so laudable . . . an institution which has relieved such a large number of destitute individuals'.[21] Another letter containing money indicated that Kincaid was treasurer of the Fund.[22] The Nourishment and Clothing Society, of which Kincaid was a committee member, was similar. In 1842 its stated objective was 'to relieve the wants of the poor. . . . The number of families relieved last winter . . . was 5,116. The food dispensed was . . . 920 quartern loaves, 7,301 quarts of soup, 21 tons of potatoes, 20 cwt of oatmeal. . . . Also various articles of clothing, 18 tons of coal, and 202 bundles of straw. *Donations of blankets or flannel, linen or calico, not made up, would be very acceptable*, as they enable the

Committee to give employment.'[23] There is no presumption that Kincaid's links with those charities brought business to Stewart & Kincaid: they probably reflected genuine concern for humanity.

Although the Stewart & Kincaid correspondence suggests that neither Kincaid nor Stewart had particularly strong religious zeal, both were associated with bodies which sought to promote Protestantism and the Established Church in particular. Kincaid was a committee member of the Hibernian District of the Church Missionary Society. Viscount Lorton, one of Stewart & Kincaid's clients, was president of the society, while two other Stewart & Kincaid clients, the Earl of Erne and Viscount De Vesci, were vice-presidents.[24]

Kincaid was auditor to the Church Education Society, which assisted schools for 'instruction in the Holy Scriptures, in addition to an improved system of secular education . . . under the tuition of teachers who are members of the United Church of England and Ireland'.[25] The Society for Promoting the Education of the Poor of Ireland (known from its address in Dublin as the Kildare Place Society) was more sectarian. According to a description of 1846, this Society was instituted for 'promoting the Scriptural and United Education of the Poor of Ireland, and is now entirely dependent for support on the benevolence of the Christian public of the United Kingdom'.[26] However, near the end of the nineteenth century T. O'Rorke wrote that the society, 'instituted in 1811 for the purpose of "promoting the education of the poor of Ireland", . . . developed through time a passion for tampering with the faith of Catholics, and lost, in consequence, its parliamentary grants'.[27] J. R. Stewart was a committee member of that society.

In the links of Kincaid and Stewart with the latter two societies, business considerations were relevant. Some of the most important landowners in the country were vice-presidents of the Church Education Society. A similar remark applies in the case of the Kildare Place Society, which included two Stewart & Kincaid clients (Viscounts De Vesci and Lorton) among its vice-presidents; furthermore, Stewart & Kincaid's client Sergeant Warren was a committee member of the same society.[28]

A Dublin directory of 1842 indicates that Stewart was a committee member of the Hibernian Bible Society. According to the same source, 'the sole object of this Society is, to encourage a wider circulation of the Holy Scriptures. . . . Funds are . . . employed . . . in making grants of the Scriptures to necessitous districts, prisons, &c.. . . . From the commencement in 1806 .. . . there had been issued from the Depository, 391,767 Bibles. . . . Members are permitted to purchase them at reduced prices. . . . Schools are supplied gratuitously, or at reduced prices'. The Earl of Roden, another of Stewart & Kincaid's clients, was president of this society, while Lorton and De Vesci were vice-presidents. The brewer Arthur Guinness, with whom Stewart &

Kincaid sometimes engaged in financial intermediation (borrowing or lending funds on behalf of third parties), was another vice-president.[29]

Stewart provided service to the Meath Street Savings Bank, which sought to encourage thrift among the poor in Dublin. It was 'open at Meath-street on Saturday evenings from 7 till 9 o'clock, and on Wednesday mornings'. It had two branch offices, and 'at each office deposits are received from one shilling upwards, which may yearly amount to £30, until the whole shall amount to £150, which is the highest the law allows'.[30] The maximum on individual deposits reflected a view that people whose financial assets exceeded that sum were not poor. A letter of 1841 informed Stewart that it was his 'turn to attend as Manager' at Abbey St on 'morn'g the 4th Feby at Nine O'ck'.[31] The bank's trustees included Arthur Guinness and other businessmen.

Involvement by the partners of Stewart & Kincaid in benevolent institutions may explain why some Dubliners, who seem to have had no links with Stewart & Kincaid's clients, applied to Stewart & Kincaid for assistance. The appeal from the widow Smith of Harold's Cross has been mentioned. Other examples could be cited from the Stewart & Kincaid correspondence.

Kincaid sought improvements in farming. Apart from being a member of the Agricultural and Husbandry Committee of the Royal Dublin Society, he was active in the Royal Agricultural Improvement Society. Letters from the secretary of that society indicate that Kincaid was expected to assign a significant amount of time in service to the society, the objectives of which included 'improvement of husbandry among the farming classes, holding under twenty-five acres Irish' and 'distribution of . . . knowledge . . . upon agricultural . . . subjects'. A genuine desire to develop agriculture was probably among Kincaid's motives in contributing to the society. But there were also issues of business. A list of the members included several important landowners. A glance at this list indicates that a rival land agent, John Ross Mahon, was active in the society.[32]

The details outlined above suggest that although they were in part motivated by concern for fellow humans, both Stewart and Kincaid participated in several organisations in order to attract business. They had contact with many of the most important people in Ireland, who could be helpful in the agency's business affairs. But Stewart & Kincaid did not merely want clients: the firm wanted its dealings to be profitable. In Stewart & Kincaid's view, the personality of clients was not important. This practical approach is revealed in remarks by Stewart about Viscount Frankfort, whom he described as in some respects 'insane'. Thus, on 13 January 1841 Stewart wrote to Kincaid: 'You were quite right to accept Lord Frankfort [as a client]. I would far rather be agent to a *Particular* man or even an *odd* man than a *distressed* one. . . . The distressed mans agency is . . . unprofitable.' (SK) Especially in the late years of the famine when much of the land under its management lay idle, Stewart & Kincaid's attitude towards tenants was similar: short-term lettings aside, Stewart & Kincaid did not merely want tenants; rather, the firm sought tenants who had good prospects of being viable over many years.

On matters of estate management, Stewart & Kincaid looked to the long term rather than the immediate future. Consistent with maximisation of the firm's expected present value, Stewart & Kincaid regarded its day-to-day decisions as part of a strategy over a lengthy horizon. Investment of time in the nurture of personal connections and in enhancing the reputation of its partners for honest dealing, as well as in its selectivity in accepting new agencies and tenants, help to explain why the firm at 6 Leinster Street perpetuated its operations until late in the twentieth century. But by then (following the Land Acts of the late nineteenth and early twentieth centuries), most of the land of Ireland belonged to descendants of former tenants and the days of traditional land agents had ended.

A few further remarks about religion and business are relevant. All or most of the religious organisations to which Stewart and Kincaid were attached promoted the Established Church. This did not reflect any obvious bigotry or grudges against Catholics by the partners in Stewart & Kincaid. Rather, it reflected the fact that most of the large landowners in Ireland belonged to the Established Church.

It should nevertheless be mentioned that the Protestant charities mentioned above, to which both Stewart and Kincaid gave support, were strongly associated with the evangelical wing of Irish Anglicanism. It could be argued that support for such bodies implied an endorsement of particular viewpoints on religion. If this was the case, it could have involved some business cost, because public association with evangelicalism could conceivably have led some liberal landowners to keep their distance from the agency. However, the fact that the firm of Stewart & Kincaid did attract business from several liberal proprietors suggests that the partners were able to separate business and personal affairs sufficiently for the latter not to be an embarrassment to liberal clients.

4 ESTATE MANAGEMENT: ISSUES RELATED TO ADMINISTRATION

The firm acted under contract to clients, and these contracts usually involved the landlord giving Powers of Attorney to Stewart & Kincaid. The Stewart & Kincaid correspondence contains only one reference to management fees. On 8 June 1848 Stewart wrote to Kincaid about a potential client: 'He wishes to know whether . . . we would undertake the Agency at the usual 5 pr. ct.' (sk).

It seems that the structure of fees remained substantively unchanged for many years: a document in the Palmerston archive at Southampton indicates that Stewart proposed to charge five per cent on receipt of rent, six per cent on all loans and further charges on other services.[33] Thus, Stewart & Kincaid usually took five per cent of rental income. But in addition to this percentage, the landlord paid the firm for its outlays on improvements, and, for example, on hiring agricultural advisers.

The 1840s were years of improvement on most of the estates managed by Stewart & Kincaid. In some cases detailed directions came from the landlord and Stewart & Kincaid were merely responsible for implementation. However, the Stewart & Kincaid correspondence clearly indicates that the firm's partners favoured rationalisation in land tenure, improvements in husbandry and projects such as drainage. Commitment to spend monies on improvements was probably stipulated in Stewart & Kincaid's contracts with clients. This may have reflected humane feelings on the part of Stewart & Kincaid towards the tenantry, though to a greater extent it probably reflected a long-term view on estate management.

Stewart & Kincaid appointed local agents for collection of rents and for supervision of improvements. In some cases a local agent received a fixed annual salary; in at least one instance his remuneration was a specific percentage of the rent which he collected. The receipts of local agents were usually remitted to Stewart & Kincaid in Dublin through the post in the form of cash, bill of exchange[34] (akin to a post-dated cheque) or letter of credit (a mechanism for transfer of funds from one bank account to another). Use of financial instruments in payment of rent was the norm on the Stewart & Kincaid client estates. Thus, the financial system was more sophisticated than has often been assumed by writers in the twentieth century. When cash was sent through the post, it was as half notes. This was to secure against loss or theft: the local agent would initially send first halves; then, following acknowledgement of receipt at Leinster Street, the local agent would send second halves. Hence, the transfer of rents to Dublin involved the intensive use of the newly reformed postal system.

Much of the rent was received on estates by Kincaid, J. R. Stewart, or Stewart Maxwell who appears to have been 'third in command' at Leinster Street. The usual practice was for one of them to visit each estate twice annually. The local agent was instructed to 'notice' the tenants to have their money ready by a certain date, and to make themselves present for payment on that date at a specific location. Kincaid, Stewart or Maxwell (typically) would be present at that date and location to receive the rents. Maxwell once referred to such a visit as a 'raid'. The 'raids' were sequential: they involved itineraries for visiting several estates in a given tour. They required careful planning, which imposed strict demands on the postal and transportation systems. Thus, Kincaid might depart from Dublin early in the morning; collect rents at a specific place and at specified times in, say, Westmeath; proceed to Longford and act likewise; do the same in Roscommon, and then visit specified locations at appointed times in Sligo. His return journey to Dublin might involve another presence on an estate which he had visited some days earlier, or it might involve carefully planned visits to other estates. When on such tours, the person from Leinster Street usually slept at the landlord's residence, at a lodge owned by the landlord, at the residence of a local agent if he were a man of comfort, or at an inn.

The rent-gathering itineraries assumed there was an efficient transport system. Given that passenger railways were not in operation outside the Dublin and Belfast districts in the early 1840s, such travel was occasionally by canal but more generally by coach. Following the development of the mail coach system by John Anderson[35] and others from 1789 onwards, and the expansion of Bianconi's passenger and mail-delivery network in the decades immediately before the famine, Ireland's internal transport system was well suited to Stewart & Kincaid's needs. Although one letter from Maxwell refers to delay due to the canal being frozen, the correspondence contains no references to inability to get from A to B due to deficiencies in transport.

Most of the letters in the correspondence which refer to internal transport are relaxed in mood. Thus, on 26 November 1843 (a Sunday) Kincaid wrote to Stewart from Longford town:

> I left Clonteem [the lodge of the Marquess of Westmeath on the western side of the River Shannon] yesterday morn'g for Strokestown & there met Ja's Nolan [Stewart & Kincaid's principal agent in County Roscommon] who . . . assisted me in the collection of Lord Westmeaths rents. We were busy till half past 6. We then dined & at 7 I started by Bianconi for Longford. . . . During the two hours I was on the road . . . the car was so comfortable . . . that I did not feel it. . . . I will go tomorrow morn'g by Bianconi to Drumsna [on the eastern bank of the Shannon, opposite Clonteem] & remain with his Lordship at Clonteem tomorrow [Monday] night after which I go over to the Kilglass property [a few miles to the south of Clonteem]. On Tuesday I hope to get into Longford in good time that ev'g & perhaps go up to Dublin that night by the mail. . . . I will not leave Clonteem on Tuesday morning till after post hour so that if you write on Monday you may address me there. (s κ)

Passenger transport aside, this letter reveals complete confidence in the reliability of the postal system.

A letter from Maxwell in Mayo to Kincaid in Dublin, 11 October 1845 (a Saturday), provides further details on transport links:

I . . . send you . . . my R/A [rent account] together with sundry bills [promissory notes and/or bills of exchange]. . . . Your instructions regarding the collecting at Scurmore [Wingfield property in west Sligo] &c are very clear and I shall attend to them and shall hope to see you on Saturday. Your best way there [from Dublin] will be by mail [coach] and mail car. . . . Go about 8 miles p[er] coach beyond Boyle where you will find a mail car on the road side which will take you to Tubbercurry [in Sligo]. . . . There will be no occasion for our sleeping at Tubbercurry as . . . I did it all already in the one day and returned to Scurmore [to sleep] at night. (SK)

Stewart & Kincaid managed the Stratford estates on both sides of the Shannon estuary – in west Limerick and near Ennistymon in Clare. Until recent years (when a car ferry across the estuary commenced operation) travel by land between these districts took many hours. Stewart proposed to visit the two estates in 1845. In this context Arthur Vincent, Stewart & Kincaid agent in County Limerick, informed him on 31 May: 'As to crossing [the Shannon estuary] from Foynes [close to Stratford's Limerick estate] to Clare it can easily be accomplished . . . by taking boat at Foynes at ½ past 6 o'clock in the morning so as to meet the day car at Kildysart by 8 o'clock at which hour it regularly starts for Ennis and arrives in time to proceed by the Miltown mail car to Ennistymon.' (SK)

Apart from collecting rents, Stewart & Kincaid were expected to respond to tenants in arrears. It might be thought that ejectment was the norm in such circumstances, but this was not the case: ejectment was a measure of last resort on the estates managed by Stewart & Kincaid. Besides, neither the landlord nor his agents could quickly remove tenants simply because they were in arrears. It is true that at any time in the 1840s ejectment decrees were outstanding, but many of them were not executed. Ejectment was an expensive and time-consuming process which normally suited neither landlord nor tenant. Undertenants (towards whom the head landlord had no responsibility) and cottiers aside, usually the formal procedure was as follows: First, a notice to quit had to be served. If the tenant did not settle arrears over some months which followed, the landlord or his agents could then arrange for a summons to be issued against the tenant. After further delays and legal expenses incurred by the landlord (and perhaps by the tenant also) the parties would go to court (the assizes), the case would be heard and an ejectment decree might be issued. But this was not the end of the matter: if a decree was obtained, it next had to be executed, as confirmed by a legal document called a Habere.

Service of a notice to quit, or (months later) issue of an ejectment decree, might induce defaulting tenants to settle; sometimes they would also agree to pay the landlord's legal costs. In many cases Stewart & Kincaid served notices to quit, or subsequently obtained ejectment decrees, against a targeted group of tenants hoping that the 'demonstration effect' would induce payment from others in arrears. For example, on 7 October 1848 Stewart wrote to Kincaid: 'I don't like . . . the wholesale noticing to quit unless we can really execute some of the proceedings already taken to show an example.' (SK)

In the 1840s, when Stewart & Kincaid sought to remove a tenant who was seriously in arrears, the firm usually sought 'voluntary' surrender of land rather than opting for formal legal procedures. This saved Stewart & Kincaid time and money and averted bad publicity. Tenants in difficulties who 'voluntarily' surrendered their holdings usually received compensation, for example part or the whole of their family's fares to America, and sometimes a contribution for clothing. Of course, such tenants knew that if they did not agree to surrender, then the landlord could probably remove them in time through the courts and execution of a decree; furthermore, because in such cases the landlord would have incurred trouble and legal costs, such tenants who refused to surrender could not expect to receive much financial compensation, if they were ultimately forced to leave an estate. Thus, 'voluntary' surrender, rather than the route toward an ejectment decree, was an alternative which could be deemed to have been simultaneously in the interests of both landlord and tenant. This observation must be qualified by noting the analogy that agreement to do something when one has a gun put to one's head is hardly voluntary in any accepted sense. Nevertheless, the chapters which follow cite examples in which the initiative to surrender land and seek compensation came entirely or mainly from the tenant.

Although rent collection was Stewart & Kincaid's primary function, the firm was also involved in other aspects of estate management. Programmes of 'squaring the land' (rationalisation in the structure of holdings), drainage, sub-soiling and road-building were among the most important of these tasks. They involved hire of surveyors and agriculturalists. Stewart & Kincaid had links with Templemoyle Agricultural Seminary in County Derry and the firm seems to have assisted in arranging enrolment of some of the sons of tenants at that college. Stewart & Kincaid's agriculturalists, who were paid from £50 to £60 a year each,[36] did not merely supervise infrastructural projects; they induced tenants to improve their husbandry. They usually urged them to grow clover in order to enhance the nitrogen content of the soil, and to plant turnips instead of potatoes. The correspondence includes many letters from agriculturalists requesting Stewart & Kincaid to arrange for supply of seed, fertiliser, and equipment such as turnip-sowing barrows.

The firm's management was correspondence-intensive. Historians have pointed to advances in transport in facilitating economic development in Ireland in the eighteenth and nineteenth centuries, but they have tended to overlook the role of the postal system. The following points are important.

First was the development of the mail coach system from 1789 onwards. In 1806 a travel-book writer observed that 'in the year 1801, there were but four mail-coaches in Ireland'; however, by the 1830s, just before the advent of railways heralded an end to the mail coaches, there were 28 routes on which they operated, some 40 coaches leaving Dublin every day.[37]

Second was the development of cross routes for the mail. With relatively few exceptions, in the early nineteenth century letters written in Ireland for delivery in Ireland passed through the General Post Office in Dublin. Bianconi first carried mail in 1815. The subsequent expansion of his passenger network led to many cross routes of postage, by which the sending of mail to Dublin for delivery in the provinces could be avoided.

Third was the cost, payable to a state monopoly (the Post Office), of having letters delivered. The two sets of developments mentioned above did *not* at first generally reduce the cost of postage; rather, *the opposite very often applied.* Irish postal rates were in Irish pence based on distances travelled in Irish miles. (Until 1826, 13 Irish pence equalled 12 British. The Irish mile equalled approximately 1¼ English miles.) In 1796 a single-sheet letter travelling over 80 miles within Ireland cost 6*d*, but in 1811 it cost 8*d*. The year 1814 brought major change under which the charge for a single sheet was calculated by the distance between post towns instead of adding the charges to and from Dublin. Under the new scheme, a single sheet cost 9*d.* for 65 to 95 miles, rising to 15*d.* for over 300 miles within Ireland. A letter of two sheets cost double, and so on. Hence, a letter of three sheets travelling over 300 miles within Ireland cost 45*d*. This was almost as much as it would have cost to hire a labourer for a week; however, given the State's monopoly in the mails, it would have been illegal to send such a person to deliver the letter. Subject to minor modifications, the revisions of 1814 applied until 1839.

Postal reform in 1839 was extensive. The uniform fourpenny post was introduced in December. It did not apply in cases in which the existing rate was under 4*d*. Also, the system of single, double and treble sheets was replaced by a weights scale. The uniform penny post began in January 1840: half an ounce prepaid to anywhere within the United Kingdom now cost a penny.

The firm of Stewart & Kincaid sent and/or received hundreds of letters weekly in the 1840s. If the postal rates of the 1830s had then applied, and if the volume of mail to and from the firm had been the same as it was in the 1840s, then Stewart & Kincaid's postal charges in the 1840s would have been equivalent to the cost of full-time employment of several unskilled workers. Stewart & Kincaid's business greatly expanded in the 1840s. The postal reforms of 1839–40 probably influenced this expansion. The cheaper postage also facilitated management of already existing agencies. Thus, cheaper information technology through postal reform may have been as important as recent advances in transport in explaining the growth of Stewart & Kincaid's business in the 1840s. But long-term forces, which involved steady decline in the middleman system of management of estates in Ireland, were also relevant.

5 STEWART & KINCAID NOT MERELY MANAGERS OF LAND

Stewart & Kincaid borrowed and lent money and acted as financial intermediary. The firm may have arranged a loan from the Dublin brewers Guinness to a business in England: in 1844 a London solicitor inquired of Kincaid whether 'Guinness will lend the £13,000 [old] Irish [currency] . . . at 4 per C.'[38] On at least one occasion Guinness borrowed from Stewart & Kincaid; on another occasion the borrowing was in the reverse direction. Such transactions are revealed in a letter of 19 October 1846, in which Guinness wrote to Stewart & Kincaid that 'on a former occasion we had the mutual advantage in your having some money for us. Now we write to say, that we could let you have 5 or 6000 for 3 or 4 months.'(sк) Stewart & Kincaid responded immediately: on 21 October, Guinness informed Stewart & Kincaid that the brewers 'can let you have £2000 . . . say 4 p. c. for 4 mo'. (sк)

The Stewart & Kincaid correspondence contains many references to efforts to raise large loans for clients, among whom was the Earl of Howth. Another client for whom Stewart & Kincaid tried to arrange such loans was the Roscommon landlord Daniel Ferrall, whose problems will be investigated in chapter 5. Stewart & Kincaid also granted some small loans from its own resources to Ferrall. In at least one case the firm was asked to lend to a client's son. Thus, at a time when Stewart & Kincaid's own resources must have been severely stretched owing to a dearth of rental incomes, on 12 August 1848 Lord Lorton requested a loan of £1,000 for his son Harman. In 1847–8, Stewart & Kincaid applied to the Board of Works for many loans under the Landed Property Improvement Act. Almost every landlord for whom Stewart & Kincaid managed affairs obtained one or more of such loans. This suggests, with long-term considerations (as well as short-term employment-creation) in mind, that Stewart & Kincaid urged its clients to seek those loans.

J. R. Stewart's cousin John Hamilton borrowed probably more under the Landed Property Improvement Act than any other proprietor among the firm's clients. The Stewart & Kincaid files for 1848 record loans of about £12,000 – probably about £1 million sterling in purchasing power at the beginning of the twenty-first century – for improvements on his Donegal estate.[39]

Stewart & Kincaid arranged insurances for several of its clients. For example, the correspondence contains letters on these topics pertaining to Lords Howth, Lorton and Powerscourt.[40] In one case, cited in chapter 5, a client could not complete an application form for life insurance because he could not remember his birth date. Sending the form to the firm, he requested Stewart & Kincaid to fill in the blank on this point. However, Stewart & Kincaid sometimes assisted on matters much more personal: as will be indicated later, Stewart & Kincaid tried to manage the consequences of the sexual activities of one client, and those of excess alcohol consumption by another.

In a few cases Stewart & Kincaid assisted in transfer of funds between America and Ireland. One communication on such transfers, written on 19 October 1846 by a person named James Ward, was addressed to 'Stuards and Kincade . . . Bankers' (sk). Ward wrote another letter to Stewart & Kincaid ten days later: 'I received a letter from my brother Francis Ward dated 28th of September stating that he paid the honerable Mr Packingham [Sir Richard Pakenham, Envoy Extraordinary to the US[41]] British Council . . . at Washingtom Sity DC . . . £20–12–10 to be paid to James Ward of Ardaghey Parrish. . . . Send the letter of credit to Mr Sleat in Company provential Banke monaghan for James Ward.' (sk) Francis Ward had paid the money to Pakenham, who sent a bank draft to Stewart & Kincaid who were being asked to use a letter of credit to transfer the money to the manager of the Provincial Bank in Monaghan town,[42] in favour of James Ward, brother of Francis in the US. It is interesting that the Wards thought that Stewart & Kincaid were bankers. The reason why Francis had paid the money to Pakenham was presumably because he was aware that Richard was a family relative of J. R. Stewart: Richard Pakenham was a cousin of the second Earl of Longford and Stewart was one of the Earl's grandsons.[43]

Before the famine, Stewart & Kincaid assisted in emigration to America of several tenants from estates under the firm's management. This was on a small scale compared with what was soon to come. The Stewart & Kincaid correspondence contains few hints about how emigrants fared in America. It does reveal details on the sad fate on one emigrant, Richard Sherlock (brother of the owner of an estate in Kildare). In the years before the famine, emigrants to America rarely returned to Ireland. Sherlock did visit Ireland, from Canada, in 1840, but the correspondence records this event only in passing. However, a letter from a young man who emigrated around 1840, from Westmeath, outlines some of his experiences during a visit to Ireland, and indicates some of his intentions for the future. The letter was written at Mullingar on 15 December 1843 by Christopher Cavanagh, and the cover was addressed to himself at Brooklyn, New York. But the content was to his 'Beloved Ellen', as follows:

> I am now in the midst of my family, with the green fields around me. . . . Neither the change of clime, nor the distance of space has caused the slightest alteration . . . in me since I left you in the land I love. . . . When I landed here . . . I was reminded

of the return of the prodigal in the Scriptures. . . . I am treated as a little God. . . . It is my intention to be out [to America] early [in 1844]. . . . My Mother . . . has my sisters . . . making linen shirts and knitting worsted socks of her own spinning for me. . . . They did not know of my engagements in America. . . . I have told them of the faithful one who resides there. . . . My occupation since I landed has been visiting my friends. . . . A tea party at one friend's house tonight, and a dancing party at another's tomorrow night. A ride through the country on one day, and a hare hunt on another.[44]

This author knows nothing more of young Cavanagh. The letter indicates that he came from a comfortable family in the Mullingar district, but Slater's *Directory* of 1846 mentions no Cavanagh under its listings for Mullingar. The letter suggests that Cavanagh came from outside the town. In the 1840s Stewart & Kincaid was agent on the lands of Edward Pakenham, Earl of Longford, to the north and east of Mullingar. It is conceivable that Cavanagh passed his early youth on Pakenham lands.

During the famine, Stewart & Kincaid organised several programmes of emigration. The Stewart & Kincaid partners felt that such schemes should have been implemented by government. Thus, on 28 July 1847 Stewart wrote to Kincaid: 'I see Lord John [Russell, the Prime Minister] will do little or nothing for emigration & with out-door relief Mullaghmore Estate [in County Sligo] will be a trying property' (in terms of the implications of out-door relief for taxation of local property) (sk). However, on the matter of organised programmes of emigration, the government remained virtually passive. Some of the programmes of emigration organised by Stewart & Kincaid during the famine years will be discussed in the chapters which follow.

The foregoing has reviewed Stewart & Kincaid's role as manager of client affairs. However, tenants of the firm's clients sometimes asked Stewart & Kincaid to intervene in the settlement of family disputes or in quarrels with neighbours. Such requests reflect the fact that the tenantry regarded Stewart and Kincaid as paternal figures.

Stewart & Kincaid dealt in substantial sums of money. It is therefore not surprising that the firm's correspondence contains allegations of misuse of funds by employees. A few of these claims, which may have reflected grudges by tenants, were against local agents. The correspondence also contains references to embezzlement at Leinster Street. Thus, in 1841 Margaret Ormsby wrote to Stewart & Kincaid in reference to 'the cause of my son Charles having left your office. . . . I hope to be able to discharge his debt to you. . . . It was only yesterday that I heard of an arrangement with the purchaser of Waltrim [Mrs Ormsby's house near Bray] to pay me. . . . You proposed to take the £541 by degrees. . . . I would venture to ask if any part of the sum could be rescinded on my settling the account at once'. Mrs Ormsby again wrote to Stewart & Kincaid a short time later: 'I . . . feel obliged by . . . your offered reduction of £100. . . . I hope in a few days to settle the account'.[45] By his mother becoming the real victim, Charles probably avoided prison.

6 AGENDA AND OMISSIONS

The Stewart & Kincaid correspondence is probably the largest single archive of its kind on the decade of the Great Famine. W. A. Maguire's study on the Downshire estates is unique in its detailed focus on the management of a specific set of rural properties in pre-famine decades.[46] One reason why so little has been published on estate management in Ireland before 1850 is that until J. R. Stewart & Son(s)closed down, the existence of the Stewart & Kincaid correspondence was unknown to historians. In November 2000 James S. Donnelly, Jr. informed me that he had 'knocked on the doors of J. R. Stewart and Sons / Stewart and Kincaid in the late 1960s' but he was 'dismissed without even discovering what kinds of records the firm actually had'.[47]

Several decades ago John Pomfret wrote, in reference to Ireland between 1800 and 1850, that 'the landlords as a class were alien and absentee, and had little interest either in the welfare of the peasants or in improvement of their property'.[48] These views are still widely held in Ireland today, though probably not to the same relative extent by historians. But the single major study hitherto published (that of Maguire) on estate management in Ireland before the famine indicates that the third Marquess of Downshire was an improving landlord.[49] And as will soon be seen, the Stewart & Kincaid correspondence indicates that Stewart & Kincaid, as well as most of the firm's clients, were committed to major improvements in the 1840s; furthermore, some of those proprietors were surprisingly charitable towards their tenantry.

The chapters which follow examine estates managed in the 1840s by Stewart & Kincaid in twelve counties. In at least five of them Stewart & Kincaid managed the lands of more than one proprietor. The choice of estates to be investigated in detail reflects the fact that the correspondence includes a sufficient amount of material to create a broad picture of what was happening on those lands in the 1840s. However, during the same decade Stewart & Kincaid had important clients whose affairs will not be discussed in subsequent chapters. The reason for their exclusion is that in such cases the letters which survive fail to yield a clear indication of developments on their estates, considered individually, in the 1840s. But the impression emerging from the material on the estates which are not individually investigated in later chapters is that, taken as a group, developments on such lands were similar to those on the estates which are investigated in detail. The following observations on some Stewart & Kincaid clients, which are excluded from further investigation, can be made.

'The Recklessly Generous Landlord'[50] John Hamilton of Donegal was one of Stewart & Kincaid's clients. As Dermot James has indicated, it can be argued that Hamilton 'probably did more for his tenants . . . than any other landlord before, during and after the Famine'.[51] Although Hamilton's son James was employed at the Stewart & Kincaid office at some stage in the 1840s in order to learn more about estate management, only a small amount of documentation on Hamilton's estate could be found among the Stewart & Kincaid files. This reflects the fact that Hamilton's estate was managed almost entirely by himself.

The material on Viscount De Vesci of Abbeyleix in Queen's County contains a few letters referring to his properties in County Dublin and in County Cork, to his annual subscriptions to the Horticultural Society in London and to a benevolent institution in Cork. A letter of 1846 indicates that De Vesci provided meal for his tenants at an early stage during the famine. Kincaid wrote to Stewart: 'Lord De Vesci did write to us to allow Mr Lyster [of Cork City?] to draw on us for a sum due for Indian meal. . . . Pay the amount'.[52]

The Viscounts Powerscourt owned about 45,000 statute acres in Wicklow and Tyrone. In 1848 William Wingfield and the Earl of Roden, as guardians to the young Powerscourt, obtained a loan of £1,800 under the Landed Property Improvement Act, for the Tyrone estate.[53] The Powerscourts resided at Enniskerry in Wicklow. A letter of 26 March 1846, written to Kincaid by John Collum of the 'Dublin Dundrum and Enniskerry Railway', concerns a branch of the proposed line crossing Palmerston lands which, Collum argued, would be enhanced in value by the railway. (sĸ) The line to Enniskerry was never laid down. However, the proposed terminus at Enniskerry may have reflected use of influence by the Powerscourts. If this was the case, it probably would not have been the first time that they used influence in order to obtain improved communications to the family's residence.[54]

The Lorton file refers to subscriptions to the Queen's County Protestant Orphan Society and to the Royal Agricultural Improvement Society of Ireland. It also includes letters of 1843–5 from Mrs Renetta Murphy at a school in London: each of these concerns a quarterly pension of £3 15s. 0d. which Stewart & Kincaid sent to her on Lorton's behalf.

A Dr O'Grady was associated with the dispensary at Swords in County Dublin, one of the subscribers to which was Sir Thomas Staples, a client of Stewart & Kincaid. Staples owned land in the district, where distress was acute during the winter of 1842–3. A letter dated 20 January 1843, to Staples from Robert Bowden of Swords, reported and solicited:

100 unemployed labourers of Swords . . . presented a Memorial . . . to the landowners . . . requesting relief. . . . Nearly 70 men were allotted to various landowners,
to provide employment. . . . A great number of men still remaining for relief, the
following resolutions were agreed to: . . . That, in order to afford those whose
circumstances do not admit of their giving employment, an opportunity to assist
us in providing it for the labourers, a subscription list be opened, to create a fund to
employ a number of men in cleaning the town & making footpaths. . . . Resolved
that Messrs. Bowden, Brangan and O'Neill[55] be requested . . . to solicit contributions. . . . About 20 men have in consequence been employed by the Committee to
take down the hill called Bellrace. (s κ)

Patrick Bowden, who was probably related to the person who wrote the above
letter, was in trouble in 1846 when, on 8 July, he wrote to Stewart & Kincaid
that he was 'under Dr O'Grady's care' and that the 'total loss of my potato crop
was much against me this year'. Given that the potato failure in the autumn of
1846 was worse than in 1845, it is likely that Bowden's position deteriorated
further in the months ahead. A letter from the Board of Works during the
summer of 1848 indicates that although Staples sought a loan of £600 for
improvements on his lands near Swords, only £300 was approved.[56]

The lands of Jane Coleman, who resided in England, were in the Kilcullen
district of Kildare. Some of her tenants were in difficulty in the autumn of 1844
when they pleaded with Stewart & Kincaid: 'We have been noticed [to meet
a representative of Stewart & Kincaid] for the rent. . . . If . . . yous would
forbear a month longer it would . . . be a great acquition [acquisition] to the
tenantry for if the[y] be compelled to sell the corn at this time they will sustain
a great loss as markets . . . is remarkably bad and the people thinks the[y] can
not remain so much longer.' In the same hand, this letter was signed in the
names of four tenants.[57] Stewart entered on it the manuscript instruction:
'These may be put off for a few weeks'.

John Burtchell was perhaps the most prosperous of Miss Coleman's
tenants. On 20 June 1846 he wrote to Stewart & Kincaid as secretary of the
recently established relief committee at Kilcullen:[58] 'It was resolved that [I]
should solicit subscriptions from the landlords and gentry of the neighbourhood to enable the committee to purchase . . . meal to sell to the poor
deserving labourer at first cost price, & to distribute gratuitously to those who
are totally destitute and for whom there is no room at the work house' (s κ).
Burtchell requested Stewart & Kincaid to send a copy of this resolution to
Miss Coleman, who had 'subscribed on former occasions'.

Jane Coleman was a subscriber to the Irish Trinitarian Bible Society, the
objectives of which included 'salvation . . . by circulating . . . Holy Scriptures'.[59]
She was benevolent. Her donations to relieve famine distress in the Dingle

district during 1842 have already been mentioned. There is no evidence that she owned property near Dingle. A letter dated 14 June 1842 from the Rev. Sherrard of Old Kilcullen Glebe, to Stewart & Kincaid 'for the Misses Coleman', refers to destitution in his own district (s k). Sherrard was then treasurer of the relief committee at Kilcullen, and he sought a contribution from the Colemans in order to abate distress.

Letters from Sherrard to Stewart & Kincaid, 14 December 1842 and 12 December 1843, refer to Jane Coleman's subscriptions to the fever hospital at Kilcullen. Another letter to Stewart & Kincaid from the same writer, 21 December 1846, refers to her 'liberal donation of five pounds in addition to her annual subscription' to the hospital. A letter from Dr William Shaw, 17 March 1846, refers to her annual subscription to the Dunlavin Dispensary (a few miles to the south of Kilcullen), while a further communication from Sherrard, 7 December 1848, confirms receipt of a donation from Miss Coleman to the Kilcullen Dispensary. In 1846 she contributed £3 towards rebuilding a school.[60]

Jane Coleman left management of her affairs largely to Stewart & Kincaid's discretion. The Stewart & Kincaid correspondence indicates no threats of ejectment from her lands; but note that the sample of letters which refer to her property is relatively small. A similar observation applies to letters about other estates, not discussed in detail in this book, for which Stewart & Kincaid were agents.

Why do the letters contain a great deal of material on some of the estates managed by Stewart & Kincaid in the 1840s but very little on others? An answer must surely lie in the probability that some files were consigned to the families or descendants of proprietors after Stewart & Kincaid (or the firm's successors) ceased to be their agents, and the firm itself may have destroyed files on extinct agencies. One would expect that in such cases only stray items would remain in the present archive. Note also that when Joseph Kincaid's son severed his connection with Stewart & Kincaid in order to set up a rival agency, he took some of the Stewart & Kincaid business (including that of Palmerston's heirs) with him.[61] He may have left only stray items on some of those agencies behind. It is known, shortly after Messrs Stewart & Son ceased operations in the 1980s, that some De Vesci material was consigned to the Pakenham residence, Tullynally Castle in Westmeath; that this material was transferred by the Pakenhams to the De Vescis of Abbeyleix; that those De Vesci files may have been acquired by the National Library of Ireland since that family sold its Abbeyleix property and moved residence to England; that Pakenham material was also consigned to Tullynally Castle around the time at which the De Vesci documents were brought there and, finally, that some of the Pakenham files, previously in the possession of Messrs Stewart & Son, were stolen from Tullynally in recent years.[62]

Other sources of omission should be noted. The chapters which follow rely mainly on the Stewart & Kincaid correspondence in my possession, but although these are comprehensive up to and including 1846, they are relatively sparse for 1847–9. This has led me to suspect that *either* the letters for those years went astray after Messrs Stewart & Son closed down *or* (as I thought more likely) Stewart & Kincaid were so overwhelmed with work in those years that they failed to keep good records of incoming or outgoing correspondence. The latter view is reinforced by the fact that the correspondence for 1847–8 was often filed by Stewart & Kincaid only by year rather than (as was earlier the case) by exact date; furthermore, several letters of 1847 were filed as having been written in 1848 and vice versa.

This same view was confirmed when I consulted the archives at Tullynally Castle. The Pakenham archive contains 253 similar volumes (a complete run from 1841 to 1946) containing copies of Stewart & Kincaid's, or Messrs Stewarts', outgoing letters to or on behalf of clients.[63] The earliest of these volumes spans 1841 to 1852. Most of those early copies are not now legible. However, the dates of those copies are very revealing: The earliest letter-book (1841–52) contains about 1,500 pages, the first 600 of which pertain to 1841–6, inclusive, while the remaining 900 pages pertain to 1851–2. Thus, it seems that the firm of Stewart & Kincaid did not usually make copies of its outgoing mail in the late 1840s. The Pakenham archive also contains a couple of hundred original letters, addressed to Stewart & Kincaid and dated 1841–6, pertaining to the Pakenham estates;[64] however, in that archive I could detect no such letters dated 1847 and only one for each of 1848 and 1849.

The Broadlands (Palmerston) papers at Southampton contain some important information on Stewart & Kincaid's activities in the 1840s which would otherwise be missing; these papers have been incorporated in the present research.

Finally on the matter of omissions, it seems that practically all detailed account books of the 1840s, on the estates to be investigated, have been destroyed by now. Only three of such account books, to which reference will be made later, were found.

TWO

PALMERSTON IN SLIGO
IN THE EARLY 1840s

—

I BACKGROUND

The links between Sligo (see maps 1 to 3) and the Palmerstons go back to the seventeenth century, when Sir John Temple was granted most of the parish of Ahamlish in north Sligo, part of Sligo town and land in Dublin. In the 1840s these properties were owned by Henry Temple, third Viscount Palmerston (1784–1865), who also had estates in England. He was British foreign secretary for most of the 1830s (until 1841) and from 1846 to 1851. A Whig, he became prime minister in 1855. In 1840, rent receipts from his Dublin properties came to over £5,000 while those from the more than 10,000 acres which he owned in Sligo also exceeded £5,000.[1] In regard to Palmerston's possessions, the primary focus in the Stewart & Kincaid files is on Ahamlish (population 8,720 in 1841) which contained only 73 Protestants in 1834.[2] Palmerston first visited that estate in 1808, 'bringing the dawn of a new era, which was to change completely the face of the land'.[3] He found a destitute tenantry renting small plots from middlemen, who set the land to tenants in *rundale*, a system of communal occupation under which an individual tenant might from time to time hold many tiny detached plots. In the early nineteenth century huge tracts of Ahamlish were destroyed by shifting sands, but Palmerston sought to bring the bogs there, as well as the lands ruined by sand, into cultivation. He also saw potential for a town to be built at Mullaghmore near the coastal centre of the estate. Up to the mid-1820s, Palmerston probably spent a few thousand pounds on improvements in Ahamlish, but he then contemplated spending at least £11,000 more on harbour and associated projects, and a similar sum spread over 22 years on land development. The expenditures of the early years were financed from rental income. But from 1826 onwards he obtained government grants of at least £5,000 and also raised considerable sums by borrowing.[4]

When some of the leases of middlemen expired in 1837, Palmerston abolished the old system of middlemen and rundale on the lands in question, and

26

set about rationalisation of landholding – 'squaring the land'. Roads and houses were built around the same time. The new roads were necessary for access to newly squared holdings. A map of Palmerston's north Sligo properties, dated 1826, suggests that there were then only four roads in Ahamlish: the coastal (mail coach) road from Sligo to Ballyshannon, the interior 'mountain road' from Sligo to Ballyshannon which ran parallel to the latter, and a road ᵗ each end of the parish linking the coastal and mountain roads.[5] Thus, the consisted of a rectangle which enclosed the core of the parish. The ᵗ of many side roads, which was mainly in the 1840s, led to a squared ds within the main roads rectangle. To stabilise the shifting sands, ntroduced a strong grass called bent. By the late 1820s he had eds of acres under it. Referring to Palmerston's 'retention of the he sea-bent', in 1854 Fraser observed that 'this has been by far ve . . . experiment of the kind yet undertaken' in Ireland.[6] In ed a plant nursery at Cliffoney. As early as August 1831, Kincaid informed Palmerston that it was the finest he had seen in Ireland.[7] A newspaper advertisement of 1832 announced 'Forest trees to be sold on Lord Palmerston's Nursery', listed an inventory of 182,000 trees, and added 'Orders to John Lynch, Rundle Cottage', Cliffoney.[8] Lynch was Palmerston's agriculturalist and agent in Ahamlish. An advertisement of 1833 indicated that about 300,000 young trees were for sale at the nursery.[9]

McGowan remarks that examination of Palmerston records (the Broadlands archive housed at the University of Southampton) would yield an impression of 'an era of landlord-tenant harmony and bliss. . . . No perusal of [such] records gives any indication of the condition of the people at any time.'[10] However, the *Poor Inquiry* of 1836 highlighted the poverty of the masses in north Sligo, and their extreme dependence on the potato.[11] The Stewart & Kincaid correspondence provides many new insights. According to McGowan, Palmerston was prejudiced against Catholics. He had built two schools, one for boys, one for girls, at Cliffoney by 1826. However, the Rev. McHugh, PP of Ahamlish, 1826–36, ordered his parishioners not to attend them until Catholic teachers were appointed. Palmerston yielded to this demand.[12] The evidence from the 1840s is not consistent with a view that Palmerston discriminated against Catholics. According to Lewis in 1837, 'three schools [in Ahamlish] are supported . . . by his lordship'.[13] A publication of 1845 reported that '6 schools [on mainland Ahamlish] had on their books 285 boys and 175 girls. Three of the teachers had each a house and garden, and respectively £15, £21 and £25 a year, from Lord Palmerston'.[14] Thus, by 1840, there were three schools in Ahamlish which were funded by Palmerston, each had male and female divisions, and the remuneration mentioned pertained to the head teachers. In 1811 Palmerston made a donation for erection of the Church of Ireland place of worship in Ahamlish cemetery between Cliffoney and Grange. But he did not neglect the ecclesiastical needs of Catholics. Around 1830 he financed the building of the Catholic church at Cliffoney. Also the parochial house, still in use, was granted by Palmerston to McHugh, and 'Palmerston and Fr. Malachi Brennan [McHugh's successor] became firm friends'.[15]

The greatest engineering achievement on Ahamlish was Mullaghmore harbour, on which work commenced in 1822 under the direction of Alexander Nimmo. In 1826 Nimmo also designed extensions to Cliffoney Inn (now a public house) where Palmerston was to stay during his visits to Ahamlish. In regard to the harbour, the original intention was to build a single pier, but about a decade after this was completed in 1827, Palmerston decided to build another, thereby creating the haven almost as it is today. In 1841 he wrote that 'my harbour . . . will be about 800 feet long and 300 wide'.[16] He sought to develop the commercial potential of Mullaghmore. In 1828 he drafted a newspaper advertisement for Mullaghmore as a trading centre, and in 1829 he considered the possibility of establishing a steam boat service between Liverpool and Mullaghmore.[17] He set up a corn store there in 1833.

An American historian wrote in 2001: 'Given the tremendous detail with which historians have scrutinised Palmerston's long career (a recently published Palmerston bibliography fills more than 300 pages), it is surprising that no detailed account of either Palmerston's Irish estate during the famine or of his emigration scheme has ever been written.' As has been indicated elsewhere, the final word in this extract should have been 'published' rather than 'written'.[18]

The administrative structure for Palmerston's Sligo estates in the early 1840s was as follows. In Dublin, Stewart & Kincaid had ultimate accountability, and James Walker was in charge of Palmerston business in both Sligo town and county. John Lynch, a Catholic who had once been employed by Lord Howth, was resident agent in Ahamlish where he arrived in 1828. His home, Rundle (Rundale) Cottage, was about half a mile outside Cliffoney. (His immediate neighbour was the Rev. Malachi Brennan in the comfortable structure which Palmerston financed.) Walker was superior in status to Lynch. From time to time the Stewart & Kincaid employee Stewart Maxwell visited Ahamlish in order to reinforce Walker's efforts to extract rent. Stevenson & Sons of Edinburgh had ultimate responsibility for the major harbour works at Mullaghmore. Their engineer in charge there was the Scotsman, William Middlemiss.

Palmerston's estates passed to his wife after his death, and then to her second son (by her first marriage) William Cowper Temple, and thence to Evelyn Ashley in 1888, who bequeathed the properties to his only son Wilfrid.[19] In 1922 Wilfrid's daughter Edwina married Lord Louis Mountbatten. Wilfrid died in 1939 leaving Edwina, amongst other assets, Broadlands House near

Southampton (which had been Palmerston's principal residence) and Classiebawn Castle at Mullaghmore.[20] It was while on holiday at Classiebawn that Lord Mountbatten was murdered in 1979. In fact, it was on board a boat at the mouth of Mullaghmore harbour that the bomb which killed him exploded.

2 ENLARGING MULLAGHMORE HARBOUR

Work on the new pier at Mullaghmore began in 1838. A letter dated 24 August 1843 from Lynch to Kincaid indicates that, excluding masonry work and stone, over £2,360 had been spent there since August 1838 on materials and on carpentry. Kincaid sent a copy of this letter to Palmerston, who responded to Lynch: 'Now that the harbour is finished all but excavation, I wish you to confine the whole expense of every kind to be incurred through you to twenty pounds a week. . . . Order no more iron or timber . . . without first writing to me, to say how much is wanted and why.' He also wished 'to know what has become of the enormous quantity of iron and timber which has been charged for' in bills to him from the Sligo merchant Thomas Kernaghan.[21] Much of the iron came from Scotland. Ahamlish itself was unable to provide the timber: in 1837 its surface had been described as 'naked and unadorned, having only one small wood'.[22]

Masonry work at the harbour was conducted largely under tender. This led to Middlemiss being accused of abuse in awarding contracts. In absolving himself of any guilt, he provided evidence of relevant tenders.[23] In regard to other charges, on 10 July 1842 Walker wrote to Stewart & Kincaid that two men 'made allegations of frauds, but not until they were removed from the works'. One of these men was a blacksmith who had been dismissed because another smith was prepared to complete specific tasks for a lower payment.[24] There were also accusations that Hugh Gilmartin's house at the harbour had been built by Palmerston's masons using Palmerston's materials. But Gilmartin produced receipts from Kernaghan and swore that he paid the masons using his own money.[25] Cash was the normal mode of payment at the harbour; however, according to Lynch, some of the men, who 'got dockets for rent', forged them, 'making 16 shillings of 6s'.[26]

The harbour works were closely monitored. Middlemiss sent regular reports to Stevensons and a monthly report to Stewart & Kincaid. But Palmerston did not leave matters to the discretion of agents. In 1841 he inspected the harbour works. After his return to Broadlands, he instructed Lynch: 'Employ the men always by the piece work for everything which is susceptible of being so paid for', but if they sought too much, Lynch was told to declare: 'There is the work to be done, and this is the price which by Lord Palmerston's directions I am authorised to give you for it. If you do not like to do the work, for that price, leave it alone.'[27] Thus, Palmerston was telling Lynch to offer work at piece-rates on a take-it-or-leave-it basis.

In mid-1842 Palmerston wrote to Middlemiss: 'If the bar which has formed at the entrance of the harbour increases, it will be well to remove it. Otherwise it will accumulate rapidly and form a dangerous obstacle.'[28] On 8 November, Stevensons sent Kincaid a report of their 'last visit to Mullaghmore harbour the works of which may now be said to be completed' (SK). But on 20 November, Palmerston instructed Middlemiss to add height to the protecting wall of the old pier so as to 'keep out the wash'. He added: 'Perhaps if you can remove by dredging . . . all the stones which have accumulated at the head of the old pier, and sink the bottom down to the same level as outside the mouth of the harbour, the sand will not settle there in future.' (SK)

In December 1843 Kincaid told the Devon Commission that about £15,000 had hitherto been spent on Mullaghmore harbour works.[29] Presumably following pressure from Palmerston, Stewart & Kincaid had earlier asked Stevensons for their views regarding the expenditure on the harbour works on the supposition that the whole had been done by contract. Stevensons responded to Stewart & Kincaid: 'We have not got the means of making a comparison. . . . We do not think that we would get a correct result by applying the prices now paid for contract work to the whole work done.' This was because 'until the men were somewhat *schooled* into the work we do not think that they could have taken it by contract at all, and if they could, certainly not at the price for which they would undertake it after the experience of such works as they now have had.'[30] This passage reveals the notion which economists call 'learning by doing'. Thus, the harbour works enhanced skills which facilitated further improvements in Ahamlish.

Palmerston did not finance the entire cost of the new harbour. On 27 August 1841 the Board of Works indicated its willingness to pay Stewart & Kincaid a sum of £500, the first instalment of a grant of £1,000 sanctioned by the Treasury. On 20 January 1843 Stewart & Kincaid wrote to the Board requesting payment of the remaining £500. But on 2 February the Board informed Stewart & Kincaid that the interior excavation was poor, and that the remainder of the grant money should not be paid until it was satisfactory. On 3 March, Middlemiss wrote to Palmerston proposing that 'from 80 to 100 men be actively employed at night and day' excavating the entrance, and on 22 March he informed Palmerston of success 'in deepening the boat channel and bar at the mouth . . . by which the boats may now go out and in, without any inconvenience'.[31] Late in March the Board made payment of £300 from the balance of £500; the remainder of the grant was paid in 1844.[32] But a problem of silting persisted. On 30 January 1846 Lynch indicated to Stewart & Kincaid that a recent storm 'increased the shingle in the mouth of the harbour and sand in the basin'. This problem was ultimately addressed by opening a gap through the new pier, thereby creating a scouring action which made the harbour less prone to silting: in 1853 Palmerston instructed that such alterations be affected.[33] By then, Mullaghmore had become the finest port in the northwest of Ireland. But absence of a railway impeded its development.

3 THE TOWN OF MULLAGHMORE, AND MILK HARBOUR

The map of Ahamlish dated 1826 does not indicate any village at Mullaghmore; however, maps of 1822 and 1825 indicate that there were then a few fishermen's cabins near the site of the first pier.[34] With one of the best man-made harbours in Ireland, Palmerston aspired to develop Mullaghmore into one of the more important places in the northwest. He intended that the corn store would become a centre for export of grain. On 7 September 1841 Middlemiss reported to Stewart & Kincaid: 'Kernaghan's vessel called the Sarah having discharged her cargo of timber from America . . . gives a lively businesslike appearance to Mullaghmore harbour'; also, 'the vessel called the Margt. left this harbour the other day with a cargo of oats from the store' (SK).

The corn store may have been successful in the late 1830s: a letter from Lynch to Edward Kelly, who rented it from Palmerston, records that between 2 October 1838 and 13 August 1839 some 322 tons weight had been bought into the store.[35] But it did not for long yield a buzz of activity. On 25 January 1841 Walker wrote to Stewart & Kincaid that the 'people are making meal of their grain and not bringing it to the store' (SK). On 8 November he reported that Kelly would 'not have more to do' with it (SK). On 5 September 1842 Thomas Kernaghan's son William wrote to Walker that his father did not wish to take the store, 'this trade paying so badly for the last two years'. Two days later, Walker forwarded the letter to Kincaid, stating: 'I was in hope of this mans taking the corn store. . . . He would be the best person to make something of trade at the harbour' (SK). On 22 November 1843 Walker informed Stewart & Kincaid that Kelly stated that there was not enough corn in the district for him to rent the store. Thus, the corn trade at Mullaghmore had declined before the famine. The *Valuation* of 1858 lists the store as unoccupied.[36] The full reasons for its poor performance in the 1840s are unclear. Publicity of allegations of theft did not help. An anonymous letter to Palmerston in 1836 alleged that Hugh Gilmartin had stolen oats from the store.[37] There were thefts in 1839 but they did not come to Stewart & Kincaid's attention until 1842, when Walker wrote that Kelly estimated his losses from the thefts of 1839 at 'from 20 to 30 tons'.[38] The writer of a letter to Palmerston dated 19 January 1843, found in the Stewart & Kincaid files, claimed that in 1839 he saw bags of oats, which had been stolen from the store, emptied 'in the front room' of Hugh Gilmartin's. But complaints of theft against the Gilmartins, who were the most prosperous residents at Mullaghmore, may merely reflect grudges against them.

By the late 1830s progress had been made into developing Mullaghmore as a leisure centre. Late in the nineteenth century there was a row of holiday apartments, rented to the well to do, facing the harbour. One of the first was built by the 1830s and was owned by, or was rented from Palmerston by, Hugh Gilmartin, who in the 1840s resided next to Pier Head House at the entrance to the old pier. The Gilmartins rented Pier Head House from Palmerston.[39] On 13 July 1841 Walker wrote to Stewart & Kincaid: 'Mrs Gilmartin who is the great building speculator of Mullaghmore wants warm baths attached to the Pier Head House' (sk). She sought a contribution of £30 from Palmerston towards the costs. These proposed baths were not built. Middlemiss had been a lodger to Mrs Gilmartin until he left in 1843; his rooms were then taken by Dr Tuthill, who was in charge of Palmerston's Ahamlish Dispensary.

Major house-building programmes were not implemented at Mullaghmore in the early 1840s: first, the land there had to be squared, and second, the harbour works deflected labour until 1843–4. But before he left, Middlemiss prepared projections. On 29 September 1842 he sent Stewart & Kincaid drawings of 'houses, baths, stables and coach houses [the latter built in 1843], also the plan of the town of Mullaghmore, accompanied by a letter to his Lordship, regarding these drawings' (sk). In regard to access to the new town, until the 1840s there was no road directly from Cliffoney into Mullaghmore. But in May 1843 Middlemiss wrote to Kincaid that he was making drawings of such a road for Lynch, who intended to present them to the Grand Jury (a unit of local government which levied taxes on property owners to finance improvements). On 11 January 1845 he wrote from Scotland to Kincaid that 'as the new road is now made into Mullaghmore' he was sure that 'you will make it an excellent watering place and pleasant resort' (sk). A letter of 1848 indicates leisure activities there. Thus Edward Smyth, who had replaced Walker, wrote to Stewart & Kincaid on 26 August: 'I suppose I may put your names down for a trifle [of money] for our [sailing and rowing] Regatta [at Mullaghmore], and [also] his Lordship.' (sk)

Improvements at Bunduff marsh near Mullaghmore and at Milk Harbour also absorbed some of the time of Middlemiss early in 1843. On 16 December 1842 he wrote to Kincaid that the marsh at Bunduff was 'constantly inundated' (sk). On 6 March 1843 he sent Kincaid a report indicating methods of draining it. On 8 March, Stevensons informed Kincaid that they had arranged for Middlemiss to take charge of lighthouse works in Scotland. But one more task awaited him before he could leave, namely that pertaining to Milk Harbour between Cliffoney and Grange. The lagoon leading to it is like a sideways U, but the entrance channel was treacherous. On 3 March 1843 Lynch informed Kincaid that 'there was a boat about coming in at the bar at Milkharbour about a month ago and six men drowned and the same number was drowned last year at the same place' (SK). Palmerston was already concerned about these tragedies. At the end of February 1843 he invited Middlemiss to indicate how 'the channel in & out would be rendered more secure', adding that it might be possible to mark out the channel by perches fixed into the sand.[40] On 22 March, Middlemiss wrote to Palmerston recommending removal of dangerous obstructions near the bar, and on the next day he suggested to Palmerston that one floating buoy be moored on each side of the channel, 'and by the boatmen being instructed to steer between these buoys', the entrance to the lagoon could be rendered safe.[41] Palmerston responded on 27 March, telling Middlemiss to go ahead with clearance of the bar and to place buoys if they were not expensive. However, on 8 April, Middlemiss informed him that a cheap alternative was that '2 small towers of common rubble masonry be built' near the entrance to the lagoon; he proposed that these would serve as landmarks for guiding boats across the bar. Palmerston replied on 10 April: 'I thought the buoys would be too expensive. . . . Your plan for towers for land marks is better.'[42] One of those towers still exists.

Having accomplished a great deal over more than three years, Middlemiss left Ireland in May 1843. Based on his plans, work at the entrance to Milk Harbour lagoon, and on draining Bunduff marsh, was continued by Lynch. Thus, on 23 June 1843 Lynch wrote to Stewart & Kincaid: 'I have Lord Palmerston's directions to go to work at Milkhaven, and I wish to have a coppy of all the plans, to clear away the bar; I also wish to have a coppy of Mr Middlemiss report as to the deepening of the harbour at Mullaghmore, and the draining of Bunduff marsh, as Lord Palmerston wrote to me on each' (SK). Work at the entrance to Milk Harbour lagoon may have been completed before the famine. But Bunduff marsh was still in a poor state in the mid-1850s.[43]

Lynch's expenditures on improvements averaged over £1,000 per annum in the twelve years 1830–41.[44] These sums certainly exceeded 20 per cent of the gross rental income from the north Sligo estate.[45] (It is doubtful whether the average of £1,000 includes all outlays during those years on Mullaghmore harbour.) Given that he then deemed the work on Mullaghmore harbour as more or less complete, on 19 September 1843 Palmerston instructed Lynch to limit his expenditures on improvements to £20 per week. Although this sum was below the amounts spent by Palmerston on improvements in Ahamlish in the earlier 1840s, it implied that outlays on improvements there would continue to exceed 20 per cent of Palmerston's gross rental receipts from that part of County Sligo. Such a ratio was exceptionally high among progressive landlords in Ireland in the decades just before the famine: Maguire has indicated that a ratio of four per cent or five per cent was probably near the average among *conscientious* landlords in those years.[46]

4 SQUARING THE LAND

Some of Palmerston's townlands were outside Ahamlish in the contiguous parish of Drumcliffe towards Sligo town. About one third of his lands in north Sligo had been squared by mid-1842. Squaring was continued through-out the 1840s. On 27 January 1843 Lynch proposed to Kincaid that some townlands still under lease should be squared among the undertenants and perhaps also among landless cottiers. Noting that 'the weather is very severe', he ended his letter with the query as to whether Stewart & Kincaid should give blankets to the cottiers, adding that 'if you do you will be encouraging them to stay. . . . The very poor tenants and widows should be the people that ought to get them.' (SK) This passage reveals a dilemma which must often have been faced during squaring: a trade-off between compassion and efficiency.

The squaring of Ahamlish led to tensions. For example, on 3 January 1841 Michael Freel complained to Stewart & Kincaid that a tenant named Patt Feeny, who held many tiny and scattered plots, refused to move to the square assigned to him; this meant that the complainant could not move to his own allotment. He also stated that some tenants gave Feeny the 'cost to bring him to England to his Lordship', as their own allotments 'did not please them', and that Feeny intended to lament to Lady Palmerston 'by crying and roaring' (SK). On 25 January, Walker wrote to Stewart & Kincaid that he had heard that Feeny had gone to London, but he was sure that Palmerston would 'not attend to him' given that 'two others went to him, within these last 2 years, without any satisfactory result' (SK). On 14 March, Lynch informed Stewart & Kincaid that Feeny 'did not return yet. They are of opinion he is lost' (SK). Feeny did find his way back, but on 29 March, Lynch wrote to Stewart & Kincaid: 'He did not come out of his house since he came home, so this tells the remainder that he must get no encouragement from Lord Palmerston.' (SK)

Another tenant named Freel may have delivered a petition to Kincaid in Dublin in May 1841, regarding strife brought about by squaring. A petition of that month, from Bryan Freel, complained that his brother James refused to go to the square assigned to him, and that when the surveyor came to mark out Bryan's square, the surveyor 'was obstructed by Jas. Freel [who] beat petrs. wife'.[47] It seems that James Freel never accepted the square assigned to him: a letter from Bryan to Stewart & Kincaid in March 1844 indicates that James had gone to America (SK).

Many other examples of strife brought about by the squaring of Ahamlish could be cited. Some tenants were unhappy because they felt that their allocation was unfair. Also, squaring often meant that they had to pull down their cabins and build new houses. Others may have felt that they were too old to have their lives reshuffled. The case of Winifred Campbell, who resided on a tiny patch, is an example. On 9 October 1845 she requested Stewart & Kincaid to let her rest in peace, 'with three orphants, in this little spot', adding that her only means of support was 'by buying eggs & fish and carrying the eggs on her back into Ballyshannon, ten miles distance' (sk). On 15 July 1845 Walker wrote to Stewart & Kincaid that 'although there is not a man on the estate that would like to remove from his wigwam', the squaring of Ahamlish was going on as well as possible (sk).

The Mullaghmore district was squared in 1846. Over-ambitious plans by Middlemiss for expansion of the town conflicted with the existing population density. Palmerston's agents may therefore have discriminated more than usual in deciding who would get what. On 26 December 1845, Walker wrote to Stewart & Kincaid: 'The plans are all on too extensive a scale. . . . There is not a spot of land unoccupied to remove the Mullaghmore farmers. . . . I enclose you a paper I got from that quarter as to the character of persons who are seeking for allotments.' (sk) Written in an uneducated hand, the paper to which Walker referred contains a list of witnesses, of accused persons, and of charges such as 'turf stealing', 'robbing lines of fish at sea', 'tretning to dround' a man, and 'stealing bed cloas'. The extent to which Walker used this list in disqualifying some of the accused is unknown. However, the 1858 *Valuation* shows that, of the 20 accusers, 15 were occupying land at Mullaghmore, but, of the 25 accused, only 10 occupied land there.[48]

In the squaring of Mullaghmore, the fishermen were assigned sites at the top of the hill behind the town. Their houses were built in 1846. The landlord provided some materials and the fishermen themselves provided labour. Their houses were slated from Welsh quarries in which Palmerston was dominant shareholder.[49] It seems that fewer than 30 were built, many of which still exist today. Down the hill in the town, Lynch was worried about Mrs Gilmartin's plans. On 11 April 1846 he wrote to Kincaid that she wanted several plots near her existing two houses, and 'she says she will build on them' (sk). But it does not seem that Mrs Gilmartin obtained all of the land which she wanted: the *Valuation* of 1858 lists only three houses in the name of her husband. A view that his wife may have been over-optimistic would be supported by noting that two of them were then unoccupied.

Resettlement during the squaring of Mullaghmore brought complaints to Palmerston. A petition to him in December 1845, purporting to come from eighty tenants, complained that they were being moved to unsuitable plots, and that the best land had been given to fishermen, 'strange lawless cotters . . . robbing everything'.[50] Another complaint, from James Williamson in England, was dated 3 June 1846. It stated that Stewart & Kincaid wished to move his father to a decaying structure without compensation for costs incurred by him in rebuilding his present house. He asked Palmerston whether this was 'by your Lordships desire' and added: 'If so, I consider it cruel usage indeed to a tenant who is bordering on eighty years' (SK). Palmerston responded by writing on Williamson's letter: 'Old Williamson ought to be paid for that portion of his house which he built at his own expense'; he then sent the letter to Stewart & Kincaid.[51] It was forwarded to Walker who, on 21 June, informed Stewart & Kincaid that Williamson would be compensated for his work on his present house, and that he had been allotted about four acres with a cabin from which the existing tenant was willing to move, subject to a payment of £10 to enable that tenant to build elsewhere (SK).

Most of Palmerston's arable land in Ahamlish had been squared by the end of 1846. In April 1846 Lynch reported that Creevykeel had just been squared but that three of the tenants there refused to move to plots assigned.[52] Around the same time, squaring on Cloonerco was slowed down by a squabble between brother and sister. The problem was compounded by two broken marriages: one of the women there had married a man 'who left her from jealousy', and another interested party had 'abandoned his wife'.[53] Lynch therefore requested Kincaid to 'give your directions how it will be squared and who it will be given to'.[54]

For many years members of the prominent Sligo family of Wynne had held Inishmurray, about five miles off the Ahamlish coast, under lease from Palmerston. The squaring there was facilitated by surrender of the lease in 1845–6. Until the mid-1840s the islanders had maintained an independent life. On 14 April 1846 John Wynne provided Stewart & Kincaid with details of their lifestyle: '[They] make a considerable sum both of sea wrack [seaweed] & lobsters annually but the great evil is their habit of illicit distillation. . . . In making the new arrangements I beg to suggest . . . allowing the schoolmaster . . . ground near his house.' (SK) On 29 June, Lynch reported to Kincaid that Inishmurray had been squared (SK).

5 OTHER PRE-FAMINE LAND IMPROVEMENTS

One historian has referred to 'Palmerston's insistence on reserving to himself a close personal oversight of every aspect of life and work on his estates'.[55] Up to 1846, when he returned to government, he was not prepared merely to issue guidelines. He sent detailed instructions and demanded detailed reports. He acquired more than a layman's knowledge of civil engineering. His approach to agricultural improvements was similar. He had probably monitored developments in Ahamlish during the late 1820s as closely as he did in the early 1840s. A document of 1829 in his hand entitled 'Memoranda for Lynch' lists 52 sets of detailed instructions for work to be done in various parts of Ahamlish.[56]

In January 1842 Palmerston wrote to Lynch: 'I forgot whether your turnips are sown upon ridges, and drilled, they should be so'.[57] In February, Lynch informed Stewart & Kincaid: 'I had a letter from his Lordship . . . about planting Dernish [island]' and he added that Palmerston had provided 'proofs to show that trees would grow on it but in my mind some of his proofs is quite opposite'.[58] But Palmerston's proofs were apparently correct: on 31 August, Lynch reported to Stewart & Kincaid that 'the pine seed sown on the island is doing very well' (s k). In December, Palmerston wrote to Lynch:

> What became of the barley which I sent in the early part of the year to be sown. . . . How much grain did the crop produce. Keep that grain so produced and sow it again next year, by which means you will probably have enough to distribute among some of the most industrious . . . tenants. How are the young plants of the Pinus Maritima looking and which have thriven the best. . . . Have the [bent] grass seeds which you sowed in the spring come up . . . and where have they succeeded the best. . . . Have you received the acorns [sent by Palmerston from Southampton] . . . and is there any difference between them and the acorns which you have got this year in Ireland.[59]

Lynch sent Kincaid a summary of his reply. In this he mentions that he sent Palmerston 'a few grains of wheat he [Palmerston, had] sent over and a few of what I got sowed that he might see the difference of the quality'.[60]

Palmerston's plantations changed the bareness of Ahamlish. In 1843 Walker reported to Stewart & Kincaid that Lynch 'has now pine seed for the whole County of Sligo', but early in 1846 Palmerston informed Lynch that he was sending 5,000 Highland Pine, and in April, Palmerston further wrote to him that he was sending, in Lynch's words, 'seed of hardy trees growing on the Himmeleah Mountains'.[61]

Palmerston's tenants were expected to follow his example. In 1842 Lynch received 'the sheet with the new form of improvement in it'.[62] Such sheets were to go into a 'Book of Improvements' indicating the achievements of each tenant on squared land.[63] On 3 March 1843 Lynch wrote to Kincaid: 'I think the only way to stimulate them is: I proclaim among the tenants that Lord Palmerston desires to have this Improvement Book in order to see how they progress . . . and that if he does not see them making exertions for the improvement of their lands . . . he will not keep them on his estate.' (s k)

In conjunction with the squaring, the tenants were responsible for building their houses, often without financial help from Palmerston, and their boundary fences were created by their own labour. The grid of access roads, built by the tenants, was financed partly by Palmerston. Before closing on pre-famine physical improvements, brief mention is made of those at Cliffoney, where Palmerston stayed during his visits of 1841 and 1845. In each case he lodged at Mrs Corrigan's inn. Improvements at Cliffoney were gradual. A few letters refer to installation of a toilet closet at the inn in preparation for Palmerston's 1845 visit. The village had at least one shop window in that year (s κ).

6 RELIGION, EDUCATION AND PUBLIC HEALTH

It has already been noted that Palmerston treated the Rev. Malachi Brennan very well (see p. 28 above). But his Church of Ireland counterpart in the 1840s, John Greene, lived in poverty. His plight is indicated by a letter from him to Stewart & Kincaid dated 25 September 1845. He commenced by referring to the 'wretched garret dwelling' at the Cliffoney Inn, for which he annually paid £21 to Mrs Corrigan.[64] He could not afford to own a horse. Greene complained of Corrigan's 'refusals at times to let us have the few promised plates and knives for dinner, obliging us to borrow from others in the village what she is receiving payment for'. He stated that 'his Lordship's kindness' to Brennan gave him hope that Palmerston would enable him 'to enjoy a holding directly under himself'. He argued that there should be a glebe house near the centre of the parish at Cliffoney. He therefore asked for a site opposite the inn. He stated that he did not expect to obtain it under the same favourable terms through which Brennan held his land and house. But if denied it as a gift, he would 'be thankful for it for purchase', which request if granted would be followed by one from Greene to the Ecclesiastical Commissioners 'for the sum required by his Lordship, together with a sum for building a glebe on it'. He hoped that Palmerston would 'free this parish from among the few exceptions of a parish without a glebe'. Having signed the letter, he added further remarks on his landlady: 'During the last two winters, she has . . . forced Mrs Greene and me to take our meals as best we could in our bedroom', and obliged them 'to sit with the window open [to facilitate exit of smoke] during the severest winter days' while repeating a promise to install a chimney top (s κ). Palmerston and his wife were to stay at the same Cliffoney Inn, just a few weeks after the above-mentioned letter was written. This meant that Greene had to be shunted off to a temporary abode elsewhere.

As far back as 1811 Palmerston had indicated that he would 'concur on any arrangement about [a] glebe that may be considered satisfactory', but in 1822 the relevant bishop declined land offered for a glebe at Cliffoney, on the grounds that it was over two miles from the Church of Ireland structure in Ahamlish cemetery. In 1839 the then vicar of Ahamlish, Charles West, wrote to Palmerston asking for land for a glebe near the church.[65] Then came Greene, who wanted land where it had earlier been rejected by the church authorities. On 25 January 1841 Walker wrote to Stewart & Kincaid: 'I have not yet heard who is to be Mr Wests successor . . . The whole income is only £83 a year & that all paid by Ld. Palmerston. . . . There is no glebe. Ld. P ought to give 10 acres.' (sk) On 7 March 1845 Greene wrote to Stewart & Kincaid that Palmerston 'declines affording me any accommodation . . . where I most require it, in Cliffony' (sk). In May 1845 Palmerston did offer a ten acre site for a glebe, rent free, adjacent to Ahamlish cemetery at Moneygold, but Greene dismissed that location.[66] For various reasons, no glebe house was built in the 1840s.[67] The *Valuation* of 1858 lists 15 acres of glebe land at Moneygold; however, there was still no glebe house. It is therefore inferred that what was once the glebe house beside Ahamlish cemetery was built after 1858. In fact, correspondence of 1866 between Greene and William Cowper Temple (a successor to Palmerston) indicates that it was probably built in the late 1860s.[68] Greene's request for a site opposite Cliffoney Inn had been refused on the basis that 'where Mr Greene wished to place himself was intended as building ground'.[69] But the real reason was probably different: if Greene had been granted that site, he would have been located next to the Catholic church at Cliffoney. This would have lowered the relative status of the parish priest and might have brought the two religions into conflict.

Turning to education, around 1840 there were three schools on mainland Ahamlish, each with male and female sections, which were supported by Palmerston. There was then also a hedge school (typically one in rural districts which was not supervised or funded by landlord, religious institution or government). By the 1840s some of the schools which Palmerston had set up were supported by both Palmerston and the Board of National Education, but the teachers looked up to Palmerston rather than to the Board. Thus they regarded him as paternalistic. Mathias Leonard was the master at Cliffoney, and in 1842 one of his daughters was mistress in the girls' school there. On 14 February 1842 he wrote to Kincaid confirming receipt of books for the school and indicating that he had received a communication from Palmerston on the same subject (sk). On 25 August he wrote to Palmerston about the school-mistress: 'My daughter has got married . . . to a young man who holds a situation . . . at Southampton. I never intended to dispose of her . . . without first obtaining your . . . permission, but he, doing business at Mullaghmore Harbour, gave me only a few hours to decide.' However, Leonard stipulated 'that she should not leave me' until a replacement was appointed.[70] She was

succeeded by Susan Tomlinson, a young Catholic who was paid £8 annually
by the Education Board.[71] On 9 February 1843 Lynch complained to Stewart
& Kincaid that there were only 44 books at the girls' school, 'which is no use
for the great number', and he enclosed a list of what was needed. He indicated
that Ms Tomlinson had arrived and was staying with the Lynchs as he had not
yet furnished her house. On 3 March, Lynch wrote to Kincaid that 'the
mistress can do very little good without the books as the school has increased
up to 176' (s k). Dressmaking was one of the subjects taught: on 11 March 1845
Ms Tomlinson requested Stewart & Kincaid to send calico for chemises,
flannel for petticoats, tape for frocks and bibs, and needles (s k).

Inland from Grange, the Benbulben schoolhouse was erected by Palmerston
*c.*1844. Its two wings were for boys and girls separately; the central portion was
the residence of Edward Ceillier, the first master. On 11 August 1845 Ceillier
wrote to Stewart & Kincaid to ask them to send books as the male school had
just been furnished. Palmerston visited the school a short time later.[72] A letter
from Ceillier dated 17 November 1845 indicates that the girls' teacher wanted
Stewart & Kincaid to send books on subjects such as spelling and geography
(s k). As at Cliffoney, prizes financed by Palmerston were awarded to the top
scholars. A hedge schoolmaster, and the master at the national school in
Grange (not on Palmerston's land) probably envied the teachers in the schools
patronised by Palmerston. On 9 October 1841 19 Palmerston tenants near
Grange wrote to Kincaid stating that a hedge schoolmaster named Giblin had
brought their children 'from darkness to light'. They requested of Kincaid 'a
set of books for the use of his school' (s k). But it is unlikely that Stewart &
Kincaid assisted him, as on 24 December 1842 Lynch informed Kincaid that
'the Head Constable called on me to know if I had any writing of Giblin's
the school master', whom he suspected of writing a threatening letter 'to a
school master named McGowan, and he would wish to see some of his
writing' (s k). The addressee of the threat was probably Terence McGowan,
master at the national school in Grange, who went to Stewart & Kincaid
in Dublin late in 1844 hoping to obtain the forthcoming appointment at
Palmerston's Benbulben school.[73]

On the question of public health, it seems that Palmerston financed
the training of a midwife for duty in Ahamlish: a letter from Lynch to Kincaid
in 1842 observed that a female 'who is to be instructed in midwifery is ready
to start for [the Lying-in Hospital in] Dublin'.[74] However, Palmerston's
main contribution to public health in the early 1840s was in funding Ahamlish
Dispensary. It appears that the first dispensary was set up in 1840 at
Mullaghmore because of 'daily occurrence of severe accidents at Mullaghmore
works' and 'fever very prevalent'.[75] It was moved to Cliffoney shortly afterwards. The doctor, Tuthill, and his wife were lodgers to Mrs Gilmartin in

Mullaghmore. Their treatment there does not seem to have been any better than that of the Rev. Greene and his wife, at the hands of Mrs Corrigan in Cliffoney. In 1843 Mrs Tuthill complained of 'the wretched comfortless state we are in here' with 'the rooms so damp that the floors are rotting. . . . Whenever it rains we have it not only down through the roof but we are ancle deep in the hall'. She was 'alarmed during the winter owing to the constant damp'.[76] These lodgings may have killed Dr Tuthill. A letter to Kincaid from Francis West at Bundoran, 5 March 1845, solicited the appointment of himself as Tuthill's replacement which, he stated, would soon be inevitable because Tuthill was very ill (sk). Tuthill was dead by early October. An enclosure attached to a letter from Walker to Stewart & Kincaid, 17 October 1845, is headed 'Subscribers to the Ahamlish Dispensary as Returned for Presentment. Summer assizes, 1845' (sk). The total subscribed came to £58, of which £30 was from Palmerston, £10 from Stewart & Kincaid, and £4 from Sir Robert Gore-Booth (whose properties were mainly in Drumcliffe parish adjacent to Ahamlish). In December 1845 the main subscribers elected West as attendant at the dispensary.

7 RENT AND EVICTIONS BEFORE THE FAMINE

Some of the leases of middlemen on the Ahamlish estate were for the life of King William IV who died on 20 June 1837. Kincaid saw this event as providing an opportunity to remove pauper undertenants. In a letter to Palmerston dated 24 June he indicated that he hoped that he would be supported by him 'in the endeavour to thin the estate of a portion of the population and create larger farms'. On the front of this letter Palmerston entered the following observations:

> Kincaid recommending me to thin the population on the townlands of which the leases have expired. . . . I have long ago made it my mind not to do so unjustifiable an act. I never yet have acted on so cruel a system and shall certainly not begin now. . . . If any [tenants] can be persuaded to emigrate voluntarily well & good; but not a single creature shall be expelled against its will.[77]

Recall that most of the middlemen's land had been in rundale, under which an individual subtenant typically had many tiny detached plots. In November 1837 Kincaid wrote to Palmerston about the lands no longer under lease and referred to amalgamation ('squaring') in order to make them sustainable. He indicated that he had offered the tenants there assistance to emigrate to America.[78]

In his *Evidence* to the Devon Commission in 1843–4, Kincaid stated that there were about 800 tenants (plus their families) on the estate in the Ahamlish district, and that 280 of them were on lands the leases of which had recently expired. These were the first of the lands to be squared, and 'Palmerston's distinct orders were, that no man should be dispossessed, unless he chose to go, and then he was to have assistance to enable him to go to America or elsewhere'; however, only a few families then decided to leave. The average size of the newly squared holdings was about 5 statute acres. Ejectment from Ahamlish in the early 1840s seems to have been rare. When Lynch was asked by the Devon Commission whether the rent paid to Stewart & Kincaid by the occupiers of the squared lands differed from what they previously paid to middlemen, his answer was evasive: 'I think that they paid more to the middlemen in some instances'.[79]

In the course of his evidence Francis Barber, who held land from Gore-Booth, stated that Palmerston 'did not put off any tenant [from squared lands] and they are in a state of beggary, and will become paupers'.[80] Barber's observations were sent to Stewart & Kincaid for comment.[81] Stewart & Kincaid rejected Barber's generalisations and added: 'His lordship does not put off any tenant holding land, when the farms are changed from the rundale system, and squared'; it was not true that those tenants 'are now "in a state of beggary": nor do we think it natural to expect, that, because they have their holdings more compact than formerly, and are now direct tenants to his lordship . . . , "they will become paupers". Many of the tenants' holdings have become very considerably improved.'[82]

The pre-famine Stewart & Kincaid letters, which are broadly consistent with the evidence of Palmerston's agents to the Devon Commission, give further details on rents and evictions.[83] But in some cases, rents charged by Palmerston on the squared lands exceeded what was previously paid. Thus, following the end of the middleman system on Dernish, Walker wrote to Stewart & Kincaid on 20 June 1842: 'The island tenants paid the middleman £42 a year for the whole island. . . . I think £80 a year would be a fair rent for it, which I intend to charge them, allowing for what Ld. P. has taken for planting.' (SK) The rents there were indeed increased: a petition signed by five of the islanders complains that they 'are deprived of a considerable part of the lands on the island, by the planting there [of Palmerston's trees], and yet the rent considerably raised'.[84]

Until the end of 1845 some tenants were evicted for theft. In one case 19 tenants requested eviction of a person who, they claimed, was guilty of 'stealing oats hay potatoes and turf'.[85] Rents were payable twice annually, on gale days, that is the dates at which the rents were due for payment, in May and November. But they did not approximate net receipts. For example, in referring to his account for November 1840, on 2 June 1843 Walker wrote to Stewart & Kincaid that his receipts from that gale exceeded his expenditures (mainly on improvements) by only £1 odd (s k). A feature of his accounts is that rent collections generally lagged a year and a half, or two years, behind the gale dates at which they were technically due. Thus, the issue of default aside, the amounts technically due on the May 1841 gale seem to have been received only in May 1843.[86] Similarly, in June 1845 Walker wrote to Stewart & Kincaid that he had just sent 'my acct. & vouchers for Nov. 1843 gale' (s k). This suggests that tenants were considered punctual in rent payments if they were technically a year and a half in arrear. But, as noted in one of the very few studies on estate management in Ireland before the famine, this practice of 'running gale' facilitated ejectment.[87] On 26 December 1845 Walker reported to Stewart & Kincaid that he had told the tenants that 'the Nov. 1844' gale would be required in February 1846. But he was not optimistic. Early stages of the famine had commenced.

THREE

THE PALMERSTON ESTATES

FAMINE AND EMIGRATION

—

I FAMINE

In January 1844 John Lynch told the Devon Commission that most of the squared farms comprised less than five *Irish* acres; this was consistent with Kincaid's evidence (in December 1843) that the average size of the 280 newly squared holdings was about five statute acres. Thus, each tenant's square was small and, as Lynch stated in evidence, the potato was the chief product of the very small occupiers. On 7 December 1845 Walker informed Stewart & Kincaid that the partial failure of that crop would be 'an excellent pretext for withholding rent'.[1] This had been invoked on 10 November by the widow O'Farrel of Grellagh, who had 'nine orphans to support', in her plea to Stewart & Kincaid against ejectment (s к). In 1847 she and her nine orphans were among those who sailed to America aboard a ship chartered by Palmerston.[2]

The arrangements made for the Ahamlish dispensary were not well suited to the treatment of famine-related diseases. Furthermore, Dr West did not for long reside near it. In March 1846 he wrote to Stewart & Kincaid from Cliffoney: 'I hope you will have no objection to my bringing my family to Bundoran and residing there . . . until such times as I may be able to procure the common necessities of life here. At present I could not . . . procure as much milk as would be required by my family.'[3] He added that 'the dispensary must be removed' because of the increased number of patients and because Mrs Corrigan was annoyed by having to keep her house open so long 'subject to diseases of every description'(s к). Thus, early in 1846 the dispensary was at Corrigan's Cliffoney Inn. West did move residence to Bundoran. On 16 April 1846 Walker wrote to Stewart & Kincaid that 'the Inn is certainly not a fit place for a mob of diseased paupers' (s к). Some days later, Lynch informed Stewart & Kincaid that West was about to relocate the dispensary to elsewhere in Cliffoney.[4] On 29 June, Lynch reported to Stewart & Kincaid that he had recently seen a new potato 'from the Revd. Mr Yates of Drumcliffe'

greatly diseased (s κ).[5] This news foreboded calamity. But the dispensary was
not right. On 8 August, West wrote from Bundoran to Stewart & Kincaid:
'Last Friday I was part of the time standing in at least three inches of water'
owing to defective plumbing at the dispensary. He added: 'On Friday when
going over from here [to Cliffoney] the fields we saw in apparent health and
bloom on my return that evening were destroyed. . . . I dread the coming
winter.' (s κ)

On 27 September 1846 Walker reported to Stewart & Kincaid that he had
just been at Cliffoney, 'the whole parish in a bad state and no great prospect of
rent' (s κ). In October, the Rev. Malachi Brennan informed Palmerston that
his tenants were 'in a very deplorable state'. With their potatoes 'all gone',
many of them were 'in a state of starvation'. He stated that 'nothing short of
general employment' could save most of them from death. He observed that
in the past Palmerston seemed to love his tenants 'as a father would love his
child', and gave them employment when other landlords did not. Brennan
now asked Palmerston to intervene immediately.[6] On 6 December, Lynch
informed Kincaid that distress 'is every day getting worse'. And on 13 December,
West wrote to Stewart & Kincaid about the poor of Ahamlish:

> There is every appearance of a dreadful disease breaking out amongst them. I
> allude to dysentry with discharge of blood from the bowels. . . . I lost a man from it
> but I think if we had at the time a soup shop. . . . [h]e would have recovered. . . . I
> really could not stand all the demands I have, nor could I think of calling on the
> priest [Brennan] for assistance as he has already done more than could be expected
> from him[7]. . . . Another disease . . . is showing itself . . . – sore mouth . . . which I
> think has been produced by the unwholesome food the poor were obliged to use . . .
> which so injured the coat of their stomachs and bowels that . . . the living mem-
> brane of the intestine is coming away. (s κ)

2 TARDINESS OF RELIEF

In 1846, Palmerston and some of his agents were subject to various kinds of
policy lags: recognition lags (in recognising an emerging problem); decision
lags (in planning response); implementation lags (between decisions and
implementation) and effectiveness lags (between implementation of policy
and its effects). At Westminster, Palmerston's party was out of office during
the first months of the crises. But in June he was foreign secretary. This meant
that he then became preoccupied with politics. Walker saw no urgency when,
on 18 June, he wrote to Stewart & Kincaid inquiring: 'What answer shall I give
to this (Mr Wynnes) letter as there is no want of provision in Mullaghmore as

Lynch says he finds it difficult to get labourers – and Sligo market last Saturday had more potato carts than was ever known . . . & many unsold' (s к). Dated 17 June 1846, the letter to which Walker referred was from John Wynne, chairman of the recently established Poor Relief Committee of the Barony of Carbury, which encompasses much of the northeastern part of the county of Sligo, including Sligo town. Wynne pointed out the urgency of opening depots for sale of meal. He stated that he had established such a depot to supply the town district at prime cost, that he sought Gore-Booth to act likewise in Drumcliffe parish, and that if Walker would 'do the same on the part of Lord Palmerston the matter is settled' (s к).

From the content of Wynne's letter of 17 June, and from Walker's initial response, it can be concluded that Walker was temporarily blind to reality. Late in April, Lynch had written that he had received directions from Palmerston, who 'intends to stick to last years expenditure' on the estate.[8] A letter dated 12 September 1846 is the earliest indication by any of Palmerston's agents that a major famine was at hand. In this letter Lynch informed Stewart & Kincaid that he was 'every hour applyed to for work'; that he feared 'an out break'; that 'the doctor says fever is setting in fast'; that Gore-Booth 'is giving employment to all his own poor' and providing them with meal, but that 'we are in the back ground altogether' (s к).

Public works had commenced in most counties by the summer of 1846, but it seems that there were then no such works on the Palmerston lands. Following the Labour Rate Act of late August, presentment sessions (meetings of rate-payers at which works were proposed) re-commenced on 4 September. In the Stewart & Kincaid correspondence the first reference to the possibility of obtaining public works for Ahamlish is in a letter from Lynch to Kincaid dated 13 September, in which he informed that a presentment sessions for the Barony of Carbury would be held on 21 September. He therefore asked Stewart & Kincaid for instructions on what should be proposed for the Ahamlish estate (s к). Lynch had already warned that the crisis was now such that there was a danger of an 'out break' of violence. On 21 September the master at Benbulben school reported to Stewart & Kincaid that a pistol shot had been fired into the portico of his schoolhouse and that he therefore felt it necessary to get 'a supply of fire-arms' (s к). Isabella Soden, who farmed and let land at Moneygold, was the only representative of the old English gentry class resident in Ahamlish during the early 1840s. She wrote to Stewart & Kincaid from Sligo town on 28 October 1846: 'Prices here are exorbitant . . . , Indian meal not to be had. The people who have conacre from me . . . say they will not pay'.[9] She believed that 'the tenants intend eating all our cattle but say they will commence with My Lords then take Mr Brennan's and thirdly mine' (s к). Destitution was now so extreme that Walker opened his eyes. On

5 October he informed Palmerston that the consequences of 'great want' in Ahamlish 'may be very dangerous'. Writing that food was needed 'to preserve property', he recommended that Palmerston allow him 'to get in a small cargo' of food for sale in Ahamlish (sκ). Early in October, Palmerston instructed Kincaid to procure meal and rice for the Ahamlish tenants, and around the middle of the month there was a depot for sale of Indian meal in Cliffoney. But the supply was nothing like what was needed to feed the 5,400 individuals on the north Sligo estate.[10] Public works under the Labour Rate Act began in Ahamlish around the end of October, and Kincaid was urged to use influence to secure appointments.

On 5 November, Lynch sent Kincaid detailed observations on these works (sκ). Several points emerging from his letter are of interest. First, Lynch wrote that most of the 550 males from Palmerston's part of Ahamlish currently engaged on public works would be unemployed in 'about a month'. Such works, which were designed so as not to benefit any particular proprietor, were providing only a temporary injection of jobs. A more sustainable approach was needed. Second, he saw that even if more public works were sanctioned for Ahamlish, they would attract labour from elsewhere. Third, he felt that to maximise employment of Palmerston tenants, Stewart & Kincaid should apply for a loan so that they could be employed in draining and subsoiling (i.e. loosening soil beneath the top soil) their lands. The costs incurred by Palmerston would then be 'reproductive' rather than 'deadweight'. The kind of loan which Lynch had in mind was under the new scheme announced on 5 October 1846 in a letter by Henry Labouchere, chief secretary of Ireland; this informed that (instead of works which would benefit no particular proprietor) reproductive works might be carried out, financed by government loans to proprietors undertaking them, provided certain conditions were met.[11] One of the stipulations was that an individual proprietor undertaking such works would have to repay the entire amount borrowed. Finally, Lynch's letter of 5 November reveals pessimism: 'As to provision all we got . . . up to this date was 5 tons [obtained in Sligo town for the depot at Cliffoney]. We cant get it in Sligo. Mr Walker says he will get some from Liverpool.' He added: 'If you don't . . . get the draining and trenching going, I don't know what the people will do. I fear much the people will suffer let you do what you will.' Thus Lynch felt that the tenantry was in any case doomed (sκ).

A letter dated 6 December 1846, from Lynch to Kincaid, mentioned further presentment sessions to be held at Sligo town on 14 December (sκ). It indicated that people regarded Palmerston as 'deserting' his tenants 'these starving times'. According to Lynch in a letter to Stewart & Kincaid dated 11 December, the Rev. Brennan estimated that it would 'take 10 tons of meal per day to feed his people' (sκ). On 12 December, Lynch wrote to Kincaid noting recent instructions from Stewart & Kincaid for establishment of soup shops (s k). On 13 December, Dr West informed Stewart & Kincaid that Lynch had told him that Stewart & Kincaid intended to spend £800 on private works, but West added: 'at 11*d*. pr. day it will pay 800 men only for one month. . . . We are only in the third month of want and can landlords be expected to do without rents and support the poor until Summer [1847] comes?' (s k)

The first indication of organised food imports for Ahamlish is in a letter of early December 1846,[12] which informed Walker that Sir Robert Gore-Booth had received a bill of lading for a cargo of 50 tons of Indian corn for Palmerston's tenants. This merely meant that the corn was on its way. But 50 tons was negligible compared to the needs of Ahamlish: it would suffice only for five days according to Brennan's estimates. Furthermore, an announcement of *c*.12 December that it was intended to set up soup shops was only an announcement: boilers had yet to be acquired.[13] On 15 December, Walker scribbled to Stewart & Kincaid that at the Sligo presentment sessions on the previous day, 'priest Brennan made . . . a frightful statement of the destitution'. He added that 'the rent of the estate will not pay the outgoings', that Indian corn 'may be expected soon for the use of the tenantry', and that 'Sir Robt. & Mr Wynne etc. have several hundred tons per same vessel' (s k). This letter from Walker was written some days after he had resigned as Stewart & Kincaid agent in Sligo.

On 18 December, Lynch reported to Stewart & Kincaid that further public works for Ahamlish had been approved at the recent presentment sessions. He also repeated his view that 'no matter what kind feeling the landlords may have a great portion will suffer'. He then turned to remarks on the ordinary improvement works on Palmerston's estate; these were the works which were supervised by Lynch and had been paid for by Walker. Lynch wrote that privately financed drainage works should be commenced as soon as possible. However, Walker had paid for labour by issue of dockets for rent or, if in cash, on a monthly basis only. On the public works labour was paid in cash, usually at short intervals. Lynch therefore feared, so long as public works were in progress, that under the existing arrangements for payment he would find it hard to recruit labour, and besides, survival required that starving workers be paid in cash on a regular basis (s k). On 26 December he complained to Stewart & Kincaid: 'I have only a few men at work for they cant support themselves when they are paid only with dockets. . . . So long as they get on the public works they will keep to it.' (s k)

Throughout Ireland public works began to be closed early in 1847, and they were replaced as measures of publicly financed relief by government soup kitchens at which food was distributed free. Some landlords, as well as the Society of Friends (Quakers), had already implemented similar schemes. It seems that Palmerston's agents had set up soup kitchens at both Cliffoney and Mullaghmore by the end of January 1847.[14] Administered by local authorities, the government soup kitchens came into operation in the spring and summer of 1847. Although central government loans were made available, virtually the entire expense of such soup kitchens was ultimately financed through local property taxes.

The Society of Friends made gigantic efforts in famine relief in 1846–7. Its account of its principal activities during the famine was published in 1852, but it provides little about Quaker assistance in Sligo town.[15] However, some details of Quaker contributions to relief there are found in a letter of May 1847 to the Central Relief Committee of the Society, from the Sisters of Mercy in Sligo town:

> The Sisters . . . will be only too happy to have food . . . for the poor starving creatures. . . . Distress is now much increased by the numbers that have been dismissed from the public works. Their wages though very small helped them to procure one poor meal in the day. . . . The Sisters . . . feel very reluctant to be so very troublesome, but the . . . deathlike countenances which are ever before them urge them to leave nothing untried. . . . The SS [Sister Superior] . . . need not say how acceptable . . . free clothing would be, as every other necessary has been pawned for food.[16]

The following directions were written on the letter after its receipt in Dublin: 'Send an order on depot for 6 sacks Indian corn meal 6 sacks barley meal and 4 bags of biscuits'. Given the responses of landlords to the financial burdens of having to feed the starving, and given the extent of destitution, 13,000 emigrants sailed to America from Sligo port in 1847.[17]

3 EMIGRATION

As was observed in chapter 2 in connection with squaring the land, Kincaid gave evidence before the Devon Commission that 'Palmerston's distinct orders were, that no man should be dispossessed, unless he chose to go, and then he was to have assistance to enable him to go to America or elsewhere'.[18] Kincaid indicated that only a small number of families took up assisted emigration during the early stages of the squaring. However, for several years before the famine, Gore-Booth had assisted large numbers of his own tenants to emigrate. But until the famine, emigration from the Palmerston lands was low. This partly explains high population density in Ahamlish, resulting in very small farms. Contiguous to Ahamlish, Drumcliffe parish was largely

Gore-Booth property. Differing attitudes to emigration were mirrored in population statistics: between 1831 and 1841 the inhabitants of Ahamlish increased
from 7,483 to 8,720, while those of Drumcliffe fell from 13,956 to 12,982.[19]

On 14 May 1841 Walker reported to Stewart & Kincaid: 'I have been
encouraging emigration, and had 2 husbands & wives shipd. off from Milk
Harbour. I have given your man from Drumfad [in Ahamlish] an order for
[£]5 to the ship broker for his passage.' (sk) Walker's next intelligible reference
to emigration from Ahamlish is dated 12 March 1845, when he informed
Stewart & Kincaid that 'I will attend to what you say on the Emigration
System. I have two widows on my list, to go – but they want to have their
children sent free also – and some men would also go on the same terms.' (sk)
On 23 March he wrote that he had '20 to 30 emigrants . . . for Quebec' (sk).

The foregoing indicates that there was a small-scale policy of assisted emigration from Ahamlish before the famine. Although not on the scale which
Lynch favoured, it was consistent with his thinking. When asked by the
Devon Commission whether tenants on newly reclaimed land were expected
to implement his recommendations on drainage, he answered 'yes', and when
asked 'What is done with them if they do not?' he replied: 'I wrote to the agent
[Stewart & Kincaid] to say, that two or three of them must go out, but it is not
done. Lord Palmerston is not favourable to harsh measures'. When asked 'Is
it your opinion that these very small farmers would be glad to get land'
conditional on making improvements, Lynch replied: 'They would be glad to
get land on any terms. . . . There was a family held about an acre. . . . Lord
Palmerston encouraged them to emigrate; I think it cost him £17 to £20 . . .
and we had a person waiting for that very small thing the very moment they
were going off.' Lynch added that 'the tenants have a great deal of confidence'
in Palmerston and that 'it would be a good thing' if he bought 2,000 acres of
land in America, 'and brought a vessel into the harbour, and took the poor
people off, and carried them out there, and let them the land as his tenants'.[20]

By the end of 1846 both Lynch and West had abandoned all hope that the
population of Ahamlish could be perpetuated. On 13 December, West wrote
to Kincaid that it would be in the interests of both Palmerston and his tenants
if Palmerston were to 'send out the half if possible of his tenantry [rather] than
have to feed them here and get no rents'. In the same context he added that 'it
is the duty of all to try . . . to alleviate the suffering' (sk). A programme of the
form recommended by West was adopted by Palmerston in 1847. A letter
from Kincaid to Palmerston, 23 March 1847, indicates some further reasoning
behind this large-scale scheme of assisted emigration. Kincaid commenced
with an estimate of the costs of the new system of outdoor relief in the absence
of emigration: 'More than three fourths of the amount will be payable by your
Lordship [through property taxes]. . . . It cannot fall much short of £10,000

for the next 7 months calculating 1000 heads of families [including those from the Ballymote district to the south of Sligo town] making 6000 [persons] at 1/- p day for 200 days.' He went on to indicate that he had recently applied for a loan of £2,000 for drainage work, but added: 'Your Lordship will have to pay the largest proportion of the expense of feeding the people whether they work or not'. Turning to the alternative of emigration, Kincaid stated that he had made a list

> of those who are desirous of emigrating from your Lordship's estates in Ahamlish and near Ballymote surrendering their holdings . . . on being taken out to Quebec. . . . The list is not yet complete but I think it . . . 150 families comprising 900 individuals who occupy 500 Irish acres of land and the expenses of their transport would be about £2500. . . . I have already chartered two vessells [which] will sail in less than a fortnight . . . and the only difficulty that now presents itself to me is . . . what 400 shall I take out of the 900 candidates all of whom are desirous to go. . . . The poor creatures . . . see nothing but misery and starvation before them if they stay where they are.

Kincaid calculated the cost of supporting 150 families 'for the next 7 months' as at least £1,500 and after that they would still be 'on the property as dead weights'. He therefore recommended that Palmerston sanction an even larger programme of assisted emigration.[21]

The fate of Palmerston's emigrant ships has been well documented by historians.[22] But in the light of the Stewart & Kincaid and other correspondence, a few relevant considerations can now be added. In 1847 nine vessels sailed from Sligo to America carrying over 2,000 emigrants from Palmerston's Sligo estates, and, according to McTernan, another vessel sailed from Liverpool to Quebec carrying about 480 Palmerston emigrants. Thus, the total number emigrated by Palmerston in that year may have been closer to 2,500 than to 2,000.[23] The average transportation cost to Palmerston exceeded £3 per adult.

The first of the Palmerston chartered ships to sail from Sligo, the *Carricks*, left around the end of March; however, she foundered and most of the passengers, mainly from the Ballymote district to the south of Sligo town, were drowned.[24] But it should not be thought that it was only vessels carrying emigrants from east to west which were wrecked in 1847. In fact, on or about the same date at which the *Carricks* left Sligo, a ship carrying food donated by Quakers in Philadelphia, for famine relief in Ireland, was wrecked in the Bay of Delaware. This is indicated by a letter from a Quaker in that city, addressed to the Quaker relief organisation in Dublin, which informed the organisation that a ship had recently departed 'for Londonderry' carrying food 'for the suffering poor of your country'; however, that vessel had 'returned in a wrecked condition to this port all her masts having been cut away during a violent storm whilst descending our bay'.[25]

Apart from the *Carricks*, each of the ships carrying Palmerston emigrants reached their intended destinations. Late in July 1847 the *Eliza Liddell* arrived from Sligo at Shippegan, a small and isolated place in the north of New Brunswick, with about 165 emigrants on board, 77 of them former Palmerston tenants.[26] Her arrival created protests that many of her passengers would spread disease. Such news did not reach Stewart & Kincaid until 13 November, when Stewart wrote to Kincaid that he was sorry that 'the shipment to *Shippegan* which Maxwell with best intention took such a fancy to has turned out a very bad business. . . . The poor fellows appear to suffer greatly from destitution and disease' (s k). But worse was to follow, and Stewart & Kincaid could not have acted from any forewarning from the case of the *Eliza Liddell* because, by the time at which news of the landings from that vessel had arrived in Dublin, the last two chartered ships carrying Palmerston emigrants were already close to, or had arrived in, British North America.

The most publicised vessel arriving in America in 1847 was the *Aeolus* which, with 428 former Palmerston tenants, berthed at St John, New Brunswick, on 2 November after the harsh winter of British North America had begun. Although Lynch had spent £59 'to clear out the ship' at Sligo,[27] its human cargo was ragged and diseased. An emigration officer at St John complained of the late arrival of 'so large a number of destitute and naked emigrants' who, before they were allowed to land, had to be provided with 'sufficient clothing to protect them from the inclemency of the season, or they will perish'.[28] Writing to Kincaid before the year's end, Stewart could only acknowledge: 'I dont know what to think of the St Johns emigrants. . . . We did not inform ourselves enough of the circumstances of the place they were sent to & the suitable seasons. But these were the very poorest cottier class & I think above £100 was laid out in getting them some clothing [in Sligo town] better than their own wretched rags.' He also remarked on 'the unpleasantness of a person in Ld. Palmerstons position being mixed with any act that may be considered careless or cruel towards the poor emigrants'.[29] Note that this second internal Stewart & Kincaid communication on unfortunate aspects of the Palmerston emigrations of 1847 mentions purchase by Stewart & Kincaid of clothing for the *Aeolus* passengers. A third letter internal to the firm refers to purchase of food: on 17 May 1848, Stewart wrote to Kincaid that 'Walker junr. of Sligo has just been here about Boyles & his fathers claim for provisions for emigrants last year. I gave him to understand we were inclined to settle these a/c's but wanted a *long day*'. (s k) The fact that Stewart wanted time to settle with the Boyles (grocers in Sligo town) suggests that Stewart & Kincaid's food bill for the 1847 emigrants was high.

The extracts from the three letters from Stewart to Kincaid, quoted above, give credibility to the content of two often-quoted[30] letters from Stewart & Kincaid to Palmerston in defence of the firm's emigration policy. However, unlike the two letters familiar to historians, the second extract from Stewart to Kincaid, quoted above, attributes some blame to Stewart & Kincaid's lack of awareness of 'the circumstances of the place [St John, which Stewart called St Johns] they were sent to & the suitable seasons' for emigration. Given information available to Stewart & Kincaid from James Miley, packet agent in Dublin,[31] Stewart & Kincaid should have been aware of the dangers to emigrants destined for British North America late in the year. Thus, on 28 September 1847 Stewart wrote to Kincaid: 'Miley can send at £3–10, & 2–10 under 14 to either New York or New Orleans, but not so late to Quebec. They all go from Liverpool. . . . New Orleans he recommends for the late season.' (SK)

Complaints about the condition on arrival of some of the emigrants from Sligo in 1847 were so serious that Palmerston was officially asked for an explanation: it was in this context that he revealed the two oft-quoted letters from Stewart & Kincaid known to historians in justification of his policy. Those letters (which seem to have been written in the knowledge that they might be subjected to public scrutiny) provided no details of the last of Palmerston's emigrant ships, the *Richard Watson*, which reached Quebec on 8 November. Thus, Stewart & Kincaid was asked for more information, which is indicated in a letter to Stewart & Kincaid from the Colonial Land and Emigration Office dated 8 February 1848, in acknowledgement of Stewart & Kincaid's 'letter of the 1st inst. offering some further explanation in reference to the people from Lord Palmerston's estate who emigrated to the North American Colonies last year in the ships *Aeolus* and *Richard Watson*' (SK).

Evidence that Palmerston intended comfortable passages for his emigrants is found in a manuscript, 'Incidents and Reminiscences of Lord Palmerston', written after Palmerston's death, by the Sligo merchant William Kernaghan. In this document (watermarked 1870) Kernaghan stated that Stewart & Kincaid contracted with him in 1847 to oversee emigration from Palmerston's Sligo estates, and that Palmerston wrote to him to request that 'if the terms were not sufficient to treat *his people well*, to rescind them & to put in a higher tender to enable them to get the best entertainment on board the ships'. Palmerston then instructed Kernaghan to 'let every man & woman have a hot tumbler of the best Jamaica rum-punch after dinner on Sundays'. According to Kernaghan, Palmerston also ordered Maxwell to give ten pounds to each captain 'to induce them to be kind to his people', and 'Maxwell also bought clothing for such poor passengers as required them. During the famine years the Marquis of Westmeath only gave half a Crown to the poor leaving his estates while Lord Palmerston's emigration cost £7–0–0 p head'.[32] (This amount presumably included the cost of extra food as well as clothing.)[33]

Apart from Kernaghan's role, the Palmerston emigrations in 1847 had been administered mainly by Maxwell and by Edward Smyth, who in January 1847 replaced Walker as Palmerston's chief local agent, but who contracted typhus 'in attending to the emigrants on board the *Aeolus*'.[34] Stewart & Kincaid had hoped that the government would intervene, but on 28 July, Stewart lamented to Kincaid: 'I see Lord John [Russell, the prime minister] will do little or nothing for emigration & with out-door relief Mullaghmore estate will be a trying property.' In making this observation, Stewart demonstrated his concern about the extra local property taxes which the new programme of feeding the poor outside workhouses would entail. This inevitably increased the anxiety of landlords to rid their estates of paupers.

In regard to the Palmerston emigrations of 1847, Tyler Anbinder has recently written that 'it was cruel to send out emigrants whose only option upon arrival in Canada was residence in an almshouse or begging', and that Stewart & Kincaid 'knew perfectly well that the emigrants' pleadings [to be taken to America] should not have been the deciding factor in determining whether or not the last ships should have sailed'.[35] However, a fair assessment should note, first, the extracts from the three letters from Stewart to Kincaid, quoted above, as well as Kernaghan's manuscript, which indicate that Palmerston and his agents had good intentions towards the emigrants. Yet in regard to the sailings to America late in the year, Stewart & Kincaid could be blamed for their ignorance. Second, the fact that many of the emigrants arrived in a diseased state is not surprising. In 1847 famine fever was widespread in Sligo and was not confined to the tenantry.

The programmes of assisted emigration in 1847 benefited Palmerston as well as his remaining and former tenants. Palmerston benefited by not having to finance the relief of those who had emigrated. Those same persons then sent substantial sums to their relatives who stayed at home, and some of those monies must have been transferred to Palmerston in rents which he would not otherwise have received. The Broadlands archive at Southampton contains copies of extracts of letters, dated late 1847 and in 1848, from former Palmerston tenants to their relatives in Sligo. The writers indicated that they felt that their decision to go to America had been wise. One of the letters, dated January 1848, was from Bridget Rooney near Toronto to her father. She wrote that good workers there 'are fed every day like on Christmas at home'.[36]

Publicity about the emigrations of 1847 must have scared potential emigrants. But although exit from Sligo was much less in 1848 and 1849, a flow to America persisted. Palmerston continued to finance some of it. The following is drawn from a petition to Stewart & Kincaid from a Palmerston tenant named John Scanlon at Tunnagh (to the east of Collooney, several miles from Ahamlish) where Palmerston had earlier granted land for a school.[37] Scanlon wrote that he had ten acres 'of which he has been dispossessed'. He had 'a family of ten persons [and] begs to recal to your recollection a promise . . . that you would give the means of emigrating to six of his family'. Scanlon indicated that some tenants on a neighbouring estate were 'going on friday next', and that he and his family 'would like to be with their former friends'. He begged the 'expense required for the passage of one of the said six, [and?] to buy clothing and necessities for the passage of the other five'. This was written on 26 December 1848, a Tuesday (s κ). Thus Scanlon indicated, if given the assistance sought, that his family hoped to leave three days later. Similar examples of the speed at which tenants sought to leave Ireland will be seen in later chapters.

The only year in which Stewart & Kincaid chartered ships was 1847. It seems that before then most of the emigration to America assisted by the firm was through Liverpool and that the emigrants went there without escort. This placed them at risk of fraud. Thus, in 1846 a government emigration agent at Liverpool informed Stewart & Kincaid: 'Bearer together with his companion had been sent over here consigned to "Keenan" [a ship's captain?] for a passage to New York'. But Keenan had been 'deprived of his licence and absconded. It will therefore be necessary for them to return to Dublin in order to obtain a return of the passage money paid to "White" in Dublin'.[38] Perhaps because the firm had become aware of the possibility of fraud, some of Stewart & Kincaid's assisted emigration in 1848 was under escort through Liverpool. On 16 June, Smyth reported to Stewart & Kincaid that 'Kernaghan has taken his departure for Liverpool with 8 or 10 of our people, and will see them on board ship for New York. I settled with him for all their passages' (s κ). On 4 November 1848 Smyth informed Stewart & Kincaid that he had just received 'a letter from Mr Coyne' (who seems to have been a Sligo grocer) 'about the persons under his charge for emigration' from Liverpool. Smyth indicated that 'it appears that the money which Tom Higgins [a Sligo publican] handed to him, £52 – he gave to the emigrants, as he was very ill himself and unable to transact their business'. Smyth therefore sent Higgins to Liverpool 'to look after Mr Coyne and the persons we sent over along with him'.[39]

Within the Stewart & Kincaid correspondence, Smyth's last reference to emigration was on 5 December 1848, when he informed Stewart & Kincaid of disaster aboard a steamer which had recently left Sligo for Liverpool, carrying 174 steerage passengers, mostly emigrants. Following the outbreak of a storm, the entrance to the steerage was secured, and that area was covered with tarpaulin to prevent the entry of water. Suffocation resulted, and many were crushed to death in the ensuing stampede. Some 72 dead humans were found

piled in the steerage after the steamer had put into Derry, and 'amongst
the survivors were three little children – all that remained of a family of
nine on their way to join their father who had already emigrated'.[40] The surnames of many of the passengers suggest that some of them may have been
Palmerston tenants.

We have no idea of how many tenants Palmerston assisted, specifically to
emigrate, in the final years of the famine (which was over by the early 1850s).
A letter of early 1851 to him from Kincaid contains a list of Sligo tenants
wishing to emigrate, and in June 1859 Stewart & Kincaid prepared a document
listing the (eleven) 'names of tenants sons sent to America [in May] at Lord
Palmerston's expense'.[41] A further letter, from Kincaid to Palmerston in
March 1862, regretted that 'there are not more than 12 or 15 young people' on
the Ahamlish estate 'who will avail themselves of your Lordship's liberal offer
of emigrating them to Canada this season'.[42] But further candidates were soon
found: in May 1862 a Sligo newspaper reported that 'in accordance with a
practice of some years' standing', about sixty persons, 'whose passages and
outfit' had been provided by Palmerston, had recently been selected for emigration from Ahamlish. The same report indicated that they consisted of 44
young people, and 'families who were wholly unable to support themselves . . .
who had asked the favour of being sent out. . . . The emigrants took their
passages . . . for Liverpool, on route for America'.[43]

4 DRAINAGE AND ESTATE CLEARANCE, 1848

On 28 April 1848 Smyth wrote to Stewart & Kincaid: 'There are some tenants
about Cliffony who are anxious to dispose of [their interest in] their land, to
the highest bidder, and go to America. Would you have an objection to let
them do so, though the neighbour would not become the purchaser – it is I
know against the usual rules of the estate.' (sk) The tenants in question may
have been allowed to sell their interest to the highest bidder – for the 'usual
rules' were beginning to change. From the autumn of 1846 the British government had taken a view that the support of Ireland's poor was the responsibility
of her proprietors, through increased property taxes. Before 1846 few of
Palmerston's tenants had been forced off his estate. In 1847 he had invested a
huge sum – probably more than £6,000 (or about £600,000 in purchasing
power at the beginning of the twenty first century) – in assisted emigration.[44]
But by 1848, in the face of high property taxes and further arrears of rent, and
given a growing realisation that estate improvement required larger holdings,
Palmerston's agents probably resorted more often to ejectments, rather than
relying on 'voluntary' landlord-financed emigration.

On 10 February 1848 Smyth wrote to Stewart & Kincaid that he feared that the fever hospital at Carney in Drumcliffe parish would shortly be closed. He pointed out that 'upwards of four hundred patients' had been admitted in the few months it had been open, and that most of them had come from Ahamlish. He added: 'There has been a report that other hospitals are likewise to be closed but the remonstrances of the neighbouring proprietors and rate payers are so strong as to afford some hope that they will be continued. . . . The same should come from our quarter.' (s κ) Unlike the workhouse, the hospital had been financed by central government rather than through taxation on local property: this was one reason why rate payers opposed its closure.[45] Stewart & Kincaid went to the top of the administration in Ireland in their efforts to keep it open. A note from Smyth to Stewart & Kincaid dated 14 August states: 'I enclose the petition for the Carney Fever Hospital . . . which you promised to lay before Mr Redington' (s κ), the undersecretary at Dublin Castle.

The programmes of assisted emigration being largely completed, in 1848 Smyth switched his efforts to improvements through drainage and consolidation. On 21 January he informed Stewart & Kincaid that he was about to commence drainage near Milk Harbour where he would employ 50 men (s κ). On 13 May he requested that an inspector be sent from the Board of Works to examine the site and it was hoped that he would approve the drainage and subsoiling near the harbour, 'as we want to plough the land for turnips' (s κ). This work was on a farm operated on Palmerston's account. The summer of 1848 also saw restocking of cattle on Palmerston's farm at Mullaghmore. Lynch and Smyth attended a fair at which, as Smyth indicated to Stewart & Kincaid on 21 June, they 'sold all his Lordships heiffers' (s κ). Contrary to threats reported by Isabella Soden in 1846, Palmerston's cattle apparently had not been seized by the starving peasants. Land improvements in Ahamlish in 1848 were financed by a £2,000 Treasury loan.[46]

Some of the improvements in the north Sligo district during 1848 involved squaring. But the pace at which they were completed was slowed owing to the manner in which labour was paid – at monthly intervals if in cash, and through issue of dockets for rent.[47] Smyth reported to Stewart & Kincaid on 16 June 1848: 'Send me £150 for drainage a/c & labr. . . . at Cliffony. . . . Our roads are going on but slowly, as the tenants are unwilling to work unless paid at the time, and say that they cannot afford their labr. to their rent account.' (s κ) On 29 June he indicated to Stewart & Kincaid that 'many of the tenants have escaped by paying up to May 46 further proceedings [against them]'.

The potato blight returned in 1848. It was against this background that Smyth stepped up population clearance. On 12 August 1848 he wrote to Stewart & Kincaid: 'The disease is appearing [in the potato]. The turnips are doing very well with the tenants and at Milk Harbr. on our own reclaimed part. . . . I have given the tenants . . . 3 weeks to pay to Nov. 46.' (s k) Some months earlier, on 23 March 1848, Smyth had announced to Stewart & Kincaid that 'tomorrow we take possession' (probably from a middleman) of a specified townland in Drumcliffe (s k). On the next day he reported that he had just been there, and had given small compensation to 3 or 4 who gave up immediate possession, leaving '16 tenants for 111 acres' there (s k). But on 7 October he wrote that the townland 'ought to be squared, and some of the tenants turned out', leaving only a few good tenants (s k). On 9 October, Smyth wrote to Stewart & Kincaid about tenants on another townland in Drumcliffe: 'They are all well aware who are to stay and who to go. Maybe some compensation wd. have the same effect, and we could arrange in this way to divide the lands among the 4 you have approved of without bringing an ejectment.' (s k) That townland was then squared.

On 11 October 1848 Smyth wrote to Stewart & Kincaid: 'At Tunnagh yesterday. . . . John and Edward Scanlon were ejected, and Richard Raycroft [also]. . . . I gave John [who was also mentioned on p. 55 above] and Edward Scanlon to Luke Scanlon and took his own part from him . . . , which I intend giving . . . to Chas. Raycroft.' (s k) In 1858 each tenant at Tunnagh had only one holding.[48] Palmerston also owned townlands southwest of Ballymote. In February 1848 Smyth wrote to Stewart & Kincaid about squaring two named townlands in that district, which involved removing people. Some £80 was given in compensation to tenants who surrendered holdings there.[49] On 9 October, Smyth wrote to Stewart & Kincaid that he had retained nine tenants, each on about 15 acres, on a third townland in the district. There was also Cloonagh to the southeast of Ballymote, where Smyth had a tenant imprisoned for nonpayment of rent. On 13 October 1848 he wrote to Stewart & Kincaid that he had 'just visited Mr Cunnane of Cloonagh in jail' but that Cunnane had refused an offer of £5, as well as being allowed to keep his crop, as compensation for giving up possession. Smyth noted that 'he now gets out of jail because he is not in for over 10£ in a decree. So we have only to wait until January next to eject' (s k). But there is evidence that Cunnane was not terminally ejected.[50]

In Ahamlish, the year of 1848 was difficult for Isabella Soden. Letters from her in that year – none of them fully dated – complain of distress. In one of them she mentioned that 'Mr Noone [the Catholic curate in Grange, near her lands at Moneygold] desired those who owed me money not to pay', and in what was perhaps her final letter in the Stewart & Kincaid correspondence she informed Stewart & Kincaid: 'I have no money!! After great loss I have some nice young cattle (not sufficient for my land). Take them! . . . I have the [Moneygold] estate on the market. . . . I sold my pig to get the enclosure.' (s k)

Mrs Soden presumably had to surrender her lease for the 100-odd acres which she held from Palmerston. In 1858 she was listed as still at Moneygold – but holding a mere acre, without house, under his lordship.[51] She seems to have recovered in status by 1860, however, when she was listed as a tenant to Palmerston at Moneygold, on land from which an annual rent of £114 was due.[52]

The profile of Ahamlish was changed by many 'voluntary' surrenders, or ejectments, arranged by Smyth in 1848. On 29 September he wrote to Stewart & Kincaid asking what he should do 'about dispossessing any of the under-tenants at Derrylehan [in Ahamlish]. . . . I shall give them some compensation' (sk). On 5 October he informed Stewart & Kincaid: 'I attended . . . yesterday the Ahamlish estate, to take possession of the sundry places under ejectment, and with the exception of two who paid up to Novr. 4 with costs, and one in Barnaderg . . . we got through all our business. We tossed all the houses under the ejectment decrees.' (sk)

Ejectment was not always simple, as the following letters from Smyth show. They pertain to Palmerston property in Ballytivnan, where the Sligo Union workhouse was located on the outskirts of Sligo town. On 26 August 1848 Smyth wrote to Stewart & Kincaid:

> I appointed this day with Mr Blair [Sheriff at Sligo] to take possession of Conor Connells house & lands. . . . The sheriff and I . . . reasoned with Connor . . . to put us to no unnecessary trouble, and I even told him that I would let him have £20 on giving up quietly, but . . . they . . . stood in the doors with grass pitchforks sticks & stones. . . . We made a charge and took possession. (sk)

On 31 August, however, Smyth was obliged to inform Stewart & Kincaid:

> The sheriff gave me possession. . . . I left Black behind me, and he left Connors house quite unprotected. . . . They afterwards took possession again, and on my having them summoned this morning before the magistrates I could not state whether there was any forcible entrance or not, as there were no doors on the houses they having I suppose taken them off . . . and the magistrates dismissed the case. (sk)

Connell was going to go but he was taking his time: on 29 September, Smyth reported that 'Connell . . . has not yet evacuated' (sk). On 5 October, Smyth informed Stewart & Kincaid that 'Connor and his cottiers have made a clearance'. The same letter observed that 'as I have heard something suspicious about W Carty of Ballytivnan I served him with a notice of distress [distraint]' (sk). Carty was still on the property in 1858.[53] In a letter to Stewart

& Kincaid dated 7 October 1848, Smyth suggested 'an ejectment against Early in case he may be as difficult to manage as Mr Con Connor. . . . What are we to do with the Ballytivnan tenants opposite the poor house' (s K). One can only wonder whether they were forced into residence across the road.

On 23 October 1848 Smyth sent Stewart & Kincaid a list of Palmerston tenants who had recently paid him. A few of those on the list had paid up to November 1846 but none of them had paid for beyond that date. Some of them had paid up to May 1844 only (s K). Some of Smyth's measures on Ahamlish, in organising with Maxwell the emigrations of 1847, and in implementing clearances in 1848 through surrender or ejectment, are mirrored in demographic statistics. Between 1841 and 1851 the population of Ahamlish fell from 8,720 to 6,499.[54]

The clearances implemented by Smyth in 1848 undoubtedly reflected a hardening of Palmerston's thinking on smallholdings. In March of that year he observed in a cabinet memorandum:

> Ejectments ought to be made without cruelty in the manner of making them; but it is useless to disguise the truth that any great improvement in the social system of Ireland must be founded upon an extensive change in the present state of agrarian occupation, and that this change necessarily implies a long continued and systematic ejectment of Small Holders and of Squatting Cottiers.[55]

In the Stewart & Kincaid correspondence, the final letter on Palmerston's Sligo estates is dated 25 March 1849. Written by Stewart to Kincaid, it indicates that although squaring may have then been completed in Ahamlish, it still remained to be implemented on some Palmerston lands in Drumcliffe, and this entailed 'a few notices to quit'. In the same letter Stewart referred to the question of how Palmerston could obtain an economic return on his investments. He observed: 'The rents on the Ahamlish estate in its unimproved state were such as could only be paid by the old [rundale] system & by poor creatures. . . . The improved value is such as a respectable tenant could pay holding a fair sized farm & living comfortably.' (s K) Having thinned the tenantry, it therefore seems, in the management of Palmerston's Sligo estates, that Stewart & Kincaid would henceforth seek to maintain larger farm sizes at rents higher than those of the past.

Judging by the events of 1848, it seems that many or most of the small-holders who left Palmerston's Sligo estates in 1849 and during the 1850s received compensation in departing peaceably, but that such sums may usually have been individually small and would only have enabled some of them to migrate to Britain. But some assistance to emigrate to America was maintained up to the years immediately before Palmerston's death.

By 1850, Palmerston's Ahamlish estate must have been almost unrecognisable in comparison to a decade earlier. In October 1850 the Marquess of Westmeath wrote to Kincaid: 'I went to Mullaghmore . . . and saw . . . enough to convince me Lord Palmerston has immortalised himself by his goodness to those people who probably would cut his throat tomorrow.'[56]

5 ON FISHERIES

Fisheries development was the main motive in building the old pier at Mullaghmore: a document of 1825 observed that 'Palmerston has contracted with the Board of Fisheries to execute the pier'. A report of 1836 describes the pier as having been 'built for the fisheries by the proprietor'. There were few fishermen at Mullaghmore when the old pier was built: in 1844 Lynch indicated that most of the fifty one fishermen there 'came in from Killibegs [in County Donegal], and other places round the coast, in the last ten or twelve years'.[57]

The report of 1836 on Irish fisheries observed that : 'The boats and gear [on the Sligo coast] are in very bad condition . . . except at Milk Harbour, where there are two or three good fishing boats. . . . The Mullaghmore fishermen sell their fish to dealers, who carry them to the markets, principally Sligo [town]'.[58] The fishing industry of Ahamlish was underdeveloped in the early 1840s. The Mullaghmore fishermen were poor: as Kincaid reported to the Devon Commission, 'they have nothing but a house or room, and have no land'.[59] Production was limited by the local market. Lynch told the Commission that in order to survive on three acres, some of the tenants 'will take a quantity of fish and travel all night as far as Mohill' in County Leitrim.[60] There may have been others like Winifred Campbell who, as already seen, claimed that she had 'no earthly means of support but by buying eggs & fish' and carrying them on her back for sale in Ballyshannon.[61] Against a background like this, with no effective means for preservation of fish and with no railway link, it could not be expected that fish could save many if the potato were to fail. Nevertheless, Palmerston did in various ways promote the local fishing industry before the famine. First, as Kincaid told the Devon Commission, there was Mullaghmore harbour upon which about £15,000 had been spent by the end of 1843, which had increased the fishing.[62] Second, there were improvements at Milk Harbour. Third, new houses for fishermen had been planned. Other evidence of Palmerston's concern for the fishermen could be provided.[63]

Efforts were made to develop salmon fisheries. A letter of 10 January 1843 to Walker, from George Robertson in Aberdeen, offered the following sums for permission to fish for salmon off Palmerston's shores: 'Fifteen pounds sterling for first year, for the second year twenty pounds sterling, the third year

twenty five pounds' (sk). However, the salmon fishery might not have been
worth the sums offered by the Scotsman: one of Palmerston's tenants, Hugh
McIntire, had earlier held the rights, and on 15 August 1843 Lynch wrote to
Stewart & Kincaid that 'as to the salmon fishery Mr McIntire complains
bitterly . . . of all the fish sold and the amount was £20–17–10 and the expense
incurred by boats water keepers and nets amounted to £33–10s.' (sk). If these
figures were correct, the salmon fishery should have been abandoned. However,
a letter from Lynch to Stewart & Kincaid dated 22 September 1843 stated that
'I am going on with the building of the piers for the salmon boxes, and getting
the boxes made.' (sk) On 26 October 1845 Walker reported to Stewart &
Kincaid that he believed 'McIntires proposal for the salmon fishing the better
one. . . . If £20 for this year can be got, perhaps it may be well to try him.' (sk) It
seems that McIntire was content. In 1846 he sent Kincaid 'by the Enniskillen
coach a salmon' in gratitude 'for the preference given me in the Mullaghmore
fishery.'[64] Hugh McIntire seems to have survived the famine: the *Valuation* of
1858 lists a person of that name holding 50 acres at Grellagh. The famine does,
however, seem to have had a harsh impact on the Mullaghmore fishermen.

In 1852 the Quakers published details of the plight of fishing communities
in the west of Ireland during 1846–7.[65] The same publication provides details
of the exhaustive assistance which their organisation provided to fishermen.
Their accounts have been well reported by historians. In discussing reasons for
the failure of their own efforts to develop fisheries in the west, the Quakers
observed: 'A main obstacle . . . to the success of the fisheries appears to have
been the absence of a local demand. . . . [Fish] is eaten with bread and potatoes.
When the people have not means to purchase both, the fish is given up. On
this account, the failure of the potato, so far from increasing the demand for
fish, greatly diminished it.'[66] If this hypothesis about joint demand was correct,
then the situation of the 50-odd fishermen at Mullaghmore must have been as
follows. Because they had no land of significance, they had little or no oats
from which to make meal. They could not have harvested many potatoes,
rotten or other. They had few assets to pawn or sell. Hence, in the absence of
a market for fish or adequate relief, they must have been among the first either
to develop illnesses from the consumption of mainly fish alone, or to starve.
Kincaid wrote to Stewart in a letter dated 28 July 1847 that 'Maxwell has written
to you that he hopes to spend Sunday in Longford . . . discussing the *Works of
Charity and Necessity* at Mullaghmore with you. . . . I quite agree with you that
we should subscribe to Mullaghmore Relief Committee.' (sk) The fact that
Stewart referred to Mullaghmore rather than to Ahamlish suggests that destitution was worst around Mullaghmore. It should be noted too that this is the
only reference in the Stewart & Kincaid correspondence to a relief committee
whose terms of reference were specific to any single place in Ahamlish.

Early during the famine, the Quakers set up fishing stations at a few points along the west and southwest coast, and a curing-house was established at one of these. Each of them was discontinued, however, either after a short trial period or after a few years. In no case was there then a railway link close to the places were the fishing stations were located. It was not until 1862 that the railway came to Sligo town.

Establishment of a fishing station at Mullaghmore, organised on commercial lines, was considered in 1848. In the summer of that year a circular from the Hibernian Fisheries Association included the following:

> The object for which this Association has been incorporated is the catch and cure of fish on the coast of Ireland. . . . The cod banks contiguous to Sligo . . . are equal to those of Newfoundland, but neither industry nor capital have been applied. . . . Dublin is now . . . twelve hours distance from London, and the extension of the railway to Galway will bring the fish caught on the west shores of Ireland to London in sixteen hours. [In 1847] the fishermen were . . . compelled to part with their nets . . . to purchase food. . . . Nor is there a single curing-house along the western coast. . . . The Association will use its own boats and nets, but will also contract with individual fishermen for supplies. (s κ)

This item was found in the Stewart & Kincaid correspondence, which also includes a letter dated 15 August 1848 from Major Creagh of the aforementioned association, informing Kincaid: 'I had . . . an interview . . . with Lord Palmerston relative to the projected establishment of the first station of this Association on his Lordships property. . . . Palmerston . . . will give all the aid in his power. . . . What encouragement might the Association expect if they established their curing station at the harbour and fishing village on his Lordships property?' (s κ)

Palmerston's fine harbour at Mullaghmore, as well as prospective railway links to Sligo town, were presumably factors in the interests of the Fisheries Association. Yet its proposals in regard to Mullaghmore were probably not implemented: in 1849 Kincaid informed Palmerston that there were not enough fish to make curing feasible there.[67]

6 ON PALMERSTON'S DUBLIN PROPERTIES

Palmerston owned land in Dublin city and county.[68] Letters from a builder, to Stewart & Kincaid and to Palmerston, sought a lease for construction of houses on the Donnybrook Road out of Dublin.[69] It appears that work commenced there in 1846. Correspondence on the Rathmines district suggests that Palmerston did not approve of non-resident middlemen. A Dr Arthur held under Palmerston about 70 acres at Rathmines Castle. He claimed that 'part' of his family farmed there on 30 acres on his own account; the remainder he sublet. The 'part' of his family to which Arthur referred was his widowed sister, a Mrs Richardson. His request in 1841 for renewal of his lease was declined. The fact that Arthur himself was resident in London seems to have been one of Palmerston's reasons for refusing renewal; however, there was also a suggestion that Palmerston had plans to lay out some of the land for building.[70]

A petition of 1843 to Stewart & Kincaid reveals that Mrs Richardson was herself a middle person. The petitioner pleaded that she was 'living as a weekly tenant of Misses Richardson these twelve years during which time while her husband was living no one could pay more punctual than she did. Since his death her daughter was employed by Mrs. Richardson untill she gave up possession since which time she has no employment for her which renders the widow unable to pay her rent. . . . Hoping you would allow her to remain in possession . . . untill the premises is pulling down'. The widow's final reference was to demolition of Rathmines Castle.[71]

When the potato failed in 1846 at Quarry Vale in the parish of Palmerstown near Dublin City, a tenant named Patrick Ternan began to quarry on Palmerston's land. But on 22 September, Stewart & Kincaid stopped him from quarrying. On the next day, Ternan wrote to Stewart & Kincaid, observing that as far back as 1829, Palmerston had visited the Quarry Vale district in the company of Kincaid, who had then indicated that 'there was verry valuable quarrys on the farm if slothfulness did not prevent me working them'. Ternan added that when he went to meet Palmerston at Gresham's hotel in Dublin in October 1845, Kincaid told him 'if I could make up any part of my rent by quarrying that he would give me leave to do so'. However, he did not commence working the quarry until 16 September 1846, when he saw 'the dreadful loss of seven acres of potatoes' (s κ). On 28 September, Ternan sent Stewart & Kincaid an account of his expenditures during the seven days he had worked the quarry. He paid labourers ten pence per day (s κ). But Ternan was not allowed to resume quarrying, and through death, surrender or ejectment, he became another victim of the famine around March 1848.[72] Stewart & Kincaid then placed his farm on the market, the first known expression of interest coming from one of his former neighbours at Chapelizod, where Palmerston had earlier donated £10 to a relief committee.[73] Thus it seems that famine distress was severe at Quarry Vale and Chapelizod, both of which are now within Dublin City. There was also distress in Rathmines, now also part of Dublin City. On 20 August 1846 Kincaid wrote to Palmerston that in County Dublin, 'the potato crop this year is entirely gone'.[74]

Many items in the Stewart & Kincaid correspondence (not only those related to Palmerston) refer to 'bills' in connection with payment of rent. In some cases these were bills of exchange; in others they were promissory notes – promises to pay by specified dates. The latter can be illustrated by letters about rent from a Mrs Smith at Chapelizod, to Stewart & Kincaid in 1846 and 1848. On 20 February 1846 she wrote to Stewart & Kincaid that she had no money, but that 'Mr Kincaid can have no objection to take my bill as he has kindly done before for my half years rent' (s к). On 12 September 1848 she wrote: 'I will not be able to take up my bill for 22 pounds due I think on the 20th of this month, owing to . . . the great loss I have had in my potatoes. . . . Give me a renewal of my bill.' (s к) It can be inferred from her reference in the first letter to *her* bill rather than a bill drawn *on her* by Kincaid, and from her request for a renewal in the second letter, that the 'bills' were promissory notes rather than bills of exchange.

Although on a smaller scale, developments on Palmerston's Dublin properties were in many respects similar to those in Sligo, Palmerston closely monitored improvements in both districts in 1841–6. Thereafter he faded out of the picture as more of the decision-making was delegated to Stewart & Kincaid. One historian has entitled a chapter, in his study on his lordship, 'Palmerston's longest "holiday", 1841–1846'.[75] In this heading the historian was referring to Palmerston's relative withdrawal from politics: it was this which enabled him to monitor developments on his Irish estates so closely during those years. But by mid-1846 he was back in government, which accounts for his fading into the background in matters pertaining to his Irish estates in the late 1840s.

FOUR

THE CRICHTON ESTATES IN SLIGO AND ROSCOMMON

—

I INTRODUCTION

The Crichton link with Ireland goes back to Sir Alexander Crichton (1763–1856) of Seal Grove in Kent, once first Physician-in-Ordinary to the Emperor of Russia, who married Frances Dodwell in 1800. Frances was heiress of Edward Dodwell, of Carrowgarry, Beltra, County Sligo, who died in 1832.[1] A descendant, also named Alexander Crichton, today resides at Carrowgarry. From the 1830s onwards, the Crichtons owned former Dodwell properties in distinct parts of Sligo, as well as over two thousand acres in or near the Parish of Kilbride in Roscommon (see map 4).[2] They also owned a sugar plantation in Jamaica.[3]

The Crichton estates in Sligo were in three principal parts of the county. First, there were properties at and around Tanrego near Beltra, west of Sligo town. Second, there was the townland of Knockanarrow near Collooney. However, most of the Crichton lands in Sligo were to the south of Ballymote.[4] A house named Somerton was the Crichton residence in this district. Sir Alexander's son, who was also named Alexander, had a farm there. In order to avoid confusion, the younger Alexander will be called Alex in what follows. He came to Ireland around the early 1840s in order to manage his family's property. Somerton is close to the Perceval family residence at Temple House. It was conveniently between the Crichton lands to the north and those to the south.

2 FAMINE DISEASE, MURDER AND FEAR

The famine hit hard and early in the Ballymote district. It was not only the poor who died from famine disease. The Rev. John Armstrong, Chairman of the Leyny Relief Committee, who lived at Chaffpool near Ballymote, wrote

66

on 8 July 1846 to Stewart & Kincaid, as agents to Daniel Ferrall, 'for a
contribution towards relieving the distressed of that district [the upper half
Barony of Leyny] in which that gentleman has landed property'.[5] However,
Ferrall's estates were almost exclusively in Roscommon. Detailed discussion
of Ferrall and his Roscommon properties is deferred to chapters 5 and 6. The
letter of 8 July bears the following Stewart & Kincaid scribble added after its
receipt in Dublin: 'Acknowledge this & say it will be forwarded to Mr F but
he is in England & his property in this Barony of Liney is very small & he has
only one tenant'. Stewart & Kincaid's unwillingness to contribute on behalf of
Ferrall did not reflect niggardliness on Stewart & Kincaid's part. Ferrall had
only one important tenant in the Barony of Leyny, and it seems that receipts
from the Ferrall lands in Sligo were seriously in arrears as early as 1843, and
that they were zero during most of 1846.[6] A letter to Stewart & Kincaid dated
14 November 1846, not in Armstrong's hand but weakly signed by him, sought
'a contribution towards relieving the most urgent distress' and elaborated:
'The poor houses of Sligo and Swinford being now quite full . . . we have
nobody to look to for assistance . . . but those land lords who have hitherto
derived incomes from their estates in this country and we can obtain no aid
from Government unless we can shew a subscription list and without some
immediate relief hundreds must die of starvation.' (sk)

Armstrong himself was dead a few weeks later. Early in December his son
George wrote from Chaffpool that his father had just died from typhus. He
added: 'Severely will his loss be felt by the poor.'[7] A letter of mid-December to
Armstrong's wife observed that 'distressed people deplore his loss very much.
He was the kindest man I ever saw.'[8] The person who wrote this was from
near Ballymote. Two bills addressed to him early in 1847 sought payment for
deliveries to Armstrong of seed wheat and meal.

Armstrong was not the only person high in social standing in the
Ballymote district to die from typhus in the winter of 1846–7. The Perceval
residence at Temple House contains a painting of Jane Perceval who died
from typhus a few weeks after Armstrong's death. It is reported that her disease
resulted from her entering tenants' dwellings delivering food and medicine.[9]

Because of the date at which it commences (late in 1847), the Stewart &
Kincaid–Crichton correspondence gives no direct indication of the extent of
distress on the Crichton lands at the peak of the famine around mid-1847. But
the subsequent letters strongly suggest that distress among those tenants was
severe during that year. Stewart & Kincaid became agents to the Crichtons
late in 1847 or early in 1848. A letter from Sir Alexander to Stewart & Kincaid,
17 November 1847, requested that: 'I wish you to do *Lady Crichton and me* the
kindness to become *our agents for our estates* in . . . Sligo and Roscommon. . . .
Lady C . . . became possessed of these estates as next of kin to her brother Edward

Dodwell who died . . . in . . . 1832. My Son Alex . . . has acted *for us* for some years as *our agent'* (s K). (For reasons that will be indicated later, emphasis has been added.)

Sir Alexander did not reveal in this letter why he wished to end the arrangement under which his son acted on his behalf in Ireland; however, later letters indicate that following several murders and attacks on landlords and their agents earlier in 1847, he feared for his son's safety. This view is reinforced when the location of the murder of Major Denis Mahon, owner of extensive lands in Roscommon, is noted. Mahon had been shot dead on 2 November 1847. Some police reports, and some modern historians, erroneously state that the murder took place in the townland of Dooherty, Parish of Kilbride, County Roscommon. The contiguous townlands of Dooherty, Leitrim and Carrownalassan are between Roscommon town and Strokestown. All or most of these lands were owned by Major Mahon and by the Crichtons. In fact, we can be certain that the shooting took place either in Leitrim townland or in the adjacent townland of Carrownalassan.[10] Mahon was thus assassinated on, or very close to, Crichton property. Sir Alexander therefore considered that his son should return to England for his own safety, and that his services should be replaced by those of Stewart & Kincaid.

Negotiations between the Crichtons and Stewart & Kincaid had actually been initiated shortly before Mahon's murder: on 24 September 1847 Alex informed Stewart & Kincaid that his father might have forgotten 'that he authorized me to treat with you in his name. It is not surprising if at the age of 84 his memory should occasionally fail him, but his judgement and reason are as vigorous as many mens at fifty' (s K). On 26 November 1847 Sir Alexander wrote to Stewart & Kincaid: '*Both my wife and I* are most anxious to withdraw our son from the . . . dangers to which . . . his zeal for *our interest*, as agent, exposes him. . . . May I request to be informed . . . if you will accept *our offer* or not' (s K) (emphasis added). On the same date (26 November), Alex wrote to Stewart & Kincaid from Somerton that 'alarmed at the state this country is in my parents have urged me to give up the agency and return to them. . . . About 25 small holdings waste two leases expired and a third broken with pauper tenants on them, require immediate attention' (s K).

Alex Crichton did not return permanently to England. He resided at Somerton throughout most of 1848. Shortly after the deaths of his parents in 1856–7, he visited his sister in Poland who had married the Baron de Chaudoir. There he met his bride to be. At some stage after his marriage in 1860 he resided at Carrowgarry[11] – in 1999 the home of his great grandson the present Alexander Crichton. Exactly when Alex moved to Carrowgarry (near the northern extremity of the Crichton properties) is unclear. Reasons for residing at Somerton rather than at Carrowgarry in 1847–8 may have been that

Somerton was close to the Ballymote district properties, and it was between his family's lands in the Beltra area (to the north) and those in Roscommon (to the south). The main point here is that in the late 1840s the Crichton estates in Sligo were under Stewart & Kincaid's management but, to some extent, jointly with Alex Crichton.

3 DERELICTION AND IMPROVEMENTS NEAR BALLYMOTE AND AT TANREGO

Some of the holdings on Crichton lands near Ballymote lay waste, and rents were severely in arrears, when Stewart & Kincaid took on their management early in 1848. Sir Alexander required income from these and other lands, not only to support his own immediate family, but also for several annuitants under the Dodwell–Crichton settlement of 1832. On 6 December 1847 he wrote to Stewart & Kincaid: 'I have to pay the many annuitants with which our estate is burthened. I always wish you to keep enough money in your hands for current expenses and the charges on the estate, but I request you as often as you have £200 or £300 overplus to spare, that you will remit . . . for my use'. (sκ) In this letter Sir Alexander was over-optimistic. On 17 April 1848 he requested of Stewart & Kincaid: 'Tell me . . . what hope there is of my receiving money. . . . It is the number of people who depend on me which fills me with anxiety.' (sκ)

Alex Crichton handed over the relevant accounts to Stewart & Kincaid early in 1848. On 24 March he wrote to them: 'The father of the Keenans [near Ballymote] divided his holding between the two sons Patk & William. . . . William has a wife & eight or nine children, without cow or pig. . . . It is hopeless to expect rent from such. Would you advise allotting him . . . an acre . . . until he can provide for the children' (sκ). Thus Alex had some compassion. William was allowed to stay: Griffith's *Valuation* lists two Keenans on the relevant townland in 1858, including William, on one and a half stutute acres.[12]

Edward Smyth, the Stewart & Kincaid agent in Sligo town, quickly applied policies on the Crichton lands near Ballymote similar to those which he implemented on the Palmerston properties. The Crichton townlands were subjected to squaring and other works of improvement, and to some clearances of their populations. On 10 February 1848 Smyth wrote to Stewart & Kincaid in reference to the tenants in the Killavil district: 'They are such a lazy and ignorant set down there. I wish you would bring down with you about 200 of Clappertons pamphlets to have circulated amongst them.[13] I wish very much we could prevail on Mr Creighton to borrow a thousand or two which wd. give much assistance to the people, and cause great improvement.' (sκ)

The squaring of Killavil was supervised by William Shaw, a middleman. The tenants were not always content with their allocations. On 24 February 1848 Shaw complained to Stewart & Kincaid that when he went to have mearings (i.e. boundaries between farms) completed in Killavil, the tenants would not co-operate. A month later, Alex Crichton wrote to Stewart & Kincaid that 'Martin Hunt of Kilavil is in dispair at your having moved James Irwins mearing wall to the gable of his (Hunts) house . . . because Irwin (he says) is a most . . . annoying neighbour.'[14] Dissatisfaction induced by allocation of squares led to violence on nearby Drumanaraher. On 11 May 1848 Shaw wrote to Stewart & Kincaid referring to 'the division that you and Woodland the surveyar settled between O Gara and Brenan in Drumanaraher. O Gara commenced working next day. Brenan came with a party with greaps [four-pronged pitchforks] and asaulted him [and] hunted O Gara off' (SK).

Compensation was given to some of the tenants or former undertenants removed from the newly squared lands. On 24 April 1848 Alex Crichton wrote to Stewart & Kincaid: 'I do not know what particular claim Jane Supple has to a holding in Kilavil or assistance to emigrate to America.' He continued: 'Biddy Davy . . . has better claim to assistance. . . . For every £5 you give, you will I think have five additional claimants. I will with your leave first try what can be done with the Misses Supple & Davy. . . . William Shaw . . . says the ladies he expects will be satisfied with two or three pounds' (SK). In a letter to Stewart & Kincaid dated the end of April 1848, Shaw referred to 'Patt Keenan and others that sent up petisians to your honer. If I got the money [for them] the[y] would go off'. In regard to 'Bridget Davey', who wanted Stewart & Kincaid to pay her passage to New York, Shaw informed the firm that 'there is a man of the name of Morrisan' from the district 'going out on the eleventh of May and Miss Davey said that nothing would pleas her beter than to be out with him'. A week later Shaw wrote to Stewart & Kincaid: 'I will give Jane Soopple two pounds. . . . There are a great deal of the cotters [cottiers who had probably been undertenants] that are speaking to me concerning compensation. Will I give it to every person that throws [down] the house and go'.[15]

Squaring and resettlement in the Killavil district having been completed, Smyth turned his attention to further improvements. On 8 May 1848 he reported to Stewart & Kincaid from Ballymote: 'I have just returned from . . . Crichtons property about here, and . . . give a favourable report of the proceedings of the tenantry. . . . If you would think well of letting them have some turnip seed, I am sure that there would be very little idle land on their holdings'. He added that the tenants were 'sowing away on their own holdings' (SK).

On 24 May, Smyth informed Stewart & Kincaid that he had bought turnip seed for the Crichton tenants at Knockanarrow near Collooney, but he reported: 'About the turnip barrow . . . , they have no such implement here. I have however directed Mr Wood the seedsman[16] to send over to Liverpool and get 3 cheap ones 25/- each which will answer for the Cliffony District, Ballymote, & Scurmore [Wingfield's estate in west Sligo]. I have received a great number of small tracts on farming . . . and will circulate them' (sκ).

During the summer of 1848 Stewart & Kincaid applied for two government loans, of £1,000 and £150, for drainage on Crichton lands in Sligo and Roscommon.[17] These works were started late in 1848.

Population decline due to the famine implied larger farm sizes. Creation of larger holdings also reflected a policy on the part of Sir Alexander's agents of having viable tenants. Such was the case on the Crichton lands near Ballymote, and the same kind of thinking was applied on the Crichton's Knocknahur North, near Sligo town. On 24 April 1848 Alex Crichton wrote to Stewart & Kincaid: 'Mattw Walsh jr a very substantial looking farmer applied for Owen Harts holding in Knocknahur [North]. He is a tenant of Ld Erne [in Knocknahur South] and his land is only separated from Harts division by the road'. He added that 'it might be desirable to have such a tenant' (sκ). On 28 April, Smyth reported to Stewart & Kincaid: 'I have set Owen Harts farm at Knocknahur [North] to Mr Mat Walsh who mears the land. . . . Will you give Owen Hart a pound or so, on leaving?' (sκ) The Griffith *Valuation* lists Mat Walsh as occupier of over 70 acres in the two Knocknahur townlands in 1858.[18]

The recent developments reported above suggest a spirit of optimism in 1848. But Sir Alexander was not optimistic for a number of reasons. First of all, there was over-reliance on the potato. Although the crop had not failed in 1847, it was feared that the failure of 1846 might be repeated. Sir Alexander wrote to Stewart & Kincaid on 22 June 1848: 'You afford me real pleasure by sending me the opinion . . . concerning . . . the crops of the tenants, and their apparently improved state of industry. Nevertheless most sincerely do I wish they would not trust so much to potatoes as they do.' He wondered: 'Do they really think in case of another visitation of the potato rot, that John Bull will willingly send them 10 or 12 millions sterling? . . . John can do no such thing' (sκ).

Second, there was fear of revolt. The early months of 1848 had seen rebellions across Europe. In Ireland, rebellion at the end of July turned out to be a farce. However, a few weeks earlier, Sir Alexander had written to Stewart & Kincaid: 'I am more alarmed than I can express at the multiplication of rebel clubs. . . . We are sleeping on the brink of a volcano'.[19]

Third, Sir Alexander's financial position had deteriorated because of events outside Ireland. In March 1848 he wrote to Stewart & Kincaid: 'I hope you are getting in some rent. . . . These are terrible times for unfortunate Jamaica proprietors whose sole dependence is on that bankrupt colony, and on Ireland!' In December he wrote to Stewart & Kincaid indicating 'loss I have just now sustained by the unexpected bankruptcy of my sugar brokers. They owe me about

£1200. . . . Have pity on my case; Think of the annuitants I have to pay this month besides the usual exigencies of my family'.[20] Very little rent was extracted from the Crichton estates in Sligo in 1848. However, the probable course of events following the harvest – distraint – is suggested by Smyth's observations in a letter of 9 October to Stewart & Kincaid that 'we cannot proceed against any of Sir A Crichtons tenants this sessions. So I suppose you intended to give them further time until they thresh their corn and make the best *fight* they can.' (sk) This indicates that ejectment, or recovery of debt through civil bill, took time.

A fourth reason for pessimism was, as Sir Alexander feared, that the potato did fail in the autumn of 1848. On 17 August, Smyth reported from Ballymote to Stewart & Kincaid: 'Alas for the potatoes, they are damaged very materially.' (sk)

The letters about the Beltra/Tanrego district span December 1847 to March 1849. The impression is one of a broken middleman and broken subtenants, of lands in decay, and of abandoned oyster beds. Late in 1847 Sir Alexander wrote to Stewart & Kincaid: 'I recd a letter from Revd John Irwin the present occupant of Tanrego west, and nephew and heir to the late Col Irwin. He proposed to give up his lease in March next provided I consented to remunerate him for the great advances of money made by his uncle for the improvement of our Tanrego. . . . I could not accede to his proposal'.[21] The matter of compensation was probably not the only issue in Crichton's rejection of Irwin's request. Given the difficulty of obtaining viable tenants at the end of 1847, it may have been the case that the head landlord felt that a tenant under lease was better than no tenant at all, better than a tenantry of paupers, and better than a hive of squatters. However, some arrangement was made with Irwin and Stewart & Kincaid did take control of his lands.

On 24 April 1848 Alex Crichton informed Stewart & Kincaid that he had heard that a grazier named Beatty 'will not retake the farm he held' under Irwin unless his rent was reduced (sk). But in mid-May, Beatty made a proposal to Smyth, and it seems that this was acceptable to Stewart & Kincaid. The *Valuation* of 1857 indicates that Richard Beatty was then the occupier of almost 100 statute acres of Crichton land in the Tanrego district.[22]

The problem of what to do with Irwin's smaller undertenants remained. On 5 October 1848 Smyth wrote to Stewart & Kincaid stating: 'I suppose I am to take the Tanregoe [under]tenants by attornment [i.e., by arranging with them that they must now pay their rents to Stewart & Kincaid rather than to Irwin], except the few . . . who are to be turned out. I go there today' (sk). Writing from Sligo town that evening, Smyth reported that he had obtained repossession from the Tanrego undertenants, three of whom he 'turned out'. However, at least two of them received small sums in compensation which, according to Smyth, 'satisfied them perfectly' (sk).

A letter from Smyth to Stewart & Kincaid dated 29 April 1848 had described a recently surrendered holding at Tanrego as 'quite worn out', while another holding in the district was 'in a terrible state from furze growing all over it' (s κ). In the Stewart & Kincaid correspondence, the final set of references to the Crichton lands at Tanrego are in a letter dated 29 March 1849, from Sir Alexander to Stewart & Kincaid, in which he wrote

> concerning Tanrego . . . I am persuaded that it will go from bad to worse at a very rapid rate except a radical remedy is found for its present defects. . . . These I consider to be the rapid growth of . . . injurious weeds . . . , also want of judicious drainage and lastly the ruin of the fences. These evils if not corrected will soon now reduce the rent of Tanrego to a small value. . . . Mr Kincaid while at the Grove [Sir Alexander's residence in Kent] . . . deemed it better to let it at a reduced rent than to ask me to undertake its improvement considering the expense. If the whole of the surface were indeed to be broken up for culture and for thoroughly extirpating the whins and weeds . . . and [if] the repair of all the fences and some drainage were to be undertaken at the same time it would require an outlay . . . which I could not afford; and yet if no improvement takes place it is clear the rent must fall every year. . . . What I am therefore most desirous of knowing is a really good and efficient plan together with an estimate of its probable cost. . . . Instruct your Sligo agent Mr Smyth to examine the condition of Tanrego . . . and to send me a report. (s κ)

Sir Alexander was 85 or 86 years of age when he made these observations. It is hard to imagine any other absentee of his age being so concerned about improvements in Ireland.

Apart from land, the Crichtons owned oyster beds at Tanrego. There may have been some theft from those beds during the famine. Early in 1848 Alex Crichton sought Kincaid's opinion: 'Do you not think it would be advisable to put a caretaker in Tanrego who would mind the oyster bed' (s κ). Several months later, Smyth wrote of the need for 'a careful person to protect the bed'. A few days later he reported to Stewart & Kincaid: 'I was at the oyster bed at Tanrego yesterday, and tried all day and caught nothing except a few'. But 'if properly watched and stocked, it might be made a very valuable bed. . . . At present it is of little value on a/c of the barbarous treatment it has been subjected to for years – it would take about £10 to put a fair stock on it. . . . Then it should be very closely protected'.[23] The Stewart & Kincaid letters do not reveal whether Smyth's proposal was implemented. What is clear is that the oyster beds at Tanrego, like much of the adjacent land, had entered a phase of severe deterioration by the later years of the famine.

Efforts were to be made to develop the oyster beds at Tanrego in the post-famine years.[24] According to a letter from the present Alexander Crichton, 'the expectation was so great that the Verschoyles who bought Tanrego East spent a fortune on oyster breeding ground and lost all. . . . My grandfather [Alexander Joseph Crichton, 1861–1934] did his best 50 years later to fatten oysters. . . . But despite building a house for a watcher' the experiment failed, for at least two possible reasons. First, it is now thought locally that the waters off Tanrego are too cold for culture of oysters on a commercial scale. Secondly, as in the 1840s, it is thought that the latent oyster venture at Tanrego was impeded by interference by parties other than the developer.[25]

The possibility of developing a salmon fishery off the Crichton shores in Ballysadare Bay was considered during the summer of 1848, when John Holliday made an inspection. He indicated that he had seen some salmon off the Crichton shores, and reported that 'the best method . . . would be a stake net the cost of which would be from £15 to £20 & a man's wages to attend same for season 11 or £12'. He indicated, however, that the season was then too far advanced for a trial, there 'being neither nets, or any other preparation made'.[26]

4 THE CRICHTON PROPERTIES IN COUNTY ROSCOMMON

The Crichton properties in Roscommon were in three districts in the centre and west of the county. First, much of the property was in the parish of Kilbride to the north of Roscommon town. Second, a little to the north of Kilbride, were the townlands of Midgefield and Clooncullaan. Thirdly, the Crichtons were the principal owners of a few townlands in the parish of Kiltullagh, located at the boundary with County Mayo, near Castlerea. Raymond Browne, PP of Kilbride, has provided details of the famine in his parish.[27] What follows complements his work.

The Stewart & Kincaid correspondence pertaining to the Crichtons and the Kilbride district begins late in 1847. It indicates that much of the land was then held under lease to middlemen, apparently on condition that it would be used for grazing. Some of them – who included Patt Taaffe and his son Chris, as well as Wynne Peyton – rented Roscommon lands not only from the Crichtons, but also from the Stewart & Kincaid client D. H. Ferrall. Some of the middlemen appear to have been non-resident. For example, at least part of the time Chris Taaffe resided in Dublin.[28] The middlemen used some of the land for grazing; however, they also rented part of it to miserable undertenants and set part of it under conacre, in some cases, it seems, in breach of conditions in their leases from the head landlord. When Stewart & Kincaid became agents to Sir Alexander, management of the Crichton lands in Roscommon was chaotic. Not only were rents from the middlemen in arrears, but it was not always clear who was responsible for payment of the rents to Stewart & Kincaid.

The Taaffes

Neither Sir Alexander nor his son was satisfied with the manner in which the Taaffes assigned Crichton lands. On 18 October 1847 Alex Crichton wrote to Kincaid about Chris Taaffe, and he remarked: 'What can be more destructive than that system of conacre so prevalent in Roscommon' (SK). On 6 December, Sir Alexander also referred to Chris Taaffe in a letter to Stewart & Kincaid:

> You represent Christopher Taaffes holding of Carrownlassan [Carrownalassan] as being *wholly* under tillage and conacre. This I believe to be quite contrary to the conditions of his lease. . . . If you are of opinion that the various holdings of Carrownlassan and especially that one of Chr. Taaffe, ought to be maintained as grazing farms, *you have Lady C's authority and mine* to use your best endeavours to maintain it as such. . . . The many wretched cabins . . . ought surely to be got rid of. . . . If . . . the conacre rent which Mr Ch. Taaffe receives for one year, is enough to pay two years of his rent, I certainly have no compassion for him and I urge you to *see that justice is done us.* (SK) [emphasis added]

Just before the famine Chris Taaffe's father, Patt, was in a hurry to have Stewart & Kincaid process a lease for him pertaining to Ferrall land. In a complaint dated 29 July 1845, about a delay in execution of the lease, Patt Taaffe wrote to Stewart & Kincaid that 'men are mortal. . . . I am anxious to get the lease' (SK). But he had less respect for leases in 1848, when viable tenants were hard to find. Both he and Alex Crichton recognised that the famine had greatly enhanced his bargaining power. On 29 September 1848 Patt Taaffe wrote to Stewart & Kincaid:

> You were pleased to tell my son you would write to Mr Ferrall & Sir Alexander Creighton relative to an abatement. I have been obliged from the impossibility of meeting the exorbitant taxes & rents to send you notices of surrender of Castletuna [Casheltauna] & Dooerty [Dooherty]. [These townlands are contiguous to Carrownalassan; Casheltauna – entirely Ferrall's – to the north, and Dooherty – mainly Crichton's – to the south.] . . . I can get . . . plenty of land if I was disposed to take land and at much reduced rents. . . . I am ready to treat for a surrender of all the land I hold under Mr Ferrall & *give them up.* (SK)

A month later, on 24 October, Alex Crichton wrote to Kincaid:

> Pat Taaffe is very provoking. He agreed to pay £200 per annum for Doorta [Dooherty] . . . but he so plagued me . . . that I reduced his rent. . . . The utmost I wd. feel inclined to allow would be 12½ per cent for cash but then the alternative in

case of his not acceding is . . . distressing. . . . With such tenants as destroy property
by putting a pauper tenantry on the land I would not show any leniency. (s k)

It seems that negotiations with the Taaffes broke down, that the lands
which they held under the Crichtons were surrendered shortly afterwards, and
that at least one viable tenant was quickly found for part of the lands which the
Taaffes had occupied. On 26 December 1848 Sir Alexander wrote to Stewart
& Kincaid: 'I am quite satisfied with all you have done for me in res. Taafe. I
hope the priest who is about to hold about 24 acres, will turn out to be a *bona
fide* good paying tenant' (s k). According to a petition of early 1849, the land
initially assigned to the priest was in Dooherty.[29] The petition also states that
one of the Taaffes was still (at the beginning of 1849) responsible for payment
of some of the rents on that townland. The priest was Andrew Quinn, the
Catholic curate at Four Mile House near Dooherty, who in 1857 held 47 acres
of Crichton land on Carrownalassan.[30] Griffith's *Valuations* do not list the
Taaffes on any Crichton lands in the late 1850s.

Peyton and Sandys

Wynne Peyton, a magistrate for Roscommon County,[31] and William Sandys,
were two other large tenants on Crichton lands in Roscommon. Peyton, a
middleman, also held land between Elphin and Carrick-on-Shannon, under
the Stewart & Kincaid client D. H. Ferrall, and by late 1846 he was deep in
financial distress. On 19 December of that year he wrote to Stewart &
Kincaid: 'I received your letter calling on me for a years rent of [Ferrall land at]
Dacklin[32]. . . . To get rent from these wretched tenants is altogether out of the
question. . . . They are a poor miserable set . . . not now able to support
themselves without the aid of Public Works. . . . I will . . . send you half a years
rent which will clear up to May last' (s k).

Peyton did honour this promise in regard to his holding at Dacklin:
on 29 December 1846 he sent Stewart & Kincaid a letter of credit for £12 odd,
six months rent of Dacklin to 1 May 1846; however, this was apparently the
final payment to be received from him (s k). Ten months later Alex Crichton
wrote to Kincaid complaining that 'Peyton . . . asked me in March [1847] to
accept his bill [of exchange] for one years rent which I acceded to but in June
he left me to take up dishonoured'.[33] A few weeks later, Sir Alexander pressed
for more strenuous efforts to extract rent from Peyton. On 6 December 1847
he urged Stewart & Kincaid: 'Use your best endeavours to obtain the . . .
arrears of rent from Peyton. The observations I have made concerning
the small tenants and cottages on Ch. Taaffes [see the passage, quoted on

p. 75, about removing many wretched cabins on his land] apply equally to Peytons' (s k).

Sir Alexander's agents did not succeed in extracting the arrears from Peyton. Apart from the fact that he was ejected, Peyton's fate is unknown to the author. However, a letter to Stewart & Kincaid from William Sandys, 3 August 1848, reveals that Peyton owed money to several other parties. The letter also indicates that Sandys and Peyton jointly held an extensive tract of Crichton land (in Carrownalassan) under a single lease, that Peyton's part was 'the half' rented to undertenants, and that Sandys assigned his own 'half' to grazing. In the same letter, Sandys stated that he was 'willing to surrender the lease which is in my possession and also to pay the rent due by me on my half of the land . . . provided I get a [new] lease . . . at the same rent'. He added that 'Sir Alexr. will loose nothing by entering into this arrangement as all the rent due to him is due by Mr. Peytons tenants' (s k). But, as will soon be seen, Sandys's business arrangement with Peyton was to get Sandys himself into trouble.

Unlike Peyton, Sandys was a resident of the Parish of Kilbride, where he owned land at Derrane near Roscommon town. Raymond Browne refers to him at three points in his research on conditions in the parish during the famine.[34] First, he observes that in September 1845 Basil and William Sandys donated a site for a new Catholic Church at Derrane, and that William Sandys also gave £10 towards building the church. Second, William Sandys was a member of the Kilbride Relief Committee when it was established in July 1846; Major Denis Mahon and the Rev. Andrew Quinn were also founding members of this committee. Third, William Sandys gave evidence at the trial of James Cummins, held in March 1849, for Cummins's part in the murder of Major Mahon. Thus, Sandys was a respected local figure. Nevertheless, in March 1848 Sir Alexander Crichton was alerted that Sandys was in prison. Crichton's full response is unknown; however, the following extract from a letter from him to Stewart & Kincaid, 11 March 1848, suggests that he had some sympathy for Sandys's case: 'Not understanding what I have to do with the accompanying notice relative to the relief of Wm. Sandys a prisoner for debt in Roscommon I beg you to inform me of what is expected from me.' (s k)

The details of Sandys's imprisonment are not recorded in the Stewart & Kincaid correspondence. One can only feel confident that the cause involved his business relationship with Wynne Peyton. A letter from Sandys to Stewart & Kincaid, 27 June 1848, indicates that he was then a free man. The following petition dated 7 February 1849, delivered by Sandys to the Crichton residence in England (and forwarded by Sir Alexander to Stewart & Kincaid), reveals details of his link with Peyton; it also shows that his business problems did not end at the time of his release from jail:

I beg respectfully to lay before you the following statement of grievous injury that I as one of your Irish tenants have suffered. In the year 1786 one of your ancestors made a lease of the lands of Carnalasson . . . to a Mr. Terence Flanegan. The interest in this lease subsequently rested in a Mr. Wynne Peyton from whom in the year 1838 I took . . . about 90 acres of the land for a term of ten years. In the year 1846 I unfortunately entered into a treaty with Mr. Peyton for the purchase of a moiety of his interest in the original lease for which I then paid him . . . £700. The failure of the potato crop came the same year . . . and every one in Mr. Peyton's situation became embarrassed. The consequence was he became unable to pay his portion of the rent reserved under the lease of 1786. . . . Although I had my portion of the rent always ready it would not be accepted without Mr. Peyton's share. The result was an eviction of the old lease, by which I have lost the entire savings of the last twenty years. I am now willing and anxious to continue [as] your tenant for the portion of the land in my own occupation. . . . I therefore . . . trust you will continue me as tenant at the same rent as that reserved in the old leases . . . and if so I am ready and willing to pay up all arrears of rent due on same since the 1st November 1846, at which time I unfortunately purchased from Mr. Peyton.

I have come a long journey from Ireland to have the honour of a personal interview which I humbly solicit. (s κ)

It seems that Sandys's petition proved effective: the *Valuation* of 1857 lists William Sands (i.e. Sandys) as occupier of 173 acres of Crichton land on Carrownalassan.[35]

The Sandys petition, along with other material discussed here, create the following picture of developments on Carrownalassan and Dooherty in 1848–51.

In regard to Carrownalassan, it seems that a Bernard Balfe (see p. 79 below) was the immediate lessor of about 225 of the 1241 statute acres in the townland; Sir Alexander was the lessor of the remaining 1,000 plus acres.[36] Contrary to Sir Alexander's wishes, Chris Taaffe's holding was wholly under tillage, instead of being used for grazing, with 'many wretched cabins' on it. Removing Chris Taaffe – which seems to have been done by 1849–50 – meant removal of the wretched cabins and their occupants. It does not seem that Peyton had used any part of his holding in the townland for grazing: Sandys referred to it as 'the half in the occupation of the [under]tenants', and Sir Alexander observed that his remarks about getting rid of the many wretched cabins on Chris Taaffe's holding also applied to Peyton's. The ejectment of Peyton meant that it was possible to implement clearance of those cabins. Sandys, by contrast, used his holding in the townland for grazing; hence, it contained few, if any, undertenants. Peyton's ejectment and the presumed departure of Chris Taaffe from Carrownalassan help explain why, although the population on the 19,287 statute acres of Kilbride parish fell by 45 per cent, from 8,578 to 4,719, between 1841 and 1851, that of the Carrownalassan component fell by 50.6 per cent, from 655 to 323 persons.[37]

In regard to Dooherty, Sir Alexander was lessor of 168 of the 310 statute acres in the townland; Henry Mahon (successor to the murdered Major Denis Mahon) was lessor of the residual 142 acres. The population of Dooherty fell by 92 per cent, from 125 to 10 persons, between 1841 and 1851. This percentage was far higher than that for any of the other 39 townlands in Kilbride.[38] The major programmes of assisted emigration, which had been implemented by Major Mahon a few months before his murder, were *not* factors behind such statistics.[39] A key to the depopulation of Dooherty is related to the fact that Patt Taaffe no longer had a holding on the townland: recall that in October 1848 Alex Crichton had referred to him as being one of 'such tenants as destroy property by putting a pauper [under]tenantry on the land' (sk). It can be inferred that those paupers were shovelled out of Dooherty shortly after Patt Taaffe's departure from the townland.

Who should pay the rent?

At the time when Stewart & Kincaid became the Crichton agents, the Taaffes, and Peyton, were not the only middlemen on the Crichton lands in the parish of Kilbride. Indeed, it seems that in some cases the structure of middlemen was so complex that it was not always clear who was responsible for payment of the rents to Stewart & Kincaid.[40] This is suggested by the following extracts from a letter written by Alex Crichton at Somerton to Kincaid, 18 October 1847:

> Is it possible that Mr Bernard Balfe has rid the farm he holds under Miss Fallon of the miserable paupers he & his father had located on it: and is land well laid down in grass as he was bound when proceeded against by Mr Baggott. He promised me a years rent the 10th inst. but as usual has not failed to keep the money. . . . Perhaps it is for the best as it will enable you to apply to Mr Baggott from whom it would be more desirable to receive the rent. . . . Upon my return from Roscommon I found a letter from one Pat Kelly . . . enclosing half notes for £22 as rent of the farm held by Richd. Payne in Carrownlassan. I wrote back to say there were three gales due to Novr. 1846. . . . Payne hearing of Kellys having sent me the ½ notes writes to request I will not send Kelly the receipt but to himself (sk)

On 6 December 1847 Sir Alexander directed Stewart & Kincaid to 'render Mr Bagot responsible for the payt. of Fallon's land' (sk). It therefore seems that at an early stage in their management of the Crichton lands in

Roscommon, not only did Stewart & Kincaid remove some of the middle-men, but it is probable that they also simplified the structure of middlemen. Getting rid of middlemen also facilitated getting rid of many or most of their undertenants. But some ejectment decrees had already been obtained around the time at which Stewart & Kincaid commenced management of the Crichton lands in Roscommon and, in many cases, no middleman had been involved. Thus, on 18 October 1847 Alex Crichton reported to Stewart & Kincaid: 'My steward whom I sent to Strokestown & Castlerea will . . . bring me word whether the decrees have been executed. But for the last two unfortunate years I think Thos. Narry would have become a good tenant. . . . Widow Nolan must be bought out. The others named by you are a bad set that must be got rid of' (sĸ). Some of the ejectments under consideration at that time were on the Crichton townland of Clooncullaan, to the north of Kilbride.[41] On 6 December 1847 Sir Alexander wrote to Stewart & Kincaid about 'weeding out the worst' tenants there (sĸ).

5 BRIEF REVIEW, AND FURTHER OBSERVATIONS ON SIR ALEXANDER

It has been shown that when Stewart & Kincaid commenced management of the Crichton estates around the end of 1847, rents were in arrears, leases had been broken, and holdings lay waste.

On the Crichton lands near Ballymote, Smyth applied policies similar to those which he implemented on Palmerston's estates. Lands were squared. Some of those removed during the clearances near Ballymote received com-pensation, including assistance to emigrate. To the remaining tenants there, Smyth distributed tracts on agriculture to encourage improvements in husbandry. Population decline due to the famine meant larger farm sizes. Creation of larger holdings also reflected the policy of having viable tenants, and was a factor in explaining why some tenants had to go.

In the Tanrego district, where both lands and oyster beds were going to waste, the famine had broken the major middleman and some of the smaller tenants. Sir Alexander's agents were reluctant to accept surrender of the middleman's lease. Given the difficulty of finding viable tenants at the end of 1847, the main reason for this was that they felt that a tenant under lease (provided he did not sublet to paupers) was better than no tenant at all, and better than a tenantry of paupers or a hive of squatters. The major middleman did leave, some of his tenants were ejected and given small sums in compen-sation, and larger farm sizes were thereby created.

In mid-1848, Stewart & Kincaid applied on Sir Alexander's behalf for two Government loans for drainage projects. The first of these commenced late in 1848.[42]

In the early years of the famine, much of the Crichton land in Roscommon was held under lease by middlemen, on the understanding that it would be used for grazing. But some of them rented it to paupers or set it under conacre. Those lands were dotted, not with cattle and sheep, but by miserable cabins. Stewart & Kincaid's policy was to revert the land to the use originally intended by Sir Alexander. This implied removing of middlemen and undertenants. Such paupers received little or no compensation: the attitude of Sir Alexander and his agents was that the small tenancies reflected unauthorised allocation by middlemen. The ruination of one large middleman, because his tenants were unable to pay him due to the potato failures, threatened to destroy one of Sir Alexander's best tenants in Roscommon, who went to England to plead his case with the landlord. But not all of the Crichton land in Roscommon was in the hands of middlemen. On those lands where there was no middleman, policy was to remove the worst of the small tenants, who might have been ejected without compensation. It should be acknowledged that in 1848 Sir Alexander's financial position was such that he could not afford to assist departing tenants on any substantial scale.

The *Valuations* of 1857 list Sir Alexander as lessor of thousands of acres in Roscommon. He would then have been about 94 years old, though he had in fact died in 1856. Although a non-resident, he had an active interest in improvements on his estates. He felt that improving tenants should be assisted, but that middlemen who destroyed land by setting it to paupers had to be removed: this involved sacrificing some middlemen and many paupers. Sir Alexander did reveal compassion. But like Palmerston, he had to address a key problem: that of selecting a zone for decision making in the trade-offs between short-term considerations of humanity on the one hand, and efficiency on the other.

Sir Alexander was a modest person who thought deeply. On 17 October 1848 he wrote to Stewart & Kincaid:

> I . . . request your attention to some observations I have been making of late. . . . They relate to the numerous holdings which have been thrown up. . . . To allow a ruined tenant to hold these in the hope of his coming round, and becoming a thriving tenant . . . appears to me to be contrary to experience. . . . I wish that you would purchase, read, and digest, a very interesting little work which has been published this year by Wm. Thos. Thornton entitled *'a plea for peasant proprietors'* as also another by a Peer of France, which country as you will know is now nearly cut up into very small freeholds and holdings. It is Mons. Passy's work *on large and*

small farms. . . . Both of these writers are in favour of small (even very small) farms, but then, they agree . . . that no man . . . who has not at command a capital of £6 or £8 per acre . . . can possibly succeed. . . . What a dismal prospect does it hold out for Ireland. . . . But this is not . . . the chief point . . . on which I beg to have your opinion. The common practice with the small tenants in Ireland when ejected, or voluntarily throwing up their holdings, is to get a substitute who will purchase the good will of the farm. . . . The new tenant begins his exertions . . . under a load of debt. No wonder that the landlords, the land and the tenant, should all go to the bad in a few years. . . . Such tenants . . . never can do justice to their farms. This appears to me to be a fearful dilemma which calls for all your experience and all your ingenuity to find the remedy. (SK)

Sir Alexander's thinking here was well ahead of his time. He seems to have been sympathetic to a system of small and prosperous tenant farmers, or to peasant proprietorship as an ideal, but he saw the policy dilemma: how could new small tenants, or new small proprietors, be enabled to start with capital rather than under a load of debt which inevitably tended to render their efforts non-viable? A resolution to this dilemma was provided only around the end of the nineteenth century: under the Land Acts, it involved the government buying out the landlords, transferring land to former tenants on holdings which were deemed to be of viable sizes, and arranging that the new peasant proprietors would compensate the government, not at once, but through payment of annuities over several decades.[43] In facilitating transfer of large blocs of land to former tenants, the Wyndham Act of 1903 was the most important.

The high levels of local property taxes, needed to finance famine relief, were probably factors in the ruination of some Irish landlords: in the late 1840s and early 1850s there was a glut of encumbered estates on the market.[44] Sir Alexander feared that such taxation would cause his own ruination. Throughout 1848 he begged Stewart & Kincaid to send him money. It seems that these requests were unsuccessful until the end of the year when, on 26 December, he wrote to Stewart & Kincaid thanking them for '£300 just now received' (SK). It seems that Stewart & Kincaid could not send Sir Alexander any monies during the first half of 1849. On 13 June 1849 he wrote stating that Stewart & Kincaid's failure to send him money 'causes me much distress and . . . it is now too late to warn the Dodwellian annuitants of my inability to pay them' (SK).

The Crichton estates were close to the doors of the bankruptcy courts in mid-1849. But it is likely that relief shortly followed. At the foot of a letter dated 13 July 1849 to Kincaid, Stewart entered as follows: '£1200 Mrs Sherlock, 500 Lord Longford, 500 Col Stratford, 400 Lord Frankfort, 300 Sir A Crichton, 400 Capt Ponsonby'. It seems that these were sums which Stewart was suggesting should now be remitted to the persons named, and that the amounts reflected rent receipts from estates recently visited. Thus, rent receipts appear to have moved in the direction of normalcy from mid-1849 onwards. It does not seem that the Crichtons had to sell any land in partial consequence of financing famine relief. An official return of 1876 lists Alex Crichton as owner of 4,021 acres in Roscommon and 2,827 acres in Sligo.[45]

In at least two respects the thinking of Sir Alexander Crichton was ahead of the times in which he lived. He had liberal views on land tenure in Ireland, but he did not see how a *viable* system of small and prosperous tenant farmers, or of small and prosperous proprietors, could be created. In this context it should be remembered that subject to relatively few exceptions, government intervention in the economy was contrary to the dominant philosophy of the age; hence, Sir Alexander could hardly have contemplated the political feasibility, in his own lifetime, of the Land Acts of the late nineteenth and early twentieth centuries. By then, social philosophy had evolved from *laissez-faire* towards pragmatic interventionism.

He also seems to have been liberal in his attitudes towards women. The *Valuations* of the 1850s refer to him as lessor of the Crichton lands in Ireland. He had married Frances Dodwell in 1800 and she 'became possessed of' the Irish properties as next of kin to her brother Edward who died in 1832. It was Sir Alexander rather than Frances who sent instructions on how the properties should be managed; however, his letters indicate that his decisions on estate management were taken in conjunction with his wife. It seems likely that most men in Sir Alexander's circumstances in the 1840s would have regarded the properties as uniquely their own, and would have given directions to their agents without referring to their wives in this manner. A legal expert in the Faculty of Law at University College Dublin has provided me with the following outline of the legal position of married women in relation to property before the Married Women's Property Act 1882:

At common law a married couple were considered to be one person. . . . On marriage the husband became entitled to the rents and profits arising from his wife's lands and acquired a freehold estate in them which lasted as long as the marriage. Thus the husband held her lands jointly with her although it was not like a normal joint tenancy, because he could dispose of the estate without her agreement. Nevertheless, he could make no disposition of her lands valid beyond his own life without her concurrence. . . . The same position applied to property acquired by the wife during marriage. . . . The only way the wife could have avoided this situation and gained control . . . was if a trust had been set up whereby the legal estate vested in trustees holding for her benefit in equity. . . . Such a trust would have had to be expressly for the *separate use* of the wife; otherwise the husband would have had the same powers over his wife's equitable estate as he had in her common law estate.[46]

The Stewart & Kincaid correspondence provides no evidence that such a trust was set up under the Dodwell settlement of 1832. In either case, it seems unlikely, in writing to land agents, that most other men in Sir Alexander's position would have referred to consultation with their wives in the manner in which he did. It therefore seems, in his references to his wife when writing to third parties on matters of business, that Sir Alexander was ahead of the times in which he lived.

Note on Alexander Joseph Crichton, 1861–1934

This book seldom refers to twentieth-century people, but some descendants of Sir Alexander Crichton are amongst the exceptions. It has been seen that the Crichton line of ownership in Ireland commenced with Sir Alexander, whose descendants became landlords only by chance (through inheritance of Dodwell properties by Sir Alexander's wife). Sir Alexander's son, who inherited those lands in the 1850s, has been called Alex. Following the death of Alex in 1888, his lands passed to his eldest son, Alexander Joseph (1861–1934). When A. J. died, the remaining Crichton lands passed to Brian Dodwell Crichton – father of the present Alexander Cochrane Crichton, a 1939 Economics graduate of King's College, Cambridge, listed in 1958 as a Director of the Bank of Ireland. He is the Alexander Crichton who today farms in the Carrowgarry district.[47]

A.J. implemented some of his grandfather's sentiments concerning the small farmers of Ireland. As already mentioned, the Wyndham Act of 1903 was the main measure which brought about transfer of land to former tenants: one reason why it had greater effectiveness than earlier Land Acts was that it offered special incentives to landlords to sell out large blocs of land. But A. J. Crichton did not need such special incentives. John McTernan, the modern historian of Sligo town and county, has written of A. J. as follows:

> Long before the Wyndham Act . . . he had put into operation a scheme whereby his tenants could purchase their holdings. Throughout his life he sacrificed time and money in his efforts to secure greater prosperity for the rural community as a whole and the small farmers in particular. . . . Crichton was one of the County Sligo pioneers of the I.A.O.S. [Irish Agricultural Organisation Society], whose aims were to assist the emancipated farmer after the passing away of landlordism. . . . He was a man before his time.[48]

Also 'a man before his time', Sir Alexander would probably have approved of the liberal sentiments and actions of his grandson, Alexander Joseph.

FIVE

THE MYSTERIOUS
DANIEL HENRY FERRALL
OF ROSCOMMON

—

I INTRODUCTION

Daniel Henry Ferrall (1788–1853) was one of the most extensive landowners in
Roscommon in the 1840s. He died unmarried and without issue.[1] Practically
nothing about the last decade of his life has hitherto been known to historians.
His lands were scattered throughout the county and they extended into Sligo
(see map 5).

Ferrall was a member of the Grand Jury of County Roscommon throughout the 1820s.[2] His nominal residence was a structure called Beechwood a
few miles outside Roscommon town,[3] but he lived in England during much of
the 1840s and it is probable that he died in France. In his absence, Beechwood
was occupied by his nephews, Edward and Daniel Irwin. It seems that Edward
resided at Beechwood in the early 1840s only; thereafter, Daniel was its
principal resident.[4]

The following are details of Ferrall's family background.[5] The first point
to note is that the Ferralls were Catholics. A grandfather of D. H. Ferrall,
Terrence Ferrall (or Farrell), was living near Roscommon town in 1749. He
was a wealthy farmer and father of Richard[6] who died in Bristol in 1799 and of
John who died unmarried in 1823. Richard had one surviving son – the Daniel
Henry of the present chapter – and four daughters, one of whom was the
future Mrs Conmee. Another daughter of Richard was named Catherine. She
died before 1854, having married E. J. Irwin. Thus, the Edward and Daniel
Irwin mentioned above (D. H. Ferrall's nephews) were sons of Catherine
and E. J. Irwin. After the death of D. H. Ferrall in 1853, his estates passed to
his sisters or their successors, including Mrs Conmee who became benefactress of the Christian Brothers schools in Roscommon town and of various
Catholic charities.

Ferrall contested the Parliamentary seat of Athlone in 1841. This did not meet the approval of J. R. Stewart who wrote to Kincaid: 'Bad as he is while in Ireland he would be far worse in London'.[7] Following a lengthy controversy during which Ferrall was ultimately elected and then unseated, the question of who was the MP for Athlone was not resolved until a by-election in the spring of 1843, which Ferrall was ineligible to contest.[8] Thus, Ferrall's absence from Ireland during the later 1840s was not related to any parliamentary representation on his part.

On initial impressions, the huge extent of Ferrall's estates suggests that he was a wealthy man. At over £9,000 per annum, the gross annual rental income from his lands was close to the £10,000 plus raised from the Palmerston properties in Dublin and Sligo. But Ferrall was not financially liquid. He had come into possession of all or most of his estates under a Deed of Trust as provided for in the will of his uncle John Ferrall in 1823. A legal document names 95 divisions of land – townlands or subdivisions of townlands – which Ferrall thereby acquired.[9]

The Deed of Trust meant that there were many claimants against the estate. In order to secure the interests of annuitants against the estate under his uncle's will, Ferrall (or, rather, Stewart & Kincaid on his behalf) was obliged to take up insurance policies for large sums on his life; these had adverse effects on his liquidity, and he resorted to substantial borrowing. As interest on his debts compounded and as legal bills increased, Ferrall's liabilities steadily advanced in the 1840s.

Ferrall was in serious financial trouble by 1843, by which time he had resorted to borrowing from some of his tenants. One of these was James Nolan, who was also Stewart & Kincaid's principal local agent in Roscommon. On 14 July 1842 Nolan informed Stewart & Kincaid that 'while he [Ferrall] was in London his bill [of exchange] became due . . . , dishonoured' (SK). The bill had been drawn by the Stewart & Kincaid agent in Longford, and had been accepted by Ferrall. Almost a year later James Nolan wrote to Stewart & Kincaid that a bill drawn by him on Ferrall had been dishonoured, and he added: 'I wont in future ask you to discount [bills accepted by Ferrall]. . . . The bank wont discount any bill with his name on it'.[10] A letter to Kincaid from Nolan on 26 August 1842 indicates that another tenant, P. O'Connor, was experiencing difficulties in extracting payment of £47 which Ferrall owed him. Another letter, written by Ferrall in 1843, indicates that he was in debt to Susan Stuart, one of his tenants near Strokestown.[11] Ferrall's indebtedness to Miss Stuart was to cause her problems during the famine, when many of those who held land from her under conacre failed to pay: this meant that she herself could not pay rent. In April 1846 she wrote to Stewart & Kincaid that her loan of £325 to Ferrall was now due for redemption, and she asked whether he had made any arrangement with Stewart & Kincaid about it. J. R. Stewart merely scribbled 'Not answered' on the letter (s к). Two subsequent communications indicate that the bill was dishonoured. In October 1846 Miss Stuart informed Stewart & Kincaid that she had recently received the firm's demand for 18 month's rent, but she replied that 'if you cannot take it out of the sum Mr Farrell owes me it is out of my power to pay'.[12] Ferrall was also in debt to one of Palmerston's Ahamlish tenants, Isabella Soden. The loan had probably been arranged by Stewart & Kincaid. In 1848 she wrote to Kincaid that she could not pay rent due to Palmerston, but she requested: 'Give me Mr Farrells address. I lent him my money for five years he has it more than double. . . . Let Mr Farrell pay principle & interest and of course I will then pay'.[13]

The Stewart & Kincaid correspondence indicates that throughout most of the 1840s Ferrall was engaged in attempts to evade litigation, that one reason why, for much of the time, he lived in England was to avoid prosecution by his creditors in Ireland, and that another reason for being non-resident was that for some years he was trying to raise huge loans in London. By 1848, when he fled to France, he was 'on the run' not only from his Irish creditors, but also from those financiers with whom he had earlier been in negotiation in London. The Stewart & Kincaid correspondence provides no evidence that he ever obtained the loans which he sought there.

The role of Stewart & Kincaid in management of Ferrall's financial affairs in the 1840s was roughly as follows. First, Stewart & Kincaid collected the rents. From such sums raised, Stewart & Kincaid paid the annuitants and other claimants against the estate, and paid the premia on several insurance policies on Ferrall's life. The firm also made monthly payments to Ferrall himself. In the mid-1840s such payments to Ferrall amounted to about £600 per annum.[14] But in the face of negligible rent receipts, in 1847 Stewart & Kincaid cut back the monthly payments to him. On 16 November 1846 Nolan reported to Stewart & Kincaid that he had received a letter from Ferrall, telling him that Stewart & Kincaid were about to reduce that part of his annual income, paid to him by his agents, to £300. In the same letter, Nolan remarked: 'I wrote him . . . that I considered him very fortunate to get so much; for that if he had the rts. [receipts] of the rents himself and were to pay all the charges you are obliged to pay, that he would not have sixpence' (sк).

In 1847–8, Stewart & Kincaid's expenditures in connection with Ferrall exceeded the income raised from his estates.[15] Ferrall's own income consisted of the remittances from Stewart & Kincaid, plus unknown sums from 'private resources'. His income from such sources presumably consisted of rental payments from his nephew(s) at Beechwood and income from the farm there. Thus, in the mid-1840s, Ferrall's net annual income – about £600 paid to him

by Stewart & Kincaid, plus what was probably a relatively small sum (not paid
through Stewart & Kincaid) from his house and farm at Beechwood – came to
an unknown sum of £600 plus.

In the first half of the nineteenth century, insurance companies rather than
banks were important sources of long-term loans to landlords in England. But
as W. A. Maguire has observed, 'such loans were difficult for an Irish landowner to obtain. . . . The lack of institutional sources for long-term loans was
unfortunate for a landowner [in Ireland] not only because it reduced his range
of choice but also because it made it difficult to consolidate his borrowings. . . .
So far as loans on mortgage security are concerned, Irish sources were local
and personal rather than institutional.'[16]

    In comparison with the years to come, for Ferrall the early 1840s must have
been relatively stress free. Although by 1841 he had already raised loans in
Ireland, at interest rates of about six per cent, these individually were for fairly
small sums,[17] and he was able to spend much of 1841–3 at Beechwood. Writing
from there on 22 August 1842, he informed Stewart that he was sending 'by
this day's [canal] boat . . . three brace of grouse shot yesterday'. Similar letters
followed in 1843 and in 1845. However, Ferrall was not at Beechwood for most
of the rest of the decade.

    Late in 1841 Ferrall and Stewart & Kincaid considered arranging a huge
loan on the security of Ferrall's estate, the proceeds from which would be used
to pay off existing claimants against the estate. It does not seem that there
were any significant developments in this context until 1843. On 15 March of
that year a person in Dublin who signed his letter 'R Newcomen' wrote to
Ferrall in London: 'A friend of mine has from *thirty* to *forty* thousand pounds
to lend. . . . I think you could have it on better terms than what is usual.(sk)'
There are good reasons for believing that this letter was not taken seriously,
because it seems that the motives of the true writer (not 'R Newcomen') were
malicious.[18] Five weeks later Ferrall wrote from Beechwood to Stewart &
Kincaid requesting that Kincaid use his contacts in the City of London to
investigate the possibility of raising a large loan there.

    In May 1843 Ferrall went to London, whence he wrote to Stewart &
Kincaid on 24 May that he had been in conversation with a Mr Browne in
regard to the possibility of obtaining a loan from the firm in which he was a
partner. He elaborated: 'I have been offered [apparently by a source other than
Browne] the money I want since my arrival – that to pay off the charges under
my uncle's will at 4 per cent per ann and a promise of the remainder at 5 per

cent per ann but I did not feel myself at liberty to treat with anyone [else while dealing with Browne]' (sk). But it seems that Ferrall was exaggerating the firmness of the 'offer' – for he again (in the same letter) appealed to Stewart & Kincaid to use contacts in the City of London.

Back at Beechwood, Ferrall wrote to Stewart & Kincaid on 3 June 1843, stating that he was optimistic of success with Browne's firm 'notwithstanding the agitation now going on in Ireland' (sk). In this he was referring to the so-called 'monster meetings' which had been organised by Daniel O'Connell from March onwards, demanding repeal of the Act of Union between Great Britain and Ireland. On the next day, however, Ferrall informed Stewart & Kincaid that he had just learned that he would not be getting a loan from Browne's firm. Again he appealed to Stewart & Kincaid to use contacts in London, adding that he must 'extirpate myself from my present position and from paying excessive interest which I at present pay for the money I have borrowed in Ireland' (sk).

It seems that Ferrall's apparent optimism in regard to obtaining a London loan on acceptable terms was pretended rather than real – that it was designed to spur Stewart & Kincaid into action on his behalf. Stewart & Kincaid did approach contacts in the City. On 3 August 1843 the secretary of the Royal Exchange Assurance Company there wrote to Stewart & Kincaid declining his firm's willingness to lend to Ferrall at five per cent annually as offered by Stewart & Kincaid (sk). The secretary's letter pointed out the following: Ferrall's estates yielded a gross rental income of £9,360 per annum; the loan which Stewart & Kincaid sought on Ferrall's behalf was £53,000; the proposed collateral was that if Ferrall died prematurely, £35,000 would be paid by the insurers on his life, and £18,000 would be raised through sale of Ferrall lands. Given that Ferrall's net annual income from his estate was only £600 plus, and given that his outlays on improvements appear to have been negligible, the information just cited indicates that payments to annuitants and other claimants against the estate, combined with the annual payments on Ferrall's life insurance policies, must have absorbed a very high proportion of his gross rental income.

The attempt to raise a loan from the Royal Exchange having failed, Ferrall looked elsewhere. It seems that he again approached the party in London to whom he had referred in his letter of 24 May 1843 and who had 'offered' him what he needed. However, the extent to which he was dependent on his agents is indicated by the following request in a letter from Ferrall to Stewart & Kincaid on 15 September: 'The party . . . with whom I have been in communication relative to the loan requires to know in what insurance offices my life has been insured and to what extent in each office. . . . Let me know (sk)'. The person with whom Ferrall was now negotiating was J. Bourdillon, an intermediary between Ferrall and the Globe Insurance Company in London. These negotiations were to accentuate Ferrall's financial problems. On 21 December 1843 Bourdillon sent Ferrall a copy of the following letter which he had just received from the secretary of the Globe, J. C. Denham: 'The Board this day . . . resolved that the proposal on the part of Mr Ferrall for the advance to him by the company of the sum of £50,000 on the security of his estates in Ireland, be proceded with on the following terms – The amount interest on the Mortgage part to be 4 p.c., and 6 p.c. in addition to the required premium of insurance . . . for the Life Annuity part'. In sending this copy to Ferrall at the Reform Club in London, Bourdillon added: 'I shall be glad to see you [so] that we may get forward with the Title for the £18,000' (s k).

Thus, with Bourdillon acting as intermediary, the Globe had agreed in principle to lend Ferrall £50,000; £18,000 of this consisted of a mortgage on Ferrall's real estate, the collateral on the residual was £32,000 in insurance policies on Ferrall's life, and Ferrall would have to provide title deeds pertaining to his lands so that the mortgage could go ahead. On 23 December 1843 Ferrall wrote to Kincaid from London: 'I have concluded the negotiation for the loan in the Globe office. . . . I had to consent that a person should be sent on the part of the insurance office to view the estate. The chairman . . . assured me . . . that the person sent shall be . . . reasonable in his demand for remuneration' (s k).

Ferrall went on to indicate that the greater part of the loan would be used 'for liquidating my personal debts'. In the same letter, he anticipated that the paper/parchment work related to confirmation of title would not be expensive: in connection with earlier loans to Ferrall, similar work had already been performed by the Dublin solicitors E. and P. Nolan. Ferrall enclosed a list indicating the documents required by Bourdillon but cautioned: 'We must have all the abstracts prepared in Ireland . . . as they will be done much cheaper'. Ferrall also stated that he intended having a Dublin solicitor named Donnelly 'apply to the persons who hold the yet outstanding bills which I endorsed for the Nolans for a letter of licence to enable me to go to Dublin' (s k). Thus, it can be inferred that Ferrall had earlier accepted bills of exchange drawn by the Nolans; that the bills had been dishonoured; that he feared prosecution for debt if he returned to Ireland; and that a letter of licence was an instrument which would exempt him from prosecution, for some definite time period, thereby enabling him to make preparations to settle the debts.

At the end of 1843 Ferrall must have thought that he would have the cash from the loan in a matter of months, and that the debts which he faced in Ireland would be speedily paid off. He was anxious to minimise costs. Just before Christmas he expressed concern about the costs (for which he would be responsible) of having a surveyor sent to inspect his estates on behalf of the Globe. On 30 December he wrote to Stewart & Kincaid that Bourdillon 'is evidently looking to have a considerable bill of costs for himself' (sk); in fact, when Bourdillon was informed that copies of the abstracts of title were being prepared in Ireland, 'he said at once that it was not fair . . . as that was his business and that he also should make copies to send to Mr Freshfield the solicitor for the Globe', whom Ferrall described as 'the most eminent solicitor in London' (sk). He may also have been the most expensive solicitor there.

Many documents on Ferrall's title to lands were needed by Bourdillon. In January 1844 it became clear that some of them could not be found. Other necessary documentation was in the custody of the Nolans (the Dublin solicitors mentioned above) but they were unwilling to hand them over to Kincaid, for dispatch to Ferrall in London. The fact was that Ferrall owed money to the Nolans. On 11 January, Ferrall wrote to Stewart & Kincaid that 'the bill of costs due to the Nolans must now be liquidated and if so how can they hesitate to deliver up [requisite documents] to me. . . . I will not submit to the extortion which they evidently contemplate practising on me' (sk). Here he was referring to the fact that the Nolans wanted not only payment for services already rendered; they also wanted further work by being involved in preparation of documents related to the proposed loan.

On 16 February 1844 Ferrall wrote from Paris urging Kincaid to send him £50. He did not feel that he could safely deal in person with the Nolans. In the same letter he mentioned: 'I shall leave this [place] immediately after the receipt of the remittance and will also get to Ireland as speedily as I possibly can but I beg of you not to mention that I have such an intention' (sk). On 2 March he again wrote to Kincaid from Paris, stating that he was now departing, not for Dublin, but for London. He instructed: 'Do not mention that I am in that town . . . until I have settled all arrangements relative to the claims against me for [the bills of exchange which he had accepted for] the Nolans. I do not wish the Dublin people to know where I am' (sk).

Back in London, Ferrall wrote to Kincaid on 18 March, hoping 'that you will be able without Mr P Nolans assistance to prepare and send over here such abstracts of the missing titles as will enable Mr Bourdillon to satisfy Mr Freshfield. . . . All the parties are calling urgently for them. . . . If those titles were furnished we should very soon know whether we could serve the 14 months notice on the creditors to whom I pay the annuities of our intentions of paying them of[f]' (sk). In the same letter, he indicated that he feared prosecution for debt in the courts of Roscommon, and pleaded with Kincaid to help him.

On 26 April 1844 Ferrall wrote from London to Stewart in connection with an extra insurance policy on his life, which he was about to take out at the Globe. He announced: 'I have as I have too frequently before done forgotten the date of my birth and you or Mr Kincaid will have to specify this part and I have left a blank in the document for the purpose of inserting it'. He

mentioned that he could not safely come to Dublin in order to have his
signature witnessed, and he therefore proposed that he would 'go to Liverpool
to meet any one you please to send over to witness my signature to the papers'.
This letter also indicates that he was now thinking of submitting to what he
had earlier described as 'extortion' by the Nolans. In it he wrote: 'I very much
fear that whether I like it or not I must employ Mr Nolan in completing the
Title I want to make out for the purpose of the loan. . . . He will give no explanations to Mr Bourdillon on the subjects on which he requires information
unless I . . . employ him' (s k).

Ferrall was in London for most of 1844 and the first half of 1845.
This presence cost money; hence, each month he urged Stewart & Kincaid to
send funds. At this stage the monthly remittances usually amounted to £50,
sometimes £60. Lack of real progress in the negotiations for the loan, and
Ferrall's continued outlays in England, must have worried Stewart & Kincaid.
Nevertheless, Ferrall remained optimistic or pretended to be optimistic.
Referring to the imprisonment of Daniel O'Connell, he reported to Stewart
& Kincaid in May 1844: 'Money is most abundant here. . . . Irish security is
more popular here than it was as I think the verdict against O'Connell has
increased the confidence of the capitalists' (s k).

Ferrall's expenses continued to mount. In the summer of 1844 he employed
a Dublin solicitor named McKeogh in connection with a search for various
deeds. He also found it necessary to give work to the Nolans.[19] On 4 June he
wrote to Kincaid in regard to the missing deeds 'as Mr Bourdillon fears that
without . . . them we may be disappointed in completing the loan' (s k). On
5 July, Ferrall urged Kincaid to bring hitherto missing deeds with him when
departing from Dublin for London early in the same month: a few days earlier
he had informed Kincaid 'you will always find me at the Reform Club about
12. . . . I will be with you at Morley's [Hotel in Cockspur St] the morning after
your arrival'.[20] But Kincaid did not bring the documents to London,[21] and
further delays therefore followed.

On 1 July 1844 Ferrall wrote to Kincaid: 'I have been obliged to submit to a
view of the estate by a surveyor employed by the Globe, a Mr Beadle. . . . I had
to yield to allow him ½ per cent [some £250, a sum close to one half of Ferrall's
annual allowance from Stewart & Kincaid] of all the money lent' (s k). Ferrall
indicated that he was worried that recent disturbances in Roscommon would
have an adverse effect on Beadle's recommendations. The same letter reveals
that Kincaid had tried to prevent Beadle's visit to the estate.

After a long absence from home, Ferrall returned to Beechwood in
August 1844. The surveyor's preliminary observations having been received,
on 5 September Bourdillon wrote to Ferrall, addressed c/o 6 Leinster Street
and redirected to Beechwood: 'Beadle has . . . surveyed your estate of which

he speaks in the highest terms . . . but he will require to state in his report the outgoings. . . . Send us a statement of them, also the arrears of the . . . rental. . . . Mr Kincaid objected to show him the rent book which renders this enquiry necessary.' (s k)

The Stewart & Kincaid correspondence contains only a few letters from Ferrall in the twelve months which followed. However, it seems that the surveyor's final report was favourable, and that Ferrall was at Beechwood for most of the year up to August 1845. The indications are that he then expected speedy release of the loan, thereby enabling him to pay off his creditors and to reside in safety in Ireland. He was in a relaxed mood on 15 August 1845, when he wrote from Beechwood to Maxwell at Leinster Street: 'My carrier will be in Dublin on Tuesday next and perhaps you would be so kind as to go over to Mr Tabuteau's[22] . . . & have the wine prepared to be delivered to here. . . . Let there be five dozen of port and the same of sherry. . . . When I hear from you [I] shall settle for it'. But Tabuteau did not receive payment until near the end of 1848.[23]

Alas, things had gone wrong! The final letter written by Ferrall from Beechwood is dated 5 November 1845: all subsequent letters from him were written from Britain or France, and many of them indicate that he was to use the name D. Fenton as an alias. Ferrall left Ireland (and probably never returned) around the beginning of February 1846. On 26 March he wrote to Stewart from Liverpool, stating: 'Let me have a ten pound note as I am . . . out of cash. . . . I propose leaving this [place] on Monday. . . . Direct [to] Mr Fenton, Post Office, Liverpool' (s k). On 22 September he again wrote to Stewart & Kincaid from Liverpool: 'I propose leaving this for London. . . . Remit me there . . . sixty pounds for the month as you did for the last and direct to me to the Reform Club Pall Mall in my own name'. This letter indicates that the monies from the proposed loan had not yet been disbursed, and that Ferrall was going to London to clarify the delay. With rental incomes in Ireland expected to fall due to the onset of famine, Stewart & Kincaid were unwilling to send Ferrall the £60 which he sought: the letter bears the Stewart & Kincaid endorsement 'Sent order for £50' (s k).

A letter to Stewart & Kincaid from Ferrall in London, 3 October 1846, provides further indications as to why he felt that he could not openly return to Ireland. In this he wrote:

My most anxious desire is to return to Ireland; but I am detered from doing so, on account of the bills which I so unfortunately accepted for the Messrs Nolan. . . . I should not, of course, be so unreasonable as to think you would pay money on my account, out of your own funds; but I . . . hope that, bad as my prospects are, still a sufficient sum may be raised from the estate to meet the claims for interest and regular charges, and to afford me . . . subsistance. (s k)

Back in Liverpool from London, Ferrall wrote to Stewart on 17 October 1846, indicating

> the particulars of my interview with the . . . Globe. . . . Denham, the secretary, assured me repeatedly that the sole cause of delay at present was the fact that they did not have the money to spare . . . and that my application stood *first* on their list for acceptance. . . . Denham . . . thought that . . . in January [1847] the business might be brought to a conclusion. . . . I feel pretty confident that it will be terminated satisfactorily. . . . I think that it might be as well to forward this letter to Mr Kincaid in Sligo, or to let him know that I am here for the purpose of [secretly] proceeding to Ireland to meet him. . . . I shall not go over to Dublin, until we fix decidedly on the day on which we are to meet. (s k)

In some respects Ferrall's position in October 1846 was similar to that of early 1844. Again he was 'on the run' and again he asserted optimism. But his indebtedness had increased in the interim, and his prospects of rental income were more bleak than ever before.

3 FURTHER DISAPPOINTMENTS AND MORE TROUBLE

Ferrall's letters from England late in 1846 and early in 1847 indicate that he was desperate for cash. Stewart & Kincaid claimed that he had 'private resources' which he should liquidate, and that if he did so, he would not have to depend on Stewart & Kincaid to the same extent as hitherto. Among those resources, Stewart & Kincaid claimed, was a store of oats at Beechwood. In response, on 3 October 1846 Ferrall wrote to Stewart & Kincaid:

> Your estimate of the value of the oats at Beechwood is overcharged. . . . I could not calculate on quite half of what you suppose it to be worth; but . . . if it were . . . ground for meal . . . it should be distributed amongst the tenants. . . . My nephew [Daniel Irwin] would not be allowed by the populace to sell any portion of it for consumption in other localities; . . . [hence] little reliance could be placed on that as a resource for supplying personal wants. (s k)

On 30 November 1846 Ferrall in Liverpool acknowledged receipt from Stewart & Kincaid of 'half notes for twenty five pounds' but he added that 'unless you augment this sum, it is quite useless for me to . . . attend to any business in London'. He claimed that Stewart & Kincaid were 'under an erroneous impression as to the value of the private resources which you suppose me to possess' (s k). But Stewart & Kincaid persisted on the question of such resources. As late as 28 July 1847, Stewart asked Kincaid 'what became of DHF £1000 worth of oats?' (sk).

On 10 February 1847 Ferrall wrote to Stewart & Kincaid: 'I would struggle, for this year to manage with forty pounds per month; and this I hope you will endeavour to allow me, but, to extricate me from the emergencies which oppress me at present', he indicated that he needed an extra once-off payment of £50; otherwise he feared that he would be subjected to 'unpleasant exposure in the County of Roscommon, an alternative which I feel confident you will do all in your power, consistent with reason, to avert' (sk). Three days later, he explained to Stewart & Kincaid that his need for the extra £50 was occasioned by the fact that he had received 'an application for poor rates for Corbo [townland] and Beechwood. . . . The sum claimed amounts to . . . £47–18 – and I am sure that the taxes on the two places for the year will amount to considerably more than one hundred' (sk). The high levels of poor rates reflected the fact that by January 1847 the workhouse at Roscommon town was full.[24]

On 2 March 1847 Ferrall informed Kincaid that he had recently been conferring with Denham of the Globe, and wrote that he had 'hopes that the board may advance at present the amount of the charges under my uncle's will' (sk). But these discussions at the Globe were not successful, and Ferrall retreated to Liverpool as the summer of 1847 approached. On 7 June he wrote to Stewart & Kincaid from that city to inform them that: 'I leave this tomorrow for Llangollen [in Wales] as fever is so rife here that I am apprehensive of remaining. So in future please to direct to . . . Mr Fenton, P.O. Llangollen' (sk). It is likely that Ferrall's fellow countrymen, the incoming Irish, many of whom were carrying typhus on their bodies, were the main source of the outbreak of fever in Liverpool. Some of those arriving there were in such wretched condition that they were refused passage to America, for fear of increasing mortality aboard ship. Because their presence in the city posed a threat to the lives of the local population, in 1847 many thousands of them were re-shipped back to Ireland.[25] Under the alias 'Fenton', Ferrall stayed mainly at Llangollen until October 1847.

It seems that around the beginning of September 1847 Ferrall was offered a large loan by a Mr Hughes of Norfolk. About six weeks later, he told Stewart & Kincaid that the money which Hughes had offered 'is vested in trustees; and one of them requires £1000 . . . for his consent . . . and . . . he expects £700 or £800 . . . for commission besides this thousand. . . . I could not afford to pay so much' (sk).[26] However, by this stage Ferrall had re-entered negotiations with Bourdillon, and on 1 October he expressed confidence of getting the money from one source or the other.

Bourdillon had recently written to Ferrall stating that he (Bourdillon) could arrange the money needed, from a source other than the Globe.[27] On

24 September, Ferrall wrote to Stewart & Kincaid that 'the party with whom he [Bourdillon] is negotiating has no doubt of being able to procure £60,000 at 5 per cent, but in the event of its being carried out to have £700 for his trouble' (sk). Ferrall was suspicious of Bourdillon's motives. He was already aware that Bourdillon was demanding payment of £700 for the costs of Freshfield in connection with the earlier negotiations at the Globe. Nevertheless, with the money market then in crisis, Ferrall went to meet Bourdillon in London early in October 1847. On 16 October he reported to Stewart & Kincaid:

> We need not hope of procuring any loan until after Christmas. I make no doubt but that the party with whom Mr Bourdillon was in communication is possessed of the money, and would have no hesitation in lending it on Irish security, but that they will do so at present, is out of the question; and the excuse given for not now entering on the business is, that I had made too much delay in consenting to pay the £700 for commission [for Freshfield's services]. . . . I trust however that the negotiation will be renewed, as soon as the present dearth of money diminishes. . . . I before mentioned to you that I thought Mr Bourdillon's anxiety to get me up to London so prematurely was to try to induce me to settle Mr Freshfield's costs; and such was the case. . . . He, I suspect, has implicated himself with Messrs Freshfield, and wishes to put me in his own place; but he shall not do so if I can help it, and my better plan is to keep out of their way until I find I have some certainty [of] the loan. (sk)

Ferrall was in fact legally liable for payment of Freshfield's costs: In February 1845 Bourdillon had written to Freshfield setting out terms which had been agreed by Ferrall: 'In reason of the Globe Insurance Company agreeing to lend [£50,000 to] our client Mr Ferrall . . . we hereby undertake in case from any cause the transaction should not be completed to pay all costs and expenses the Company may incur.'[28] This letter, and the fact that Ferrall had agreed to the terms therein, were unknown to Stewart & Kincaid until Ferrall informed the firm of those facts on 30 November 1847. In the same letter of 30 November, he wrote to Stewart & Kincaid: 'I do not hope to do more than parry off, for some little time, the payment of the costs; as I apprehend that they must be paid in the end' (sk). Bourdillon's next moves – in the second half of 1848 – will be considered shortly. But first, it is interesting to note some apparent discoveries related to Ferrall's estate, made early in 1848.

Ferrall does not appear to have made any further real efforts to raise a loan through Bourdillon, whom he now feared. Again he looked elsewhere, and in February 1848 he wrote from London informing Stewart & Kincaid that he had commenced negotiations with another party (sk). In the course of these negotiations he submitted his uncle's will to legal experts in London. Until then, it seems, both Ferrall and his advisers in Ireland had been under the impression that the Deed of Trust under his uncle's will prevented him from selling part of the estate, and imposed constraints on the extent to which it could be mortgaged. However, the legal opinions obtained in London early in 1848 suggested otherwise. On 25 March 1848 Ferrall informed Stewart & Kincaid that the recent opinion which he had obtained on his uncle's will 'was more favourable to me than I had expected; and . . . according to it, the ultimate fee of the estates devised by the will is vested in me, and I may dispose of them myself, by will, in any manner I may think proper' (s k). Early in the summer of 1848 Ferrall took more expensive legal advice, the content of which, it seems, was similar to that obtained in March.[29] He still wanted to raise a large loan. The recent legal opinions, if correct, would have given him greater flexibility on the question of how he might secure a creditor. However, what happened next in this context is not revealed in the Stewart & Kincaid correspondence. But late in 1848, actions by the London financiers caused Ferrall to flee to France.

Ferrall resided at Liverpool for most of the second half of 1848. However, his creditors in England were not aware of this fact. In his correspondence to them, he pretended that he was writing from Ireland (to which he could not then safely return). Thus, his letters to those in England seeking money from him were, in the first instance, sent as enclosures to Stewart & Kincaid from Liverpool; Stewart & Kincaid then re-entered them in the mails, so that they bore a Dublin postmark. Letters to Ferrall from creditors in England were sent to either Beechwood or c/o Stewart & Kincaid, from which sources they were dispatched to his true place of residence.

On 2 October 1848 Bourdillon wrote to Ferrall: 'There can be no doubt that the costs [claimed by Freshfield] must be paid & on the 24th inst the time will have arrived when the Plaintiff will be entitled to proceed with the Action – this is a position in which I am sure you will not suffer me to be placed on account of a liability purely for your benefit & in full reliance on your honor that I should not be called upon for the payment' (s k). Thus, Bourdillon was stating that Freshfield was about to sue him (Bourdillon) for the costs. It may in fact have been the case, as Ferrall believed, that Freshfield and Bourdillon were colluding. It could only be expected that if Ferrall did not now pay him, Bourdillon would sue Ferrall. On 9 October 1848 Ferrall sent Bourdillon's letter, quoted immediately above, as an enclosure to Stewart, and added:

The enclosed letter is that which you forwarded to me . . . and is from Mr Bourdillon, and, from it, you will learn that, unless some arrangement with Messrs Freshfield be speedily effected, the suit for recovery of the costs, on account of the loan [sought] from the Globe, will be proceeded with; and, as it is probable that an adverse verdict will be obtained, that further heavy costs will be added to those already incurred. It may possibly be very soon an object of importance to us [in negotiations for a loan from some other source] to get us the papers in Mr Freshfield's hands, and the opinions . . . on my Titles. . . . I [therefore] submit it to your consideration . . . to propose to discharge the claim by instalments . . . on the express conditions of having all the papers in Mr Freshfield's hands . . . delivered into our possession. (sk)

On 23 October 1848 Ferrall addressed a letter to Bourdillon 'offering under certain conditions therein specified to pay Messrs Freshfield one hundred [pounds] per ann until their claims against you were discharged in order to relieve you from any responsibility to them on my account' (sk). This offer of payment by instalments was not accepted, and on 26 December 1848 Ferrall felt it necessary to write from London to Stewart & Kincaid: 'It is imprudent for me to remain here on account of Mr Bourdillon who is about to take proceedings against me for the amount of the . . . costs to Messrs Freshfield. . . . I propose proceeding to Paris' (sk). Finding it now safe to abandon his alias, he added in the same letter that Stewart & Kincaid should now send him his monthly remittance to 'Monsieur Ferrall, Rue de Lille No 17, a Paris'. We can be sure that he was deep in financial indebtedness to Stewart & Kincaid by the beginning of 1849; yet he maintained his optimistic facade. On 17 January 1849 he wrote to Stewart & Kincaid from Rue de Lille: 'Your account of the state of Ireland at present is most melancholy; but, let us hope that the great activity now visible in trade in England will cause better prices for agricultural produce. . . . Every mill in the northern manufacturing districts in England is at work and the manufacturers will be enabled to purchase beef and mutton, and thus rich us.' (sk)

There is no evidence that Ferrall ever obtained the loan from the Globe: he remained in France until the end of 1849, or beyond. The final letter from him is dated 22 December 1849, written from Rue de Lille. The Stewart & Kincaid correspondence provides no evidence that he ever returned to England or Ireland. The Griffith *Valuations* of County Roscommon in 1857–8 contain many references to 'Reps. Daniel Farrell [Ferrall]' as immediate lessors of land, and his nephew Daniel Irwin was then listed as occupier of some of those lands around Beechwood. Daniel Irwin appears to have inherited Beechwood and some of the land in its vicinity. He died, at Beechwood it seems, in 1866.[30] A publication of 1876 lists James Nolan Irwin (presumably son of Daniel Irwin) of Beechwood as owner of 1,849 acres of land in the County of Roscommon.[31]

It can only be assumed that Ferrall's creditors were ultimately paid. If so, lawyers and financiers, whose honesty in some cases was dubious, must have been major beneficiaries of his difficulties. However, his own financial problems and his ensuing absence from Ireland during the famine years accentuated the hardships of his tenants. What happened on his estates during the 1840s will be investigated in the next chapter.

SIX

FERRALL'S ROSCOMMON ESTATES

—

I INTRODUCTION

The Ferrall estates in Roscommon were scattered (see map 5). First, in the southeast of the county there were the impoverished holdings of the Grange Lyster district in the Barony of Athlone.[1] Second, Ferrall's holdings included many townlands near the centre of the county in the Union of Roscommon.[2] (Amongst others, these included Casheltauna, Corbo and Grange.) Third, to the north and northeast of Roscommon town, Ferrall owned lands in the Union of Strokestown.[3] (These included parts of Ballyfeeny.) Fourth – and further to the north – Ferrall had lands in the Union of Carrick-on-Shannon.[4] Fifth, to the west of Carrick, Ferrall had properties in the Union of Boyle.[5] (These included Dooneen and Runnaboll.) Sixth, Ferrall had extensive holdings in the northwest of the county, in the Union of Castlerea.[6] (These included parts of Aghacurreen, Ballyglass, Lissian and Lissergool.) Ferrall also owned some land across the Roscommon boundary in southern Sligo.

At an annual salary of £80,[7] James Nolan was Stewart & Kincaid's chief local agent for Ferrall's Roscommon estates. He resided at Runnamede (now called Runnamoat) near Roscommon town. Although he farmed on Ferrall land, he also acted for the county in collecting cess (a tax). The north of the county was too far from his residence to enable him in detail to oversee matters there; hence, Patt and John Sharkey (father and son) attended to details on those Ferrall lands.

2 FINANCE AND RENT COLLECTION BEFORE THE FAMINE

For both Ferrall and James Nolan, Stewart & Kincaid often performed some of the functions of a financial institution. In the early 1840s it was not unusual that bills of exchange, accepted by Ferrall, were made payable at 6 Leinster Street, and in other cases, Stewart & Kincaid were asked to ensure that payment was made on Ferrall's acceptances, elsewhere in Dublin. For example, on 25 October 1842 Ferrall wrote to Stewart & Kincaid from Beechwood stating that 'two bills of mine [to an amount of £348] will be due on Friday next and will be called for at your house [i.e. office]' (s k). On 16 November, he again wrote to Stewart & Kincaid, informing them and requesting that 'there will be a bill of mine due tomorrow . . . and I beg of you to send that sum . . . to . . . Fleet Street at No 9' (s k). Stewart & Kincaid also facilitated financial transactions for James Nolan. On 30 October 1842, for example, Nolan wrote to Stewart stating that he 'would feel obliged by your giving directions to have my acceptance . . . due at your office tomorrow, paid, amt £60'. Stewart & Kincaid arranged a £500 loan for Nolan in the winter of 1841–2.[8] And as has been observed in chapter 5, in the early 1840s Stewart & Kincaid discounted bills of exchange drawn by Nolan on Ferrall.

Much of the Ferrall land was held under lease by graziers. Although the leases had clauses discouraging tillage, several of the large tenants had under-tenants, and many in conacre. Among the substantial graziers was James Nolan and, apparently unrelated to him, Michael Nolan. There was also Patt Taaffe, who in 1842 became a member of the Grand Jury of the county.[9] The Stewart & Kincaid correspondence indicates that there were also Edward, James and Dominick Corr; the latter was another member of the Grand Jury. There was George Knox of Strokestown who was government agent on the troubled Crown townland of Ballykilcline, near the Ferrall lands of Ballyfeeny. Shortly before his death around the end of 1847, and under orders from the Crown, Knox supervised the initial stages of mass eviction of virtually every occupant on Ballykilcline, and was responsible for the initial stages of their shipment to America.[10] John French, brother of Lord de Freyne whose mansion was at Frenchpark, was also one of Ferrall's tenants. Thus, Ferrall's larger tenants – the list of whom also included P. O'Connor (probably the Pat O'Connor who was a member of the Grand Jury in 1842) – included some of the most prominent names in the county.

James Nolan attended the most important fairs in Roscommon and in adjacent counties. He kept a close eye on prices obtained by Ferrall's other tenants, and reported them to Stewart & Kincaid. On 3 October 1842 he wrote to Stewart & Kincaid stating that he feared 'from the fair of Boyle being so bad on Saturday, the rt [i.e. rent receipts] will not be as good as last year' (s k). Next day he wrote from Ballinasloe, to report that 'the sheep fair was, at least, 5/- a sheep under last years price' (s k). About three weeks later, he wrote that 'it is impossible to get a shilling from the gentlemen farmers', as those who tried to sell their heifers at the fairs 'could not sell a beast'.[11] The fact that prices at the autumn 1842 fairs were low must at least partly explain why the year which followed was one of greater distress than usual.

The larger tenants on the Ferrall estates usually paid rent by, in the first instance, accepting draft bills of exchange, payable in three or four months, drawn on them by Nolan. The bills were sent to Stewart & Kincaid. The use of bills of exchange as instruments through which the larger tenants paid rent reflected initiatives by Stewart & Kincaid: such bills could be used to ensure that the rent was paid on time, by making redemption dates coincide with the dates at which payment of rent was due. Ferrall's smaller tenants, who usually did not have a lease, were expected to pay in cash, though some of them accepted bills of exchange drawn on them by Nolan. As on Palmerston's Ahamlish, their payments usually lagged behind gale dates. For example, late in 1841 Nolan sent £417 to Stewart & Kincaid and informed that he hoped that he would soon send 'another return which will nearly wind up the Nov. 1840 collection'.[12] But the November 1840 account was not closed until the second half of February 1842. As Nolan explained early in that month, this was mainly because of difficulties on 'Grange Lyster as usual' and on Ballyfeeny; however, he added: 'I have no doubt the B'feeny tenants will make a good payment after the fair of Lanesboro which will be the 12th of this month'.[13]

In the company of the local agent, Stewart or Kincaid or Maxwell usually made a 'raid' on the various parts of the estate twice a year, demanding rent. The local agent would 'notice' the tenants to have their rents ready at a named location on a specific date, and he would work out the itinerary. For example, on 16 September 1841 Nolan wrote to Kincaid:

> I have fixed our route as follows. . . . Commence at Roscommon for B'feeny, Islands[14] . . . , on Saturday the 25th. The Ballyfeeny men will have the benefit of the market at Strokestown on Friday. Monday, Knockcroghery for the Barony Tenants, who will have the market of Athlone on Saturday. Tuesday visit Ballyglass. Wednesday, Castlerea. . . . Thursday visit Dooneen. . . . Saturday Elphin tenants, who will have the benefit of Boyle fair the day before.

Nolan wrote similarly to Kincaid on 9 September 1842:

> Monday 26th at Ballyfeeny. We can receive the rents at John McGuires.[15] . . . Return to Beechwood. Tuesday Barony [of Athlone] at Patt Kellys. . . . Wednesday 28th visit Dooneen & return to Runnamede, or sleep at Castlerea. Friday 30th visit Mayo estate [presumably meaning the Castlerea district] and return to Runnamede. Saturday Roscommon & Monday Elphin. . . . We must not forget laying out a list of any bad tenants . . . and have them process'd [summoned to court] for the next sessions. . . . It will increase the rent in Jany very much, as they will have means, and the decree against those persons will bring them to convert it into money. (SK)

Note, in this passage, that Nolan indicated that he intended to seek ejectment decrees against some 'bad tenants'; however, it seems that he expected that the existence of such decrees would induce payments, and that therefore ejectment decrees might not need execution.

3 DISTRESS, EVICTION, DISTRAINT AND VIOLENCE BEFORE THE FAMINE

Those on the townland of Grange Lyster in the Barony of Athlone were among the most miserable of Ferrall's holdings. On 19 February 1841 Nolan reported to Stewart & Kincaid that the people there 'are in a sad way with poverty & sickness. There are no less than 14 families now in fever' (s κ). A few weeks later he indicated that 'the Barony tenants have been in . . . spotted fever. . . . I dare say 5 or 6 of the tenants [there] are dead, together with losing many of their children'.[16] He also pointed out that Ballyfeeny was another problem townland. Tenants on Ballyfeeny and in the Barony were still distressed at the end of 1841. Some of those on Ballyfeeny may have been served with notices to quit and summonses to court: on 16 October, Nolan wrote that 'the Ballyfeeny lads are really frightened'. And on 31 December he informed Stewart & Kincaid that he had just 'come to [Roscommon] town to attend the sessions, where I hope to rid you of some of our Barony folk' (s κ). It seems likely that Nolan obtained ejectment decrees against tenants on other townlands early in 1842: on 4 January he wrote to Stewart, requesting: 'Send me the Power of Attorney you have from Mr Ferrall as I have some ejectments at Strokestown sessions against some of the Lyssine [Lissian] and Aghacurreen lads' (s κ).

Ejectment for rent arrears was an alternative of last resort on the Ferrall estates in the early 1840s. Early in 1843 Nolan considered a summons for nonpayment of debt as preferable to seeking an ejectment decree. In this context he wrote to Stewart & Kincaid on 13 March: 'I find it impossible to get those defaulters in Grange [Lyster] & B'feeny to pay their rents. It has just occurred to me, that the cheapest, and best mode of bringing them to rights would be to process for all rent up to Nov. last. A decree in that case w'd only cost 5/- and we w'd get the possession of the land a year sooner than by ejecting, or be paid up the rent, which is all we want.' (s κ) Observe in this passage that Nolan indicated that if he were to follow the route leading to ejectment, he would expect about a year to elapse before the landlord were restored to full possession. But it does not seem that Nolan's suggestion was then implemented on any extensive scale. In fact, when the tenant had means, distraint was the preferred solution in the first half of the 1840s. In the same letter of 13 March 1843,

Nolan stated that 'in serving processes on the defaulters, I would only serve those that had nothing to distrain' (s k).

While on a rent-collecting tour of the Ferrall properties, on 13 January 1843 Stewart wrote to Kincaid that he 'found the poor law valuation in every case under the rent but not very much perhaps about 10 p. ct.' (s k). This does not mean that such rental levels were 'unreasonable', relative to those on other estates. As W. A. Maguire has written with reference to the early 1840s, 'on most estates Griffith's [poor law] valuation was considerably below the letting value of the land': on those of the Marquess of Downshire, rents seem to have exceeded Griffith's valuations by about 30 per cent. R. B. MacCarthy has observed that the poor law valuation was 'generally accepted as below the fair letting value' of land.[17] Nevertheless, a collapse in prices – such as occurred late in 1842 and which extended into 1843 – was likely to induce a substantial increase in rent arrears. After that collapse in prices, Nolan wrote early in 1843:

> The Aghacurreen [and] Lyssin [Lissian] . . . tenants have left me in a bad way. I had to pay most of the bills they passed for the May rents. Even the Lyssergooles [Lissergool tenants] and Ballyroe[18] did not pay more than half . . . and I cannot blame them. They did their best, but the prices are so low for everything that it is impossible for them to pay rents, until the fairs come on. I had 30 head of [distrained] cattle belonging to them at the fair of Ballaghadireen, & could only sell one horse.[19]

This passage is curious in its reference to the bills which the tenants 'passed'. It seems that a sequence of events such as the following had taken place: the tenants had accepted bills of exchange drawn on them by Nolan; Nolan had discounted them at a bank on the understanding that he would be liable for payment to the bank should they be dishonoured by the tenants at redemption date; the bills had in fact been dishonoured and Nolan had to pay the bank.

Stewart wrote to Kincaid on 13 January 1843: 'We had a very bad days receipt yesterday. . . . Evidently a combination among the Dooneen tenants to force an abatement by offering short payments which I . . . refused and left Sharkett [Sharkey] orders to distrain.' (s k) Two days later, Stewart reported to Kincaid from Runnamede: 'I was obliged to take bills [probably promissory notes] from a great part of the Castlerea tenants. It was out of the question getting cash.' (s k)

On 16 February 1843 Nolan informed Kincaid: 'I have keepers on Ballyfeeny and the Barony and will not take them off until most of them have paid' (s k). The purpose of placing keepers was to ensure that produce remained safe as collateral for rent arrears, and that it could be sold by Nolan whenever he deemed appropriate. Nolan wrote to Stewart & Kincaid on 14 June: 'I am just returned from Strokestown, where I expected to have got some of the Ballyfeeny arrears after the fair, but . . . [only] two of them . . . p'd. . . . I intended processing . . . some of them, but there w'd be an outcry against us all, if I did, as there are so many landlords giving abatements.' (s k)

John McGuire was probably the most important of Ferrall's tenants on Ballyfeeny. On 23 June 1843 Nolan wrote to Stewart & Kincaid:

> I regretted much the return which I sent up being so very small and the number of defaulters being so many particularly on the B'feeny and Barony Estates. The former . . . will be more satisfactorily paid, than heretofore, as I have entered into an agreement with John McGuire to do the business of that estate. He resides on the land, and will see that any man having means, will sell it, and pay his rent. . . . He will distrain them. (s k)

The pre-famine Stewart & Kincaid correspondence refers to only one large tenant on Ferrall land whose acceptance of a bill of exchange for payment of rent was dishonoured. Nolan responded by distraining. On 21 July 1843 he reported to Stewart & Kincaid: 'I put two keepers on his land for 14 days and on the day previous to the sale a notice was served on the keepers stating that the people [undertenants] having grazing cattle on the land, would bring a party that night and take away their cattle by force. I then thought it more prudent to remove the keepers, as we w'd lose the grazing cattle which was the only stake for the years rent.' (s k) This passage illustrates the fact that, even if they themselves were up to date in rent payments, the property of undertenants could be distrained if their immediate landlord (a middleman) was in arrears. (In such cases the undertenants were legally empowered to take action against their immediate landlord.[20])

Unusual hardship persisted on the Ferrall estates until late in 1843. Kincaid was in Roscommon on 28 September, when Stewart wrote to him: 'I have rec'd your letter with bank order for £350 & bill £135–10–0. I am sorry you have not better success in Roscommon. I think from Ferrall estate alone you used to send up £1400 at this season.' (s k) However, the fairs of late 1843 revealed recovery in prices: in October, Nolan reported that a fair which he had just attended was 'very dear'.[21]

Distress among the tenants during the hungry months of 1843 may have contributed to violence. On 8 June, Nolan wrote to Kincaid: 'They are burning houses of those that wont reduce the conacre rents. They have gone so far as to threaten the priests'. On 14 June he informed Stewart & Kincaid that 'in the Parish of Kilglass [of which most of Ballyfeeny formed part] they are swearing the people not to pay county cess. I fear I will have to get the police.' (s k)

It seems that violence was increasing in Roscommon in the months before the famine. On 29 March 1845 Patt Taaffe wrote to Stewart & Kincaid: 'Should

the present state of things continue . . . it would be better hold no lands. . . .
Fellows are out every night and many armed' (sK). Maxwell was on a rent-
collecting tour of Roscommon when, on 25 September, he reported to Stewart
& Kincaid: 'Night after night outrages are taking place. On Sunday night
last 16 of James Nolan's best heifers were stabbed within 40 yards of the
police barrack of Castleplunket. . . . Nolan talks of his being obliged to leave
Runnamede for the winter and live in Roscommon [town].' (sK)

The Molly Maguires were an agrarian secret society, members of which
sometimes dressed like women when engaged in violence. But in the 1840s,
perpetrators of any form of agrarian crime were often described as Molly
Maguires. On 28 September 1845 Maxwell wrote to Stewart & Kincaid referring to how they were treating Daniel Farmer, a land surveyor at that time
engaged by Stewart & Kincaid in connection with drainage and road building:

> Molly Maguire . . . has kindly selected a wife for him [Farmer] and began by
> serving him with a notice that he must obey under pain of death, but as this would
> not marry the young lady . . . about 20 of them went to his house lately with a horse
> and pulled him out of his bed and would not let him dress . . . and off they set to the
> house where the fair lady lived. They . . . put him to bed with her. (sK)

Maxwell sent further details to Stewart & Kincaid on 30 September:

> This country is in an awful state. . . . Michl. Nolan was stopped . . . when on his car
> coming out of Roscommon [town]. We were on another one within 300 yards of
> his and knew nothing about it and very fortunately for the gentry who did it as we
> had 4 well loaded barrels. Mr Hanley the priest[22] hinted to me . . . that he wished
> very much that one or two of them were shot. . . . The reason James Nolan's cattle
> were stabbed is that he dismissed his herd lately. . . . Molly Maguire . . . insists on
> his taking him back. James Nolan told me . . . that the *clergy* in this county had
> written to Rome to consult the Pope upon . . . whether it would not be well to
> excommunicate all parties allied to Molly. (sK)

A letter from Maxwell to Stewart on 7 October 1845 suggests that there
may have been more to the relationship between Farmer and 'the fair lady'. It
reported that Farmer had been 'attacked again by the Molly Maguires and
given one week to marry the girl under pain of death. I understand that the
priests in his neighbourhood have all denounced him from the altar.' (sK) The
Stewart & Kincaid correspondence does not indicate whether Farmer opted
for marriage, but we know that the death threat was not implemented: on
12 August 1846 James Nolan wrote to Stewart & Kincaid that 'Farmer is
employed by the Board of Works as inspector' (sK).

4 SLOW PACE OF IMPROVEMENT, AND DETERIORATION, ON THE FERRALL LANDS

The Castlerea Agricultural Society was active in the early 1840s. Two Stewart & Kincaid clients – Ferrall and the Marquess of Westmeath – had estates near Castlerea. The society was funded by voluntary contributions and by fees charged for the services of an agriculturalist. In 1842 Ferrall's subscription to the society was £5; the Marquess also subscribed a similar sum. Robert Blundell was the society's treasurer. In a letter to Stewart & Kincaid dated 1 December 1843, requesting a renewal of Ferrall's subscription, Blundell observed that he found 'great apathy among the landlords . . . respecting our agriculturalist's services' and he feared that 'from want of funds we shall have to discharge him' (SK). The advisory service was terminated early in 1845, and it seems that the society ceased to exist a short time later. The agriculturalist, John Kirkpatrick, was unemployed in 1845: on 27 October of that year he requested Kincaid 'to keep me in your eye [as] a person . . . to act as . . . agriculturalist. If I had continued at Castlerea I could have made something of the people. . . . They were just *beginning* to begin' (SK).

Given that Ferrall was in a state of increasing financial crisis in the years just before the famine, it is not surprising that improvements on his lands were few. Furthermore, whatever improvements were made were implemented mainly by the larger tenants rather than by Ferrall. Thus, very few decent houses were built and there were few drainage projects. Admittedly, the scattered character of the Ferrall lands made improvement more difficult than would have applied had his estate been in a single composite bloc. Also, the fact that a high proportion of his acreage was held by graziers meant that there was less need to square holdings. However, Ferrall's absences from Ireland, as well as his inability to honour whatever expectation those tenants with leases might have had in regard to compensation for improvements, militated against progress. Let us consider the case of Patt Kelly, who occupied part of Grange Lyster.

On 4 November 1841 Kelly wrote to Stewart & Kincaid enclosing a bank order for £80 odd 'together with a recpt. for twenty five pounds . . . for the building of the house' (SK). The Stewart & Kincaid correspondence contains very few similar references to building on Ferrall land. Kelly also drained his land, but he was to be disappointed when the matter of compensation arose. On 4 May 1844 he complained to Stewart & Kincaid: 'I am very badly treated, particularly by Mr Ferrall, who told me he would inspect the work that was done and allow full compensation. . . . I must suspend the work . . . until I am alowed for what I have done.'(SK) Kelly again referred to his claim in 1846, when he wrote to Stewart & Kincaid that 'Mr Ferralls absence . . . left me unable to establish my claim upon him which is only three years due'.[23] With Ferrall on the run from his Irish creditors, in hiding in England, there was then little prospect that he could come to inspect the work and validate Kelly's claim.

It seems that 'squaring' of land was implemented on only one Ferrall town-land – Runnaboll – in the 1840s before the famine. This brought protest. On 5 August 1845 Farmer the surveyor wrote to Ferrall that 'the mearing [boundary] between Bern'd Rock and the widow Ferrall remains unsettled. She would not allow me to take the half acre from her and give it to him. She says she will loose her life before she parts with it.' (sk) The same letter indicates that some drain-age was probably implemented on Runnaboll following the allocation of squares.

It does not seem that there were any publicly financed drainage works on Ferrall lands in the first half of the 1840s. On 21 February 1842 Nolan wrote to Kincaid: 'We are fighting ahead to get the drains passed [at a presentment sessions] for taking away the water off Ballyfeeny.' (sk) The project would have involved drainage of the Scramoge river, the flooding of which affected Ferrall lands, as well as lands of two other proprietors, Richard Irwin and one of the Mahons of Strokestown. The application was not passed.[24] Some drainage of the Scramoge was in fact implemented shortly afterwards. But the initiative came from Irwin and Mahon: Ferrall knew little about the details. However, because the drainage improved his lands in the Ballyfeeny district, Ferrall did subscribe – 'liberally' according to a letter from him to Stewart & Kincaid dated 27 May 1844 (sk) – to the project.

Drainage of the Scramoge was amongst the public works carried out late in 1846. Mindful that a second year of potato failure had begun, Ferrall wrote from London to Stewart & Kincaid on 30 August: 'There may be difficulty in obtaining rents this season but I hope that those of our people who are worst off viz those at Ballyfeeny will be able to pay somewhat decently in conse-quence of the work going on for the drainage of the Scramoge River. The[y] will be all no doubt employed.' (sk)

On Ferrall's behalf, Stewart & Kincaid applied to the Board of Works in 1848 for a loan of £1,550 under the Landed Property Improvement Act. The sum finally sanctioned was only £800.[25] This served two functions: on 7 August 1848 the Stewart & Kincaid agent in northwest Roscommon, John Sharkey, wrote that 'the potatoes are partially diseased', and he added that he was 'proud you have succeeded in getting the means to begin the drainage as it will not only benefit the property but I hope mend the condition of very many of the tenants' (sk). Bad housing and lack of farm offices were general throughout the Ferrall estates. In 1848–9, when substantial tracts of his land lay idle, Ferrall recognised that such deficiencies militated against finding large and viable tenants. There can be no presumption that there was any *net* improvement on the Ferrall estates over the 1840s. As will be indicated later, there is evidence that much of the land deteriorated.

5 THE FAMINE ON THE FERRALL ESTATES, 1846

The partial failure of the potato in 1845 did not have immediate effect on receipts from Ferrell's tenants. On 25 September, Maxwell wrote to Stewart & Kincaid from Strokestown that his rent receipts in that district were 'much as usual' (sk). On 30 September he wrote from Castlerea: 'My receipt has hitherto been very successful, as usual not much money from the Barony and Ballyfeeny but here and in Roscommon we have done very well. Rather more *cash* here than usual and less bills. The tenants who went to England got plenty of work and some of them brought home £7 in gold.' (sk) In his next recorded letter, from Beechwood on 7 October, he informed Stewart & Kincaid: 'I enclose . . . bank order for £800 and expect to send you about £200 more from Ballinasloe [fair] tomorrow. The money I have is almost all gold. . . . I came here yesterday evening with Mr Ferrall from Runnaball where we had a field day'. (sk) Two days later he sent Stewart & Kincaid 'another bank order for £230' (sk).

Early in 1846, Maxwell and Stewart went to Roscommon to extract money. On 16 January, Stewart wrote to Kincaid:

> At Elphin . . . payments were made few & grudgingly, not more that day than £300. . . . [However] after going thro Dooneen & scholding a good deal we sat down at Sharkeys house & there recd. another £100 . . . , so that on the whole that district will be nearly as well paid as usual. . . . After threatening ejectments against the Lissergools we made them pay part in cash . . . & took bills from the rest payable after fair of Frenchpark 20th May. . . . The potato crop . . . is very bad. . . . Assistance in work or money may have to be given this summer. The Aghacurreen men also stood out for bills due in September but in the end we took bills from the whole estate payable at the same period (21 May). . . . The people do not deny having means but state they will have to use the corn for their own support. (sk)

On 21 January 1846 Stewart reported to Kincaid: 'Very few rents from Ballyfeeny'; there was, however, 'a good receipt on Beechwood estate' (sk). On 27 January, Nolan wrote to Stewart & Kincaid indicating that developments on Grange Lyster were worse than those on Ballyfeeny. He stated that Patt Kelly was in trouble 'in consequence of not having been paid his conacre' and added that 'they have scarcely one [potato] safe' (sk). Thus, the partial failure of the potato in 1845 began to have major impact on Stewart & Kincaid's receipts only from early in 1846 onwards. Almost all classes were affected. In the case of the small tenants, those who had produced grain, which had previously been a cash crop, now sought to deflect it for their own consumption. Most of the large tenants, who used the land mainly for grazing, had set part of it under conacre, but the collapse in conacre payments moved them also towards financial ruin. The situation became worse as the summer of 1846 approached.

Apart from Grange Lyster and Ballyfeeny, some of the Ferrall lands in the Castlerea district were severely distressed in the months before the 1846 harvest. Among them were Aghacurreen and Ballyroe. These were in the northwest of Roscommon near the boundary with Mayo; hence, they were in the district for which John Sharkey was responsible. On 30 March 1846 Nolan informed Stewart & Kincaid that 'Sharkey . . . was obliged to distrain the defaulters' (s k). And writing to Nolan from Dooneen on 16 April, John Sharkey stated: 'It will be quite out of my power to either receive or return any thing satis-factory. . . . After the service of the Notices to Quit I will be able to make one satisfactory return of all I expect to pick up among them for this season' (s k).

On 1 June 1846 Nolan reported to Stewart & Kincaid: 'I send an order for £209–10–0 in part paymt. of the bills [promissory notes]. . . . I had hard work to bring the Aghacurreen tenants to paymt. . . . I ordered Sharkey to seize every beast. . . . I told them I wd. sell if they did not . . . pay their bills. Some then did so . . . Sharkey says that by Saturday all will be paid up, except about £20, and those are really distressed people, who only ask to get their portion of the bills renewed.' (s k)

The Castlerea Relief Committee had been established by mid-1846. In response to a request for a contribution, on 13 July Ferrall wrote from Wales instructing Stewart & Kincaid to respond as thought fit (s k). It does not seem that Stewart & Kincaid made a contribution on Ferrall's behalf: in response to a petition from the Ballyroe tenants, Nolan had suggested on 23 June: 'It wd. relieve every person in distress on the Castlerea Estate if Mr Ferrall gave £25 for improving the lands. . . . There are about 16 on Aghacurreen in absolute want. . . . The £25 will be better disposed of by giving the employment ourselves than putting it in the hands of a relief committee.' (s k)

Ballyfeeny persisted as a problem townland. Developments there were influenced by those on the nearby Crown townland of Ballykilcline. A 'rebellion' on Ballykilcline against payment of rent had perpetuated from the 1830s onwards; indeed, 'by 1846, none of the tenants owed less than nine and a half years' rent'.[26] The duration of this 'rebellion' and the fact that the military was unable to quell it induced emulation on Ballyfeeny. On 22 December 1845 Nolan wrote to Stewart & Kincaid stating that along with Ferrall, he would be proceeding to Ballyfeeny next day. He observed that he had '6 processes fill'd for the most formidable of our opponents . . . if we find them still inclined to persevere' (s k). On 19 March 1846 Nolan reported that processes had been served on those of the Ballyfeeny defaulters who he knew had means, and he felt sure that such action would scare them into paying. He added: 'One or two of them told me they had the money but were afraid to pay – and said they wd. be glad that I wd. process them.' Thus there was intimidation on Ballyfeeny against those paying rent. Nolan was happy to inform Stewart & Kincaid on 26 May that 'the Ballyfeeny tenants are beginning to show a disposition to pay.... I will proceed with the processes against such as I think are able to pay – there are some I know who cannot'. But on 8 July, Nolan wrote to Stewart & Kincaid that 'the process server could only serve 9 of the Ballyfeeny tenants all of whom I decreed for 1 years rent. The decrees are now in the hands of the bailiff to ... have them executed.... I have no doubt when one or two of the Ballyfeeny lads are arrested, that a great many of them will pay'. He also observed that 'there is a fine prospect of the harvest' (sκ); however, disaster was soon obvious. On 23 July he informed Stewart & Kincaid that 'the potato crop will, I fear, be a failure.... I know of several places where the stalks are as withered as you wd. see them in December' (sκ). On 12 August he wrote to Kincaid: 'There is a total loss of the potatoe crop' (sκ).

Drainage on Ballyroe, advocated by Nolan in June 1846, commenced in August. Patt Sharkey of Lissian (father of John Sharkey of Dooneen) was the overseer. The outlay of £25 on these works had been recommended before the 1846 potato failure was known. It was now obvious that they were on a trivial scale compared to what was needed. On 21 August, Nolan reported to Stewart & Kincaid: 'I left [Patt Sharkey] ten pounds to pay them a weeks wages.... This country presents a melancholy appearance, not a vestige of a green stalk.... If it had not been for the public works ... hundreds would have starved all the summer.' (sκ)

Kincaid came on a rent-gathering tour of Roscommon late in September 1846. On 9 September, Nolan wrote to him outlining the proposed itinerary, and warned: 'Our prospects ... are very gloomy' (sκ). Some income was raised from the Ferrall lands in the autumn of 1846, but we do not know how much. Some defaulting tenants were brought to court. Thus, on 8 October John Sharkey wrote to Maxwell: 'The civil bills have been timely served on the old defaulters.... There can be nothing better done to forward the approaching collection than to proceed against the few for example to the many' (sκ). A few weeks later, Nolan reported to Stewart & Kincaid that 'the processes have frightened both the Dooneen and Aghacurreen lads, the Aghacurreen men wanting [to sign] a bill, and the Dooneen men to get time until after Croghan fair'. He also proceeded against some of the Ballyfeeny tenants, about whom he wrote, in the same letter, that he would 'if possible have some of them arrested, and that may do some good'.[27]

The Stewart & Kincaid correspondence of 1846 contains only one petition from a Ferrall tenant seeking abatement. It was written by a woman near Carrick-on-Shannon, who stated that her husband had recently died, and that he had left her with 'eight infant children'.[28] The letter bears Stewart's manuscript note, 'Not answered'. Another of Ferrall's tenants near Carrick sought deferral of rent in 1846. In November, John Golrick of Knockadalteen delivered a plea addressed to Nolan and Kincaid at Elphin. He wrote of his 'truly wretched' distress, 'not having as much as would sustain one of my nine children'. He stated that death had recently deprived him of his wife, 'and afterwards it has pleased an all wise providence to blast our hopes, by depriving us of our potatoe crop, the only sustenance we had'. He therefore sought 'an extension of time' for payment of his rent, and added that he was 'not the only applicant that the universal cry of misery and distress . . . has urged some relief of their agents'.[29] No person named Golrick was listed on Knockadalteen in Griffith's *Valuation* of 1858.

The Union of Carrick-on-Shannon included part of the Barony of Boyle. This district contained all or parts of four parishes – among them Ardcarn and Tumna – within which there were several Ferrall townlands (including Knockadalteen). By late 1846 distress in this district was extreme.[30] On 24 October the secretary of the relief committee for Ardcarn and Tumna wrote to Ferrall seeking a subscription, in view of the starvation and the absence of public works in the district (SK). Ferrall sent this letter to Stewart & Kincaid, whose response is unknown.

One could reasonably ask, how could the smaller tenants in Roscommon possibly have paid their rents in the autumn of 1846? The public works were one possible source of income, and Nolan tried to ensure that Ferrall's tenants benefited from them. On 13 September he informed Stewart & Kincaid that a presentment sessions was about to be held at Frenchpark, which he proposed to attend 'in order to get public works for the Aghacurreen and Dooneen tenants'. He indicated that he intended 'to apply for a continuation of Mr Ferralls new road thro Dooneen out to the Frenchpark road', which, he believed, would 'give the tenants a great deal of employment – and be of great use to the estate also' (SK). Similarly, two months later Nolan informed Stewart & Kincaid that he would be attending another presentment sessions at which he would press for public works on a Ferrall townland near Beechwood.[31]

Apart from the possibility of paying rent from public works income, there was also a possibility of demanding works of improvement from the tenants, on their own holdings, in lieu of rent, and this was suggested by Stewart in a letter to Kincaid, 26 September 1846. Stewart wrote: 'Your account of the *payments* out of Ballyfeeny & Kilglass does not at all surprise me. . . . If we employ . . . them by *allowance out of the rent* we lose *nothing* & get the work done, but I should not be inclined to pay away any cash in that district.' (SK) This would have amounted to a policy of starvation. The Stewart & Kincaid correspondence provides no evidence that it was implemented.

It was not only the small tenants, and those who held land under conacre, who fell victim to developments in 1845–6. Middlemen experienced loss of conacre income, and some of them were quickly edged into financial collapse. Among them, it seems, was the magistrate George King[32] in the Barony of Athlone, who was in trouble by the end of 1845. It appears that he was ejected early in 1846. George Knox, the Crown agent on Ballykilcline, was another grazier in trouble. In June 1846 he wrote to Stewart & Kincaid that he could not yet pay the May gale on Casheltauna, as he had 'no rents coming in'. In October he requested of Stewart & Kincaid 'to let the May gale remain over a little longer until I ascertain will the people release their conacre oats. . . . [Otherwise] I hope . . . you will agree to take the land off my hands'. The land formerly held by Knox lay idle in April 1848, when Nolan wrote to Stewart & Kincaid that 'Knox's land is so much out of heart that I fear it will be hard to get grazing for it'.[33]

Ferrall owned small tracts of land in southern Sligo. These were largely in the Barony of Leyny, where Charles O'Connor, a middleman, was his tenant. On 17 August 1846, O'Connor wrote to Stewart & Kincaid from Roadstown[34] that 'last year I lost considerably by the conacre and this year from the total failure of the potatoe crop. . . . I'll be unable to make out any rents' (SK). On 27 October he again wrote to Stewart & Kincaid: 'I find it impossible to get any rents owing to the great *distress*' (SK). It seems that O'Connor's difficulties persisted for some years. In his final letter in the Stewart & Kincaid correspondence dated 8 August 1848 he wrote: 'I have a greater part of the land set to tenants [but] it is impossible now to get a shilling from them. . . . Most of them are gone to England to seek for work' (SK). He closed this letter with the remark that 'this country is most peaceable' (SK). Two points are relevant here. First, as will be indicated below, the Ferrall lands a few miles to the south of O'Connor's holdings were also depopulated in 1848. Second, life on those lands to the south was not 'most peaceable'.

6 THE FAMINE ON THE FERRALL ESTATES, 1847

On at least three occasions during the summer of 1846, Ferrall received requests to subscribe to local relief committees in districts where he had land. In each case he directed Stewart & Kincaid to use discretion. It does not seem that Stewart & Kincaid made any such contributions on Ferrall's behalf in 1846.

Ferrall was in financial distress at the beginning of 1847: in the face of falling rental incomes, Stewart & Kincaid had reduced their monthly allowances to him. However, at about that same time, he altered his views in regard to relief committees: he now felt that, if possible, Stewart & Kincaid must make contributions on his behalf. On 2 February 1847 he wrote from London to Stewart & Kincaid:

> With respect to the subscriptions to the relief committees I think it is not only a duty to do so but also . . . advisable. . . . But now how can I ask you to do it . . . when you can not afford myself . . . reasonable maintenance. . . . The agitators in this country will be publishing lists of those who have not contributed and I perceive that a notice of motion was given in the House [of Commons] last night . . . for . . . a return of any subscriptions for the relief of the poor in every union by the pro-prietors of the estates therein. . . . This . . . will bring great contempt on all those who have not so subscribed. . . . But what can I do circumstanced as am at pre-sent. . . . I have not ten shillings in my pocket. (s k)

The correspondence contains no evidence that Stewart & Kincaid responded to the sentiments expressed in this extract; but of course the firm might not have been financially able to do so. In fact, financial considerations led Stewart & Kincaid and Ferrall to alter their policies in 1847: they decided to clear the Ferrall lands of their excess population. Thus, on 27 January 1847, Ferrall wrote to Kincaid:

> Give moderate sums to such of the tenantry as are willing to . . . quit . . . and, if we can by such means remove a part of the overpopulation, we can then borrow money from the Government as you propose, or devise other modes of improving the land, and recovering the losses we may sustain by those advances etc to defaulting tenants, who may emigrate. . . . I . . . hope you may get rid of [a certain named tenant] for the £6 or £7 which you have desired Sharkey to offer him. As to the other tenants on Dooneen, who have not paid any thing, I would commence mea-sures at once to get rid of them. . . . Commence the preliminary proceedings for getting rid of a very great proportion of the unsatisfactory tenants on Aghacurreen and Clooncur. . . . The population on those townlands is quite beyond what the quantity of land in them can sustain. . . . You seem . . . to have already determined to eject [from] the Lissergools. (s k)

Two points should be noted in regard to the lengthy passage reproduced above. First, the 'dirty work' was to be overseen by the Sharkeys who, Ferrall assumed, would not need police protection. Second, the objective was to clear the estates of the defaulting *small* tenants.

It seems that within a short period following service of notices to quit, many of the small tenants surrendered their holdings. Those tenants were apparently given small sums of money in compensation, instead of being summoned ('pro-cessed') to court, while Ferrall was spared legal costs and unpopularity attached to ejectment. On 7 June 1847 Ferrall wrote to Stewart & Kincaid: 'I hope you will . . . mention [in your next letter] if during your visit to Roscommon you get any proposals for a letting of [specified townlands] which were surrendered' by small tenants. Further depopulation was implemented in the autumn of 1847. On 14 September, Ferrall instructed Stewart & Kincaid: 'If you find that the rents in Aghacurreen are not likely to be well paid . . . , get rid quietly if practicable of as many as possible. . . . The place is so overcrowded that it will be a benefit to themselves as well as to us to leave it.' (s k)

Most of the above details pertain to the small tenants, relatively few of whom had livestock. In his letter to Stewart & Kincaid of 7 June 1847, Ferrall expressed confidence in the prospects of the large tenants (many of them graziers) who, he remarked, 'ought all to pay their rents now as surely they can have no cause of complaint for meat . . . was never dearer'. But contrary to Ferrall's optimism, Irish livestock prices collapsed in both 1848 and 1849.[35] The policy announced in January 1847 implied consolidation of holdings. But Ferrall's plans for large solvent farms began to be undermined by late 1847, when many of the large tenants sought to surrender their leases. The danger then was, having got rid of many of the smallholders, that very substantial tracts of land would become untenanted and abandoned.

On 25 October 1847 one of Ferrall's most important tenants, the Rev. John French, boldly wrote to him: 'I will on the first day of May next surrender . . . Ballyglass [Union of Castlerea].[36] Ferrall was angry. On 29 October he wrote to Stewart & Kincaid: 'French's agreement . . . was for a tenure of 21 years. . . . Not more than ten can have elapsed. . . . I can not be made accept his surrender. . . . The land . . . might lay on our hands for a year. . . . Probably too the land is now out of heart; as, to my own knowledge, he had the greater part of it in conacre.' In the same letter, Ferrall wrote that another tenant under lease had sought to surrender. Thus, he continued: 'as to Mr Burke I will not take up his land either . . . , nor will I take up the land from any of those who hold [leases] under us unless absolutely constrained to do so' (s k). Within a few weeks, however, Ferrall was informed that the large tenant Pat O'Connor wanted to surrender his lease.[37] Around mid-December 1847 Stewart & Kincaid sent Ferrall a list of the larger leaseholders whom he might lose. Ferrall replied that they 'occupy such a position in society that they must pay. . . . All those you have alluded to in your letter are perfectly solvent, unless it be the Featherstones [graziers on Grange in the parish of Kilbride]; and even they will pay, for they have too good an interest in their lease to lose it'.[38]

Ferrall received further bad news in letters from Stewart & Kincaid late in December 1847. He deferred his response until 3 January 1848, by which time he had digested their content, which induced 'the most disheartening anxiety of mind'. He then observed to Stewart & Kincaid:

The amount of the arrear for 1846 . . . appears to be nearly £3000 . . . [which] amount would absorb nearly the whole of the rental of that portion of the estate occupied by the poorer description of tenantry. . . . I thought that most of the land that had been surrendered had been let in conacre, or for grazing; and that it would have produced some income . . . but, from what I collect from your letters, I am induced to fear that . . . last year [1847] these farms have been wholly unproductive. . . . You say that you have 'looked at the *agreements*' of those [large] tenants who have served notice surrendering their farms, but, do you not recollect that they have executed leases? and that, under these, we can enforce a continuation of their occupation. . . . Let us make every ostensible resistance. . . . Retain the tenants who are solvent. (s k)

At the end of 1847, considerable acreages previously occupied by defaulting tenants remained abandoned. Furthermore, Ferrall was in danger of losing the larger tenants who, he claimed, were solvent. However, in his letter of 3 January 1848, he optimistically added: 'You may not experience so much difficulty in inducing graziers to hold on their farms in the spring. . . . Trade is steadily reviving in all the manufacturing districts of England, and I confidently hope that there will be a far better demand for the products of grazing farms.'

7 THE FAMINE ON THE FERRALL ESTATES, 1848

The year 1848 was highlighted by the following developments on the Ferrall estates:

1 Massive depopulation and great hardship, especially in northwest Roscommon where the depopulation was supervised mainly by the Sharkeys.
2 Violence against the Sharkeys.
3 Persistent efforts to keep those larger tenants who, it was believed, could pay their rents, or would ultimately be able to pay them, in continued possession.
4 Efforts to find solvent tenants for depopulated lands.
5 Some drainage projects, financed mainly by a government loan.

Depopulation

The beginning of 1848 saw the ejectment of one of the larger (middlemen) tenants, the magistrate Wynne Peyton, whom we have already met in chapter 4 and who had become hopelessly insolvent. On 11 January, John Sharkey reported to Stewart & Kincaid that like others who had debts all around them, 'Peyton is unfortunately shut up for the last three months guarding against services & executions' (SK); however, he left the Ferrall lands a short time later.

On 27 February 1848 Ferrall wrote to Stewart & Kincaid from London:

> Of the Lissergools [east and west] . . . an empty house is preferable to a bad tenant, & I would discretely diminish the population on the two Lissergools as much as possible. . . . Self preservation renders it imperative . . . to consolidate. . . . [In regard to Lissian] . . . all the farms now to be relet should be increased to 20 acres, or even more than that, if we could procure tenants for them. . . . By the proposed outlay on the land by means of the loan from the Board of Works, and the drainage . . . before the end of spring, you may have a better class of tenant. . . . As to the Aghacurreen tenants I would almost wish that they had not paid so well . . . for we must get rid of at least half of them. . . . I hope you will be able to dispose of all the waste land in Dooneen amongst the old tenants who remain. . . . Let us try to induce as many of them as we can to add portions of it to their present holdings. If however we can even make the taxes & charges of the waste portions by grazing, as you hope, it will be better to keep it unlet for a time than to get bad or indifferent tenants. . . . [On Ballyfeeny], it will require your utmost caution to select a tenantry for such portions of it as you can relet. . . . Clooncur must be cleared. . . . All I can say of the tenants in the Barony . . . is that . . . we must endeavour to diminish their number as much as possible. . . . I hope, with you, that the worst is past. (SK)

For many of the tenants, the worst was not past. Some of them received compensation on surrendering. On 2 March 1848 Owen Sheridan of Ballyfeeny wrote to Stewart: 'I did not enter an appearance [in court] to the ejectment. . . . I beg you will remit me the five pounds you promised' (SK).

On 3 March 1848 old Patt Sharkey wrote to Kincaid: 'James Bruin is dead. [Hence] the life of [the lease of] Lissergool est and west [is expired]. . . . Let me know about what will be don with the tenants' (SK). The fact that the lease of the Lissergools (and of another district called Cashel near Carrick-on-Shannon) had expired, made it easier for Stewart & Kincaid to depopulate those lands of undertenants on them.

On some of the lands mentioned in Ferrall's lengthy letter of 27 February, a campaign of 'voluntary' surrender, or other forms of depopulation, was applied during the spring and summer of 1848. These were supervised by John Sharkey of Dooneen, and to a smaller extent by his father, Patt Sharkey (and by his other son Pat) of Lissian. On 5 April, John Sharkey informed Stewart & Kincaid that he had borrowed money 'to pay those bought out . . . in my district' (SK). On 27 May, young Pat Sharkey wrote to Kincaid: 'I had to go to the petty sessions of Frenchpark to indite the tenants of Aghacurreen that took forciable possession after there houses been trown doown. I had also to go to Aghacurreen to excicute the decrees that was got last June. . . . Send me a list of both Aghacurreen and Ballyroe as I think we ar better serve them with sevil bil processes as it would be a good time to hurry them pay.' (sκ)

On 15 June, John Sharkey described to Stewart & Kincaid his operations in districts to the west of Carrick-on-Shannon:

> We . . . got through Meera . . . and Cashel. We leveled the houses on the latter . . . but the sheriff refused throwing down at all in Meera. He got up the possession and put back the several tenants for six months under an attornment. . . . The tenants [on Meera] are . . . wretchedly poor. . . . They must be turned out. . . . We propose being at Lissergool on tomorrow . . . executing the . . . Habere against the west village. . . . The other village should be done again as there are many of the paupers who are very unruly still in possession. I must remain in Lissian and Lissergool district until Saturday evening trying to let some grazing which those paupers have prevented my brother to let since [they] themselves were dispossessed. (sκ)

In a letter to Kincaid on 19 June, John Sharkey again referred to the operations at Cashel, and then proceeded to describe the work at Lissergool:

> We have rid Cashel of the wicked fellow who overheld in the middle of the nine acres held by the undertenants who lived in the old village. Besides of others who lived on the road side and disputed to pay any rent . . . for the use of the houses which we have levelled. . . . The Lissergool tenants with the exception of three or four are equally poor and destitute. . . . I should be very sorry to recommend any further dealing with a lot of paupers. We had therefore . . . to throw down about 34 houses . . . including ten of those thrown in Lissergool east in April last . . . and which were since rebuilt by the evicted tenants who were living in them back again in possession same as they are still in Aghacurreen. But I shall in future guard against this . . . by frequently visiting the lands same as I did this morning, and . . . succeeded in knocking about several huts which were built by the ditches since Saturday evening. And had to employ two men . . . as caretakers . . . not only to . . . secure the crops but to prevent rebuilding and those paupers of coming in again. (sκ)

In a letter of 23 June, Sharkey reported further to Kincaid:

> There are now about 30 of the Lissergool families lying by the ditches in a most wretched condition & I have done all in my power to get some of them taken in to the poor house not only for the sake of relieving them but to get rid of such a plague and of the extreme trouble of preventing them of building hovels – but unfortunately it is so crowded that there cannot be one more recd. They are getting

out door relief. . . . I shall obey your generous order and give them £1 to 10/- [£1 10s 0d] each according to the family and distress. (s k)

John Sharkey wrote an addendum to this letter, concerning his brother Pat who, he complained, 'is encouraging the evicted tenants at Lissergool to go in to some of the . . . houses in order to make himself popular. . . . Write him a line saying you will not allow any of the tenants turned out by me back again.' Pat's probable motive will be indicated later.

On 25 June, John Sharkey explained to Stewart & Kincaid:

> I forgot to mention . . . who those families turned out at Lissergool are. . . . They were under tenants and cottiers and people of worthless character the dregs of Lord Defreynes tenantry and those of different other estates . . . who were . . . turned out for nonpayment and misconduct and then harboured in Lissergool. . . . We have the original tenants or their offsprings there still. . . . How was it possible we could enter into any arrangement for a continuance with those paupers without involving you in future trouble. . . . The safest way was to get rid of them . . . in this season of the year as if they were to remain until November the case would be very much worse if then turned out and exposed to . . . the winter. . . . No solvent tenant could be had to take one of the intended farms in this townland while . . . paupers continued to live on it. . . . Many of them . . . will clear off on getting such small sums as you have allowed and will go to England. (s k)

Ferrall was genuinely disturbed by the plight of those removed from Lissergool and was upset by adverse publicity. On 3 July he wrote from London to Stewart & Kincaid: 'I regret exceedingly that we have been obliged to resort to such extremities with the tenants of Lissergool [who, according to the Sharkeys, had been squatters, or undertenants to a person whose lease had expired on his death], for it is a melancholy reflection that one should be obliged to consign his fellow creature to such misery.' (s k) On 12 July, Ferrall wrote to Stewart & Kincaid that 'the fact of your having sent pecuniary relief to the poor people who were ejected, should satisfy the public that you were activated by kind feelings towards them.' (s k)

According to a letter dated 6 July from old Patt Sharkey to Stewart & Kincaid, the lands which had been cleared in Aghacurreen and Lissergool were speedily set for grazing and conacre (s k); however, this claim must be discounted in view of the fact that it was made in a context in which old Sharkey was denying John Sharkey's complaint that young Pat was permitting the return of those who had been removed from the land. In fact, much of Lissergool remained untenanted throughout the late summer of 1848. This is revealed by John Sharkey's letter to Stewart & Kincaid on 11 September: 'The crops on the ejected holdings at Lissergool will be in a few days fit for cutting, and I fear if not sold uncut they will be stolen . . . by the evicted tenants notwithstanding all the exertions of the caretakers.' John Sharkey continued: 'Our safest plan is to sell those crops immediately . . . uncut, and let the buyers deal with the thieves in the best manner they can. I have advertised the sale to take place by auction.' (s k)

Resumption of distraint

The desired depopulation of the Ferrall lands was largely completed by mid-1848. For the most part, policy towards defaulters reverted to what it had been in the years before the famine: distraint tended to replace 'voluntary' surrender or ejectment. The cost of compensation to tenants who surrendered in 1848 is unknown. However, in the summer of 1849 Stewart & Kincaid sent accounts, presumably for 1848, to Ferrall in France. In response, in mid-1849 he referred to 'costs of ejectments and compensation to tenants – £450'.[39] In 1847 and early 1848, efforts to distrain tenants who had no means would have been pointless, but from late June 1848 onwards, there were fewer of them. On 27 June 1848 Patt Sharkey wrote to Stewart & Kincaid:

> I have distrained all of the tenants that had means in Aghacurreen & Ballyroe as the[y] had closed their doors against the services of the sivil bills except three [from whom] I have received some rents. . . . I hope all the arreares due in Aghacurreen & Ballyroe will be paid before the first of august except four tenants in Aghacurreen that has no means. . . . Give each of them 3 pound [to leave] as you have done with the Ballyroe tenants that had no means. (s k)

On 18 October, John Sharkey wrote to Stewart & Kincaid that several tenants 'thrashed all their corn on the pretence of making up their rents', but if not immediately distrained, 'they surely will not pay a penny' (s k). However, a threat to distrain, or leniency on distraint, often undermined its purpose of extracting monies for rents due. The option of distraint worked best when it was implemented with unanticipated speed. In this context, on 4 October 1848 Ferrall wrote to Stewart & Kincaid: 'As to those in Dooneen who have endeavoured to steal away their crops [because they anticipated distraint], I would get rid of them at once' (s k). Need for speed in obtaining distraining orders is clear from a communication from John Sharkey to Stewart & Kincaid, 29 October 1848, in which he reported that a named tenant 'is at enmity with his former wifes children and got married to a handsome young woman . . . and . . . has thrashed out & sold his corn and is determined on selling all his other effects & going to America. If not immediately distrained the rent due on his holding will be surely lost' (s κ).

Leniency in distraint could be futile. Let us consider the case of the Sweenys on Lissian. On 2 November they complained to Stewart & Kincaid that John Sharkey had seized their cattle, and drove them off to Frenchpark 'and after putting them to pound, he . . . allowed the cattle to be taken from out of the pound by [the Sweenys] first paying 2/6 each, together with poundage fees'. The same letter added: 'Poor tenants really had enough to do . . . to endeavour to pay their rents and not to be trampled upon by the like tyranny' (s κ). But a few days later, Sharkey explained to Stewart & Kincaid that he had been deceived by the Sweenys, about whom he wrote: 'If you send me a distraining order agt. them I promise to send you their half years rent'. Sharkey continued: 'I distrained them under your last but unfortunately afterwards gave them time to make up their money at the fair of B'rine on Wednesday last, rather then leave the cattle in pound, but contrary to their promise they now refuse to pay'.[40] Stewart & Kincaid did not immediately send the requested (second) distraining order. On 13 November, Sharkey wrote to Stewart & Kincaid that the Sweenys 'spent the entire of last week looking for a farm elsewhere. . . . They intend to carry away their effects and leave Lissian' (s κ).

Anticipation of distraint led to a bargaining game on the part of tenants on Grange, north of Roscommon town. On 15 November, John Sharkey informed Stewart & Kincaid that Patt Flynn, the Featherstone brothers and John Neilan, who 'hold their farms quite separate' but were co-tenants on Grange, 'proposed to pay three years rent . . . provided you give time'; however those 'solvent' tenants 'pretend quite careless to settle at all' but in Sharkey's view, they would 'pay rather than give up the farms with their comfortable houses'. They had 25 undertenants 'who are a wretched group of paupers'; Sharkey requested Stewart & Kincaid 'to give them £1 or 30/- each to help them go' to Britain (s κ). However, on 23 November he wrote to Stewart & Kincaid stating that he had been deceived by Flynn and the Featherstons who had 'carried away all their effects, I fear with the intent to cheat you of the rents. . . . Those fellows are . . . determined to retreat their arrangement with me [under which] they seemed well inclined to pay 3 years rent.' Sharkey went on to state that 'their apology . . . is that . . . by paying 3 years rent they could not possibly hold afterwards to any advantage and that they thought it more prudent to go at once with their means to America. . . . But in my opinion . . . the fellows are only trying to get off for two years rent.' (s κ) Their game plan paid off: early in December, Sharkey reported that he was 'proud we have at last settled with the Grange men and that we have recd. the two years rent'.[41] Each of those tenants mentioned was listed on Grange in 1857.

Stewart & Kincaid softened their treatment of tenants late in 1848. One reason for this was that the firm would otherwise have had even more idle lands on hand; another was that both Ferrall and Stewart & Kincaid were anxious to minimise adverse publicity. Thus, in mid-November 1848 John Sharkey wrote to Stewart & Kincaid: 'I understood . . . that both you and Mr Ferrall were disposed to be as lenient as possible . . . among the defaulters. I have therefore been in the habit lately of giving them from one fair to another hoping them to pay quietly rather than you should be plagued by complaints.'[42]

Rent abatement on large holdings, and finding viable tenants

It has already been observed that late in 1847 several of the larger tenants wanted to surrender their leases, and that there was then a danger that Ferrall and Stewart & Kincaid would have more idle land on hand. At the same time, the high levels of local taxation would have to be met. These problems were carried forward into 1848, and were accentuated by the fact that in April of that year Patt Taaffe sought an abatement in his rents. Ferrall's immediate response to Stewart & Kincaid, on 15 April 1848, was that if Stewart & Kincaid decided to grant him the abatement, it must be on the strict stipulation that he would continue to hold Casheltauna as well as other Ferrall lands. But Taaffe wanted to surrender Casheltauna late in 1848. The Stewart & Kincaid correspondence on the Ferrall lands contains no further reference to Taaffe's request for an abatement, or to Ferrall's conditions pertaining thereto, until 22 October 1848, when Ferrall wrote to Stewart & Kincaid that Taaffe's lease of Casheltuana 'ended last May; and, as he did not then surrender the land, I do not suppose you are bound to take it from him now, unless he serves you with a 6 months notice of surrender' (SK). Several letters of November and December 1848 refer to the tactics to be adopted to force Taaffe to continue as tenant on all of the lands he then held under Ferrall. Taaffe's existing leases, combined with a demand that he must give at least six months' notice for surrender of Casheltauna, were the technicalities involved in attempts to force him to continue each of his tenures until 1849.

Throughout 1848 both Ferrall and Stewart & Kincaid continued to try to prevent any tenants deemed solvent from surrendering their lands; however, they continued to try to remove those who were not solvent. Thus, on 22 October 1848 Ferrall wrote to Stewart & Kincaid: 'Burke can not give up his part of Lismurtagh, nor will I take it from him; but . . . I would consent to a small abatement in the rent as I would also for Farmer's portion. They are both solvent tenants and we should not lose either' (SK). Late in October 1848 Pat O'Connor sent Ferrall a 'notice of surrender', in response to which Ferrall informed Stewart & Kincaid that 'the idea of taking up the farm from him is out. . . . The question therefore is whether he should get an abatement'.[43] Ferrall again referred to O'Connor in a letter to Stewart & Kincaid dated 3 November: 'He has . . . laid out . . . £2000 . . . in improvements. . . . We should not lose him. . . . If you let him go the very least loss you can escape with will be that of the half years rent to May next, for it will be impossible to let the land before then.' (s κ)

On 11 November 1848 Ferrall wrote to Stewart & Kincaid that in regard to 'Pat O'Connor, Mr Burke and Mr Farmer, I will give the abatements you suggest, as also to Mr Hugh Byrne, if you consider that he will be able to hold the land.' Thus, by late 1848, Ferrall was happy to offer abatements in order to induce solvent tenants to stay. These were measures of desperation: the alternative was to leave the lands idle, and Ferrall recognised this when he wrote to Stewart & Kincaid on 14 November: 'Do all in your power to . . . retain the [solvent] tenantry, for without them [the land] will produce nothing, and I shall be ready to sanction any abatement' recommended by Stewart & Kincaid. (s κ).

Reference has already been made to the manner in which the Rev. John French, in October 1847, gave notice of surrender of his lease of Ferrall lands on Ballyglass, and that Ferrall would not accept the surrender. The Stewart & Kincaid correspondence of late 1848 contains much detail on this issue. On 17 August 1848 Ferrall wrote to Stewart & Kincaid that French's brother, Lord de Freyne, 'had come to the determination of seizing on his [Rev. French's] stock, for rent he owes him'. Ferrall added that 'if his brother adopts this course, I do not think we should be prevented by any feelings of delicacy from following the example' (s κ). Kincaid inspected the farm some days later, and reported what he found when he met Ferrall at Liverpool in September 1848. Ferrall was furious. On 19 September he wrote to Stewart that the farm 'is now in such a state . . . that [if surrender were to be accepted] the whole of next year's rent of it will be lost. . . . The farm is now totally unproductive from his mismanagement'; hence, it 'would lay on my hands were I to accept a surrender of it; and, as I can not afford the loss of the rent . . . I must decline doing so.' (s κ)

Late in September 1848 Stewart & Kincaid agreed to take the farm from French, provided he paid the rent arrears as well as £300 for damage he had done. No settlement was reached during the two months which followed. However, the possibility of a change in strategy was posed on 22 December, when Ferrall sent Stewart & Kincaid news that French 'has come to a settlement with his brother Lord de Freyne. . . . He is to get from him twelve thousand pounds in cash . . . [which] will . . . render him a most desirable tenant.' (s κ) On 5 January 1849 Ferrall wrote to Stewart & Kincaid from Paris: 'John

French . . . must be by £12,000 a better man now. . . . Take it into your
consideration whether you ought to take up the land from him or not.' (s κ)
The Stewart & Kincaid correspondence does not reveal whether he was
forced to continue to abide by his lease for Ballyglass.

Following depopulation of the Ferrall lands and with large tracts idle, in
1848 both Ferrall and Stewart & Kincaid hoped to attract viable farmers from
England in order to develop those lands.[44] On 23 March 1848 a recently returned
migrant named Sheridan, who seems to have saved a lot of money in England
and who may have come back to Ireland in the hope of buying idle land at
bargain prices, wrote to Stewart & Kincaid: 'I beg to make application to you
for a farm of about 100 acres Irish measure - or more. . . . I have plenty of
capital to go on with 2 or 3 hundred acres. I don't care what county the land
may be situate in.' (s κ) In response, Stewart & Kincaid offered Sheridan lands
at Mullymux near Roscommon town.[45] These were owned, not by Ferrall, but
by Dean Pakenham, for whom Stewart & Kincaid were agents; however, those
lands were close to Ferrall properties. It may be the case that Stewart & Kincaid
offered Sheridan tracts of Pakenham rather than Ferrall land because the
former had decent buildings on them whereas the latter did not.

The level of rent which Stewart & Kincaid would have required Sheridan
to pay for Mullymux is unknown. However, on 6 April he informed Stewart
& Kincaid: 'I would not give more than 16*s* per Irish acre for Mullymux. . . . I
am well aware that the competition for land in Ireland has been so great that
people were found to offer more than . . . their returns warranted.' (s κ) In
making his offer (which seems to have been low by standards of the recent
past) Sheridan must have been aware of his bargaining power. It is likely, in
reaction to whatever level of rent Stewart & Kincaid asked for Mullymux, that
Sheridan's reference to 'competition for land' was an expression of sarcasm.
Nevertheless, following his return to England, Sheridan indicated what appears
to have been a real interest in the Ferrall lands of Corbo near Beechwood.
Thus, on 16 June 1848 he wrote to Kincaid inquiring: 'Shall I send a surveyor
over to Corbo to lay out' a large farm so that he could 'commence building'.
(s κ) Sheridan was not listed on Corbo in 1857.

Early in 1849 Henry Brennan, PP of Kilglass, applied to Ferrall for financial
aid. On 17 January, Ferrall wrote to Stewart & Kincaid: 'About Mr Brennan the
clergyman. I am sensible of the distressing difficulties' but 'I cannot afford to
alleviate them'. He continued: 'I would however cheerfully, if you are willing, & can afford it, give him a moderate contribution' because 'he might be a
useful auxiliary in the neighbourhood of Ballyfeeny, either in influencing the
payment of rent, or in procuring solvent tenants for some of the land that
is waste there.' Ferrall therefore suggested: 'From £5 to £10 would be a fair
contribution from us.' (s κ)

With much of his land going to waste, Ferrall seemed optimistic when he wrote from Paris to Stewart & Kincaid on 25 January 1849: 'I see by one of the last numbers of the [Dublin Evening] Post . . . that, at a . . . leting of some lands in Roscommon, there was a good deal of competition . . . and that the lands were let at . . . £1–10–0 per acre. . . . I hope you may have had offers for some of our lands. . . . If we could only let them from year to year, at even that rent, it would be . . . desirable to do so.' (s κ)

On 12 February 1849 Ferrall expressed the following opinions in another letter to Stewart & Kincaid from Paris:

> If we can let the lands temporarily, it would be better accept of almost any rent than to leave them unlet; but I would not, at present, let any land for a longer time than from year to year, as the general aspect of mundane affairs convinces me that, 'ere the lapse of another year, you will see a considerable improvement in the prices of all agricultural products, and that the present depression on the land in Ireland can not continue; and, if I could afford it, or could manage to turn the lands held by Mr P Taaffe, or Mr P O'Connor, to any good account for the next season, I would not hesitate to take them off their hands. . . . The whole of the manufacturing population of England is now in full . . . activity, and the influx of gold into England, which is likely to take place in consequence of the recent discoveries in America, must . . . raise the price of all manufactures; and a corresponding rise in the price of agricultural products must follow. (s κ)

Ferrall's letter from Paris on 31 March 1849 was less optimistic in tone. In this he informed Stewart & Kincaid that he considered 'the English farmers who are over looking for land . . . cheering; but I fear that the want of dwelling houses on the farms will provide an insurmountable obstacle to their taking any' of his idle lands (s κ).

On 3 April, Ferrall again wrote to Stewart & Kincaid referring to the possibility of attracting English farmers: 'I have been apprehensive, since the receipt of your . . . letter intimating that the Norfolk farmers had visited you, but the want of residences on our different farms would prevent them from dealing with us. . . . As to letting the waste lands, at the prices which you say have been offered, I would not think of it as a permanency; but for the present any rent would be better than having them entirely unproductive.' (s κ)

8 VIOLENCE DURING THE FAMINE

Violence in Roscommon seems to have been increasing in the mid-1840s. This trend extended into the famine years. On 22 December 1845 James Nolan wrote to Stewart & Kincaid stating that he feared trouble in the Ballyfeeny district, partly because of recent events on the nearby estate of Lord Castlemaine. As Nolan put it: 'Castlemaine sent a man to serve ejectments . . . and the man was attacked by about 200 men, many of whom were armed. He had to fly for his life.' (sĸ) A similar event occurred a few months later: in March 1846 Nolan, whose life, it seems, had recently been threatened, informed Stewart & Kincaid that he had 'sent out 50 processes against the Ballyfeeny tenants but the man who serves them was attackd' and that the processes had been taken from him.[46]

There were many arrests in Roscommon early in 1846 under legislation designed to curb agrarian crime. These were reflected in Nolan's news to Stewart & Kincaid from Roscommon town, 1 March 1846: 'We had six convictions under the White Boy Act, and there are 26 more to be tried' (sĸ). The convictions may have had their desired effects in setting examples: the Stewart & Kincaid correspondence pertaining to the Ferrall estates contains only one reference to violence during the summer of 1846. This was on Ballyfeeny, and the disturbed state of the nearby Crown townland of Ballykilcline [also in Kilglass parish] was held partly responsible for it. On 20 May, Nolan wrote to Stewart & Kincaid about tenants on Ballyfeeny, where Susan Stuart was one of Ferrall's most important tenants, and where 'there are some I know who are not able to pay. But there are a great many who can, and are taking advantage of affairs in Kilglass. They attacked Miss Stewarts [Stuart's] house on Friday night, beat her severely, and made her give them 12/- to drink'. Nolan indicated that they attacked two other houses, 'and got money from them also' (sĸ).

Ferrall owned lands very close to the place (briefly discussed in chapter 4) where Major Denis Mahon was murdered on 2 November 1847. On 18 November he wrote to Stewart & Kincaid: 'I should like much to have my name put down as a subscriber to the fund for discovery of the murderers of Major Mahon, & I hope you will be so good as name me as a subscriber for any respectable sum you think you can afford to pay for me.' (sĸ) The murder must have terrified Nolan, who fled to Dublin. On 30 November, Ferrall wrote to Stewart & Kincaid: 'In reference to James Nolan's conduct I can guess at no cause for it; unless that he is afraid . . . to bring himself . . . in collision with the lower classes . . . and that he therefore wishes to relinquish the office which he held from you.' (sĸ) Nolan formally quit the agency a short time later.

One month after Mahon's assassination, Ferrall referred to the murder of the Rev. John Lloyd of Elphin, whom he described 'as inoffensive a gentleman as ever was & one who had very little landed property at all so that I can guess no reason'. Ferrall added: 'I hear Dominick Corr [a magistrate of Roscommon[47]] is on the list for assassination'.[48] On 18 December, Ferrall wrote to Kincaid: 'Before you go down [to Roscommon] you ought in my opinion apply at the Castle for an order for 2 or 3 policemen to attend you while travelling on the roads in that county.' (s k)

The fact that old Patt Sharkey of Lissian and his son John of Dooneen played significant roles in the population clearances of 1847–8 placed their lives at risk. Of the two, Patt Sharkey was the first against whom revenge was exacted: around the end of 1847 his house was attacked. In February 1848, those found guilty for this attack were sentenced to transportation.[49] The convictions led to fears of further revenge attacks on Patt Sharkey and his son Pat (who resided with him). This was despite the fact that, under legislation of December 1847, Stewart & Kincaid had arranged special police protection for them. On 1 March 1848 young Pat wrote to Kincaid, to inform him and to plead: 'Those who attacked my fathers house were transported for seven years. We [Patt and Pat] did knot think it would be so severe as transportation but if you had the kindness of interfering for them to get them off for confindment it would oblige us as we live in the middle of their friends.' (s k) On 3 March 1848 Patt the father wrote a barely intelligible letter to Kincaid, stating: 'As it is my sons procution that has found them gelty he is afaird . . . so I hop your Honour will get him som bisness to go in the castle of Dublin or som wheare eals that he will have a lving by for a few years untill the crim is out of their friends mind as I do not wish to send him to america' (s k).

The two extracts reproduced immediately above explain why, in June 1848, Pat Sharkey was encouraging tenants removed from Lissergool by his brother John, to go back to houses there: he feared for his safety and therefore sought popularity. John Sharkey was also a target for revenge. On 16 February 1848 he wrote from Dooneen to Stewart & Kincaid, complaining:

Bryan Flanigan and his connections have determined . . . to be revenged on me for the . . . proceedings taken by me when I decreed him in March last. This wicked man and his Molly McGuire connections . . . assembled in Ballinameen [about two miles from John's house] as usual on last Sunday week where they drank. . . . My eldest daughter had unfortunately an occasion to come by Ballinameen on her way home. . . . These ruffians . . . forced her off the high road into a house where they shut her up with one of the party for the purpose of . . . destroying her character and . . . have revenge for . . . their Molly McGuire leader. . . . I fortunately succeeded in entering the house and risking my daughter out of their hands. I lost no time in sending for the police who . . . succeeded . . . in the arrest of the principal and two more of the party who have been . . . committed to Roscommon goal and likely to be transported. . . . Our Molly McGuire adversaries are now more enraged and surely will do me more harm if not . . . protected. The law authorities here are quite determined to punish these ruffians as far as possible but none of them have . . . the friendly feel for me that I see you have had in my fathers case . . . owing to the [police] protection afforded him through . . . your influence in high quarters. (s K)

Thus, it seemed that John Sharkey's daughter had been sexually assaulted. On 25 February he wrote more generally to Stewart & Kincaid from Roscommon town, to which he had come for the assizes:

> I . . . feel exceedingly obliged . . . for the [police] protection you kindly propose to send me. . . . The Roscommon jurors are doing their duty and in almost every case as yet have given their verdicts of guilty. . . . Donogho of Derm near the Four Mile House has been tried and found guilty of the murder of the Revd. Mr Lloyd. Another man named Flynn is also found guilty of the murder of Dignan. (s K)

On 5 March 1848 Sharkey informed Stewart & Kincaid that the case involving his daughter was being withdrawn, 'as we fortunately sustained no loss of character on the part of the female' (s K). But it does not seem that the threat of violence against John Sharkey had subsided by late in 1848 when, on 4 October, Ferrall wrote to Stewart & Kincaid that he hoped 'that Sharkey's exertions to . . . secure the rents for us may not subject him to . . . vengeance' (s K).

9 BRIEF OBSERVATIONS IN CLOSING

It has been seen that both Ferrall and his overpopulated tenantry were in severe difficulties even before the famine. Given his own problems, there was probably little he could have done to ease the plight of his tenantry. Maintaining the small defaulting tenants on his lands in 1847–8 might have forced him into the Encumbered Estates Courts at the end of the decade. In several letters written between 1846 and 1848, he expressed a desire to return from England. But had he done so, it is likely that he would have been imprisoned for debt. For the same reason he fled from England to France at the end of 1848, and it seems that he stayed there until his death.

Among his tenantry, it is difficult to avoid the view that the greatest hardship during the famine years was borne by those in the north of Roscommon, where John Sharkey was agent. However, it should not be forgotten that according to Patt and John Sharkey, many of those removed from Ferrall land were squatters, while others were undertenants towards whom neither Ferrall nor his agents had the same legal responsibilities as they would have been obliged to respect if those removed had been tenants to the head landlord.

John Sharkey, who was a practising Catholic,[50] was an intelligent man, dedicated to the service of his employers. His letters suggest that he had little sense of compassion: but he was not employed to be compassionate. Ferrall (who seems to have been a practising Catholic and who at times did show compassion) defended Sharkey's actions, regarding them as necessary for his own economic survival. It seems that most of Ferrall's small tenants who left his lands during the famine years were given financial assistance, though such sums were usually small. These amounts were paid by Stewart & Kincaid who, during the famine years, probably received less from the Ferrall lands than their expenditures on Ferrall's behalf: that was why Stewart & Kincaid reduced his monthly allowances during those years. Thus, Ferrall himself could not have eased the hardship of the mass of his tenantry to a significant extent.

One has an impression of John Sharkey as a giant of a man, greatly feared by the tenants. He may in fact have been small in stature: in April 1997 the author visited his great grandson, Patrick Sharkey, who resides in the house at Dooneen built by John Sharkey in the 1830s. Aged 73 (in April 1997) the present Patrick Sharkey is about five feet tall, but sturdy. John Sharkey felt that he had had enough of Dooneen when, at the end of 1848, he requested of Stewart & Kincaid:

> Take me out of this remote place to some other quarter under your agency . . . for the safety of my substance and family. . . . You are already aware of the many risks and disagreeable occurrences which happened to us here for the last three years. Now we anticipate a renewal of some of these matters if we remain . . . and we have therefore determined to leave Dooneen after all my struggling with improvements for the last 15 years. . . . It is my wish to obtain a residence in the Carrick district. (SK)

Stewart & Kincaid somehow managed to convince John Sharkey to stay at Dooneen.

SEVEN

WINGFIELD'S SLIGO ESTATE

—

I INTRODUCTION

Edward Wingfield, a son of the third Viscount Powerscourt, was born in 1772.[1] A colonel in the army, he owned substantial tracts of land in west Sligo and, to a smaller extent, across the county boundary in Mayo (see map 4).[2] Most of his properties were close to the river Moy: moving from north to south, amongst others they included all or most of the townlands of Scurmore (where he had a residence, a farm and a salmon fishery), Carrowcardin, Ballymoghany, Dooneen, Rinroe, Newtown, Ballyholan (near Ardnaree, a suburb of Ballina) and Breaghwy. Within a few miles from Breaghwy, in Mayo he owned all or most of the townland of Lissard More. All of the above are in the Inniscrone/Ballina districts of Sligo/Mayo. Tracts of land to the east were also among the possessions of Edward Wingfield. The largest of these was Coolrecuill, a few miles west of Tubercurry. The manner in which these lands became Wingfield properties goes back to about the year 1600, when some of the Wingfields came to Ireland with the army.[3] One of them was Lewis Wingfield, who obtained a Crown grant of lands in County Sligo. In 1788 Edward Wingfield became entitled to them under the will of his father. In the 1840s, Cork Abbey near Little Bray in County Dublin was his main residence in Ireland. Until the early 1840s he sometimes resided at his house called Moyview on the aforementioned Rinroe townland. In the late 1840s he was occasionally resident at his newly enlarged structure, Scurmore House, which overlooked the mouth of the Moy. Wingfield also spent much time in England where his twin brother had property. He was a Tory in politics.

The Sligo/Mayo estate of Edward Wingfield was one of the first agencies of the firm which, in the 1840s, was known as Stewart & Kincaid. It was seen in chapter 1 that Henry Stewart was Dublin agent for the estate as early as 1791. However, the firm's function then consisted of little more than collection and forwarding of rent. A letter dated 22 February 1803 from Arthur Knox at Ardnaree to Henry Stewart in Dublin enclosed a bill of exchange and half notes to a total value of £271. These probably constituted rent due from a middleman.

In the early nineteenth century Wingfield caught salmon off Scurmore. Three stake nets were set up there in 1854, when they yielded 4,800 salmon valued at £600. Wingfield is known to historians mainly due to litigation in 1857, the matter at issue being a claim by Little and Clarke against him: the plaintiffs contended that they alone had a right to fish for salmon in the tidal part of the Moy, and that Wingfield was therefore a trespasser. The jury found for the plaintiffs; thereby ended Wingfield's profitable fishery at Scurmore.

In 1802 Wingfield's twin brother, John, a lieutenant colonel, assumed the additional surname of Stratford (and was known as Colonel Stratford). He had lands in Clare and Limerick, developments on which are considered in chapters 9 and 10. The present chapter concentrates on the properties of Edward Wingfield; references to his twin brother will be under the surname of Stratford. There was some interchange of overseeing personnel between the Stratford estates in the southwest and the lands of Edward Wingfield in the northwest

Wingfield was keen to promote the Established Church. Thus, in January 1846 he wrote to Lieutenant Clifford, RN, secretary of the Loochoo Mission near Dingle in Kerry, stating that he would soon place '£5 at yr. disposal towards the support of the Loochoo Mission and a like sum for the Ventry and Dingle Institution':[4] Stratford too was a contributor to the Mission as well to the other institution in the Dingle district, the objectives of which were to convert Catholics to the Established Church. That wealthy Protestant land-lords supported the dissemination of their own religious beliefs is not surpris-ing; indeed, the same was expected of Catholics who had means. However, evidence provided later indicates that Wingfield and Stratford were bigots opposed to Catholicism.

2 IMPROVEMENTS ON THE SLIGO ESTATE

Wingfield took an interest in the health and education of his tenants. Writing in 1837, Lewis noted a dispensary on his lands of Dooneen.[5] The structure, now a residence, may have cared for at least one in-patient at a time. This can be inferred from a letter of 20 May 1846 from Wingfield at Scurmore in which he requested of Stewart & Kincaid: 'Write to Vincent [sκ agent on Stratford's Limerick estate] to pay to the wife of the poor man who was sent by [John] Stewart [an agriculturalist] from Shanagolden [in Limerick] to his farm near me, & who broke his leg & thigh, £2–10–0 . . . which will be some assistance to her & children 'till he is able to return to them. . . . I called twice to see him at the dispensary & found him . . . carefully attended to.' (sκ) On 16 July 1846 Wingfield wrote to Stewart & Kincaid that the son of one of his tenants had been 'hurt severely by the same mare by which the other man had his limbs broken. He is still at the dispensary' (sk). Apart from making annual contributions to the Dooneen dispensary, Wingfield also subscribed to that at Tubercurry, which catered for his tenants on Coolrecuill.[6]

Close to Scurmore House, Wingfield erected a forge and converted a residence into a schoolhouse.[7] He sought a strong and permanent police presence on his lands. On 16 August 1845 he informed Stewart & Kincaid that a new police barrack 'is now in a forward state' and he added that this 'has disconcerted Mr [Patrick] Howley & his *faction*' because 'we shall now be able to keep out the Molly Maguire family from settling in our district'. On 24 August he wrote to Stewart & Kincaid stating: 'I have got the building for the constabulary covered in' (sk). It is inferred that Wingfield built the structure and rented it to the police. It was probably on Ballymoghany: a police barrack was there in 1848.[8] On 31 May 1848 he wrote to Stewart & Kincaid from Cork Abbey: 'It would not be unreasonable to have a moderate sized turf shed built adjoining the privy for the constabulary. . . . I had to report one of the detachments that occupied the barracks for gross neglect in permitting the garden which I manured & cultivated for them to remain in a very foul & filthy state full of weeds.' (sk) Perhaps the most substantial single work of improvement on the estate in the mid-1840s was enlargement of Scurmore House. That a residence had already been there is indicated in a publication of 1845, but facilities at the older structure were probably basic.[9] On 9 July 1846 Wingfield wrote that his farm offices at Scurmore 'are now almost up to the ceiling joists which will make this a comfortable residence', and that 'the addition to the house is now pretty well forward' (sk).

Wingfield preferred to have Protestants in positions of responsibility below him. Throughout most of the 1840s his farm at Scurmore was managed by a man named Burrow, who was probably a son of the vicar of the parish church located two miles away.[10] Liverpool was an important market for cattle fattened by Burrow.

Throughout the 1840s, Scurmore fishery was managed by Wingfield's most important tenant, a Scot named William Holliday; in fact, Holliday was joint partner with Wingfield in this enterprise. The ice-house, still visible at Scurmore, may have been erected around 1840: a letter of 16 August 1845 from Wingfield to Stewart & Kincaid refers to buildings which Holliday had erected at the fishery. Between 1839 and 1850 the value of Holliday's annual catch of salmon, most of which was exported to Liverpool, ranged from £380 to £560.[11]

Leases to middlemen on Palmerston's north Sligo estate delayed improvements there. A similar situation applied on Wingfield's lands: on 19 September 1848 he referred to 'the terms of lease which kept my brother out of possession of his Limerick estate for 60 ys, . . . & me from my property in Sligo for nearly as long'. Rationalisation of Wingfield lands – squaring the land – was implemented in the early 1840s. A letter to Stewart & Kincaid from Wingfield at Scurmore dated 16 July 1842 reported that 'everything here is flourishing & there are no hands unemployed' (SK): this indicates improvements in progress. Wingfield's schemes of squaring were on a less extensive scale than those on Palmerston's Ahamlish: perhaps a smaller proportion of the Wingfield lands had previously been farmed under rundale. The process of squaring meant that tenants had to level their old houses, they had to move from one place to another and build, and some of them were removed from the land. Thus, addressed to Stewart & Kincaid on 7 February 1844, the 'petition of Barthol. Morrison of Moyview . . . showeth' that 'petr. is one of the persons whom you were pleased to dispossess when you were dividing the lands. . . . Petitioner [reminds you] that you . . . promised to give as much money as would bear the expense of him and family [in all eleven persons] to America. . . . Petitioner thinks that £40 would . . . do so'. But 'petitioner would prefer remaining at home' (SK). This passage indicates that, like Palmerston, Wingfield provided assistance to emigrate even before the famine; however, such emigration was probably on a small scale. The Stewart & Kincaid correspondence also suggests that tenants who surrendered land received compensation. For example, on 13 March 1845 William Ormsby, local agent for Stewart & Kincaid, reported to the firm that Reid of Lecarrownaveagh had 'given up his holding. . . . I . . . told him I would give him £10–10–0 for his improvements which he consented to'. (SK)

Squaring of land and related construction programmes peaked just before the famine. Wingfield sometimes assisted in erection of the new houses. Thus, on 14 February 1845 Ormsby wrote to Stewart & Kincaid from Moyview: 'I am sorry Colonel Wingfield has not given you an answer with regard to my getting the land outside Moyview. . . . Mr Joynt [a land surveyor in Ballina[12]] has laid out all the new squares as we arranged. Some of the tenants . . . are satisfied and some not.' He added that a tenant 'was here today and said he would build a good slated house if he got encouragement. I said we would give him the roof and slates.' (SK) On 24 August, Wingfield wrote to Stewart & Kincaid from Scurmore: 'The tenants are on the move to their localities bringing the materials for building to the places I have marked out for them & many of the old houses are pulling down. . . . Now that the road is travelable, they have brought down all their tillage to it.' (SK) This passage indicates that, as on other estates, road works were necessary for access to newly squared holdings.

Wingfield removed some small tenants during the squaring. A letter of February 1845 refers to land in Newtown which had been 'taken from . . . small tenants' who may have received some compensation: a note from Ormsby in August observed that he had to pay about ten cottiers one pound each.

However, squaring did not always result in large farms: referring in March 1845 to Reid's departure from Lecarrownaveagh, Ormsby reported: 'If the land was striped [i.e. squared] it would now give the present tenants [there] 7 acres each'.[13]

Squaring of land near the Moy was extended into the early months of the famine: at the end of 1845 Wingfield wrote that he had heard from Ormsby 'that he had got Lecarrownaveagh & Breafy [Breaghwy] striped & laid out by Joynt but he made no mention of Ballyholan which requires it.[14] Squaring, and associated house-building programmes, seem to have been nearly completed by 14 February 1846, when Wingfield wrote from England informing Stewart & Kincaid that '8 of the new houses are already occupied & others in forwardness' (sĸ). The final reference to squaring on the lands near the Moy estuary is in a letter of 25 August 1846 from Wingfield at Scurmore to Stewart & Kincaid, in which he wrote that there was 'full employment here & most of the new cottages thatched & inhabited & the old ones eradicated' (sĸ).

Wingfield had further improvements in mind on the eve of the famine. At the beginning of April 1845 John Stewart, the agriculturalist on the Stratford estates in Limerick and Clare, came to the Scurmore district for about two months. He supervised the deepening of some streams. Shortly before his return to the southwest, he rode with Wingfield over part of the estate and pointed out the improvements which he considered the most urgent. He was again in that district in November 1846 and in July 1848.

William Holliday, perhaps the most progressive tenant on the Wingfield estate during the 1840s, was hard working and had a spirit of entrepreneurship. Unlike Wingfield, the repeal of the corn laws, which had imposed duties on the import of grain to the United Kingdom (and raised prices), did not greatly bother him. For a few years the prime minister, Peel, had been moving towards a view that the corn laws must go. His Tory cabinet split fundamentally on this issue early in December 1845, and later in the same month Wingfield wrote of 'the untoward situation in which that *Traytor* Peele has placed us'.[15] On 4 March 1846 he noted to Stewart & Kincaid: 'We lost our Battle of Protection' (sĸ). Holliday's response was that in the face of free trade in grain, domestic farmers would have to increase their efficiency. With a degree of objectivity which may have upset his landlord, he wrote to Wingfield on 18 February 1846: 'This consummation of the corn law was to be expected. . . . Agriculturalists must [now] lay their account with more activity and management. . . . Unless a farmer improves every acre of land that he holds . . . he has no chance of doing any good.' (sĸ) Holliday added that in order to further improve his farm: 'I wrote Mr. Kincaid that I would be willing to pay for £500 to be so laid out should he know of any one who might be inclined to lend for three years certain. His reply is in the negative'. (sĸ)

Holliday had come to the Wingfield estate in 1839. Another recent arrival, before famine distress became extreme, was Arthur Fry, who was also an improving tenant. Observing that he was 'late of the constabulary', he had been recommended to Wingfield by the Rev. John Garrett, vicar of Emlaghfad near Ballymote.[16] He was the kind of tenant Wingfield, who wrote that Fry 'is a Protestant & has means', wanted.[17] On 30 July 1846 Wingfield reported to Stewart & Kincaid that 'Fry has his House slated. . . . He is also doing much in making drains' (s к). Fry's fine house is still in good repair on the lands of Newtown.[18]

On the Wingfield lands, the few years before the famine must have been an era of optimism. On 18 February 1846 Holliday wrote to Wingfield: 'I am glad you are coming over [from England]. Unless you are here soon you will not know the place with all its changes and improvements.' (s к)

3 DISTRESS AND FAMINE

Some of Wingfield's tenants were in financial trouble in the months immediately before the partial failure of the potato in 1845. But ejectments seem to have been few. In June 1845 Wingfield wrote to Stewart & Kincaid from Scurmore that 'Ormsby served the ejectment yesterday. . . . It had the effect of getting possession from one or two others.' (s к) In this he was referring to the 'demonstration effect' of threatened ejectment: it encouraged others who were in arrears to pay or surrender their holdings 'voluntarily', and thereby saved the landlord time and money. 'Voluntary' surrender might also have been in the interests of the tenant in obtaining compensation upon departure.

On the eve of the famine, Patrick Howley was one of Wingfield's largest tenants. For many years he resided at a substantial house called Seaville (near where Wingfield built the police barrack) in the Ballymoghany district.[19] In Wingfield's view his politics were 'wrong': recall Wingfield's remarks on Howley and the Molly Maguires. The fact that Howley had fallen into arrears of rent by the autumn of 1845 gave Wingfield an opportunity to try to remove him. On 16 August, Wingfield wrote to Stewart & Kincaid that 'Patsey Howley has got some of his friends to walk him into gaol [apparently for debt] but I hear he cannot leave it without a surrender of his lease which we must get from him. . . . Take the necessary steps . . . as speedily as possible' (s к). But it took a long time to remove Howley. It seems that Wingfield was rid of him only through his death. In March 1846 Wingfield in England informed Stewart & Kincaid: 'I had a letter from Mr Pat Howley a few days ago, telling me he had been served with the ejectment, with an application [for Wingfield to use his influence] to get his *two* sons into some militia regt'.[20] Nevertheless,

on 24 April 1846 'Richard M. Howley for Patrick I. Howley' wrote to Stewart
& Kincaid: 'I expect . . . to be able to pay three half years rent next November.
. . . I lost all my potatoes with the exception of some early seed'. He complained:
'The few tenants that were here made off with the rent and seed oats I gave
them last year. . . . The failure of the potatoe crop was the cause of it. . . . Bailiffs
came and seized all the grazing cattle. . . . I was making up the rent . . . and would
have it only for this seizure'. Howley added that he had got 'two compitent
persons to . . . value the improvements which come to £1841-18-2½' (sк). This
sum was probably an exaggeration, for purposes of bargaining. On 30 July 1846
Wingfield instructed Stewart & Kincaid to 'get rid of Howley . . . by ejectment' (sк). On 6 September he again directed Stewart & Kincaid: 'Do not
neglect to take steps to get rid of Patrick Howley' (sк). However, on 15
December, Howley wrote to Stewart & Kincaid: 'I will have the £35 the
balance of the rent next week. . . . I wish to know if I am to get the 80 acres you
laid out for me as I intend sowing' (sк). Two days later Ormsby wrote to
Stewart & Kincaid: 'What am I to do with Mr P Howly. I think he will never
pay the rent. I told him yesterday I would have to put him out. . . . He wants
some compensation for all his improvements.' (sк) What happened next is
unknown. But Howley was dead by mid-May 1848, when a letter from
Edward Smyth (the Stewart & Kincaid agent in Sligo town) indicated that
the letting of 'the late Patt Howlys farm', was under consideration.[21] The
correspondence on Patrick Howley illustrates how difficult it could be to
remove an unwanted tenant.

Pat Manning was also troublesome. On 22 February 1846 he wrote to
Wingfield that he would have difficulty if he were then to repay a loan of £25,
which Wingfield demanded, while simultaneously paying rent to Stewart &
Kincaid, as was demanded by Stewart & Kincaid. In the same letter he pleaded
that if he were to bring these accounts up to date, 'it will distress me . . . for I
will not have a single potatoe for seed nor any to eat after May day [1846]. . . .
I have not one single potatoe without a black spot. . . . I therefore trust to your
accustomed . . . generosity to write to Mr. Kinkaid not to press me' (sк). In
March 1846 Wingfield wrote from England stating that he was still 'trying . . .
to get a repayment of £25 from Manning which I advanced him when he took
the farm at Dooneen'.[22] On 30 July he instructed Stewart & Kincaid :'Get rid
of Manning' by ejectment. The final reference to Manning is in a letter to
Stewart & Kincaid dated 6 September from Cork Abbey, in which, describing
Manning as a 'drunken idle vagabond', Wingfield repeated that he must be
got rid of (sк).

Howley and Manning blamed the potato failure of late 1845 for com-
pounding their difficulties. The failure seems to have been extensive on the
Wingfield estate. On 24 December 1845 Ormsby wrote to Stewart & Kincaid

that 'as to their [the tenants'] potatoes they are getting worse every day. In a short time they will have none. What am I to do about the arrears' (SK). Thus, the impact of the potato failure on rent receipts seems to have been more immediate on Wingfield's estate than on the Ferrall lands in Roscommon.

Following the first potato failure, Wingfield was genuinely concerned for those of his tenants who were industrious. But he expected them to support the law. In February 1846 he informed one of his agents then staying at Scurmore: 'I wrote to Mr Kincaid some days ago about the potatoes. Pray let me have your opinion what is best to be done as to the failure amongst those who have been industrious. I was disappointed at not seeing Hollidays & Ormsbys names to the reward offered for apprehension of those concerned in the outrage on . . . Dunbars sheep in which all my tenants should go hand & heart with me to prosecute offenders'.[23]

Among Wingfield lands, it seems that distress was worst on isolated Coolrecuill near Tubercurry. Much of that land is between two rivers – the upper Moy and the Einagh. No decent road had been engineered through the townland by the early 1840s, and access was further limited by the absence of any bridge.[24] Sheets 36 and 37 of the Ordnance Survey map of County Sligo, surveyed and engraved in 1837, show only a short spur into the townland; this disappeared into the bog, then resumed a further short stretch, and came to an end when it met the Einagh.

Late in December 1845 Wingfield wrote to Stewart & Kincaid stating that he was anxious to hear of 'the new road I have in at Coolrecul being approved of at the Road Sessions early next month'.[25] Writing to Stewart & Kincaid again on 11 February 1846, he expressed his concern: 'I was sorry to find Ormsby's report from Colleracul so very distressing. . . . Propose what you may think best to be done towards the relief of the tenantry both personally & by application to Government.' (SK) On 17 April 1846 Wingfield wrote to Stewart & Kincaid 'about the new road I proposed to run thro' Coolrecul which would give seasonable relief by employment to the distressed tenantry . . . & which I beg you will direct Mr Maxwell & Mr Ormsbys particular attention so that the work may be put in board as soon as possible after the Presentment is granted' (SK). In regard to the expense of the proposed road, Ormsby wrote to Stewart & Kincaid on 4 July that 'the board of works were to pay half and the Colonel the other half' (SK).

In the summer of 1846 the kind of projects which might be undertaken as public works (then in receipt of central government funding of one half of the cost) was restricted to works which would not benefit individuals more than the rest of the community. It was on this point that the proposal for the road through Coolrecuill failed. The entire townland was owned by Wingfield: therefore he would have benefited disproportionately. Hence, although the road would have been useful, it is not surprising that on 17 July 1846 the Board of Works informed Stewart & Kincaid that it 'cannot recommend this road, being as it is, more for the benefit of the proprietors, than the public, and . . . a large bridge should be built'.[26] In spite of the rejection of the request for financial support from the Board, some outlay was in fact incurred on the Coolrecuill road, on Wingfield's own account. Thus, on 8 September 1846 Ormsby wrote to Stewart & Kincaid: 'I will look after the Coolrecuill road' (sk). It seems that the road was completed in 1847.

The correspondence provides no evidence that many of Wingfield's tenants benefited from public works in 1846. Therefore, relief had to take other forms. On 14 July 1846 Ormsby wrote to Stewart & Kincaid: 'I am very busy giving out meal to the tenants. Our potato crop is universally attacked [by disease]' (sk). The meal in question was provided at Wingfield's expense. On 5 September, Ormsby wrote to Stewart & Kincaid that 'McHale called on me for one hundred pounds as part payment for the meal Colonel Wingfield desired me give the tenants. I got from McHale £163 worth.' (sk)

Substitution of meal in the diet of the peasants created opportunities for others. In the autumn of 1846 Wingfield received applications for a site for a corn mill. Religion may have been a factor in deciding which applicant was successful. On 25 August he wrote to Stewart & Kincaid: 'I send you . . . a proposal from a man in Ballina of some substance & character tho' a Holy Roman. . . . He is not a bigotted man & would engage to vote as I wished or not to register at all. He would . . . commence building forthwith if accepted on speculation of a great demand for meal in spring [1847] from the failure of the potato' (sk). This applicant was Michael Howley, a corn merchant in Ardnaree. There was also an application from Evans Grose, a calico dealer in Ardnaree.[27] On 8 September, Ormsby wrote to Stewart & Kincaid that Grose 'is a protestant' (sk). In regard to the other applicant, Wingfield had tempered his views by 6 September when he wrote to Stewart & Kincaid: 'I have more Howleys than I wish on the estate & would much prefer Grose even at a lower rent than the other' (sk). The Griffith *Valuation* indicates that the corn-mill was on Ballyholan, which was owned by Wingfield. It indicates that in 1856, Evans Grose was in occupation of 92 acres of land, which included a then unoccupied corn-mill, on Ballyholan.[28] However, the mill may have proved worthwhile during the famine: on 11 May 1848 Edward Smyth informed Stewart & Kincaid that Grose 'has received the 15 tons of barley and paid forty pounds as yet to Burrows for it', and on 5 June, Wingfield wrote to Stewart & Kincaid stating that he had 'heard that the tenant at our mill is going on very spiritedly' (sk).

William Holliday also gained from the distress of 1846. On 25 August, Wingfield wrote to Stewart & Kincaid that he had been 'at Hollidays this day

who has reaped . . . nearly 40 acres of wheat & oats. The turnips will be good'
(sk). On 26 October he informed Stewart & Kincaid: 'The poor people are
taking to the turnips so much that Holliday is selling his . . . as fast as he has
hands to supply them & it is well to dispose of them in this way. . . . It will
prevent their being stolen & supply food to the lower classes' (sk). According
to Wingfield on 4 November, for the turnips Holliday charged 'a penny a
stone which allowing 30 tons to the acre will pay him well. He is also thrashing
out & selling his oats at 26 shillings a barrel' (sk). On 2 November, Holliday
himself reported to Stewart & Kincaid that 'the people . . . buy the turnips
most readily. About 30/- daily sale'. In the same letter Holliday wrote: 'I have
kept on my men at odd jobs rather than pay them off to go home and starve'
(sk); thus, some of what he took with one hand, he returned with the other.

   Early in the autumn of 1846 the government announced new schemes of
famine relief. Public works were again to be undertaken, and these were to be
on a large scale. But the government now announced that it would no longer
pay half the cost. It was initially intended that the entire expense was now to
be paid by taxation of the districts in which the works took place. Presentment
sessions would be convened as before, but instead of reflecting purely local initiatives they would now be summoned at the discretion of the lord lieutenant;
thus, they were called 'special' sessions. Proposed projects had to be approved
by the Board of Works and, if acceptable, had to be implemented by the Board.
Presentment sessions under the new legislation began early in September, and
over the months which followed, the Board was deluged with applications
which it did not have the capacity to handle. Hence there were delays in getting
works approved and, if approved, started. As under the schemes earlier in
1846, no works from which an individual gained disproportionately could be
undertaken as public works. This eliminated many badly needed drainage
programmes. However, at later stages in the famine – mainly in 1848 – the
owners of almost every estate managed by Stewart & Kincaid borrowed public
monies to conduct 'reproductive works' on their lands.

   That some roads which were useless (apart from creating employment)
were built as public works is well known. However, it may also be the case that
the sheer administrative burden of assessing hundreds of submissions from
presentment sessions led to rejection of proposals which would create employment, while simultaneously being otherwise useful. On 7 November 1846
Thomas Redington, under-secretary to the lord lieutenant, wrote to Edward
Howley (deputy-lieutenant of County Sligo[29]) of Belleek Castle, Ballina, that
'the immediate attention of the Board of Works has been called to your
communication . . . relative to the want of employment' (sk). A letter from
Howley to Kincaid dated 9 November indicates that what Howley specifically
sought for employment creation was the construction of a major road through

specified townlands in which there was a 'vast amt of destitution' (sk). The proposed road, to the east of Ardnaree, would have traversed Ballyholan and other Wingfield lands, as well as some further townlands. Howley indicated: 'The estimate for it including a small bridge was £650. It was surveyed . . . by the *Deputy Co. Surveyor* who *declared it a most useful and necessary* road. . . . It opens an immense tract of country now quite land locked – very thickly populated.' (sk) He added that 'the want of a bridge frequently obliged the poor people to keep in their dead *for 4 or 5 days*, and the clergyman is *often obliged to return*, not being able to visit *the dying* for the want of a road to travel over.' (sk) Howley therefore asked Kincaid to go immediately to the Board of Works, where he was sure Kincaid would find an engineer's report in favour of the road. Wingfield referred to the same road on 4 November, when he wrote to Stewart & Kincaid urging use of influence at the Board: 'As to the road at Ballyholan . . . I will trouble you to expedite by a personal representation to Col. Jones [the chairman] & the other members of the Board of Works, that they may send down an order to have it proceeded on forthwith, so that work may be given to the poor & starving people.' (sk)

The Stewart & Kincaid correspondence includes a further letter from Edward Howley, addressed to Kincaid and dated 16 November. Written from Belleek Castle, it related that he was about to go to Dublin hoping to influence the Lord Lieutenant in favour of the proposed road and also 'to press upon the Board of Works the absolute necessity of having this work reconsidered, and undertaken at once, as the people are in the most awful state of destitution' (sk). It is inferred that the Board had rejected the proposal. This might have reflected overwork at the Board; alternatively, it might have been in recognition that Wingfield would have been a major beneficiary of the proposed roadworks.

Apart from delays in getting public works started, there were also problems in speedily commencing private reproductive works such as drainage, partly because of delays in obtaining government loans for the financing of such works. Furthermore, because individual proprietors had to repay government loans financing reproductive works on their properties, it followed that in the case of major reproductive works which substantively benefited more than one proprietor, the consent of each of them had to be obtained. A letter from Wingfield to Stewart & Kincaid on 4 November 1846 indicates that he (along with Holliday) was then preparing an application to the Board of Works for a loan of £1,000, which would be used to finance reproductive works (sk). Holliday anticipated problems. On 2 November he wrote to Stewart & Kincaid:

The machinery in these government [loan] schemes seems at best most cautious. . . . We want immediate work for the people and not less so for our [own proposed] operations, because draining . . . if longer delayed will come into the season for our next years crop culture, and thus be unavailable. It was in anticipation of these difficulties that I proposed Colonel Wingfield should . . . take with me a fair proportion of drainage cost, and I still consider a private mode of raising the money would be infinitely more simple, quick, and efficious. (sk)

It was not only in the Ballina district that problems arose in quickly implementing public or reproductive works. Recall that Wingfield also owned the impoverished townland of Coolrecuill near Tubercurry in the Barony of Leyny. On 15 December 1846 John Hamilton, who was probably the acting secretary of the relief committee in that district, wrote to Wingfield. He enclosed a copy of a resolution adopted by the committee, dated 28 November 1846, and requested Wingfield's co-operation. The resolution was as follows:

That public works hitherto sanctioned for the Upper Half Barony of Leyny are altogether insufficient to afford employment to the numerous destitute poor within the district, and that even for the portion of the population provided for by these works, there will not be employment for more than two or three months longer and that under these circumstances we feel it our duty to direct the attention of the landed proprietors . . . to the . . . absolute necessity of providing works of a reproductive kind . . . for the employment of the poor within the district, for the first six or eight months of the ensuing year [1847]. (sk)

In the same letter of 15 December, Hamilton indicated that an application had been made for a presentment sessions for the Upper Half Barony of Leyny. What happened at the ensuing sessions is indicated in a letter of 24 December 1846 in which Ormsby informed Stewart & Kincaid: 'The gentlemen of that Barony were not willing to undertake reproductive works [presumably, as provided for under Labouchere's letter, mentioned on p. 47 above]. I thought to get the Coolrecull road finished but could not succeed.' (sk)

Most of the Wingfield townlands were in the Barony of Tireragh, in north-western Sligo. On 15 December 1846, Holliday informed Stewart & Kincaid that 'the Tireragh Sessions will be held in Easky on Tuesday the 22nd., and an endeavour is being made to have the proprietors unanimous in presenting for drainage' (sk). The drainage projects were in fact accepted, and some of these were on the Wingfield estate. The projects agreed at the Easky sessions were expected to provide two months employment for 4,000 men, but Holliday felt that the drainage programmes were coming too late in the year.[30] On 25 December, he wrote to Stewart & Kincaid: 'This presentment is calculated to last only till February. That is our wetest season. . . . I conceive it to be a radical error . . . to take main drains & river deepening now in the teeth of the physical difficulties of the season and with . . . starved & naked men as workmen' (sk).

Neither Ormsby nor Holliday, who was about to take an appointment as local drainage inspector under the Board of Works, was optimistic at the end of 1846. In the last letter from him in the Stewart & Kincaid correspondence (24 December 1846), Ormsby observed to Stewart & Kincaid that 'the poor are in a wretched state' (s k). Holliday added a postscript to his letter to Stewart & Kincaid dated 21 December: 'Daily deaths in the poor house 13 to 15. Numbers are dropping from want' (s k).

4 LATER FAMINE YEARS

The Stewart & Kincaid correspondence of 1847 on Wingfield's estate is missing. However, we know that he assisted emigration in that year. Some of the evidence is contained in a letter from Wingfield of 20 December 1848 in which he referred to a request that he sign a document proposing a project on the Moy near his lands. The proposal may have been to make the Moy navigable up to Ballina, through use of public funds (which probably would have entailed further local property taxation). Wingfield's response to Stewart & Kincaid on 20 December 1848 was as follows:

> Was this project to advantage the property or give any permanent or reproductive employment . . . I should certainly sign it. . . . Some years ago Mr Nimmo [who built many harbours in the west of Ireland] expended several thousand pounds . . . to establish a harbour there & a main road to it & also to cut away ledges of rock to make the Moy navigable from the Quay[31] near Bunree to the town of Ballina which proved to be a complete failure & throw away of money & what was then done suffered to get into decay & be carried away by the seas. . . . A grant for such a purpose would be the means of bringing back the idle population which I paid so much to get rid of by transporting to America the year before last. (s k)

Wingfield should have written 'about a year and a half ago' (which would have been in 1847) instead of 'the year before last' (1846). This inference is made for the following reasons: First, the elderly Wingfield was inaccurate elsewhere about dates.[32] Second, the Stewart & Kincaid correspondence of 1846 does not refer to assisted emigration from the Wingfield lands in that year. Third, MacDonagh has noted that Wingfield implemented a programme of assisted emigration in 1847, while McTernan indicates that families from Wingfield's estate sailed for British North America on board the *Marchioness of Perth* in June of that year.[33]

We can be confident that most of the assisted emigration from the Wingfield estate to America was in 1847. The Sligo merchant William Kernaghan (see chapter 3) participated in arranging the Palmerston emigrations from Sligo in 1847, and some of the food for the voyages was obtained by Stewart & Kincaid's agents from a grocer named Boyle in Sligo town. A letter from J. R. Stewart to Kincaid, 17 May 1848, contains the following passage: 'I postponed sending Thos Kernaghan [father of William Kernaghan] an account due to him by Col Wingfield . . . thinking that we might stop it towards the Cols share of Boyles demand' (on account of provisions which Boyle supplied for emigrants in 1847) (s κ). Thus Wingfield shared with Palmerston the costs of the emigrations from Sligo in 1847: hence an inference that some Wingfield emigrants may have been on board one or more of the vessels which carried Palmerston's emigrants to America.

The Stewart & Kincaid correspondence provides no further details of the Wingfield emigrations in 1847. However, a letter from Wingfield to Stewart & Kincaid, dated 22 April 1848, indicates that emigration from the port of Sligo was then so brisk that it interfered with the cattle export trade. In this letter Wingfield informed Stewart & Kincaid that 'there was as usual a great disappointment about sending the fat cattle to Liverpool. The steamer was so crowded with emigrants, but two of them . . . were sold in Sligo for £34.' (s κ)

A letter to Kincaid dated 5 December 1848 from a tenant named Wills indicates that there may have been some assisted emigration from the Wingfield lands in 1848–9. In this he stated that some of his property had recently been distrained because of rent arrears. Wills added: 'Allow me what you said you would for sending my sisters to America. . . . I wrote [to Wingfield] a letter by this post, requesting of him . . . either to give me imployment or to allow you to let me go as you are letting part of the tenants go with the littel things they have.' (s κ) But it seems that the only assistance received from Wingfield by most of the tenants to whom Wills referred was that although they were in arrears of rent, they were allowed to sell whatever property they had in order to finance their departure.

In the Stewart & Kincaid correspondence of 1848, most of the many items on the Wingfield estate concern drainage and, following the departures of 1847, efforts to find viable tenants for lands which were going to waste. Major programmes of drainage commenced in January 1848. On 18 January, John Stewart the agriculturalist reported that he had been ten days at work in the Moyview district, where he had devised 'a very cheap way of providing materials for the drainage' by setting 'a lot of boys and girls to collect the small stones along the strand' (s κ). John Stewart paid the workers in cash every two weeks. The average fortnightly labour bill in the spring and summer of 1848 came to over £50. This was usually sent down from Dublin; however, Stewart sometimes drew on an account at the Provincial Bank in Ballina. On 31 January he provided details of daily rates of pay: excavators, 10*d* to 1*s* 4*d*; horses and carts, 1*s* 3*d* to 3*s*; stone collectors, 1½*d* to 4*d*. In the same letter he indicated that he had commenced work on Dooneen. The works were financed by a government loan of £2,000.[34] Wingfield's tenant William Holliday inspected the drains on behalf of the Board of Works. He did not always approve of them.[35]

On 14 February 1848 John Stewart indicated that he had commenced work on Ballymoghany, and that a second agriculturalist, Peter Bridgeman, had just arrived from the Stratford estate in Limerick. Stewart sent Bridgeman to supervise drainage on Coolrecuill, which had recently fallen out of lease. For many years the entire townland of Coolrecuill had been leased to a man who, according to Wingfield, kept 'the profitable part of it . . . in his own hands, & letting off the remainder at I dare say double the rent he paid to me for the whole'.[36]

John Stewart did not merely supervise drainage works: he sought to encourage improvements in tenants' husbandry. Thus, on 11 May 1848 Edward Smyth informed Stewart & Kincaid that Stewart 'would wish for turnip seed and will induce the tenants to sow a good breath of them if he gets it. Mr Holliday has a good quantity to sell'. Referring to Coolrecuill in the same letter, Smyth reported that 'Bridgeman says that if you allow turnip seeds for the tenants, there will be about 14 acres under them.' (SK)

In consequence of emigration, death and other forms of depopulation ('voluntary' surrender or actual ejectment), many of the holdings on Wingfield's properties lay idle by early 1848. On 7 March, Wingfield wrote to Stewart & Kincaid that 'Burrow's last report . . . says that none of the waste holdings have yet been set & that he fears the fever is getting more prevalent.' He added in the same letter: 'Since I came over [to England] I have not drawn on Puget [a banker in London] for a single farthing but I must soon get some cash from him' (SK). By early in 1848 Wingfield had fallen into deficit in his accounts with Stewart & Kincaid. Still in England, he wrote to Stewart & Kincaid on 28 March: 'Thank you very much for the report. . . . It is a sad thing to find such a quantity of land lying waste but as to letting unless at a great undervalue, it cannot be accomplished at present. You must manage therefore in the best manner you can for me about it & give the necessary direction, to Burrows and Stuart [meaning John Stewart] to attend to it. I was in hopes you would have got sufficient rent to put me on the right side of your books.' (SK)

Treatment of the waste lands meant that John Stewart had other work to do, 'on the Colonel's account', apart from drainage (under the Board of Works loan account). On 4 April he informed Stewart & Kincaid: 'I would like to know the actual sum that you would wish to be expended in tilling the unoccupied farms'. Having indicated that 'Howlys old farm . . . is a great eye sore', he went on to state that 'as to Ballymoghany there is very little land in it that I would recommend to be tilled. What I would recommend . . . is to . . . lime and top dress the land. . . . There is a fence round every two acres of the land at present but by treating it . . . it would make a good sheep farm.' (s K)

On 8 May 1848 John Stewart informed Stewart & Kincaid that he expected that 'all the unoccupied grassland will be set next week' (s K). He let some of the untenanted land under conacre.[37] Wingfield and his agents did not simply want tenants: they had to be solvent tenants. On 13 May, Stewart indicated to Stewart & Kincaid that he had met a man named Collran, who 'asked if I would set [to him] Pat Howlys farm and house. . . . He would be a very good tenant and . . . a very solvent one' (s K). A few days later, Edward Smyth came to the Wingfield lands and on 19 May he wrote to Stewart & Kincaid: 'I set the grass of the farm Mrs Atkinson lately surrendered called Lessermore [Lissard More] to Higgins[38] today. . . . It is in a very poor state. . . . He engages to build a good 2 story house on it, provided you allow slates and timber, and give a lease. . . . I have set Pat Howlys farm to a Mr Callorin . . . for £1 per acre and to give a lease' (s K). But the negotiations with Collran appear to have broken down. There is no mention of such a person in the subsequent correspondence; furthermore, no person of such (or similar) names is listed on Wingfield land in the Griffith *Valuations* of the 1850s. In the absence of a viable tenant for Howley's farm on Ballymoghany, Wingfield's agents decided to stock it with cattle. On 11 May 1848 Smyth informed Stewart & Kincaid: 'There are at present on the [late Howley] farm between 40 and 50 . . . cattle' (s K).

In 1848, apart from those grazing on untenanted lands, cattle were also fattened on Wingfield's farm at Scurmore. Some of them were sent to Liverpool; others were sold locally. Referring to those from Scurmore in his letter to Stewart & Kincaid dated 11 May, Smyth reported to Stewart & Kincaid that 'twelve of the stallfeds [i.e. cattle fed from stalls rather than by open grazing] have been sold at Liverpool and twelve more are to be shipped on Tuesday next. They ought to bring about 23£ each. I must remain in Sligo to see them on board' (s K). On 7 October, Stewart & Kincaid instructed John Stewart to send 'another score [of] heifers to Ardnaree fair' outside Ballina (s K).

Apart from stocking Ballymoghany with cattle, John Stewart spread guano and ashes as fertiliser and planted barley on Carraun townland. He also supervised the digging of lands in preparation for grass seed.[39] However, although Stewart & Kincaid offered prospective tenants financial assistance for building, some of the land remained unproductive. Few new tenants were found in 1848. One potential tenant was rejected on non-financial grounds. On 28 September, Wingfield wrote to Stewart & Kincaid: 'It is very troublesome to have so much land in my own hands, yet I believe the old saying to be true "that it is better to have an empty house than a bad tenant". . . . You acted very judiciously by putting such a rent on the 40 acres priest Duffy wants to get into his clutches, as to prevent any further application from him, for you know they are not the description of persons I would think of having as tenants.' (sk)

In 1849 D. H. Ferrall had sought to attract English farmers to idle lands in Roscommon. Wingfield sought likewise. In September 1848 David Bellamy of Durham in England expressed an interest in settling on the former Howley farm in Ballymoghany. On 29 September 1848 he wrote to Wingfield: 'A good English farmer might . . . be of infinite service to his landlord, by . . . improved implements & herds of cattle, as well as by his example' (sk). In a letter to Stewart & Kincaid dated 28 September 1848, Wingfield observed that 'it would be very advantageous to have a substantial Durham agriculturalist who could manage a farm of two or three hundred acres settled upon the estate' (sk). But there is no evidence that Bellamy ever came to Ireland: no person of that name is listed on Wingfield land in the Griffith *Valuations* of the 1850s. Wingfield's inability to attract suitable tenants extended into 1849. On the first day of that year, he wrote to Stewart & Kincaid: 'I hope you may succeed in getting me some good tenants for the waste lands, preferring the Protestants at all times.' (sk)

Some of Wingfield's larger tenants were financially distressed in 1848. On 7 March, Wingfield wrote to Stewart & Kincaid: 'I shall be anxious to know how Holliday & Ormsby have paid their rent & if they are . . . getting over their difficulties. . . . Keep a strict watch over them.' (sk) The problems of Holliday and Ormsby extended into the summer of 1848. On 25 June, Wingfield wrote to Stewart & Kincaid that he had 'heard from Burrows that ten keepers have been placed on Hollidays farms at Newtown & Dooneen, & I fear the same may be the case with Ormsby at Moyview' (sk). Wingfield was more nervous on 26 July when he wrote to Stewart & Kincaid: 'I hope you will look well after both Ormsby & Holliday, the latter of whom should have sent you up the amount for *one half* of the fishery money before the season ends which will be before the end of next month. Should you not get it before then he may pocket the whole.' (sk) The financial difficulties of Holliday and Ormsby in 1848 were related: Holliday's problems arose because he provided security for some speculative venture on Ormsby's part, which apparently failed.[40] Ormsby's fate is unknown: he is not listed on Wingfield land in the Griffith *Valuations* of the 1850s which indicate that in 1857, Holliday held about 470 acres of Wingfield land.[41]

5 CONCLUDING OBSERVATIONS

The foregoing has indicated that Wingfield was an improving landlord. On 16 May 1848 John Stewart wrote to Stewart & Kincaid that 'all the tenants are asking me if they will get turnip seed this year. . . . What is very much wanted is two or three small turnip sowing barrows. If you send them they will be very useful.' (s κ) In response, Stewart & Kincaid wrote to Edward Smyth in Sligo town, who on 24 May replied: 'Allow the small tenants at Scurmore the turnip seeds. . . . I made inquiry about the turnip barrow, but they have no such implement here. I have however directed Mr Wood the seedsman to send over to Liverpool and get three cheap ones . . . which will answer for the Cliffony District, Ballymote, & Scurmore.' (s κ) The encouragement of tenants to grow turnips may have provided a cushion against the potato failure of 1848. In this context John Stewart reported to Stewart & Kincaid on 12 September: 'The turnip crop on this estate is doing remarkable well. As for the potatoe crop . . . they are every day getting worse.' (s κ)

Although he spent much of his time with his brother in England, or at his home in County Dublin, Wingfield maintained an active interest in his Sligo tenants. He informed himself of their individual characters. He respected the industrious but had no time for idlers, especially if they were heavy drinkers. Thus, it may be recalled that in September 1846 he referred to Pat Manning, whom he wanted to 'get rid of', as a 'drunken idle vagabond' (see p. 136 above). On 31 December 1846 a person named William Maundy wrote to Stewart & Kincaid requesting that he be confirmed as a tenant. Stewart & Kincaid forwarded the letter to Wingfield, who returned it to Stewart & Kincaid with the manuscript observation: 'He [Maundy] did not do a days work . . . the whole summer & is continually drunk' (s κ). Thus, Maundy's aspiration to tenancy was apparently denied.

To an extent, Wingfield was a paternal figure on his Sligo estate. This is illustrated in his views in regard to the marriage of one of his farm labourers at Scurmore, a man named Lewis. Writing to Stewart & Kincaid on 28 September 1848, Wingfield explained:

> He wants to bring his wife to live in the yard [at Scurmore House] which Burrows thinks would not be desirable & therefore it would be much better to get another in his place. I did as much as I could to disuade him from marrying any person that would not bring him some suitable means . . . , but he took his own way and that should not make him dictate to me [for an increase in pay]. His wages are certainly very small, yet if I added a couple of pounds to it, I think he would still remain dissatisfied. (s κ)

Although Wingfield was in financial distress in 1848, he continued to subscribe to dispensaries and other bodies on or near his estate. On 7 March 1848 he complained to Stewart & Kincaid that despite 'the situation in which all the landlords are placed, I am plagued with as many applications for charity as if I was in great affluence' (s κ). However, on 15 March he requested Stewart & Kincaid to pay my annual subscriptions . . . to the fever hospital at Ballina, the dispensaries there & at Killanley[42] & also at Tubbercurry that there may be no delay in making out the presentments [for public funding, matching the sums raised through private subscriptions] for them & poor as I may be I wish you would leave £5 with Mrs Joyner[43] for me as a donation to the ladies Industrial Institution in Ballina. (sk)

EIGHT

THE ROSCOMMON ESTATES OF
THE MARQUESS OF WESTMEATH

—

I INTRODUCTION

In the 1840s George Nugent, Marquess of Westmeath, owned land in two districts of Roscommon. The major part consisted of about 6,000 statute acres in the parish of Kiltullagh in the northwest of the county near Castlerea. In the northeast, close to the Shannon and to the east of a line drawn from Strokestown to Carrick-on-Shannon, he owned about 4,000 statute acres in the adjacent parishes of Kilmore and Kilglass, both of which suffered extreme distress during the famine.[1] See map 6. To avoid confusion with the county of Westmeath, most of the references to the proprietor in this chapter will be to 'George Nugent' rather than to 'Westmeath'.

Nugent's main residence was at Clonyn in Westmeath. He was also occasionally resident in Kilmore at Cloonteem Lodge, near Drumsna across the Shannon in Leitrim. Writing from Drumsna on 20 May 1845, the Stewart & Kincaid employee Maxwell reported that 'his Lordship was with me this morning and yesterday he had the lady with him walking about the street. . . . She goes by the name of his wife'.[2] The firm of Stewart & Kincaid commenced as his agent c.1843. On 11 September of that year, John Taylor, the steward at Cloonteem wrote to Stewart & Kincaid: 'I have got all the tenants warned to meet Mr Kincaid at the tims [times] and pleses [places] appointed, and I am sorey Mr Kincaid cannot be accomadated with a bed in the Lodge, as his Lordship dos not hire out any sheets or blankets fit for a gentleman, but Drumsna is only a short mile from the Lodge, and there is a good inn in it'. Despite this unenthusiastic introduction, Kincaid met tenants at Cloonteem Lodge, and he slept there, in November 1843.[3]

For at least two reasons, George Nugent had persistent financial problems. First, the family estate 'was burdened with debt, much of which went back to 1796', when George's father had divorced his mother for adultery.[4] Second, financial consequences of his sexual adventures and of litigation followed his first marriage. He wed Lady Emily Cecil in 1812. However, he had already fathered a child by a mistress (whom he once described as 'of the lower order') in Ireland, and he sired a second by the same woman around the time of his marriage. Emily resented the financial support which he continued to give this second family. In 1818 George and Emily parted beds. In consequence, a gigantic 15-year legal battle began in 1819. In 1857 Nugent claimed that this 'war' with his first wife had cost him £30,000 in legal fees. In the 1840s he openly kept a French mistress by whom he had further offspring. Within a month of Emily's death in 1858, and then aged 73, he married again (not to the French woman). But four years later he resorted to litigation in order to obtain a divorce because of his young wife's adultery. He married once more in 1864. Neither of his two late marriages produced an heir, so that on his death in 1871 his only surviving legitimate child was Rosa (by Emily), who inherited his estates.

2 DEVELOPMENTS IN KILMORE AND KILGLASS, MAINLY IN 1843–5

Michael Johnston (in Kilglass) and Michael Dowd (in Kilmore) were the Stewart & Kincaid bailiffs in northeast Roscommon. Weak in literacy in the English language, they were immediately responsible to the Stewart & Kincaid agent in Longford town, John Crawford.

Until 1843, some of the land in Kilmore had been leased to a middleman who probably let the land under the rundale system. The firm of Stewart & Kincaid then undertook direct management of those lands. Early in 1844 Stewart & Kincaid implemented some restructuring of holdings – squaring – in Kilmore.[5] During the same year a surveyor came to divide bogs in Kilglass among the tenants, and to show them how to drain. According to Johnston on 24 June 1844, 'there is no person aloud to coot any turf until the drains are finished' (SK). In November 1844 another surveyor, Daniel Farmer, came to the 500 (statute) acre townland of Carrigeen in Kilglass. As he explained to Stewart & Kincaid on 12 November, he told the tenants of 'the advantage of having their detached holdings in one and properly laid out. 24 willingly agreed and signed the document for this but 14 dissented: those 14 would not agree to be shifted.' (SK) The document (reproduced in Farmer's letter to Stewart & Kincaid) signed by the majority stated: 'We . . . on the lands of Caragans [Carrigeen] being desirous to have our present holdings . . . consolidated . . . hereby refer the same to his Lordship's agents . . . and do hereby bind ourselves to abide by such arrangements as they may make, and to accept such new holdings . . . in lieu of our present detached holdings and our several rights of grazing in common, . . . each class of equal holdings to be . . . drawn by lot' (sk). But resettlement on the newly squared land was slow. Thus, on 14 February 1846 Crawford wrote to Stewart & Kincaid: 'I thought it well to allow [against rent payments] whatever portion Mr Farmer approved of on account of the ditches already made in Carrigans & also to direct Johnston to put all the tenants that were satisfied into possession of their new holdings.' (sk) On 29 October 1846 Johnston reported to Stewart & Kincaid that in Carrigeen, 'the men ar now setled and evrry one in possessions of his new division' (sk). Road works were also in progress in Kilglass late in 1845. According to Johnston in August: 'Crawford gave me a parsle of tools' for road building and drainage by the tenants there. In the same month Dowd informed Stewart & Kincaid that tenants in Kilmore 'requested that I should ask some picks and two sledgess and two crow barrs of you. The[y] would wish ... to quarry stoans to burn lime. ... If you give them [tools] the[y] will pay for them in six months'.[6]

Much of the land in Kilglass is poor and even today a large part of Kilmore is liable to flooding. These features accentuated the difficulties of extracting rent. But there was a further problem: the then Crown townland of Ballykilcline is in Kilglass and, as mentioned in chapter 6, a rebellion on Ballykilcline against payment of rent was extended from the mid-1830s until the eve of the famine. The success of those tenants in avoiding rent inevitably affected the willingness of tenants elsewhere in Kilglass, and in Kilmore, to pay. It may also have induced disregard for the Law in other respects. To keep their jobs under such circumstances, the Stewart & Kincaid bailiffs in Kilglass and Kilmore had to be firm. However, at least one tenant complained that Johnston's actions reflected personal hostility. On 31 December 1843 his neighbour Peter Donnelly wrote to Stewart & Kincaid: 'I was distrained for £5-10-9 of an arrear that I do not owe at all. But Michl. Johnston [has] enmity to me because my brother ... reported him ... to the Marquis for ... fraud' (sk). Johnston's efforts to seize Donnelly's assets to the value of £5 odd were unsuccessful. He therefore sued Donnelly for nonpayment of debt. A consequence is indicated in a letter from Donnelly in Roscommon jail to Stewart & Kincaid, 2 May 1844: 'I have been here since the 15th april last ... when I ought be sowing something that might support me. ... Take pity on me and release me'. He wrote that if Stewart & Kincaid insisted that he pay the debt for which he was in jail, he would 'sell the cow and pay' but he added: 'I now trust you will allow me to keep my cow' so that he could pay Stewart & Kincaid from money obtained from milk sales (sk). Only one reference to Donnelly was found in subsequent correspondence: On 29 October 1846 Johnston wrote to Stewart & Kincaid that (possibly in order to avoid distraint) 'peter donely sold his horse and cart and his two cows and three cags of buttur' (sk).[7]

As on other estates, 1843 was a difficult year. On 29 April, William O'Brien wrote to Stewart & Kincaid from Kilglass, stating that 'its . . . out of my power to have the rent for you sooner than the autumn. . . . The distresses . . . and the difficulty in getting money for anything . . . are unprecedented' (SK). On 4 October, O'Brien sent Stewart & Kincaid a bill of exchange for £20, 'in lieu of rent due'. But in anticipation of the next gale he stated: 'I do not know how we shall exist or make rent, the times are so dreadfully bad.'[8] The hard times of 1843 affected arrears in 1844. Several tenants in Kilglass were processed (summoned to court) during the summer of 1844 because of rent arrears.[9] On 6 July one of them, Andrew Finn, wrote to Kincaid that 'if your honour was as human as to give me a stay of execution untill harvest I would be able to pay' (SK). Almost a year later on 18 June 1845, Finn again petitioned Kincaid stating that he 'was decreed in June 1844 for an alledged arrear of £3–11s. He being unable to pay was sent to the County Goal [*sic*] and remained there untill he paid £2 . . . to John Craford [Crawford] Esq & had to give security for the ballance . . . to Michl Johnston. And petr. is processed for the 26th of June 45 for the £1–11. Your petr. hopes your Honour will . . . indulge him until harvest, as he has no support for his family to the number of 10.' (SK) Finn's fate is unknown.[10]

On 7 September 1844 Johnston wrote to Stewart & Kincaid that 'the crops are much better than usual. . . . There are several of the tenants that went to England to the harvist and promised to pay when the[y] return and the[y] are now at home and paying none' (SK). On 1 November he wrote to Stewart & Kincaid requesting 'some Distraining Notices as I expect to make those that are able to pay again [i.e. by] the fair of Strokestown which will be on the 12th' (SK). Relative prosperity in the autumn of 1844 seems to have had a favourable effect on rents collected in the following summer: On 20 May 1845 Maxwell wrote to Stewart & Kincaid from Drumsna: 'I sent last night by Mr Crawford £270 for my R/A [rent account] and as far as I have gone . . . the receipt this year is double that of last year' (SK).

Even before the potato failure of 1845, tenants threatened with ejectment were offered money to leave. Thus, on 27 June 1845 Dowd wrote to Stewart & Kincaid that two tenants in Kilmore had indicated, 'if the[y] get three pounds that the[y] will go'. He stated that 'there is a great many tenants that did not pay there rent' (SK). For many, the coming harvest was to make such payments impossible. Nevertheless, the end of 1845 saw several cases of distraint against those who had assets. On 10 December, Johnston reported to Stewart & Kincaid that in Kilglass he had recently distrained assets of two tenants but that two others had 'locked up there cattle in there houses' and he 'could not get them'. He had also impounded the bed of another tenant but this had been 'rescued' from Johnston, who added: 'There is no landlord in this country demanding any rents. . . . The disase of the potatoes in this country is still

increasing and I think there will not be a potatoe in it the 1st of February' (SK).
On 19 December 1845 Dowd reported to Stewart & Kincaid: 'I have seven
cows in the pound' (SK).

Unauthorised burning of land (for the fertilising effects of ash) seems to
have been the main form of breach of law on Nugent's properties in the early
1840s. For example, on 1 November 1844 Johnston wrote to Stewart & Kincaid
that he had 'seen a leter that Lord Westmeath rote . . . to no how many was
convicted for burning land in the year 1842 and 43 . . . and how many was sent
to gaol'.[11] Reports of burning land can be found in other letters from Johnston
in 1844. The correspondence contains only two references to violence in Kilglass
or Kilmore before 1845. What seems to have been the first is in an undated letter
to Stewart from Kincaid at Cloonteem Lodge, which reported that a notice
'was posted on the gate this morn'g threatening death to anyone that would
take any of the waste lands' (in Kilmore). Another letter, dated September 1844
to Stewart & Kincaid from a tenant in Kilglass, complained that he had been
'compelled to give a portion' of his holdings to the former occupants in order
'to evade a premature death'.[12]

Many acts of violence were reported from Nugent's townlands in 1845.
Early in the year John Clancy complained that his son had taken forcible
possession of his house in Kilmore. On 22 February he wrote to Stewart &
Kincaid: 'I found myself obliged to resort to the strong arm of the law, for the
safety of my person, from which course I was diverted by the advice of . . . the
Roman Catholic rector of the parish [and another person], who undertook to
settle the case by arbitration.' (SK) Arbitration did not favour the son, and
threats against the father, who sought intervention by Stewart & Kincaid,
continued.[13] However, other acts of violence in 1845 were more serious. On 4
April, Crawford wrote to Stewart & Kincaid from Longford that 'two troops
of . . . Hussars have arrived this day. . . . Our neighbouring counties are the
cause' (SK). Maxwell was more explicit when he wrote from Drumsna on 20
May: 'This part of the world is in a most *unsatisfactory* state. On Sunday
evening Mr Hoggs[14] steward was shot at and wounded and the same night
200 Molly Maguires walked into this town and posted notices on the chapel
door threatening death to any person who should charge above a certain rate
for meal' (SK). On 29 June, Johnston reported to Stewart & Kincaid that the
process server in the Strokestown district had 'processes taken from him'.
Also, Johnston had just heard 'that there came four boats loaden with Molly
McGuire men from the County Leitrim in to Moyglass' near Cloonteem (SK).
On 11 August he informed Stewart & Kincaid that 'there is a grait dale of this
county in a bad state . . . since I was attacked' (SK). On 16 August, Dowd wrote
to Stewart & Kincaid: 'Seven men well armed . . . came to Cloonteem [Lodge]
about 12 or 1 oclock in the day and . . . took three guns and a baynet. . . . The[y]

were pursued by Fransis Waldren[15] and the police but none of them was taken.' (s k) The attack on Cloonteem Lodge caused great concern. On 19 August, Waldron wrote to Stewart & Kincaid: 'The Govt. have offered a reward, of £40, but . . . it would be . . . expedient that as large a *Private* reward as possible would be offered, for the apprehension of the robbers.' (s k) Waldron and another magistrate in the Drumsna district were each assigned two policemen for protection. Waldron wrote again to Stewart & Kincaid a few days later: 'There would be little use in advertising the reward in any of the papers, but, circulating hand-bills amongst the poor . . . in the immediate neighbourhood where the arms went [probably meaning the Ballykilcline district] will I think answer the purpose. It would be . . . advisable to buy for Dowd a small double pistol . . . for the defence of his person.'[16] The Stewart & Kincaid letters do not reveal whether those who attacked Cloonteem Lodge were arrested. However, tranquillity did not quickly return to the district. On 10 December, Johnston informed Stewart & Kincaid: 'There is not a night but there is sum outrage committed' and that in Kilglass, a property owner had 'his horse shot and himself and his brother draged out of his gig and got several wonds on the head and a notice posted in the chapple door that the next visit is to shoot him. All about his rents.' (s k).

3 THE FAMINE YEARS IN KILMORE AND KILGLASS

Further serious offences were committed in 1846, particularly in Kilglass. On 2 January, Johnston wrote to Stewart & Kincaid that 'the prosis server of that district would not serve any prosis for rent', due to fear (s k). On 22 June, Johnston reported that he had received 'three parcels of prosises . . . and delivered them to the prosis server [who] said he was sick and if . . . he atempted to serve them he would loose his life'. He indicated that 'in the different townlands there was an armed party of men with cloacks and bonnets on them and posted notices . . . against the prosis server and me and where my mare was working . . . tretened to shoot her'. He added that when a local Board of Works official and Captain Blakeney (sub-inspector of police at Strokestown) heard of such matters, they said that they 'would put a stop to all the public works in the parish of Kilglass and Captain Blakeney told me he would send me . . . pulice to protect me if the prosis server would serve' (s k). Three weeks later – on 15 July – Blakeney wrote to a solicitor in Roscommon town: 'I have received . . . processes to be handed to Michael Johnston . . . and if he will give intimation to the constables in charge at Kilglass and Ruskey, when the process server is going to serve, I will give directions that a day patrol shall be out so as to prevent interruption.' He added: 'You know the description of persons that are to be found in Kilglass, and if Johnston or McGarry the process server, promulgates their intention of serving on any particular day they will be . . . probably deprived of the processes by armed Mollys in female attire, as we had them in that dress in Kilglass some time ago.'[17] That the process server did ultimately succeed in serving the summonses is suggested by a letter of 29 October, in which Johnston informed Stewart & Kincaid that he had 'notice[d] the tenants for . . . the third of November to meet Mr Maxwell with the rents in Strokestown and also the tenants that were decreed [for ejectment] to be prepared to pay on that day' (s k).

In 1845 Stewart & Kincaid had sought to remove a tenant named Carney from Kilmore.[18] Michael Doyle then became tenant on the land, but Carney did not promptly leave the district and he pointed anger towards Doyle. Also in 1845, Maxwell had reported to Stewart & Kincaid: 'Several shots have been fired around Doyle's house'.[19] On 14 March 1846 Dowd informed Stewart & Kincaid: 'Doyle . . . must take off his stock evrry night lest the[y] be enjured by Carney and he says that he is often treatened by persons that he dos not know.' (s k) A letter of 31 March 1846 to Stewart & Kincaid from Patrick McGrevy in Kilmore contained an enclosure threatening death. In this McGrevy expressed his fears 'in consequence of the holding of land formerly held' by two others. He was 'constantly anoyed by those villains called Molly Mcguires and has put up on my door several notices threatening to shoot me and my family'. He enclosed one of those notices and remarked: 'Nothing here . . . but shooting horses and maltreating every man that lately took a holding . . . to give it up to the former tenant. I am not sure of my life or my family.' One side of the enclosure warned: 'Take notice Patt McGrievy not to commence tilling any of that disputed land between you and Molly Mcguir or if you do my children are in duty bound to civilize in the most excruciating manner. . . . If you do not comply with . . . this notice or the terms made by my sons I will shoot you by day or consume you by night. Wrote by captain starlight and signed by Molly Mcguir'. A sketch of a coffin and spade was drawn below this passage. The other side of the enclosure was as follows:

> I am a young fellow
> both airy and free
> I shot two in tullamore
> I came to shoot Mc
> Grevy and two more

The 'two more' were presumably McGrevy's wife and child (s k).[20]

In October 1846 some of Nugent's tenants, including one named James Farrell, were imprisoned for an armed attack on a group of men in Kilglass (but just off Nugent's property there).[21] The Stewart & Kincaid correspondence contains no subsequent reference to violence in Kilmore/Kilglass during the famine.

Turning to rent collection, there were significant arrears early in 1846, when Johnston wrote to Kincaid that Crawford 'came to the land . . . and got very little. . . . McDonell of Caragin [Carrigeen] is served with six pare of prosises up to Novimber 1845. He paid owenly one half years rent since you comminsed' as agent.[22] Dated 13 January 1846, a petition to Stewart & Kincaid from James Farrell 'prays your honour will . . . forgive [his] rent. No person shall be the wiser of any thing which shall transpire between [us]. . . . There is no crop this year' (SK). As has been seen above, Farrell was still one of Nugent's tenants in October 1846.

Stewart came on a rent-collecting visit to Kilglass early in January 1846. On 21 January he wrote to Kincaid that the fields and pits of potatoes which he inspected in the townland of Culleenaghamore were 'the very worst' he had ever seen. The tenants there stated that 'they would starve if they parted the oats' and he added that Johnston 'says he is himself hard up for provision for his little family of 14' (SK). On 19 May 1846 Henry Cline wrote to Stewart & Kincaid from Kilmore: 'I have no means to pay the present rent save that of selling one cow which I have and if you insist on the rent I will sell same' (SK). In the Kilmore/Kilglass districts, several ejectment decrees were outstanding late in the summer of 1846. However, it does not seem that any of them were executed at that time. On 19 July, Crawford wrote to Stewart & Kincaid: 'Widow Beirne [apparently in Kilmore] was not served as she gave up possession before the ejectments came. . . . Her most industrious boy . . . has lately gone to America. It would create a great excitement to execute the ejectments at this most distressing period of the year' (SK). On 26 August, Dowd wrote to Stewart & Kincaid that although the potatoes in Kilmore 'are all destroyed', he had distrained cattle of four tenants (SK). He was in a quandary a few days later when he informed Stewart & Kincaid: 'I have sold Frank McNons cow at three pounds which I have and the purcheser has given the cow to McNon again. . . . Can I distrain the cow'.[23]

A letter from Johnston to Stewart & Kincaid on 29 October 1846 refers to 'combination' against rent (SK). On 25 November, he wrote to the firm that he was about to demand possession from some tenants in Kilglass. Referring to the 'demonstration effect', he noted that 'by serving a few ejectments their [there would] be a good deal of rents paid' (SK). On 10 December, Dowd informed Stewart & Kincaid of 'the tenants [in Kilmore] that was to be prossessed and them that had effects to distrain'. He listed 56 tenants on the various townlands, and observed that three of them had 'nothing', 28 were to be distrained and the other 25 were to be processed for ejectment (SK).

Consultation of the relevant *Valuation*[24] indicates that in 1858, the three who had 'nothing' appear to have gone, 13 of those who were to be distrained were still there, and five of those who were to be processed for ejectment were still tenants on the townlands on which they had holdings in 1846. Thus, it was not the case that almost all ejectment decrees sought were terminally executed. On 29 December 1846 Dowd wrote to Stewart & Kincaid that 'some of the tenants that is prossessed requesed that I would let you know that the[y] would pay one half years rent and the cost of prossess' (s K).

The firm of Stewart & Kincaid encouraged depopulation in Kilglass in 1847. This is illustrated in letters from Stewart to Kincaid dated 17 April and 9 September 1847. Stewart's letter of April observed: 'You give indeed a most distressing account of the poor creatures in Kilglass', and in reference to assistance for migration or emigration, he noted that it was 'indeed a charity to help them away from the scene of death and destitution'. He thought that 'probably more will soon go'. He also indicated that he had 'got a ton of beans' and would send a sack of them, and perhaps 'some grey peas', to Crawford in Longford (s K). Stewart's letter of September reported that he had just been to Kilglass, where Stewart & Kincaid had recently appointed an agriculturalist named Wilson to oversee improvements. Some of the holdings on Carrigeen had recently been 'given up'. However, Stewart felt that 'there must be a great clearance of tenants' there 'before it does any good' as 'the crop on the land . . . would not half feed the population if they paid nothing for rent'. In regard to Mullaghmacormic townland, he indicated that Wilson had sketched a plan for 'laying out' a large farm to be operated directly by Stewart & Kincaid, and that he had instructed Wilson to extend its projected size. He added: 'This with the entire of Mullagh[macormic] except the corner including Michl. Johnston & two or three other farms makes one large stretch . . . & contains about 500 statute acres which Wilson thinks would cost [in projected improvements] £4,000. . . . [It] might then be laid down in grass with one corn crop which would repay'. Stewart also observed that on Culleenaghamore townland, two families 'who got compensation for giving up & leaving are living on the adjoining farm' but he hoped that 'with a little decision . . . these may be sent off'. Near the end of the letter Stewart reported: 'I am sure many more must give up before *any good* can be done. . . . Every one is clearing that part of the country & the people are willing enough to go.' (s K) Stewart again wrote to Kincaid on 24 October 1847. He noted that some tenants in Kilglass were talking 'about going to America', and he remarked: 'The more we press for the rent the more they will be inclined to move away' (s K).

Many of Nugent's tenants who surrendered their holdings received compensation on leaving. What might be the earliest reference to assisted emigration from Nugent's estates in the Kilglass district appears in a letter to

Stewart & Kincaid from John Mills in Longford town, 5 February 1846. It contains a curious request: 'As I understand your paying Johnston and his family passage to New York, . . . be good enough to have the money remitted to . . . Liverpool as Johnston has a friend there that would be able to get the passage cheaper. That would leave him something when he would land in a strange country with his poor and helpless family.' (sK) Whether or not the aforementioned Johnston was related to Michael Johnston, Nugent's bailiff in Kilglass, is unknown.

The amount normally given in compensation to Nugent's former tenants was probably small – in most cases only enough to enable them to migrate to Britain.[25] This is suggested by the case of John Shannon, whose name appeared on Dowd's list in December 1846 of those to be processed for ejectment. On 11 February 1848 Shannon wrote to Kincaid that he hoped 'you will . . . allow me the compensation as I am determined to go to [his brothers in] America. . . . It would inable me to go myself and my family' (sK). He wrote again, less than two weeks later, asking Kincaid to inform him what he had decided 'to do with me concerning the giving up my land. I hope you will luck [look] to me as well as the tenants that owed from forty to fifty pounds'.[26] Following its receipt in Dublin, Stewart wrote on this letter: 'Write . . . & say that we will give 3£ but no more'. The only explicit reference to assisted emigration in the few surviving letters from Nugent to Stewart & Kincaid appears in one dated 15 May 1848, in which he requested 'the accounts of the expenditures including sums given for emigration' (sK). One of the last letters in the Stewart & Kincaid file on Nugent's lands is from Stewart in Longford town to Kincaid on 27 October 1848. Apparently in reference to tenants in the Kilglass district, Stewart reported: 'Several applicants for emigration who would give up some land. Shall we start them off?' (sK)

In regard to programmes of public works implemented (mainly in 1846) in response to destitution in the Kilglass/Kilmore district, on 21 June 1846 Dowd informed Stewart & Kincaid that 'all your tenants [in Kilmore] is imployed' on such works (sK). The road network in Kilglass was underdeveloped until the famine years. Hence, some of the roads which were built as public works in the parish were useful in providing access. These can be recognised today by their long and narrow stretches. A petition of 20 October 1844, to Stewart & Kincaid from the Culleenaghamore tenants, 'sheweth' that they needed a road to their land 'to draw home turf, to go to fairs & markets with our cattle and grain, or to draw lime', and as they were 'precluded from the benefit of man-uring their lands by burning', it would be 'impossible that your petitioners can with any propriety cultivate the land' without such a road (sK). The same tenants again wrote to Stewart & Kincaid on 8 March 1846, to inform the firm that a local magistrate had told them that if Stewart & Kincaid 'would write to him on the subject' of the proposed road he would use his influence in favour of the road, which was 'necessary to all the tenants' (sk). Stewart & Kincaid did write to the magistrate, who quickly responded by informing Stewart & Kincaid that at a forthcoming sessions, 'he will bring forward' the proposed road.[27] The road in question, between two and three miles long, was constructed during the summer of 1846. By intersecting Culleenaghamore, and by crossing two roads to Strokestown, it greatly improved access.

That the huge extent of public works in 1846 gave rise to abuses is known to historians.[28] Tenants who were refused employment appealed to Stewart & Kincaid to use influence. For example, on 23 June 1846 Michael Fox of Culleenaghamore requested Stewart & Kincaid to intercede with a local Board of Works official for employment, 'as the line of road is now passing thro memorialists land' (sk). On 10 July, Pat Sheridan also appealed to Stewart & Kincaid: 'There is a new line of road running through my land and strangers are earning in it and myself . . . did not earn a penny'. He asked Stewart & Kincaid to use influence 'to have me a time keeper on the road'. Sheridan also complained of irregularities to the Board of Works (sk). On his behalf Stewart & Kincaid contacted both the Board and the local official, who responded to Stewart & Kincaid on 19 July stating that 'Sheridan is a very troublesome man [who] keeps a Shebeen house [for sale of alcoholic drink] and is the cause of much irregularity on the Works. . . . I cannot help thinking him a subject for punishment, rather than . . . assistance.'[29] In contrast to the response of the local official, Colonel Jones, Chairman of the Board, did treat Sheridan's allegations seriously. On 20 July, Jones wrote to Stewart & Kincaid that he had 'very little doubt' but that Sheridan's complaint was correct, 'and if so, it will only be an additional case to corroborate the reports we almost daily receive from our engineers of . . . forcing upon the Works by the relief committees as well as by individuals of a much greater number of men than ought to be employed. . . . Our overseers have been forced by threats to take on a greater number of hands' (than they were authorised to hire). However, Jones added that 'with upwards of 50,000 men daily employed I am sure you will feel the difficulties [the Board faced]' (sk).

Road works were not the only improvements in Nugent's Kilglass/Kilmore during the famine years. Further rationalisation of holdings on Carrigeen was also implemented in 1846. Population clearance paved the way for more improvements. On 9 September 1847 Stewart wrote to Kincaid about proposed projects in Kilglass: these involved drainage, subsoiling, and conso-lidation (sk). Drainage and subsoiling were commenced, at first on a small scale, late in 1847: a letter of 24 October from Stewart lists implements for drainage and subsoiling to be sent to Crawford in Longford 'for Lord Westmeath' (sk). A letter to Stewart & Kincaid from the Board of Works dated March 1848 indicates that a loan of £2,000 had been agreed, to finance improvements in Kilglass. Late in 1848 the Board agreed to another loan, of £300, for drainage on Clonteem.[30]

Wilson the agriculturalist spent most of 1848 in Kilglass supervising improvements. On 17 March he wrote to Crawford that it was 'an idle day for the rifraff', but added that the work 'is going on to my entire satisfaction'. The work which Wilson supervised consisted mainly of ploughing, laying drains and spreading guano fertiliser, for which the labourers were paid in cash.[31] On 3 August, he reported to Stewart & Kincaid that he had 35 men at work on Culleenaghamore 'levelling old fences' in order to create larger farms (SK). Wilson was replaced by a man named E. Skinner. In 1848 and 1849, some of the Mullaghmacormic district was cultivated on Nugent's own account. Thus, on 26 October 1848 Skinner wrote to Stewart & Kincaid: 'I have been ear [here] onley a few days. . . . Two fields ar sawn [sown] without aney mene-war [manure] and the next field we ar going to saw it would be well don to get sum lime. . . . We have 18 men woman and children in the privet work at present. . . . Now they ar getting in the oats. . . . The horses ar in number 9' (SK). On 5 November 1848 he wrote that his progress in sowing wheat was impeded by the weakness of the horses, which rendered them unfit to plough; in fact, he added the postscript: 'Befor I post my lettar this day the tow [two] horses abov mentioned ar both dead' (SK). The last recorded letter from Skinner is dated 31 December 1848, to Crawford in Longford. In this he wrote that he had recently sold two tons of turnips, that he was engaged in drainage, and he requested two new ploughs (SK).

In 1848 Nugent informed Stewart & Kincaid that he would write to a cousin in Scotland to 'get some men over with capital if you will tell me how many farms you think the land in Kilglass will make'.[32] Thus, given the depopulation of Kilglass, one of Nugent's immediate objectives was to obtain viable tenants on larger farms. We do not know whether he succeeded in attracting any farmers from Scotland.

Stewart & Kincaid's account book on Nugent's properties in Kilglass and Kilmore, for the half year ending May 1848, shows the following. It lists the names of 147 heads of households in Kilglass. However, four pages of the book pertaining to that parish are almost entirely missing, but it seems that they listed about 55 further heads of households there. Most of the holdings were extremely small – they probably averaged about four or five statute acres. Another feature to note from the accounts is that in May 1848, many of the tenants on Kilglass were in considerable arrears – in several cases their deficit in payments went back about three years. Finally in regard to Kilglass, many of the tenants had recently surrendered their holdings, implying that their arrears would never be recovered. The accounts for Kilmore list the names of only 85 heads of households, but they seem to be complete. Again, almost all of the holdings were very small, several tenants were some years in arrears, and about seven had recently surrendered their holdings.[33]

4 DEVELOPMENTS IN THE PARISH OF KILTULLAGH, 1843–5

A publication of 1845 observed that Nugent's Kiltullagh estate 'comprises a considerable proportion of waste.[34] Nugent rarely (if ever) visited the district in the 1840s. The only reference in the Stewart & Kincaid correspondence to his possible presence there is in a letter to him dated 20 September 1843 from Robert Blundell, the rector at Ballinlough, in which Blundell wrote: 'I was in quiet hopes of seeing your Lordship in this neighbourhood having heard you were coming to Mr Wills shooting lodge'. In the same letter Blundell added: 'I have the pleasure of forwarding to you the Report of the Castlerea Agricultural Society for the year ending March 1843 to which you were good enough to become a subscriber. . . . I think when the fruit of good management in those who have listened to the advice of our agriculturalist is shown, that others will follow their example. . . . The drains made by your Lordship in the distressed season have . . . enabled the people to reclaim. . . . Your property might be much enhanced in value by [further] draining' (s k).

It seems that Stewart & Kincaid's first visit to Kiltullagh was in September 1843. On 2 October, Stewart wrote to Kincaid: 'The Marquis has . . . a numerous & pauper tenantry near Castlerea & I fear little can be done for them. He should give us the £400 a year which he loses by his lands not being let, to lay out on the property' (s k). Contrary to what might be inferred from Stewart's letter, subsequent correspondence suggests that competition for arable land in Kiltullagh was brisk.[35] Thus, it seems that much of the land there was not arable.

Patt Naghtin was Stewart & Kincaid's local agent in Kiltullagh, where he was himself a tenant. He always sent his rent receipts to Dublin by means of a letter of credit. Until the first potato failure, he recorded no unusual difficulties in collecting rents. None of his pre-famine letters refer to ejectment and only one mentions distraint. Thus, on 7 February 1844 he wrote to Kincaid: 'I distrained the defaulters according to your Honours orders. There is a good many of them that has no cattle nor even a sheaf of oats.' (s k)

Rent collections seem to have been satisfactory when Maxwell visited Nugent's estates in October 1845. On 7 October he informed Stewart & Kincaid that he had received £800 from Westmeath's townlands in Kilmore, Kilglass and Kiltullagh. On 10 October he wrote to Stewart: 'You seem surprised at the amount of allowances [for drainage by tenants] made by me on the Kiltullagh estate. . . . I got a great deal of cash there this time which is chiefly oweing to the fine season for the reapers in England'. In the same letter, he indicated that he had obtained 'upwards of £400' from the Kiltullagh tenants (sk). However, on 27 October, Naghtin reported to Stewart & Kincaid: 'I send you . . . a letter of credit for £13–10–8. . . . I could get no more money. . . . Their answer was that they were sorry for paying any the last time. . . . The loss of the potatoes . . . is shoking' (sk).

Turning to the matter of improvements, on 18 December 1843 John Kirkpatrick, the agriculturalist employed by the Castlerea Agricultural Society, wrote to Stewart & Kincaid that 'it was resolved to continue my services here in consequence of a letter from you engaging ¼ of my time on the Westmeath Estate' (sk). On 29 December he informed Kincaid that 'the Marq's property has hitherto been the most neglected part of the [Castlerea] Union' (sk). Kirkpatrick's connection with the Society ceased in 1844, when he was replaced by a younger man. But on 28 March 1845 Blundell wrote to Stewart & Kincaid: 'It being found that no one would engage the services of the agriculturalist except you on the part of Ld. Westmeath it was decided [by the Society] not to engage him for the year beginning March 17 1845. . . . [However] if you wish to continue the work that is now . . . done so well on his Lordship's estate I think he would be disposed to act for you at the same rate of payment per day.' (sk)

The person who replaced Kirkpatrick was Bernard Timothy. In 1843 Kirkpatrick had written that Timothy 'speaks Irish etc. He is about the best practical farmer I know'.[36] Timothy was employed by Stewart & Kincaid, on a part-time basis, in 1845–6. On 13 August 1844 he wrote to Kincaid: 'I have made an estimate of the expense of deepening the Clooncrim River. . . . It is quite impossible to drain the lands adjoining it until it will be done. If you . . . give me the necessary directions I will see it properly executed.' (sk) On 20 March 1845 Timothy reported to Stewart & Kincaid: 'An astonishing improvement has taken place both in the habits of the people, & on the face of their holdings. The course of drainage in progress has been rendering the property immense service, and I have no doubt of being able to persuade nearly every one of the tenants to sow turnips this year – a step which . . . is one of vast importance in the improvement of any property.'[37] For their drainage work in 1844 and 1845, the tenants were remunerated, not in cash, but in rent allowances.[38] Referring to the Kiltullagh tenants, on 10 October 1845 Maxwell wrote to Stewart: 'I very nearly had the whole of the estate about my ears for not allowing enough. . . . Many of the tenants did not earn 2 pence a day at the draining'. (sk)

5 FAMINE IN KILTULLAGH

On 23 January 1846 a tenant on Kiltullagh, Andrew McDermott, wrote to Stewart & Kincaid that 'the times are indicative of no other than a famine among the poorer classes' (s k). Timothy wrote to Maxwell on 18 April, indicating what should be done on Kiltullagh 'both for its permanent improvement and to give full employment to the tenantry'. One of his suggestions involved squaring the land. Thus, he wrote that although access passages and drainage were required, the system of rundale would first have to be abandoned. He remarked: 'A tenant improves his small farm more in 3 years when he has it to himself than he otherwise would or *could* do in 20' and he urged that the near future 'ought to see every tenant on the property working on his own holding, newly squared'. There is no evidence that the proposed squaring was implemented in 1846. Other suggestions in the same letter refer to seed and fertiliser. Thus, Timothy continued:

> The tenants . . . have been most urgent in their entreaties to get *guano* to plant potatoes, sow turnips, topdress oats, etc.. . . . Lend them a sufficient supply of *this*. . . . A person on the estate has asserted that some of the tenants have been selling their *straw* . . . to buy seed potatoes: such tenants as *these* can't have manure. I have been also told that tenants on the estate have been obliged to pledge their *beds* for money to be converted to the same purpose! This is awful. . . . 'Good tenants' have been obliged to do it. . . . The country every where here is in a wretched state. . . . Supply them with useful works so as to put it in their power to purchase food. . . . They will cheerfully work if they get work to do – they *must* do so or *starve*. I have urged on them . . . the great necessity of planting what potatoes they intend putting down, *at once* . . . & in case of failure . . . they could resow the land with turnips. . . . *Guano* . . . can be [got from] a Galway merchant [named Persse]. . . . I have directed P. Naghtin to go around all the tenants, & furnish me with a list of all they'll require. . . . I think they'll take about 5 or 6 tons. . . . Most of the landlords . . . in this locality have been lending their tenants *guano* this year. (s k)

A letter from Timothy to Stewart & Kincaid on 17 May 1846 indicates that the guano had arrived from Galway, and that Timothy had signed a promissory note, guaranteed by Stewart & Kincaid, for which payment was due on 20 November. He indicated that '3 tons of it was intended for myself, but being encouraged by Pat Naghtin to give it all to the tenants, I have done so without hesitation as I am most certain that they will pay all punctually. P. Naghtin himself took nearly a ton of it, & so, in proportion, have all the tenants – those who can pay best having taken by far the greater part.' Timothy added: 'I'll have to send for about 2 tons more for the tenants . . . & also for the turnip seed' (sk). On 24 June, Timothy wrote that he could not get the turnip seed 'about here to my satisfaction', and he therefore requested Stewart & Kincaid to arrange with Drummonds, seed merchants in Dublin, to send him 60 pounds weight of turnip seed for the tenants. He indicated: 'I got my own from Drummonds last week at from 9*d* to 1*s* a lb, & any where here I should pay about 1*s*/6*d*. . . . They can be sent by . . . canal (Mullingar & Ballymahon) & by Bianconi's car to Ballymoe'. (sk)

In May 1846 Timothy was confident that the tenants would be able to pay for the guano. However, for many of them, the total failure of the potato in the autumn of 1846 made such payments impossible. On 27 November, Timothy wrote to Stewart & Kincaid: 'I have been . . . at the tenants for the guano money' but he had not got 'one farthing of the money from any of them. . . . Very many of the tenants cannot possibly pay a penny until they get it . . . on the public works. There is nothing more certain than that they are *panting* to pay it as they are all under the impression that there will be nothing done for them on yr. part . . . until they first pay me.' He continued: 'I thought well of writing to Mr Persse requesting of him to renew the Bills [promissory notes] for 2 or 3 months. . . . 3 months wd. be best as works may not be in good progress before that time. I have no . . . estimates relative to the drainage of any part of the estate. . . . I fear there will be too much *bungling* . . . [at] the Board of Works' (sk). This passage suggests that an application for a government loan, to finance drainage on Kiltullagh, was under consideration late in 1846. But it seems that such an application was postponed because of an expectation that large-scale public works would soon commence. At the end of 1846 Timothy got tough in regard to the guano money, when, on 31 December, he wrote to Stewart & Kincaid: 'Some of the tenants have paid me . . . but I have got *80* of them processed for . . . 5th of January [1847]. I expect the greater portion of them will settle with me before then'. But he added: 'There are some, & a decree against them would be useless as they have *no-thing*. . . . Many of the tenantry . . . are in a most wretched condition. . . . They . . . must inevitably starve I fear – indeed they are *half-starved* already.' (sk)

Proposals for public works in the Kiltullagh district were passed at a presentment sessions in Castlerea around the end of April 1846, by which time a relief committee had been established there. During the summer of 1846 it was the local relief committees – rather than Board of Works officials – who decided which people would be given work. In May, Naghtin requested Stewart & Kincaid to use influence in getting his son employment whenever the works commenced. Indicating that small-scale public works (the cutting of two hills) had just begun in the Kiltullagh district, Blundell wrote to Stewart & Kincaid on 1 July that 'this beginning of work has brought us [on the relief committee] a host of wretched applicants', many of whom 'could not be employed on the small works but no steps have been taken as respects the large work' (sĸ). The latter was a proposed road from Ballinlough to Ballymoe, which had been approved by the Board. Blundell therefore asked Stewart & Kincaid 'to call at the Board of Works and as you are known there . . . urge . . . speedy commencement' of the road. He added that 'the Board have acted in the same manner in Castlerea' where they ordered 'a few petty works . . . which has excited the whole pauper population and they cry for food or work' (sĸ).

Public works in Kiltullagh during the summer of 1846 were suspended shortly after they started. Hence, they could not have provided much employment. There were complaints of discrimination. Thus, on 2 July, John Winston of Kiltullagh wrote to Stewart & Kincaid: 'I applied for work but was refused. The cuting of them hills began this day within five perch of my house where I see men at work and the tenants of the neighbouring estates who were by far less in need of it than I was and myself standing idle and a good many of your honours tenants who were also in want were refused too.' He had 'little or no means left to support my family [of twelve]' (sĸ).

There were no public works in Kiltullagh at the time of the 1846 harvest. On 17 August, Naghtin informed Stewart & Kincaid: 'There is no sign of getting any money at present. There [their] cry is that they will actually starve. The potateoe crop . . . is no use' (sĸ). The total failure of the potato led to further public works, which were on a larger scale than those of the summer, and which commenced towards the end of the year. A priest in Kiltullagh wrote to Stewart & Kincaid in October:

> You wished to know the population of this parish. . . . It contains near 1600 families. . . . Each family contains about 5½ members. . . . There are about 600 families who would require permanent employment until August next [1847] to preserve them from starvation, and to that number, we must add before Christmas [1846] at least 300 more, so that from the beginning of Spring [1847] the most part of our population will be deprived of all means of support, except what they may earn on public works. That there are many families striving to live on a scanty meal in the day I am well aware of, and many more, who have only some cabbage and salt to eat.[39]

Resumption of public works late in 1846 led to further complaints of unfair discrimination in regard to those given employment. This was despite the fact that the system of selection of those employed had been changed: local relief committees were now to have less influence than they had earlier, and the decisions on who would be employed were to be made by Board of Works officials. On 13 October, Pat Caulfield wrote to Stewart & Kincaid asking the firm to use its influence with the Board engineer, Buck, in order to obtain for him an appointment as steward on the road works (s k). On 4 November, Andrew McDermott wrote to Stewart & Kincaid:

> The publick works being now commenced in our parish, . . . all [jobs are] distributed, by Thomas Wills [chairman of the Castlerea Relief Committee] among his own tenantry . . . as independently as if the whole money to be expended had been entirely contributed by himself & as if he, solely, were to render an acct. of it, at the repayment of these expenditures. It does not appear that . . . the Marquis of Westmeath or his tenantry are, at a future time, to pay to the Treasury any part of the money. They are like a flock without a shepherd, defenceless as orphans, without any person to speak for them. . . . We were, at all times, obliged to pay rent [and] taxes. . . . Still we are denied any situation, whatsoever, in these Government works. . . . I make no allusions to Mr Henry Buck regarding this statement, who is the Government Engineer & with whom rests the appointment of persons to these employments, because this Wills is grasping at every thing that can be had & recommending his own tenantry. Therefore, having a son qualified to fill any of these situations . . . I'll expect from you . . . a letter of recommendation to Mr Buck, or Mr Wills asking the situation of cheque clerk or the like, in the name of Martin McDermott. (s k)

Andrew McDermott sent a similar letter to Stewart & Kincaid, on behalf of his son Martin, on 14 December 1846 (s k).

The Stewart & Kincaid correspondence from Kiltullagh in 1847 is missing. There are, however, a few letters for 1848. One of them reveals that in this year, Nugent applied to the Board of Works for a loan of £1,000 for drainage in Kiltullagh, and that payment of the first instalment of the loan was authorised in mid-November.[40]

Stewart & Kincaid's accounts for the half-year ending May 1848 list the names of close to 200 heads of households on Nugent's Kiltullagh estate. Judging by the rents charged, it seems that many of the holdings were tiny, and that almost all of the tenants were in arrears of payment, in some cases to a considerable extent. At least nine of them had recently been ejected, and a few had 'gone' (s k).

Close to 50 of them had recently been served with, or would soon be served with, notices to quit. About eight were under distraint, or were soon to be placed under distraint. At least three of them had recently been granted, or were about to be granted, rent abatements. A few of them had recently surrendered their holdings, while another four had been granted 'compensation', or were shortly to be granted 'compensation', presumably in exchange for peaceable surrender and departure.[41]

NINE

THE STRATFORD LANDS IN CLARE

—

I INTRODUCTION

John Wingfield (1772–1850) was a son of the third Viscount Powerscourt.[1] A lieutenant-colonel, he was twin brother of Edward, whose Sligo estate was discussed in chapter 7. In 1802 he assumed the additional surname of Stratford and became known by that name. The Griffith *Valuation* of 1855 indicates that he owned over 2,000 statute acres in northwest Clare between Ennistymon (spelt Ennistimon in the *Valuation*) and what is now the town of Lisdoonvarna.[2] This district was remote: in the mid-1840s Lisdoonvarna had not yet become a village. On the other side of the Shannon estuary he owned over 2,000 acres in the Robertstown-Shanagolden district of west Limerick. See map 7.

The Stratford townlands were mainly in a square-shaped cluster in the Union of Ennistymon. All but two of them (which were in the parish of Kilfenora) were part of the parish of Kilshanny. Amongst these townlands, Tooreen is at the northwest of the cluster and Boghil is at its northeast. Smithstown is in the centre of the cluster. To the east of the cluster, Stratford owned property in the village of Kilfenora.

The Wingfields obtained their Clare estate in the seventeenth century. In 1788 Stratford inherited the family's properties there and in Limerick. During the 1840s he dwelt in London and at Maidstone in Kent. Documents in the Stewart & Kincaid archive, dated 1752 and 1761, indicate that his holdings in Clare and Limerick in the 1840s were almost certainly the same lands as those owned by Lord Powerscourt in those counties in the mid eighteenth century. The relative valuations of the two estates are suggested by noting that in the mid eighteenth century, annual rent receipts from that in Limerick were close to £600, while those from Clare were less than £400.[3] The difference in receipts reflected the fact that the quality of land in Clare was generally inferior to that in Limerick.

In 1761 the Clare estate was held under leases by twelve tenants, probably middlemen. There were still middlemen there in the early 1840s, but by then most of the occupants were tenants, without lease, to the head landlord.

Stewart & Kincaid commenced active management of the Stratford lands in Clare in 1841.[4] The firm implemented many improvements on the estate and paid Stratford's annual subscription (£3) to the Kilfenora dispensary.

In the years just before the famine, Stratford's Clare tenants were peaceful and hospitable. In 1843 Arthur Vincent, Stewart & Kincaid's agent resident at Shanagolden in Limerick, wrote about a recent visit to the Clare estate: 'I heard Mrs Considine [probably the wife of James Considine, who may have been Stewart & Kincaid's most important tenant resident there] was greatly disappointed I did not call in as she had lunch prepared for me. I find the people remarkable for their hospitality'.[5]

An obvious link with the Powerscourts can be found in Clare today. This is the house called 'Wingfield' (the Powerscourt family name) near Kilfenora. As indicated by Weir:

> A seventeenth-century house . . . stood on the site of the present residence. . . . Honora . . . , wife of Richard Wingfield . . . was the eldest daughter of Teige O'Brien of nearby Smithstown Castle. Their son, Sir Edward Wingfield, was progenitor of the Lords Powerscourt of County Wicklow. . . . Honora's Will was dated 1650. Her . . . descendent, Edward Wingfield-Stratford . . . was declared bankrupt in 1886 when his estates passed to his principal creditor [who] held them until they were . . . re-distributed amongst the tenants between 1915 and 1920. Wingfield Lodge has been in the hands of the Caher [Cahir] family ever since.[6]

2 THE BLACKWELLS

Himself a tenant on Stratford's Tooreen, John Blackwell, a Catholic whose forebears had long been on the estate, was Stewart & Kincaid's local agent in Clare from 1841 onwards.[7] Until his death in 1840, a man named Shawe had been Stratford's agent in Clare. Blackwell had been employed by both Stratford and Shawe. On 28 February 1841 Blackwell wrote to Stewart & Kincaid: 'I have no doubt but that you . . . will continue me in the same employment. My salary was but low, £10-10: £5-5 from Col Stratford for acting as land bailiff and £5-5 from Mr Shawe as acting under agent' (sk). Blackwell's role under Stewart & Kincaid's management was similar to what it had been when Shawe was alive: he was both bailiff, and under-agent to the aforementioned Arthur Vincent.

There was no road through the townland of Tooreen in the early 1840s. However, a side road entered Tooreen from the northeast, but it ended at Blackwell's house beside the stream called the Tooreen river.[8] Roadworks during the famine years were to ease Blackwell's access to the rest of the estate.

Blackwell usually sent rents to Stewart & Kincaid in the form of half notes. The Stewart & Kincaid letters refer to two instances (both in 1843) in which a half note, sent from Clare, was lost in the post. However, the fact that half notes were missing probably did not cause Stewart & Kincaid any financial loss: following presentation to the banks of the other halves, the banks (the Provincial Bank and the National Bank at Kilrush) seem to have paid the full amounts. Sending money as half notes could be awkward in another respect: in 1846 the serial numbers on two halves sent by Stewart & Kincaid to Blackwell's son Thomas (then at an agricultural college in Derry) did not match.[9] At least once, Blackwell transferred rents to Dublin by means of a letter of credit. This method of transfer involved going to a bank in Ennis (a round trip of about 35 miles).

There were a few families named Blackwell on the Clare estate in the 1840s. One of the earliest letters from there to Stewart & Kincaid was from Mrs Henry Blackwell of Smithstown, whose husband had recently died. Dated 10 February 1842, it requested a waiver of £6 in rent arrears (sk). Margaret Blackwell of Tooreen was another Blackwell widow. The fact that other Blackwells on the estate were related to him made the job of John Blackwell more difficult. Thus, on 30 January 1843 he informed Stewart & Kincaid that he had recently distrained property of his brothers, James and Robert. On 18 May 1843 John Blackwell sent Stewart & Kincaid half notes for rents, part of which pertained to James Blackwell who was then seriously ill: in the enclosed letter, John informed that 'my brother James is confined to the bed . . . with a lump on his belly' (sk). But tension between James and John was mounting as James approached death. Early in 1844 James sent a petition to Stewart & Kincaid stating that his late father lived several years on the lands of Smithstown and that he (James) 'got a part of his father's holding as a marriage portion'; however, 'some evil disposed persons are endeavouring to get his land and to through [throw] petitioner and his poor helpless wife and children out. . . . These evil persons are his own nearest relatives'.[10]

James was dead by 3 May 1844, when John Blackwell informed Stewart & Kincaid: 'I demanded possession', which 'Widow [Anne] Blackwell refused to give'. She was the wife of James. John threatened to distrain her property. On 30 September 1845 Anne wrote to Stewart & Kincaid:

The widow of the late James Blackwell . . . begs . . . to express an astonishment at the treatment she has received from John Blackwell. . . . Ill-will prompted that man . . . to be cruel against her. . . . What private motives this would-be-tyrant has, is unknown, but the common say of the country is 'to oblige her . . . to flee her holding, in order that some one of his family, or well-wishers may get it'. . . . The rent . . . is forthcoming. . . . The price of three pigs and a cask of butter will be ready

... on about the tenth of October next. She is mother of six orphans ... and it is evident that their uncle must be absolutely of an unfeeling disposition, when he acts against their mother ... [like] a wolf. ... God ... rescue your poor applicant from the grasp of him, who means to ... send her a beggar on the wide world. (s k)

Anne Blackwell did pay, close to the amount promised, in October 1845.[11] But on 28 April 1846 Stewart & Kincaid sent John notices to quit to be served on her, and some months later he indicated that he wanted her land. On 29 October 1846 he wrote to Stewart & Kincaid: 'I was told ... that the widow J Blackwell is preparing to go to America. ... I trust your Honrs. will have the kindness of not allowing any strange name in my brothers place but have myself the possession of it. ... I suppose she will [go] if she be in the family way as reported from that unfortunate man she is keeping in spite of her brother & friends. A man that is married before & his wife still living.' (s k) John Blackwell again expressed his desire for the land held by Anne in a letter to Stewart & Kincaid dated 7 November 1846:

She ... told me there were two or three messages sent her to know whether she would sell her [interest in her] holding when the report went about that she was talking of going abroad. ... I trust your Honrs. will have the kindness of giving me some money to enable me to settle with her. ... I would repay back the money by instalments. ... Mrs James Blackwell requested of me to tell you that she expected your Honrs. would ... let her know which would be the best place to go with her helpless family. ... The poor unfortunate creature is an object of charity now abandoned by her friends & relations. (s k)

John was worried when he wrote to Kincaid on 23 November 1846: 'The widow of James Blackwell is disposing of her [interest in her] holding'. John therefore desired 'your kind interference from prohibiting her from disposing of it to strangers. ... I am willing to pay her as much as any other bidder.' (s k)

In 1844 John Blackwell's son Thomas informed Stewart & Kincaid that he intended 'going to the Templemoyle Seminary', an agricultural college in County Derry. He therefore sought a loan from Stewart & Kincaid. The firm did provide some form of assistance. Thomas Blackwell attended Templemoyle in 1845 and 1846.[12] It may be the case that there were two students from Stratford's Clare estate at Templemoyle in 1846. The second of these – son of the tenant James Spellissy – may have later become an attorney in New York.[13]

Only two Blackwells were listed on Stratford's Clare estate in the Griffith *Valuation* of 1855. They were John, who held about 160 acres in Tooreen and 4 acres in Smithstown, and Thomas, who held 42 acres in Smithstown. It seems that the Blackwell line on Smithstown ended long ago, but a field there is locally known as 'Blackwell's meadow'. The presence of Blackwells in the entire parish of Kilshanny seems to have ceased around 1950. The remains of John Blackwell's house can today be seen beside the road, completed during the famine, which cuts through Tooreen.[14]

3 DEVELOPMENTS ON THE ESTATE,
MAINLY BEFORE THE FAMINE
Distress and improvements

Early in 1842 Stewart & Kincaid sought to have the sparse roads on the Clare estate repaired. The work was done by the tenants themselves who, in return for their labour, were given rent allowances. The summer of 1842 was a time of distress among the tenants. On 15 June, John Blackwell wrote to Stewart & Kincaid that 'some of them were in a state of starvation'. Stewart & Kincaid responded with works of improvement: it was hoped that the resulting employment would enable them to buy food. Blackwell indicated that he was about to commence drainage beside his own holding. Also on 15 June he reported to Stewart & Kincaid: 'It is a real quagmire. . . . There was a cow of mine drowned there a few years ago & another cow of mine nearly drowned there last spring. . . . The usual wages in this country is 8*d.* @ day. . . . The tenants are complaining of the wages. . . . I'll give but 8*d.* until I hear from yr. Honr. again & find what is given in other places.' (sk) This passage indicates that on the Stratford estate in Clare, no significant works of improvement, involving the hire of labour, had been implemented in the years immediately before Stewart & Kincaid actively commenced as Stratford's agent.

On 19 June 1842 Blackwell informed Stewart & Kincaid that he had '15 men of the most distressed each day [on drainage]. The tenants are in such distress that they are pushing for work. Would you allow more than 15 men @ day. . . . There are some of the tenants that's not able to come forward to work through weakness for want of provision. . . . I am in want of provision 2 [too]' (sk). He did get permission to increase numbers employed. Furthermore, late in June, Stewart & Kincaid sent (from the Stratford lands in Limerick) John Stewart the agriculturalist, to plan further drainage as well as roadworks on the estate.[15] In August, Arthur Vincent came and laid out further work.[16] On 17 August, Blackwell sent Stewart & Kincaid details of work in progress and works which were planned, and added 'now that there are jobs . . . if your Honr. thought fit to allow those in arrear to work in part payment of it I am sure they would be glad to do so' (sk). His suggestion does not seem to have been implemented. In fact, most of the work came to an abrupt halt late in August.[17]

Many of the tenants were distressed in the summer and autumn of 1843, when the prices of their produce were lower than usual. On 14 May, Blackwell informed Stewart & Kincaid that he had been 'expecting to get a good deal [of cash] after the fair day of Ennistymon [but] such of the tenants as had a beast for sale must wait for the fair of Kilfenora' (s κ). On 6 October, Blackwell wrote to Stewart & Kincaid that both he and the other tenants had been selling butter in Kilfenora, but that the price 'is remaining very low' (s κ). On 16 November the Stewart & Kincaid employee W. V. Griffith wrote to Kincaid that Blackwell 'fears the potato crop is "slack", that many of them are rotten & will not keep.' (s κ) And at end-year a middleman sought a waiver of rent, on account of 'the depressed state of the times'.[18]

John Stewart, the agriculturalist, returned to the estate in March 1843. On 4 April he wrote to Stewart & Kincaid: 'I have been here for the last fortnight during which time I have gone through the tenants and advised them to alter their system of husbandry & . . . to turn . . . to the draining of their land. . . . They are busy sowing their oats & planting their potatoes & most miserable tillage it is . . . , the land in general so wet that they could not dress it but even where there is a dry field they dont do it. . . . I brought . . . turnip . . . seed & gave a little to each of the tenants who I find has a spot for such.' (s κ)

John Stewart left Clare around the middle of April 1843 but he was back on 11 August, when Blackwell informed Stewart & Kincaid that Stewart was 'measuring roads . . . & teaching the tenants how they would drain. . . . He brought some tools. Five crow bars, three sledges, three hammers & six picks'. In the same letter, Blackwell indicated that the tenants probably had to pay for the tools. (s κ) Thus, it seems that many of the improvements on the estate circa 1843 were implemented by the tenants themselves. In some cases they received allowances in their rents for their labour on such improvements.[19] It appears that in one case, Stewart & Kincaid agreed to allow a tenant who had a lease the sum of £35 for building 'a substantial residence'.[20] John Stewart was staying at 'Wingfield Lodge' on the Clare estate on 1 June 1844 when he reported to Stewart & Kincaid that 'most of the subsoiled plots [there] have been treated [by the tenants] according to my directions' (s κ).

By the eve of the famine there had been very considerable improvements in both the infrastructure and the practice of husbandry on the estate. On 3 May 1845 John Stewart wrote to Stewart & Kincaid from the Wingfield estate in Sligo: 'It is now near the time I usually go to the Clare estate for to measure and inspect the drains and other works . . . & to give the tenants instructions [on] how to drill & prepare their turnip. . . . I dont see such lasting improvements going on in any part of the country as . . . on the Clare estate, that is as regards thorough draining & subsoiling and the growing of green crops. . . . There was as good a crop of turnips, potatoes & clover on plots on the Clare

estate last year as there was in any part of the count..
Kincaid correspondence of 1845 contains references tc
on the estate.[21]

The then recent improvements in Clare suggest an atn.
mism on the eve of the famine. However, the abundant pota
started to rot early in 1845. Thus, on 7 April 1845 Blackwell wrote .
Kincaid that he wanted 'to buy potatoes for seed as I would no.
to sow any of my own in consequence of the rot. I'll come short c
potatoes too' (SK). On 28 April he asked Stewart & Kincaid for financi. aid.
By mid-year, disease had broken out in the Blackwell household. On 20 July,
Blackwell informed Stewart & Kincaid that his twelve-year-old daughter
had 'a low typhus fever. She is speechless' (SK). On 31 August he wrote to
Stewart & Kincaid that 'the rot in potatoes in many parts of this neighbourhood is dreadful' (SK).

Distraint, surrender and emigration

Distraint on the estate in the years immediately before the famine was frequent. In fact Blackwell, in one of his earliest letters in the Stewart & Kincaid
correspondence, suggested that the properties of certain tenants should be
distrained.[22] Formal ejectment, by contrast, may have been non-existent in
those years: the pre-famine letters on the estate do not provide a single reference
to any ejectment decree. However, in the face of rent arrears, Blackwell asked
several tenants to surrender their holdings. On at least one occasion the
initiative came from a tenant. Consider the case of Thomas Reidy. On 31
January 1842 Blackwell wrote to Stewart & Kincaid: 'Riedy of Toureen has his
mind made up to remove to Van Diemans land with his family, ten in number. . . . If he had his portion of Toureen rent free he could badly support &
clothe his long family by the produce of it. That being so he expects your
Honrs. will have the kindness . . . of sending off himself & family. He has no
means. . . . His brother . . . is satisfied to be under the arrear & keep the holding.'
(SK) Stewart & Kincaid responded favourably to Thomas Reidy's request for
assistance to emigrate. On 9 April 1842 Blackwell informed Stewart & Kincaid:
'Thomas Riedy . . . requested that I would state to your Honr. as vessils were
not going out to Australia; that he has his mind made up to enjoy the offer
your Honr. was very kind to promise, to send himself & family to America
which is only 8 now, as two of his children died since he wrote first to your
Honr. on the subject' (SK). The departure of the Reidy family is the only case
of emigration from the Clare estate mentioned in the pre-famine Stewart &
Kincaid letters. Although Stewart & Kincaid did organise a programme of

₃ation from the estate in the spring of 1847 (see below, p. 179), the correspondence yields only one other case of a *named* tenant on the estate – Marty Considine – whose emigration was definitely assisted by Stewart & Kincaid.

Early in 1846 Marty Considine, who held eight acres of land on Gortnaboul townland, announced that his family of seven and his sister wanted to go to America. Blackwell wrote to Stewart & Kincaid on his behalf requesting assistance. Marty's brother Michael, a tenant on adjacent land, offered him £40 for his interest in the eight acres. It was from this £40 that Marty expected to pay the passage to America. Stewart & Kincaid agreed to lend the money to Michael. Marty Considine and his family sailed to America from Galway on 1 April 1846.[23] His brother was probably the Michael Considine who was buried in Kilshanny churchyard in 1890. Today another Michael Considine resides in Gortnaboul, on 50 acres.

Following the distress of 1842, assets of several tenants were distrained early in 1843. One of them, James Considine, wrote to Stewart & Kincaid on 4 January 1843 requesting that he be allowed to defer sale of his hay until the price increased, and he added: 'Should you give directions to sell it by auction . . . it would not sell [at a sensible price]. . . . In case you give directions to sell the hay, and the four head of cattle, what would become of myself and my poor family . . . I will conclude in imploring your mercy' (s κ). Considine again wrote to Stewart & Kincaid in 26 April 1843, claiming that he had spent 'upwards of £500 during the past 14 years' improving his farm. He stated that his harvest in 1842 had been poor, and that he now feared ejectment because of rent arrears (s κ). But he was still on the estate on 2 November 1843 when Blackwell reported to Stewart & Kincaid: 'I got no money yet from . . . James Considine' (s κ). It seems that Considine did manage to settle with Stewart & Kincaid: on 27 September 1845 Blackwell wrote to Stewart & Kincaid that the agriculturalist 'Stewart is [staying] at James Considine's' (s κ).

On 28 April 1843 Blackwell wrote that he had 'served [notices to quit on] Corbits wife in her own cabbin, Hallinan & [his own brother] James' (s κ). Six months later he informed Stewart & Kincaid: 'I demanded possession of James Blackwell, Hallinan & the widow Corbit. . . . They all said that they would sooner sell what they had . . . than go out of their houses this time of the year'.[24] In his letter of 28 April he indicated that he hoped to serve notices to quit on two other named tenants, but there was a problem. He wrote: 'I am on the watch & prepared to serve them but it is unknown what part of the country they are in. . . . O'Connor's door is locked & no smoke in it but I saw smoke in old Davises house now & then but no way of puting in a notice & even if a man got an opportunity of puting in the notice it is unknown who is inside' (s κ).

Blackwell continued to threaten distraint up to the time of the potato failure in the autumn of 1845. He also placed keepers on land in order to prevent clandestine sale of produce. For example, on 12 September 1845 James Spellissy requested Stewart & Kincaid to 'write Blackwell to take the keepers from me, and not to put me to the expense of paying them' (SK). On 27 September, Blackwell wrote to Stewart & Kincaid about Anne Blackwell's produce: 'My brother Robert is watching it for me not wishing to put the creature to the expense of keepers. She came here yesterday to tell me that she would have what she promised by the time you would come to Clare, £18.' (SK)

4 FAMINE

On 1 November 1845 Blackwell reported to Stewart & Kincaid that 'the general accounts of the potatoe crop are dreadful. Oatmeal . . . in Ennistymon . . . is now so high as 2/4 [2s 4d] @ stone'.[25] Thus, the price of a stone of oatmeal was then so high that it required about three and a half days of work by a labourer (if he could obtain work) to buy it. Blackwell sent Stewart & Kincaid further details on 16 November: 'I travelled through the estate . . . to take a view of the potatoe crop which is dreadful. . . . The people . . . would be satisfied if the seed remained alive but I am much in dread it will not.' (SK)

The failure of the potato in the autumn of 1845 had little immediate effect on rent receipts. On 4 December, Maxwell wrote from Ennistymon to J. R. Stewart: 'This day I began work here and have got as much as usual say in round numbers £400 and £300 cash out of that. I expect to get about a hundred more. The potatoe rot among the small tenants I hear has done great damage and I suppose that as the spring comes on we will have to give them work to keep them from starving. . . . This country is very quiet and I dont see any turn out against paying rents.' (SK)

The 'hungry months' – usually those of summer – began early in 1846. On 14 March, Blackwell inquired of Stewart & Kincaid: 'Let me know what your intentions are respecting relieving the tenants in want. . . . There are a great many tenants now trusting to the handful [of potatoes] they are striving to preserve from roting by . . . keeping them dry. I am sorry to have to state that I am one of those in immediate want of provision.' (SK) Blackwell again wrote to Stewart & Kincaid three days later: 'The . . . tenants . . . are out of provision except what [seed] they intended to sow. . . . The Parish Priest and the flock met after mass last Sunday & he pointed out a decent man out of every quarter in the parish to take a list of the families in their own neighbourhood. He called on me to take a list of the families in my own locality in order to have characters to produce before the [relief] committee' [which, until the autumn of 1846, issued employment tickets for engagement on public works]. (SK)

Arthur Vincent came to the estate at the end of March 1846 in order to prepare a report for Stewart & Kincaid on the condition of the tenantry there. He informed Blackwell that John Stewart, the agriculturalist, would come soon 'to lay out work for the tenants to enable them to earn the price of provision'.[26] But Blackwell saw a problem of timing: On 3 April he wrote to Stewart & Kincaid that 'the people could not attend the work this time of year, the spring business [of sowing] interfering'. He therefore suggested an alternative: he recommended that Stewart & Kincaid should send money 'to be given to such of the tenants as are in immediate want & to distribute it among them' (sk). The view of John Stewart, who came to Clare around mid-April, was similar. On 17 April, he reported to Stewart & Kincaid:

> There is a few of them very badly off and I am sorry to think that a part of that few will never be better. There is 4 or 5 tenants on the estate that are in want of immediate relief in the way of a loan as they could not attend any work that you might set on until they have their crops sown. . . . After they have that done they will be in want of relief in the way of work. . . . The best way to give relief to the few above mentioned would be to send them some money to be repaid in work when they had their tillage done. . . . Send the money to John Blackwell as the most of them are in Toureen and he is in the number himself, and let them join and send a horse & car to Ennis for meal and perhaps some of them might want to get some seed potatoes. . . . If they got meal from you they would be under the impression that they would never have to pay for it as they got it before for nothing. (sk)

John Stewart went on to mention various improvements which could be commenced in May, after the tenants had completed their tillage. Stewart & Kincaid did send some relief – initially, £10 – which, on 26 April 1846, Blackwell indicated to Stewart & Kincaid was 'to be lent & distributed among the most distressed'. Blackwell added that he would 'distribute it without either favor or affection . . . but as I see them in immediate want the sum you sent will go but very short' (sk). In a letter to Stewart & Kincaid dated 1 May 1846 Blackwell listed the (seven) beneficiaries of the above-mentioned £10. They included his brother Robert and the widow Anne Blackwell. However, he added that 'a few pounds more will be wanted shortly' (sk). The same letter indicates that he had just received a further £10 from Stewart & Kincaid, for relief of himself and family.

It seems that the works of improvement on the Clare estate, laid out by John Stewart, commenced in May 1846. On 17 July he wrote to Stewart & Kincaid: 'I . . . paid the men a fortnight wages. . . . The [private] work on the Clare estate [financed by Stratford] could not be going on more regular than it is. . . . Toureen hill is cut down. . . . The Toureen road will be graveled early

next week and the [private] Carronnebohel [i.e. Boghil[27]] road going on very
well. . . . The Board of Works are running a new line [of road] across it which
will make your road of very great use to the tenants.' (sĸ) The privately
financed roadworks, along with the Board's road, greatly improved access for
Stratford's tenants.

The public works in the vicinity of the Clare estate, which commenced in
July 1846, were extended into the autumn and winter. Thus, both public and
private works were in progress during the summer. However, given that one
half of the cost of the public works would ultimately have to be financed by
local property taxes, early in August Blackwell indicated to Stewart & Kincaid
that he was alarmed by their scale.[28]

The failure of the 1846 potato crop was apparent by 5 August, when
Blackwell informed Stewart & Kincaid: 'There will not be a potatoe hardly alive
next Christmas. . . . It is . . . melancholy to see whole gardens of potatoes black
looking that were fine looking a few days ago. . . . Some gardens that were
green looking last Sunday were black on Monday.' (sĸ) The suddenness with
which the blight took effect elsewhere has already been observed in chapter 3.

Private works on the Clare estate ended in September. More of Stratford's
tenants therefore sought employment on public works. On 1 October 1846
John Blackwell's brother Robert, who had been a steward on private works
during the summer, wrote to Stewart & Kincaid requesting use of influence to
obtain employment for him on public works. On 2 October, John Blackwell
wrote to Stewart & Kincaid: 'Most of the tenants are in great distress just now.
[More] than they were last July as being earning then & not earning any now.
There are lots of respectable people runing about here . . . to get situations
under the Board of Works & I was informed yesterday that it was the Head
Engineer that could do it. . . . So [I] trust your Honrs. will have the kindness
of speaking to him for me . . . so that I will get some employment.' (sĸ) Stewart
& Kincaid responded by providing the Blackwells with letters of recommendation. However, on 26 December, John informed Stewart & Kincaid that his
application to the head engineer at Ennis had not been successful (sĸ).

Early in October 1846 the tenants petitioned Stewart & Kincaid to send
them meal, for which they were expected to pay.[29] Blackwell went around the
estate asking them how much they wanted, and on 11 October he wrote to
Stewart & Kincaid requesting that three tons of meal be sent to Clarecastle.
He added: 'The times are very disturbed. . . . There was a horse belonging to a
man from this parish shot near Ennis yesterday. . . . There is a man . . . from
Ennis selling . . . meal & flour in Ennistymon & always when a cargo is
coming to Ennistymon it is escorted by some of the policemen. Do you think
would it be expensive for you to order a few of them up with the carmen as far
as Ennistymon [?]' (sĸ)

On 25 October 1846 Blackwell sent Stewart & Kincaid half notes for
£35–10, this sum being most of the cost (£42, excluding cost of delivery from
Clarecastle to Ennistymon) of the three tons of meal sent by Stewart & Kincaid.
In the enclosed letter he stated:

> Its a loss that we had not more of it. It is now 2s/2d @ stone in Ennistymon. Did
> you Sirs buy any more than the 3 tons you have sent. The 3 tons did not go far on
> the tenants. . . . A good many of them were between two minds when you men-
> tioned £14 a ton, for it was selling at the time for 1s/10d @ stone in Ennistymon. . . . I
> would much want 3 tons more. . . . If some [more] relief does not come half the
> people will starve . . . as the public work is not getting on in this parish. . . . I am
> much surprised that men of property & learning did not put a stop to the opening
> of unnecessary lines of roads, & [instead] fence, drain & subsoil the land which
> would be of use to both landlord & tenant, as all these unnecessary lines are
> nothing but snares & instruments to destroy both landlord & tenant [through
> taxation]. (s k)

This letter reveals that the savings due to bulk purchase and bulk delivery of
meal by Stewart & Kincaid were smaller than might have been expected. The
cost per ton on arrival at Ennistymon was £14 plus the cost of carriage from
Clarecastle. By way of contrast, the price of meal in Ennistymon at the
beginning of October – 1s 10d per stone – was (on a pro rata basis) equivalent
to £14 13s 4d per ton. On the other hand, the Ennistymon price of 2s 2d per
stone at the end of October was the equivalent of £17 6s 8d per ton; hence bulk
purchase by Stewart & Kincaid at £14 per ton to Clarecastle would then
certainly have been worthwhile. Given the destitution of the tenantry, every
penny mattered. Blackwell's letter of 25 October closed with a list of the
amounts of meal bought, at original cost price to Clarecastle, by each of 31
named tenants.

Presumably with a view to spurring Stewart & Kincaid to re-commence
private works, Blackwell again referred to injurious effects of large-scale
public works in his letter to Stewart & Kincaid dated 29 October 1846:

> There are already too much public works laid out in this Barony. As much . . . as
> will be injurious yet to both landlord & tenant. Taxes will I fear amt. so high as
> that it will be next to impossibility to get over them. It is very extraordinary that
> there is no public works going on yet in this parish [Kilshanny] & men at work in
> the surrounding parishes. The most of the inhabitants of this parish marched to
> Ennistymon last monday to the resident engineer to know the reason they were
> kept back & the chief part of them in a state of starvation. . . . There were plenty
> of roads already. Lay out the money in draining & subsoiling. (s k)

Although we can be sure that arrears of rent accumulated, it seems that few (if any) of the tenants who farmed on Stratford's Clare estate were removed from the land in 1846. Those whose possession was terminated seem to have been middlemen. Thus, on 14 March, Blackwell wrote to Stewart & Kincaid: 'I received the parcel of ejectments. . . . You are quite right to think that I will get no opposition, for the tenants would be very glad to get under the head landlord' (SK).

In 1846 Stewart & Kincaid's agents seem to have been fully aware that many of the tenants could not pay. Maxwell came to collect rents in June. Some days before his arrival, Blackwell wrote to him, at Shanagolden in Limerick, informing him that: 'I could not see the [Boghil] tenants at [Kilshanny] chapel as the Carrownbohilly [Boghil] tenants goes to mass at Kilfenora, but I sent for them last Monday morning & told them you would take so small a sum from the whole of them as £20. They all spoke one man after another to say that unless they could borrow it they could not pay.'[30]

The Stewart & Kincaid correspondence on the Clare estate contains only a single letter written in 1847. But the information which it contains is important: it indicates that a programme of assisted emigration from the estate was implemented in the spring of that year. Thus, on 5 May 1847, J. R. Stewart wrote to Kincaid: 'You see by the enclosed . . . the numbers sent from Col Stratfords Clare estate. Vincent gives a piteous account of their wretched appearance & want of clothing. I only wonder. He did not venture on two or three pounds to get them some, but he dont venture far *without order.*' (SK) One wonders whether these emigrants included Denis Spellissy, who appears to have been a son of the Stratford tenant James Spellissy, and who was an attorney in Manhattan in the 1880s.[31]

The Stewart & Kincaid correspondence pertaining to the Clare estate in 1848 is sparse. The letters reveal that during the summer of 1848, following some depopulation, Stratford obtained a government loan in order to finance drainage works on the estate.[32]

5 CONCLUDING OBSERVATIONS

It can be concluded from the foregoing that, on Stratford's behalf, Stewart & Kincaid's response to distress on the Clare estate in the 1840s was humane. Although many notices to quit were served, the correspondence provides no evidence that any tenant who farmed on the estate was formally ejected in the 1840s. It seems that works of improvement, involving hire of labour, were first implemented on the estate (in 1842) in response to destitution. Following instructions from the Stewart & Kincaid agriculturalist John Stewart, the practice of husbandry greatly improved in 1843–5. In the spring of 1846 Stewart & Kincaid sent small sums of money for relief of the most distressed tenants, and again implemented works of improvement during the summer. Failure of the potato crop in the autumn of 1846, combined with termination of private works in September, accentuated distress. However, Stewart & Kincaid responded by arranging a shipment to the estate of three tons of meal, for which the tenants were expected to pay. It seems that by early 1847 Stewart & Kincaid had come to the conclusion that (as on other estates managed by the firm) the existing population on the Clare estate could no longer be maintained. The firm therefore organised a programme of assisted emigration from the estate, which was supervised by Arthur Vincent. It must, however, be recognised that those who then emigrated were wretched in appearance, and in want of clothing.

That huge numbers of tenants were dispossessed in the Poor Law Union of Kilrush (in the southwest of Clare) – especially during 1847–8 – has been well documented.[33] A small number of them did manage to get to America. However, in the Kilrush district, landlord assistance to enable them to emigrate seems to have been rare or non-existent. The Stewart & Kincaid correspondence on Stratford's Clare in the same period is very thin, but it can reasonably be inferred that Stratford's treatment of tenants was more humane than in the case of the thousands of destitute and dying in the Kilrush district. Stratford did organise a programme of assisted emigration from Clare in 1847, though the number involved is unknown.

TEN

STRATFORD'S LIMERICK ESTATE

—

I INTRODUCTION

Apart from his lands in Clare, Stratford owned over 2,000 statute acres in the Barony of Shanid, County Limerick.[1] Most of these were opposite Aughinish Island on the Shannon estuary. See map 7. With the townland of Robertstown in its centre, it was common to refer to these properties as constituting the Robertstown estate. The tidal part of the Robertstown River separates Aughinish Island from the mainland. The fact that some of the estate was contiguous to the Robertstown River meant that it could be subject to severe flooding at times of high tides: hence, adequate protective embankments were essential.

Between the late eighteenth century and around 1840, the Robertstown estate was held under a lease for the life of Lady Clonbrock, who resided in County Galway.[2] The existence of this lease meant that even if he had wished to do so, Stratford could not have implemented improvements on the estate during those years. All or most of the estate was held by a middleman named Stephen Dickson, who died c.1840.[3] On 10 February 1841 his brother Richard wrote to Stewart & Kincaid: 'Having rec'd no answer to my letter to Col. Stratford except through you, I beg to know whether it is his intention to entertain my proposal of taking a lease [forever] of Robertstown during Lady Clonbrocks life, & receiving a sum of money to fine down the rent. I have laid by a sum of 5000 £ for this purpose'. He added that he wished 'to remove the excessive population of paupers by sending them to America'. (SK)

Lady Clonbrock died in May 1841. Probably on the advice of Stewart & Kincaid (who commenced as active managers of Stratford's Limerick estate in 1841), Stratford decided not to grant a lease to Richard Dickson, whose tenancy ended. On 5 June 1841 Dickson wrote to Stewart & Kincaid:

During the short time the [tenancy of the] property was mine . . . I was particular in the removal of obnoxious characters. . . . I had the advantage of the . . . excellent agent I employed (Mr Arthur Vincent, son of the [Church of Ireland] Clergyman of Shanagolden Parish) whose local knowledge of the property & of every individual upon it enabled him to select such as would be good tenants, while he removed the bad. . . . It would be impossible for you to obtain the services of a person better qualified. (s k)

Three days later Dickson wrote to Stewart & Kincaid recommending James Moran, 'a most respectable & intelligent tenant at Ardaneer, to you for the situation of driver [i.e. bailiff] . . . as he has acted in that capacity for me with zeal & . . . is a . . . fearless person in the discharge of his duty'.[4] In line with Dickson's recommendations, Stewart & Kincaid appointed Vincent as local agent, and Moran as bailiff, on the estate. Vincent's salary was about £55 per annum.[5]

Although Stratford never visited his Robertstown estate in the 1840s, he did subscribe to the dispensary at nearby Shanagolden.[6] Like his brother Edward, he was a Tory who opposed repeal of the Act of Union between Britain and Ireland. During the spring and summer of 1843 Daniel O'Connell held a series of 'monster meetings' urging repeal of the Act. Colonel Stratford expected his tenants to stay clear of agitation for repeal. On 31 July 1843 Vincent wrote to J. R. Stewart from his residence, Shanagolden House: 'I apprised the tenants of the Col's sentiments "with regard to the repeal". And although there was an immense meeting near this [place] on Sunday last, not a tenant on the estate attended it, and they said, if Ireland had many such landlords, no repeal would be wanted: as the crowds were marching through, the tenants were groaned, and hooted, at for not following them. . . . The priests headed each party'. Vincent again referred to the tenants' stance when he wrote in August in regard to 'Stratfords pleasing answer about his tenants not joining the Repealers. They are all very happy at not doing so.'[7]

Stratford's views on religion were similar to those of his twin brother: he seems to have been a bigot. On 14 October 1841 he wrote to Stewart & Kincaid that 'approval of the parish priest has little weight on me' (s k). In 1843, when J. R. Stewart first visited the estate, the parish priest sent or handed to him a letter requesting that he use his influence with Stratford 'regarding the chapel of Robertstown' which had 'no gate, no yard, wall, no fence . . . to defend it from the intrusion of animals', and the priest added: 'At the time of its being built, I refrained from making any application to the Hon'ble proprietor of the soil, knowing the income accruing to him *then* out of Robertstown was inconsiderable: but I hope he will not consider it in any way intrusive *now* to request . . . that he will have . . . the chapel yard to be walled in for us'.[8] The Catholic church at Robertstown today has three old walls surrounding its sides and rear. The Stewart & Kincaid correspondence provides no evidence on whether Stratford assisted in their construction. However, the letters do indicate that he assisted the Church of Ireland, both on and off his estates. Thus, on 13 April 1848 the Rev. David Whitty wrote to Stratford from the vicarage in Foynes:

> I have established a school in the parish of Shanagolden . . . in connection with the Church Education Society. The opposition to the project was so great that I could only get one person in the whole place to set a house to me for the purpose. . . . Thirty four children attend it daily. . . . Had we [larger] accommodation we should have had upwards of seventy. The Reformation Society is going to assist me to build [a schoolhouse] and therefore knowing you to be disposed to promote Scriptural education among the peasantry . . . I hope you will not refuse to assist. . . . Since I came here thirty seven have left the church of Rome. (sĸ)

On 17 April 1848 Stratford wrote to Stewart & Kincaid to tell them that the clergyman's letter 'ought to be attended' (sĸ). And writing on his brother's behalf on 5 June, Edward Wingfield instructed Stewart & Kincaid to donate 'about £5, which is one 6th of the sum required'. Stratford donated a further £5 in July, and it may be the case that he granted another £5 in August.[9] On 13 August, Whitty informed Stewart & Kincaid that 'the school is going on well . . . the converts generally standing resolute tho' greatly persecuted' (sĸ).

Stratford assisted Church of Ireland missioners elsewhere. As mentioned in chapter 7, in the early 1840s he contributed to the Ventry and Dingle Institution, and to the Loochoo Mission, in Kerry. Late in 1848 he informed Stewart & Kincaid that he had 'written to the Rev'd Edward Nangle to call on you for ten pounds, as a subscription to the Charitable Achill Mission [in Mayo]'.[10]

2 SQUARING THE LAND AND OTHER PRE-FAMINE IMPROVEMENTS

One of Vincent's first tasks as Stewart & Kincaid agent was to oversee squaring of the land. This implied the removal of several small tenants. On 9 October 1841 he wrote to Stewart & Kincaid: 'I have just received the ejectments and shall have them served. . . . From the number of cottiers . . . those you sent will not be sufficient'. Vincent again referred to ejectment a few weeks later: 'I am most anxious to get rid of those wretched paupers. . . . I am sorry the Habere [a writ issued by a plaintiff after obtaining judgment in ejectment[11]] runs out so soon as the 11th Jan'y [1842], as it will be dreadful if we are obliged to turn them on the world at that inclement season. If it ran to March at which time emigration commencing we would have no pity for them.'[12] In view of the considerations just outlined, on 11 January 1842 Vincent requested Stewart & Kincaid to have the Habere (which may have applied to the entire tenantry of the estate, thereby giving Stewart & Kincaid power to quickly eject any tenant) renewed. If the Habere did apply generally, it would have made it easier to shift tenants from one location to another during the squaring.

Many of those who left the land during the squaring received assistance to emigrate. There had, in fact, already been some emigration from the estate before Stewart & Kincaid started to provide assistance: a letter from Vincent late in 1841 refers to a tenant who had nine children and a wife at home; Vincent advised him to go to America, 'where he has two sons already'.[13] The sums which Stewart & Kincaid provided to individual families in assisted emigration from the Robertstown estate were probably small. Thus, on 22 December 1841 Vincent wrote to Stewart & Kincaid: 'Although you have given me the liberty of assisting those poor cottiers to emigrate I should like to have your advice . . . as to what . . . to give. What has struck my mind to offer, is, one pound to each member of the family. . . . £100 or £150 in this way would clear off a good many paupers' (sk). But the levels of payment contemplated by Vincent did not satisfy the cottiers. He therefore suggested that some of them should be offered more. On 29 January 1842 he wrote to Stewart & Kincaid: 'There are six families on Srulawn [Sroolane townland] comprising in all 37 individuals who look to us for assistance to emigrate'. He 'told them that they might expect £1, each'. However, 'they say we may keep this much as it would be of little or no assistance to them [to get to America]. The very least which I think will quiet them is £2 each. . . . I would be for giving it' (sk). The sums paid to emigrants from the estate in 1842 are unknown.

Late in 1841, a surveyor came to the estate to plan squaring of the land and new roads for access. Not all of the tenants were content with the squares assigned to them. Two of them indicated their objections in petitions which they sent to Stratford.[14] In December 1841 Vincent wrote of 'that horrid fellow James Bridgeman' who 'wants all his former holding',[15] and on 1 January 1842 he reported to Stewart & Kincaid that 'James Bridgeman brought a plough & pair of horses yesterday and commenced sowing wheat in a part of the farm which is not intended for him. I went to the ground & . . . ordered the plough-man to desist. . . . He did not stop for me so I had him summoned for the next Petty Sessions.' (sk)

It seems that Bridgeman, along with others on the lands to be squared, had an ejectment decree outstanding against him, but that it had not been executed. The existence of such a decree would have given Stewart & Kincaid leverage in inducing tenants promptly to move to their newly assigned squares. On 11 January 1842 Vincent wrote to Stewart & Kincaid: 'I this day took the bailiff and a party of the tenants with me to dispossess [Bridgeman]. . . . He James

refused to give up; and just as I was setting the men to pull down his house . . .
his friends broke in his door . . . and brought him out, and they begged of me
there to grant him his pardon. His wife clung to me and cried mercy. I could
not resist the call and stopped further proceedings. . . . I gave the possession to
those the farm was divided out for.' (sk)

Following the events of 11 January 1842, it is likely that James Bridgeman
moved peacefully to his newly assigned holding: in the early 1850s there was a
James Bridgeman farming Stratford land on Robertstown.[16] Another tenant
refused to move. This probably meant that he was given no land, and it probably benefited a widow. Thus, in January 1842 the surveyor wrote to Kincaid
that certain fields in Sroolane, comprising not much more than an (Irish?)
acre, 'are yet to be disposed of', one named tenant having refused them. He
proposed giving them 'to Widow Maddigan who was removed from Dysert,
where she had held about two acres *for upwards of forty years*. She has in
consequence of her removal been reduced to great distress and . . . I would be
glad of it *as I recommended her removal from Dysert*.'[17]

Although some of the land was not to be squared until the autumn of 1843,
it seems that most of the tenants had moved to their new holdings by the end
of February 1842. This meant that access roads had to be built. Many of the
tenants also sought assistance from Stewart & Kincaid to build on their new
holdings. In a letter of 29 January 1842 to Stewart & Kincaid, Vincent proposed 'that we will give slate and timber which they will buy as cheap as they
can and bring us the dockets for payment' (sk). This was the practice which
was most often adopted. Most of the new houses were slated rather than
thatched. Apart from the fact that they would last longer, an advantage of this
practice, as Vincent pointed out, was that straw could be saved for manure (sk).
Thus, on 1 August 1842 he wrote to Kincaid: 'Thos. Kelly . . . who we arranged
should remove to his brother Mich'ls farm has been with me respecting his
house which is ready for roofing. Mr [John] Stewart [the agriculturalist
recently hired[18]] made an estimate of the cost of slate and timber. . . . About
£7–10 would do all and as the poor man is now living in the wretched cabin
you saw his brother in which is not fit for pigs, it would be a great act of
kindness to give this allowance, and more particularly so, as it will spare straw
. . . to make manure'. Vincent again referred to dilapidated housing in a letter
to J. R. Stewart on 5 July 1843. Referring to two tenants in Dysert, he wrote:
John Barrett's house 'is in a very tottering state and is not worth losing to
repairs. He has a large family and is greatly inconvenienced not having room.
John Lynch has a small house, only the kitchen and one room. This house is a
good one for the size but having a family of twelve he is obliged to have them
all nearly sleeping in one room. . . . Should you sanction their building they
could do so now' (sk).

Apart from receiving assistance in building their houses, some tenants obtained financial aid for construction of farm offices. For example, on 17 March 1843 Vincent informed Kincaid that 'John Connors offices are 60 feet long and 16 broad . . . containing a dairy, stable and barn. The timber, slates and laths cost £32–8–2' (s k). On 20 July 1843 Vincent recommended to J. R. Stewart that another tenant be allowed £12 for slates and timber on a stable and cowhouse which he wanted to build (s k). Writing from Shanagolden on 27 April 1843, J. R. Stewart reported to Kincaid: 'I am not I confess satisfied about the houses, as I think they might have been much better . . . without any additional cost to Col Stratford . . . and I suspect they have been more lavish of timber in the roofs than if they paid for the timber themselves' (s k). Apart from the planting and harvesting seasons, building was in progress from early 1842 until late 1843. On 19 October 1843 Vincent wrote to Stewart & Kincaid: 'I think we wont have many more applications for building' (s k).

Along with house building, 1842 was a year in which new roads were laid down. On 29 January, Vincent informed Stewart & Kincaid: 'I will order the roads to be commenced immediately' (s k). These had been planned by the surveyor as works of utility rather than as devices for employment creation. Some of the work was performed directly by the tenants themselves, for which they received allowances against rent; however, it appears that most of it was conducted by hired labour under the supervision of John Stewart the agri - culturalist.[19] The labourers were probably paid about one shilling a day: on 14 June 1842 Vincent wrote to Stewart & Kincaid that 'the usual wages given to labourers in this country is a shilling a day'. (s k) The road works were virtually completed by September 1842. Their construction meant that in 1846, when many roads were built elsewhere as public works, Stratford's Limerick estate was amply endowed with useful roads. Thus, some of his improvements in 1842 were to have adverse effects on his tenants during the famine.

On 5 March 1842 Vincent informed Stewart & Kincaid that the tide had broken the banks along the Robertstown River and had 'inundated all the low lands' (s k). John Stewart first arrived on the estate in 1842. One of his first tasks was recruitment of labour for clearance and widening of the river, and during the summer of 1843 he supervised repairs to embankments.[20] However, in mid-October 1844 he wrote to Stewart & Kincaid that the tides had again come over the embankments. He therefore supervised 'a good repairing' late in 1844.[21]

In the autumn of 1842 John Stewart turned to drainage. It seems that most of this work was by the tenants on their own lands under Stewart's super-vision. On 11 February 1843 Vincent wrote to Stewart & Kincaid that 'the tenants are draining . . . and the drains appear to be all well done' (s k). On 27 April, J. R. Stewart reported to Kincaid: 'I have been over a good deal of the estate and like very much what Stewart has been . . . getting done by the tenants' (s k). More extensive drainage works during the winter of 1843–4 involved employment of hired labour.

John Stewart oversaw other improvements on the estate. Shortly after his arrival he marked out two places for sinking water pumps which, according to Vincent, the tenants were 'in the greatest need of, being completely run dry'.[22] But it is likely that his most important contribution to the estate was in inducing tenants to change their methods of husbandry. In April 1842 he wanted Stewart & Kincaid to send a turnip barrow because, as reported by Vincent, he 'could not get it in Limerick'.[23] Unlike the potato, which was mainly for human consumption, the turnip was a multiple purpose crop which was relatively free from disease. On 7 June, Stewart informed Stewart & Kincaid that 'most of the farmers are sowing a few turnips. I got a good many of them to sow rye grass and clover', to enrich the nitrogen content of the soil. (s k)

On 1 August 1842 Vincent reported to Stewart & Kincaid that 'if this lovely weather continues a great deal of wheat will be fit for the sickle next week. Everything is looking most cheering' (s k). However, referring to the wheat on 19 August, he wrote to Stewart & Kincaid that 'never did I see farmers more disappointed. From its appearance before being ripe all expected a full average crop but now the fields show the quantity far short' (s k). On 7 September, John Stewart explained to Stewart & Kincaid as follows: 'The cause of the bad wheat is this. Where they find a good spot of ground they crop it with potatoes and wheat alternatively for 10 or 12 years and not giving the land good manure . . . [they] will never have good wheat until they change their way of farming' (s k). On 31 December 1842, Stewart wrote to Stewart & Kincaid that 'what I am afraid of is that the ground is exhausted. . . . When there is not sufficient nourishment in the ground to ripen wheat, the stalk loses the sap and falls. . . . This I am sure to be the cause of such a bad crop of wheat. . . . The only remedy is to get the tenants to sow as much as possible of their lands with clover and grass seeds. . . . I have tried to impress [this] upon the whole of the tenants.' (s k)

There was a lime kiln on the estate. John Stewart's letter of 31 December 1842 indicates that several tenants had been supplied with lime earlier in the same year, and that they were expected to pay for it (s k). A letter of 1 March 1845, from Vincent to Stewart & Kincaid, indicates that those tenants who obtained lime at the kiln were then in receipt of an allowance from Stewart & Kincaid (presumably against rent) of 2½ *d.* per barrel purchased by them. (s k)

Consistent with a desire to encourage improvements in husbandry, it seems that Stewart & Kincaid provided assistance to Joseph, son of one of Stratford's Limerick tenants named Patrick Bridgeman. Joseph Bridgeman studied agriculture between 1842 and 1846. The nature of Stewart & Kincaid's assistance is not clear.[24]

John Stewart was optimistic when, on 8 June 1845, he wrote from Robertstown to Stewart & Kincaid: 'Crops . . . are looking very well here. I am sure when Mr Kincaid see[s] the clover crops . . . that he will say that he saw no better this year. . . . Yet they are grumbling to pay for the seed I got them last year. . . . There is a good many of the tenants sowing turnips . . . and some of them are using guano. . . . The nursery [which seems to have been set up by Stewart] is doing very well. I shall have 40000 Thorns fit for planting out [for fencing] next winter'. (sk)

3 RENTS AND DISTRESS, 1842–5

The reader may have inferred that the pre-famine years under Stewart & Kincaid's agency must have been a period of prosperity on the estate, but this was not the case. On 5 March 1842 Vincent wrote to Stewart & Kincaid: 'The tenants I fear will not be able to *meet* us *well* as they made money of almost every grain of corn they had to clear off Mr Dickson's arrears.' (sk) Following a recommendation by Vincent, Stewart & Kincaid granted rent abatements in the spring of 1842.[25] But these could not have been of much use to landless labourers. On 4 June 1842 Vincent reported to Stewart & Kincaid the plight of 'many poor labourers who were in great distress . . . from the want of general work and the high price provisions have risen to' (sk). He added that the timing of the start of some works of improvement, which involved hire of labourers, was fortunate.

Vincent's rent receipts remained poor throughout 1842. This meant that during the summer he had to write to Dublin asking for money to be sent to pay labourers. On 14 June he sought £40 'to meet the next pay day and pay off other emergencies' (sk) and on 22 June he asked for £100 (sk). On 12 December he informed Stewart & Kincaid that one reason why he was 'very unsuccessful in collection of the arrears' was that although some tenants had wheat, oats and pigs, they were keeping them 'expecting a rise in the markets' (sk).

For one tenant in 1843, a marriage settlement was the source of the rent. On 11 February 1843 Vincent wrote to Stewart & Kincaid: 'James Dempsey who buried his wife on Xmas Eve, I hear is going to be married and is getting £150 fortune. . . . I hope it is the case as he is deeply in arrear.' (sk) A letter from Vincent to Stewart & Kincaid dated 3 March indicates that Dempsey was then again married (sk).

Rent receipts remained poor in 1843. On 12 October, Vincent wrote to Stewart & Kincaid that 'wheat is very bad and prices low. Loud calls on all sides for abatements' (sk). On 19 October 1843 he explained to Stewart & Kincaid: 'You think that I have not exerted myself to make the tenants pay their balances of the Septr. 1842 rents. . . . I did not like, from the agitation and the excited state of the country all last summer, to distrain as I feel quite certain we could not get bidders for a single beast.' (s k) Vincent was here referring to the agitation, including O'Connell's 'monster meetings', for repeal of the Act of Union. It may also be the case that he was scared by tales of events in neighbouring Tipperary of which J. R. Stewart might have informed him. In the spring of 1843 Stewart wrote to Kincaid from Limerick City, stating that a passenger on the coach upon which he had travelled had provided him with 'details of murder and outrages as we came from Roscrea to Nenagh, every turn in the road opening a view of some hill or house where there had been a scene of violence. . . . I start at 9 o'clock . . . & hope to be at Mr Vincents at 1 o'clock'.[26]

Vincent again referred to distraint in a letter of 1 March 1845 in which he wrote: 'I have been endeavouring as much as possible to get rent . . . without going to extremes but as I cannot succeed by quiet means I find I must have recourse to distraining which I will do immediately everywhere I find means.' (s k) The Stewart & Kincaid correspondence provides no evidence that any tenant was ejected from the estate between the spring of 1842 and the end of 1845. Nor is there any evidence, over the same period, that any of Vincent's threats of distraint were implemented.

On 7 July 1845 John Stewart wrote to Stewart & Kincaid from Robertstown describing an experience, the form of which was to be repeated on many occasions and in many places during the famine. He reported that he had commenced deepening a small river but had to stop the work 'on account of so many men crowding about me for work. Some of them wanted work right or [w]rong. . . . The poor about here are very ill off.' (s k)

On 7 June 1843 Vincent wrote to Stewart & Kincaid that in the Robertstown district, 'numbers are complaining of a failure in the . . . potatoe' (s k). The earliest indication in the Stewart & Kincaid correspondence of the partial failure of the potato on the estate in 1845 is in a letter from John Stewart to Stewart & Kincaid on 29 October, in which he reported: 'I cannot find a single field that the rot has not made its appearance in. . . . Mr Vincents potatoes were reported to be all gone. I went to examine them and found the above statement to be the fact. When the potatoes are dug dry and the pits well ventilated I think puts a check to the rot. In low damp wet situations here-abouts the rot is much worse.' (s k). Vincent wrote to Stewart & Kincaid on 8 November indicating his concern about 'the state of the potatoes. . . . All will be lost before Xmas. . . . Famine stares us in every quarter if the corn is not left in the country.' (s k)

The potato failure of 1845 did not immediately affect rent receipts. On 18 November, Vincent sent Stewart & Kincaid £165 in half notes, and

Maxwell was elated when he wrote to J. R. Stewart from Shanagolden on 13 December: 'We have got a splendid receipt on this estate £1250 and perhaps may get a little more' (s k).

4 FAMINE
Relief

A relief committee, of which Vincent was both vice-chairman and treasurer, was formed in 1846. As explained by him in a letter to Stewart & Kincaid dated 18 April, on the second of that month the committee first met at Shanagolden 'for the purpose of getting subscriptions to purchase Indian Meal . . . to be disposed of at prime cost to the distressed. . . . [This] will keep down the high price which huxters generally take advantage of . . . when a scarcity prevails. . . . The only steps taken as yet by the committee . . . is their having taken a house to store and sell Indian Meal . . . & directing the secretary to apply to the different landed proprietors for subscriptions.' Vincent added that 'several meetings have been held to promote public works [but] none of the intended works come at all near our Robertstown district as the roads about the neighbourhood are all so good [. Hence] we will have to make out some work on the property' (s k).

Because few (if any) of the Robertstown tenants were employed on public works early in the summer of 1846, Stewart & Kincaid's agents sought to contrive schemes of useful employment on the estate. A high tide had flowed over the embankments of the Robertstown River in February, causing much flooding. On 24 February, John Stewart recommended to Stewart & Kincaid that 'the whole of the banks on this estate wants a thorough repairing except the few breaches that was repaired last year' (s k). On 7 May, Vincent wrote to Stewart & Kincaid recommending major works on the lands contiguous to the river (s k). But there is no evidence that any of these proposals was implemented during the summer of 1846. On 1 June, however, the Commissioners of Drainage indicated to Stewart & Kincaid that they intended to implement improvements at the Robertstown River, and they requested Kincaid to send them any relevant plans which Stewart & Kincaid might have prepared. The absence in the Stewart & Kincaid files of any further details of relevance suggests that the Commissioners' proposal was almost certainly abandoned or substantively postponed.

In June 1846 John Stewart recommended a new road in Robertstown, work on which was in progress by 9 July, when he wrote to Stewart & Kincaid that 'the road could not be better laid out to suit all parties'. On 7 October, Vincent informed Stewart & Kincaid that many new programmes of public works had been granted for the barony of Shanid (of which the Robertstown estate was part). However, they had not yet commenced. He added that the works were urgently needed because 'the potatoes are all gone from the labouring class and nothing can equal the awful state they are in' (sĸ). On 10 October, Vincent wrote to Stewart & Kincaid that 'the Indian Meal has risen to 2/- per stone this day. What a mistake it was in Government allowing the merchants such a monopoly in trade. A starving population will never be content with this state of affairs' (sĸ). If a labourer, with a wife and five children, was fortunate in obtaining employment, the most he could expect to earn was about 1*s* a day.[27] Given the price of meal, with this sum he could buy only seven pounds weight of it – only one pound of meal per day for each person in his family (assuming that he worked seven days each week). Vincent feared that there would be outbreaks of violence on the estate. On 25 October he wrote to Stewart & Kincaid:

> There have been two large meetings of the people in Askeaton. . . . The bakers shops have been plundered of all bread. . . . Discontent is beginning here but no outrage as yet. Several houses have been visited within the last week and deprived of arms, among the rest Moran [the bailiff] whose gun was taken. [The home of] a Mr Massy . . . was attacked. . . . They took his gun. . . . A woman in her fright leaped out of a window and broke her back. She is in a dying state. There was a very large meeting here this day by Proclamation for employment of the poor. . . . Captain Kennedy attended on the part of the Board of Works. . . . If [the people are] not immediately set at work nothing will keep them quiet. . . . We have very serious times before us. (sĸ)

On 31 October 1846 Vincent reported to Stewart & Kincaid:

> I wish . . . the Govt. would set the Robertstown Embankment in progress. . . . There are no works of any kind struck off near Robertstown and the poor are in much distress. I was obliged to employ a few men to stop the heavy breaches on the banks lately broken. . . . I went to Limerick this week to purchase Indian Meal for the relief committee and could only get 5 ton in all the city. . . . The people are getting into despair and a resort to the stock [of animals] is greatly to be apprehended. Numbers leaving this [district] are selling off so much that stock have fallen greatly. The fairs are thronged with cattle and no buyers to be found for them. . . . God only knows when this calamity will end. (sĸ)

It seems that, pending provision of employment, Stewart & Kincaid tried to buy meal for the Robertstown estate. A letter to Stewart & Kincaid, dated 1 November from W. H. Hall in Limerick City, reported that 'there is no corn

meal here of any kind for sale. . . . Supplies are daily expected & with your
sanction I will purchase 2 ton the first opportunity'.[28] Public works on a large
scale were not in progress in the Robertstown district until around mid-
December 1846 when Vincent wrote to Stewart & Kincaid asking the firm to
use influence at the Board of Works to secure an appointment for him.[29]

The need for seed potatoes

Early in 1846 John Stewart wrote that he was worried 'about the potatoes
having the seed decaying. . . . Failure of the growing crop is greatly dreaded.
Numbers of the poor are now quite out of provision. . . . We have no pleasant
prospect before us this summer'.[30] On 18 April, Vincent asked Stewart &
Kincaid to intervene on the matter of seed potatoes. Thus, he wrote that 'the
first and most important step . . . would be to send if possible a supply of good
seed to be distributed in small portions among the tenants' (sk). Stewart &
Kincaid immediately contacted W. H. Hall who, on 24 April, informed the
firm that 'there are not any sound seed potatos for sale at our quays [in
Limerick]. A cargo is daily expected. . . . On arrival I will communicate with
you & Mr Vincent' (sk). Vincent next considered the possibility of getting
seed from the Society of Friends in Cork City. On 27 April he wrote to
Stewart & Kincaid: 'We have no chance of procuring seed potatoes from Cork
. . . as there are no boats plying or sufficiently seaworthy to employ at Foynes
for the trip' (sk). On the next day, however, W. H. Hall informed Stewart &
Kincaid that 'the cargo of seed potatos . . . arrived. . . . She [the ship] has 100
tons of apparently fine seed & which is selling @ 10 pence per stone' (sk). Early
in May, Vincent sent for two tons of this seed for the Robertstown tenants.[31]

Rents

On 10 February 1846 Vincent informed Stewart & Kincaid: 'I sat at home this
day waiting for the Robertstown tenants to pay after the fair of Rathkeale,
but . . . only [one] person . . . paid. . . . I know they can pay well but the fear of
a scarcity is keeping them all back. I gave them to next Monday, the fair of
Askeaton which after that some do not come forward I shall have to distrain'
(sk). A letter from Vincent to Stewart & Kincaid, 19 February 1846, is the only
definite indication that he had distrained properties on the Robertstown
estate. This action paid off: on 28 February he was able to send Stewart &
Kincaid first half notes for £135 from the tenants there. On 10 October 1846
Vincent wrote to Stewart & Kincaid that he feared 'rents will be very hard to

get in this year' (s k). Referring to the tenants on 31 October, he informed Stewart & Kincaid that he was 'not getting in any rent from them' (s k). In December he indicated that Maxwell had just visited the estate on a money-gathering tour, and that 'Maxwell was wild with the tenants which I hope it may have the effect of bringing in more of the defaulters on tomorrow'.[32]

The Stewart & Kincaid correspondence does not contain any letters from the estate in 1847. However, rent receipts in that year may have been satis-factory, given hard times. This is inferred from a letter of 1848 from Stratford to Stewart & Kincaid inquiring 'whether the tenants are likely . . . to pay their rents, as last year [1847] tho I cannot expect to the same extent'.[33] It may be the case that some of the tenants felt that Vincent pressed too hard in 1848: on 7 September of that year, Stratford wrote to Stewart & Kincaid that he was 'very sorry to see in the papers some time ago that Mr Vincents house was attacked & plundered' (s k). On 20 December 1848 J. R. Stewart, who had just come from Shanagolden, sent from Limerick City a letter of credit for £320 as an enclosure. In the accompanying letter he stated: 'I think a good deal more will be paid to Vincent' (s k).

The Stewart & Kincaid correspondence does not reveal any cases of ejectment from the Robertstown estate during the famine years. Furthermore, the letters contain no evidence of distraint after February 1846. But these remarks must be qualified by the fact that the letters for 1847 are entirely missing, while those for 1848 are thin.

Emigration

There was probably some assisted emigration from the estate early in the famine. On 19 February 1846 Vincent informed Stewart & Kincaid: 'A few of the cottiers on the Robertstown Estate are inclined to emigrate. Will you allow me to give them some allowances on getting their holdings thrown down. I think it would be well to lessen them.' (s k) On 6 March 1846 Vincent again referred to cottier emigrants. He explained to Stewart & Kincaid that 'they never had any land more than a cabbage garden. . . . I should think that £20 should cover the whole' (s k). However, the latter sum was not acceptable to the cottiers, as a group. On 17 March, Vincent reported to Stewart & Kincaid:

> With respect to the allowances you would give the cottiers on giving up their cabins I cannot get one who will accept of £5, as all their other effects when sold would not make as much as would pay their passage to America. What they look for is £2 for each member of the family. In former years the people had their potatoes which afforded them great assistance towards emigrating. . . . The few

who want to sell can hardly get buyers as in less than a fortnight half the barrel of
potatoes will be decayed. . . . The landlords will have to give assistance . . . to the
support of their tenants this summer and I think £100 could not be better
converted than in thinning the poorer portion of cabins on this property. (s k)

Apart from the cottiers early in the year, emigration to America from the
Robertstown estate in 1846 seems to have been low. A letter from Vincent to
Stewart & Kincaid, dated 26 April, mentions two tenants who had recently
gone to America (s k), but the letters for 1846 provide no further mention of
emigration from the district. However, it is likely that there was some assisted
emigration from the estate in the spring of 1847: recall from chapter 9 that
early in that year, Vincent supervised emigration of some of Stratford's
tenants in Clare. The only subsequent reference to emigration from
Stratford's lands is in a letter dated 20 December 1848, posted in Limerick
City by J. R. Stewart. In this he indicated to Kincaid that he had just come
from Shanagolden, and he added: 'I have arranged for exporting 3 or 4 families
& if we were merely wanting to get people off could send lots more. But of
course I only send those who have land & whose rent which they are unable to
pay would [from new tenants] soon come to the cost of emigration.' (s k)

5 CLOSING OBSERVATIONS

Many of the tenants on the Robertstown estate regarded J. R. Stewart and
Joseph Kincaid as paternal figures who wielded great influence. One such
person was Cornelius O'Shea. Early in 1842 he wrote to Kincaid describing
himself as of 'a numerous and helpless family on 3½ acres' in Robertstown. He
asked Kincaid to help him obtain an appointment in the Water Guards, but
added that 'if this cannot be obtained anything which your goodness may
deem proper is acceptable to me'.[34] On some date (probably early) in 1843 he
decided to try J. R. Stewart. He again sought 'a situation in the Water Guards
or any other situation that your Hon'r would be pleased to place him'.[35] On
13 November 1843 he delivered a letter to Shanagolden House, addressed to
J. R. Stewart. It read: 'I . . . call to your mind the promises you made me on
your former visit to this estate which was that you would get me a situation in
the Dublin Police' (s k). Young O'Shea was still on the estate early in 1846,
when he went to London to see Stratford. On 10 March of that year, Edward
Wingfield wrote to Stewart & Kincaid from Stratford's London residence: 'A
gosing lad of the name of Cornelius O'Shea called here at 6 o'clock in the
morn'g with a letter from Mr Vincent recommending him for a situation in
the Custom House. A greater simpleton you never beheld, nor a more foolish

act could anybody do than to send a poor booley [a seasonal cow-herd] like him . . . without a penny in his pockett'. Wingfield added: 'I hope he got safe back with . . . the assistance my brother . . . gave him to pay for his return. I mention this that you may write to Mr Vincent, who ought to have more sense than . . . put the poor young fellow to such fruitless trouble & expense.' (s κ) It appears that there were no O'Sheas residing on Robertstown town-land in 1852.[36]

On 17 March 1846 Vincent replied to a communication from Stewart & Kincaid in regard to O'Shea's visit to London: 'I regret much having sent Cornelius O'Shea to London but as Col. Stratford interested himself about a journeyman [a qualified mechanic or artisan who works for another] named Fleming last year, the people here think he can get anything he asks. I will be more cautious in future.' (s κ)

But Vincent was not consistently 'more cautious'. In a letter from London to Stewart & Kincaid dated 17 April 1848, Stratford noted: 'With this I send you . . . an application from a Michael O Connor for a situation under Government, with a certificate from Mr Vincent, which I returned to O C. telling him I had no Interest with Government, of which Mr Vincent sh'd have mentioned to him, & not have encouraged him to come here at con-siderable . . . expense.' (s κ)

It was not the case that all of the requests by Robertstown tenants for use of 'influence' to obtain employment ended in failure. Thus, on 22 December 1841 Vincent wrote to Stewart & Kincaid: 'Cornelius Madigan & Philip Stack begged I would mention to you how much obliged they feel for all the trouble you have taken to get them provided and . . . they will join the City of Dublin Police. They will call upon you the second Thursday in January.' (s κ) But Madigan failed to pass examination by the police doctors in Dublin.[37]

Stratford and his Dublin agents received several petitions from the Limerick tenants concerning matters other than employment. An example is that addressed to J. R. Stewart at Shanagolden House in 1846 (no exact date provided). It was written by a tenant named Conor Kinane who 'Humbly Sheweth':

> That his three orphan sisters are . . . for the last ten weeks labouring under a malignant fever during which time he has lost all his little means to nourish them. . . . The small quantity of potatoes which . . . had been intended for their support these hard times he had to sell, also a pig which he intended to have helped him to pay his rent . . . had to be sold in order to nourish [the sisters].
>
> That they are now in a surviving state if they had sufficient nourishment. But the little means being exhausted renders them truly miserable. . . . May it therefore please Mr Stuart [Stewart] to take petitioners case into his humane consideration

by representing the state of these unfortunate beings to the Honourable Wingfield
Stratford for some relief.

How Stewart responded to this particular petition is unknown. However, a
letter from Stratford to Stewart & Kincaid dated 25 October 1846 indicates
that he was prepared to assist individual tenants who were really in a state of
destitution. In this he wrote as follows:

> I have just rec'd the enclosed [petition]. I think it right to know from you or
> Mr Vincent, whether the petitioner is in the situation she represents herself to
> be. . . . Sh'd she however turn out to be greatly in want I am willing to assist . . .
> but . . . at this time [of] distress . . . many imposters will . . . misrepresent the con-
> dition they are in. . . . Consider where charity is to be dispensed, among my tenants,
> & the lower classes & assist them accordingly everywhere, in the best manner. (SK)

ELEVEN

ON TWO ESTATES IN
SOUTH LIMERICK

—

I INTRODUCTION

Apart from managing that of Stratford, Stewart & Kincaid were agents on two other estates in Limerick – that of Mrs Gertrude Blakeney Fitzgerald and that of a person known as Sergeant Warren.

The Fitzgerald lands were between Charleville in north Cork and Kilmallock in Limerick (see map 7). They included most of Mount Blakeney (563 statute acres) and the contiguous townland of Thomastown (953 statute acres).[1] These lands, some or all of which had been granted to William Blakeney at the time of the Cromwellian plantation in the seventeenth century,[2] were generally known as the Mount Blakeney estate. Mrs Fitzgerald resided about 60 (English) miles away, at Whitegate House near Cloyne in southeast Cork. Stewart & Kincaid commenced as her agent at Mount Blakeney around 1843 and appointed John Murnane, a tenant on a nearby estate, as bailiff on the property.

Sergeant Warren's lands were within a few miles from, and to the south and southeast of, Ballingarry in Limerick. They included all or most of the 436 statute acres on the townland of Kilmihil outside Ballingarry, and all or most of the 1,561 statute acres on Ballinruane to the south, as well as other properties.[3] The Stewart & Kincaid correspondence variously refers to these as comprising the 'Ballinruane' or 'Ballyroan' or 'Ballingarry' estate. Stewart & Kincaid commenced as Sergeant Warren's agent around the end of 1843.

Links between Stewart & Kincaid, Gertrude Fitzgerald and Sergeant Warren involved more than business alone. In June 1841 Thomas Stewart wrote to Kincaid: 'Tell me if there is any proper legal form of appointing an Agency & if there is pray send me one directed to Whitegate House Cloyne, for . . . my young Lady'. The writer was a brother of J. R. Stewart of Stewart & Kincaid. The person whom he described as his 'young Lady' was not young.[4] She was born as Gertrude Blakeney Leon. She wed Robert Uniake Fitzgerald in 1807. Their marriage was childless. Robert's sister married James Penrose, and their daughter Anne married the aforementioned Thomas Stewart in 1855. Through Anne, J. R. Stewart's brother Thomas thereby succeeded to the Mount Blakeney estate in 1855. Gertrude had died *c.*1850. In the 1840s, a close bond between Gertrude Fitzgerald and J. R. Stewart was indicated by the fact that her letters to Stewart & Kincaid were almost always directed to him, whom she usually addressed as 'my dear friend'.

In regard to the Warren family, a Dublin directory for 1848 lists R. B. Warren, Sergeant at Law, at Leeson Street.[5] He was Richard Benson Warren, the person known as Sergeant Warren. J. R. Stewart had married his daughter Martha in 1835;[6] thus, Sergeant Warren was J. R. Stewart's father-in-law. The same directory, but for 1849, lists Robert A. Warren, barrister, at the Leeson Street address, but it does not mention Sergeant Warren, who almost surely had died recently: he was definitely dead by 1852.[7] We can be confident that Robert A. Warren was Sergeant Warren's son.

The Dublin directory for 1849 also lists another Robert Warren, at Rutland Square.[8] This Robert Warren, who was Stewart & Kincaid's solicitor,[9] was almost certainly related to the Warrens of Leeson Street. In 1860 Walford indicated that Robert Warren, Stewart & Kincaid's solicitor, was 'eldest son of the late Robert Warren' of Dublin, 'by Barbera, dau. of Joseph Swan', and that his heir was also named Robert, who had been born in 1820.[10]

Taken together, the above details and those in the supporting notes indicate that the wife of (the late) Robert Warren, senior (the father of Stewart & Kincaid's solicitor), was daughter of Joseph Swan; this Swan was probably related to Graves Swan of the land agency of Stewart & Swan in the 1820s, which had evolved into the firm of Stewart & Kincaid by the 1840s; the Warrens of Leeson Street and the Warrens of Rutland Square were almost surely related; finally, J. R. Stewart had family and/or other close ties with all of the above-mentioned Warrens. The foregoing details again illustrate how family and other social links facilitated expansion of Stewart & Kincaid's business interests in the 1840s.

2 REALLOCATION OF LAND ON THE MOUNT BLAKENEY ESTATE AND THE CASE OF JOHN CALLAGHAN

On the Mount Blakeney estate in the early 1840s, there was some 'pyramiding' in the structure of middlemen: in at least one case there were two middlemen between the head landlord and the ultimate tenants.[11] Stewart & Kincaid decided to remove the middlemen whose leases had expired, and to rationalise the structure of holdings. This meant that the firm could remove undertenants, at least some of whom were compensated for surrendering their land. It seems that most of those who left at the time of squaring had been undertenants to former middlemen.[12] There were also some adjustments in the boundaries of those who were allowed to stay. Thus, on 29 March 1844 James Donnovan, who was hungry for land,[13] wrote to Mrs Fitzgerald that Kincaid had recently been on the estate and that he had 'taken from me the best two acres I had of my former holdings . . . and has given them to my brother' (SK). In order to facilitate squaring among the tenants who were allowed to stay, Stewart & Kincaid insisted that certain tenants would have to compensate other tenants for their transfer of interest in holdings.

In 1844, abatements in rent were granted to some of the tenants on the new holdings: presumably, it was intended that these would partly offset 'restart' costs.[14] In at least one case an ejectment decree, which does not seem to have been executed, was obtained, apparently in order to expedite resettlement on the estate. Thus, on 16 April 1844 John Russell wrote to Stewart & Kincaid: 'I did not think that the costs of ejectment [£13 odd] would be so high' (SK). Russell agreed to pay these costs, and he was allowed to stay on the estate.[15]

A policy of population reduction was recognised among the tenantry early in 1844. On 18 March, John Walsh wrote to Mrs Fitzgerald that he had 'paid twenty five pounds sterl. in advance for that part of Mt Blakeney lately occupied by Michl. Fitzgibbon . . . and most humbly implores your compassion and mercy towards him, and not have him now removed from this place' (SK). On 20 March he sent a similar plea to Stewart & Kincaid, in which he added that both his father and grandfather had been tenants on the estate, and that his land amounted to about five acres. Walsh's letter of 18 March contained an addendum in his support written by his parish priest; that of 20 March contained a similar addendum written by the local Church of Ireland rector. But he was not allowed to stay. On 26 March 1845 Murnane the bailiff wrote to Stewart & Kincaid that 'Walsh gave up the possession immediately without any trouble' (SK).

In at least one case in 1844, a tenant leaving the estate appears to have received assistance to emigrate to America. On 29 April, Michael Bernard, who had surrendered his land and had received money from Stewart & Kincaid, wrote to Stewart & Kincaid that he had 'not words to express my gratitude for your kindness. I have also received the enclosed from C Grunshaw and Co. [passenger agents[16]], Liverpool with whom I had engaged to carry us out.' (SK) He indicated that he did not have enough money to buy clothes, and hoped that Stewart & Kincaid would send him instructions.

In connection with squaring the lands, John Callaghan was most troublesome. Early in 1844 he received £15 from Stewart & Kincaid on the understanding that he would promptly surrender his land. Around the same time,

John Bernard was assigned a portion of Callaghan's land. Furthermore, it was agreed that John Bernard would pay Callaghan £4 for having planted crops there. But by March 1844 Callaghan had changed his mind: he now refused to surrender his farm. On 21 March, Murnane reported to Stewart & Kincaid: 'I got possession from Keefe and Michael Bernard and paid them their money. I gave Bernards part to his brother. . . . Callaghan will not give up the possession. . . . If you send me Walsh [who has already been mentioned above] and Reddy's money I think the[y] will give up.' (SK) Callaghan wrote to Mrs Kincaid, c/o 6 Leinster Street, Dublin, on 24 March: 'I am now deprived of any future hope for my poor wife and six helpless children'. He stated that he 'did not think it imprudent to solicit your Ladyship's intercession on my behalf to Mr Kincaid', and begged Mrs Kincaid to 'say something in my favour' to her husband (SK).

On 31 May, Murnane wrote to Stewart & Kincaid stating that he had arranged settlements with or between certain named tenants; however 'John Callaghan would not settle. . . . Therefore you must follow the ejectment against him' (SK). On 9 August, Murnane reported to Kincaid that 'Callaghan was up with Mrs Fitzgerald this week' (SK). Two days later Callaghan sent Kincaid a petition, which 'Sheweth':

> That . . . petr. went and saw Lady Fitzgerald at Whitegate. . . . Memorialist stated to her Ladyship that the fifteen pounds handed by your honour to Memorialist at the surrendering of his lands that he would now return the same to your honr. . . . Her Ladyship has referred Memorialist to your honrs. consideration. . . . Memorialist most humbly pray yr. honr. will . . . continue Memorialist as tenant. . . . Otherwise Memorialist and six helpless children has no other resource but the workhouse. (SK)

Apart from receiving £15 from Stewart & Kincaid conditional on surrendering his land, Callaghan had agreed to accept £4 from the incoming tenant on part of his land, John Bernard. However, Callaghan refused to allow Bernard to occupy the land assigned to him (Bernard). Bernard therefore sought legal action against Callaghan, who wrote to Kincaid on 11 August 1844: 'Bernard summoned him to Kilmallock Petty Sessions on friday last for malicious trespass, and a second charge for being in dread of killing him and setting fire to his house. But memorialist [Callaghan] was at once acquitted.' (SK)

On 12 August 1844 John Bernard wrote to Stewart & Kincaid: 'I am now ready to pay Callaghan the four pounds that you ordered me to give him', but Callaghan 'has his horse on the land still and positively forbids me to turn my cow on the land' (SK). On 3 September, John Stewart the agriculturalist wrote to Stewart & Kincaid from Mount Blakeney: 'This morning . . . Callahan (that is the man that got £19 for to leave the land) and his brother in law got a party of about 200 men and cut a field of oats and carried it off. Murnane was there & three of the police but they struck the police with stones. . . . They have taken the ringleader & three others of the rioters & 17 police have come since and taken more' (s κ). Although it differed in details, Murnane's report to Stewart & Kincaid on the next day was broadly similar (s κ). A letter from him to Stewart & Kincaid, 27 September 1844, reported that 'John Bernard caut [caught] Callaghan a second time by night taking his oats' (s κ).

On 26 March 1845 Murnane wrote to Stewart & Kincaid that he had just gone to Callaghan and begged of him to surrender possession, but 'Callaghan took a pike in his hand and swore he would run any person that would come near him' (s κ). Little had changed in regard to Callaghan by 12 May, when Murnane reported to Stewart & Kincaid that 'he told me . . . not to dare come inside the farm' (s κ). Callaghan made a further plea to Stewart & Kincaid on the next day when he wrote: 'Is there anything more unfair . . . than to take the part of one man having a large family and whose ancestors have lived on this estate for the last century, and hand it over to another [John Bernard] . . . who has no original claim, save his being a lot holder . . . to the late Thomas White [a middleman]. . . . Leave me my little holding and you shall be honestly repaid what money you gave me.'(s κ)

On 12 June 1845 Mrs Fitzgerald wrote to Stewart & Kincaid about Callaghan, stating that she hoped Stewart & Kincaid would 'conquer him peaceably'. Murnane, however, was soon contemplating more drastic action: on 10 July he wrote to Stewart & Kincaid that 'I think I will be able to have Callaghan in Limerick snug [prison]' (s κ). Upon the receipt of this letter in Dublin on 11 July, Stewart & Kincaid noted on the back of it: 'We wrote to him [Murnane] yesterday on the subject of a compromise with Callaghan' (s κ). Details here are unclear. However, on 10 July, Mrs Fitzgerald's solicitors in Cork City, Colburne and Bennett, had written to Stewart & Kincaid that 'Limerick assizes are fixed for the 17th inst.' and they indicated that Kincaid had 'got up possession from Callaghan' but had 'put him back again' on the land (s κ). On 13 July, Murnane wrote to Stewart & Kincaid, presumably in response to the firm's proposal of a compromise with Callaghan: 'He give no settlement unless he got his crops together with £10–0–0 which of course I would not consent to. I will have him arrested' (s κ). Callaghan was in prison on 16 July, when Murnane wrote to Stewart & Kincaid from Limerick City: 'I lodged Callaghan in the County prison. . . . He told me he would sooner be hanged than settle. . . . I have arrested him [more accurately, had him arrested] in his bed this morning.' (s κ) [17]

The exact charges against Callaghan are unknown. But the plaintiffs did seek an ejectment decree. Maxwell, who attended at Limerick on behalf of Stewart & Kincaid, decided to visit Callaghan in jail, where 'he at last consented to take 15£ and to get his potatoes' in return for quietly giving up possession. It seems that the case against Callaghan was then struck off the list. Although the case does not seem to have gone before the court, the legal costs incurred in July 1845 were at least £14.[18] On 30 July, Mrs Fitzgerald wrote to Stewart & Kincaid that 'although I deeply regret your having had so much trouble with Callaghan . . . you but carried out my wishes in expelling him *quietly*' (SK).

On 7 August 1845 Murnane informed Stewart & Kincaid that he had 'got the possession from John Callaghan and turned every farthings worth belonging to him out off [of] the house and lands and left seven men in care of the place last night.' (SK) On 10 August he wrote to Stewart & Kincaid indicating the state of Callaghan's former lands, as follows:

'2 acres of bad oats, 1½ ditto of potatoes, ½ meaddowing, 3¼ ditto pasture or waist land' (SK).

News of Callaghan's surrender spread quickly. As early as 26 July 1845 Edmond Kelliher, who described himself to Stewart & Kincaid as 'the most solvent tenant on the estate', sought Callaghan's farm. On 31 July, John Bernard wrote to Stewart & Kincaid: 'Some of the tenants . . . are tampering with your Honours respecting Callaghans holdings, which your Honour told me I was to get, when I before paid Callaghan four pounds for the seed and labour for same, besides being watchful day and night. Nothing could induce me to believe any other person would get it.' (SK) But on 10 August, Murnane recommended to Stewart & Kincaid that a person named John Hickey be assigned an acre of Callaghan's farm. Thus, it can only be assumed that John Bernard became tenant on part of Callaghan's land.

Maxwell subsequently indicated sympathy for Callaghan. On 6 December 1845 he wrote to Stewart & Kincaid from Limerick City: 'Stewart [the agriculturalist] hints throughout [a letter received from him] of John Murnane being behaving very ill . . . and states . . . that poor John Callaghan against whom we had to bring ejectments last assizes was put up by Murnane to set the part he did. I trust that Mr Kincaid will be there to investigate the matter and if he is not I shall do my utmost to get at the truth and have already taken active steps at coming at it.' (SK) Callaghan was, however, still on the estate early in 1846, though not as an immediate tenant of Mrs Fitzgerald: on 23 March, Murnane reported to Stewart & Kincaid that 'Callaghan . . . lives in one of John Keeffes cabins' (SK).

3 OTHER PRE-FAMINE DEVELOPMENTS ON MOUNT BLAKENEY

The tenants on the estate usually paid rent in the form of cash. There were also instances in which they paid rent through bank transfers to Stewart & Kincaid. Murnane also used the banking system to remit to Dublin, and Stewart & Kincaid used letters of credit to transfer rental income, dispatched to Dublin, to Mrs Fitzgerald's bank account in Cork City.[19]

The pre-famine Stewart & Kincaid letters do not provide a single example in which we can be certain that an ejectment decree was executed in connection with non-payment of rent on the Mount Blakeney estate. There were several cases of 'voluntary' surrender of land. In a sense, this suited both the tenant (who usually received compensation, and who avoided possible legal costs associated with formal ejectment) and the landlord (who avoided the time and financial costs of obtaining ejectment decrees and of having such decrees executed). Distraint, and placement of keepers on tenants' lands in order to prevent clandestine sale of farm produce, were the usual means of extracting rents due from those in arrears. Thus, on 9 August 1844 Murnane wrote to Stewart & Kincaid: 'Would you advise me to put keepers on Sullivan for crops is near at hand'. On 21 August he reported: 'I distrained Sullivan. . . . He has but two acres of oats. . . . I have . . . liberty to thrash the oats and will go and send to market. . . . I have laid one man by day and two by night [as keepers]. . . . By these means I will be able to get one years rent from him.'. (s k) On 27 September, Murnane wrote to Stewart & Kincaid: 'If you allow me to place two or three keepers on all the defaulters I would be able . . . to send you all the back rents.' (s k) Distraint and placement of keepers in 1844 – a year in which the harvest on the estate was poor – seems to have borne fruit: in January 1845 Stewart & Kincaid transferred £400 to Mrs Fitzgerald's bank account.[20]

On 27 September 1844 Murnane informed Stewart & Kincaid that 'the potatoes are very bad with most of the tenants'. A letter from John and James Keeffe of Thomastown, 28 October 1844, reported 'the total failure of five acres of potatoes. . . . We are . . . sending a Memorial to her Ladyship.' (s k) The Keeffes were not the only tenants who petitioned Mrs Fitzgerald in October 1844. On 30 October she wrote to Kincaid: 'I enclose a letter which I received . . . from Maurice Foley. . . . I am persuaded you will both act *impartially*, and allow the tenants any reasonable indulgence you may think them entitled to. Since I wrote the above I received the accompanying petition from John and James Keefe . . . which I leave to your better judgement.' (s k)

On 12 March 1845 Murnane informed Stewart & Kincaid that he had 'offered to take one quarters rent from the Keffes which the[y] are not able to pay. The[y] have not one single potatoes to put in the ground nor for their own use' (s k). On 13 April he wrote to Stewart & Kincaid that 'the defaulters

on the estate is worse off now. . . . There is no means' (sκ). Thus, following a
partial failure of the potato crop on the Mount Blakeney estate late in 1844,
distress seems to have been severe early in 1845. Because certain tenants in
arrears had no means, an attempt to distrain them would have been pointless.
However, during the summer of 1845 keepers were placed on the lands of some
of those who did have means. For example, on 14 June 1845 Murnane informed
Stewart & Kincaid: 'I put keepers on Duane, James Donovan and the Twohys
for the balance of May 44 [rents]. . . . I have broken up the combination
[against payment of rent] and will be able to remitt a large sum before long.' (sκ)
    Distraint and placement of keepers annoyed tenants, who were obliged to
pay costs. Thus, on 14 June 1845 James Donnovan sent Stewart & Kincaid 'an
Order on the National Bank of Ireland for £13 [odd] being the ballance due of
the last Nov. rent'. He added that there had been 'a Notice served on me by
Mournane stating my being distrained. . . . Mournane has compelled me to
pay six shillings cost. Will your Honors allow such conduct'. (sκ)
    Murnane was correct in his anticipation that placement of keepers early in
June 1845 would speedily yield results. As already indicated, James Donnovan
paid up immediately, and the representatives of 'Joseph Keeff' (to May 1844),
the representatives of 'John Twohy' (to May 1844), as well as 'Jeremiah Keeffe',
paid within two weeks. On 24 July 1845 Stewart & Kincaid sent a letter of
credit for £500 to Mrs Fitzgerald's bank account. [21]
    As crops ripened, Murnane placed keepers on other holdings in the autumn
of 1845. However, there was little danger that the widow Ambrose would be able
to sell her crops clandestinely. On 4 November, Murnane informed Stewart &
Kincaid that he had employed 'a keeper on the widow Ambrose effects as she is
in a dying way. . . . There is two years rent due of her the first of November'.[22]
    The only other interesting developments on the Mount Blakeney estate,
recorded in the Stewart & Kincaid letters of the pre-famine period, are about
improvements. Until the summer of 1845 these consisted of small-scale drainage projects for which tenants were granted allowances against rent. In the
autumn of 1845 John Stewart the agriculturalist was on the estate supervising
repairs to a road. Arthur Vincent came from Shanagolden to inspect it, and on
2 September he wrote to Stewart & Kincaid stating that 'it will be a very great
convenience to the tenants' (sκ).
    Following the poor harvest in 1844, John Stewart was optimistic in regard
to that of 1845. In a letter from Mount Blakeney to Stewart & Kincaid dated 1
September 1845, he stated that 'the crops on this estate are very good' (sκ).
However, in a letter of 10 October to Stewart & Kincaid, the Cork solicitor
Bennett expressed a view that 'the failure of the potatoe . . . will rather militate
against your success in obtaining next March gales from the poorer class of
subtenants' on the estate (sκ).

4 THE YEAR 1846 ON THE MOUNT BLAKENEY ESTATE

Following the partial failure of the potato in the autumn of 1845, many proposals were made for treating the rot. John Stewart thought that keeping potatoes dry and ventilated would prevent further decay. On 26 February 1846 he reported to Stewart & Kincaid that the tenants at Mount Blakeney were 'worse off' than those at Robertstown, and he criticised them for covering potatoes with 'heavy coats of earth' rather than with straw to facilitate ventilation. On 5 December 1845 Mrs Fitzgerald wrote to J. R. Stewart: 'I send you a receipt [recipe] . . . for boiling the diseased potatoes . . . whereby they are rendered perfectly good'. (SK)

The Farmers' Gazette and Journal of Practical Agriculture was published in Dublin every week. Early in 1847 it contained many advertisements offering defence against potato blight. On 1 May 'Two Essays on the Potato, containing the Cause, and Simple Remedies for the Disease' were advertised. Another advertisement in the same issue was for a 'Remedy for the Potato Disease . . . which entirely arrests this terrible national calamity . . . by a scientific application of chemical knowledge'. The latter advertisement, or a variant of it, appeared in every issue of the *Gazette* for 1847 until 31 July, inclusive. Subsequent issues of the *Gazette* in 1847 carried no such marketing. None of the many proposals, advanced in the late 1840s for counteracting the potato rot, had significant effect.

It does not seem that the partial failure of the potato in the autumn of 1845 had much immediate impact on rent receipts from the Mount Blakeney estate. Similar observations have already been made in connection with other estates. In January 1846 Stewart & Kincaid was able to send £500 in the form of half notes to Mrs Fitzgerald's bank account and, using a letter of credit, the firm transferred a further £500 to the same account on 29 July.[23] But in comparison with the same period in 1845, receipts from the estate almost certainly declined in the second half of the year. The Stewart & Kincaid correspondence indicates very few cases of distraint on the estate in 1846. The fact that it contains only one such reference, until the harvest months, possibly reflects a lack of means among those in arrears. In a letter to Stewart & Kincaid dated 23 September, Elizabeth Twohy of Thomastown complained:

There was keepers placed on me by John Murnane . . . with the advice of my co-tenants. I had one load of corn fit for market . . . to buy some provision, to feed myself and my six young fatherless children. But the keepers would not allow me dispose of it and consequently myself and themselves are starving. . . . I am so distressed . . . in consequence of the entire failure of my potatoe crop last year and this year and the expense as well as the loss of burying my husband. . . . I am trusting that your honors kindness will remove the keepers from me and . . . will forgive me the eight pound arrears. (sk)

This letter contains an addendum by David Nagle, PP, confirming 'great distress' of the widow and her family. But it does not seem that the keepers were withdrawn until the rent was paid: on 3 October she sent Stewart & Kincaid 'eight pounds together with a receipt of work for £1[-odd] which . . . makes up my half years rent' (sk). The only subsequent reference to keepers on the estate in 1846 is in a letter of 18 November, in which Murnane informed Stewart & Kincaid that 'Russell . . . is not inclined to pay. . . . If you permit me . . . I will lay keepers on him and . . . he will pay instantly.' (sk)

The Stewart & Kincaid correspondence for 1846 contains no references to ejectment from the estate, and only a single instance of voluntary surrender there. This was the case of John Hickey of Mount Blakeney townland who, on 7 March, informed Stewart & Kincaid:

The time appointed for me to give up that part of Bernard's house which I have occupied some years past is just at hand. . . . I am the father of six helpless children, and have no means whatever to provide the common necessaries of life. . . . Famine is staring me in the face. I have neither clothing for day or night nor even the most remote prospect of a house to shelter my poor family, from the morning of the 25th Inst., as on that day I am fully determined to give up the house. . . . Mr Kincaid . . . had the kindness of holding out some encouragement to me, in the event of my giving up . . . peaceable possession of the house. (sk)

Hickey did receive compensation: On 23 March, Murnane wrote to Stewart & Kincaid that 'Hickey is leaving the estate . . . so you may send me the five pounds and I will not give him one penny until he is off.' (sk)

On the Mount Blakeney estate in 1846, Stewart & Kincaid intervened against market forces in two principal respects: first in the provision of lime and probably seed potato; second, in improvements in the topography of the landscape.

John Stewart the agriculturalist visited Mount Blakeney and Ballinruane in February 1846, and on the 24th of that month he recommended to Stewart & Kincaid that the tenants on those lands should be encouraged 'to draw some lime for to assist the scanty supply of manure' (sk). On 27 March, Mary Hannan in Kilmallock provided him with a tender for supply of £100 worth of lime at 1s 2d per barrel. This represented more than 1,700 barrels of lime. It is probable that the Mount Blakeney tenants obtained the lime on easy terms from Stewart & Kincaid: John Stewart had written from Robertstown to Stewart & Kincaid on 21 March, stating that he knew that many of the tenants on the Mount Blakeney estate 'could not buy 5 barells lime'. He had added the recommendation: 'Let the Mt. Blakeney tenants have lime' (s κ).

On 5 March 1846 Murnane informed Stewart & Kincaid that 'the potatoes are getting very bad. . . . It is . . . feared the seed will fail' (s κ). Letters to Stewart & Kincaid from Vincent, dated 7 and 13 May, considered the question of supplying seed potatoes to the most distressed tenants on the estate. He suggested that either the seed should be supplied gratis, or 'allow it in any work which may be carried on this summer' (s κ). The amount (if any) of seed potato supplied by Stewart & Kincaid is unknown.

John Stewart spent about two weeks on the Mount Blakeney estate in February 1846 'inspecting drains and laying out drains for some of the tenants that are beginning'. He reported to Stewart & Kincaid: 'A good many of the tenants are thro. [thorough] draining and they are doing the work very well'.[24] It seems that they received rent allowances for this labour. On 1 April he informed Stewart & Kincaid that 'most of the drains on Mt. Blakeney are finished by the tenants'; he added, however, that 'the potatoes are going very fast. . . . There is no exception among them. They are all alike bad' (s κ).

A relief committee with responsibility for the Mount Blakeney district was established on 26 April 1846. David Nagle, PP, was treasurer. He solicited subscriptions from local landowners, 'to relieve the awful distress'. In a letter to Mrs Fitzgerald seeking a subscription, he stated: 'The farmers of the parish tho suffering most severely from losses in their potatoes . . . have cheerfully subscribed a cess [tax] of one shilling per acre to meet the present alarming crisis. . . . I request . . . a reply at your earliest convenience, as the government grant will be in proportion to the paid up subscriptions in each locality.'[25] On Mrs Fitzgerald's behalf, Stewart & Kincaid sent Nagle £20 on 6 May. Given the prospect of a very hungry summer, on 13 May 1846 Vincent wrote to Stewart & Kincaid referring to the Mount Blakeney tenants. He ended his letter with the view that provision of employment by Stewart & Kincaid 'will be necessary particularly where it can be found both for the advantage of landlord and tenant' (s κ).

A tenant on the estate named Catherine Blakeney sent Mrs Fitzgerald the following petition on 26 May 1846:

> At a former period, I took the liberty of humbly addressing you through the medium of petition, handed to you by one of my sons. It contained a statement of these distresses peculiar to the forlorn widow to which helpless class it has pleased an . . . omnipotent God to class me. . . . God has added another affliction to these already felt and suffered. He . . . deprived a . . . good son of health. . . . At the period alluded to you had the kindness to make my son a promise that you would . . . remember me in the plenitude of that bounty that distinguishes and exalts you

above the generality of your sex and upon which my poor brother Robert Blakeney
is a pensioner for years back. . . . Humbly beseeching you to whom the helpless
never applied in vain, to remember the widow who has no other anchor. (s κ)

Mrs Fitzgerald forwarded the petition to Stewart & Kincaid. Although it bore
the signatures of two Catholic clergy, there is no evidence of any response
from the firm. However, Mrs Fitzgerald did continue to assist Catherine
Blakeney's brother Robert. In a letter dated 31 March 1847 she instructed
J. R. Stewart to 'please give Robt. Blakeney a couple of pounds *extra* for *this*
year only' (s κ). Why Mrs Fitzgerald gave a pension to Robert Blakeney is
unknown. He may have been a distant blood relative: her full name was
Gertrude *Blakeney* Fitzgerald.

On the Mount Blakeney estate in the summer of 1846, relief works
organised by Stewart & Kincaid commenced around the end of June. On 9
July, John Stewart reported that he had road and river works in progress on the
estate. The workers were paid every two weeks in cash, thereby enabling them
to buy food.[26] The road works were near completion on 27 July, when Stewart
wrote to Stewart & Kincaid: 'I can only employ 10 men from this [date] forward to spread the gravel. . . . It will be a very good road. . . . I have . . . trouble
in turning the men off as every one of the small tenants crowd about me and
says they are entitled to get work' (s κ). Similar examples of overcrowding at
sites of work have been seen in earlier chapters.

The river works on the Mount Blakeney estate, for which the men were
paid about a shilling per day, were completed around mid-August.[27] The
remaining period before the harvest was difficult. In response to a call for rent
payments, Maurice Foley wrote to Stewart & Kincaid on 18 August:

It is too early for you to expect it, as no one here has done any reaping yet, and my
own corn will not be fit for the sickle sooner than 8 or 10 days, but as soon as I reap,
I will begin to thrash and sell . . . and I surely will send up a satisfactory remittance
by the 20th of next month. You cannot . . . think how bare I am . . . after buying
food for a large family for the last 3 months, since my potatoes rotted, and the
prospect before us is worse, as the new crop is failing fast. (s κ)

It seems, during the hungry months of mid-1846, that the Limerick Protestant
Orphan Society assisted destitute Catholics, conditional on their conversion
to Protestantism. The Stewart & Kincaid correspondence contains a letter
dated 21 August 1846 from Godfrey Massey, Vicar of Bruff (about eight miles
from Mount Blakeney) and secretary of the Society, seeking financial aid from
the firm. Some extracts from this letter are as follows:

Permit me . . . to request . . . in behalf of 260 protestant children . . . & of many converts from the Church of Rome . . . under the care of the Limerick Protestant Orphan Society. . . . The Work House affords no or eligible asylum for Protestant children & they must therefore perish or become Romanists.[28] Hence the necessity for the protestant Orphan Society which educates the children in the pure Word of God. . . . For 13 years The Lord has enabled us to maintain this charity. . . . Now that the universal distress of our R. C. fellow country men absorbs all our resources . . . our balance in hands . . . has been exhausted. (SK)

Massey went on to list five 'donations already rec'd' from England, totalling £167. It does not seem that Stewart & Kincaid made any contribution to the Society.

The Stewart & Kincaid correspondence contains no reference to any public works in the Mount Blakeney district during the first nine months of 1846. The almost total failure of the potato in the autumn made such works imperative. On 3 October, Murnane informed Stewart & Kincaid that 'publick works will begin nex[t] week' (SK), and on 18 November he requested Stewart & Kincaid to use influence with the Board of Works in order to obtain 'some respectable situation' for himself on the works (SK).

Destitution in the Mount Blakeney district at the end of 1846 was extreme. On 22 December, David Nagle wrote to Stewart & Kincaid that one of his clergymen was 'in the greatest possible danger of death from a most malignant and contagious fever' (SK). By the end of the year, there was little prospect that rents would be paid. In his last letter in the Stewart & Kincaid correspondence, Murnane reported on 30 December: 'There is no thinking of paying any rent in this country at present. The mob of Charleville [three miles from the estate] is . . . breaking opened the shops and taking away everything' (SK). Murnane died early in 1847. On 31 March, Mrs Fitzgerald wrote to J. R. Stewart: 'Give Murnane's widow the half year's salary, £4, that would have been due to her husband had he lived this month' (SK). Edmond Bourke replaced Murnane as bailiff.

5 THE YEARS 1847 AND 1848: EMIGRATION FROM
THE MOUNT BLAKENEY ESTATE

Much of the Stewart & Kincaid correspondence pertaining to the estate in 1847 and 1848 refers to emigration. It seems that by the spring of 1847 many of the tenants had lost hope for their future if they were to stay in Ireland. Some of them did not therefore take good care of the lands which they held. On 31 March 1847 Mrs Fitzgerald wrote to J. R. Stewart: 'I was glad to hear that you were encouraging the tenants to cultivate their ground, and that you had ordered a turnip sowing barrow for their use. . . . You should enable any of the tenants who wished it to emigrate provided the expense to me would not be very great, & that you thought it would be advantageous to both parties.' (s κ)

Mrs Fitzgerald's finances constrained the extent to which she could assist tenant emigration. Her receipts from Mount Blakeney were probably very small in the spring of 1847. She also depended on the degree of prosperity in the Whitegate/Cloyne district of southeast Cork: she was the beneficiary of a jointure, the financing of which depended on rent receipts there. In the spring of 1847, ability to pay rents in that district depended on programmes of public works. However, on 1 May 1847 Mrs Fitzgerald wrote to Stewart: '400 labourers have been dismissed from the public works in this vicinity and an attack on Cloyne is expected . . . but I suppose they will not do more than take bread from the shops, which happened once already'.[29] Mrs Fitzgerald again wrote to Stewart on 14 August 1847, indicating her financial difficulties:

> I send you an accompanying letter which I received yesterday from some of my tenants [apparently, seeking assistance to emigrate]. Requesting you to act for the best, but at the same time must inform you that I have *not yet* got a farthing of my last half years jointure. Therefore feel almost afraid to incur such an expense *this* year as sending a family to America. . . . I have not heard if you and Mr Kincaid have been successful in collecting my rents, and your silence on the subject makes me fear the worst. I shall thank you to answer the accompanying letter, as I always send such letters to you, besides my not liking to *interfere* between my agents & tenants. (s κ)

A letter from Mrs Fitzgerald to Stewart, 21 August 1847, indicates improvement in her finances. In this she thanked Stewart & Kincaid for receipt of £300 'and your advice respecting the Misses Russell [who sought assistance to go to America], whom I commit to your *discretion*. I have not yet been paid any part of my last half year's jointure, Mr P [Penrose[30]] Fitzgerald [a person related to Gertrude] having found much difficulty in collecting his rents.' (s κ)

The 1847 correspondence on the Mount Blakeney estate contains only one other letter. Again Mrs Fitzgerald had a visit from one of her tenants, and again she asked J. R. Stewart to deal with the matter. Thus, on 7 September she informed him of a visit by a tenant, who 'came here [to Whitegate House] a few days previous, but I would not go to hear his complaint knowing that I should be tormented by them all if I did so' (sκ). She instructed the tenant '*not* to *come* here, but to write if he pleased' and she indicated that she would refer such tenants for Stewart & Kincaid's decision, 'knowing that you would act *justly always*, and *leniently if* you considered the tenant was *really distressed*' (s κ).

One of the earliest letters from the Mount Blakeney estate in 1848 was from Mary Sullivan, an undertenant. Dated 15 March and addressed to Mrs Fitzgerald, it stated that 'Memorialist her two sons and one daughter were lying in sickness for the last six months when it pleased the Almighty God to take her daughter aged fifteen. . . . Memorialist has no way of supporting her two sons . . . and rather than put them in the poor house Memorialist most humbly prays your Ladyship may take them into your Ladyships school' (s κ). Mrs Fitzgerald did support education at Whitegate.[31] In effect, Mary Sullivan wanted her to provide for her sons' maintenance. Mrs Fitzgerald forwarded the letter to Stewart on 20 March 1848. In her accompanying letter from Whitegate House she mentioned that 'Mrs Sullivan . . . wants me to admit her two sons into my school. . . . Let her know that if I had one at Mount Blakeney she would be welcome to send them to it, but that I could not undertake the care of them here.' The same letter contained details of three sisters who sought assistance to emigrate. Thus, Mrs Fitzgerald's letter of 20 March continued:

> Miss Russel arrived, to say that you & Mr Kincaid had signified your intention of enabling *two* of her sisters to emigrate to America, and that there is a third sister *most exceedingly anxious* to accompany them, that she wants nothing but her passage money (Miss R said it was £5) and that if you approved of it her brother [presumably, the tenant on the Mount Blakeney estate named John Russell mentioned earlier] would *advance* it, provided you allowed him to deduct *half* from the *next* payment he makes of his rent, & the remainder the *payment after*. Please write by return of post as Miss R said that the packet is to sail for Dublin on Monday & that she & her two sisters (the 2 that are going to America & the one that wants to go) will come down to me from Cork on Saturday to know your decision. (s κ)

This letter was written on a Monday. The fact that the Russell sisters hoped to leave Cork one week later indicates the speed with which emigrants were willing to leave. Similar examples have been noted earlier.

Two of the Russell sisters seem to have left Cork, en route to America, close to the date which they had planned for their departure. They were probably content with whatever assistance they received from Stewart & Kincaid on behalf of Mrs Fitzgerald who, on 27 March 1848, informed Stewart: 'I have just had a second visit from *Miss Russell* the *elder*, & one of her sisters, they are well satisfied now with your decision, as a relative of theirs has taken the 3rd sister to reside with her. You will smile when I deliver a message from the elder Miss R, namely to request that you will desire the physician on board the ship in which her sisters are going to America, to take particular care of the eldest of the two as her health is delicate.' (s κ)

On 8 March 1848, Stewart wrote to Kincaid: 'I must send Sankey [an
employee of Stewart & Kincaid] to spend a week on Mt Blakeney & Sergt
Warrens estates as there are . . . emigrants to be got off & Haberes to execute'
(sk). The reference to Haberes strongly suggests that there were some ejectments on the Fitzgerald and/or Warren estates in 1848. The emigration of
the Russell sisters was not an isolated event: in the spring of 1848 Stewart &
Kincaid organised programmes of emigration from the two estates in south
Limerick.

On 18 March 1848 Stewart wrote to Kincaid: 'Sankey getting out a lot of
the Mt Blakeney people, but it will cost a good deal' (sk). Two days earlier,
Sankey had reported to Stewart:

> I went . . . to Mt Blakeney yesterday and reserved my visit to Mr Saunders' farm
> until today when I think he will accompany me and see that the tenants [Saunders'
> undertenants on Thomastown] give proper possession. John Bernard and his wife
> are ready to go but want 30/- for clothes. They certainly are very poor and must get
> some assistance. . . . David Fitzgibbon is anxious to go but his wife being in the
> family way he will not be ready to start for 6 weeks. He will require some money
> for clothing as he and his family (in all 4) are naked. . . . I next visited Finns and saw
> Thomas' family in all 7. I offered £10 on the part of Mrs Fitzgerald if the brothers
> would give the balance . . . of cost of sending them out. They seem ready to assist
> but I fear when the cost of clothing be added, that £40 will hardly cover all. . . . I
> think I may increase Mrs F's donation to £15. . . . As the 2 [Keeffe] families number
> 14 it will take about £70 to send them out. . . . Money must be given for clothing
> but I think a small sum in this way will induce many to go. (sk)

On 17 March 1848 Sankey informed Stewart & Kincaid that he was
'surrounded by emigrants'; that he had arranged with the 'Keeffes to go . . . to
Dublin to be shipped to America';[32] that he had 'arranged with the Finns to
give me Bills for £25 towards sending their brother out, Mrs F to bear the
balance of expense'; that 'the Mahonys will not be ready till Tuesday week so
that the only ones leaving this now are the 2 Fitzgibbons, J Bernard and family
and the Ambroses' (sk). Within the Stewart & Kincaid correspondence, the last
letter requesting Stewart & Kincaid for assistance to emigrate from the Mount
Blakeney estate is dated 4 April 1848. Written by Thomas Sullivan, it states:

> Tho it is a grievous thing to leave the land of my birth . . . I have determined to
> leave this ill fated country but fear I have not the means of doing so without your
> generous assistance. I am ready to hand you over your lands provided you give me
> assistance. My family consists of seven children myself and wife . . . and of course
> we could not be pennyless on landing in a strange country. . . . My farm is well

circumstanced with a comfortable house near an acre cropped with barley and wheat and near three acres prepared fit for oats and the rest for potatoes. (s k)

Issues of compassion aside, it seems that the thinning of the population on the estate in 1848 was part of a programme of improvements. On 15 March, Stewart & Kincaid applied to the Board of Works for a loan of £700 to finance improvements on the estate. Towards the end of the year the Board sanctioned the loan, only a small proportion of which was spent in 1848.[33] In other respects, progress on Mount Blakeney in the second half of 1848 was slow. Stewart & Kincaid encountered difficulties in finding solvent tenants on lands which had badly deteriorated. On 10 June, Sankey reported to Stewart & Kincaid that a new tenant named Bennett 'has already put a new face on the Keeffes farm. In another year it will be all right again. He intends writing about J Bernards and Moloneys[34] lots which are quite run out. If you could get him to give £2 p. acre by offering some allowance towards putting the land in heart it would be the best. At present it is not worth 30/- p. a.' (s k)

J. R. Stewart was not optimistic when he visited the estate late in 1848. On 13 December he wrote to Kincaid: 'I fear Russel [Russell] & Foly [Foley] will not stand [solvently] but I hesitate in forcing them away while land is so depressed. . . . Bennett declares he would not give the rent he does for Keeffes if now to be let.' Thus, developments on the Mount Blakeney estate in 1847 and 1848 were in many respects similar to those on other estates under Stewart & Kincaid's management. The foregoing sections have mentioned the names of several tenants on the Mount Blakeney estate in the 1840s. Griffith's *Valuation* indicates that few of them were there in 1851.[35] Among those still there were Henry Bennett, who then held 173 statute acres.

6 THE BALLINRUANE ESTATE, 1845–8

The Stewart & Kincaid correspondence pertaining to Sergeant Warren's townlands near Ballingarry is relatively sparse. It contains no letters dated before January 1845, very few for 1847, and ends with a letter of December 1848. Many of the tenants on the Ballinruane estate were very poor. On 24 February 1845, Vincent wrote to J. R. Stewart that 'a large portion of them are run to the lowest ebb of poverty' (s k). On Warren's behalf, Stewart & Kincaid made subscriptions to two dispensaries which his tenants attended.[36]

Improvements

In January 1845 John Stewart went to Ballinruane and reported that he 'never saw such exhausted lands' and that he 'met all the tenants together and gave them a lecture on the utility of thorough draining and on the use of lime'.[37] He recommended that Stewart & Kincaid should give the lime free of charge. Stewart & Kincaid responded quickly: on 24 February, Vincent informed J. R. Stewart that he had 'agreed this day with one of the Rathkeale lime-burners for 500 barrels @ 9*d* per [barrel]. . . . The barrel contains 42 imperial gallons'. It seems that the tenants did get the lime free of charge: in the same letter, Vincent stated that he thought the Ballinruane tenants 'with few exceptions unable to bear the cost' (SK).

Following John Stewart's recommendations, some of the tenants on Ballinruane worked on drainage in the spring of 1845. In his letter of 24 February to J. R. Stewart, Vincent wrote that 'those tenants who intend to drain asked me for crows and picks and a few sledges. I said I would ask you to allow me get them a few, at their paying half price' (SK). Further drainage was conducted by tenants late in 1845. They were remunerated through rent allowances. In a letter to Stewart & Kincaid, 10 February 1846, Vincent mentioned three tenants who had 'a good deal of drains made which when surveyed by [John] Stewart will amount to more than their balance due' (SK). On 24 February, John Stewart wrote to Stewart & Kincaid that the Ballinruane tenants wished 'to know if they will get lime this year'. He added: 'If they do get it . . . give a greater allowance [of lime] to the tenants who have thoro. drained most'. Stewart & Kincaid did provide them with a fresh supply of lime in the spring of 1846.[38]

On 1 April 1846 John Stewart wrote to Stewart & Kincaid that the tenants on the Ballinruane estate were 'in a very bad way with potatoe rot', and he added that 'it would be a charity to do something for them in the way of giving them employment. There is a river along the bottom of that estate that wants to be sunk' (i.e. to have its bed deepened) (SK). Stewart & Kincaid's major project providing employment on the estate during the summer of 1846 was the sinking and straightening of the 'Ballyruane River'.[39] This involved access to lands of contiguous estates, for which the tenants on those lands were compensated. On 9 July, Stewart wrote to Stewart & Kincaid: 'I have some days a 108 men at work. . . . I am oblige[d] to employ more men than I want so as to be allowed [to trespass] to cut off the short turns on the river' (SK). The labourers on the river works were paid in cash.[40] The river work was near completion by mid-August 1846, when Stewart explained to Stewart & Kincaid that its final cost would be a little above his original estimate, partly because 'Warrens tenants forced themselves into the work both old and young and showed me a letter from Sergt. Warren promising them support and the fact is they should be supported or they would starve and I am afraid that they will be as bad next year for the potatoes are beginning to look very bad'.[41] On 24 September, Vincent sent Stewart & Kincaid a summary of the work on the river during the summer, stating: 'I consider it a work of the greatest benefit to the property and not only to Sergeant Warrens' but also to neighbouring lands. He indicated that about two miles of river work had been completed, at a cost of about £100, and he remarked that low lands 'which have hitherto been perfect swamps . . . will now if drained become . . . most valuable' (s k).

The Stewart & Kincaid correspondence provides no indications of improvements organised by the firm on the Ballinruane estate after the autumn of 1846. The correspondence for 1847 pertaining to the estate is very sparse, and much of what survives for 1848, a year at the end of which J. R. Stewart reported that 'the Ballingarry Estate is in a most wretched state',[42] pertains to emigration. Some improvements (drainage, buildings and fencing) were implemented by tenants during the summer of 1848. Recall that on behalf of each of the landlords, whose estates have hitherto been investigated in detail, during 1847–8 Stewart & Kincaid applied to the Board of Works for a loan, or loans, to finance improvements. The correspondence provides no evidence that the firm sought such a loan on Sergeant Warren's behalf. But he was probably dead by the end of 1848.

Rent collection and distress on the Ballinruane estate

On 1 July 1845, Vincent wrote to Kincaid: 'If you have a list of the Ballyroan defaulters made out send it to me as Friday [next] will be the fair day of Ballingarry' (s k). On 25 July he wrote to Kincaid: 'Dont be disappointed about the Ballyroan tenants as you know they are very generally poor, and they made great promises . . . until harvest when I expect they will meet us better'. He added that he had recently received £20 odd from four tenants on the estate (s k).

On 12 November 1845 Vincent informed Stewart & Kincaid that he feared that the potato crop on Ballinruane 'will turn out as bad as in all other quarters where the lumper is the kind chiefly planted' (s k). It has been seen in earlier chapters that the partial failure of the potato in the autumn of 1845 had little immediate effect on rent payments from other estates managed by Stewart & Kincaid. The same kind of lags may have also applied on the Ballinruane estate: on 15 November, Vincent sent Stewart & Kincaid first half notes for £165 received from the tenants there. In the accompanying letter, he mentioned the name of only one tenant on the estate 'who did not come in with his balance' (s K). However, the rents had not been otherwise fully paid up: in a communication to Stewart & Kincaid dated 27 December, he referred to defaulters on Ballinruane and asked: 'How do you wish I should proceed against those who are so deep in arrear as I fear we will not find enough of means on the land if we go to distrain' (s K).

On 7 January 1846 Vincent sent Stewart & Kincaid £59 odd in cash received from the Ballinruane tenants. He informed the firm that: 'The defaulters begged time until the 7th of February the fair day of Rathkeale. . . . Collins has paid more than his land made as he was obliged to give a large abatement to his conacre tenants in consequence of the disease' (s K). This reference to Collins is the first clear indication that the partial failure of the potato in the autumn of 1845 was beginning to have an effect on rent receipts on the Ballinruane estate. It has earlier been observed that middlemen tended to be early casualties of the failure.

On 10 February 1846 Vincent was able to send Stewart & Kincaid £57 odd in cash, which sum he had just received from the Ballinruane tenants. In an accompanying letter, he indicated that he did 'not see any chance we have of getting much more out of them as they are I am sure keeping up some of their money fearing a scarcity . . . as the potatoes are every day rotting' (s K). Properties of some tenants on the estate were distrained within the few days which followed. It can therefore be inferred that the potato failure of 1845 began to have a serious impact on rent receipts on Ballinruane in the spring of 1846 – as was also the case on other estates already investigated.

During the summer of 1846 some of the Ballinruane tenants complained to Stewart & Kincaid in regard to the operations of the local relief committee. The secretary of that committee responded in a letter to Stewart & Kincaid: 'We grant tickets, entitling the holders to purchase . . . meal at our depot, to a certain amount according to the number of individuals in each family, at a rate per lb. *considerably under* first cost. . . . Such tickets are confined to the destitute'. He added: 'To *all other* parties we sell the meal in *any* quantities at the rate of 1*s*/9*d* per st., being a fraction over the first-cost, carriage etc.'[43]

The river works in Ballinruane during the summer of 1846 helped some tenants to pay rent arrears. However, those works were largely completed by mid-August. They were not immediately offset by public works. The almost total failure of the potato in the autumn of 1846 greatly accentuated the existing crisis, which Warren tried to abate: on 26 September, J. R. Stewart observed to Kincaid: 'Sergt. Warren is willing to forgive the quarters rent – I wish we had the other ¾ '(s K).

Vincent was not optimistic late in 1846. On 2 October he went to Kilmihil in order to ask the tenants there to sign promissory notes for their rents. Back at Shanagolden that night, he wrote to Stewart & Kincaid stating that the

Kilmihil tenants 'told me if I delayed coming until tomorrow when a public meeting takes place they could not answer for their own lives or mine if it was known they consented to sign Bills for rent. Mr Gubbins [the Rev. George Gubbins of Ballingarry] also told me the same.' Vincent also referred to the prospect of public works in the Ballingarry district, and rates of pay thereon. Thus, he continued:

> Mr Devonport [?] had a great escape of his life at a meeting on Monday last as it was reported he said 8*d* per day was enough to pay labourers. The[y] overpowered the police to get hold of him and were it not for [certain named gentlemen] nothing could have saved his life. *But he never* said so. An adjourned meeting takes place tomorrow for the purpose of arranging some works which is expected to be very turbulent. The dragoons & soldiers are ordered out. . . . Several [public] works are expected to open immediately which will give only partial relief which if they are only to get 8*d* per hire . . . will drive them to madness. . . . How can the widow with a helpless family *subsist*. How can an aged man with a family unable to earn their hire and himself infirm get on. . . . How can a man of 8 or 9 in family support his charge on 8*d* per day. (s k)

It seems that Warren's tenants obtained little employment on the public works which commenced in the Ballingarry district late in 1846.[44] On 24 October, Vincent informed Stewart & Kincaid: 'I hear even the liberality of Sergeant Warren [in waiving one quarter's rent] will not bring them forward' to pay. On the next day he reported to Stewart & Kincaid: 'I have written to notice the Kilmihil tenants to meet me in Ballingarry [to pay rent]. . . . There have been two large meetings of the people in Askeaton [less than ten miles from Ballingarry] within the last week. The bakers shops have been plundered of all bread.' (s k)

Vincent's 'notice' to meet him with their rents frightened the Kilmihil tenants, and on 4 November ten of them signed a petition addressed to Warren at Leeson Street in Dublin: 'We . . . have passed our [promissory] notes, payable on the 18th Nov Inst. . . . Our provision has been gone from us, our familys solely dependent on the portion of corn which we now have. Want and destitution day after day threatens us. . . . Help us in this time of distress and calamity by not looking after the amt of the aforesaid notes.' Warren forwarded the petition to Stewart & Kincaid. Around the time at which Stewart & Kincaid received it, J. R. Stewart wrote to Gubbins in Ballingarry, seeking information. In his reply to Stewart & Kincaid dated 9 November 1846, Gubbins informed them: 'We expect to have a company of infantry placed here. Provisions are so high now farmers are frightened to part with their corn.' (s k)

Vincent was in a giddy mood on 6 November when he wrote to Stewart &
Kincaid: 'I am just going up [to Ballinruane] to meet the boys there. . . . I fear
my purse will not be very heavy returning.' (sk) He reported to Stewart &
Kincaid on the following day: 'I returned . . . without receiving *one shilling*.
The tenants are in such fear of famine that they will not sell their small store
of oats'. He added: 'I told them if they showed an inclination to pay . . . , their
landlord was inclined to carry on works on his property and send meal for their
support but from their not making any payments I could not recommend
them. . . . They begged I would make no bad report of them until after the fair
of Rathkeale the 18th of this month.' (sk)

It is clear from the petition which the Kilmihil tenants had addressed
to Warren, that the promissory notes which they had signed were due for
payment on 18 November. A few of them did pay in full on that date. Vincent
allowed others to renew their notes, and by the end of 1846 most of the
Kilmihil tenants had paid the full amounts which they had promised.[45] Such
payments exposed them to great dangers in 1847: following the potato failure
of the autumn of 1846, by what means could they be expected to acquire food
in the months which followed?

Departures from the Ballinruane estate

Some holdings on the estate were vacant during the summer of 1847. This may
have been through death, 'voluntary' emigration, or formal ejectment. Stewart
& Kincaid organised a programme of emigration from the estate in 1847: in a
letter to Kincaid dated 4 May of that year, J. R. Stewart wrote that he feared
that 'we shall have to pay the increased rate [of transatlantic passage] for Sergt
Warrens people' (sk). In at least one case, Stewart & Kincaid showed sympathy
towards a tenant against whom an ejectment decree had been obtained. Thus,
on 1 June 1847 J. R. Stewart wrote the following letter, to be brought by a
tenant who had come to Dublin from the estate, to Warren in Leeson Street:

> The Bearer Michl. Fitzgerald is one of your tenants in Ballyroan under ejectment
> who foolishly came up to Dublin about his farm. . . . He is rather a decent
> industrious man & were he clear from law cost [presumably incurred in defence of
> ejectment] & from his brothers & sisters I dare say he would be able to pay up the
> rent. . . . The rest of the family will not be easily induced to go to America. . . . I
> should be glad if you would see him. . . . With respect to Jas. Guiry . . . , I heard . . .
> that he made opposition to Quiltys getting the 19 acres given up by his father in
> law, but we have the Habere ready to issue & perhaps when he finds that he may
> withdraw his opposition. I would be very glad they would also go to America. (sk)

The Stewart & Kincaid correspondence pertaining to the Ballinruane estate in 1845–6 mentions three tenants named Guiry (Michael, Patrick and James). In the *Valuation* of 1852, only one of those Guirys – Michael on about 50 acres – is listed as a tenant on the estate of the late Sergeant Warren.[46] The same listings omit the aforementioned Michael Fitzgerald. It is therefore inferred that each of those missing names had left the estate by 1852. The same volume of the *Valuation* indicates that John Quilty was then a tenant on Ballinruane townland.

It is likely, in 1847, that the firm of Stewart & Kincaid was selective in reallocating lands which had become vacant on the estate: Stewart & Kincaid wanted solvent tenants, not merely tenants. Letters dated 7 and 23 June 1847 from two local farmers (not Warren tenants) offered £1–5–0 per acre for the lands of a former tenant on Ballinruane townland.[47] The *Valuation* of 1852 omits these names in its listings of tenants on the estate.

Departures from the estate continued in 1848. John Scollard was one of the tenants on Kilmihil who had signed promissory notes for payment of rent in November 1846. By 24 November he had made partial payment of £10. He renewed his note for the balance, to be paid on 10 December.[48] But it seems that he was one of three tenants on Kilmihil whose notes were not fully settled by 26 December 1846,[49] and that Stewart & Kincaid subsequently had him imprisoned for non-payment of debt. On 7 March 1848 he solicited Stewart & Kincaid's 'goodness for mercy . . . as I am now come out of goal. . . . By giving me liberty to carry on business I do promise to satisfy your demands. . . . By giving me another trial [as tenant] I hope I will follow the rules of my ancestors who lived in Kilmihil these 70 years past . . . until they left me the oldest of five orphans'. In the same communication, Scollard indicated that he saw 'by the ejectment' against him that Stewart & Kincaid claimed that he was £85 in arrears. But Scollard argued that he owed Stewart & Kincaid only £42 odd, which was, nevertheless, a substantial sum (s k).

On 14 March 1848 Scollard wrote to Stewart & Kincaid that he would 'give you up the possession of my part of the lands of Kilmihil by your assisting me and family in going to America. . . . I would wish to prepare for the first of April, in procuring some clothes' (s k). Stewart & Kincaid's response was favourable. This may be regarded as surprising, in view of the extent of Scollard's debt to the firm. However, Stewart & Kincaid recognised that 'chasing losses' did not make commercial sense. On 22 March, Scollard informed Stewart & Kincaid: 'I have made up my mind with Mr Sankey . . . to go to America. . . . He told me that you would not give us any clothing until we would go to Dublin. We are to[o] naked and we could not leave home without the clothing', but he hoped that his family would be 'redy from the 10th to the 12th of April if we get the clothing and some cost' (s k). This letter was signed by John, Edmond, William and Eliza Scollard.

On 22 March 1848 Sankey wrote to Stewart & Kincaid stating that 'David Dunworth [of the Ballinruane estate] has been with me begging to be sent to America. I offered to send 6 of his family' (s κ). Sankey's letters make no further reference to him until 14 June 1848, when Sankey wrote to Stewart: 'I know he wants me to send out 6 of his family which will cost £35 and then I calculate £10 for James Dunworth & his wife. Shall I do this?' (s κ)

Sankey was on the Ballinruane estate on 23 March 1848, when he received possession from Patrick Guiry and from some other tenants. In a letter of that date to Stewart & Kincaid, he reported: 'I know not whether you will think I have gone too far but when I looked over his [Patrick Guiry's] farm and saw the good state it is in at present I settled on giving him £40 and £10 to Brosnaghan'. He also indicated: 'Fitzgeralds gave up quietly and I have arranged with Michl. [apparently, the person who had visited Stewart & Kincaid in Dublin in June 1847, and who, in Stewart's words, was then "under ejectment"] in case he does not go to America that he is only to get £20. His brother Patt will not go so I gave him £8 and £5 settled the two cottiers'.[50] In the same letter of 23 March 1848, Sankey added: 'I understand that many good men are on the lookout' for Patrick Guiry's farm (s κ). A letter from Sankey on the next day indicates that he had agreed to pay £10 each to two tenants when they surrendered their holdings.[51] Possession was obtained from other tenants on the estate, who received compensation, later in 1848.[52]

Most of the tenants on the Ballinruane estate in 1845–6 seem to have died or left by the end of 1848. This is inferred from the following considerations: First we know, on behalf of the landlords throughout Ireland whom Stewart & Kincaid represented, that the firm engaged in large-scale programmes of assisted emigration in 1847–8, and that such assistance must have been on a much smaller scale thereafter. Secondly, the Stewart & Kincaid correspondence on the Ballinruane estate lists the names of about fifty tenants on the lands of Sergeant Warren, mainly in 1845–6. It is probable that these included almost all those heads of households who were immediate tenants to Warren. The Griffith *Valuation* indicates that only about nine of them were still on the estate in 1852.[53]

It has been seen that there were major changes in the composition of the tenantry on the Ballinruane estate between 1845 and late 1848. However, it was not the case that all of those on the estate in the autumn of 1848 promptly paid their rents. On 12 September 1848 Sankey informed Stewart: 'I have put keepers on several of the Kilmihil tenants as I found they were carrying away the crops as fast as they could cut them' (s κ). One of the final letters in the Stewart & Kincaid correspondence on the Ballinruane estate is dated 14 September 1848, when Sankey indicated to Stewart & Kincaid that the bailiff on the estate intended to distrain.

7 CONCLUDING OBSERVATIONS ON THE MOUNT
BLAKENEY AND BALLINRUANE ESTATES

It has been seen in earlier chapters that the partners in Stewart & Kincaid, as well as proprietors whom Stewart & Kincaid represented, were regarded by the tenantry as paternal figures. Tenants thus sometimes asked Stewart & Kincaid to use influence in order to secure employment, for themselves or their relatives, off the estates. The schoolmaster at Cliffoney in Sligo, referred to in chapter 2 (see p. 39 above), felt obliged to write to Lord Palmerston, explaining the circumstances of his daughter's marriage. It was seen in section 5 above that a tenant on the Mount Blakeney estate asked Mrs Fitzgerald to take her two sons into her school at Whitegate. In earlier chapters, instances have been cited in which a tenant asked Stewart & Kincaid or the landlord to intervene in family disputes. Only one case of such a request is recorded in the correspondence on the two estates investigated in the present chapter. This is in a letter dated 27 November 1846, to Kincaid from the widow Margaret Keeffe of Thomastown on the Mount Blakeney estate, in which she reminded him: 'When you were here about twelve months past I made a complaint to you of my son James who has given nothing to his sister although his father charged his part of the farm with £10 for her use. You then was pleased to desire me to try and get her married and that you would make him pay the money his father left her by his will, namely the £10 above mentioned.' She added that she 'did get' the daughter married to a son of another tenant; however, 'James did not give her one shilling, nor has he done so since'. She therefore expected that Kincaid would 'make him act justly towards her' (s k). Kincaid's response is not known.

The material surveyed in the present chapter yields the following conclusions.

Both Mrs Fitzgerald and Sergeant Warren were caring landowners who sought to improve their estates. They sought such improvements for two reasons: from the standpoint of their own self-interest, and because works of improvement gave employment to distressed tenants. Works of improvement enabled tenants to buy food. But it is also recognised that they also enabled some tenants to pay rents which would not otherwise have been forthcoming; thus, by means of productive works, landowners recouped some of what they spent, not only in the long run, but also in the short run.

Mrs Fitzgerald and Sergeant Warren received petitions from tenants. They usually passed these on to Stewart & Kincaid. Mrs Fitzgerald, however, indicated that although the ultimate decisions in regard to such petitions should generally be at Stewart & Kincaid's discretion, she expected her agents to be fair and caring to those in genuine distress. It may have been in response to petitions, or in response to pressure from his son-in-law J. R. Stewart, that Sergeant Warren waived one quarter's rent following the potato failure of 1846.

One of the tenants against whom an ejectment decree had been obtained (but not executed) came to Dublin to plead his case to Stewart & Kincaid. His journey involved a round trip of about 300 miles. J. R. Stewart expressed sympathy for him and asked Warren to talk to him. At Whitegate House in southeast Cork, Gertrude Fitzgerald had several visits from tenants on her Mount Blakeney estate. These involved round trips of over 100 miles. She actually refused to meet some of these supplicants. This may seem harsh, but she feared setting precedence which would lead to much pestering, with aggrieved or distressed tenants arriving at unexpected times.

Many ejectment decrees were obtained against tenants on the Mount Blakeney and Ballinruane estates during 1845–8. It seems, however, that few (if any) of them were terminally executed. On behalf of Mrs Fitzgerald and Sergeant Warren, Stewart & Kincaid sought to thin the populations of those estates, especially in 1847–8 when solvent tenants were wanted. The firm sought to persuade the financially weaker tenants peacefully to surrender their holdings. Most of them received financial incentives to leave. Compensation often involved payment of a family's passage to America along with sums for purchase of clothing. In some cases tenants themselves asked to be sent to America. Instances have been cited in which the financial packages offered by Stewart & Kincaid seem to have been surprisingly generous. In regard to the treatment of the tenants on the Mount Blakeney and Ballinruane estates, neither Stewart & Kincaid, nor Mrs Fitzgerald, nor Sergeant Warren, fit the caricatures often portrayed of Irish landowners or their agents in the 1840s.

TWELVE

THE FRANKFORT ESTATES IN KILKENNY AND CARLOW

—

I INTRODUCTION

Lodge-Raymond de Montmorency, second Viscount Frankfort, was born in 1806.[1] In 1876 he owned 636 statute acres in Carlow, 1,045 acres in Cavan and over 4,600 acres in Kilkenny.[2] The Stewart & Kincaid correspondence contains only six letters from him, each of them from England. They indicate that he was ignorant of the extent of distress throughout the famine years. The Frankforts were absentees who resided in England.[3] Stewart & Kincaid commenced as the Viscount's agent in Ireland in the early 1840s. The correspondence contains little on the Cavan estate.[4] On Frankfort's behalf, in 1846 Stewart & Kincaid contributed to the dispensary at Freshford, County Kilkenny, and sent at least £10 for relief of the poor on his Rathrush estate in County Carlow.[5] See map 8.

On 24 November 1843 Stewart wrote to Kincaid: 'Frankfort is becoming as oblivious in matters of business as he is insane in other matters' (sk). Stewart & Kincaid were aware of Frankfort's idiosyncrasies when they first agreed to act as his agent; however, Stewart emphasised that personality should not be confused with business. On 13 January 1841 he wrote to Kincaid: 'You were quite right to accept Lord Frankfort [as a client]. I would far rather be agent to a *particular* man or even an *odd* man than a *distressed* one.' (sk)

Frankfort's largest property was in the townland of Coolcullen near Castlecomer in Kilkenny. He owned almost all of the 3,234 statute acres there.[6] His interest in Coolcullen derived from his marriage in 1835 to the heir to the property.[7] In 1844–8, his local agent there was Major Diamond, who was also one of his tenants. At a salary of £25 per annum,[8] Diamond had been one of Frankfort's agents on Coolcullen for some time prior to Stewart & Kincaid's commencement of the agency. A person named Devereaux also acted on Frankfort's behalf on Coolcullen up to the early 1840s.

223

2 MURDER AND OTHER ACTS OF VIOLENCE ON COOLCULLEN

Among rural townlands in the south of Ireland, a striking feature of Coolcullen in the 1840s was the large number of Protestant tenant farmers. Some of these families came in the early eighteenth century; others arrived from County Wexford around 1800.[9] Traces of their former presence in Coolcullen are easily found. There are some fine period houses, and a Church of Ireland place of worship, Mothel parish church. Opposite the former rectory there is a thoroughfare called Protestant Road, on which Prospect Hall was the home of William Tyndall, who was almost certainly a grandfather of the famous scientist John Tyndall, FRS (1820–93).[10] Today the decline in the Protestant population is reflected in the fact that only about 15 persons attend Sunday services at Mothel.[11]

Coolcullen was subject to violence in the 1840s. The most serious case was the murder of Matthew Brennan in 1844. Along with his brother, he had in the early 1840s taken a holding previously occupied by Thomas Purcell who had been ejected. It seems that this ejectment was executed very shortly before Stewart & Kincaid commenced the Frankfort agency. In the Stewart & Kincaid correspondence, the earliest mention of the murder is in a letter to Stewart & Kincaid from Matthew's brother Michael dated 26 November 1844. The letter complained that 'the murder was plotted' locally at the house of Michael Purcell, brother of the ejected Thomas; that the locals knew 'the guilt of the parties' but would not give evidence to convict them on account of 'the bad feeling of the majority of the tenants . . . whose native sympathy is for the assassins'; that 'very few attended the funeral'; that 'the demons rejoice'; that he did not believe that 'their thirst for blood is yet satisfied' as he heard 'trets daily'; that 'the land is under continual trespass' and that he could not go there (from his residence which seems to have been at the boundary between Coolcullen and County Carlow) 'without the police under the sneers of every person I meet'; that the matter did not seem to bother Frankfort (SK).

Where the Brennan brothers had originally come from is uncertain. That they had not hailed from some other part of Coolcullen is suggested by Michael's observation, in the same letter of 26 November 1844, that 'the courpse [corpse] was delayed in Coolcullen for one night'. Furthermore, the fact that the letter is postmarked Leighlinbridge rather than Castlecomer suggests that they may have originated in County Carlow. The murder of Matthew Brennan, who was sickle-slashed, is remembered in the folklore of Coolcullen. However, although some locals can point out the location of Michael Brennan's house, and exactly where the murder of Matthew took place, it seems that nobody in the district knows when the murder was committed – it was merely 'a long time ago'.[12]

Background to the enmity against the Brennans is revealed in a letter sent to Stewart & Kincaid on 1 October 1845 by Thomas Purcell, who, in about 1840, had been ejected from his holding on Coolcullen 'by the late agent Mr Devereaux'. In this letter Thomas referred to

that farm in Coolcullen out of which Mr Devereaux ejected me, at which time my father lay on his death bed, being . . . worn out with age. He was then dragged from his bed, and laid on the dunghill. . . . Death relieved him of his suffering. . . . My father . . . settled his children leaving me . . . the Coolcullen farm. . . . My [subsequent] arrears were not more than that of very many of my neighbours . . . some of which were ejected . . . as well as me, but they were allowed compensation for the improvements they made, while . . . I received no allowance whatsoever. But Mr Devereaux held out the promise of giving the land to me again. . . . After Brenan got possession of my land, Mr Devereaux . . . requested of Brenan to give up the land to me. . . . My request of you is that you will . . . do me justice in restoring to me my farm. . . . If not, I request of you to give it . . . to another tenant which I will propose. (SK)

Note that these complaints of the evicted tenant, Thomas Purcell, were dated October 1845, and that this was close to a year after Michael Brennan (in his letter of 26 November 1844) had informed Stewart & Kincaid that 'the four Purcells were together the night before the murder at Michael Purcells house' and that they were implicated in the murder. The essence of Thomas Purcell's letter was that if the lands were not to be returned to him, then they must not be left in Brennan's hands. This reveals a sense of hatred, or merely local unity against aliens who sought to rent land which had previously been held by a local who had been ejected. But Michael Brennan's problems did not end with his brother's murder.

The fact that one of the Purcells – Michael – held land which was surrounded by Brennan's holding (the former holding of Thomas Purcell) accentuated enmities between Brennan and the Purcells, and led to further confrontations. On 14 December 1844 Diamond wrote to Stewart & Kincaid stating that Michael Brennan (who was not yet residing on the holding under dispute) had recently complained: 'He lost a two year heiffer in value about £6 off his farm. . . . He also states that his fence is thrown down [and] gates thrown open & broken. [He] can get no man to herd on the farm. He says if Michl. Purcell is allowed to live as he is in the centre of his lands he cannot hold the farm as it was in his house that the murderers of his brother lodged the night before. . . . [They] are daily lurking after his own life' (SK). Diamond's suspicions on the identity of the murderers were similar to those asserted by Brennan. Diamond also saw that Frankfort's authority might be undermined

if intimidation or murder were tolerated. On 31 December 1844 he wrote to
Stewart & Kincaid:

> Respecting the murder of Mattw. Brenan . . . the parties concerned are well known
> to all in our neighberhood and are *backed* by manny on the estate. . . . It is reported
> that Ed. Holbrook made an offer to you of ten shillings per acre of Willoughbys
> bog and he is in great *fier* of his person on account of such report, as Samuel
> Willoughby is in the habit of keeping lowar *company*. . . . Serve Ml. Purcell with a
> notice [to quit]. . . . It will show your determination to support Ml. Brenan and to
> maintain Lord Frankforts rights. . . . I do not go out without being prepared to
> meet friend or *foe*. . . . Ml. Brenan has got a gun and has a police man with him
> when he visits his farm. (s к)

On 8 January 1845 Diamond wrote to Stewart & Kincaid that the police
sergeant at Coolcullen had taken Patrick Purcell to Castlecomer where, when
'Capt Roberts [Justice of the Peace[13]] read his inditement, Purcell fainted'.
Diamond added that 'Patk. Purcell is lodget in Kilkenny goel for the murder
of Mattw. Brenan' (s к). On the following day Diamond informed Kincaid
that 'Ml. Brenan had engaged a man to herd . . . his farm and before the man
came he was served with a notice not to go on pain of his life, the figure of a
coffin on the notice and marked with blood.' (s к)

Two people – Patrick Purcell and a 'servant boy' – were arrested in connection with the murder. Kilkenny solicitor John Maher was anxious to obtain
convictions but Frankfort's lack of interest disgusted him. Like Diamond,
Maher saw that such indifference was contrary to Frankfort's interests. On 7
February 1845 Maher informed Stewart & Kincaid: 'I wrote a very strong
letter, to Lord Frankfort, about this murder. . . . The tenantry, seeing Lord
Frankfort takes no notice of it . . . are glad it occurred in the hopes that no one
else will interfere with ground, if they should refuse to pay rent.' (s к) In a
communication dated 16 February to Stewart & Kincaid, Maher observed
that 'Frankfort has not answered my letter' (s к). On 28 February he expressed
his frustration to Stewart & Kincaid: 'Roberts . . . has being doing all man
could do, to get information, but when persons see the Lord of the soil, indif-
ferent, to such cold blooded murder . . . they all become the same. . . . Roberts
has the two men in custody, who committed the murder, but none of the 9
men, that were looking on, will speak.' (s к) Unwillingness of witnesses to give
evidence led to abandonment of the case. On 4 March 1845 Maher wrote to
Stewart & Kincaid: 'Roberts was obliged to discharge Purcell, and the other
prisoner, charged with the murder' (s к).

Michael Brennan again had problems with one of the Purcells during the
summer of 1845. As Brennan's holding surrounded that of Michael Purcell,

this led to conflict in regard to access. Thus, on 12 May, Diamond reported to Stewart & Kincaid:

> Ml. Purcell summoned Brenan to cort for not allowing him to pass through the midst of that field [Brennan's holding] that Mtt. Brenan was murdered in. Ml. Brenan summoned me and I took him to an aturney and asked him to have it left to an arbitration. . . . Mr Gordon [an important tenant] was named by Purcell and I by Brenan. . . . We could not agree and called John Comerford [another tenant] who . . . said that he was in fier to speak his mind freely and beged leave. (s k)

Both Brennan and Purcell swore that they would abide by any decision which the arbitrators, Diamond and Gordon, might ultimately reach. On 26 May, Diamond informed Stewart & Kincaid: 'We allowed Purcell to take his manure through that field that Mat Brenan was murdered in through a part that was not ploughed. . . . [But] when Purcell came to draw his manure he took it through the potato land and not in the place we apointed regardless of his oath' (s k).

At the end of May 1845 Brennan had not yet moved into the house on his holding, but he intended to do so soon. Fear for his life meant that he wanted police protection, which Stewart & Kincaid seem to have arranged. Thus Diamond, in his letter of 26 May 1845 to Stewart & Kincaid, continued: 'Brennan has not got his house in full repair to live in it yet but will in a few days. He was very thankful to you for your goodness to him. He has spoke to Capt. Roberts who will send the police. . . . Roberts also told him to summons Purcell for the breach he made in breaking his oath.' (s k) What happened next is indicated in a letter from Brennan to Stewart & Kincaid, 30 July 1845, in which he reported:

> Some time since I took the liberty of writing to you . . . of my intention to live here [on the holding once occupied by Thomas Purcell] . . . I have two police with me. . . . I have to find them only with fuel and candle light. . . . As to the difference with Purcel it was arranged by the magistrates that he should not trespass on my land again but he . . . continued to do so, for which he was fined or in default thereof to go to jail for one month which he chosed and on tomorrow he returns home. Two of his brothers are . . . employed by John Clear on my bounds. . . . The police and me are apprehensive of an attack from them. (s k)

The Stewart & Kincaid correspondence provides no more references to intimidation against Michael Brennan, who was apparently on the estate in 1850.[14] As already indicated, both Diamond and Maher feared that Frankfort's indifference to the murder, and the failure to convict, would weaken his authority and that of his agents. This seems in fact to have been the case. Thus, on 1 September 1846 Diamond reported to Stewart & Kincaid: 'Last night [a] son to James Comerford came to me for arms to protect his fathers house & I gave him three pistols loaded' (sκ). In November 1848 the Stewart & Kincaid employee Matthew Sankey wrote that he hoped that Diamond's 'fears for his personal safety are only imaginary'. Earlier in the same year (1848) William Sherriff, another Stewart & Kincaid employee, had written from Coolcullen: 'I was but a short time here when I was led to think the tennantry . . . were regularly combined against . . . rents. . . . Since the murder of Brenan, at which revolting deed many of them still rejoice, they seem to think Coolcullen their own'.[15] It seems that Stewart & Kincaid removed some of the Purcells in 1848, when Frankfort wrote to Stewart & Kincaid on 21 March: 'I assent to your recommendaytion for giving £50 to get rid of them' (sκ). The *Valuation* of 1850 lists two Purcells on Coolcullen. They were William and Michael. The latter was probably the person with whom Michael Brennan had been in conflict.

3 OTHER DEVELOPMENTS ON COOLCULLEN
Improvements

In the Stewart & Kincaid correspondence, the earliest letters from Diamond date from the summer of 1844. Their main concerns were assignment of turf banks to the tenantry and repair of bog roads. Diamond reported that some of the tenants were cutting as much turf as possible, not only for their own use, but also for sale. However, with rent payments in mind, on 3 July he wrote to Stewart & Kincaid: 'If you are pleased to allow the tennants to sell turf this season all will go well' (sκ). Improvements on Coolcullen in 1844 were negligible.

Early in 1845 Stewart & Kincaid sent William Cathro, an agriculturalist, to the estate. He stayed for three months, supervising small-scale drainage works. On 15 January he wrote to Stewart & Kincaid: 'I have been through most of the ground but I find it in a very bad steat [state] with water' (sκ). The implements for drainage were sent by Stewart & Kincaid and were given on loan to the tenants, who received work allowances in their rents.[16] Diamond was worried that some of them might be stolen. On 29 January he informed Stewart & Kincaid: 'I am troubled verry much by a grope . . . that lives near the bog. All thieves & beggers' (sκ). Some implements were missing a few months later, when Diamond wrote to Stewart & Kincaid: 'I have went through the tenantry and cannot make out all the draining tools'. In August he reported to Stewart & Kincaid: 'There was four picks given out that I could get no account of'.[17]

Apart from drainage, Cathro also sought improvements in the crops sown by tenants. On 7 February 1845 he wrote to Stewart & Kincaid: 'I have proposed to the tenants that I would get an early kind of oats for them. . . . I wrote to Mr Drummond [seedsman in Dublin] about them' (SK). Cathro had turned his attention to turnips by 10 March, when he wrote to Stewart & Kincaid: 'The tenants . . . have all promised to sow turnips. I have got a box made for them that will sow turnips for them very handy. It is impossible for them to farm there [their] land [properly] as they have nothing to work it with. . . . I hope you will allow them turnip seed from Dublin' (SK). Early in April, Diamond reported that 'Cathro [is] now making ready to go [off from Coolcullen] and he asked me to say something of him. . . . He knows his business well'.[18]

During the summer and early autumn of 1845 Diamond supervised roadworks on bogs as well as small-scale drainage. It seems that the tenants were still remunerated for labour by means of rent allowances.[19] However, following the failure of the potato in the autumn of 1845, men working on a private road were paid in cash. Early in November they were paid ten pence per day.[20]

Cathro returned to Coolcullen, for a few months, in March 1846. One of his main tasks was construction of useful roads. At the beginning of May the workers hired by him were paid one shilling per day. On 22 March Cathro wrote to Stewart & Kincaid that most of the tenants 'will sow turnips if you incurage them by sending down seed. . . . Send down the quicks [for hedgerows] as fast as possible' (SK).

Cathro left Coolcullen, and the private road works were suspended, in July 1846.[21] The Stewart & Kincaid correspondence does not reveal why the works were stopped at a time when they were needed most. But it may have been the case that Frankfort felt that he could not afford such works. It does not seem that any works were in progress on Coolcullen during the last five months of 1846. Thus, distress was extreme in the weeks immediately before the usual period for harvesting, and following the potato failure. Around the time of the cessation of private road works during the summer of 1846, the Rev. Richard Graves of Mothel rectory had written to Stewart & Kincaid 'on behalf of the tenants and labourers on Lord Frankfort's estate', requesting that those useful works be recommenced.[22] On 5 October, Samuel Gordon, one of Frankfort's most important tenants, wrote to Stewart & Kincaid: 'Public works can be had for Coolcullen . . . if timely application be made by proper agents. . . . It is therefore hoped you will not disregard this important business, and if such grant be obtained, . . . a continuation of the line of road made last summer by Mr Cathro . . . would open a communication thro' some hundred acres now nearly barran for want of means of improvement' (firstly, access) (SK). On 17 October 1846 Graves informed Stewart & Kincaid that 'a sum of twenty thousand pounds was presented [i.e. proposed] at the [presentment] sessions of Castlecomer, yesterday, for the purposes of drainage and other agricultural improvements, in addition to a very large sum for public roads'. He continued: 'You are aware of the steps to be taken by each proprietor, to avail himself of the benefit of this presentment. . . . Your application should be made as soon as possible.'(sk) On 2 December 1846 Gordon wrote to Stewart & Kincaid: 'Distress prevails here to such extreme that my neighbours came to me for work and if I did not give employment . . . intimating [that they] would take my cattle. . . . I am forced to employ to make drains. . . . We have lost some fowl and most likely, [they] shall take our cattle as they have already done to our neighbours. . . . We have not yet been nor likely to be favoured with [public works] employment.' (sk) Another important tenant, James Woodcock, wrote to Stewart & Kincaid on 26 December:

> There will be an extraordinary presentment sessions held in Castlecomer on the 31st. . . . You should deem it prudent to present to move at the same sessions for the drainage of the land, which of course would benefit the landlord & tenant, and also the unemployed who are on the verge of starvation. . . . They are not tolerated to work out of the townland, being opposed by other labourers, and as there has been no public work commenced here yet, property is not save [safe]. . . . It is therefore requisite that public works be presented for at the ensuing sessions to avert this impending danger. . . . Those works may prove of very little benefit to the land-holders, who are to feel the smart [i.e. cost] of it by & by. . . . Drainage is what will prove advantageous. . . . I have been influenced by the feeling of humanity to give money out of my pocket every day to prevent persons from falling victims to hunger. (sk)

From the foregoing, in the autumn and early winter of 1846 (a period in which no private works of significance were in progress on the estate), it seems that Stewart & Kincaid failed to press for publicly financed works on Coolcullen. This may have been because Frankfort was concerned about the property tax implications of public works, if they were to be implemented.

The Stewart & Kincaid letters provide no evidence of improvements on Coolcullen in 1847. But the year which followed probably saw more improvements on the estate than in any earlier year. William Sherriff came in 1848 to supervise those works, which were completed in September. On 19 February he wrote to Stewart & Kincaid about the neglected state of Coolcullen: 'I was quite ignorant of the wretched state of misery and privation of both labourers and occupiers. . . . Never have I . . . witnessed the existence of such a state of neglect and want of improvement as the entire of Coolcullen.' (sk) At first, Sherriff found difficulty in hiring labour. This he attributed to combination, and to the adverse effects of outdoor relief on incentives. On 12 February 1848 he reported to Stewart & Kincaid: 'I cant get enough of labourers to do the work. There is employment for 50 men at present. Several of them tryed it, and when they found that they could not get money without working hard for it, walked off. . . . I will give notice to the person who gives out the relief money to give no more to any one in Coolcullen.' (SK) A week later Sherriff informed Stewart & Kincaid that he had 'got the combination broken up completely. . . . At first I was inclined to think that the cause of the labourers not pressing on to the work proceded from a lazy disposition, but I now find . . . they are . . . good labourers.'[23]

The improvements on Coolcullen in 1848 consisted of drainage and subsoiling. They were financed mainly by a government loan of £550. But the extent of the work should be placed in context. There were over 3,200 acres in Coolcullen, and Frankfort owned almost all of them. The sum spent – about £570 – probably had an overall impact that was not substantial. The Board of Works inspector allowed from £3 15s 0d to £4 11s 0d per acre of improved (mainly drained) land.[24] Thus, not much more than 150 acres of Coolcullen could have been *directly* affected by the improvements of 1848.

Rent receipts

The *Valuation* of 1850 lists the names of about 70 of Frankfort's tenants on Coolcullen.[25] Many of those names appear in the correspondence of 1844–8. The letters contain no references to distraint on Coolcullen. Until 1848, they provide no evidence that Stewart & Kincaid ejected any tenant from the townland.

On 2 June 1845 Diamond wrote to Stewart & Kincaid: 'You may not expect . . . good payments in future from manny of the tenantry for . . . manny would wish to run further in arrears, as the[y] say that there is an act to pass for no tenant to be evicted' (SK). On 12 June he reported: 'I visited everry house on the estate and told those who did not pay me what the[y] might expect' (SK). On 18 June he informed Stewart & Kincaid: 'I will do all I can to get the rents but I am of opinion that I will get but littel until the piggs and butter is selling'. He was optimistic on 14 August when he wrote that 'the tennants are all prepairing to pay their rents. . . . Potatoes never looked so well since I came to this country' (SK). But on 23 September he reported to Stewart & Kincaid that 'the potatoes are in many places blasted' (SK).

In mid-December 1845 Diamond informed Stewart & Kincaid that he would 'meet the tennants in Kilkenny [City] as they come home from the fair of Bennets Bridge and will send in all the rent'.[26] The potato failure of the autumn of 1845 began to have a significant impact on rent receipts in the first half of 1846. This is apparent in the earliest letter from Frankfort in the Stewart & Kincaid correspondence. On 2 July 1846 he wrote to Stewart & Kincaid: 'I am . . . short of money and find you have made but two remittances on the 2 of Feb & 27 of April. . . . Remitt as soon as possible & make good the regular periodical two monthly remittances' (sk). The decline in rent receipts, which had become obvious by mid-1846, probably explains why the private works, supervised by Cathro on Coolcullen, were abruptly suspended in July 1846. This was presumably in response to instructions from Frankfort. On 5 August 1846 Diamond reported to Stewart & Kincaid: 'Our potatoe crops are almost all distroyed' (sk). Rent receipts further deteriorated following the potato failure of 1846. On 24 September, Frankfort complained to Stewart & Kincaid: 'The usual remittances for this year have all been long after the periods agreed. . . . Also they have fallen short of the averages of last year' (sk). On 10 November 1846 Stewart & Kincaid informed Frankfort: 'We have very recently been on your estates in Cavan and Kilkenny & . . . in both the rents were very badly paid. This time twelve month we got in Kilkenny £800 this time only £300' (sk). On 12 November, Frankfort responded by asserting that 'the tenants must not be allowed to humbug – it is only the poorest that are suffering & that not so bad as is stated.' (sk) Thus, his Lordship did not understand what was happening in Ireland.

On 9 September 1848 Sankey wrote to Stewart & Kincaid: 'With respect to the 3 tenants in Coolcullen against whom we have ejectment decrees, I do not think any of them will be able to hold & would therefore advise your giving them the following sums: Mrs Clear £15, Ja's Brennan £10, Peter Quirk £10' (sk). Neither James Brennan nor Peter Quirk are listed as tenants to Frankfort on Coolcullen in the *Valuation* of 1850. It does, however, list a person named Anne Clear on the estate. That Peter Quirk was in fact ejected is indicated in a letter to Stewart & Kincaid dated 6 November 1848 from the Rev. Delany, Catholic curate responsible for Coolcullen, who wrote as follows:

> I am directed by the Rev Mich'l Birch . . . to request of you to inform him thro me, if Quirk . . . who had been lately put out by the sheriff, would have any chance of his land again by paying up all arrears & cost of ejectment process. Quirk has stated that he proffered the money required by a Mr Sankey & that he still w'd not be allowed to continue the possession. . . . Mr Birch is not inclined to believe him tho he produced a slip of writing . . . requiring the sum of 9£ 19s 3d. It appears to us that there must be *more* arrears due, as Viscount Frankfort & you his agents enjoy (from the *industrious* portion of the tenantry . . .) the character of humane . . . gentlemen. (sk)

Calculations entered on this letter, following its arrival in Dublin, suggest that at the time of his ejectment Quirk was almost £22 in arrears. The letter also suggests that any tenants ejected from Coolcullen during the late famine years were in substantial arrears, and were not considered viable in the long run.

On 7 November 1848 Sankey wrote to Stewart & Kincaid: 'I think that Dimond should try & make those who are now left as caretakers leave the estate and pay the money agreed upon [as compensation]. The case of Shirley . . . should also be considered. . . . Unless his rent is reduced he has determined to leave. . . . Being a Protestant & a respectable man he should be encouraged [to stay]' (sk).

At least one important tenant on Coolcullen, Samuel Gordon, was in serious difficulties early in 1849, when Stewart wrote to Kincaid: 'Get rid of old Gordon or come to some settlement with him'.[27] The *Valuation* of 1850 indicates that Gordon was then still a tenant to Frankfort, on 61 acres in Coolcullen.

The Stewart & Kincaid correspondence contains only two references to emigration from Coolcullen. On 27 March 1846 Diamond informed Stewart & Kincaid that 'Leary says that he will go to America' (sk). The *Valuation* lists no person named Leary on the estate in 1850. On 13 May 1847 Stewart wrote to Kincaid: 'Has Major Diamond ever reported if Crowe will give up and go to America. If not we should eject him.' (sk) This passage indicates that 'voluntary' surrender of tenure, combined with financial assistance to emigrate, were not independent of a decision to seek ejectment. No tenant named Crowe is listed on Coolcullen in the *Valuation* of 1850.

4 OTHER FRANKFORT PROPERTIES IN KILKENNY AND THOSE IN CARLOW

Apart from Coolcullen, Frankfort owned properties in Kilkenny City and County. He owned buildings in the city as well as land at Keatingstown, a couple of miles to the north.

Keatingstown is 733 statute acres in extent. In 1845, and at a salary of £12 per annum, Mark Shearman was the local agent on the townland.[28] He was assisted by his son Robert, who became local agent in 1847 or 1848. One of the earliest letters in the Stewart & Kincaid correspondence, which appears to pertain to Keatingstown, refers to an attempt to obtain an ejectment decree against a middleman. In this letter of 28 July 1845, John Maher reported: 'I sent you a newspaper, where the report of the tryal of this ejectment was reported of Lord Frankfort against Costello. . . . One service of the copy of the ejectment [was rated] to be bad, because, the person served was a sister of one of the undertenants, and as she was served outside the dwelling house, and

Shearman not been able to swear whether the woman resided in the house or not, the barrister . . . held the service . . . to be bad.' (s κ)

On 5 October 1846 Sankey informed Stewart & Kincaid that 'several of the Keatingstown men asked if you would allow for drains as they intend spending their time at that work having no potatoes to dig. . . . A large number of labourers collected in Kilkenny [City] on Friday demanding work.' (s κ)

The Shearmans experienced severe distress during the famine. On 23 November 1846 Robert Shearman wrote to Stewart & Kincaid requesting use of influence at the Board of Works 'for me to get employment . . . as one of the clerks or gangers on any of the roads here as I am totally idle' (s κ). On 16 December he informed Stewart & Kincaid: 'My father and family are in great want. . . . Unless gentlemen your so kind as to send some relief to us or a quarters salary [in advance] we must starve.' (s κ) Stewart & Kincaid immediately sent £3 to Mark Shearman. On 20 December he wrote to Stewart & Kincaid expressing his thanks. In the same letter, he stated that his son Robert had just obtained employment as an overseer on the public works. In this context too, he thanked Stewart & Kincaid. How long Robert Shearman was employed on the public works is unknown. They ceased early in 1847.

On 7 April 1848 Robert Shearman wrote to Stewart & Kincaid stating that he had '3 quarters of an acre of lands without crops. I trust you will consider me & assist me with a quarters salary for provision and seed. . . . I am totally idle . . . not earning one shilling but depending on a small salary.' (s κ) Stewart & Kincaid quickly responded by sending the Shearmans £1 to purchase seed. On 12 April the Shearmans explained to Stewart & Kincaid that this money would have to be used to buy food for the family 'consisting of seven', some of whom 'had to forfeit their clothes to get food' (s κ). A further letter to Stewart & Kincaid, dated 19 April, requested advance payment of 'the quarters salary to the 1st August' in order to enable the Shearmans 'to get some seed potatoes' (s κ). Stewart & Kincaid's response is unknown. However, it seems that Robert Shearman did survive the famine. The *Valuation* of 1849 lists him as a tenant to Frankfort on Keatingstown.

There was some distraint on Keatingstown in 1847. Thus, on 1 September 1847 Robert Shearman reported to Stewart & Kincaid: 'I send you an inventory of the stock & crops destrained on 30th . . . : James Houghrahan [Hourigan], 2 cows, 1 heifer & 27 stacks of wheat . . . , 12 stacks of oats. . . . John Bergin, 9 cows of grazing stock which were removed on the night of the 31st' (s κ). Both Hourigan and Bergin are listed as tenants on Keatingstown in the *Valuation* of 1849. Properties of at least one of Frankfort's tenants on Keatingstown, and of at least one in Kilkenny City, were distrained in 1848.[29]

Some ejectment decrees against tenants on Keatingstown were obtained in 1848. Whether they were executed is unknown. In one case an attempt to obtain a decree again failed on a technicality. On 12 July 1848 Robert Shearman wrote to Stewart & Kincaid: 'The process cases went on well here. . . . All were decreed. Except Lawrence Nearys. . . . On his attorny producing all his mothers receipts . . . the barrister on this dismissed the process on the grounds that he was not the real tenant but his mother which is dead since March last. He . . . boasts now that he will not pay a penny rent out of this [year's] crop. So what is to be done now. He has 2 cows, 2 horses & 5 pigs, besides 3 acres of wheat & 4 of oats' (sk). On 16 September 1848 Robert Shearman informed Stewart & Kincaid: 'I have distrained Lawrence Nearys property' (sk). It seems that Neary managed to remain on the estate: he is listed on Keatingstown in the *Valuation* of 1849.

There was some emigration from Keatingstown in 1848. In February, Robert Shearman wrote to Stewart & Kincaid that 'John Kavanagh . . . & Patt Campion is . . . going to America. Kavanagh is offered 40£ for his good will & Campion is offered 80'.[30] On 14 August, Shearman informed Stewart & Kincaid that Campion and his family had left the estate (sk). On 25 September, Shearman reported to Stewart & Kincaid: 'Kavanagh has given me possession of his land. . . . He has scarce as much as will pay his passage' (sk). It is not known whether Campion or Kavanagh received assistance from Stewart & Kincaid to emigrate. Nobody of those names was a tenant to Frankfort on Keatingstown in 1849.

In County Carlow, Frankfort owned about 630 statute acres at Rathrush.[31] A person named James Brennan was Stewart & Kincaid's representative in the county. In the mid-1840s, John and Sylvester Coughlan, Thomas Kinsella, and the Rev. William Kinsella were Frankfort tenants on Rathrush. Thomas Kinsella sent his rent to Dublin by means of letters of credit. Brothers John and Sylvester Coughlan, who also sent rent to Dublin through letters of credit, were substantial farmers.[32] Letters from November 1841 to February 1843 indicate that the Coughlans' payments were in arrears throughout that period.[33] Stewart & Kincaid therefore distrained some of their property. On 13 February 1843 Brennan wrote to Stewart & Kincaid: 'I reached Silvester Coughlins . . . about nine o'clock this day. [I] caught them taking away about 24 barrels of threshed oats, which I stopt. . . . I enclose you a copy of the seizure. . . . I have two men on [as keepers]. . . . Coughlin says there is an arrear . . . totalling £263' (sk). The following is the inventory of goods distrained:

1 Cow and calf his own property. Value	£4– 0s–0d
2 grazing cows	.8– 0–0
4 horses	.12– 0–0
1 Large pit of potatoes	.10– 0–0
1 Large heap of dung	.5– 0–0
1 Heap of threshed oats in barn about 24 bs [barrels]	.10– 0 -0
2 Stacks of barley about 30 bs	.15– 0 -0
2 Stack of oats about 30 bs	.15– 0 -0
1 Winnowing machine	.1– 0–0
1 Large cock of hay	.4– 0–0
Household furnitures.	.1– 0–0
10 Small pits of potatoes belonging to tenants	.5– 0 -0
1 Cow and heiffer belonging to tenants.	.6– 0–0
30 geese	.1–10–0
2 Cars and several other small articles	.2– 0–0
	99–10–0

It can be seen that the distraint involved seizure, not only of Coughlan assets, but also some of those of their undertenants. The Coughlans were expected to pay costs, including those of keepers. On 2 March 1843 Sylvester Coughlan requested Stewart & Kincaid to 'be kind enough to interfere in having the costs attending the seizure as reasonable as possible' (s k).

James Brennan sometimes sent Kincaid a hamper of butter.[34] He expected reciprocation. As will be indicated below, when Brennan was sent to prison in 1845, he sought Stewart & Kincaid to use influence to secure his release. The background to his imprisonment involved a dispute between Brennan and John and Sylvester Coughlan on the one side, and their younger brothers and a sister on the other side. Brennan disapproved of the younger Coughlans. On 18 August 1843 he wrote to Stewart & Kincaid: 'Silvester Coughlins three brothers namely Richard, Owen, and Francis and their sister all remains in part [of Rathrush House, where it seems that Sylvester also resided] locked up by day and out by night. . . . They must be removed, as they do not attempt to do anything to support them' (s k).

In 1844 the three younger Coughlan brothers took legal action against James Brennan and their two older brothers, John and Sylvester. The following is an account from the Tullow petty sessions, 31 August 1844, as reported in *The Carlow Sentinel* at the beginning of September:[35]

The defendants were summoned by complaints for taking forcible possession of a part of the mansion house of Rathrush[36]. . . . It appeared that old Mr. Sylvester Coughlan (the father of the Coughlans before the court) held . . . part of the lands of Rathrush . . .; that by lease, in 1832, he sublet a portion of said lands to his two sons, the complainants, Richard and Francis . . . and they (the complainants) continued in possession of the land until 1839. Old Mr. Coughlan died in 1835, and upon his death his two sons John and Sylvester became possessed of the residue of the farm not leased to the complainants; these two defendants allowed their portion of the lands to go in arrear, the consequence of which was an ejectment brought by the head landlord for the recovery of the possession of the entire farm . . . , and in 1839 the ejectment was put into force by the defendant, James Brennan, sheriff's bailiff; and after the possession of the house and lands were taken from all the brothers (the Coughlans) by the direction of the agent of the head landlord, the complainants and their sister . . . were allowed to . . . go back into the possession of a portion of the dwelling-house . . . until . . . the 23rd of August last, when Brennan, with a troop of his bailiffs . . . rushed into the apartments occupied by the complainants, and in the most savage manner assaulted complainants, drove them out . . . and still retains forcible and illegal possession. . . . Brennan and his party . . . are to be tried for the forcible entry, and assault.

On 8 January 1845 Brennan wrote to Stewart & Kincaid from prison in Carlow town: 'The [younger] Coughlins swore all before them yesterday. . . . They would not take any money. Revenge they wanted. I am sentenced to two months. . . . But the young lads [Coughlans] are a terrible set. I hope you can get me turned out [from prison] by your interest . . . with the Lord Lieutenant. . . . I am only indighted for a common assault. Richard Coughlin swore I hit him' (s k).

Stewart & Kincaid had offered the younger Coughlans £20 to leave and Sylvester had offered them furniture.[37] On 11 January 1845 Brennan informed Kincaid: 'They [John and Sylvester] have kept out all the brothers and sister and never will let them in again' (s k).

The four younger Coughlans felt that the sentence of two months' imprisonment was insufficient revenge. They wrote to the Lord Lieutenant complaining that the governor of Carlow prison was treating Brennan too lightly.[38] Brennan used various means to try to secure his early release. On 15 January 1845 he prepared a petition addressed to Henry Hutton, assistant barrister for County Carlow, 'emploaring and beeseeching that you would . . . take his case in your consideration and either shorten my duration in this painful prison or recommend me to . . . the Lord Lieutenant that he may look with compassion on me and grant me my liberty.' (s k) Brennan sent the petition to Kincaid: he requested Kincaid to deliver it to Hutton in Dublin.[39] Brennan prepared another petition, which he sent or gave to Henry Bruen, MP for County Carlow. According to Brennan on 15 January, Bruen agreed to send it to the Lord Lieutenant along with his own favourable recommendation.[40]

On 22 January, Brennan wrote to Kincaid: 'I hope you will do all you can for me at the Castle [in Dublin]'. The Stewart & Kincaid correspondence provides no evidence that Brennan's attempts to use 'influence' secured an early release from jail.

During the summer of 1845 Brennan was again in court in a case involving the younger Coughlans. On 8 July he informed Kincaid: 'This day I have succeeded against the three young Coughlins. . . . and I was honourably acquited. And the three young Coughlins proved perjerous. . . . John and Silvester and all my party proved loyal and true to me. . . . They will be well able for the next rent now they are quite clear of the night walking robbers.' (s k)

John and Sylvester Coughlan were still on Rathrush late in 1846. However, their problems increased as the famine progressed. In the Stewart & Kincaid correspondence, Sylvester's last letter is dated 1 October 1846. He is not listed as a tenant to Frankfort in the *Valuation* of 1852. It may be the case that he went to America in 1849, or he may have died by then. On 29 January of that year, Stewart wrote to Kincaid: '[Sylvester or John?] Coughlan has not taken defence, so press Reeves [a solicitor] to get out the Habere [to execute eject-ment]. . . . I offered to assist him out to America but he rejected the offer' (s k). The *Valuation* indicates that John had left the estate by 1852. It does, however, list him as renting 118 acres on a nearby townland.

Apart from the Coughlans, there were at least two other tenants to Frankfort – Thomas Kinsella and the Rev. William Kinsella – on Rathrush in the 1840s. In 1852 Thomas held 185 acres of the Frankfort lands at Rathrush.[41] One of his descendants resides in Rathrush House today.[42] William Kinsella was a Catholic priest. He resided at Rathrush House. In the early 1840s he farmed many acres of Frankfort land: his annual rent was £173.[43] He appears to have been consistently punctual in payment. It also seems that he was an improving tenant. Thus, on 22 August 1845 he wrote from Rathrush to Stewart & Kincaid: 'I left a paper at your office some time back, stating the expense I had in draining some of this land. You kindly promised to lay it before Vis. Frankford. . . . Is he inclined to encourage such improvements on his estate.' (s k) This passage suggests that William Kinsella had a long lease, that he had engaged in drainage, and that he now sought aid from his landlord in order to finance more drainage.

On 17 July 1842 William Kinsella wrote to Kincaid 'hoping you would induce Lord Frankford to subscribe to our fund for the relief of the poor' (s k). Whether Frankfort made the subscription is unknown. However, on 6 June 1846 Kinsella wrote to Stewart & Kincaid acknowledging receipt of a 'liberal donation of £10 for the poor of Rathrush' (s k). The *Valuation* lists him as occupier of 296 acres of Frankfort lands on Rathrush in 1852. A plaque in the

Catholic church at Rathoe observes of him as follows: 'He laboured . . . in this parish for 52 years the last 43 of which he was parish priest'.

5 JANE TYNDALL, HER SON JACOB, AND JOHN TYNDALL, FRS

In 1844 and for most of 1845, the widow Jane Tyndall, a Protestant, lived at Leighlinbridge, County Carlow. There is no evidence, in the Stewart & Kincaid correspondence or in the *Valuations*, that Frankfort owned property in Leighlinbridge. But his lands of Coolcullen were only about five miles to the west of Leighlinbridge. Jane Tyndall was in receipt of an annuity from Frankfort – £20 per annum, payable on the 25th of the month at the end of each quarter. The Stewart & Kincaid correspondence does not reveal the reasons for this pension. But it seems that Jane's late husband had been a tenant on Frankfort's Coolcullen.

On 23 February 1845 (a Sunday) she wrote to Stewart & Kincaid stating that she wanted to prepare her son Jacob, with whose family she then resided, 'to meet . . . the undertakers, of the rail road, in the middle of this week, in Carlow [town]. They are to commence the rail road on the first of March. The Dean [of Leighlinbridge, the Rev. Richard Bernard] is to get him a situation and desired him to prepare himself to go on that day, and it would be impossible for him to go in any kind of a decent manner being so long out of a situation [employment] without getting some articles [of clothing]'. She accordingly asked Stewart & Kincaid to send her 'this quarters salary which would be due on the 25th of next month' (SK).

On 27 May 1845 Jane Tyndall wrote to Stewart & Kincaid: 'It is 3 months . . . since I rec'd the last quarters salary. I would not trouble you for this quarters only the rail road did not commence . . . yet.' (SK) This letter suggests that during the summer of 1845, the Tyndall household had no source of income other than the quarterly payments from Stewart & Kincaid on behalf of Frankfort.

Along with her son Jacob and his family, Jane Tyndall moved to Dunleckny Cross, Bagnalstown, County Carlow, near the end of 1845. A letter from her to Stewart & Kincaid, 17 December 1845, provides details: 'I and my son . . . live within a quarter of a mile of the Revd. Mr Grogan,[44] brother to the Member of Parliament. . . . My son . . . has a school since the 1st of this month. . . . We will live on the profits of the school, along with the firing & provision I shall buy. If your Honours will be so kind as to send me this quarters salary in advance . . . never [again] will I be a trouble to your Honours until the proper time, the next not until the 25th of June next, for during the summer [when sowing will have ceased] he will have a large school' (SK). Jane Tyndall wrote

another letter to Stewart & Kincaid on 23 December 1845, again requesting
payment in advance. In this she added: 'The school will be able to support us
after Christmas. . . . May God Almighty bless your Honours and send it on
Christmas Day' (s k). Jane Tyndall received this advance payment [due to be
paid to her on 25 March 1846] early in 1846. On 11 March 1846 she asked
Stewart & Kincaid to send her, in advance, the payment due to her on 25 June
1846. The same letter indicates both optimism and distress:

> My son . . . will have a large school all summer [when he will receive] 2½d per week
> from each scholar. . . . The potatoes is rising [in price] every week. We have about
> a quarter [of an acre] of land to our house. . . . We had no opportunity these many
> years to sow until now and if we could get this next quarters salary we could buy
> provision and sow it and it would keep us going until the school w'd be strong and
> I hope then we would not have occasion to be a trouble until next September. . . .
> Think what must be a parents sufferings, to hear his [Jacob Tyndall's] little innocent
> children crying with hunger and have nothing to give them. (s k)

This is the last letter from Jane Tyndall in the Stewart & Kincaid correspondence. In mid-April 1846 the Rev. Grogan informed Stewart & Kincaid
that she had died. Jacob Tyndall's response was rapid: he abandoned all hope
for the school and decided to take his family to Quebec, the costs to be paid by
Stewart & Kincaid on behalf of Frankfort. On 30 April he wrote from
Dunleckny Cross to Stewart & Kincaid:

> I rec'd your kind Letter . . . and we return Lord Frankfort and you gentlemen our
> sincere thanks. . . . The names of my family who will go to America are –
>
> Jacob Tyndall
> Hannah Tyndall. Wife to Jacob
> Children,–
> William Tyndall, aged, 8 years
> Elizabeth Tyndall, aged, 6 years
> Montgomery Tyndall, aged, 2 years
> James Tyndall, aged, 6 months
>
> Oh Hon'ble Sirs, when you are sending any one to pay the passage to *Quebec*, may
> I humbly beg you will give orders to use the greatest economy. I have nothing to
> depend upon in a foreign land but what shall be left on the passage. . . . I am ready
> to leave this [place] the second day after I receive your answer, as I have nothing to
> live upon here . . . as no one belonging to me since my dear mother died would
> hardly speak to me, but all wishing me to leave the Kingdom for fear I should be a
> disgrace to them in my poverty, as they are all in a comfortable way of life.[45]

Hon'ble Sirs, I owe upwards of £2–10s for the medicine & funeral expenses of my dear mother, and £2–6s for to release my clothes & my wife's &c. out of the pawn brokers. . . . If your Honours would please to send me £6, I would be in Dublin with my family the second day after. . . . Be so kind not to pay for the passage in any vessel, that would sail by the 11th of May as my wife would wish to stop in Dublin for 3 or four days with her brothers whom she did not see these 12 years. (SK)

This passage gives interesting details of intra-family relationships. Note also that the Tyndalls were willing to leave County Carlow on the second day after they had received a letter, as well as money, from Stewart & Kincaid. Similar hastiness to leave what appeared to be a hopeless country has been noted in earlier chapters. As has been argued elsewhere, we can be virtually certain that the Jacob Tyndall who emigrated to Quebec from Carlow in 1846 was a son of William Tyndall of Frankfort's Coolcullen in Kilkenny, and an uncle of the famous scientist, John Tyndall, FRS.[46]

6 BRIEF OBSERVATIONS ON BURTON LANDS IN CARLOW AND KILKENNY

Apart from managing the Frankfort lands in Carlow and Kilkenny, in the late 1840s Stewart & Kincaid also managed the lands of Sir Charles Burton in those two counties. This estate consisted of about 380 statute acres at Pollerton Big (on which was sited the family residence, Pollacton House) on the outskirts of Carlow town, and about 160 acres in County Kilkenny.[47] On 15 June 1842 a firm of solicitors in London, Walker & Grant, wrote to Stewart & Kincaid: 'We have been requested to recommend a land agent to undertake the management of the small property of Sir Charles Burton Bt in the County of Carlow. We have named your firm. Sir Charles Burton . . . will attain the age of 21 in Jan'y 1844. . . . An uncle of Sir Charles is the present receiver [of rents], having been appointed . . . during the lunacy of the recently deceased baronet Sir Charles Burton' (SK). Stewart & Kincaid wrote to Walker & Grant three days later, expressing thanks for that firm's recommendation.[48]

Young Charles Burton, who had been educated at Eton and was in the army, did not reside at Pollacton during the 1840s. In 1851 he was appointed High Sheriff of County Carlow, and he resided mainly at Pollacton from about that time onwards. A letter dated 17 June 1844, to Stewart & Kincaid from Walker & Grant, indicates that 'Sir Charles Burton will shortly sail with his regiment to India', and in 1860, Walford indicated that Burton then had an address in London as well as at Pollacton. In 1893, Walford listed Pollacton as Burton's sole place of residence.[49]

Pollacton moved into decay early in the twentieth century. The author of *The Carlow Gentry* has reported as follows: 'The baronetcy, created for Charles Burton of Pollacton in 1758, became extinct . . . with the death, aged 80, in 1902, of Sir Charles William Cuffe Burton'.[50] Except for the walls which surrounded it, three gates, a gate lodge and some farm offices, today there is little trace of the Pollacton demesne. The house was demolished in the 1970s.

Stewart & Kincaid's management of the Burton properties was closely monitored by Walker & Grant, which firm acted as intermediary between Burton and Stewart & Kincaid. The Stewart & Kincaid correspondence contains no evidence of any direct communication between Stewart & Kincaid and Burton. Rather, the Dublin firm received directions from Law Walker, of Walker & Grant in London, who allowed Stewart & Kincaid little discretion. During the summer of 1844 Walker instructed Stewart & Kincaid to rent Pollacton House to a specified tenant for seven years. In regard to the lands immediately surrounding the house, these were to be rented to two specified tenants. But the rigid terms laid down by Walker seem to have been unattractive to the prospective tenants. Pollacton House remained untenanted in December 1844. On 6 January 1845 Walker wrote to Stewart & Kincaid: 'Charles Burton will be obliged by your having the family portraits at Pollerton carefully packed & removed to your care in Dublin' (SK). The Stewart & Kincaid correspondence provides no indication that a suitable tenant for the house was found in 1845.

In January 1845 Walker instructed Stewart & Kincaid to spend money on repairs at Pollacton House. These were completed by January 1846. On 15 May of that year, Walker wrote to Stewart & Kincaid: 'There are . . . matters in your cash account . . . on which I must trouble you to afford me a little explanation' (SK). The explanations sought pertained to details on the cost of the repairs. Walker's letter of 15 May is close to accusatory in tone: it suggests that Stewart & Kincaid may have been negligent, or that the manner in which the firm spent Burton's money may have been inappropriate. (SK)

Walker was rigid on the matter of punctuality of rent receipts. On 25 February 1845 he wrote to Stewart & Kincaid: 'Sir Charles Burton requests me to ask you when he may expect to receive his accounts & the rents due November last. There appears no reason . . . why the rents should at any time be more than a few days in arrear.' (SK) It seems that Walker knew little about payment of rents in Ireland, or of the 'running gale' often attached thereto.

Following the partial failure of the potato in 1845, Walker again expressed his disapproval to Stewart & Kincaid on 12 September: 'I shall be glad to receive Sir Charles Burton's accounts. . . . I understood from Mr Kincaid that you furnished your accounts yearly on the 31 January & so told Sir Charles. He is displeased & in my opinion justly so at not having received his accounts.' (SK)

Apart from a letter from three tenants early in 1846, the Stewart & Kincaid correspondence contains little else of interest on Burton's Carlow estate. The letter pleaded: 'We the tenantry on the Pollerton estate have been noticed to meet you on the 21st' for extraction of rent; however, 'should you gentlemen feel it your duty to persevere we fear all our efforts will be frustrated, as we shall be compelled to sell our corn [or] to part with our stock'. The three tenants added: 'The kindness we have always experienced as tenants to the *Burton* family, have induced us to lay the circumstances before you, as a respectful humble petition, to postpone your visit. . . . We propose on the 5th May next to forward the rent'.[51]

Given the firmness of the stance of Law Walker as indicated in earlier letters, it seems unlikely that the firm of Stewart & Kincaid was able to show much leniency to the Pollerton tenants in 1846. Letters of January 1846 indicate that some tenants on Burton's small estate in Kilkenny had been summoned to court for ejectment.[52] Whether decrees were obtained and executed is unknown.

THIRTEEN

PROPERTIES OF PONSONBY, PAKENHAM AND ST LAWRENCE

—

I INTRODUCTION

The Stewart & Kincaid correspondence contains a relatively small amount of material on the three principal estates investigated in this chapter. On each of them in the early 1840s, the recipients of rental income had one characteristic in common: each had a title, one of them being a bishop, while the other two were earls. The main estates to be investigated here are those of the Ponsonbys in the Philipstown district of King's County, now named Offaly, of the Earl of Longford (Edward Pakenham), and of the Earl of Howth (Thomas St Lawrence). This chapter also contains a brief section on the lands of E. J. Nugent near Ballymahon, County Longford, for which Stewart & Kincaid were agents. See map 9.

It was noted in chapter 1 that late in the eighteenth century J. R. Stewart's father married a daughter of the second Lord Longford: it was presumably through this connection that the firm which became known as Stewart & Kincaid obtained the Longford account. Stewart & Kincaid's management of the estate of the Earl of Howth probably predates the 1840s. Stewart & Kincaid's account with the Ponsonbys in King's County commenced early in 1841.[1]

2 THE PONSONBY ESTATE AT PHILIPSTOWN

The Ponsonby estate included about 2,000 statute acres – much of it bog – in the neighbourhood of Philipstown (now named Daingean). Of these and contiguous lands, a report of 1836 observed: 'It must appear an extraordinary anomaly that so many thousand acres of bog . . . should remain within view of Philipstown untouched. . . . The proprietors of the bog in the neighbourhood of Philipstown are . . . and Lord Ponsonby [Richard, Lord Bishop of Derry], to whom, in my opinion, it would have been by this time a source of great profit, if they had permitted and encouraged its cultivation.'[2] The Ponsonby estate also included houses in Philipstown. The number of Ponsonby tenants in the Philipstown district came to 329 (exclusive of their dependents) in December 1842.[3]

One of Stewart & Kincaid's first actions following commencement of the Ponsonby agency was to seek a large loan in London on the security of the estate. Such a loan was declined in 1841 'on the ground that the rental arises from small sums paid by a numerous tenantry'.[4] At the end of 1842 a firm in England wrote to Stewart & Kincaid: 'We have found the money wanted at the Philipstown estate at 4½ per c. provided the security be considered eligible. It is not what in this country is called a first rate security.'[5] It seems that the security was not then considered 'eligible', that the sum sought was £19,000 and that the money was not provided until 1844.[6] Some of the funds may have been provided by the Dublin brewers, Guinness; however, most of the money was provided by a person named Adelaide Burton.[7] Why the loan was needed is unknown.

No member of the Ponsonby family resided on the estate. Until 1844, Stewart & Kincaid paid net incomes, and submitted relevant accounts, to Richard Ponsonby, Lord Bishop of Derry. Thereafter, Stewart & Kincaid's communications on such matters were to Captain William-Brabazon Ponsonby's solicitors in London, Walker Grant & Co. Stewart & Kincaid also dealt with this firm in connection with the Burton estate in Carlow. Captain Ponsonby was Richard Ponsonby's only son. Upon the death of a cousin, he became the fourth Lord Ponsonby of Imokilly in 1861.[8]

Provision of pensions

On 15 April 1841, shortly after Stewart & Kincaid commenced the Philipstown agency, 'Elenor Kenedy' sent a petition to Richard Ponsonby expressing her hope that he would continue payment of a pension to her – £4 per annum for life – as it was 'the only means of paying her lodging' (sk). Ponsonby forwarded the petition to Stewart & Kincaid, instructing that 'the prayer of this memorial ought to be complied with'. She was not the only person at Philipstown in receipt of a pension. On 20 April 1841 Elizabeth Hopkins applied her mark to the following petition addressed to Richard Ponsonby: 'Memorialist has during the last twenty two years been in the enjoyment of an annual pension of two pounds from the Ponsonby family. . . . Mr Kincaid . . . has directed your memorialist to apply to your Lordship for permission to him to continue the payment to her of the said pension', as she was 'not able to support herself' (s K). On 23 April 1841 Richard Ponsonby instructed Stewart & Kincaid that Elizabeth Hopkins's pension should be continued. A person named Catherine Kennedy also received income from Stewart & Kincaid. On 6 October 1844 she wrote to Stewart & Kincaid indicating 'thanks for . . . sending me my half yearly annuity'. In the first two cases mentioned above, the beneficiaries of pensions were dependents of former agents on the estate. It seems that the third beneficiary was also in that category.

Rents and related matters

Rent receipts from the Philipstown estate in 1842 seem to have been regarded as satisfactory. Early in 1842, the Stewart & Kincaid employee, Stewart Maxwell came to extract rents. He may have travelled by the Grand Canal, which passes through the place now called Daingean. On 6 January he reported to J. R. Stewart: 'I may not be able to be in Dublin as soon as I proposed tomorrow as the canal is frozen over & there is some talk of the boats not being able to get on. I have received as I thought upwards of £400 which is not bad considering that there are a good many of the large tenants to pay yet.'[9]

In March 1842 Michael Grogan senior, who was then Stewart & Kincaid's local agent, sent Stewart & Kincaid half notes amounting to £112. Nevertheless, Stewart & Kincaid decided to press on those in arrear by having notices to quit served on them. Some of them responded by paying quickly.[10] Michael Grogan's last communication to Stewart & Kincaid – a list of tenants from whom he had recently received rents – is dated 10 February 1843. Next day he died. He had three sons: Michael, Joseph and James. On 14 February 1843 Joseph wrote to Stewart & Kincaid requesting the appointment held by his late father. Shortly afterwards Stewart & Kincaid appointed Joseph Grogan as local agent. Himself a Ponsonby tenant, he was not popular with others on the estate.

Several tenants sought rent abatements in 1843. One of them was James Grogan. On 2 March he wrote to Maxwell stating that he held 'a small bit of ground at the rate of £3 per acre. . . . You were good enough to promise my poor father . . . that you would go out on it with a view to an abatement' (s K). A short time later, an attempt was made to force abatements by sending an announcement to the *Freeman's Journal* stating that abatements had been granted on the estate. Thus, on 25 April, Henry Quinn of Philipstown, who was a baker[11] and a Ponsonby tenant, wrote to Stewart & Kincaid: 'Seeing an advertisement in the Freemans Journal of the 16th instant purporting to be from me stating particulars with regard to reductions of rent to the tennantry on the Lord Bishop of Derry estate . . . I disclaim any knowledge of it. . . . There are parties here [who] by these fictitious advertisements would wish to press an abatement.' (sk)

Stewart & Kincaid agreed to rent abatements in 1844: on 13 December of that year Captain Ponsonby's solicitors in London, Walker Grant, informed Stewart & Kincaid: 'We have not received the schedule of abatements at Philipstown' (sk). The abatements might explain why Maxwell's receipts there in January 1845 were below the £400 received in January 1842. On 9 January 1845 he wrote from Philipstown indicating that he had received £367, and he added: 'The receipt may be up to what I thought before I left Dublin. I am off to dine with Father Rigney' (PP at Philipstown) (sk).

Up to 1846, the many letters from Joseph Grogan to Stewart & Kincaid contain no references to ejectment, and only a passing reference to contemplated distraint which was not implemented. On 13 February 1845 he wrote to Stewart & Kincaid: 'I call'd to James Rourke for his rent and he told me that he was not able to pay. . . . He has a boat load of turf which I would distrain but it was not on Cap't Ponsonbys land.' (sk)

Stewart & Kincaid's stance on rents at Philipstown hardened in 1845–6. This reflected the fact that in 1845 Law Walker began to monitor closely Stewart & Kincaid's activities on the estate, and imposed demands on the Dublin firm. In April 1845 Walker wrote to Stewart & Kincaid: 'How does Capt Ponsonbys account with you stand? He has returned from the Mediterranean & is in want of money' (sk). Walker had become more demanding by September 1845 when he wrote to Stewart & Kincaid about 'your letter. . . . The account only includes rent to Lady Day 1844. Have you nothing in hand on account of the subsequent rent? Or do the tenants owe not only the arrear due at March 1844, but 1½ years rent in addition. If this be so we must desire some means to alter such a state of things. It will not answer Capt Ponsonbys purpose to have his income two years in arrear.'[12] Walker thus wanted Stewart & Kincaid to end the system of 'running gale', under which rent payments were considered punctual if they were a year or thereabouts behind the nominal date for payment.

The earliest reference to ejectment on the estate is in a letter from Walker to Stewart & Kincaid of 20 November 1845, which inquired: 'Inform me in what state of forwardness are the ejectments as to the town plots' (sk). Whether many ejectment decrees were obtained and executed is unknown. The first indication of distraint on the estate is in a letter of 23 March 1846, in which Joseph Grogan reported to Stewart & Kincaid: 'I enclose ½ notes for £22 – a ballance of Pat'k Hill's rent. I distrained his premisis . . . and very little was to be found there' (sk).

Stewart & Kincaid usually sent someone to Philipstown to extract rents in January of each year. On 9 January 1846, Sankey wrote from Philipstown to

Stewart & Kincaid: 'I send you 1st halves of notes amt £333–5–0 and will bring the seconds up with me tonight. I do not expect to get above £400 this time as the tenants are not . . . anxious to make money of their crops. Great complaints still about the potatoes' (s k). Thus, at Philipstown the partial failure of the potato in 1845 did not have much immediate effect on rent receipts. Note also that in the winter of 1845–6 many of the Philipstown tenants were keeping grain for their own consumption, rather than selling it. Similar observations have been made in earlier chapters.

There is no evidence that Stewart & Kincaid made a rent-collecting 'raid' on the estate in January 1847. Receipts there in July 1847 were higher than might have been expected. On the 22nd of that month Stewart wrote to Kincaid: 'Sankey got near £400 at poor Philipstown' (s k).

Ejectments were executed on the estate in 1847 or early in 1848, but in some cases the tenants involved were allowed to remain on the properties, at least for a while, as caretakers. This is inferred from correspondence about a house built around 1790 by Matthew Walsh, then PP at Philipstown. Relevant details follow.

The Rev. Matthew Walsh built his house on Ponsonby land. He had a brother, U (U for first name unknown). This brother had two sons, Patrick and U' (U' also for unknown first name). U' Walsh married and resided in the house built by the Rev. Walsh. Over time his positions in the social ordering were in descent. However, his brother Patrick moved upwards. In 1846 Patrick was listed as 'surgeon' at Naas in County Kildare, where he was also medical attendant at the dispensary, at the prison and at the workhouse.[13]

Patrick's brother, U', had two sons, Matthew a tradesman and Thomas. In the mid-1840s Matthew resided at the house built by the late Rev. Walsh. In the late 1840s Thomas was self-employed at Mary's Lane, Dublin, at which address he was listed as 'clothes broker' – probably a dealer in secondhand clothes.[14] Although Dublin was his principal place of employment, Thomas maintained an interest in the family homestead at Philipstown.

In the Stewart & Kincaid correspondence, the earliest letter pertaining to this Walsh family was written to Stewart & Kincaid by Patrick Walsh at Naas who, in January 1848, wrote as follows: 'I have been requested by Mr. Ths. [apparently meaning Matthew] Walsh of Philipstown, whose premises are now under ejectment, to intercede with you on his behalf. He is in fact the son of a late brother of mine. . . . This young man tells me that himself and a brother of his, an industrious tradesman of Dublin, are . . . putting the house in repair. This house was built about 60 years ago by an uncle of mine, who was Parish Priest.' (s k) Two days later Matthew Walsh himself informed Stewart & Kincaid that he proposed to 'repair and slate the house in Philipstown' and he agreed 'to give 2 years rent at the present rate' (s k). But

Matthew's offer (which suggests that he had access to more financial resources than might be expected of a tenant under ejectment) did not immediately yield the results which he desired. On 15 May 1848 he wrote to Stewart & Kincaid 'relative to the house of which I have been dispossessed last week. . . . I fell into arrears, but where is the poor man with a large family in Ireland who had to undergo the ordeal of the two or three last years that is not similarly circumstanced. I am now . . . precluded from any possibility of earning bread for a large and helpless family, as my workshop was in that house and I have not *now* a spot to put up my bench in.' He hoped that Stewart & Kincaid would 'extend to me the indulgence which others experienced by permitting me at least the use of my workshop and house even as a *care taker*. The others were permitted to re enter their houses.' (s k)

It seems that Matthew Walsh had to leave the family homestead at Philipstown, but that his departure was only temporary. On 22 November 1848 Thomas Walsh wrote to Stewart & Kincaid from Dublin: 'I hereby propose for the house . . . lately occupied by Mathew Walsh . . . and to pay one years rent on the 8th January next' (s k). Stewart & Kincaid's immediate response, and the fate of Thomas Walsh, are unknown: his name was not listed in the Dublin directory for 1850. However, financial aid from him may have enabled his brother Matthew to renew tenancy of the family homestead. The *Valuation* of 1854 lists a Matthew Walsh in occupation of a house in Philipstown.[15]

In 1848 Captain Ponsonby's net income from the Philipstown estate was probably negative. His net income reflected not only the level of rent receipts, but also the need to pay, to Adelaide Burton, interest on a loan of £12,000 which had been negotiated by Walker Grant & Co in 1844 on security of the Philipstown estate.[16] It seems that the rate of interest on the loan was initially set at 4.25% or 4.5%, and that it was subsequently reduced to 4%.[17] According to Law Walker, the low rate of interest was 'in consideration of . . . a promise of punctual payment'.[18] Thus, some £480 of the rental income from the Philipstown estate was pre-empted for payment of interest. A letter dated 22 February 1848 from Walker to Stewart & Kincaid, which requested the Dublin firm to remit the interest to Miss Burton's London bankers 'early in each month of January and July', suggests that the payments were then in arrears (s k). On 11 August, Walker informed Stewart & Kincaid that 'the half years interest due the 1st July . . . has not yet been paid' (s k). This breach in the conditions of the loan probably reflected difficulties in extracting rents from the estate in 1848.

The correspondence provides no evidence that Stewart & Kincaid organised a programme of assisted emigration from Captain Ponsonby's estate during the famine years.[19] Gráinne Breen has reported that at some time before June

1847, 'Ponsonby on his Cloghan estate' in King's County spent £350 on assisted emigration;[20] however, the 'Cloghan estate' was many miles from Philipstown, and the Ponsonby to whom Breen refers was Frederick, who was one of Captain Ponsonby's uncles. The Stewart & Kincaid correspondence contains only a single reference to apparent emigration from the Philipstown district. This was around the end of 1846, when a tenant wrote to Stewart & Kincaid seeking a small plot of land held by a person who was 'leaving this country'.[21]

Family strife

It has been seen in earlier chapters that the landlord, or Stewart & Kincaid his agents, were sometimes asked by tenants to intervene in family disputes. The correspondence on the Philipstown estate contains similar requests. A letter dated May 1843 indicates strife among the Grogans. It reported that Joseph Grogan 'is boasting he will take [his mother's] bit of grazing land as their [there] is another son or two belonging to Michael Grogan *diseased* [*deceased*]'.[22]

Following his mother's death about two years later, on 23 July 1845 Joseph Grogan wrote to Maxwell in Dublin: 'In consequence of the death of my mother . . . my two brothers [Michael and James] is looking for the land and any other property that she might have at the time of her death and my eldest brother Mich'l told me that he would . . . take the whole thing to himself'. He added: 'You have seen the will of my mother. She has left me all the land that she had in her possession her cattle and house and furniture reserving one cow and a part of the furniture for my sister. . . . But not one word about any other person. . . . I intend going to Dublin next week and would thank you to have some honest atturney that I would consult on the matter.' (sᴋ)

Three days later – on 26 July 1845 – three females named McCeland wrote from Philipstown to Stewart & Kincaid, complaining that they wished 'to let you know the ungrateful behaviour of Joe Grogan to his brothers. His father died . . . without making a will and had he lived to do so every one on the estate knows he would cut him away to nothing. . . . His mother was buried on this day week. . . . He says she made a will in favour of him and tretens his brother James with Mr Maxwell that . . . he will get him to put him out of his place' (sᴋ).

On 18 August 1845 Joseph Grogan's eldest brother, Michael, sent a memorial to Stewart & Kincaid, which 'Sheweth':

> Memorialists father died intestate leaving money to the am't £520 houses lands &c. . . . The money was divided between your mem'st and his three brothers and one sister & his mother. . . . At that time your memorialist & his brothers, Joseph & James, agreed to leave the land with their mother . . . with distinct

understanding . . . that at her death . . . the ground should be divided between them. . . . In violation of the above agreement your memorialists brother, Joseph, after having caused my mother to make a will leaving him everything she possessed is holding and intends to keep possession of the houses & lands. . . . Memorialist humbly hopes & prays your honours will . . . bring all the parties before you and your memorialist will be perfectly satisfied to abide by whatever decision which you may . . . come to. (s k)

Whether Stewart & Kincaid intervened is unknown. However, none of Joseph Grogan's brothers are mentioned in later Stewart & Kincaid letters. It seems that James Grogan was forced to leave the estate. In the *Valuation* of 1854 only one person surnamed Grogan was listed as a tenant there. That person was Joseph Grogan, who then occupied about 52 statute acres of Ponsonby land.[23]

The Stewart & Kincaid correspondence contains one other letter referring to a family dispute on the estate. In June 1849 Anne Sheill tried to explain her problems, as follows:

I am a poor distress woman destitute of all friends and my husband the only . . . enemy that I have. . . . I hold a portion of Mr Ponsonbys land. . . . It is got into debt on me. But if it was in your power to spear me until harvest I would [be] able to pay you what is due on it. But I understand that my husband Denis Shill is striving to take it. . . . Doe with me as you please if it is youre wishes to turn me outside of the door [and] I will give you up the quiet and peacable possession. And if youre kindness allows me to stop in it I will pay you the rent that is due on it. But my unkind husband would take the land over my head to turn me to the wave of the world. The thruth of the subject is I am living to long. I am a stumbling block in the way I prevent his youngest brother [who] wants [to] get married and to bring in the wife into the father house. . . . But my husband is in the way and I am in all there [their] way. When he [her husband] could not dispatch [me] out of the way for three years he spent with me he thought to poison me. I trow myself at youre feet. I crave for mercy. (s k)

The *Valuation* of 1854 does not list Anne Sheill on Ponsonby land. It does, however, indicate that Denis Sheill (her husband) was then a tenant to Ponsonby.

Education and other improvements

On 14 April 1842 the master at the endowed school in Philipstown wrote to Stewart & Kincaid:

The inspector of the Erasmus Smith Schools visited here on Monday, and desired me communicate to you that the following school requisites were wanting . . . : Short tablets, spelling & reading. Parables, miracles and history of Our Saviour. School register. Outlines of geography, one dozen. Cheap grammars, one dozen. One ream of ruled paper. Daily report book. . . . The rear of the house has been striped, and the rain consequently comes down in many parts. The ceiling over the lobby is ready to fall, and makes it dangerous for the children to pass up and down to the girls school room. . . . There are beyond 120 children attending the schools. (SK)

Stewart was in Philipstown on 18 May 1842, when he wrote to Kincaid: 'The books for the school have been forgotten'. He accordingly asked Kincaid to send them promptly, by canal (SK).

An estimate for repairs to the school includes the cost of work on the kitchen and that of whitewashing inside and outside the schoolhouse. The board of governors of the Erasmus Smith Schools contributed one half the cost; the other half was paid by Stewart & Kincaid on behalf of Richard Ponsonby. A similar arrangement applied when a stable and store-house were built at the school early in 1845. In regard to the cost of the school requisites, it seems that these were obtained by Stewart & Kincaid from the Kildare Place depository in Dublin at half the usual retail price.[24]

It seems that some of the Catholics who attended the school sought exemption from having to read the approved versions of the Scriptures. However, in 1843 the registrar of Erasmus Smith Schools informed Stewart & Kincaid that 'the governors cannot dispense with the rule that *all* children capable of reading, shall read the Holy Scriptures'.[25] Apart from financing part of the costs of the school, Richard and later Captain Ponsonby subscribed £5 annually to the Philipstown dispensary.[26]

In the years immediately before the famine, physical improvements on the estate seem to have been few. The Stewart & Kincaid correspondence of 1842–3 contains some requests from tenants for aid to repair houses and a request for assistance to plant quicks (for fencing). In 1843 a tenant was granted an allowance for small-scale drainage on his holding, and in the same year Joseph Grogan supervised repairs to a road.[27]

There is no evidence, at any stage during the 1840s, that Stewart & Kincaid sent an agriculturalist to the Philipstown estate. The Stewart & Kincaid agriculturalists encouraged cultivation of the turnip, a good rotation crop as well as a substitute for potatoes as animal feed. One tenant on the estate did switch to turnips: in a letter to Stewart & Kincaid dated 11 July 1846, John Murray stated that 'from the missed crop of potatoes I am trying turnips, as it may answer to feed bullocks' (SK). Given that the potato failure of the autumn of 1846 was virtually total, his decision seems sensible.

On famine relief

On 27 October 1846 Joseph Grogan in Philipstown informed Stewart & Kincaid that 'there is some public works going to commence about this town' (s k). The Stewart & Kincaid letters do not reveal the form which those works took. However, a proposal passed at a sessions in Philipstown for a new road, conditional on £120 being contributed by Ponsonby, was probably not implemented. On 7 November, Stewart & Kincaid wrote to the Board of Works 'to know if the Board will advance the whole sum, taking security from Capt. Ponsonby'. On 26 November the Board informed Stewart & Kincaid that it 'cannot advance the money to Captain Ponsonby or take the security proposed' (s k). It is probable, contrary to the guidelines for public works, that the proposed road would have benefited the Ponsonby properties disproportionately.

Throughout Ireland, relief through public works was abandoned in 1847. Under new arrangements of that year, distressed persons could be classified as paupers, could be placed under the Irish Poor Law and, when necessary, they could be given outdoor relief by the local authority. The cost of such relief was to be financed by taxation of local property. But some local relief committees continued to exist, financed largely by voluntary subscriptions. It seems, in the Philipstown district in 1847, that the provision of outdoor relief did not increase the tax burden: it was provided by the local relief committee rather than by the local authority.[28] For some weeks at least, this situation changed early in 1848, when John Walsh, a member of the local relief committee and chairman of the board of guardians of the Poor Law union of which Philipstown formed a part, wrote to Stewart & Kincaid on 25 January:

> By means of the funds entrusted to the charge of the relief committee & by the very meritorious conduct of the landholders of the E[lectoral] Division [of Philipstown] the proprietors have been preserved since the new act [providing for outdoor relief under the Poor Law] came into operation to the present day, from any cost whatever for the support of the poor entitled to out door relief. . . . But as the subscribed fund was exhausted last week the poor entitled to out door relief have been transferred from the books of the [relief] committee to that of the relieving officer [of the Poor Law union] & the patience of the landholders in supporting the able bodied without the aid of the proprietors must be now exhausted. . . . The rate payers [which body included the larger tenants as well as owners of land] have well deserved the liberal cooperation of the proprietors to relieve all parties from burthensome rates. (s k)

On 31 March 1848 Daniel Sullivan, a baker in Philipstown who was secretary of the relief committee, wrote to John Walsh: 'All the labourers that are able to work are in employment on the land. None are breaking stones. When the funds [of the relief committee] closed there was a rush on the relieving officer . . . as money was given. But by representation of the committee to the vice guardians [of the Poor Law union], to change the relief to meal, which the[y] have done there is not . . . the same temptation to remain idle. Enclosed is a statement how Capt'n Ponsonbys subscription [to the relief committee] was disposed of' (s κ).

In the Stewart & Kincaid correspondence, the final letter relating to famine relief in the Philipstown district is from John Walsh to Stewart & Kincaid. Dated 17 December 1848, it reported: 'I have this day received from you half notes for thirty pounds to be applied in giving employment to the able bodied destitute . . . as last year. . . . The scale on which you have contributed would I think suffice for employing the able bodied destitute during the slack season' (s κ). The same letter gave details of planned expenditures, on projects of employment creation, by landlords in the Philipstown district other than Captain Ponsonby.

One historian's assessment of Ponsonby's contributions to famine relief seems unfair. Timothy P. O'Neill has written:

> The wealthy in Offaly could also have done more [in famine relief]. . . . Captain Ponsonby had an estate in Philipstown from which he collected in the region of £800–00 per annum. The only incumberance on his land was a mortgage of £12,000 on which he paid £240 per annum. He did help during the famine but his agent's correspondence shows that he was constantly looking for his money. 'How does Captain Ponsonby's account with you stand?' his solicitor wrote to his agent, 'He has returned from the Mediterranean and is in want of money'.[29]

Initial impressions which this passage may have generated should be amended in the light of the following considerations:

1 Although the Stewart & Kincaid correspondence indicates that for much of the 1840s the Philipstown estate did yield an annual rental income in a region of £800, it would not be plausible to argue that in the second half of 1847, or in 1848, receipts were in line with that annual sum.

2 O'Neill's statement that Ponsonby paid £240 annually in interest on the Philipstown mortgage is in error. Such a sum would have reflected an interest rate (2 per cent) which is not credible. In fact, on 23 February 1848 Law Walker wrote to Stewart & Kincaid: 'The only incumbrance upon the Philipstown estate upon which interest is payable is the £12,000 due to Miss Burton & upon that interest at 4 per c is payable' (s κ); hence, the annual interest on Ponsonby's mortgage in fact came to £480.

3   The quotation provided by O'Neill in support of his statement that Ponsonby 'was constantly looking for his money' was drawn from a letter (the relevant part of it is reproduced above on p. 247) written by Walker to Stewart & Kincaid dated April 1845: the passage reproduced by O'Neill was not written by Captain Ponsonby and it was not written during the famine.

Taking considerations 1 and 2 above into account, and bearing in mind Ponsonby's expenditures on relief, it can be inferred that Ponsonby's net income from the Philipstown estate was almost certainly negative in 1848 and low in other years of the famine period. There is therefore no presumption that Captain Ponsonby could have done much more to relieve the needy on his estate at the peak periods of famine and famine-induced distress. During the famine years, it seems that some of the local proprietors, including Ponsonby, were quite generous in subscribing to relief in the Philipstown district. Note that not only did this ease hardship of the smaller tenants; it also eased the burden of taxation on the larger landholders (some of whom were themselves subscribers to the relief committee).

3 THE ESTATES OF THE EARL OF LONGFORD

In the 1840s Edward Pakenham, third Earl of Longford, owned at least 4,500 statute acres in Longford and 14,000 acres in Westmeath.[30] He sat in the House of Lords. Pakenham Hall (now called Tullynally Castle) near Castlepollard, County Westmeath, was his residence in Ireland. The County Longford properties were mainly in, or in the vicinity of, Longford town. Those in Westmeath were concentrated in the parish of Killucan, to the east of Mullingar. A letter of 1841 indicates that Pakenham supported a school on his Killucan estate. The master's annual income was £15 from Pakenham and £5 5s 0d from a Mr Crampton, besides contributions from the children, which were stated to have been insignificant. The master also had a rent-free house and garden.[31] The fact that the school-house was unoccupied in 1854 may have reflected depopulation during the famine.[32]

Rents and related matters

A person named Ramage was Stewart & Kincaid's agent on the Killucan estate. On 27 November 1840 he wrote to Stewart & Kincaid: 'I have called upon Matthew Hetherston & have explained the purpose of your letter, which was by his giving up possession immediately & paying a years rent, his pension w'd commence immediately, but if the rent was not paid his pension would not commence until next January twelvemonth' (s k). Ramage did not provide details of the pension which Stewart & Kincaid were to pay. Hetherston was not the only person to whom Pakenham granted a pension in the 1840s. A cash book in the archive at Tullynally Castle, which lists current expenditures in the Castlepollard district, contains the following entry dated 31 October 1848: 'To pensioners, this quarters pension – (£)18–3–10'.[33]

On 27 March 1841 a person named Carroll wrote to Stewart & Kincaid that 'being served with ejectment . . . for 2½ years rent of my plots in Longford [town], I . . . solicit your kindness, in accepting for the present, one years rent. . . . I . . . hope you'l prevent . . . proceedings' (s k). Whether Carroll was ejected is unknown.

In 1842 a tenant near Longford town claimed that she lost her rent money, and she pleaded for time. On 18 April she sent a petition to Stewart & Kincaid, which 'Sheweth': 'Y'r pet'r . . . on coming to Longford with a 5£ note in her pocket and also a promissary note lost her pocket before she came to the road. . . . Y'r pet'r had ample means to pay the present demand of rent notwithstanding this loss by pigs but hath been visited by the disease'. She hoped that Stewart & Kincaid would grant her 'time untill the present crop now sown and tilled shall come forth' (s k). In regard to the pigs, it is not fully clear from this passage whether the pigs had eaten the pocket containing rent, or whether the pigs were ill.

Another strange event is reported in a letter written on 2 September 1843 from near Mullingar, addressed to Stewart. In this letter one James Wilson wrote as follows: 'What steps ought to be taken by the owner of Bank of Ireland notes that have been gnawed by mice (almost *devoured*!). . . . A poor woman . . . laid bye two thirty shilling notes in a box, *near the bread*, in a village shop, and, yesterday morning, was horrified to find her notes in the condition you will see, if you look into the enclosed packet.' (s k) The letter reveals much about hygiene in the shop.

In the early 1840s there was at least one case of 'voluntary' surrender of Pakenham property in Longford town. On 28 November 1842 James and Sarah Martin sent a petition to Stewart & Kincaid, according to which

They . . . [were] always expecting some remuneration or compensation for the serious loss they have sustained in the surrender of their holding . . . without litigation . . . , and since that melancholy occurrence took place they have been thrown upon the mercy of the worthy and respected Doctor Fleming[34] who has kindly . . . afforded them shelter of his house these eighteen months past. . . . He wants our room . . . for . . . two of his cousins that are going to the seminary here. They must leave the place and be thrown out on the world. . . . The Earl of Longford . . . promised that they . . . would be considered for their . . . disappointments. . . . Pet'rs now humbly implores that you will . . . afford them some place of residence in or near Longford [town]. (SK)

It is conceivable that Stewart & Kincaid did provide the petitioners with accommodation free of rent: in the previous decade of the 1830s, it may have been the case that there was a tenant on the Pakenham estates from whom rent was not demanded. This is suggested by the following extracts from a letter dated 9 March 1845, in which Mary Cooper informed Kincaid from near Mullingar:

> I am the widow of thomas cooper. . . . My eldest son has . . . been my only support. His means . . . derived from teaching the neighbouring farmers children but death has also deprived me of him. . . . I have now no person to provide for me and my three children. The produce of the two gardens that is attached to my house together with our own little industry is all the support I now have. I am informed in consequence of the ground where my home and gardens are being thrown in to Andrew Releghan farm that I will lose them. . . . I hope that your honour . . . will not suffer me and them [the children] to be driven from the small place of residence. . . . During the late Earl of Longfords lifetime [he died in 1835] he never charged any rent for my little place but did annually . . . remit my husband . . . two pounds. (SK)

Note that the person named Andrew Releghan in the above passage was a blood relative of Mary Cooper.[35] Perhaps Stewart & Kincaid expected him to provide for her family.

In 1846 Daniel O'Donnell wrote to Kincaid from Longford town seeking the use of a house; this, he hoped, would be in reward for his loyalty. O'Donnell wrote as follows: 'I am absolutely bereft of . . . means. Neither can I pay rent. I applied to your Honour for a place in one of the widows houses. There is two old men living in each house. . . . These . . . could live in one house & leave the other to me. If this should meet your approbation I will feel ever gratefull.' He added: '[I] voted for the Conservatives at the struggle of 38. The clergy turned against me & ordered the people not to enter my house or speak or leave any money with me. My windows were broken, myself abused.'[36] The *Valuation* of 1854 does not list O'Donnell as tenant to Pakenham in Longford town.[37]

Rent receipts in parts of the Longford district were down in the autumn of 1846, when Stewart wrote from there to Kincaid: 'I send £550 for my R/A [rent account] and close not much short of the usual receipts, but not a single March rent' from two named townlands belonging to Pakenham.[38] It is possible that the £550 was obtained from more than one estate (not only that of Edward

Pakenham) in the district. Thus, it may have included receipts from the estate of the Stewart & Kincaid client E. J. Nugent near Ballymahon (about 15 miles from Longford town).

It seems that Stewart & Kincaid were firm on the matter of payment of rents in County Longford in 1848. Stewart wrote to Kincaid on 15 December: 'I hope you have ordered the Longford ejectments' (s k). There was also some distraint in the same district. John Williams was a bailiff who worked under John Crawford, Stewart & Kincaid's agent in Longford town. On 7 December he sent Stewart & Kincaid a long list of household furniture including beds, farm equipment and farm produce, which he had distrained on the holdings of two tenants (s k)

The Stewart & Kincaid correspondence gives an impression that elderly and long-standing tenants on Pakenham's estates were well treated. It might be expected, therefore, that acts of violence on his properties would be infrequent.

Violence

In contrast to life on some estates west of the Shannon, life on the Pakenham lands seems to have been relatively peaceful in the 1840s. However, in 1841 the surgeon to the county jail in Longford town wrote to Stewart & Kincaid: 'My gardener . . . was visited at one o'c a.m. by Capt. Rock . . . , dragged from his bed & severely beaten. . . . He has been in hospital since this occurred & is now afraid to return home for he thinks they will *kill him*'.[39] The aforementioned 'Capt. Rock' was a general term often used to describe the leader of any group involved in agrarian crime.[40]

In a letter to Stewart dated 17 May 1844, Kincaid referred to an outrage which involved a widow in or near Longford town, and he indicated that the government had probably granted her police protection. Another letter of 1844, dated August, is amusing. In this, Captain William Pakenham (Edward's brother, who later became his successor as fourth Earl of Longford) wrote to Stewart & Kincaid: 'McCutcheon has opened a public house at Castlepollard and established an orange lodge in it where all the young Protestants meet, drink, fight, etc etc. It is quite a brothel.'[41]

In the Stewart & Kincaid correspondence, the only indication of strife in the Killucan district is in a letter to Stewart & Kincaid dated 15 December 1845, in which Patrick Bray informed Stewart & Kincaid: 'There was a house burned on my land in July. . . . It was rebuilt on the 2nd of this month against my will and I was afraid to stop them. . . . It is in the middle of my land and I wish to let your Honours know of it and to direct me what I will do.' (s k) Stewart & Kincaid's response is unknown.

Emigration

There was some emigration to America from the Killucan estate in the early 1840s. On 11 March 1842 Ramage wrote to Stewart & Kincaid about 'Pat Keirnan who I hear is about going off to America', and he added that 'I think it was ten pounds that was promised him on giving up his land'. In fact, as indicated by Ramage on 24 March, Keirnan was paid £16, £8 of which was paid by four incoming tenants. Ramage explained to Stewart & Kincaid as follows: 'The agreement Mr Kincaid made *was* Whatever sum the tenants paid he would pay the same, & they paying eight pounds will make 16 pounds in the whole.' (sk)

The earliest indication of emigration from Pakenham property in Longford town is in a petition of 1846 from Catherine Curran, which 'Showeth': 'Pet'r is under ejectment for nonpayment of rent. . . . With the depressed state of times, my husband and son were obliged to go to America . . . which left your pet'r and eight helpless children. . . . Pet'r humbly prays for mercy as she does not know the day or hour she may have relief from her husband and son and stay the execution [of ejectment] and not throw herself . . . on a merciless world.'[42] On Pakenham's behalf, Stewart & Kincaid assisted Curren and her children to emigrate – presumably to join her husband in America. On 12 November 1846 she wrote from Longford town to Stewart & Kincaid: 'I beg . . . that ye will be pleased to remit me 3£ in addition to the 2£ already given. I had to release some articles I had to pawn'. She added: 'Myself and children are in want of clothing to fit us out for the voyage and to procure some sea store and to pay our travelling expenses to Dublin. God willing we will be in Dublin on Tuesday or Wednesday next. . . . We cannot leave here unless ye are pleased to send us the sum now claimed which will be the last till I am in Dublin.' (sk)

Emigration from Pakenham's Longford estate was probably low until 1847, when, on an unspecified date, Stewart wrote to Kincaid in Longford town: 'I hope you got on . . . well in Longford but some there the small farmers will not be able to pay up. Get some of them off to America if you can & soon. The price to New York now is only £3 or £3-3 for adults.' (sk) Early in 1848 Stewart & Kincaid implemented a programme of assisted emigration among Pakenham's tenants. This can be inferred from the fact that on 4 February of that year Stewart informed Kincaid: 'I accepted a bill [of exchange] for Miley [American packet agent in Dublin] for £400 . . . for L'd Longfords emigrants.' (sk)

On April 1848 John Slevin, a Pakenham tenant near Longford town, wrote to Stewart & Kincaid requesting a rent abatement. He indicated that if this were not granted he would have to surrender his farm. In December he again wrote to Stewart & Kincaid: 'I have been haunted by Mr John Williams [bailiff] demanding rent and . . . tretning to seize. . . . In fact if there was no anoyance in the case I would not be able to hold and pay the present rent. . . . Grant an abatement. Otherwise take the possession, giving me a fair consideration for my expenditures, and his Lordships bounty, as in the like former cases to assist the emigration of myself and family'.[43] It seems likely that Stewart & Kincaid assisted in emigration of Slevin and his family. No person named Slevin was listed on the relevant townland in the *Valuation* of 1854.

Improvements

Stewart & Kincaid's agent on the Killucan estate sought to encourage tenants to rotate their crops and to sow turnips. Thus, on 24 March 1842 Ramage wrote to Stewart & Kincaid that 'the principal object is to draw the small tenants . . . into the culture of turnips & house feeding. By a regular rotation of crops it would . . . give employment to every member of their families every day in the year.'

There was some restructuring of farm size on Pakenham's Killucan in the mid-1840s. That this did not mean creation of large farms is suggested by a letter dated 28 January 1845 to Kincaid from J. T. D'Arcy in England, who made the following request: 'Having been informed by my nephew Francis D'Arcy, that you intend leting out Clonreigh [Clonreagh] into small farms, or about making exchange of grounds with the different tenants, if so I will feel obliged if you will let F. D'Arcy have eight acers of Clonreigh' (sk). In 1854 Francis D'Arcy was listed as holding 11 statute acres on Clonreagh.[44]

It seems that in 1846 Stewart & Kincaid supplied guano fertiliser to a tenant on the Killucan estate: in February a tenant there wrote to Stewart & Kincaid expressing thanks for 'the very kind manner in which you have express'd your approval of my industry, as well as the kind concession to my request of the guano'.[45]

Private works were in progress on the Killucan estate during 1846 and 1847. Details are vague, but those of 1846 seem to have involved purchase by Stewart & Kincaid of a ton of lead and construction of a bog road.[46] A letter of 11 May 1847 from Stewart to Kincaid refers to the 'Killucan Improvement a/c'. Around the end of 1847, on Pakenham's behalf, Stewart & Kincaid applied for government loans for drainage. Sums of £400 and £1,000 were approved. That of £400 appears to have been spent on the Killucan estate; that of £1,000 pertained to drainage affecting two rivers near Longford town.[47]

Only a single ledger – a cash book – of relevance to the present study could be found in the Pakenham archive at Tullynally Castle.[48] Most of the entries pertain to lands in the vicinity of the castle. Many of the entries for 1847 and 1848 were for 'extra labourers this week', those sums usually amounting to about £20 in a given week. The nature of the work is not recorded. However, two other entries are curious: an entry for March 1848 records: 'To John Cook for killing rats 41 @ 2*d* each'. A similar entry for March was for killing 21 rats (s k). Thus, surviving rats were probably well fed.

During the famine years Stewart & Kincaid encountered great difficulty in attracting viable tenants to depopulated lands on various estates under the firm's management. It seems that most of the Pakenham townlands of Lisduff and Cooleeny, both a short distance outside Longford town, lay idle late in 1848. One of Stewart & Kincaid's immediate tasks was to try to find viable tenants for those lands.

On 23 September 1848 David Wakefield, a businessman in County Galway, wrote to Stewart & Kincaid stating that he had recently opened 'an establishment' in Longford town, which induced him 'to look at some farms at present on hands in that neighbourhood'. He explained that he had offered Stewart & Kincaid's local agent '25/- per [Irish] acre for the two farms Lisduff & Cooleeny', that he needed about 80 acres upon which he would build and improve, and that he could obtain 'any reference you please from the Earl of Clancarty down . . . and at least 12 or 14 merchants of the most respectable protestant class in Dublin'. On 28 September, Stewart in Dublin wrote to Kincaid: 'Wakefield . . . was here today. . . . He is a good Protestant & I would expect would make an improving tenant. . . . I am inclined to deal with him if you don't think the price much too low.' (s k) However, it does not seem that Wakefield became a tenant to Pakenham on either Lisduff or Cooleeny: no person named Wakefield is listed on those townlands in the *Valuation* of 1854.

4 BRIEF OBSERVATIONS ON NUGENT LANDS IN LONGFORD AND WESTMEATH

The Stewart & Kincaid correspondence contains some letters about the lands of E. J. Nugent near Ballymahon, County Longford. Matthew Higgins was the most important tenant – on the townland of Clooncullen – there. He usually paid his rent by, in the first instance, signing promissory notes, against which he made payment at the Bank of Ireland in Longford town. However, his notes often had to be renewed. E. J. Nugent's smaller tenants in the Ballymahon district paid rent to Peter Farrell, Stewart & Kincaid's local agent there, and occasionally to Stewart & Kincaid's agent in Longford town.

In 1842 Higgins was in dispute with other tenants (not Nugent's) on Clooncullen townland. The quarrel was about a passage between Higgins' two farms. On 26 April he complained to Stewart & Kincaid: 'Those very persons . . . had Rockite notices posted near their dwellings for no person to assist me with men or horses and as a pretext for depriving me of the passage mentioned in their notices for no one to let me through their land.' (sκ) Other controversies in regard to access to individual holdings have been noted in earlier chapters.

Between 1841 and 1845 Higgins consistently complained of hard times. On 22 December 1845 he explained to Stewart & Kincaid that he could not promptly pay his rent arrear of about £35, and he added: 'My potatoe crop suffered so much from the rot that I could not with safety to my family part with what corn I have. . . . All the landlords of this neighbourhood are making allowances to their tenants in consequence of the rot.' (sκ) In a letter to Stewart & Kincaid dated 4 October 1846, Higgins stated that he was a member of the local relief committee and that he had spent a lot of time collecting money for it. He stated that public works would shortly commence in his parish and he indicated that he wanted to obtain employment as overseer: he therefore requested Stewart & Kincaid to use influence for him at the Board of Works. In the same letter he explained: 'I have a large family and unfortunately their principal support gone. Potatoe [conacre] rent which paid half years rent for me every year gone.' (sκ) It seems that Matthew Higgins did survive the famine: the *Valuation* of 1854 lists a person of that name as a tenant on 183 statute acres in Clooncullen townland.[49]

E. J. Nugent, the proprietor of the lands on Clooncullen discussed above, owned other properties in the Ballymahon district. It seems that he was the same person named Nugent who, in the 1840s, owned property on townlands located a few miles to the northeast, in the Union of Granard, County Westmeath: the firm of Stewart & Kincaid was Dublin agent for the two blocs of property, and in each case, the aforementioned Peter Farrell was the local agent. Apart from Matthew Higgins and a middleman named O'Brien, it appears that the Nugent tenants on both blocs of property were very poor.

On 16 August 1843 Farrell informed Stewart & Kincaid that he had recently been around E. J. Nugent's Ballymahon and Westmeath estates, but that he could extract little rent from the small tenants. He added: 'For the [Clooncullen] lads there is a great part of them that has no stock. . . . I'll go round on these that has no cattle & tell them that they'l all be processed [unless they] get their rents out of the loan fund. . . . It would be a good plan to process them for a years rent then they'd soon get at least half a years rent.' (sκ) Referring to the small tenants in Westmeath, and presumably with distraint in mind, on 13 September 1843 Farrell reported to Stewart & Kincaid: 'The[y] have not stired anything as yet but the flax'. Early in 1844 he wrote that he had 'treatened them . . . I'd leave keepers on them & take all they had. . . . However the[y] came forward [in payment] better than I expected'.[50]

Difficulties in extracting rent created a financial crisis for the landlord at an early stage during the famine. On 1 August 1846 Stewart wrote to Kincaid: 'I am sorry to hear that E. J. Nugent's affairs look so hopeless' (s κ). The Stewart & Kincaid correspondence on his estates contains some references to eject- ment decrees, but there is no definite evidence that any of them was executed.

5 THE EARL OF HOWTH AND HIS ESTATES

In the 1840s, Thomas St Lawrence, Earl of Howth, owned several thousands of acres in north County Dublin and in Meath.[51] Around 1843 the annual rental income from the Dublin properties approximated £9,000 while that from Meath was about £2,000.[52] He was born in 1803 and resided at Howth Castle and in England.

A quarrel over land

The greater part of the earl's land was rented to large tenants, many of whom seem to have sublet. The Stewart & Kincaid correspondence contains three items pertaining to intimidation in a dispute over land in the parish of Lusk, County Dublin. Thus, on 19 February 1846 John Cole, sub-inspector of the police at Balbriggan, wrote to the earl about

> two threatening letters being sent through Balbriggan post office to two men named Mich'l Boylan & M Sweetman the former residing on your property [in the townland of Jordanstown]. . . . I beg to forward [copies of] the letters in question (which I have reported to government) written . . . for the purpose of intimidating any person on your estate from giving land or houses to McDonnell . . . in all probability [written] by the Smiths, from whom some portion of ground . . . was to be taken for McDonnell, to build a house on. (s κ)

The earl passed on this letter, and the copies which accompanied it, to Stewart & Kincaid, presumably with instructions to deal with the matter. The 'Smiths' mentioned by Cole were probably Charles and William Smyth, who were listed as tenants to the Earl of Howth, on the townland of Jordanstown, in the *Valuation* of 1852.[53] One of the letters reported by Cole warned: 'Boylan. We hear you are about . . . to build a house for . . . McDonnell. . . . If you attempt to do any work for him mark the consequence, for if you do we intend to give you a Tipperary touch. . . . He must get it if he does not draw back his horns'. The other letter was similar: 'Sweetman. We understand that you have got a new tennant, and since you do not know your duty . . . we intend to let you know it. I am sorry that you could not find better use for your house than to give it to McDonnell or any other land shark. But I hope we wont be disappointed in finding you and him one of those nights shortly. For your own sake I hope you will not give us the trouble of finding him there.' Following the arrival of Cole's letter (with copies of the threats) at Stewart & Kincaid's office, an employee noted on it: 'The Jordanstown tenants required to be at Leinster Street at 12 oC on Thursday' (sk). The person named McDonnell in Cole's letter was probably Edward McDonnell who, in 1852, held a house and about 18 acres on Jordanstown.

Trying to raise a large loan

The earl's properties were heavily encumbered: in January 1844 he sought 'a loan of £45,000 to £50,000 upon his Irish estates at 4 p c' from a firm in England.[54] The greater part of these monies was sought in order to pay off an existing mortgage on which an interest rate of five per cent was charged. Negotiations for the loan were tactical. On 8 February 1844 St Lawrence wrote to Stewart & Kincaid from England: 'I think the parties who were to advance me the money @ 4 per cent are holding back until they can see what will be the result of Dans [Daniel O'Connell's] trial. The general opinion in this country is that he will be acquitted, but if found guilty they have a fancy there will be a rebellion in Ireland.' (sk) The loan had not been approved by 2 August 1844, when the earl informed Stewart & Kincaid: 'I highly approve of the [draft] letter which I return to you. Pray send copies of it off to the creditors without delay' (sk). The draft letter to creditors, which St Lawrence returned to Stewart & Kincaid, was as follows:

> By desire of the Earl of Howth we beg to state that we have recently been nego-tiating a loan for his Lordship in England upon the security of his Irish estate for the purpose of reducing the interest . . . upon his estate, and we find that the sum necessary for the purpose can be obtained from respectable parties in London at 4 p cent. Before however concluding a treaty for the loan his Lordship is desirous of ascertaining from his present creditors whether they will consent to reduce the interest upon the securities they hold to 4¼ p cent as he would be unwilling to take any steps for paying them off without first asking them this offer & he would prefer paying ¼ p cent additional to his present creditors rather than make a change. (sk)

Following his trial Daniel O'Connell went to prison, but he was released in September 1844. This may not have created a favourable impression at Roy Blount & Co, the firm in England with which Stewart & Kincaid was trying to negotiate the loan. On 3 October the English firm informed Stewart & Kincaid, that if the loan were approved, the rate of interest would have to be 4¼ per cent.

Stewart & Kincaid again tried to raise a loan for St Lawrence early in 1846 when a Dublin barrister wrote to Kincaid declining to lend at 4¼ per cent (as proposed by Stewart & Kincaid); he did, however, indicate that he would sanction a loan to the earl if the rate of interest were 4½ per cent. The earl sought further restructuring of his liabilities when, in 1848, he informed Kincaid that he was 'sorry to hear that you have not as yet been successful in obtaining a loan of £6,000 for me'.[55]

Pre-famine requests for donations

The Stewart & Kincaid correspondence related to the Earl of Howth contains several requests for financial assistance. The earliest is dated November 1842, when a curate at Kells in County Meath wrote to Stewart & Kincaid: 'As treasurer of the Kells dispensary I . . . request that you will . . . solicit Lord Howth to become an annual subscriber . . . , his properties of Gravelstown and Drakerath being contiguous to this town. . . . In a very few days our account for the year must be closed, previous to the usual application for a grant [as counterpart to the amount raised by private subscriptions] from the county.'[56] A letter to Kincaid in 1843 from the parish priest at Castletown, near Nobber in Meath, suggests that St Lawrence granted land for building a school.[57] In 1845 the earl was asked to contribute to building at Navan. Other local landlords contributed. Thus, the Rev. Eugene O'Reilly, PP, wrote to St Lawrence on 11 June: 'I am at present engaged in building a Parochial House [and] have been obliged to apply to all the landlords holding property in this parish to assist us. . . . From the Duke of Bedford we received £30, from the Earl of Essex & Baron de Ros £30, from JJ Preston £10 in cash & to the amt. of £30 in building materials. . . . May I hope your Lordship will be so kind as to assist us in this undertaking.' (sk)

Late in 1845 it was the Church of Ireland rector at Lusk who sought assistance. On 9 December he wrote to Stewart & Kincaid stating that he had been 'obliged to solicit aid . . . to rebuild our much wanted church. . . . I ask your intervention on this occasion with Lord Howth, who is the largest landed proprietor in this parish' (sk). Annexed to his letter, he listed the names of landowners who had already agreed to subscribe a total sum of about £400. The names and the individual amounts included: Edward Taylor, £100; George Woods, JP, £100; Charles Cobbe, £100; James Hans Hamilton, MP, £25; George Alexander Hamilton, MP, £10.

On 11 December 1845, Edward Bullen, the secretary of the Royal Agricultural Society of Ireland, wrote to Kincaid soliciting his own subscription, as well as those of the Earl of Howth and Lord Lorton, to the society. As was indicated in chapter 1, Kincaid was an important member of the society, the objectives of which included 'the improvement of husbandry among the farming classes holding under twenty-five acres Irish' (SK).

Famine

The impact of the potato failure in the autumn of 1845 was severe among the earl's Meath tenants. This was mirrored in several requests for aid, addressed to Stewart & Kincaid as the earl's agent. The fact that all of such letters pertained to Meath, rather than to the part of the estate in County Dublin, suggests that the effects of the potato failure of 1845 were much more severe in Meath.

On 17 January 1846 a person named John O'Connor wrote to Stewart & Kincaid stating that 'a meeting . . . will be held at Nobber . . . to take measures affording employment. . . . There are many cases of distress upon the Earl of Howths property in this neighbourhood.' (SK) On 23 January, O'Connor reported to Stewart & Kincaid:

> The unanimous opinion of . . . [the] meeting was, that distress and want of food existed to a very great extent, and that the exertions of all persons were required for the relief of the labouring classes.
>
> We have at length obtained from government a pledge to forward our exertions . . . which I hope will prove effective towards the obtainment of public works. . . . Such works if judiciously carried on will I hope avert a crisis. . . . Special sessions [have been] called for the purpose. . . . It will be necessary for the parish committees to have funds to a small amt in their hands to enable them to supply provisions to labourers at lowest possible rates. (SK)

On 27 February 1846 Samuel Garnett, of the relief committee for Morgallion and Lower Slane in Meath, informed Stewart & Kincaid that the committee 'have succeeded in procuring employment for the necessitous poor on your [the Earl of Howth's] estate, and its immediate vicinity'. He added: 'In addition to employment, the committee find it to be imperatively necessary to provide funds, to form a depot for provisions, in the different localities, and also to enable the committee to give provisions at a lower rate, to such persons as are not able to earn sufficient wages, to support their families. You are therefore requested to forward your subscription.' (SK)

A further request for aid followed on 18 April 1846, when the Rev. Stevenson wrote from Kells to Stewart & Kincaid: 'In consequence of . . . the failure of the potatoe crop & the high rate of provision, the relief committee for this parish . . . take the liberty of calling on the landlords to aid them by contributing to the fund to be expended on the purchase of food. Mr Thomas Farrell[58] has most liberally given £50. . . . Use your influence with Lord Howth.' (sk) Robert Skelly was secretary to the local relief committee at Navan. Early in May 1846 William Stanley, the secretary to the Central Relief Commission at Dublin Castle, wrote to him requesting 'that a detailed list of the local subscriptions . . . be forwarded to this office, on [receipt of] which, they will be submitted to the Lord Lieutenant for his Excellency's donation.' (sk) Skelly sent a copy of this letter to the Earl of Howth on 9 May 1846, and in the same communication, he pleaded: 'The Navan relief committee beg again . . . your Lordship's kind subscription for the relief of the numerous distressed poor of this town. The committee are most anxious to have the honor of your Lordship's name placed on the list that is to go before the Lord Lieutenant, as it will enable the acting members to meet the distress of the poor in the coming months.' (sk) Stewart & Kincaid responded quickly: on 22 May, Skelly wrote to Stewart & Kincaid confirming 'receipt of a half note of £10, this sum (£10) being the Earl of Howth's contribution to the relief committee at Navan' (sk).

Destitution was extreme in Meath following the second failure of the potato in the autumn of 1846. On 26 October, Patrick Lynch, one of the earl's tenants near Kells, wrote to Stewart & Kincaid enclosing a letter of credit for £115, this amount being one half year's rent due from him. He indicated: 'The relief committee of this district are making arrangements to collect subscriptions from the landed proprietors to assist the poor . . . reduced to the lowest state of wretchedness. . . . The Board of Works have commenced employing the people but at such a low rate of wages that they cannot possibly subsist if relief be not given them. . . . I merely mention this for his Lordship's consideration.' (sk) On 4 December 1846 Lynch again wrote to Stewart & Kincaid: 'A presentment sessions for this barony (Lower Kells) will be held . . . on Monday next. . . . I will not consent to admit the Board of Works to enter on my farm for draining but would most willingly make arrangements with Lord Howth to drain it under my own inspection & by that means give more employment' (sk). What Lynch's motives were is unclear. However, he may have felt that by supervising drainage work himself, employment could be restricted to tenants (probably including undertenants to Lynch) on lands owned by the Earl of Howth.

Further indication of famine destitution in Meath appears in a letter from the rectory at Dunshaughlin to Stewart & Kincaid, 26 December 1846, in which the Rev. John Low stated that many of the people in his district 'are absolutely starving'; he therefore asked Stewart & Kincaid to send a contribution on behalf of the Earl of Howth (s κ).

In the autumn of 1846 Stewart & Kincaid were anxious to encourage the earl to implement privately financed improvements. Thus, Stewart wrote to Kincaid: 'I hope you will be able to attend the Balrothery [presentment] sessions and that Lord Howth will have courage to undertake a good quantity of drainage say £1000'.[59] On the earl's behalf, and in conjunction with other proprietors, Stewart & Kincaid may have supervised drainage in Meath and in County Dublin late in 1846.[60] An attempt to develop a salmon fishery at Howth was a failure: it was abandoned by mid-August 1846.[61]

The Stewart & Kincaid correspondence pertaining to the Earl of Howth in 1847 consists of a single letter of little interest. In 1848 he obtained a loan of £1,000 from the Board of Works. All or most of this was spent on improvements in County Dublin.[62] A letter from the Dublin-based stockbroker George Symes refers to famine fever in the Artane district (now a suburb of Dublin City). Symes resided at Artane. On 13 January 1848 he wrote to Stewart & Kincaid from his office, about one of his neighbours, a tenant to the earl: 'Corcoran the man who holds the ground from Lord Howth has sent me half a years rent. His family & himself are all bad in fever. If you insist on the half year due 1 Nov., send me a note . . . that I may send it.' (s κ)

Probably the most important improvements affecting the earl's lands around the time of the famine were partly independent of action by the earl or by Stewart & Kincaid. The projects in question were the building of the Dublin and Drogheda railway, and its extension (a spur) to the town of Howth. The railway terminus at Howth (located opposite the main gate to Howth Castle) was in use by 1848, when the earl sent a message to Kincaid: 'Will you dine with me today. You can return by ¼ past 9 o'clock if you wish.'[63]

The Stewart & Kincaid correspondence provides no evidence that any of the earl's tenants were ejected during the 1840s, but it does contain three sets of references to distraint, in each case in County Dublin. The more interesting of these involved Charles Frizell, who in 1847–8 held 238 statute acres at Stapolin, Baldoyle.[64] The famine – perhaps the plight of undertenants – seems to have ruined him. On 3 June 1848 St Lawrence wrote to Stewart & Kincaid from England: 'It is my determination to get possession of Stapolin without further delays' (s κ). On 10 June he wrote to Stewart that 'Frizell is likely to force us to have recourse to legal proceeding to get possession of Stapolin' and that he expected Stewart & Kincaid 'to take the most prompt and determined steps . . . to eject him'. He added that 'now that Mr Frizell sets me at defiance I shall not hesitate to have recourse to what may be considered an unpopular act.' (s κ) It seems that Stewart & Kincaid responded through distraint. On

15 July the earl wrote to Kincaid: 'The removal of the cattle from off the lands will show Mr Frizell that we are not to be trifled with any longer. Cutting the meadows is taking possession of the land . . . & when the hay is made up it should be disposed of by auction or removed to my farm yard' at Howth Castle (s k).

Late in July 1848 the earl wrote to Kincaid: 'If we are to commence fresh proceedings by ejectment again against Mr Frizell it will be very unfortunate & it will end of course by my giving £250 & losing another years rent out of Stapolin.'[65] The £250 seems to have been offered to Frizell if he were to surrender his lease promptly. Thus, on 13 June 1848 Stewart in Dublin had written to Kincaid: 'Miss Frizell called again alone + I was ingallant enough to tell her we would withdraw the proposed gift of £250 . . . & that we were preparing in the most legal manner to take possession by forcible means.' (s k)

The earl returned to Ireland around the beginning of August, and it seems that he agreed to a compromise with the Frizells. On 28 August he wrote to Kincaid:

> I cannot at present hold out any hopes to the Messrs Frizell of my being able to procure appointments for them in any of the colonies. Situations in the colonies are much sought for by persons who have political claims & I have no political claims. When the Messrs Frizell have established themselves in any of the colonies if I can be of any service to them through my private friendship with some of my political friends it will afford me pleasure to do so. (s k)

Presumably the Frizells did receive the £250 from the Earl of Howth and it is likely that they did emigrate.[66] However, the Stewart & Kincaid correspondence reveals no more on their fate.

FOURTEEN

THE SHERLOCK AND THE
BATTY ESTATES

WINE, WOMEN AND SADNESS

—

I INTRODUCTION

Both the Sherlocks of Kildare and the Battys of Westmeath were commoners. The owners of the estates of the two families – see map 10 – shared another feature: their lifestyles led them into deep personal problems, and the firm of Stewart & Kincaid was called upon, not only to manage their estates, but also to manage more personal affairs. His interest in alcohol was a cause of William Sherlock's problems. Those of Fitzherbert Batty were related to his interest in women. It is not to be inferred that the owners of estates discussed in earlier chapters were immune from problems associated with alcohol or extra-marital sex. In fact, the handwriting styles of George Nugent (the Marquess of Westmeath), and of Viscount Frankfort, suggest that they were in or on the verge of *delirium tremens*. Furthermore, it may be recalled from chapter 8 that Nugent's relationships with women got him into financial difficulties and that while at Drumsna in 1845, Stewart Maxwell saw Nugent (then aged about 60) with a woman who he pretended was his wife. However, the firm of Stewart & Kincaid was not called upon to manage any very personal affairs of either the Marquess or Frankfort.

Palmerston was lover of Lady Emily Cowper for almost the last thirty years of her husband's life (and in 1839 he became her husband).[1] At Buckingham Palace he was known as 'Cupid'. It has been reported that while staying at a royal palace he made 'a violent and brutal' attack on a Mrs Brand; the source states that 'her piercing screams were heard by half the inmates at Windsor Castle and she was rescued in the nick of time just as her knickers were being torn off'.[2] It seems that in 1865 his excessive arousal – reportedly with a maid on a snooker table – brought about his death.[3] None of Palmerston's interests of intimacy became the business of Stewart & Kincaid. It was owing to the

fact that Stewart & Kincaid were asked to manage consequences of very personal matters among the Battys and the Sherlocks that we know about them.

In the early 1840s William R. Sherlock owned at least 867 statute acres near
Naas in County Kildare. These included Sherlockstown and Sherlockstown
Common.[4] Both the Grand Canal and the Great Southern and Western
Railway cut through the latter property. William resided on the estate at
Sherlockstown House, which still stands. He was a blood relative of the
Pakenhams of Pakenham Hall by virtue of the marriage of his grandfather
to one of that family. The firm of Stewart & Kincaid became his agent in the
1830s or earlier.[5]

The Stewart & Kincaid correspondence indicates an unusually close relationship between the Sherlock family and Stewart & Kincaid. It can reasonably
be said in regard to the Sherlocks that the firm of Stewart & Kincaid was as
much engaged in management of personal affairs as in management of the
Kildare estate. Stewart & Kincaid's involvement in such personal affairs is the
main focus of the present section.

The correspondence provides no definite evidence that William Sherlock
ever married. He had no recorded children. He had two brothers, Richard
Thomas, and Frank. The early 1840s were unfortunate for the three male
Sherlocks: each of them died tragically between 1840 and 1843. William was
deemed a lunatic shortly before his death.

The earliest letter pertaining to the Sherlocks in the Stewart & Kincaid
correspondence is dated 20 February 1841. Addressed to Stewart & Kincaid,
this was written from England by a person named Walker, and it enclosed a
receipt for half a year's interest of £150 paid to Walker 'by the Trustees of
Sherlock Esq'. Thus, the Sherlock estate had to pay Walker interest of £300
annually: this reflected a claim against the estate on a principal of about
£6,000. Several similar letters from Walker followed up to October 1848. The
loan was probably negotiated by Stewart & Kincaid: a letter of 1842 indicates
that another of Stewart & Kincaid's clients, Palmerston, also borrowed from
Walker.[6]

In May 1841 Sherlock was confined to the Sheriff's Prison in Dublin,
probably for debt. He was then both physically and mentally ill. Letters of
January 1842 to Stewart & Kincaid, from a doctor in Naas, indicate that a
bill of exchange for £50 odd, which had been accepted (signed) by Sherlock,
had been dishonoured. Similarly, in March 1842, Pierce Doyle wrote from
Sherlockstown to Kincaid complaining that a bill of exchange which he held,

and which had been accepted by Sherlock, had been dishonoured.[7] Referring to Sherlock on 1 June 1841, William Harty, physician to prisons in Dublin, reported to Kincaid that he had just visited Sherlock in jail, 'where he is *now* sober & under strict surveillance with two keepers'. However, Harty had also visited him on the previous night, and 'found him grossly drunk & kicked up such a row with the governor & turnkeys for permitting such scenes in the prison that matters were today speedily redressed' (sκ).

William Sherlock was a violent prisoner. On 28 June 1841, Harty wrote to Stewart & Kincaid: 'Michael Reilly was Mr Sherlock's attendant in the Sheriff's Prison, whose health has seriously suffered by Mr Sherlock's violence.... He was useful in assisting the two men I had placed over Mr S.' (sκ) Referring to Reilly in a second letter, also dated 28 June, Harty informed Kincaid: 'As I promised him remuneration for his special attention to Mr S. at night (before the men were placed over him) with a view to keeping Mr S. as sober as possible, I will with your concurrence let him have 10/- more & think him at the same time entitled to compensation from Mr S. for the injuries he has sustained.' (sκ)

The firm of Stewart & Kincaid paid Sherlock's legal and medical bills. Thus, on 28 July 1841 Richard Meade, a Dublin solicitor, wrote to Kincaid: 'Upon examining the probable expense of ... the ... inquiry agst Mr Sherlock I apprehend they will fall very little short of £100' (sκ). And later in 1841 a retail firm in Dublin informed Stewart & Kincaid: 'We are supplying Mr Sherlock (at present in the Sheriff's Prison) with medicine, and we will consider you accountable for the same.'[8] Whether Stewart & Kincaid received bills for the alcohol supplied to Sherlock while in prison is unknown.

On 2 February 1842 Stewart wrote to Kincaid that a surgeon had told him that 'poor Wm Sherlock had been very ill indeed & scarcely takes any nourishment ... & seems anxious if we can so manage to have him moved' from jail. Stewart added: 'There would be no trouble in taking charge of him now in his present weak state if the wife can be kept away but she will become restive when she loses the £10 a week' (sκ). The reference to 'the wife' should not be taken as evidence that William had once married. In all other cases in the Stewart & Kincaid correspondence, letters to or from Stewart & Kincaid refer to the spouses of the firm's clients in a respectful manner; those which refer to mistresses are subtle. Stewart's reference to 'the wife' seems to have been to a mistress.

William Sherlock was freed from prison early in February 1842. Stewart & Kincaid assigned him to the care of a Mrs Ormsby in Kingstown, County Dublin, who seems to have received £12 per month in remuneration. A doctor named Swan resided close to her. He attended to some of Sherlock's medical needs. On 24 February 1842 he wrote to Stewart: 'Sherlock is ... much worse than I had any idea of. He is but skin and bone. . . . He has a severe cough and his strength completely gone.' On 18 March, Mrs Ormsby wrote to Kincaid: 'Send out a few bottles of port wine today for Mr Sherlock. I have still four bottles of the sherry which you sent before but he prefers port and will not drink any but Kinnahans.[9] I did not know the last decanter I sent up was drunk when Mr Sherlock sent down for more and . . . I tried to get the best in Kingstown for him. He instantly perceived it was not Kinnahans and said he could drink no other. . . . Mrs Sherlock [William's mother] dined with him the day before yesterday. He has not been out of bed for three days.' (sk)

On 5 March 1842 Dr Swan wrote to Kincaid indicating that the Ormsbys would soon be leaving Kingstown. He added that if Stewart & Kincaid wished that Sherlock should continue to reside in the Kingstown district, he would try to find 'a suitable place for him' (sk). However, Swan feared that Sherlock's right lung was 'extensively diseased'. Swan did find new lodgings for Sherlock, and on 14 March he requested Kincaid to come to inspect the place (sk).

The foregoing details indicate that following Sherlock's release from prison, Stewart & Kincaid tried to make his life as comfortable as possible. But he was dead before the end of May 1842.

It does not seem that William Sherlock's mother, Matilda, resided at Sherlockstown House at any stage during the 1840s; rather, along with her daughter, she lived at Warrington Place, along the banks of the Grand Canal, between Lower Mount Street and Upper Mount Street in Dublin. As is indicated by Dublin directories, she had been at this address since 1836. For the period during which Sherlock was in prison, Pierce Doyle acted as caretaker of Sherlockstown House. On 4 October 1841 he reported to Kincaid: 'Mrs [Matilda] Sherlock is about to take some things out of Sherlockstown House. Before they are taken I wish you to know' (sk).

In 1842–8 the lands of the Sherlock estate were rented. Stewart & Kincaid supervised some improvements. In May 1843 Stewart & Kincaid received a proposal for 'scouring and cleaning up all the ditches and drains . . . in the bottoms of Sherlockstown . . . to draw off the water from them' and also to scour and deepen a small river.[10] The proposed improvements appear to have been implemented. In 1845 there were dangers that construction of the railway would damage the estate. Thus, on 3 February, John Mitchell wrote on behalf of his father James (an important tenant), informing Stewart & Kincaid that 'they contractors has commenced they railroad at Sherlockstown. The[y] had a great deal of men working last week. . . . They damage will be very great. . . . Mr Kincaid asked me . . . did we get any notice and to let him know when we would. We have received no notice.' (sk) On 22 March 1846 James Mitchell complained to Stewart & Kincaid that because it divided his farm, construction of the railway was causing problems of access to part of the land which he rented. It seems that his complaint was ineffective: today there is no evidence of a pass under the railway on the farm at Sherlockstown Common.[11]

Stewart & Kincaid offered to rent Sherlockstown House to the railway contractors for use as offices, workshops and stables. Ireland's great builder of railways, William Dargan, fortunately declined. On 22 February 1845 he wrote to Kincaid: 'I do not require Sherlockstown House, indeed it is too good for our business, and would no doubt be injured by our occupation' (s k). It seems that Stewart & Kincaid advertised the letting of Sherlockstown House in May 1845.[12]

As already indicated, Richard Thomas Sherlock was William Sherlock's brother. Richard emigrated to Canada, probably in the early 1830s. He visited Ireland in the autumn of 1840. In this context, a letter to Kincaid dated 17 April 1841, from Thomas Daniell at Carrickmacross in Monaghan, reported: 'I received a letter from my son from Toronto in which he states that he remitted a sum of £20 by the hands of . . . Richard T. Sherlock who was coming to Dublin in September last, who states he directed his agent . . . Kincaid . . . to send to me enclosed in a letter sent with him by my son. . . . If you have the money will you . . . give it to Charles C Gibson Esq're [an attorney in Dublin] who will forward it to me.' But the £20 sought by Daniell remained unpaid in June 1843.[13]

Richard was on close terms with Kincaid and his family. On 22 April 1841 he wrote to Kincaid from Seneca, Grand River (about 60 miles from Toronto), as follows: 'We have great hopes of a war with the United S. on account of the affair of Mc Leod.[14] I am living entirely on the hope as I shall then have a chance of some employment. . . . I suppose that William [Richard's brother, discussed above] is as usual and that he has almost run the length of his string by this time. I expect to see Frank [Richard's other brother, mentioned again below] some of these days if there should not be a war with America. . . . If you have any influence with our *She Queen* (as the Indians call her Majesty) . . . persuade her to give the Yankeys a good beating.' (s k) Frank Sherlock, an army lieutenant, was in fact dead when these lines were written. A letter to Mrs Matilda Sherlock from the War Office indicates that he died in Jamaica of yellow fever on Christmas Day, 1840.[15] Frank's death helped to improve Richard's finances. On September 1841 he wrote to Kincaid from 'the bank' in Toronto: 'I have this day drawn on you for £200 part of the four hundred which will be coming to me on Franks account' (s k).

Richard Sherlock did not survive for long after the death of his two brothers, William and Frank. On 13 June 1843 his uncle, Colonel Francis Sherlock, wrote to Kincaid from England: 'I was truly sorry to hear of the melancholy death [by drowning] of my poor nephew Richard, and of the distressing state in which it must have left his widow and infant children, coming so totally

unexpected on them. Poor Mrs [Matilda] Sherlock has had many severe trials
of late years, and now the melancholy death of her only surviving son in a
distant country and leaving a widow and infant children . . . must occasion her
much anxiety.' Col. Francis Sherlock added: 'I suppose Mrs R Sherlock's
family are residing in her neighbourhood, as I understand he [Richard]
married a young lady of a family that had left England in order to settle in
Upper Canada.' (s k)

The person whom Richard Thomas Sherlock had married (in 1835) was a
daughter of Thomas Galer, who had emigrated from England. On 6 November
1844 Galer wrote from Seneca in Canada to 'Mrs RT Sherlock' at Haddington
Road in Dublin. (This address is very close to Warrington Place, where
Matilda Sherlock, the mother of the late Richard, resided). Galer's letter
enquired: 'As administrator for Mr [Richard T.] Sherlocks property in
Canada, I would wish you to send me word how I am to proceed with the
creditors here. . . . There are between three and four hundred pounds standing
debts here.' (s k) Mrs R. T. Sherlock passed this letter on to Stewart &
Kincaid, which firm presumably advised on the matter.

The most substantive claims against the property of the late Richard
T. Sherlock were those by Mr Daniell of Toronto, son of Thomas Daniell of
Carrickmacross in Monaghan (mentioned earlier in the present section) who,
as was stated in a letter of November 1846, had paid 'a considerable sum as
security for the deceased Mr [R.T.] Sherlock'.[16] It can be inferred that the
gross assets in Canada of the late Richard Sherlock were insufficient to settle
the claims of Daniell in Toronto, who responded by making claims against
the Sherlockstown estate.

Richard Thomas Sherlock's eldest son, who was born in Canada in 1836,
was named William. The passages immediately above suggest that his mother
brought that son to Dublin shortly after his father's death. Dublin directories
of 1845 and 1846 list 'Mrs Sherlock' at Haddington Rd.[17] Where she and her
son William resided during the next few years is uncertain. However, this
William inherited all or most of the Sherlockstown estate. He was educated at
Trinity College, Dublin, and became a Church of Ireland clergyman. In 1860
he married a daughter of the aforementioned Colonel Francis Sherlock, of
Nottinghamshire in England. Thus, he married one of his cousins. Resident
at Sherlockstown House, he was in 1893 the vicar of Clane.[18] A publication of
1876 lists him as owner of 1,202 acres in Kildare.[19]

A directory of 1816 lists Colonel Francis Sherlock at Lower Mount Street
in Dublin, and at Sherlockstown.[20] The Stewart & Kincaid correspondence
does not indicate when he moved to England. However, he was in the 1840s
in receipt of income from the Sherlockstown estate. On 6 October 1843 he
wrote to Kincaid stating that he would be 'obliged by your looking over

my account and transmitting the balance to Hopkinson's' (London bankers) (sk). He died in January 1848. Most of the subsequent letters related to Sherlockstown are from his widow, Emma.

Following the death of Colonel Sherlock, Emma Sherlock quickly turned her mind to matters of business. On 1 February 1848 she wrote from England to Stewart: 'I wish to call in the twelve hundred pounds from Lord Palmerston [which loan was presumably arranged by Stewart & Kincaid]. . . . I also wished to consult you & Mr Kincaid on the subject of the Grand Canal debentures. I should like to dispose of them'. She mentioned that her late husband 'was always anxious that I should bring all his money matters to England. . . . There is one half year's annuity due on Sherlock's Town, besides the different interests which have been accruing since the last settlement.' (sk)

Payment of the annuity on Sherlockstown ceased with the death of Col. Sherlock. This consideration, combined with the fact that Emma Sherlock sought to liquidate her financial assets in Ireland, came close to breaking the link between the Sherlocks of Nottinghamshire, and Sherlockstown. In a letter to Kincaid dated 3 August 1848, Emma stated that she and her children wanted 'to have all our affairs concentrated [in England] as we are not likely ever to visit Ireland' (sk). But the link with Sherlockstown did not end in the late 1840s: as already indicated, in 1860 a daughter of Francis and Emma Sherlock, married Richard Sherlock's eldest son, William, who inherited the estate in Kildare. That daughter came to Ireland and lived at Sherlockstown House. William Sherlock, the vicar of Clane, had four daughters. When one of them died in 1953, the estate was sold and passed out of Sherlock hands.[21]

In the Stewart & Kincaid correspondence, letters pertaining to the Sherlocks are different in content from those on the estates discussed in earlier chapters. They contain little about rent collection, nothing about distraint or ejectment, and nothing about the famine or landlord-assisted emigration.[22] However, they do provide insights into activities of an Irish land agency which are generally different from those reported in earlier chapters.

3 THE BATTYS OF BALLYHEALY

The Batty family of Westmeath came from England and settled at Ballyhealy, near Delvin, in about the year 1690.[23] In the early 1840s the big house and surrounding lands there were owned by Fitzherbert Batty, a magistrate for Westmeath.[24] The estate was at least 2,400 statute acres in extent.[25] It consisted of lands which were together known as the Ballyhealy estate.

Management of personal affairs

In the 1840s the Batty family maintained a close relationship with Joseph Kincaid and his family.[26] It seems that there was a marital link between Kincaid and Edward, one of Fitzherbert Batty's three brothers: Edward's second wife was a daughter of a person named John Kincaid, MD. It also seems that this John Kincaid resided in County Armagh, and that he was Joseph's father.[27] If that was the case, then Edward Batty's second wife was Joseph Kincaid's sister, and this connection would account for both the close personal relationships between the two families as well as the allocation of the Batty account to the firm of Stewart & Kincaid. In the late 1840s Kincaid dealt with consequences of the sexual adventures of both Fitzherbert Batty and his brother William.

In the nineteenth century, relationships between males of the Batty family and women were in many cases unhappy. Fitzherbert Batty's eldest brother, Espine, married at least twice – in 1832 and 1835.[28] But Walford records that a person named Espine Batty, who died in 1883, married three times.[29] Several months before his death *c*.1847, Fitzherbert Batty got into trouble with a woman named Brigid Gaffney. On 23 January 1846 Fitzherbert wrote to Kincaid requesting assistance:

> A person named Brigid Gaffney has lately commenced an action against me for the alleged breach of an agreement said to be contained in some letters of mine in her possession. . . . She is a pauper. I have deemed it prudent to compromise the matter, which she has offered through her attorney to do, upon payment by me of the sum of fifty pounds & the costs . . . , in consideration of which she would drop all proceedings and grant me a general release of all claims. . . . I have agreed to these terms, upon condition that all my letters should be delivered up & be destroyed. The attorney in the action is Mr Richard Walsh. . . . The favour I have to ask you is to settle this business for me. . . . It will be necessary for you to see Mr Walsh as early as possible to prevent further proceedings & costs in the action & to pay him the £50 & the amount of the costs, upon his delivering to you on my a/c, a general release . . . and also my letters to be destroyed. (SK)

Kincaid did act along the lines requested but the letters were not then destroyed. On 9 April 1846 Fitzherbert wrote to Stewart & Kincaid: 'Thank you for . . . the attention you paid to my wishes in the affair of the Gaffneys. The letters are of no consequence. . . . As a full release has been given, I fancy no further use can be made of them.' (SK) However, in a letter to Stewart & Kincaid dated 27 October 1846, Fitzherbert again sought Kincaid's assistance, due to the necessity of 'defending of a second action . . . which that woman

Brigid Gaffney, notwithstanding her release, as she had kept my letters, has
again renewed against me. . . . The release is still in your possession and Mr
Fitzgerald [Batty's solicitor] will require it for the defence. [Please] see him &
advise with him what it is best to be done.' (s k)

The Stewart & Kincaid correspondence reveals nothing more about Ms
Gaffney. The *Valuation* of 1854 lists no Gaffney on the estate. But the correspondence does indicate that Ms Gaffney was not the only woman with whom
Fitzherbert Batty had association around the mid-1840s. Shortly after his
death, a woman named Mary McNally wrote to Stewart & Kincaid stating
that she had 'lived with . . . the late F Batty . . . by whom she has a child, a boy
now nine months old and in consequence of the sudden death' of Fitzherbert,
both she and child 'are plunged in the greatest distress'. She trusted that Stewart
& Kincaid would not allow her and the child 'to be cast upon the world' and
added that her name 'appears in the books of the deceased gentleman as
having received various sums of money from him'.[30] The *Valuation* of 1854
provides no evidence of any person named McNally on the Ballyhealy estate.

On Fitzherbert's death the estate passed to his brother Espine, a barrister
with an address at Stephen's Green in Dublin. His sister Catherine resided
there. In the late 1840s he resided in London. He had, at that time, two surviving brothers, Edward and William. Edward was the Church of Ireland
vicar at Duleek in Meath. William had been a tenant to Fitzherbert on the
Ballyhealy estate. Following Espine's succession, he became a tenant to Espine.

One of Espine's first tasks as owner of the estate was to face the question of how to deal with a woman named Monaghan, who had been another
associate of Fitzherbert. It seems that Fitzherbert had fathered several illegitimate children; this was a further problem which Espine had to face.
On 28 February 1848 he wrote to Stewart & Kincaid: 'With regard to . . .
[Monaghan] I believe it would be right to give her the means of going to
America. . . . As to 2 children if they were the *only ones* to be dealt with, it
would make a material difference. . . . I had heard surnames of more. . . . Have
an inquiry made . . . whether there are prospects of more turning up as claimants. With regard to . . . Monaghan . . . the sooner she is enabled to go the
better.' (s k) The *Valuation* of 1854 does not list any person named Monaghan
on the estate.

Espine Batty still had the affairs – meaning business as well as possibly
matters more personal – of Fitzherbert in mind when he wrote to Stewart &
Kincaid on 19 April 1848: 'I believe you generally furnish annual accounts
about this time & I shall be glad to receive from you the usual statement of
affairs of the estate when ready. Also a statement . . . as to my late brothers
affairs. . . . Mrs Ruxton is to receive from you only £33–6–8 annually . . ., the
sum arranged with her by my late brother.' (s k) The reasons for Fitzherbert

Batty's arrangements with Mrs Ruxton, who was probably a widow in 1848, are unknown.[31]

At the time that Espine sent to Stewart & Kincaid the instructions indicated above in regard to Ms Monaghan, he was probably not aware that his brother William was in trouble with a female named Caffrey who resided on the estate. She appears to have been a young widow.[32] On 21 July 1848 Espine wrote from London to Kincaid:

> My brother William has written to say he would propose to give up . . . the . . . Cloughmore farm . . . so as to give up included therein the buildings in which the *objectionable person* [the woman Caffrey] resides. . . . I presume he means by this that as he could not personally use force in putting out that person, he would give up that farm & thereupon remove her. . . . She I presume might be treated as his servant remaining as an intruder, & not as a tenant. If William will give it up cleared of her, & if you see no difficulty in getting her removed from the house & estate & if on your consulting Edward [the clergyman brother of Espine and William], you & he see that that object can be attained without throwing on you any unpleasant difficulties, I should be ready to acquiesce in William's proposal. (s k)

On 21 August 1848 William's sister, Catherine, wrote to Kincaid:

> William has been staying here with me & left me this morning. . . . He gave me leave to endeavour by every means in my power to put an end to a most unhappy & disgraceful connexion . . . with a person of the name of Caffrey at Ballyhealy. He says he has done his best to get rid of her . . . He is willing to give her £300 [probably the equivalent of about £30,000 sterling in purchasing power at the beginning of the twenty-first century] to get rid of her. . . . I think £50 or £60 would suffice to induce her to set out for America or Australia. . . . I *depend on your friendship* that you & Edward will put your heads together & try to *emancipate* the unhappy young man who is convinced of the sin of such a connection, & yet has not strength or power to shake her off. . . . She has children . . . from whom she says she will not be separated, so that I think the best thing that could be done, would be to send her & them to Australia. . . . *I leave it to you & Edward* to do your best & to *strike the iron while it is hot*, lest her wishes should get the better of him when he sees her again. (s k)

Catherine herself probably delivered this letter to Kincaid. A letter dated 22 August 1848, from William to Catherine, indicates that Kincaid immediately agreed to intervene. In this letter, William wrote as follows: 'I feel greatly obliged to Mr Kincaid for his kindness in undertaking so disagreeable an office. . . . You seem to doubt the sincerity of my willingness to put an end to this connexion. I know not how else to prove it than by . . . putting into Mr Kincaid's hands £300, any part or the whole of which, he shall be at liberty to use if he can effect by gentle means her and her childrens emigration.' (s k)

Ms Caffrey was still on the estate on 28 October 1848, when Catherine wrote to Kincaid: 'I *depend* on your using *every effort* to get *the person to depart from Ballyhealy*, as I dread his being exposed to her wiles every time he *goes to his farm* where she lives' (s k). It seems that she did leave: the *Valuation* of 1854 provides no evidence of any Caffrey on the estate. The *Valuation* indicates that in 1854 William Batty held almost 300 acres on Ballyhealy townland, plus 70 acres (which may have comprised the farm known as Cloughmore on which Ms Caffrey had dwelt).

The *Valuation* of 1854 names the Rev. Edward Batty as lessor of the Ballyhealy estate. It indicates that it was then at least 2,400 acres in extent. An official publication of 1876 lists Edward Batty as owner of 1,216 acres of land in Westmeath.[33] It also indicates that he was the only person named Batty who then owned land in the county. It can therefore be inferred that substantial tracts of the estate passed out of Batty ownership between 1849 and the 1870s.

Management of the estate

Earning a commission of five per cent on what he collected in rent, Henry Morgan was between 1841 and 1848 Stewart & Kincaid's local agent at Ballyhealy. The earliest surviving letter from him to Stewart & Kincaid indicates that he was active in distraint. Dated 24 February 1843, it reported as follows:

> I have made the following seasures, Patt Kearnan . . . , Luke Kearnan . . . and widow Nugent. . . . James Corcoran and Wm. Kelly has got time unto Patrickmass [Patrick's Day]. Peter Seerey is to pay tomorrow, if not I will distrain his property. James Seerey on Munday the fair of Kildalkey. James Glennan was married on Wednesday and is to receive £60 in 10 or 12 days and to pay. . . . Denis Nail has drew money this day from the loan fund and will pay ½ years rent. . . . John Geeland promis'd shurely at the fair of Kildalky. . . . John Divine is to settle. . . . There was not sufficient stock of cattle with those I distrained to make up the amount of rent due and I seized their property on the ground. I have placed Read as keeper. (s k)

Morgan again distrained properties of several tenants – in one case for the large sum of £109 – in October 1844.

The Stewart & Kincaid correspondence refers to instances in which Fitzherbert Batty assisted tenants. Kincaid was a director of the Midland

Great Western Railway of Ireland, a company formed for the construction of a railway, by Mullingar in Westmeath, to Athlone and Longford.[34] On 31 March 1846 Fitzherbert wrote to Kincaid in regard to a tenant: 'This note will be handed to you by Pat. Gough [Goff], son of the late Mat. Gough [Goff], a mason who tells me you were good enough to promise, on his producing a letter from me, that you would get him employment on the Mullingar Railway' (sk). Goff did gain the employment which he sought but, as work on the railway progressed westward, his employment may not have lasted for long. On 25 May 1846 widow Goff wrote from Ballyhealy, apparently to Fitzherbert Batty, stating 'thanks . . . with respect to obtaining imployment for my son, at Corbitstown [Corbetstown, near Killucan]. I understand there is the most of the masons to be broke on Saturday next. . . . The[y] are advising my son to go to Dublin but that would not answer me. . . . I further pray you to spake to Mr Farrell who will be in Corbitstown this day that he may keep my son Patt'k in the work.' (sk)

Following the partial failure of the potato in the autumn of 1845, Fitzherbert reported from Ballyhealy to Stewart & Kincaid on 9 April 1846: 'The tenants in general here have not been badly off, but some half dozen families I have been obliged to support & since January by orders for meal and giving them work on the new road. . . . I fear a good many of the poorer sort will plant no potatoes this year, & that there will be a greater scarcity next year . . . unless seed potatoes be supplied to the people.' (sk)

Rent receipts from Ballyhealy were surprisingly high in the autumn of 1846. On 27 October, Fitzherbert wrote to Stewart & Kincaid: 'Yesterday . . . Griffith [an employee of Stewart & Kincaid] . . . collected a larger sum than usual. . . . We are likely to have abundance of work in this neighbourhood immediately, not only from presentments at Extraordinary Sessions, of which I have obtained grants for £340, to be worked on this property & the immediate neighbourhood, but also by the draining & sinking of the Lisclogher River, on which £8,000 is to be expended very shortly, so that we may expect the smaller tenants to make payments.' (sk)

Subsequent letters suggest that the drainage and deepening of the river were not implemented during the winter of 1846–7. The Stewart & Kincaid correspondence reveals little about economic conditions on the estate in 1847 – almost certainly the year in which Fitzherbert Batty died. However, the Battys obtained a large loan in that year. A letter dated 19 April 1848, from Espine Batty in London to Stewart & Kincaid, requested: 'As the time has passed when the first half yearly gale of interest became due to Messrs Fuller & Yates [in London] under the deed signed by myself & my two brothers, I write to apprise you of it . . . as due on the 13th of April on £6400 at 5 per cent.' (sk) Espine went on to refer to interest on another loan outstanding from a

Mr Hawkins. The purposes for which those liabilities were created are not revealed in the Stewart & Kincaid correspondence. It appears that Stewart & Kincaid simultaneously borrowed and lent money for members of the Batty family. In the same letter as that in which Espine referred to interest due to Fuller & Yates, and to Hawkins, he added: 'I should thank Mr Kincaid to tell me whether he succeeded in getting [the Stewart & Kincaid client] L'd De Vesci to take my sister's money at 5 per cent.' (s κ)

It seems that rent receipts in 1847 were very low: by February 1848 Stewart & Kincaid had a net claim against the estate. This reflected the fact that in the then recent past, Stewart & Kincaid's expenditures on behalf of the Battys exceeded the firm's rent receipts, less its charges for management. In 1847, Stewart & Kincaid's expenditures on behalf of the Battys included payments under a jointure, possibly payments to women who were induced to leave, payment of interest on at least one outstanding loan and, it seems, outlays on purchase of meal for the tenants. On 10 February 1848 Espine Batty wrote to Stewart & Kincaid requesting an estimate of the assets of his late brother Fitzherbert, excluding '[rent] arrears not likely to be recovered', and 'also a rough estimate as to how much of the assets may be applicable to the reduction of your claim on the estate'. As an enclosure in the same letter, Espine sent Stewart & Kincaid 'a leaf out of a report on the Lisclogher Drainage District sent by the Board of Works to me for *my assent* to drainage works in that district from which it appears there are 64 acres of Ballyhealy likely to be benefited.' (s κ) Given that the cost of the proposed drainage would ultimately have to be paid by those landlords who benefited from it, Espine sought Stewart & Kincaid's advice on whether he should indicate his assent to the scheme. On 28 February 1848 he wrote to Kincaid: 'I was glad to find by Mr Stewarts letter that you had signed my assent to the Lisclogher Drainage' (sκ).

Although, early in 1848, Stewart & Kincaid encouraged Espine Batty to incur further liabilities on works of improvement, neither Stewart nor Kincaid was happy in regard to the Batty finances. On 8 March 1848 Stewart wrote to Kincaid: 'I quite agree as to Espine Battys letter being far from satisfactory as to our balance. . . . We must put our balance on a better footing than at present.' (sκ)

Given that Stewart & Kincaid had a net claim against the estate by early 1848, it seems that both Espine Batty and Stewart & Kincaid then adopted a firmer stance in dealings with tenants. There was a squatter to be removed. At an unknown date early in 1848, Espine wrote to Stewart & Kincaid: 'There is a cotter who was allowed a year ago or more to build a hut [on a bog]. He is a stranger & a bad character & it is absolutely necessary to get him out. . . . He is not a tenant at a rent. . . . A small sum of money given to him would be better than Law. Will you consider this' (sκ). There also seems to have been a case of a tenant who was not being charged any rent for one of two lots which he held. On 18 March 1848 Espine wrote to Stewart & Kincaid that a tenant named Kelly 'had been distrained by your order for a very large amount of rent' and that 'it has always been my conviction that he ought not to be allowed to retain that portion of the ground adjoining my brother William's farm', as 'he appears never to have paid more rent than would cover the demand for the lot at his dwelling house & . . . he . . . continued to keep the other lot without paying any rent for it'. Espine urged Stewart & Kincaid to consider whether Kelly should be required 'to give up that other lot in consideration of the remission of a large sum of irrecoverable arrear' (s K). In a letter to Espine dated 22 March 1848, Kelly stated that 'as matters stand at present the rent is set at £40 p year', and that he had been distrained for £122. Thus, he was three years in arrears. However, Kelly went on to state that the value of the land held by him had been reduced 'by the cutting it received by roads by which all the land of any value . . . was frittered away' (s K). Those roads were probably built to create employment in 1846 or 1847. Espine's suggestion on how to respond to Kelly's 'irrecoverable arrear' was probably implemented: in 1854 Kelly had only a single holding on the estate.

Despite the hard times, Espine Batty continued his family's support of a school, about which he sought to avoid any misunderstanding. On 18 March 1848 he instructed Stewart & Kincaid: 'Enter on the rental of the estate the schoolhouse lot', including 'the garden allowed by our family to be used by the schoolmaster not as tenant but simply as our schoolmaster while we keep him as such, by way of an annual subscription to the school. . . . Act on the principle that the house & the garden are in my full possession & that [the master] uses it only by permission & at will.' (s K)

Stewart came to Ballyhealy early in 1848. On 4 February he reported to Kincaid: 'I returned last night from Ballyhealy. . . . My whole time was occupied with dirty little accounts for labour and allowances for meal and corn. . . . There appears very little appearance of getting cash rents from the small folk . . . & I fear there will be very considerable loss before these fellows are cleared away or made to pay. I also doubt whether Morgan [s K's local agent] is a good person to deal with these small tenants. A good sharp bailiff to whom we might give the 5 p cent on the small rent might squeeze something out of them.' (s K) This passage indicates that the tenants had been given food in 1847, and that they paid for at least part of it by providing labour for work on the estate. It also reveals, because Morgan was not sufficiently aggressive in extracting rents, that Stewart contemplated having him replaced. It seems that Kincaid came to the estate in April 1848 in order to collect rent. On 20 April, Stewart wrote to him stating: 'I enclose some blank notices to quit in case you think well of serving 10 or 12 of the Ballyhealy fellows with notice . . . as some high pressure must be brought to bear on them.' (sκ) Although, in this letter, Stewart contemplated having notices to quit served on some tenants, assistance to the distressed was provided around the same time. On 19 April, Espine Batty wrote to Stewart & Kincaid: 'I sent a small sum of £10 to Ballyhealy for seed potatoes for a beginning to be sold at half price & the half price to be laid out in more potatoes in like manner, as a help to the smaller holders' (sκ). Thus, although the smaller tenants at Ballyhealy were paying little or no cash in the spring of 1848, Espine Batty nevertheless subsidised some of them in provision of potato seed.

The Stewart & Kincaid correspondence up to late 1848 does not provide any indication that any person was required to leave the Ballyhealy estate for reasons of arrears in rent. Morgan was replaced as local agent by George Witton who arrived early in December. Witton was probably tougher. The last recorded letter to Stewart & Kincaid pertaining to the estate is from him. Dated 12 December 1848 it reported: 'I gave over possession of the land and house . . . lately held by the widow Nugent to Mr Tho's McEvoy. . . . I also got the enclosed proposal signed by Andrew Devine and gave him possession of the land given up by widow Pakenham, and the house held by Hegarty, and I took down the other house as directed. The Corcorans I cannot get off without giving them 20 or 25 shillings so I must take the course of Law.' (sκ)

The sexual activities of the Battys in perspective

Although Fitzherbert's sexual activities were irresponsible, the Stewart & Kincaid correspondence indicates that in their dealings with the tenantry in the 1840s the Battys were sympathetic landlords. The correspondence shows that in 1846 Fitzherbert helped to obtain employment off the estate for the son of a widowed tenant; that in the same year he provided food and road work to some needy tenants; that Espine subsidised the provision of seed potatoes in 1848 and that he presumably borrowed from government in order to finance a drainage project in that year; that the Battys provided financial support for the school on the estate. It is of course true that some of the children at the school may have been illegitimate offspring of Fitzherbert and/or William Batty. As also noted, the Stewart & Kincaid correspondence up to late in 1848 provides no evidence that any (legal) tenant on the estate was forced to leave because of arrears in rent. It also indicates that Stewart & Kincaid had a net claim against the estate by early 1848; that in the same year a small sum may have been paid to a squatter in order to induce him to leave; that Stewart & Kincaid's attitude towards defaulting tenants hardened toward the end of 1848; that around the same time, a few tenants appear to have surrendered their holdings but that any compensation of such departing tenants seems to have been very small.

It is likely that the Batty file is of more interest to social rather than economic historians. What is particularly interesting is the light it casts on the sexual behaviour of some members of a landed family vis-à-vis the women below them in the economic and social hierarchy. Although tales and rumours abound, surprisingly little is known to historians about the sexual behaviour of landlords in Ireland vis-à-vis their tenants. Seamus MacPhilib has investigated the recorded folklore and other evidence on the subject.[35]

As indicated by MacPhilib, 'among those . . . traditions which present Irish landlords in an unfavourable light is the tradition that they had the right to sleep with brides on the first night of marriage'.[36] MacPhilib consulted 44 folklore accounts, involving Irish landlords and others in authority, on the supposed right of the first night. He found that many of the supposed male participants in such sexual acts were of Catholic and indigenous Irish origin, rather than landlords whose progenitors had come from Britain. He went on to consider 96 records, obtained from folklore, concerning a more general perception of landlord sexual activity (not merely on the 'first night'). He noted that 'the most common theme among recorded oral traditions of other types of sexual activity of landlords is that they were often the fathers of illegitimate children. . . . There are several related . . . traditions concerning the maintenance of mistresses by landlords'.[37] MacPhilib concluded that 'the Irish folk tradition of *ius primae noctis* is not borne out by other types of sources to any significant extent'; however, 'there is a much greater degree of concurrence between folk tradition and other types of sources with regard to other forms of sexual behaviour of the landed classes'.[38] Some of these 'other types of sources' cited by MacPhilib express suspicions or mere allegations rather than well documented facts. For example, the most celebrated case of murder of a nineteenth-century landlord in Ireland allegedly because of his sexual adventures with tenants is that of the third Earl of Leitrim in 1878. MacPhilib reports that the Earl

is depicted in a lustful light in . . . some contemporary accounts.[39] . . . Leitrim's bachelorhood undoubtedly lent itself to imputation of lasciviousness on his part. Otherwise it appears that there was nothing in particular in his diaries to suggest this, nor indeed is he accused of it in the reports of police and of poor law inspectors who accuse him of a host of other malpractices. It may be that the imputation of lasciviousness to him is primarily a way of denigrating him, of underlining and illustrating his oppressive character in the minds of many and of lending some justification for his assassination. . . . There may be some significance in the fact that in his will Leitrim bequeathed £20 to each of his female servants but made no similar bequest to his male servants.[40]

The Stewart & Kincaid files on the Battys provide facts rather then allegations in regard to the sexual activities of an Irish landlord and his brother. It is interesting to observe that in the period reviewed in the present chapter, the cost of removing former sexual associates of the Battys must have been greatly in excess of that involved in removing any 'ordinary' tenants. The costs to Fitzherbert of settlement with Brigid Gaffney were certainly more than £50. Her name is not listed among those on the estate in 1854. Shortly before his death *c.*1847, Fitzherbert lived with Mary McNally, to whom he paid money, and by whom he had a child. No person named McNally was listed on the estate in 1854. A woman named Monaghan was another sexual associate to Fitzherbert. It seems that Stewart & Kincaid paid for her passage to America. The *Valuation* of 1854 provides no evidence of any person named Monaghan on the estate. Finally, there was William Batty's 'disgraceful connexion' with the female named Caffrey. It will be recalled that he was willing to pay as much as £300 to have Ms Caffrey and her children emigrated.

The number of illegitimate children fathered by the Battys is unknown. It is probable that there were many. In regard to Fitzherbert, Espine referred to two illegitimate children but he thought that they were not 'the *only ones*', as he had 'heard surnames of more' and he feared 'prospects of more turning up as claimants'. In revealing some details of the sexual activities of the Battys, the Stewart & Kincaid correspondence yields insights into an aspect of Irish social history about which virtually nothing else is firmly known. The details on these matters in the Stewart & Kincaid correspondence probably represent the mere tip of an iceberg: the details were provided, not in admiration of the sexual prowess of the two Batty brothers, but in efforts to minimise the costs associated with consequences of their sexual activities.

FIFTEEN

CONCLUSIONS

—

Several years after starting research on the Stewart & Kincaid correspondence, my views on the parties mentioned therein are now very different from my initial expectations. I had anticipated that the letters would reveal heartless landlords; a system in which most of the owners did not care about improvements; mass poverty among the tenantry; a system in which tenants were ejected upon a whim of the landlord; a legal system which left them defenceless; an environment in which compensation was not usually given to tenants leaving an estate; a general 'sink or swim' attitude amongst landlords who rarely assisted tenants in emigration; a primitive financial system; and that the Dublin district escaped the direct effects of the famine. As general propositions to which confidence can be attached, I now adhere to only one of those views – that large sections of the tenantry lived in great poverty. Conclusions here will be confined to matters relating to the expectations mentioned above. Some of the quotations used in the following discussion have been presented more fully, but in a few cases more briefly, in earlier chapters; these have been indicated with a page reference to the earlier citation.

The past few decades have seen publication of many books on the famine.[1] The present work complements them. But it also suggests a need for revision of some of the recent research on the famine years. Popular views on that period concern matters of a general character while others are on very specific issues. Among those of a general character is a view that landlords as a group failed to respond to destitution in a humane manner; an example of those on specific points is a view that the financial system was primitive. Two views expressed by Lynch and Vaizey need clarification and/or correction.[2] The first is that non-monetisation of the economy made the famine more severe than it would otherwise have been. The second point concerns the impact of the famine on Dublin City and its neighbourhood.

I A NON-MONETISED NON-MARKET ECONOMY?

On the first set of points, Lynch and Vaizey state that for many decades up to the famine, Ireland was a dual economy: a maritime economy which was monetised and market-oriented, and a non-monetised subsistence economy, and that 'perhaps rather more than 6.0 million people lived in the subsistence economy when the Great Famine came in 1845, and about 2.0 million in the maritime economy around Dublin, Belfast, Cork, Waterford, Limerick and Galway'.[3] Although it seems to have been now largely discredited, the Lynch–Vaizey view of dualism has had some influence among historians. In 1974 E. D. Steele cited their work and remarked that 'the scarcity of money was indicative of the backwardness then of a vast area, containing over three-quarters of the population'.[4]

Lynch and Vaizey state that the subsistence economy was 'a society without a market' and in that society 'when famines occurred the precariousness of a non-monetary economy . . . became apparent with startling rapidity. . . . The rural economy was founded on subsistence and barter. . . . A day's cart-journey from any town the use of money was rare. . . . By the suppression of paper money in 1826 the tragic effects of the Great Famine twenty years later were made inevitable. . . . As the economy of the areas where absentee landlords had their estates was almost exclusively of a subsistence kind, the rents paid in money cannot have been substantial.'[5] The key points in the Lynch–Vaizey argument seem to be as follows.

Outside the maritime economy, people relied mainly on barter (of goods for goods, and of labour–services for land use) rather than on use of financial instruments; in the second half of the 1840s those with food to sell were unwilling to barter; even if those in the non-maritime sector seeking food had substantial assets, they had no means of converting such assets into money and then into food because for them the use of money and markets generally did not exist; therefore those in the huge subsistence sector were virtually doomed to starvation when their subsistence crop, the potato, failed. This reasoning relies on two assumptions: first, that outside the maritime sector the economy was effectively non-monetised; secondly, that individuals outside the maritime sector, who possessed non-financial assets, could not convert such assets into money, or had great difficulty in doing so. If either of these assumptions were invalid, then the Lynch–Vaizey conclusions in regard to the link between non-monetisation and the severity of the famine are logically invalid.

Turning to the first – and the dominant – assumption, one has only to look at the frequency and locations of fairs in rural Ireland on the eve of the famine to see that the picture created by Lynch and Vaizey exaggerates reality. For example, Pettigrew and Oulton's 'list of fairs in Ireland for the year 1845' has about 270 fairs scheduled for the County of Clare, and well over 100 in the County of Roscommon, in that year.[6] The earlier chapters have contained many references to use of fairs by tenants in order to enable them to obtain cash to pay rent.

I am not claiming that the Lynch–Vaizey interpretation of the rural economy is wrong in all respects. The Stewart & Kincaid correspondence indicates that landlords sometimes paid for private works by means of allowances towards rent. The earlier chapters have cited instances during the famine in which Stewart & Kincaid's agents recommended that tenants involved in such works should be paid, at frequent intervals, in the form of cash in order to enable them to buy food, and in order to avoid deflection of labour, away from works of improvement on a landlord's estate, towards public works projects where payment in cash, at short intervals, was the norm.[7] But in contrast to the picture which Lynch and Vaizey create, the Stewart & Kincaid correspondence indicates a sophisticated financial system in rural Ireland during the 1840s. The evidence is, more often than not, that Stewart & Kincaid tenants paid rent in cash; that to a considerable extent they signed promissory notes against which they usually made settlement in cash; that tenants (as well as Stewart & Kincaid's agents) often sent rents directly Dublin by forwarding half notes through the post; that sometimes a tenant used a letter of credit (a mechanism for reallocation of bank deposits) to transfer monies to Dublin; that some of the larger tenants accepted drafts of bills of exchange a few months before their rent was due; that Stewart & Kincaid sometimes (or always) had such bills discounted, thereby giving the Dublin firm liquidity prior to the redemption dates of the bills. Thus, although the Lynch-Vaizey distinction between the 'maritime' and the 'subsistence' economies may have had some elements of validity, the Stewart & Kincaid correspondence indicates that in itself it had little relevance to the many districts in which Stewart & Kincaid managed estates. Given the failures of the potato, in the case of many tenants the real problem was not that they had no assets in the form of money; rather, it was that they had virtually no assets. A fundamental assumption behind the Lynch–Vaizey analysis of why, given the potato failures of the late 1840s, the famine was so severe, is therefore refuted.

2 ON THE EFFECTS IN DUBLIN OF THE FAMINE

The second context in which the Lynch–Vaizey discussion requires clarification and/or correction is their statement that 'the areas unaffected directly by the Great Famine were the maritime economy centred on Dublin, Cork and Belfast'.[8] The important words to note here are 'directly' as well as 'unaffected'.

Thus, in the view of Lynch and Vaizey, the Dublin district was *not directly* affected by the potato failures; however, their statement is perfectly consistent with a view that Dublin (like the English port of Liverpool, which was the most important immediate destination of Irish emigrants) was *indirectly* affected by the famine.

A view that the *direct* impact of the potato failures was weaker in the Dublin district than in rural Ireland is plausible, given that Dublin City was the commercial and administrative centre of the country, as well as its principal port. Most households in rural Ireland grew potatoes and depended on that crop for their consumption. In many cases it was virtually the only solid foodstuff which they consumed. Such extreme dependence on the potato did not apply in and immediately around Dublin City, where production of services rather than tangible goods predominated. However, the Stewart & Kincaid correspondence indicates that the Lynch–Vaizey view that the Dublin district escaped the direct effects of the potato failures is inaccurate. It may be recalled from chapter 1 that in July 1846 Patrick Bowden wrote to Stewart & Kincaid from Swords (about nine miles north of the city centre): '[the] total loss of my potato crop was much against me this year' (p. 23). In chapter 3 it was seen that on the Palmerston lands at Quarry Vale, 'the dreadful loss of seven acres of potatoes' (p. 64) in 1846 led Patrick Ternan into confrontation with Stewart & Kincaid; it may also be recalled that Ternan's neighbour, a Mrs Smith at Chapelizod, informed Stewart & Kincaid in September 1848 that she could not pay her rent promptly owing to 'the great loss I have had in my potatoes' (p. 65). (Quarry Vale and Chapelizod are only a few miles from the centre of Dublin City.) Finally, it was observed in chapter 13 that by early 1846 the potato failure had caused severe distress on the lands of the Earl of Howth in County Meath (contiguous to County Dublin), that in the autumn of 1846 many of the earl's tenants there were 'reduced to the lowest state of wretchedness', in consequence of the total failure of the potato crops (p. 267), and that a letter of December 1846 reported to Stewart & Kincaid that many of the people near the Meath boundary with County Dublin were 'absolutely starving' (p. 268).

That the potato failures of the late 1840s had *indirect* effects on the Dublin district is not denied by Lynch and Vaizey. In fact, on the basis of earlier experiences, by the mid-1840s it was recognised that a severe potato failure would be followed by outbreak and spread of famine-related diseases. As summarised by Woodham-Smith: 'The moment when the epidemic broke out in any locality depended on when infection was brought there. . . . The Warrenpoint-Rostrevor area, in County Down, appears to be the only district recorded as having escaped fever entirely. . . . The explanation, in all probability, is that the Warrenpoint–Rostrevor area lay off any main route to a large town and was therefore not inundated by wandering paupers who brought fever'.[9] Chapter 5 observed that during the summer of 1847, the Irish landlord D. H. Ferrall left Liverpool out of fear of fever then rife there, and that the incoming Irish, many of them hoping to be in transit to America, were probably the main cause of the outbreak there. It is likely that most of these potential emigrants had earlier arrived from Dublin. It is also likely that many of those who arrived in Dublin stayed there indefinitely, in crowded environments; this must have accelerated the spread of 'famine fever' there. The Stewart & Kincaid correspondence refers to the case of the Corcoran family, 'all bad in fever' in January 1848 (p. 268), a few miles from the city centre. The absence of further references to fever within the city or in the district immediately surrounding Dublin City reflects the fact that almost all of the lands for which Stewart & Kincaid had responsibility were located beyond that district.

The statements by Lynch and Vaizey on the impact of the famine on the Dublin district have been misinterpreted by one researcher. Recall that their statement about the famine's impact on 'the maritime economy' pertained to direct effects; of indirect effects they had practically nothing to say, and they certainly made no reference to effects of induced migration to Dublin, whether by individuals in transit through the port or those of a more permanent character. In a recent publication, Cormac Ó Gráda has provided a useful analysis of such indirect effects in Dublin city.[10] He quotes the same passage from Lynch and Vaizey as that quoted at the beginning of the present section. He classifies the induced spread of fever in Dublin as an indirect effect, and he shows that 'mortality in Dublin rose during the famine'; however, he adds: 'Were Dubliners largely immune [from famine-induced diseases] as Lynch and Vaizey claimed?'[11] But Lynch and Vaizey made no such claim: while not denying them, they did not investigate such indirect effects.

It is probable that a high proportion of the excess mortality in Dublin during the famine is attributable to deaths among migrants from elsewhere in Ireland. Many of the would-be emigrants from Ireland arriving in Liverpool were in such wretched condition that they were refused passage to America, and because their presence in Liverpool posed a threat to the lives of the local population, in 1847 thousands of them were shipped back to Ireland, where Dublin was the closest port to Liverpool. It is very likely that deaths among such individuals were largely responsible for a huge level of excess mortality among paupers in Dublin in that year. This consideration should be borne in mind in interpretation of statistics presented by Ó Gráda.

3 ON EVICTIONS IN THE 1840S

Although historians have written much about evictions during the famine years, I am not aware that any of them have clearly defined what they meant by 'eviction'. In an oral communication to me, a lawyer has described 'eviction' as 'a sociological term' in contrast to the legal term 'ejectment'. Historians have tended to refer to eviction rather than ejectment. Eviction is here defined as *involuntary (on the part of a tenant) termination of tenancy, usually following action in court*. The main reason for the qualification 'usually' is to allow for the circumstances of cottiers (small tenants with agreements for short periods, such as month to month): in most cases, a head landlord did not need to make any special application to the courts in order to remove individual cottiers (who were often undertenants to middlemen, and who were often removed around the same time as the departure of a middleman). According to the above definition of 'eviction', voluntary surrender of land held by a tenant in arrears, against whom a notice to quit had been served, did not constitute eviction.

An understanding of law pertaining to ejectment is essential for sensible interpretation of the figures on famine-period evictions relied upon by many historians.[12] Tim P. O'Neill has provided a convenient summary of the estimates of historians in regard to the number of evictions during the famine years. He also provides his own estimates.[13]

Taking O'Neill's contributions into account, along with consultation of nineteenth-century parliamentary papers[14] and the Stewart & Kincaid correspondence, leads to the conclusion here that although some historians have estimated the number of famine-period evictions with apparent confidence, we have no real idea of the number of evictions in Ireland during those years. Reasons for this view will be indicated near the end of the present section. But first, a summary from the Stewart & Kincaid correspondence of findings related to eviction is as follows:

Chapter 1 included references to some of the lands (not discussed in subsequent chapters) for which the firm of Stewart & Kincaid was agent in the 1840s: those of De Vesci in Cork and Dublin; of the Powerscourts in Wicklow and Tyrone; of Viscount Lorton whose seat was in Roscommon; of Thomas Staples in Dublin; of Jane Coleman in Kildare; of John Hamilton in Donegal. Some of those owners were benevolent. The Stewart & Kincaid letters indicate no threats of eviction on the aforementioned lands; however, the sample of correspondence which refers to those properties is too small to justify any firm conclusions in regard to eviction: all we can say is that the Stewart & Kincaid correspondence contains no reference to eviction from those lands.[15]

Developments on Palmerston's Sligo estates have been surveyed in chapters 2 and 3, where it was observed that there were few evictions in the early

1840s. As Kincaid explained to the Devon Commission in December 1843, at the time of squaring and resettlement in Ahamlish parish, 'Palmerston's distinct orders were, that no man should be dispossessed, unless he chose to go, and then he was to have assistance to enable him to go to America or elsewhere'.[16] Kincaid stated that there had been a few cases of distraint on the Sligo estate, and that (several months) after service of notices to quit, some tenants had been ejected. It seems that most of the Palmerston tenants evicted up to the end of 1845 had very lengthy arrears of rent, and that others were evicted because they were accused of crime. Thus, three tenants were evicted in 1842 in connection with theft of oats, and in 1841 19 tenants urged Stewart & Kincaid to evict a tenant whom they accused of stealing various items. A document sent to Stewart & Kincaid in 1846 contains a list of tenants accused of theft. Some of them may have been forced to leave.

Chapter 3 indicated major changes in Palmerston's thinking in the late 1840s: he was seeking to depopulate his Sligo estates thereby creating more viable farm sizes. Many of his tenants were taken to America in 1847. The cost of getting them there was deemed compensation for 'voluntary' surrender of their holdings. In 1848 the Stewart & Kincaid agent Smyth sought 'voluntary' surrender or ejectment in further reducing the population on Palmerston's lands. Much of this depopulation was related to further squaring of lands (at this time mainly outside Ahamlish), in which context Palmerston's earlier orders no longer applied. Smyth's letters suggest that all or most of those who made life easier for Stewart & Kincaid, by promptly giving up possession, received compensation. Some of them were cottiers who had earlier been undertenants to a middleman or middlemen who had gone, rather than direct tenants to Palmerston. Ejectment decrees were obtained against others, though not all of those decrees were executed.

Palmerston's agents sought and terminally executed ejectments only as a measure of last resort. In October 1848 Smyth sent Stewart & Kincaid a list of tenants who had recently paid him. He indicated that a few of those on the list had paid up to November 1846 but none of them had paid for gales beyond that date, and that some of them had paid up only to May 1844. Although ejectment was a time-consuming task to which legal expenses were attached, it was not always simple. Recall the case of a tenant at Ballytivnan outside Sligo town. It seems that following a physical fight, an ejectment decree was executed against him, but that he took possession again, and that the case against him was then dismissed at court.

Stewart & Kincaid commenced management of the Crichton properties around the beginning of 1848, when rents seem to have been greatly in arrears. Smyth implemented policies on the Crichton lands near Ballymote in Sligo similar to those which he applied on the Palmerston properties: townlands were subjected to squaring and population clearance. In many cases the clearances were facilitated by 'voluntary' surrender rather than by resort to the courts. Compensation was given to at least some of those who gave up possession of lands about to be squared. To the north of Ballymote a few tenants were evicted. However, those people had previously been undertenants to a middleman, and Stewart & Kincaid gave them only small sums in compensation.

The Crichtons also owned land in Roscommon. Much of this was held by middlemen, apparently on condition that it would be used for grazing only. But some of them rented tracts to subtenants, and set plots under conacre. It seems that such allocations breached conditions in the middlemen's leases. The potato failure of 1846 meant that the undertenants and those on conacre to one of the middlemen, Peyton, could not pay their rents; therefore Peyton could not pay Stewart & Kincaid. Wynne Peyton was ejected. He had a business agreement with another large tenant on Crichton land, William Sandys. Peyton's financial distress, combined with his business arrangement with Sandys, appear to be the main reasons why Sandys was sent to prison for debt, and was evicted, early in 1848. Peyton's eviction made it easy for Stewart & Kincaid to remove his undertenants. A similar observation applies to Crichton lands held by the middleman Patt Taaffe.

The ejectment of Peyton from Carrownalassan, and the ensuing 'shovelling out' of his undertenants, help to explain why the population of that townland fell from 655 to 323 persons between 1841 and 1851. Similarly, the departure of Taaffe from the contiguous townland of Dooherty, where he had a pauper tenantry, helps explain why the population there fell from 125 to 10 over the decade. Some of the tenants on those townlands may, however, have been evicted because of suspicions that they were implicated in the murder of Denis Mahon in 1847: this took place in a neighbourhood of those townlands (though not where some historians have stated). However, the extent of depopulation should be placed in context. First, most of the victims were undertenants to Peyton or Taaffe who, in setting Crichton lands to paupers for tillage, appear to have violated conditions in their leases. Second, Crichton himself was in distress in 1848.

Chapter 5 examined the financial problems of the Roscommon landlord D. H. Ferrall. For much of the 1840s he was an absentee, not by simple choice, but out of fear of being imprisoned for debt in Ireland or in England. John Sharkey was his principal agent in north Roscommon, where programmes of depopulation were implemented in the late 1840s.

Several ejectment decrees appear to have been obtained against Ferrall's tenants in the years immediately before the famine. Whether many of these were executed is unknown. However, until the second half of the 1840s, Stewart & Kincaid and the firm's agents seem to have been as much interested in the 'demonstration effects' of such decrees as in any prospect of last-moment settlements. Thus, as late as October 1846, Sharkey wrote that he thought that 'there can be nothing better done to forward the approaching collection [of rents] than to proceed against the few for example to the many' (p. 111). Until 1847, distraint was the preferred measure against defaulters on the Ferrall estates.

By the beginning of 1847 Stewart & Kincaid believed that in a great many cases there was no prospect of collecting arrears, and that the population of small tenants was unsustainably high. Ferrall therefore concurred with Stewart & Kincaid's recommendation of a new policy: that as many as possible of the small tenants be given 'moderate sums' in order to encourage them to surrender their holdings and depart from his lands. Many of them did receive small sums of money to leave. Ferrall believed that such departures were in their own interests: he wrote that some of his land was 'so overcrowded that it will be a benefit to themselves as well as to us to leave it' (p. 115). Defaulting large tenants – mainly those with leases – would have been in a better financial position to go to America; however, both Ferrall and Stewart & Kincaid regarded many of them as viable in the long run, and therefore sought to retain them. The immediate alternative would have been to leave huge tracts of land idle.

On several townlands in north Roscommon, the policy of depopulation was accelerated in the first half of 1848. The fact that one large middleman had been ejected, and that other leases had expired through death, made it easier to rid the lands of former undertenants. On 19 June 1848 Sharkey wrote that he had thrown 'down about 34 houses . . . including ten of those thrown in Lissergool east in April last . . . and which were since rebuilt by the evicted tenants who were living in them back again.' He added that he had 'succeeded in knocking about several huts which were built by the ditches' (p. 118). On 23 June he reported to Kincaid that 'there are now about 30 of the Lissergool families lying by the ditches in a most wretched condition & I have done all in my power to get some of them taken in to the poor house not only for the sake of relieving them but to get rid of such a plague and of the extreme trouble of preventing them of building hovels. . . . I shall obey your generous offer and give them [small compensation]' (pp. 118, 119). It should be noted that it seems that those to whom Sharkey referred were not legitimate tenants to Ferrall; rather, according to Sharkey, all or large numbers of them were squatters who had been ejected from other estates, and Sharkey expected that the small sums of money which he gave would induce many of them to go to England. Furthermore, Ferrall himself was genuinely disturbed: in July 1848 he wrote to Stewart & Kincaid that 'it is a melancholy reflection that one should be obliged to consign his fellow creature to such misery' (p. 119) and that 'the fact of your having sent pecuniary relief to the poor people who were ejected, should satisfy the public that you were activated by kind feelings' (p. 119). The desired depopulation of the Ferrall lands was more or less completed by mid-1848. Policy on defaulters then reverted to what it had been in the years immediately before the famine: distraint tended to replace 'voluntary' surrender or ejectment. A letter from Ferrall in 1849 refers to 'costs of ejectments and compensation to tenants – £450' (p. 120). A breakdown of the £450 (probably the equivalent of about £45,000 sterling in purchasing power at the beginning of the twenty first century), distinguishing between sums spent on compensation and sums spent on ejectment, is not available.

No moral opinion is offered in regard to the depopulation of the Ferrall lands in 1847–8. But it is suggested that those expressing such views might bear the following considerations in mind: Ferrall's financial problems became desperate during those years; Sharkey acted responsibly in the interests of his employers; the partners in Stewart & Kincaid had their own financial survival to worry about; although the sums involved in individual cases were small, most of those leaving the Ferrall lands in 1847–8 were given financial assistance; some of those who were given small sums of money by Stewart & Kincaid were squatters rather than legitimate tenants to Ferrall; finally, note that the evidence is that both Ferrall and Sharkey were Irish Catholics.

Many of the developments on Wingfield's lands in west Sligo were similar to those on Palmerston's Ahamlish. The limited programme of squaring Wingfield lands in the pre-famine 1840s appears to have been accompanied by few evictions. It seems that relatively small numbers of tenants and former undertenants were 'dispossessed', or they surrendered their holdings; these were financially 'assisted' or 'compensated' upon departure. An ejectment decree was obtained against at least one tenant during the summer of 1845. Whether this was executed is unclear; however, in Wingfield's words, 'it had the effect of getting possession [ie. surrender, presumably combined with compensation] from one or two others' (p. 135). It seems that some of Wingfield's small tenants 'voluntarily' surrendered their holdings in 1847 in exchange for the same kind of 'compensation' as that given to departing Palmerston tenants in that year. An inference that their numbers were significant is consistent with the observation that many of the holdings on Wingfield's property lay idle early in 1848.

Some of the discussion on threatened eviction in chapter 7 concerned the case of Patrick Howley. He held a lease from Wingfield, who disliked him. The fact that Howley had fallen into arrears of rent by the autumn of 1845 gave Wingfield an opportunity of trying to get rid of him. But it took a long time to remove Howley: it seems that this was realised only through his death in 1847 or early in 1848. The case of Howley is one of several which illustrate that ejectment was not necessarily a simple or inexpensive matter.

Chapter 8 surveyed developments on the Roscommon estates of George Nugent. It seems that relatively few ejectment decrees were executed on his lands up to the end of 1846, but that even before the famine, some of Nugent's tenants received compensation for surrender of their holdings. Many ejectment decrees were outstanding on his properties in east Roscommon late in the summer of 1846. However, it does not seem that any of them were executed at that time. Stewart & Kincaid recognised that execution of decrees would have created bad publicity at that hungry time of the year. Some decrees may have been executed around the end of 1846. Referring to the 'demonstration effect', one of Stewart & Kincaid's agents on the Nugent lands wrote in November 1846 that 'by serving a few ejectments their [there would] be a good deal of rents paid' (p. 156)). In December 1846, another of Stewart & Kincaid's local agents listed 56 of the tenants on Nugent townlands, and he observed that three of them had 'nothing', 28 were to be distrained and the residual 25 were to be processed for ejectment. The *Valuation* of 1858 indicates that the three who had 'nothing' seem to have gone, 13 of the 28 who were to be distrained were still there, and five of the 25 who were to be processed for ejectment were still on the townlands on which they had holdings in 1846. It is probable that several of the latter 25 were among those who surrendered their holdings in 1847–8, in exchange for financial assistance. Thus, it was not the case that almost all ejectment decrees were terminally executed.

Stewart & Kincaid implemented a programme of depopulation on Nugent properties in 1847–8. Many of his tenants were induced to surrender their holdings, for which all or most of them received probably small sums in compensation. In September 1847 Stewart wrote to Kincaid: 'Every one is clearing that part [of east Roscommon] & the people are willing enough to go' (p. 157). The Stewart & Kincaid correspondence strongly suggests that although the number of evictions on the Nugent estates was small, the depopulation of those lands brought about by 'voluntary' surrender of holdings in 1847–8 involved hundreds of persons.

Chapter 9 indicates that Blackwell, the Stewart & Kincaid agent on Stratford's Clare estate, exercised widespread distraint. The correspondence provides no evidence that any tenant who farmed there was evicted in the 1840s. However, in the face of arrears of rent, Blackwell asked several tenants to surrender their holdings. In two known cases the initiative for surrender came from tenants, who received assistance to leave. Apart from impoverished cottiers, it seems that there were very few evictions on Stratford's Limerick estate in the 1840s. Some ejectment decrees seem to have been obtained in the early 1840s for possible execution on his Limerick lands. However, these may have been obtained in order to give Stewart & Kincaid leverage in shifting tenants from one location to another during squaring. The evidence is that in

1841–2, and again in 1846, many cottiers were induced to leave. All of the cottiers induced or forced off the estate seem to have been given compensation in order to enable them to go elsewhere.

The leases of some middlemen expired around the time at which Stewart & Kincaid commenced management of Mrs Fitzgerald's Mount Blakeney estate in south Limerick. One of the firm's first tasks was to rationalise the structure of holdings, which involved the removal of former undertenants, at least some of whom were compensated for surrendering their holdings. In one case an ejectment decree – which was not executed – was obtained. It seems that expedition of resettlement during the squaring was the motivation behind this. In connection with squaring of the land, John Callaghan was the most troublesome tenant on the estate. Early in 1844 he received £15 from Stewart & Kincaid on the understanding that he would surrender his land; however he changed his mind and refused to go. Assisted by police, in September 1844 Stewart & Kincaid's local bailiff unsuccessfully tried to remove him by force. Further efforts to remove him were also unsuccessful. However, it seems that a compromise was ultimately reached, that Callaghan surrendered possession, and that the case against him was struck off the legal list late in July 1845. Callaghan was still on the estate in March 1846, though not as an immediate tenant to Mrs Fitzgerald. Thus, it proved very difficult to get rid of him.

The Stewart & Kincaid correspondence for 1846 contains no references to ejectment from the Mount Blakeney estate, and only a single instance (involving £5 in compensation) of voluntary surrender. It seems that some tenants sought to surrender their holdings in 1847 in exchange for financial assistance. But Mrs Fitzgerald's own financial position militated against such assistance on any large scale in that year; nevertheless, in September she wrote to Stewart 'knowing that you would act *justly always*, and *leniently if*' Stewart considered that a tenant was '*really distressed*' (p. 210). Several of Fitzgerald's tenants surrendered their holdings in the spring of 1848. In compensation, Stewart & Kincaid made significant contributions in financing their departures. The *Valuation* of 1851 indicates major changes in the tenantry on the estate. Apart from the removal of some former undertenants *c.*1844, there is very little evidence to suggest that many of those changes were brought about by eviction.

Developments on Warren's Ballinruane estate in 1845–8 were similar to those on Mount Blakeney. The property of some defaulters was seized for rent; however, probably most of them had no assets which could have been distrained. Many of the tenants surrendered their holdings in 1847–8. At least two of them had ejectment decrees outstanding against them, which appear not to have been executed. Compensation given to those who surrendered was generous. Very few (if any) tenants seem to have been formally ejected. The letters on the estate list the names of about fifty tenant heads of households, mainly in 1845–6. The *Valuation* of 1852 indicates that probably no more than nine of them were still there. It is likely that most of the others had then surrendered their holdings and left Ireland.

Chapter 12 examined developments on Frankfort's lands in Kilkenny and Carlow. His Kilkenny properties were mainly in two districts – at Coolcullen in the north and at Keatingstown towards the south near Kilkenny City.

There were some ejectments from Coolcullen in the early 1840s. According to one of the ejected tenants, Thomas Purcell, most of those evicted received compensation for improvements. However, these developments occurred before Stewart & Kincaid commenced as agent on the estate. Shortly after the firm's commencement there, a person who had accepted the tenancy of land formerly occupied by Purcell was murdered. There is no evidence that Stewart & Kincaid ejected anyone from Coolcullen until 1848. Some of the Purcells appear to have surrendered their land, and to have received compensation, in 1848, when Frankfort wrote to Stewart & Kincaid 'relative to the Purcels', indicating 'I assent to your recommendaytion for giving £50 to get rid of them' (p. 228). There were three tenants on Coolcullen who had ejectment decrees outstanding against them in September 1848. One of Stewart & Kincaid's agents recommended that they be given specific sums (£10 to £15 each) to leave (p. 232).

The Stewart & Kincaid letters pertaining to Keatingstown and to Frankfort lands in Carlow differ in three respects from those about Coolcullen. First, distraint in those districts was more frequent. Second, there are two letters, both of which appear to refer to Keatingstown, which report applications for ejectment decrees which failed due to technical points of law. Third, the letters on the Carlow estate refer to imprisonment of one of Stewart & Kincaid's agents. These cases of failure to obtain decrees, and that in which one of Stewart & Kincaid's agents was sent to prison, illustrate that the Law did not always favour the strongest.

Chapter 13 contains relatively little about eviction. It seems that some ejectments were executed on the Ponsonby estate in 1847 or early in 1848, and that in some cases the tenants involved were allowed to remain on the properties, at least for a while, as caretakers. In 1842 a Pakenham tenant surrendered his holding, for which Stewart & Kincaid gave him £8. In August 1846 an ejectment decree was outstanding against another Pakenham tenant – a woman whose husband (and a son) had already gone to America. It seems that the decree was not executed, that the woman surrendered her holding, and that Stewart & Kincaid financially assisted her and eight of her children to leave. It seems that 'voluntary' surrender of holdings on the Pakenham lands was on a considerable scale in 1848. Chapter 14 on the Sherlock and the Batty estates contained practically nothing about eviction. It will be recalled, in the case of the Battys, that the primary people to be removed were women whose sexual connections with family members were costing the estate a great deal of money and embarrassment.

It is concluded that eviction of legitimate tenants to the landlords whose estates were managed by Stewart & Kincaid was relatively infrequent. This was the case for a number of reasons, which are set out below.

1   The procedures leading to an ejectment decree consumed time and money. In most cases they would have involved service of a notice to quit and, some months later, service of a summons or summonses to court proceedings which cost the plaintiff money. There was no guarantee that such proceedings would lead to terminal ejectment.

2   Those ejectment decrees which Stewart & Kincaid did obtain were not always executed, for a number of reasons. First, Stewart & Kincaid was aware that execution of decrees could cause bad publicity. Second, there were cases in which tenants paid rent arrears, as well as Stewart & Kincaid's legal costs, at the last moment. Third, there were cases in which tenants surrendered their holdings shortly after the issue of an ejectment decree, but prior to its execution. Some of such departing tenants under ejectment received compensation from Stewart & Kincaid, prior to any need to have decrees executed (involving extra costs). Fourth, on any given estate where many tenants were in arrears, the firm of Stewart & Kincaid was aware of the 'demonstration effect' of obtaining decrees against a few tenants only, for the example of many.

3   In the case of tenants in arrears who had assets, and who in Stewart & Kincaid's opinion were viable in the long run, Stewart & Kincaid preferred to distrain rather than lose them. In many cases Stewart & Kincaid's agents placed keepers on the lands of distrained tenants in order to prevent clandestine removal of farm produce. There was little point in replacing an ejected tenant by an insolvent tenant. Hence, even when they were in arrears during the famine years, Stewart & Kincaid sought to keep those tenants considered viable in the long run. Distraint meant some income for Stewart & Kincaid. In many cases during 1847–8, a decision to eject would have amounted to a decision to leave land idle, or occupied by new tenants who had no assets or who could not pay any rent.

4   Especially during the famine years, there were a great many tenants who Stewart & Kincaid deemed non-viable in the long run. The firm therefore sought 'voluntary' surrender of their holdings, usually in return for compensation. *This was the optimal solution from Stewart & Kincaid's point of view: the firm thereby avoided costs of time and legal expenses in getting rid of tenants who were paying no rent, and (directly or indirectly) of financing their*

*relief if they stayed on the estate. It was also arguably optimal from the tenants'
point of view.* Many of them must have recognised that they might be
doomed if they forced on the landlord the costs of waiting to go to court
and of court proceedings, and they might not have expected compensation
on their departure under such circumstances. Many of them therefore
regarded it as optimal to surrender the land without court proceedings, in
return for 'compensation', or 'assistance' upon departure. This reasoning
reflects simple economic calculus: it is therefore surprising that the points
just raised appear to have remained unnoticed by economic historians.
Note that cases in which the initiative in surrender came from a tenant
were not rare.

Given the considerations in 1 to 4 above, it is not surprising that the bulk of
departures from estates managed by Stewart & Kincaid in 1846–8 appear to
have reflected surrender of land in return for financial aid, rather than formal
ejectment. Such surrenders did not constitute eviction, as that concept was
defined at the beginning of the present section. But given that the alternative
must often have been terminal ejectment, most of the surrenders probably did
constitute a form of 'quasi-eviction'. However, use of such a classification
raises a problem for which no resolution can be offered here: if initiative for
surrender in return for compensation came from a tenant, should one really
classify such a departure as 'quasi-eviction'?

It was stated earlier that although some historians have estimated the
number of famine-period evictions with apparent confidence, we simply do
not know the approximate numbers of evictions in Ireland during those years.
Further comment relevant to the above summary of findings from the Stewart
& Kincaid correspondence will therefore be brief. As summarised by O'Neill:

> Estimates of the scale of evictions for the period 1846 to 1854 have varied widely
> from W. E. Vaughan's 70,000 families or 250,000 persons to J. S. Donnelly's
> estimate of over half a million persons. Mary E. Daly, while acknowledging
> that the [official] statistics present difficulties, gave a figure of 19,283 families
> evicted in the years 1846 to 1848 inclusive. These figures were cited with approval
> by Christine Kinealy. All historians appear to agree on the accuracy of the police
> eviction returns that began in 1849 and recorded permanent evictions of 47,511
> families from 1849 to 1854. Adding the police returns for the years 1848 to 1854
> inclusive to Daly and Kinealy's returns for 1846 to 1848 gives a figure of 66,794
> families evicted between 1846 and 1854.[17]

The main problems with the official statistics, used in modified or original
form by some historians, are given below.

First, the official statistics for 1846 to 1848 inclusive refer to ejectment cases brought for the attention of the courts.[18] They do not purport to indicate the number of families or persons terminally ejected. The set of persons encompassed by such statistics intersects with the set of persons who eventually surrendered land and accepted compensation to leave 'voluntarily'. We do not know how significant these intersections were in 1846–8.

Secondly, the official statistics for 1849–54 are almost entirely drawn from 'evictions which have come to the knowledge of the constabulary'.[19] Thus, as compared to the official statistics for 1846–8, the police statistics involve an important change of classification. The figures for the earlier period pertain to ejectments sought; those for the later years purport to pertain to 'evictions'. But much more problematic is the fact that we do not know, in the compilation of their returns, how the police defined 'evictions'. If notices to quit were served on tenants, and if they then voluntarily surrendered their holdings in exchange for compensation and left an estate, did the police include them in their eviction statistics? If ejectment decrees were obtained but not executed against tenants because they voluntarily surrendered in exchange for compensation, were they included in the police returns of 'evictions'? In either case, the answer probably is that large numbers of them were included in the police returns. However, given the definition of eviction at the beginning of the present section, those in the two last-mentioned categories were *not evicted*. Thus, it is likely that in an important respect the police returns for the late years of the famine overstate evictions. But on the other hand, if there were many evictions which did not come to the attention of the constabulary, then the police returns could arguably understate the extent of evictions.

The real problems in the works of those who have tried to estimate levels of eviction during the famine years are, first, that they have generally failed to define what they meant by eviction; secondly (and this is an unsurmountable problem) there is the difficulty of assigning numbers on a spectrum, from 'mainly voluntary' surrender of land, to 'mild forms of quasi-eviction', to 'severe forms of quasi-eviction', to terminal execution of ejectment decrees. In view of the immediately foregoing discussion, it is surprising, in O'Neill's words, that hitherto 'all historians appear to agree on the accuracy of the police eviction returns'.[20] Note that O'Neill himself had reservations (though quite distinct from those raised here) on this point.

Surprisingly, the Stewart & Kincaid correspondence does not seem to contain a single reference to the (Gregory) 'Quarter Acre Clause' of 1847. This legislation stated that any occupier of more than a quarter acre of land would not be deemed destitute, and was therefore not eligible to receive relief financed by the poor rates. The high levels of 'voluntary' surrender of land in 1847–8 may have been in part induced by this notorious piece of legislation.

4 ON ASSISTED EMIGRATION

About 13,000 emigrants sailed for America from the port of Sligo in 1847. Many of them left under some form of landlord assistance. More than 2,000 of those brought from Sligo to America in 1847, at landlord expense, were former Palmerston tenants, and it is possible that hundreds in the same category came from the Wingfield estates.

It was seen that on behalf of Stewart & Kincaid, James Walker implemented a small-scale programme of emigration from Palmerston's Sligo estates in the years immediately before the famine, and that Quebec was the destination of at least one batch of such emigrants. John Lynch, the Stewart & Kincaid agent in Palmerston's Ahamlish, recommended a large-scale programme of emigration as early as January 1844, when he stated that 'it would be a good thing if Lord Palmerston bought 2,000 acres of land on the other side in America, and brought a vessel into the harbour, and took the poor people off, and carried them out there, and let them the land as his tenants' (p. 50). By the end of 1846 both Lynch and Dr West (the attendant at the dispensary in Cliffoney) seem to have abandoned all hope that the existing population of Ahamlish could be perpetuated. Late in 1846 the doctor wrote to Kincaid: 'It would be much less expensive for Lord Palmerston to send out the half if possible of his tenantry than have to feed them here and get no rents' (p. 50). A few days later, Lynch informed Kincaid: 'Gore Booth asked me to write to you to know if Lord Palmerston would join him in a vessel or vessels to send out a great portion of the people, who would give up their small farms, as he thinks nothing else will save them but sending them to America'.[21] Kincaid sent the relevant arithmetic – a cost-benefit analysis – to Palmerston on 23 March 1847. In this communication he stated that he had made a list 'of those who are desirous of emigrating from your Lordship's estates . . . 150 families comprising 900 individuals who occupy 500 Irish acres of land and the expenses of their transportation would be about £2500. . . . I have already chartered two vessells. . . . The only difficulty that now presents itself to me is . . . how to make the selection out of my lists – what 400 shall I take out of the 900 candidates all of whom are desirous to go by the first ships. . . . The poor creatures . . . see nothing but misery and starvation before them if they stay where they are'. Kincaid recommended that Palmerston sanction an even larger programme of emigration. In regard to the above-mentioned persons, he wrote that if they were to stay on the Palmerston lands 'the cost [to Palmerston] of supporting these 150 families for the next 7 months would be at least £1500' (p. 51).

The emigration of over 2,000 persons from his lands in 1847 cost Palmerston a sum approximating £6,000. Through direct and indirect mechanisms, he probably recouped that cost in a few years. Thus, Palmerston gained from emigration. So too did many of his former tenants. Some passages in Kincaid's letter to Palmerston, 23 March 1847, suggest that a great many of them desperately wanted to get to America.

Severe hardship among those who travelled on board some of Palmerston's emigrant ships in 1847 has been documented elsewhere. The Stewart & Kincaid correspondence, as well as the Palmerston archive at Southampton, give new insights of relevance, which are set out below.

1 Both Palmerston and Stewart & Kincaid wished the emigrants well. The documents mentioned in what immediately follows, which were not written for publication or propaganda, help to put the issue in sensible perspective. First, it may be recalled that before the end of 1847 Stewart wrote to Kincaid in regard to those who had arrived in New Brunswick from Sligo on board the *Aeolus*: 'I think above £100 was laid out in getting them some clothing better than their own wretched rags', and he went on to refer to 'any act that may be considered careless or cruel towards the poor emigrants' (p. 52). Second, another letter, from Stewart to Kincaid, suggests that the food bill incurred in Sligo town in connection with the emigrations was a large one. Third, further evidence that Palmerston intended comfortable passages for his emigrants to America is contained in a document written by the Sligo merchant William Kernaghan, from which extracts were drawn in chapter 3.

2 A key cause of the hardships of those who travelled on the ships which left Sligo for British North America late in the emigration 'season' of 1847 was that Stewart & Kincaid did not realise the harshness of the North American winter, which had already set in by the time some of the vessels reached their destinations. A letter of late 1847, from Stewart to Kincaid, attributes blame to Stewart & Kincaid's own lack of awareness of 'the circumstances of the place they were sent to & the suitable seasons' for such emigration (p. 52).

In 1848, at least some of Stewart & Kincaid's assisted emigration from Sligo to America was under escort, in small batches, through Liverpool. The petition of John Scanlon, quoted in chapter 3, is particularly interesting because Scanlon indicated, if given the assistance which he sought, that he and his family would seek to emigrate three days later (p. 55). Similar examples have been cited in later chapters.

It was noted in chapter 4 that compensation, or assistance to emigrate, appear to have been given to tenants who surrendered their holdings/cabins on the Crichton estates in 1848. *But it is impossible to make a clear distinction between the two groups – between those 'compensated' and those 'assisted'.* Especially when relatively large sums of money were involved, the amount paid to a tenant departing from an estate managed by Stewart & Kincaid was sometimes in recognition of the tenant's improvements. However, in most cases it probably did not reflect any improvement: in such cases it was intended merely to induce the tenant to leave peacefully, without forcing Stewart & Kincaid to incur other expenses. In referring to a Crichton townland which was being squared, in 1848 William Shaw wrote to Stewart & Kincaid: 'There are a great deal of cotters that are speaking to me concerning compensation. Will I give it to every person that throws [down] the house and go' (p. 70). It was assumed that those who received 'compensation' would leave the estate. The same assumption was made in regard to those who were 'assisted'. We can only assume, in many cases, that those in receipt of 'compensation' used the monies in order to finance their own departure. If the compensation was not for improvements, it consisted of assistance to migrate or emigrate. Because 'compensation' monies paid to Crichton tenants who surrendered were in most cases very small, if many of them did use such sums to leave Ireland they probably went to Britain rather than America. (Note that in the 1840s migration from Ireland to Britain was not usually described as emigration.) In April 1848 two women on Crichton lands sought assistance specifically to enable them to go to America. There was no programme of assisted emigration from D. H. Ferrall's estates. The depopulation of 1847–8 was to be attained mainly by 'voluntary' surrender and departure, *to anywhere* off the Ferrall lands, in exchange for small sums of money. It seems that hundreds of families were involved, and that Stewart & Kincaid gave most of those families from £1 to £1 10s 0d each. At best, such sums would have represented small help to go to Britain.

In regard to Wingfield's lands, it seems that Stewart & Kincaid assisted the emigration of a tenant whom Stewart & Kincaid had been 'pleased to dispossess'. But he did not really want to go: in 1844 he wrote to Stewart & Kincaid that 'you . . . promised to give as much money as would bear the expenses of him and family to America', but he 'would prefer remaining at home, if he had wherewith to purchase a small farm to encountering the dangers of a long voyage to a foreign land with a numerous and helpless family' (p. 133). There is no other evidence of Wingfield-financed emigration to America before the famine. In 1847 Wingfield did finance a programme of emigration. That this was on a significant scale is suggested by his observation in 1848 which referred to the dangers he perceived of inducing 'back the idle population which I paid so much to get rid of by transporting to America' in 1847 (p. 142).

The financial position of a majority of those cleared off the Roscommon estates of George Nugent was similar to that of Ferrall's small tenants: in most cases, the sums given to them were probably just about enough to get them and their families to Britain. In April 1847 Stewart wrote to Kincaid referring to assistance which enabled 'poor creatures in Kilglass' to get 'away from the scene of death' (p. 157). In October 1847 he reported that some of Nugent's tenants were talking 'about going to America'. In May 1848 Nugent requested Stewart to send him 'the accounts of the expenditures including sums given for emigration' (p. 158). Finally, in apparent reference to Nugent's tenantry in the Kilglass district, Stewart wrote to Kincaid in October 1848: 'Several applicants for emigration who would give up some land. Shall we start them off?' (p. 158) Thus, whereas it seems that many of Nugent's tenants probably went to Britain through the small sums which they received in 'compensation', an unknown number of them emigrated to America.

The Stewart & Kincaid letters refer to only one case of assisted emigration (in 1842) from Stratford's Clare estate in the years before the famine. This involved eight persons in the family of Thomas Reidy. The initiative to surrender in exchange for assisted emigration came from Reidy himself. Also, in April 1846 Marty Considine, his wife and their five children sailed to America from the port of Galway. Payment of their passage was made possible by a loan from Stewart & Kincaid to Marty's brother. In the spring of 1847 Arthur Vincent administered a programme of emigration from the estate. This is indicated in a letter in which Stewart referred to 'the numbers sent from Col Stratfords Clare estate'. He added: 'Vincent gives a piteous account of their wretched appearance & want of clothing. . . . He did not venture on two or three pounds to get them some, but he don't venture far *without order*' (p. 179). It can be inferred that these emigrants left from the port of Limerick, and that Stewart disapproved of Vincent's failure to buy clothing for them.

The treatment of cottiers on Stratford's Limerick estate at the time of the squaring there in 1841–2 seems to have been unusual. On other estates under Stewart & Kincaid's management, cottiers who were induced to go were given only small sums in compensation. Many of Stratford's Limerick cottiers were more demanding: they wanted enough money to get to America. Chapter 10 provided evidence that Stewart & Kincaid assisted the emigration of a small number of cottiers from the estate in 1846. There may have been some assisted emigration from the estate in the spring of 1847 (at the same time as the emigration of a batch of Stratford's tenants in Clare). At the end of 1848 Stewart, who had just come from the Stratford lands in Limerick, reported: 'I have arranged exporting 3 or 4 families & if we were merely wanting to get people off could send lots more [indicating that many tenants really wanted to emigrate]. But of course I only send those who have land & whose rent they are unable to pay would [from new tenants] soon come to the cost of emigration' (p. 194). It is inferred that in 1849 Stewart & Kincaid-assisted emigrants from Stratford's Limerick lands were farmers in arrears rather than cottiers who, as described by Vincent, 'never had any land more than a cabbage garden' (p. 193).

At the time of the squaring of Mrs Fitzgerald's Mount Blakeney estate in 1844, Stewart & Kincaid assisted at least one tenant to go to America. Much of the correspondence about the estate in 1847 and early in 1848 refers to assisted emigration. In 1847 there were some requests for assistance to go to America; however, Fitzgerald's financial position militated against any large-scale programme in that year. Many tenants were assisted to America in 1848. An unusual request was made in connection with one of them. In March 1848 Fitzgerald wrote to Stewart: 'You will smile when I deliver a message from the elder Miss R[ussell], namely to request that you will desire the physician on board the ship in which her sisters are going to America, to take particular care of the eldest of the two as her health is delicate' (p. 211).

Stewart & Kincaid's agent Sankey came to Mount Blakeney in mid-March 1848. He sent Stewart details of several tenants and their families whose emigration was to be assisted. He noted that 'money must be given for clothing'. He observed that one tenant 'is anxious to go but his wife being in the family way he will not be ready to start for 6 weeks. He will require some money for clothing as he and his family (in all 4) are naked' (p. 212). On 17 March, Sankey wrote that he was 'surrounded by emigrants' (p. 212). The last recorded letter requesting assistance to emigrate from the Mount Blakeney estate is dated April 1848. It was written by Thomas Sullivan who wrote: 'It is a grievous thing to leave the land of my birth. . . . I have determined to leave this ill fated country but fear I have not the means of doing so without your generous assistance. My family consists of seven children myself and wife . . . and of course we could not be pennyless on landing. . . . [Therefore] we should have something to carry us into the interior and not leave us in the town where we would land' (p. 212). Sullivan's foresight was unusual: many of the famine Irish became trapped in slums on the east coast of America; Sullivan was probably aware of this problem and he hoped that Stewart & Kincaid would help him avoid it.[22]

According to MacDonagh, there was an organised programme of assisted emigration from Warren's Ballinruane estate in 1847.[23] The Stewart & Kincaid correspondence contains only a passing reference to it and we have no idea of the numbers involved. More followed in 1848. The background to the departure of one of those families was unusual. Early in 1848 Stewart & Kincaid caused a tenant named Scollard to be imprisoned for non-payment of debt. Stewart & Kincaid claimed that he was £85 in arrears; but Scollard claimed that he owed the firm only £42–odd, which was nevertheless a substantial sum. In mid-March Scollard wrote to Stewart & Kincaid: 'I will give you up the possession . . . by your assisting me and my family in going to America. . . . I would wish to prepare for the first of April' (p. 219). Stewart & Kincaid's response was favourable. This may be regarded as surprising, in view of the extent of Scollard's indebtedness to the firm. On 22 March, Scollard informed Stewart & Kincaid that Sankey had 'told me that you would not give us any clothing until we would go to Dublin. We are to[o] naked and we could not leave home without the clothing' (p. 219).

In regard to Frankfort's estates, chapter 12 indicates that 'compensation' or 'assistance' appear to have enabled a small number of tenants to emigrate. There was also the assistance to America on Frankfort's behalf of the immediate family of Jacob Tyndall, who was not a tenant to Frankfort, and who was almost certainly an uncle to the famous scientist John Tyndall, FRS.

Apart from observations about some tenants of the Earl of Longford, chapters 13 and 14 contain little about assisted emigration. There may have been several of such cases from Longford in 1847, when Stewart wrote to Kincaid in reference to tenants there: 'Get some of them off to America if you can & soon. The price to New York now is only £3 or £3–3 for adults' (p. 259). There was apparently some assisted emigration from the earl's lands in 1848. This is inferred from the fact that in February of that year Stewart informed Kincaid: 'I accepted a bill [of exchange] for Miley [American packet agent in Dublin] for £400 . . . for L'd Longfords emigrants'. This sum paid to Miley would have covered the cost of transporting up to 200 persons (including children as well as adults) to America.

The Stewart & Kincaid correspondence does not enable us to make any firm estimate of the number of persons from estates under the firm's management whose emigration was 'assisted' during the famine. It has been seen that large numbers of Stewart & Kincaid tenants were 'compensated' for surrender of holdings, and that in many cases such compensation did not reflect any improvements on the part of the tenants. Some of those 'compensated' presumably used the monies to migrate to Britain, and an unknown number used them to emigrate to America. It seems that most of those who left estates managed by Stewart & Kincaid in 1846–8 received 'compensation' or 'assistance'. But a distinction between 'compensation' and 'assistance' is nebulous.

It is difficult to see how one can sensibly attach confidence to estimates of 'assisted emigration' presented by some historians. MacDonagh was cautious when, in the 1950s, he wrote that 'in 1846–52, landlord-assisted emigration must have been very small; it can scarcely have exceeded 50,000 in extent'. In a note, MacDonagh was careful to add: 'This . . . estimate . . . is put forward most tentatively. . . . It must be remembered how difficult it was to decide exactly what amounted to 'assistance'. MacDonagh also remarked that 'an offer of "assisted emigration" often meant no more than eviction and a small sum' of money; thus, whether he regarded some of the 'compensation' as a form of 'assistance' remains an open question. The generality of such payments to those departing from the Stewart & Kincaid lands in 1846–8 causes serious doubt on MacDonagh's upper bound estimate of 50,000 for 'landlord-assisted emigration' over the seven years 1846–52.[24]

Some of the more recent writings of historians have expressed no caution or less caution on 'assisted emigration' during the famine. In 1994 Kinealy wrote with apparent certainty that 'landlord-assisted emigration accounted for only about 5 per cent of the total'.[25] In 1999 Ó Gráda referred to 'emigrants whose passages were paid by landlords or by the state' and he added: 'Only a small share of all passages overseas were so financed, certainly no more than 4 or 5 percent'.[26] Ó Gráda cites MacDonagh's estimates, and research by David Fitzpatrick, as his sources. Fitzpatrick had reported in 1989 that 'references were found to about 175 cases of assistance by individuals (usually landlords) or groups, who probably aided at least . . . 22,000 [emigrants] between 1846 and 1850'.[27] It seems likely that if the Stewart & Kincaid correspondence had been available to him at the times at which he revealed his research results, examination of its contents would have induced Fitzpatrick to raise his lower bound estimate,[28] and that this consideration, along with appropriate attention to MacDonagh's caution, would have led those who wrote on the subject in the 1990s to express less of a sense of precision.

5 PROGRESSIVE LANDLORDS?

The 1840s saw major improvements on the estates managed by Stewart & Kincaid. First, there was rationalisation in the structure of holdings. This 'squaring of the land' facilitated and required other improvements. New roads had to be constructed for access to the new squares, and houses had to be built to accommodate tenants shifted from one place to another. The landlord usually paid the cost of the roads, often through rent allowances for labour. The tenants were expected to build their houses, though in many cases the landlord made contributions for materials. On at least two estates (Ahamlish and Robertstown) the road-building programmes in connection with squaring in the early 1840s militated against the welfare of tenants in 1846–7: the existing network of roads then weakened arguments for public works in those districts. Rationalisation in the structure of holdings did not make sense unless the tenants were sufficiently skilled in husbandry. Kincaid's interest in agricultural progress is indicated, among other things, by the fact that he was active in the Royal Agricultural Improvement Society, which sought to induce improvements among those 'holding under twenty-five acres Irish' (p. 11). Stewart & Kincaid was willing to assist sons of some tenants to attend an

agricultural college. More important, Stewart & Kincaid employed agriculturalists who sought to induce the tenants to plant clover (which improved the
nitrogen content of the soil), and turnips instead of potatoes. They also
assisted in provision of seed, fertilisers, and equipment such as ploughs and
turnip-sowing barrows. Throughout most of the 1840s Stewart & Kincaid
organised sub-soiling and drainage works.

Improvements during the pre-famine years

The most substantial pre-famine changes on any of the estates managed by
Stewart & Kincaid were those on Ahamlish. Apart from squaring holdings
and associated construction programmes, these included: completion of a
major harbour; building the town of Mullaghmore and implementation of
measures aimed at developing it into a commercial centre; improvements to
navigation; development of a plant nursery; planting of bent grass in order to
prevent lands from being destroyed by shifting sands; creation of forest plantations; various agricultural experiments; promotion of Palmerston's three
schools and the construction of a fourth; the sending of a local woman to
Dublin to train as a midwife, etc. In fact, in the early 1840s Palmerston sought
to improve almost every aspect of the estate. Up to 1846 he was not prepared
merely to issue general directions to his agents. He sent detailed instructions
and demanded minute detail in progress reports. In connection with the engineering works, he made a point of acquiring much more than an intelligent
layman's knowledge of civil engineering. Some of his letters were like those of
a site engineer. His approach in matters relating to agriculture was similar. His
tenants were expected to follow his example. In 1842 a 'Book of Improvements'
was under preparation: each tenant on the squared lands was to be assigned a
section in the book, into which records of improvements made by the tenant
would be recorded.

   Distress on Ferrall's Roscommon estates was probably more extreme than
on the lands of any other owner for whom Stewart & Kincaid was agent. This
situation was partly attributable to the fact that for much of the 1840s Ferrall
was absent, 'on the run' from creditors in both Ireland and Britain. The
Castlerea Agricultural Society was active in the early 1840s. Although Ferrall
subscribed to the society there is no firm evidence that he ever made use of the
services of its agricultural adviser. Given that Ferrall was in a state of increasing
financial crisis in the 1840s, it is not surprising that improvements on his
estates in those years were few.

   Like Palmerston in the early 1840s, Edward Wingfield closely monitored
developments on his estates. Although his improvements were on a smaller

scale, a summary of their form and sequencing would be similar to those on the Palmerston properties. But after 1846 Wingfield played a more active 'hands on' role than did Palmerston.

Pre-famine improvements on Nugent's lands in the east Roscommon were few. But there was some rationalisation in the structure of holdings (squaring) there in 1844–5. In 1844–6, Stewart & Kincaid employed Bernard Timothy to supervise improvements on Nugent's properties in northwest Roscommon. In March 1845 he reported to Kincaid : 'An astonishing improvement has taken place both in the habits of the people, & on the face of their holdings. The course of drainage in progress has been rendering the property immense service, and I have no doubt of being able to persuade nearly every one of the tenants to sow turnips . . . which . . . is . . . of vast importance in the improve-ment of any property' (p. 162).

Chapter 9 provided evidence that on the Stratford estate in Clare, no significant works of improvement, involving hire of labour for money, had been implemented in the years before Stewart & Kincaid commenced active management there. Such works commenced in 1842. At around the same time John Stewart the agriculturalist came to the estate to plan drainage and road works. In 1843 Stewart wrote that he had given turnip seed to tenants (p. 172). By 1845 there had been considerable improvements on the Clare estate. On Stratford's Robertstown estate in Limerick, one of Vincent's first tasks as Stewart & Kincaid agent was to oversee rationalisation in the structure of holdings. This meant that roads had to be built for access. Tenants received financial assistance from Stewart & Kincaid to repair or build houses. In 1842–4 John Stewart supervised drainage, and repair of river embankments against flooding. But perhaps his most important contribution to the estate was in inducing the tenants to change their methods of husbandry.

One of Stewart & Kincaid's first tasks following its commencement of management of the Mount Blakeney estate was to rationalise the structure of holdings, mainly in 1844. In 1844–5 there were also some small-scale drainage projects. In the autumn of 1845 John Stewart came to the estate to supervise useful roadworks. The Stewart & Kincaid letters on the nearby Ballinruane estate of Sergeant Warren commence in January 1845, when John Stewart went there and reported to Stewart & Kincaid that he 'never saw such exhausted lands'. He 'met all the tenants together and gave them a lecture on the utility of thorough draining and on the use of lime'. He recommended that Stewart & Kincaid should give lime free of charge (p. 214); Stewart & Kincaid's response was immediate. Further drainage was conducted by tenants late in 1845.

Apart from demanding rent, Frankfort paid little attention to management of his estates. Thus, policies pertaining to long-term development of his lands reflected initiatives by Stewart & Kincaid. Major improvements on his

Kilkenny estates (mainly at Coolcullen) commenced at the beginning of 1845, when Stewart & Kincaid sent the agriculturalist Cathro, who supervised small-scale drainage works. Like John Stewart, he sought improvements in the crops sown by the tenantry.

One of Stewart & Kincaid's first tasks when the firm commenced management of the Ponsonby estate at Philipstown in 1841 was to seek a large loan in London. The application failed 'on the ground that the rental arises from small sums paid by a numerous tenantry' (p. 245). On behalf of Richard Ponsonby, Stewart & Kincaid contributed to costs of repairs to a school in 1842. Stewart & Kincaid also sent annual contributions to the local dispensary. But in the years before the famine, improvements on the estate were few. The Stewart & Kincaid correspondence contains some requests for assistance for repair of houses and for fencing there. In 1843 a tenant was granted an allowance for drainage on his holding, and in the same year Grogan, the local agent, supervised repairs to a road on the estate. Chapter 13 indicates that, like Ponsonby, Pakenham also supported a school on his lands. In the early 1840s the local agent on the Pakenham lands in Westmeath sought to encourage small tenants to rotate their crops properly, and to sow turnips. There was some restructuring of holdings on the Pakenham estate in 1845. Although the Stewart & Kincaid letters mentioned in chapter 13 indicate some requests for subscriptions from the Earl of Howth for various purposes (support of a dispensary and of a school, repairs to a church and a subscription to the Royal Agricultural Society), they reveal nothing about pre-famine improvements on his lands.

Improvements: from 1846 onwards

A view that the existing population density in some districts in the mid-1840s was unsustainably high, and was inconsistent with maintained economic development of estates in the long run, is plausible. Thus, some of the depopulation measures implemented in 1847–8 should be considered as features of development programmes. For example, recall the letter to Palmerston dated 23 March 1847 in which Kincaid referred to 'those who are desirous of emigrating from your Lordship's estates . . . 150 families . . . who occupy 500 Irish acres' (p. 51). Those 500 Irish acres amounted to about 800 statute acres. This meant that on average, and at the best of times under the existing system, the 150 families would have had to subsist on land of poor quality on holdings of slightly less than six statute acres each. It is hard to see how such tenures could have enabled much further development on Palmerston's Sligo estate.

In regard to management of his estates in Ireland, Palmerston faded into the background following his return to government in 1846; for the remainder of the decade authority was assigned to Stewart & Kincaid without much surveillance from his Lordship. With public works in Ahamlish on an inadequate scale, late in 1846 Lynch wrote to Kincaid: 'If you don't . . . get the draining and trenching going, I don't know what the people will do' (p. 47). Thus, Lynch was advocating private works, not for the sake of improvement alone, but because they would give employment. It was not until over 2,000 of Palmerston's tenants (including their dependents) had been taken to America that major programmes of drainage and sub-soiling were executed in 1848. The same year saw further squaring of Palmerston land. The major improvement works in Ahamlish in 1848 were financed largely by a £2,000 government loan.

Like Palmerston, Crichton was an absentee but he maintained an active interest in improvements. In several respects, developments on his lands were similar to those on Palmerston's but they were implemented on a smaller scale. In May 1848 Edward Smyth indicated that he had received 'a great number of small tracts on farming', and that he was about to distribute them in the Ballymote district (p. 71). Crichton wrote to Stewart & Kincaid in June: 'You afford me real pleasure by sending me the opinion . . . concerning . . . the crops of the tenants, and their apparently improved state of industry. . . . I wish they would not trust so much to potatoes' (p. 71). There were attempts to develop fisheries off the Crichton shores in 1848. In 1848 Stewart & Kincaid obtained two government loans for drainage on Crichton lands.

Aimed at relieving distress, small-scale drainage works were executed on one of D. H. Ferrall's Roscommon townlands in 1846. The poor quality of houses and lack of farm structures was general on his lands. In 1848–9, when substantial tracts of his land lay idle following depopulation, Ferrall himself recognised that such deficiencies militated against any prospect of being able to find large and viable tenants. He wanted to attract substantial farmers from England, but it seems that none came. On his behalf, early in 1848 Stewart & Kincaid applied for a government loan of £1,500 for drainage. The sum finally sanctioned was smaller – £800. Although Ferrall did of course have to indicate his assent, we can be confident that initiatives in seeking the loan for improvements came from Stewart & Kincaid. However, there can be no presumption that there was any net improvement of the Ferrall estates over the 1840s.

The network of roads affecting the lands of George Nugent in Kilglass in east Roscommon was underdeveloped until the famine years. Some of the roads in the parish which were built as public works in 1846 were useful in providing access to recently squared holdings, as well as access to markets. It was the depopulation of 1846–7 which paved the way for further improvements. From 1847 onwards, Stewart & Kincaid amalgamated small holdings into more viable farm sizes. Nugent wanted to attract capitalist farmers from Scotland to settle on his lands. There is no evidence that he succeeded in doing so. It seems that drainage and sub-soiling in Kilglass were commenced in 1847. In March 1848 the Board of Works agreed to lend Nugent £2,000 for improvements there, and towards the end of the year, the Board agreed to a smaller loan for drainage in Kilmore. On Stewart & Kincaid's behalf, William Wilson spent most of 1848 in Kilglass supervising improvements. In 1848–9, some of the Kilglass lands were cultivated on Nugent's own account. The alternative would then have been to leave the land idle.

In regard to Nugent's properties in northwest Roscommon, in April 1846 Bernard Timothy wrote a letter in which he proposed projects of improvement. He regarded squaring of the land as by far the most important. Thus, he wrote that other 'things I would not advise to be proceeded with until the system of "rundale" will be entirely done away, & every tenant on the property have his holding to himself. Experience forces me to advise *this* as I have constantly observed that a tenant improves his small farm more in 3 years when he has it to himself than he otherwise would or *could* do in 20' (p. 163). The squaring probably took place in 1847. A letter from Timothy in mid-1846 indicates that several tons of fertiliser had arrived, for use by himself and the tenantry. In 1848 a government loan of £1,000 was authorised for drainage on the estate. Nugent seems to have maintained little active interest in the development of his estates. It can be inferred that the several improvements on his lands in 1845–8 primarily reflect initiatives on the part of Stewart & Kincaid.

Works of improvement on Stratford's Clare estate, laid out by John Stewart, recommenced during the summer of 1846. Much of the work – for which the participants were paid in cash – involved construction or improvement of useful private roads. In 1848 Stratford was granted a government loan in order to finance large-scale drainage on the estate.

John Stewart returned to the Mount Blakeney and the Ballinruane estates in February 1846. On Mount Blakeney, Stewart & Kincaid intervened against market forces in that year in two respects: first, in the provision of lime, and probably seed potato; second, in drainage, including river works, as well as road works, for which it appears that the men were paid a shilling per day. Stewart & Kincaid's major project providing employment on Warren's Ballinruane estate in 1846 was the deepening of a river and straightening of its course, which works Vincent regarded as 'of the greatest benefit to the property' (p. 215). Further improvements were implemented by the remaining tenants on Ballinruane in 1848. In March 1848 Stewart & Kincaid applied for a government loan for improvements on the Mount Blakeney estate. The loan – £700 to finance drainage and/or sub-soiling – was approved near the end of the year.

In March 1846 Cathro the agriculturalist returned to Frankfort's Coolcullen in Kilkenny. One of his tasks in the spring and early summer was the construction of useful roads. At the beginning of May the workers hired by

Cathro were paid a shilling per day. However, he left the estate, and the private road works were abandoned, in July 1846. It seems that there were neither private nor public works on Coolcullen during the last five months of the year; thus distress was extreme. There is evidence suggesting that the private works were stopped because Frankfort was annoyed by the fact that he was receiving little in rental income. At the same time, it seems that Stewart & Kincaid failed to press for publicly financed works on Coolcullen. The firm of Stewart & Kincaid was presumably acting under Frankfort's general instructions: he may have been concerned about the local property tax implications of public works. However, the year 1848 witnessed probably more improvements on Coolcullen than in any earlier year. William Sherriff came in January 1848 to supervise those works. Shortly after his arrival he wrote to Stewart & Kincaid: 'Never have I . . . witnessed the existence of such a state of neglect and want of improvement' (p. 230). The improvements supervised by him consisted mainly of drainage, as well as a small amount of sub-soiling. The work was financed by a government loan of £550.

Chapter 13 was the last to provide much detail on improvements. In the Philipstown district in 1847–8, it seems that schemes of employment-creation – financed through the local relief committee in part by Stewart & Kincaid on behalf of Captain Ponsonby – consisted of, or included, useful works on the lands of various proprietors in the district. Some private works were in progress on Pakenham's Westmeath estate in 1846 and 1847. A letter of May 1847 refers to the 'Killucan improvement' account. In 1848 Stewart & Kincaid obtained two government loans for improvements on Pakenham properties. In the autumn of 1846 Stewart & Kincaid encouraged the Earl of Howth to implement privately financed works. There is strong evidence that on his behalf, Stewart & Kincaid supervised drainage projects in counties Meath and Dublin in 1846 or early in 1847. In 1848 a government loan of £1,000 was obtained for improvements on the earl's estates. Early in the same year Stewart & Kincaid signed documents from the Board of Works which committed Espine Batty to expenditures on drainage on his Westmeath estate.

The reader might have concluded that, taken as a group, those landlords who were clients to Stewart & Kincaid comprised a progressive set of people who were keen to develop their estates. This view should be qualified by noting that the initiative for many of the improvements must have come from Stewart & Kincaid. It was hardly coincidental that squaring of lands was implemented on several of the estates very shortly after Stewart & Kincaid had been appointed as agents; indeed, the partners in the firm seem to have regarded such rationalisations as preconditions for further progress. Nor does it seem to have been coincidental that a large majority of the firm's clients obtained government loans in 1848 in order to finance large-scale improvements. As indicated in chapter 1, Stewart & Kincaid took a long-term view in regard to development of estates under the firm's management; furthermore, a commitment to accept expenditures on improvements may have been embodied in Stewart & Kincaid's contracts with client proprietors. But it was up to the landlords to accept or reject whatever proposals for improvements emanated from Stewart & Kincaid.

6 LANDLORDS AND AGENTS: DID THEY REALLY CARE?

It is probably accurate to state that, in Ireland early in the twenty first century, a majority of people believe that the landowners of Ireland, and their agents too, were generally uncaring and inhumane in their treatment of the tenantry during the famine years. The Stewart & Kincaid correspondence creates a very different picture of reality. However, before proceeding, the following observations should be noted.

1   In coming to an overall judgement as to the true thinking of landlords and their agents, it should be borne in mind that the Stewart & Kincaid letters were not prepared for use in propaganda. If a given letter does contain serious deception in regard to the true thinking of its author, it is likely that the letter was composed by a person who was seeking favours or expressing grievances. Much of the correspondence is internal to the firm of Stewart & Kincaid, and it is unlikely that the firm could have survived as the leading land agency in Ireland if the information available to its top decision-makers (as often expressed in letters) had been serious distortions of reality. Furthermore, in his letters to partner A in the firm of Stewart & Kincaid, partner B had no obvious reason for disguising his true attitudes towards tenants.

2   The dangers of drawing inferences from the particular to the general should be kept in mind. Stewart & Kincaid was only one of many firms of land agents. There is no presumption, just because Stewart & Kincaid thought in such-and-such a manner, that all other land agents in Ireland thought likewise.

3   Observations similar to those in (2) apply to the landlords. Perhaps the attitudes of the landlords on Stewart & Kincaid's books were not representative of those of landlords in general. It was not necessarily the case that the criteria applied by Stewart & Kincaid in accepting accounts were the same as those of most other firms of land agents. For example, Stewart & Kincaid may have insisted that its clients commit themselves to improvements; other land agencies may have been less demanding in this

respect. For similar reasons, the attitude of Stewart & Kincaid's landlords on the question of ejectment may have differed from those of proprietors of estates managed by other firms.

4   Similar remarks apply to local agents. It could be argued that in making such appointments on an estate, Stewart & Kincaid was anxious to avoid bad publicity generated by excessively tough behaviour on the part of agents, and that the same level of concern did not necessarily apply to other firms.

What immediately follows pertains only to evidence from the Stewart & Kincaid correspondence.

Were the Dublin agents humane?

An impression emerging from chapter 1 is that Stewart and Kincaid cared about the welfare of those of their fellow humans far below themselves in the economic and social ordering. Kincaid was connected with a large number of organisations, some of them charitable, some religious and some educational. Links with many of those bodies must have been indirectly good for Stewart & Kincaid's business. However, there is no presumption that Kincaid's association with charities, which assisted Dublin's poor, brought any business to Stewart & Kincaid: an inference is that they reflected genuine concern for humanity. Stewart's involvement in the Meath Street Savings Bank, which encouraged thrift among Dublin's poor, probably reflected similar concerns.

In support of a view that the partners in Stewart & Kincaid really cared about the well-being of the tenantry, one might be tempted to invoke the firm's policy decisions: its emphasis on improvements; its hire of agriculturalists; its purchases of meal at times of distress; its tardiness to eject; assistance in emigration including outlays on food and clothing. There are two problems in such an approach. First, many of Stewart & Kincaid's policies did not assist tenants alone – they also enhanced the long-term viability of its clients' estates. They therefore improved the well-being of landlords which, after all, was the landlords' main objective in appointing Stewart & Kincaid to look after their interests. Secondly, it is not always clear where the initiative for a particular policy decision came from – whether it reflected discretion within the firm itself, or whether it followed an instruction by the landlord. The letters between Stewart and Kincaid provide more reliable indicators of their thinking.

In several of their references to tenants or former tenants, the very choice of words used by Stewart and by Kincaid in their letters from one to the other indicates much about their true feelings towards those in distress. It will be recalled that the *Eliza Liddell* arrived in New Brunswick from Sligo in July 1847 carrying 77 former Palmerston tenants who were then in a state of extreme destitution. Referring to these people, Stewart wrote to Kincaid that they had been taken to north America 'with best intention' and he added: 'The poor fellows appear to suffer greatly' (p. 52). In a letter to Kincaid concerning the Palmerston emigrants who arrived in New Brunswick aboard the *Aeolus*, Stewart remarked on 'the unpleasantness of a person in Ld. Palmerstons position being mixed with any act that may be considered careless or cruel towards the poor emigrants' (p. 52). The choices of adjectives in these letters indicate feelings of compassion. None of the letters between Stewart and Kincaid express disrespect towards the tenantry. Several letters indicate that very many of the tenantry were poor, but none expresses a view that the people were an inferior breed who did not deserve respect.

On the local agents

Stewart & Kincaid's local agents usually commanded detailed knowledge of the circumstances of each tenant and some of them wrote to Stewart & Kincaid pleading a case on a tenant's behalf. But exercise of their primary function – rent collection – meant that they often had to act toughly. Thus, most of them displayed features of firmness as well as sympathy. On Stratford's Clare estate in 1843, Blackwell distrained assets of his own brothers. However, a year earlier, he had written to Stewart & Kincaid on behalf of Thomas Reidy: 'If he had his portion of Toureen rent free he could badly support & clothe his long family by the produce of it. That being so he expects your Honrs. will have the kindness of tender feeling of sending off himself & family [in assisted emigration]' (p. 173). During the early famine years some of the local agents worked tirelessly to relieve distress.

The personalities of some of Stewart & Kincaid's local agents might be deemed unattractive. Walker in Sligo was a bigot who seems to have had little genuine concern for the well-being of the tenants. Two of Stewart & Kincaid's local agents might be considered 'land-grabbers'. In 1844 and 1845, complaints were sent to Stewart & Kincaid because Blackwell sought to add to his holdings by obtaining the land held by his late brother and his sister-in-law. Grogan at Philipstown was involved in similar family strife. But quarrels caused by some members of a family seeking to increase the size of their holdings, thereby causing allocations to other family members to be reduced or not increased, was not confined to families in which one member was a local agent. Such was the general obsession for land in an over-populated country.

The choice of words in some of Sharkey's letters suggests that he did not have much respect for some of the people on Ferrall lands. In June 1848 he informed Stewart & Kincaid that he had removed a 'wicked fellow who overheld', and a few days later he indicated that he wanted to get rid of 'a plague' of about 30 families (p. 118). It should be remembered, however, that it seems that none of those to whom Sharkey referred were legitimate tenants to Ferrall. He did display some pity toward squatters about whom he complained. Unpopular as some of his actions were, Sharkey's policies merely reflected what he was employed to do.

In spite of their incomes from Stewart & Kincaid, many of the local agents suffered severe distress during the famine. Some of them asked Stewart & Kincaid to use influence with the Board of Works in order to obtain employment for them on public works in 1846–7. But such requests were not confined to local agents alone: the correspondence includes many cases in which ordinary tenants requested Stewart & Kincaid or their landlord to use influence in their favour in order to obtain work. On balance, and taken as a group, it seems that Stewart & Kincaid's local agents were reasonable people. Some of them held the welfare of the tenantry high in their priorities. As in most other professions, some of them were humane, while others were less caring. Of course they were not very popular among the tenantry, who did not enjoy having to pay rent.

On the landlords

Much of the initiative in seeking government loans in 1847, to finance improvements, came from Stewart & Kincaid rather than the landlords. Tardiness to eject, and programmes of assisted emigration, also seem to have reflected Stewart & Kincaid's thinking. In fairness to the landlords, it should not be forgotten that Stewart & Kincaid acted on their behalf and required landlord consent. But even if we were to infer that the Stewart & Kincaid landlords were progressive as a group, we could not infer with certainty, on that count alone, that tenant welfare was high among their priorities. However, the overall impression is that although they pursued mainly their own long-term economic interests, many of them indicated good feelings towards their tenants. The paternalistic views of tenants on some of the estates towards their landlords, as well as the choice of words in letters from proprietors to Stewart & Kincaid, indicate some of the thinking of landlords and tenants vis-à-vis each other. On several occasions tenants wrote to their landlord expressing grievances and requesting appropriate action, or seeking a favour (such as acquisition of employment). The recipients usually forwarded such letters to Stewart & Kincaid, often adding a note suggesting how the firm of agents might respond. Some tenants adopted a more direct approach by travelling to their landlord's residence where, in most of the cases recorded, their arrival was unexpected.

The first reference in the Stewart & Kincaid correspondence to a visit by a tenant to his landlord in England is dated early in 1841. This involved the problems of Patt Feeny who disagreed with the manner in which Palmerston lands were to be squared. According to another tenant, Feeny was 'determined to make his lamentation to his Lordship's Lady by crying and roaring in her presence' (p. 34). As Walker indicated to Stewart & Kincaid in January 1841, two other Sligo tenants had earlier gone to plead with Palmerston in England 'these last two years, without any satisfactory result to their mission' (p. 34). It seems that Feeny's visit was unsuccessful. William Sandys also went to England to plead his case with his landlord. It may be recalled that Sandys was imprisoned for debt and was ejected shortly afterwards in 1848. Early 1849 saw him seeking an interview with Crichton in England. Sandys's journey may have been worthwhile: in 1857 he was listed as a tenant on 173 statute acres of Crichton lands. The journey to London of Cornelius O'Shea, from the Stratford estate in Limerick, seems to have been less successful. Chapter 10 indicated that Edward Wingfield – Stratford's twin who was on a visit to his brother in London – complained to Stewart & Kincaid in March 1846 that the 'gosing lad [O'Shea] . . . called here at 6 o'clock in the morn'g with a letter from Mr Vincent recommending him for a situation . . . without a penny in his pockett. I hope he got safe back [to County Limerick] with his bag of cloaths & the assistance my brother compassionately gave him to pay for his return' (p. 195). In 1847 Mrs Fitzgerald in County Cork wrote to J. R. Stewart informing him that she recently had a visit from one of her tenants, but that she 'would not go to hear his complaint knowing that I should be tormented by them all if I did so' (p. 210). Stewart & Kincaid's clients did not wish – either through letters or through personal interview – to deal directly with tenants: this was one reason why they had employed Stewart & Kincaid. They did not want to be pestered. Although landlords did not welcome visits by tenants to their homes, the fact that some tenants went to such trouble indicates that they did not regard their landlord as an uncaring despot.

Among all of the landlords whose estates have been investigated in detail in the present work, Viscount Palmerston seems to have been the most committed to expenditure on improvements. It is reasonable to assume that he expected to obtain an economic return on most of such outlays. However, it is not clear that he was the principal beneficiary of his expenditure on education and public health, or of his financial contributions to the Catholic Church. That Palmerston regarded the welfare of his departing tenants in 1847 as important is revealed by Kernaghan's manuscript, 'Incidents and Reminiscences of Lord Palmerston' (see pp. 53, 54). That Crichton also had genuine concern for tenant welfare is suggested by his lengthy letter dated 17 October 1848 to Stewart & Kincaid (see pp. 81, 82). Ferrall was genuinely disturbed by the plight of those removed from his lands of Lissergool by Sharkey in 1848. Some of the wording in letters from Edward Wingfield regarding his tenants in Sligo suggest coldness. But the overall impression is that he was compassionate toward those who were industrious. Although Wingfield was in financial difficulties in 1848, he continued to subscribe to dispensaries, etc., on or near his Sligo estate. Stratford seems to have been similar in disposition to his twin Wingfield. In assessment of his true attitude in regard to his tenants, his guideline to Stewart & Kincaid in October 1846 – to 'consider where charity is to be dispensed, among my tenants . . . & assist them accordingly everywhere, in the best manner' – needs no elaboration (p. 196). The guidelines sent to J. R. Stewart by Mrs Fitzgerald in September 1847 were similar in tone. But it is difficult to assess how much compassion the proprietors of some other estates managed by Stewart & Kincaid showed towards the tenantry. One receives an impression that Frankfort was far more concerned about rent receipts than for tenant welfare. George Nugent may also have been among the less compassionate of Stewart & Kincaid's clients.

Closing observations

It is concluded that taken together, Stewart and Kincaid and the group of landlords which their firm represented were both progressive and humane in the 1840s. It might be argued that both Stewart & Kincaid and the firm's clients could have done much more to alleviate distress during the famine years. But it should be remembered that Stewart & Kincaid was primarily a business – not an aid agency financed by charitable donations – which operated subject to budget constraints. It might be argued that the firm's clients should have sold some of their land, and that such actions could have made more money available for tenant assistance. But two crucial considerations should be noted here.

First, large tracts of land in Ireland lay idle in the late 1840s. Reduction in incomes inevitably meant that the effective demand for land, and hence its price, fell. Economic analysis indicates that if substantially more land had been placed on the market, then the price of land would have fallen even further. Indeed, given that the market demand for land in Ireland in the late 1840s was almost certainly what economists call price-inelastic (a measure indicating relative insensitivity to changes in price), economic analysis tells us

that even small increases in the supply of land on the market would have
induced substantial reductions in price. Furthermore, it is easy to see that in
the face of price-inelastic demand for any good (such as land), any increase in
the market supply of that good must cause a *reduction* – not an increase – in
total receipts from sales of that good. Thus, it is concluded that if, as a group,
landlords had responded to famine distress by selling parcels of land, then the
sellers of land would, as a group, have been worse off rather than better off, [29]
in the sense that total receipts from sales of land would have fallen rather than
risen.[30] Besides, the question of who would have been willing to finance
massive land purchases in the circumstances of the late 1840s remains unclear.
It seems that these points have been overlooked by economic historians.

Secondly, and very much subsidiary to the first set of points above, until
the Encumbered Estates legislation at the end of the decade, it was difficult or
impossible to sell parts of an estate which had financial claims against it – and
even before the famine many of the estates managed by Stewart & Kincaid
were heavily encumbered by debt.[31]

No study of the 1840s along the lines of the present work has been
published.[32] One of those which comes closest is Maguire's work (1972) on the
Downshire estates.[33] Maguire in his preface indicated that he was providing 'a
detailed study of the management of a single property, the kind of study that
did not exist for any Irish . . . estate' before the famine, and he went on to
observe that 'comparative material from a variety of sources has been used as
far as possible, but in some areas of inquiry – the structure and practice of
estate administration, for instance – little could be found of use'.[34] The focus
in Maguire's book is on the 40 years preceding the famine. He shows that, like
many of Stewart & Kincaid's clients, the Downshires were progressive
landlords, and like the present author, he questions 'the folk memory [in
Ireland] of the agent as the heartless oppressor of the tenantry'.[35] It is hoped
that this book has helped to fill some of the gaps in our knowledge to which
Maguire refers.

Two more recent studies should be mentioned. One of these is MacCarthy's
work on the estates of Trinity College, Dublin.[36] His findings are very different
from those reported in this book: throughout the nineteenth century, Trinity
relied on the 'middleman system' of management. Huge tracts of land were
leased directly by the college to middlemen who rented parcels of their holdings
to other middlemen. There was in many cases a pyramid of middlemen
between the owner of the land and those who farmed it. MacCarthy reports
that before 1850 the middlemen 'were regarded as the landlord by the tillers of
the soil who could only have been dimly aware of the college's connection with
the land'.[37] It is interesting to observe that the Catholic 'liberator' Daniel
O'Connell was one of the middlemen on the college lands in Kerry, where it

was alleged in the 1840s that he charged his undertenants three times the amount of his own head rent, and that he made no improvements.[38] In general, there was very little progress on the Trinity estates before the famine.

Gerard Lyne has provided a scholarly study of the huge Lansdowne estate in Kerry, under the agency of William Steuart Trench. Trench was appointed as agent to the Lansdownes in 1850. In many respects, during the 1850s and 1860s the Lansdownes acted as Palmerston did in the years after 1846. Like Palmerston during those years, they delegated much of their authority to their agent's discretion. The improvements implemented by Trench in Kerry during the 1850s and 1860s were similar to those administered by Stewart & Kincaid on Palmerston's behalf in the 1840s. Trench also organised a programme of assisted emigration: as reported by Lyne, between December 1850 and February 1855 he arranged for shipment of some 3,900 destitute persons from the Kerry estate to America. According to Trench, such former tenants had made 'wholly and entirely voluntary' surrender of their holdings.[39] As Lyne observes, 'the parallels between the Palmerston and Lansdowne emigrations are striking'.[40]

Coming back to the main thrust of the Stewart & Kincaid archive, it was warned earlier that the dangers of drawing conclusions from the particular and applying them to the general should not be forgotten. The behaviour of landlords and agents on estates managed by Stewart & Kincaid in the 1840s – which together comprised a relatively small proportion of the land mass of Ireland – might not have been indicative of what was then typical in Ireland. It is probable that the correspondence archives of many land agents in the 1840s have been by now destroyed. However, in reference to estates not under Stewart & Kincaid's management, thousands of letters pertaining to management of land in Ireland in the 1840s do survive. But it is very unlikely that most of these will ever be researched along the lines of this book: most of them are the scattered properties of postal history collectors in Ireland and abroad.

Notes

INTRODUCTION

1   James S. Donnelly, Jr, *The Land and the People of Nineteenth-Century Cork* (London and Boston, 1975), pp. 9 and 52.

2   Writer's name not identified. Written 20–30 July 1821 and posted at Coleraine. Letter in possession of the author but not part of the Stewart & Kincaid correspondence.

3   Mary E. Daly, *The Famine in Ireland* (Dundalk, 1986), p. 35. For details on potato acreage, yield and production between 1844 and 1849 see ibid., pp. 53–6.

4   A manual of the early forties observed that 'great failures have taken place in the potato crops within the last few years in every part of the United Kingdom': see *The Farmer's Guide*, 2nd edn (Dublin, 1842), p. 95.

5   I thank Monsignor Ó Fiannachta of Dingle for information on Gayer. Following the death of Gayer's wife in 1846, he himself died in 1848, aged 42. See the report on the trial for libel on Gayer, in Charles Gayer, *Persecution of Protestants* (Dublin, 1845); D. P. Thompson, *Brief Account of . . . Change in Religious Opinion . . . in Dingle* (London, 1846); Desmond Bowen, *Superism: Myth or Reality* (Cork, 1970); plaque to the Gayers in the church of St James, Dingle.

6   Charles Gayer to Stewart & Kincaid, 18 Mar. 1842, Stewart & Kincaid Papers in possession of the author. Subsequent references to this archive in the chapter will be given in the text as (SK).

7   What follows here draws on the summaries in George Nicholls, *A History of the Irish Poor Law* (London, 1856), pp. 222–404.

8   Ibid., p. 226.

9   Ibid., p. 228.

10   'Summary of the 6th and 7th Vict. cap. 92. For the further Amendment of the Law for the Relief of the Poor in Ireland', quoted in Nicholls, *Poor Law*, p. 291.

11   The Ricardian theory of economic rent (which must have been familiar to many landlords in the 1840s) tells us that if the equilibrium market rent of land and the actual rent coincide, it would make no difference whether the tenant or the landlord was made *administratively* liable for payment of a land tax: in either case the *burden* of the tax - the question of who *ultimately* pays it – would be on the landlord. Thus, suppose that there were no rates (lump sum taxes on assets such as land) to begin with and that the market equilibrium rent, as determined by supply and demand, was £x per annum. Next, suppose that a rate of £y per annum is introduced, and that it is administratively payable by the tenant. As a group, tenants are now willing to pay £(x–y) for the land. (The demand curve shifts down a distance of £y). With the total stock of land fixed implying a vertical supply curve, the rent would fall by £y, and the burden of the tax would be on the landlord. If, however, the landlord was administratively liable for payment of the tax, the demand curve for land would be unchanged and with the total supply of land fixed, the rent of land would remain £x, but out of this the landlord would have to pay the £y. *The burden is the same in either case.* To argue otherwise is to claim that equilibrium and actual rents do not tend to

coincide. In the early 1840s an overwhelming majority of the small tenants on estates managed by Stewart & Kincaid had no lease. Furthermore, competition for land was brisk. It is therefore reasonable to assume that equilibrium and actual rents tended to coincide, in which case landlords had little or no reason to respond to the legislation of August 1843 by clearing their estates of small tenants. Some historians have asserted to the contrary. See, for example, the study by Donnelly *The Land and the People*, p. 112, and in apparent agreement with Donnelly on this point, Tyler Anbinder, 'Lord Palmerston and the Irish famine emigration', *Historical Journal* 44: 2 (2001), p. 445. The theory of economic rent is outlined in many economics text-books. See, for example, Desmond Norton, *Economics for an Open Economy: Ireland* (Dublin, 1994), pp. 535–9 (on economic rent), and pp. 69–72 (where it is shown that in a competitive market the burden of a per unit tax is independent of whether it is administratively payable by the suppliers or the demanders). The existence of middlemen and of leases (not usually held by the small tenants) complicates the reasoning outlined above. But they do not substantively change the conclusions in regard to the incidence of land taxes in the long run: if markets are competitive, the burden of a land tax tends to be on the head landlord, regardless of who administratively pays it. I am, however, willing to concede that some landlords did assert that the legislation of 1843 induced them to remove some of their small tenants in the late 1840s.

12 Nicholls, *Poor Law*, pp. 313, 320; Cecil Woodham-Smith, *The Great Hunger* (London, 1962), p. 172; Christine Kinealy, *This Great Calamity* (Dublin, 1994), pp. 134–5.

13 Nicholls, *Poor Law*, p. 330.

14 Ibid., p. 335.

ONE: MESSRS STEWART, STEWART & SWAN, STEWART & KINCAID

1 *Wilson's Dublin Directory . . . 1788*, p. 85.

2 James O'Donnell to Lord Powerscourt, 24 Apr. 1791, Stewart & Kincaid Papers in posses-sion of the author. Subsequent references to the archive in this chapter will be given either in the text or in notes as (SK).

3 Edward Pakenham to the second Viscount Palmerston, 19 June 1788, Broadlands (Palmerston) Papers, Hartley Library, University of Southampton, BR 141/20; Henry Stewart to the second Viscount Palmerston, 22 July 1789, Palmerston Papers, BR 141/22.

4 *Wilson's Dublin Directory . . . 1809*, p. 92.

5 Henry Stewart to the third Viscount Palmerston, 23 Nov. 1805, Palmerston Papers, BR 144/1/1.

6 James Watson Stewart, *Gentleman's and Citizen's Almanack*, published annually in Dublin.

7 Beatrice Butler, 'John and Edward Lees, Secretaries of the Irish Post Office, 1774–1831', *Dublin Historical Record* III (1952–4), pp. 138–50.

8 The postal rates applicable in each year can be found in the *Gentleman's and Citizen's Almanack*. F. E. Dixon, *Irish Postal Rates before 1840* (Munich, 1986), provides a useful compen-dium of rates. On Swan's apparent abuse of his position of Treasurer of the Post Office, see Desmond Norton, 'Irish postal history circa 1660 to circa 1860', *Genealogical Society of Ireland Journal* 6: 1 (Spring 2005), pp. 20–38.

9 Rob Goodbody, 'Obelisk Park', *Blackrock Society*, vol. 7 (1999), pp. 24–33.

10 Joseph Kincaid to Palmerston, 29 Dec. 1827 and 20 June 1829, Palmerston Papers, BR 149/10/29 and BR 144/7/41.

11   Lord Longford, a relative of the Stewarts, owned land in this district. Kincaid was a director of the Dublin and Kingstown Railway, the city terminus of which was near Stewart & Kincaid's office.

12   *Thom's Official Directory . . . 1883*, p. 1430.

13   Stewart & Kincaid to Evelyn Ashley, 4 Jan. 1883, Palmerston Papers, BR 148/7/11; *Thom's 1884*, pp. 1433 and 1711.

14   Enclosure in Priscella Nugent to Stewart & Kincaid, 29 Jan. 1848 (SK).

15   Dermot James, *John Hamilton of Donegal, 1800–1884* (Dublin, 1998), p. 22.

16   W. Woods to Kincaid, 28 July 1848 (SK).

17   I. Slater, *National Commercial Directory of Ireland* (Manchester and London, 1846), section on Leinster, p. 83.

18   Martha Ellis to Stewart & Kincaid, 13 Sept. 1846; Robert Cornwall to Stewart & Kincaid, 16 Sept. 1846 (SK).

19   *King's County and County Westmeath, Valuation . . . Union of Tullamore* (Dublin, 1854), p. 24; *Thom's 1850*, p. 422.

20   William Brooke to J. R. Stewart, 23 May 1843 (SK).

21   William Whitsitt to Kincaid, 5 Feb. 1841 (SK).

22   William Furlong to Kincaid, 19 Jan. 1843 (SK).

23   Pettigrew and Oulton, *The Dublin Almanac . . . 1842*, p. 335.

24   Pettigrew and Oulton, *Almanac 1846*, p. 316.

25   Ibid., p. 320.

26   Ibid., p. 321.

27   T. O'Rorke, *History of Sligo*, vol. II (Dublin, n. d.), p. 441.

28   Pettigrew and Oulton, *Almanac 1846*, pp. 320–1.

29   Pettigrew and Oulton, *Almanac 1842*, pp. 293–4.

30   Ibid. p. 291.

31   John Warham to J. R. Stewart, 28 Jan. 1841 (SK).

32   Edward Bullen to Kincaid, 3 Jan., 13 Feb. and 18 Oct. 1843; 19 Dec. 1846; Pettigrew and Oulton, *Almanac 1846*, p. 185.

33   'Mr [Henry] Stewarts Terms of Transacting Agency Business 1791', Palmerston Papers, BR 141/26/1.

34   Acceptance (by signature) of a draft bill of exchange in recognition of indebtedness makes the acceptor liable for payment. Issued by the drawer, a bill of exchange is an order to pay a certain sum of money to the bearer at a specified future date; its acceptance is what makes it like a post-dated cheque. Following its acceptance and its return to the drawer, the drawer might not keep it until maturity; rather, the drawer could have it discounted (converted into cash), usually at a bank. The ultimate bearer (e.g. the bank) would demand payment from the acceptor on redemption date.

35   Niall Brunicardi, *John Anderson, Entrepreneur* (Fermoy, 1987).

36   Stewart & Kincaid to Col. Stratford, 21 Feb. 1842, Pakenham archive, Tullynally Castle, Castlepollard, County Westmeath, PAK M/33.

37   Quoted and reported in Brunicardi, *Anderson*, p. 151.

38   Law Walker to Kincaid, 9 May 1844 (SK).

39   Board of Works to Stewart & Kincaid, 18 Feb., 12 and 13 Apr, 17 May, 7 June, 15 July, 10 Aug., 26 and (?) Sept. 1848 (SK).

40 Royal Exchange Assurance to Stewart & Kincaid, 17, 22 and 26 June 1841, 12 July 1843 (s k); National Assurance Office to Stewart & Kincaid, 22 June 1841 (s k).

41 Edward Walford, *The County Families of the United Kingdom* (London, 1860), p. 490.

42 Slater, *Directory*, section on Ulster, p. 497.

43 Walford, *Families*, p. 490.

44 Letter in author's private collection.

45 Margaret Ormsby to Stewart & Kincaid, 5 and 18 Nov. 1841 (s k). Ambrose Leet, *Directory to the . . . Noted Places in Ireland*, 2nd edn (Dublin, 1814), lists Michael Sandys as resident at Waltrim. The Stewart & Kincaid correspondence indicates that in the 1840s Robert Sandys (probably Michael's son) acted as local agent for the Stewart & Kincaid client Edward Wingfield, near Bray.

46 W. A. Maguire, *The Downshire Estates in Ireland 1801–1845* (Oxford, 1972). But see also P. J. Duffy, 'Management problems on a large estate in mid-nineteenth century Ireland: William Steuart Trench's Report on the Shirley Estate in 1843', *Clogher Record* XVI: 1 (1997), pp. 101–22.

47 James S. Donnelly, Jr, *The Land and the People of Nineteenth-Century Cork* (London and Boston, 1975), refers to Stewart & Kincaid on three occasions, but those references are for the 1860s–1880s. W. E. Vaughan, *Landlords and Tenants in Mid-Victorian Ireland* (Oxford, 1994), contains details on estate management from the 1850s to the 1880s, but does not mention J. R. Stewart or Joseph Kincaid, or their successors. Gerard J. Lyne, *The Lansdowne Estate in Kerry under the Agency of W. S. Trench 1847–72* (Dublin, 2001), is also almost entirely about post-famine years. Trinity College, Dublin relied on middlemen to 'manage' its agricultural properties: see R. B. MacCarthy, *The Trinity College Estates 1800–1923* (Dundalk, 1992). Unlike the above-mentioned studies, Lindsay J. Proudfoot, *Urban Patronage and Social Authority* (Washington, DC, 1995), concentrates on management of town properties in Ireland – those of the Dukes of Devonshire between 1764 and 1891.

48 John E. Pomfret, *The Struggle for Land in Ireland 1800–1923* (Princeton, 1930), p. 27.

49 Downshire's motives in developing the village of Dundrum in County Down, into a leisure and commercial centre, were similar to those of Lord Palmerston at Mullaghmore (discussed in chapter 2 below).

50 This is the subtitle of James, *Hamilton*.

51 Ibid., p. ix.

52 No exact date given, but marked Sept. 1846 (s k).

53 Board of Works to Stewart & Kincaid, 24 July 1848 (s k).

54 For letters circulating within the city limits, the Dublin Penny Post commenced in 1773. In 1774 the limits for the Penny Post were extended to four Irish miles from the General Post Office. These limits were increased to 6 Irish miles in 1819. Under the extended systems, letters delivered to places beyond the (1773) two-mile radius from the GPO, but within four (and subsequently six) miles, were charged 2*d*. This resulted in what was known as the Two Penny Post. Enniskerry was beyond the six-mile limit. However, it was made an exception: it was serviced by the Two Penny Post. This special treatment was probably due to influence of the Powerscourts. For details see J. Stafford Johnson, 'The Dublin Penny Post, 1773–1840', *Dublin Historical Record* IV: 3 (Mar.–May 1942), pp. 81–95; David Feldman and William Kane, *Handbook of Irish Postal History to 1840* (Dublin, 1975); Norton, 'Irish postal history', pp. 20–38.

55 James Brangan and Terence O'Neill, both millers at Swords, listed by Slater, *Directory*, section on Leinster, pp. 88–9.

56   Board of Works to Stewart & Kincaid, 27 May 1848 (s k).

57   Thomas Bermingham, William Bermingham, William Dowling and Patrick McDonald to Stewart & Kincaid, 12 Oct. 1844 (s k).

58   It seems that the famine was much more severe in the Kilcullen district than in some other parts of Kildare. See Kildare County Council, *Lest we Forget Kildare and the Great Famine* (Naas, n. d.), pp. 11–13.

59   Pettigrew and Oulton, *Almanac 1843*, p. 289.

60   C. W. Doyne at Fenagh rectory to Stewart & Kincaid, 6 May 1846 (s k).

61   See Congested Districts Board to Messrs Kincaid & Matthews, 16 Apr. 1914, Palmerston Papers, b r 148/11/20).

62   This information draws on oral communications from Thomas Pakenham, the present Lord Longford.

63   Pakenham archive, PAK m/33–286.

64   Pakenham archive, PAK h/2.

TWO: PALMERSTON IN SLIGO IN THE EARLY 1840S

1   Broadlands (Palmerston) Papers, Hartley Library, University of Southampton b r 146/10/10. As compared to 1828, the aggregate increase in 1840 was about 20 per cent, that in Sligo being slightly higher than in the case of the Dublin properties. In 1857 his rent receipts from Sligo came to £7370: see Kenneth Bourne, *Palmerston, The Early Years 1784–1841* (London, 1982), pp. 258–9.

2   *The Parliamentary Gazetteer of Ireland*, vol. a (Dublin, London and Edinburgh, 1845), p. 24.

3   Joe McGowan, *In the Shadow of Benbulben* (n. p., 1993), p. 159.

4   Bourne, *Palmerston*, p. 258. A document in Palmerston's hand, 'Expenses incurred in Ahamlish in 1825–26–27' lists £2,853 on Mullaghmore harbour works, £125 on bent planting, £358 on embankment and sluice at Bunduff marsh and nearby roadworks, and £976 on bog cultivation: see Palmerston Papers, b r 139/24. Details on some government loans are provided later. Letters to Stewart & Kincaid in the 1840s refer to loans to Palmerston from individuals in Ireland.

5   Draftsman unknown, 'A Sketch of Lord Palmerstons Sligo Estate' (1826), Palmerston Papers, b r 152.

6   James Fraser, *Hand Book for Travellers in Ireland*, 4th edn (Dublin, 1854), p. 449.

7   Palmerston Papers, b r 145/4/12.

8   McGowan, *Shadow of Benbulben*, p. 165.

9   Palmerston Papers, b r 145/4/9.

10   McGowan, *Shadow of Benbulben*, pp. 169, 170.

11   See, for example, *Poor Inquiry (Ireland), Reports from Commissioners* (London, 1836), appendix e, pp. 7–8, and supplement to appendix e, p. 38. For a summary of the Commissioners' findings relevant to living standards in north Sligo in 1836, see Tyler Anbinder, 'Lord Palmerston and the Irish famine emigration', *Historical Journal* 44: 2 (2001), pp. 441–69.

12   Note T. O'Rorke's observations on the Kildare Place Society cited in chapter 1, p. 10. O'Rorke indicated that in 1826 the society assisted two schools in Ahamlish: one at Mount Temple with 20 scholars, of which Palmerston and Mrs Soden were patrons; the other at Cliffoney with 350 scholars, of which Palmerston and Graves Swan were patrons. The society's support for these schools was terminated shortly afterwards. Palmerston's response to controversies

over religious instruction was sensible. In reaction to a complaint that the Protestant children at the school in Cliffoney were no longer reading the Scriptures, in November 1827 he noted on a letter from the mistress there: 'Saturday to be declared no school day, & Catholics to come at one time to be instructed in their Catechism + Protestants at another to read Scriptures.' See Palmerston Papers, B R 147/1/26.

13   Samuel Lewis, *A Topographical Dictionary of Ireland* (London, 1837), p. 22. Two of these schools were those mentioned in note 12 above. It seems that the third was at Castlegal: see B R 149/4/6 and 7.

14   *Parliamentary Gazetteer*, vol. A, p. 24. In 1845 Kincaid wrote to Palmerston that Stewart & Kincaid paid Leonard, the master at Cliffoney, 20 guineas a year, and that Leonard had no other income. Kincaid added that the female school there had been placed under the Board of National Education, which paid the mistress £8 a year 'in addition to what she is paid by you': see Palmerston Papers, B R 148/3/4.

15   McGowan, *Shadow of Benbulben*, p. 177.

16   Ibid., p. 199.

17   Palmerston Papers, B R 139/12 to 15 and B R 145/1/10.

18   See Anbinder, 'Lord Palmerston', and Desmond Norton, 'Lord Palmerston and the Irish famine emigration: a rejoinder', *Historical Journal* 46: 1 (2003), pp. 155–65.

19   Richard Hough, *Edwina Countess Mountbatten of Burma* (London, 1985), p. 27.

20   W. E. Vaughan, *Landlords and Tenants in Mid-Victorian Ireland* (Oxford, 1994), p. 1, is apparently incorrect in stating that 'Palmerston at Classiebawn was one of the few landlords whose front door could be seen from the public road'. Although the castle had been planned before he died in 1865 aged about 80, most of it was built in 1868 or later (Palmerston Papers, B R 149/13/4 and 5). According to McGowan, *Shadow of Benbulben*, p. 206, work on Classiebawn was completed in 1874.

21   Copy sent by John Lynch to Kincaid, 22 Sept. 1843, Stewart & Kincaid Papers in possession of the author. Subsequent references to the archive in this chapter will be given either in the text or in notes as (S K).

22   Lewis, *Topographical Dictionary*, p. 22.

23   William Middlemiss to James Walker, 19 July 1842 (S K).

24   Lynch to Kincaid, 29 Jan. 1842 (S K).

25   Walker to Stewart & Kincaid, 25 July 1842 (S K).

26   Lynch to Kincaid, 13 July 1842 (S K).

27   Copy of Palmerston to Lynch, 25 Jan. 1842, contained in Lynch to Kincaid, 29 Jan. 1842 (S K).

28   Copy in Middlemiss to Kincaid, 6 June 1842 (S K).

29   *Evidence taken before Her Majesty's Commissioners of Inquiry into the State of the Law and Practice in respect to the Occupation of Land in Ireland*, pt I (Dublin, 1845), p. 32.

30   Messrs Stevenson to Kincaid, 8 Nov. 1842 (S K).

31   Copies in Middlemiss to Stewart & Kincaid, 7 and 28 Mar. 1843 (S K).

32   Board of Works to Stewart & Kincaid, 24 Mar. 1843 and 12 July 1844.

33   Kincaid to Palmerston, 9 Feb. 1853, and Palmerston's instructions, both in Palmerston Papers, B R 148/4/2. It seems that this work was not completed until the 1860s: see B R 148/4/10.

34   Palmerston Papers, B R 139/6 and B R 139/7.

35   Lynch to Kelly, 2 July 1842 (S K). Kelly was a provision merchant in Sligo town: see I. Slater, *National Commercial Directory of Ireland* (Manchester and London, 1846), section on Connaught, p. 140.

36 *Valuation of the Several tenements in the Union of Sligo* (Dublin, 1858), p. 2.

37 Palmerston Papers, B R 145/8/8.

38 Walker to Stewart & Kincaid, 16 Jan. 1842 (s κ).

39 Walker to Kincaid, 28 Oct. 1845 (s κ). A map of 1824 indicates a structure on or close to the site of Pier Head House: see *Sixth Report of the Commissioners of the Irish Fisheries; for the Season of 1824*, fig. 2, in *House of Commons Parliamentary Papers 1825*, vol. 15. Letters of 1826 and 1827 refer to the Gilmartin residence at Mullaghmore pier. Letters of 1827 and 1828 refer to Pier Head House. See BR 145/6/3; 146/6/27; 147/10/26 and 27; 149/10/1.

40 Palmerston to Middlemiss, 27 Feb. 1843 (s κ). Copy in Middlemiss to Kincaid, 7 Mar. 1843 (s κ).

41 Copies in Middlemiss to Stewart & Kincaid, 28 Mar. 1843 (s κ).

42 Copies of the letters dated 8 and 10 Apr. can be found in Middlemiss to Kincaid, 14 Apr. 1843 (s κ).

43 Palmerston Papers, B R 148/4/3.

44 Palmerston Papers, B R 146/3/19.

45 The following details are given in Palmerston Papers, B R 146/10/10. In 1840 Palmerston's unsettled estates in Dublin yielded a gross rental income of £5,123 while those in Sligo yielded £5,030. The same document does not reveal how much of the figure of £5,030 pertained to the Palmerston lands in north Sligo (as distinct from his properties in Sligo town and to the south of the town). However, in December 1843 Kincaid told the Devon Commission that of the 800 families on the north Sligo estate, 280 – those on the newly squared lands – paid rent of about £1,500 a year. An inference that annual rent receipts due from Palmerston's north Sligo estate came to about £4,000 in the early 1840s is further supported by the following figures for the year to May 1860. The year's rent due from Palmerston's unsettled estate in County Sligo (outside Sligo town) was £4,306. The accounts indicate that most of those lands were in the Ahamlish district. The year's rent from Palmerston's unsettled properties in Sligo town was £1,634. Year's rent due from Palmerston's settled estate in County Sligo, £1,738. The latter lands were outside Sligo town and largely to the south of Ahamlish. See account book, *Rental of the Estates of the Right Hon. Visc. Palmerston in the County of Sligo for one years Rent /Arrears to May 1860*, document no. 558, Local History Dept, Sligo County Library.

46 W. A. Maguire, *The Downshire Estates in Ireland 1801–1845* (Oxford, 1994), pp. 70–8. Cormac Ó Gráda has reported: 'It seems safe to say that there was more landlord investment in the 1850s and 1860s than in the preceding decades'. Nevertheless, he concludes that in the relatively prosperous decades immediately after the famine, proprietors of Irish estates 'ploughed back from 3 to 5 per cent of their rental incomes in improvements related to agriculture': see Ó Gráda, 'The investment behaviour of Irish landlords 1850–75: some preliminary findings', *Agricultural History Review* 23 (1975), pp. 139–55. For 1850–80, Vaughan, *Landlords and Tenants*, pp. 122–3, is in broad agreement with Ó Gráda's estimates.

47 There is no evidence that this petition was sent through the post. No exact date indicated (s κ).

48 *Valuation*, pp. 2–8.

49 Bourne, *Palmerston*, p. 260; McGowan, *Shadow of Benbulben*, p. 162.

50 Palmerston Papers, B R 146/7/55.

51 Palmerston had appointed Williamson senior, a Protestant fisherman, as water bailiff at Mullaghmore in 1825 and as harbour master in 1829. Palmerston appears to have paid the cost of

slating his house *c.*1828. In January 1842 Kincaid wrote to Palmerston: 'The annual payment of £4 a year to old Williamson will be discontinued henceforward.' See Palmerston Papers, BR 144/7/47, 145/1/44, 146/4/5, 147/10/13, 150/5/6, 150/9/30, 150/16/10 and 150/16/32.

52 Lynch to Kincaid, no exact date provided (SK).

53 Walker to Stewart & Kincaid, 16 Apr. 1846 (SK).

54 Lynch to Kincaid, n. d., late Apr. 1846 (SK).

55 Bourne, *Palmerston*, p. 257.

56 Palmerston Papers, BR 137/52/1.

57 Palmerston to Lynch, 25 Jan. 1842 (SK). Copied in Lynch to Kincaid, 29 Jan. 1842 (SK).

58 Lynch to Kincaid, 15 Feb. 1842 (SK).

59 Palmerston to Lynch, 14 Dec. 1842 (SK). Copy in Lynch to Kincaid, 24 Dec. 1842 (SK).

60 Lynch to Kincaid, 24 Dec. 1842 (SK).

61 Walker to Stewart & Kincaid, 2 Apr. 1843 (SK); Lynch to Kincaid, 17 Feb. 1846 (SK); Lynch to Kincaid, n. d., late Apr. 1846 (SK).

62 Mary Anne Lynch to Kincaid, 11 July 1842 (SK).

63 John Lynch to Kincaid, 13 July 1842 (SK).

64 Hugh Corrigan and his wife Mary seem to have become Palmerston's tenants at the inn *c.*1814 (Palmerston Papers, BR 147/5/16). In 1833 Walker informed Palmerston that Hugh 'is in the last stage of paralysis from whiskey drinking' (BR 145/5/9). Hugh was dead by October 1835. For Mary's defence in her dispute with Greene see her letter of January 1845 to Palmerston (BR 149/8/32).

65 Palmerston Papers, BR 146/1/3, 147/3/19 and 147/7/51.

66 Bishop of Kilmore to Stewart & Kincaid, 13 May 1845 (SK).

67 One reason was that the church authorities did not have requisite financial resources: see Bishop of Kilmore to Stewart & Kincaid, 13 May 1845 (SK), and Rev. H. Hunt to Stewart & Kincaid, 7 July 1845 (SK).

68 Palmerston Papers, BR 148/5/9.

69 Walker to Stewart & Kincaid, 15 July 1845 (SK).

70 Letter forwarded by Palmerston to Stewart & Kincaid (SK).

71 Board of National Education to Stewart & Kincaid, 24 July 1844 (SK).

72 Edward Ceillier to Stewart & Kincaid, 16 Aug. 1845. Lot 160 in MacDonnell Whyte philatelic auction, Dublin, 13 Dec. 1997. Not in the author's possession.

73 Terence McGowan to Kincaid, 2 June 1845.

74 Lynch to Kincaid, 15 Feb. 1842 (SK).

75 Palmerston Papers, BR 146/3/1, 3/3 and 3/25.

76 C. Tuthill to Stewart & Kincaid, n. d., 1843 (SK).

77 Palmerston Papers, BR 145/9/15.

78 Palmerston Papers, BR 145/9/42.

79 *Evidence*, pt I, pp. 30–9, 60–76, 148–53; pt II, appendix B, p. 10.

80 *Evidence*, pt II, pp. 203–7. Francis Barber was himself a model as an improving tenant. However, in the face of bad luck, his entrepreneurship led him to financial disaster in the 1880s. See John C. McTernan, *Sligo Long Ago* (Sligo, 1998), pp. 491–6.

81 Captain Kennedy, Secretary, Land Commission, to Stewart & Kincaid, 14 Dec. 1844 (SK).

82 *Evidence*, pt II, appendix B, p. 10.

83 The Stewart & Kincaid correspondence contains many references to rents per acre, which are stated to have been about £2 in parts of Ireland. But it is not always clear whether such rents pertained to the statute acre or the larger Irish acre.

84   James and Peter Mulligan, and Michael, John and Pat Gillen to Stewart & Kincaid, n. d., *c.* May 1842 (s κ)

85   See enclosure in Walker to Stewart & Kincaid, 15 Apr. 1841 (s κ).

86   Walker to Stewart & Kincaid, 2 June 1843 (s κ).

87   Maguire, *Downshire Estates*, pp. 52–61. Maguire states that on estates in Ireland the running gale usually lagged six months.

THREE: THE PALMERSTON ESTATES

1   James Walker to Stewart & Kincaid, 7 Dec. 1845, Stewart & Kincaid Papers in possession of the author. Subsequent references to this archive in the chapter will be given either in the text or in notes as (s κ).

2   Broadlands (Palmerston) Papers, Hartley Library, University of Southampton, B R 146/9/6.

3   Dr West to Stewart & Kincaid, n. d., Mar. 1846 (s κ).

4   Lynch to Kincaid, n. d., Apr. 1846 (s κ).

5   Yates was great-grandfather of the poet William Butler Yeats who received a Nobel prize. See William Murphy, *Prodigal Father: The Life of John Butler Yeats (1839–1922)* (Ithaca, 1978), pp. 132–3.

6   Malachi Brennan to Palmerston, 24 Oct. 1846, Palmerston Papers, B R 148/3/15.

7   Catholic priests made gallant efforts in famine relief and many of them died from diseases thereby contracted. See Donal Kerr, *'A Nation of Beggars'? Priests, People and Politics in Famine Ireland, 1846–1852* (Oxford, 1994), ch. 2, and idem, *The Catholic Church and the Famine* (Blackrock, County Dublin, 1996), ch. 1. Similar observations apply to Protestant clergy.

8   Lynch to Stewart & Kincaid, n. d., late Apr. 1846 (s κ).

9   Letting land in conacre was an arrangement under which the immediate landlord sold the use of land from planting to harvest.

10   Palmerston Papers, B R 148/3/13 and 14.

11   The 'Labouchere Letter' is reproduced in John O'Rourke, *The History of the Great Irish Famine of 1847*, 3rd edn (Dublin, 1902), pp. 549–51.

12   James Gulley to Walker, 9 Dec. 1846 (s κ).

13   Dr West to Kincaid, 13 Dec. 1846 (s κ).

14   Palmerston Papers, B R 146/9/11.

15   *Transactions of the Central Relief Committee of the Society of Friends during the Famine in Ireland* (Dublin, 1852). For a modern survey see Rob Goodbody, *A Suitable Channel, Quaker Relief in the Great Famine* (Bray, County Wicklow, 1995).

16   Sisters of Mercy to the Society of Friends, 6 May 1847. (Not part of the Stewart & Kincaid correspondence, but in the author's possession.) Mercy Sisters came to Sligo in June 1846 and commenced charitable work there. In 1847 they resided in a house owned by William Kernaghan, 'a Protestant . . . who refused to take any rent' from them. See Patricia Kelly, 'Sisters of Mercy in Sligo during the Great Famine', in Raymond Browne (ed.), *The Destitution Survey, Reflections on the Famine in the Diocese of Elphin* (Boyle, 1997), pp. 86–95. On Quaker relief in County Sligo, see Liam Swords, *In Their Own Words, The Famine in North Connacht, 1845–49* (Blackrock, County Dublin, 1999).

17   John McTernan, *Memory Harbour, The Port of Sligo* (Sligo, 1992), pt 2, p. 67.

18   *Evidence taken before Her Majesty's Commissioners of Inquiry into the State of the Law and Practice in respect to the Occupation of Land in Ireland*, pt I (Dublin, 1845), p. 33.

19   *The Parliamentary Gazetteer of Ireland*, vol. D–G (Dublin, London and Edinburgh, 1845), p. 82.

20   *Evidence . . . State of the Land . . . in Ireland*, pt I (Dublin, 1845), pp. 152–3.

21   Palmerston Papers, BR 146/9/3.

22   Cecil Woodham-Smith, *The Great Hunger* (London, 1962), may be the most accessible. See also McTernan, *Port of Sligo*, pt 2, pp. 26–35 and appendices.

23   McTernan, *Port of Sligo*, pt 2, pp. 29, 31, implies that about 2,500 people were emigrated by Palmerston in 1847. Woodham-Smith, *Great Hunger*, p. 228, states that in 1847 nine ships left Sligo carrying Palmerston emigrants, 'and additional passages were booked from Liverpool, about 2,000 persons leaving in all'. According to a letter of December 1847 from Stewart & Kincaid to Palmerston, reproduced in McTernan, pp. 76–7, 'the numbers sent out last season from your Lordship's estate exceeded 2,000, all of whom were conveyed . . . chiefly to Quebec, and a few to St John's [St John] and Shippegan'. See the earlier document dated June 1847 filed by Palmerston as 'List of Emigrants from my Sligo Estate', Palmerston Papers, BR 146/9/6. It seems that everyone on this list travelled in a family group. The document describes those emigrants as '136 families averaging 6⅓ in each'. See also Tyler Anbinder, 'Lord Palmerston and the Irish famine emigration', *Historical Journal* 44: 2 (2001), pp. 441–69, n. 42.

24   See 'List of Passengers sent to Quebec from Lord Palmerston's Sligo Estates in April 1847', Palmerston Papers, BR 146/9/4. The *Carricks* may have been ill fated in another respect. Dated June 1832, the following appeared in the diary of Philip Hone, once mayor of New York: 'The cholera . . . has crossed the Atlantic and made its appearance first in Quebec', to which it had been brought 'in a vessel called the Carricks, with a cargo of Irish emigrants'. It quickly spread to New York where it caused hundreds of deaths. See Ric Burns and James Sanders, *New York* (New York, 1999), p. 77, for which I thank my daughters Chantelle, Shevawn and Emma.

25   G. Justice to Joseph Bewley and Jonathan Pim, 30 Mar. 1847. 'Per Steamer', this letter arrived in Dublin on 16 April. It was among a collection of letters from Quakers in America in relation to their donations for Irish famine relief, acquired by me at auction in 1996. Not part of the Stewart & Kincaid archive.

26   BR 146/9/17; McTernan, *Port of Sligo*, pt 2, p. 83.

27   Edward Smyth to Stewart & Kincaid, 5 Aug. 1848 (SK).

28   This complaint, by an officer named Parley, is reproduced in McTernan, *Port of Sligo*, pt 2, appendix 2.

29   Stewart to Kincaid, n. d., but marked 1847 (SK).

30   For example, McTernan, *Port of Sligo*, pt 2, pp. 76–9; Woodham-Smith, *Great Hunger*, p. 230.

31   Pettigrew and Oulton, *The Dublin Almanac . . . 1846*, p. 549.

32   Palmerston Papers, BR 138/19.

33   See 'Weekly rations to passengers', dated Dec. 1847 in Palmerston Papers, BR 146/9/17.

34   Kincaid to Palmerston, 24 Nov. 1847, Palmerston Papers, BR 146/9/14.

35   Anbinder, 'Lord Palmerston', pp. 468–9, according to whom about 300 emigrants from Palmerston's Sligo properties had settled in the Five Points slum in New York before the American Civil War. Anbinder describes the Five Points as 'the most notoriously crowded, decrepit, and disease-ridden district in North America'. For confirmation of this, see Luc Sante, *Low Life* (New York, 1992). But Anbinder's contribution unfortunately contains errors: see

Desmond Norton, 'Lord Palmerston and the Irish Famine Emigration: A Rejoinder', *Historical Journal* 46: 1 (2003), pp. 155–65. A more recent study is subject to problems similar to those in Anbinder, as well as statistics which seem to be inconsistent. See Thomas Power, 'The Palmerston estate in County Sligo: improvement and assisted emigration before 1850', ch. 5 in Patrick J. Duffy (ed.), *To and From Ireland: Planned Migration Schemes c.1600–2000* (Dublin, 2004), and Desmond Norton, 'On the Sligo estates of three proprietors in the 1840s', unpublished paper presented to Group for the Study of Irish Historical Settlement, Annual Conference, Sligo, 6–8 May 2005, esp. the lengthy note 2 (obtainable from the author).

36 The copies of extracts from letters by emigrants can be found in Palmerston Papers, BR 146/10/13.

37 Luke Cullinan to Stewart & Kincaid, 15 Feb. 1846 (SK); Education Office to Stewart & Kincaid, 25 Nov. 1846 (SK). There are two townlands named Tunnagh in County Sligo. The other Tunnagh is south of Ballymote.

38 T. E. Hodder to Stewart & Kincaid, n. d., 1846. 'White' was probably Michael White, listed as a ship agent in Pettigrew and Oulton, *Dublin Almanac 1848*, p. 598.

39 On the identities of Coyne and Higgins, see I. Slater, *National Commercial Directory of Ireland* (Manchester and London, 1846), section on Connaught, pp. 139, 140.

40 McTernan, *Port of Sligo*, pt 2, p. 40.

41 Palmerston Papers, BR 146/11/4 and BR 148/4/11.

42 Palmerston Papers, BR 148/4/20.

43 Quoted by McTernan, *Port of Sligo*, pt 2, p. 53.

44 Some of these monies were obtained by borrowing: see Palmerston Papers, BR 146/9/7, 11 and 12.

45 Woodham-Smith, *Great Hunger*, p. 201; George Nicholls, *A History of the Irish Poor Law* (London, 1856), pp. 319–20.

46 Board of Works to Stewart & Kincaid, 22 Dec, 1847; 11 May, 13 July, 19 Sept., 11 Oct. and 18 Dec, 1848 (SK); Smyth to Stewart & Kincaid, 29 June and 26 Sept. 1848 (SK); Stewart to Kincaid, 25 Mar. 1849.

47 Smyth to Stewart & Kincaid, 5 Aug. 1848 (SK).

48 *Valuation of the Several Tenements in the Union of Sligo* (Dublin, 1858), pp. 228–9. Descendants of Luke Scanlon and of Charles Roycroft stayed undisturbed for a century. In 1996, Mrs Kearns of Tunnagh informed me that the Roycroft line died out, on the land now farmed by her family, c.1945, and Michael Healy, who once resided at Tunnagh, stated that the Scanlons also died out c.1945. The ruins of the Scanlon homestead can be seen near the lake.

49 Smyth to Stewart & Kincaid, 29 Apr. and 9 May 1848 (SK).

50 A person named Michael Cunnane farmed on Palmerston land at Cloonagh in 1858: see *County of Sligo, Valuation . . . Union of Boyle* (Dublin, 1858), p. 56. There are four townlands named Cloonagh in Sligo: see *General Alphabetical Index to the Townlands and Towns, Parishes and Baronies in Ireland* (Dublin, 1861), p. 261.

51 *Valuation, Union of Sligo*, p.15.

52 See account book, *Rental of the Estates of the Right Hon. Visc. Palmerston in the County of Sligo for one years Rent/Arrears to May 1860*, document no. 558, Local History Dept., Sligo County Library. The Sodens had been granted lands in the Grange district in the mid seventeenth century. As magistrates and administrators, the family was influential in Sligo town in the

eighteenth and early nineteenth centuries. An early directory lists Capt. James Soden, of the Sligo Militia, at Moneygold. Isabella was probably his wife. A directory of 1846 lists Mrs Isabella Soden at Stephen Street, Sligo town. In the late nineteenth century, the principal representative of the Soden family was Capt. G. Eccles, JP, of Moneygold House, a large structure which was demolished about twenty years ago. See J. Pigot & Co., *City of Dublin and Hibernian Provincial Directory and Directory of London* (London and Manchester, 1824), section on Connaught, p. 214; Slater, *Directory*, section on Connaught, p. 138; T. O'Rorke, *History of Sligo* (Dublin, n. d.), vol. I, pp. 336–7, and vol. II, pp. 52, 600.

53   *Valuation, Union of Sligo*, p. 119.

54   *Census of Ireland 1851*, pt I, vol. IV (Dublin 1852), p. 220.

55   Extract from Palmerston in G. P. Gouch (ed.), *The Later Correspondence of Lord John Russell 1840–1878*, vol. I (London, 1925), pp. 224–5.

56   Kincaid to Palmerston containing a letter from the Marquess of Westmeath to Kincaid, 7–12 Oct. 1850, Palmerston Papers, B R 144/11/40.

57   *Sixth Report of the Commissioners of the Irish Fisheries; for the Season of 1824*, p. 20, in *House of Commons Parliamentary Papers 1825*, vol. 15; *First Report of the Commissioners of Inquiry into the State of the Irish Fisheries, with Minutes of Evidence* (Dublin, 1836), p. 221; *Evidence, Land in Ireland*, pt I, p. 153.

58   *First Report . . . with Minutes of Evidence*, pp. 71–3, 221.

59   *Evidence, Land in Ireland*, pt I, p. 31.

60   Ibid., p. 150.

61   Winifred Campbell to Kincaid, 9 Oct. 1845 (S K).

62   *Evidence, Land in Ireland*, pt I, p. 32.

63   See the communication dated 2 October 1843 from the Shipwrecked Fishermen & Mariner's Benevolent Society in London to Palmerston, requesting that he use his influence for 'formation of branch societies in your Lordships neighbourhood'. On 24 November, Palmerston sent this communication to Stewart & Kincaid: 'I shall be glad to subscribe to this institution'.

64   Hugh McIntire to Kincaid, 14 July 1846 (S K).

65   *Transactions*, pp. 78–84, 107–9, 390–404.

66   Ibid., pp.108–9.

67   Kincaid to Palmerston, 1 Feb. 1849, Palmerston Papers, B R 149/8/34.

68   Several roads in Dublin bear the name Palmerston. Some older thoroughfares bear the Palmerston family name, Temple. For example, 'Temple-bar acquired its name from having been the site of the mansion and gardens of the family of Temple, the first of whom settled in Dublin was William Temple . . . the Provost . . . of the College of Dublin, 1609': see J. T. Gilbert, *History of the City of Dublin*, vol. II (Dublin, 1859), pp. 315–16.

69   John Hoskyns to Stewart & Kincaid, 16 Jan., 18 May, 20 July and 26 Oct. 1846 (S K); to Palmerston, who forwarded the letter to Stewart & Kincaid, 22 May 1846 (S K).

70   Dr Arthur to Stewart & Kincaid, 22 Mar. and 7 July 1841 (S K).

71   Catherine Conless to Stewart & Kincaid, 14 July 1843 (S K). In 1837 there were two structures named 'Rathmines Castle'. The reference in the text is to 'Old Rathmines Castle', south of what is now Palmerston Park. See Christopher Haden and Catherine O'Malley, *The Demesne of Old Rathmines* (Dublin, 1998), p. 8. My thanks to John Lennon for a copy of this reference. See also Palmerston Papers, B R 144/9/29.

72   W. Walker to Stewart & Kincaid, 18 May 1848 (S K).

73   William Willcocks to Stewart & Kincaid, 31 Dec. 1846; W. Walker to Stewart & Kincaid, 18 May 1848; J. Walker to Stewart & Kincaid, 28 May 1848; M. West to Stewart & Kincaid, 28 May and 14 July 1848 (SK).

74   Palmerston Papers, BR 144/11/9 and 148/3/7.

75   Herbert Bell, *Lord Palmerston*, vol. 1 (London, 1966), ch. XV.

FOUR: THE CRICHTON ESTATES IN SLIGO AND ROSCOMMON

1   L. G. Pine (ed.), *Burke's Landed Gentry of Ireland*, 4th edn (London, 1958), p. 189.

2   *Valuation . . . Union of Roscommon in the Counties of Roscommon and Galway* (Dublin, 1857), pp. 79–86. The only official holdings of records on Crichton lands in the 1840s which I could find were maps of Killavil and Knockanarrow, in Sligo County Library.

3   According to the present Alexander Crichton, one of the Dodwells obtained the Jamaican property in settlement of a debt, and it passed to the Crichtons in the same manner as their lands in Ireland.

4   *County of Sligo, Valuation . . . Union of Boyle* (Dublin, 1858), pp. 39–52.

5   Rev. John Armstrong to Stewart & Kincaid, 8 July 1846, Stewart & Kincaid Papers in possession of the author. Subsequent references to the archive in this chapter will be given either in the text or in notes as (SK).
Several letters dated 1846 from Armstrong in connection with famine relief survive in the National Archives of Ireland. Extracts from some of them can be found in Liam Swords, *In Their Own Words: The Famine in North Connacht 1845–49* (Blackrock, County Dublin, 1999).

6   In April 1843 a Dublin solicitor wrote to Stewart & Kincaid indicating that he had claims, which were not being honoured, on Ferrall's Sligo rents. In December 1846 he wrote to Stewart & Kincaid seeking a year's rent from Ferrall's lands in Sligo, to March 1846. Either Stewart or Kincaid instructed a clerk: 'Civil answer – No rents paying in that district. No funds.' See Robert Simpson to Stewart & Kincaid, 27 Apr. 1843 and 2 Dec. 1846 (SK).

7   George Armstrong to Edward Armstrong, 3 Dec. 1846, found in an accumulation of Armstrong documents acquired by the author *c*.1988.

8   Thomas Rice to Eleanor Armstrong, 13 Dec. 1846. From the Armstrong correspondence.

9   When I visited Temple House in 1996, Sandy Perceval recounted that in 1969 an old IRA man told him that the circumstances surrounding Jane Perceval's death were the reasons why the house had not been burnt down by republicans circa 1922.

10   Desmond Norton, 'Where was Major Denis Mahon shot?', *County Roscommon Historical and Archaeological Society Journal* 9 (2003), pp. 54–8, and references cited therein.

11   Details here have been drawn from a communication from the present Alexander Crichton of Carrowgarry, and from Pine (ed.), *Landed Gentry*, p. 189.

12   *County of Sligo, Valuation, Union of Boyle*, p. 47.

13   John Clapperton, *Instructions for the Small Farmers of Ireland, on Croping and Culture of their Farms* (Dublin, 1847). Priced at one penny.

14   Alex Crichton to Stewart & Kincaid, 24 Mar. 1848 (SK).

15   William Shaw to Stewart & Kincaid, 30 Apr. and 7 May 1848 (SK). The *Valuation* of 1858 does not list any Supple on Killavil. It lists a Briget Davy on Drumanaraher. See *County of Sligo,*

Valuation, Union of Boyle, p. 49. Patrick J. Duffy of Killavil has written to me that 'descendants of many of the families mentioned [in an earlier draft of this chapter] are still around'.

16 William Woods of Sligo town: see I. Slater, *National Commercial Directory of Ireland* (Manchester and London, 1846), section on Connaught, p. 140.

17 Alexander Crichton to Stewart & Kincaid, 22 June 1848 (sk); Board of Works to Alexander Crichton, 9 Sept., and to Stewart & Kincaid, 11 Sept. 1848 (sk).

18 *Valuation . . . Union of Sligo* (Dublin, 1858), p. 117 (sk).

19 Crichton to Stewart & Kincaid, 22 June 1848 (sk).

20 Crichton to Stewart & Kincaid, 11 Mar. and 6 Dec. 1848 (sk). A letter from him to Stewart & Kincaid, 26 Dec. 1848, indicates that the firm which had become bankrupt was Vendewell & Co., listed under 'Brokers', London, in J. Pigot and Co.'s *City of Dublin and Hibernian Directory and Directory of London* (London and Manchester, 1824).

21 Crichton to Stewart & Kincaid, 6 Dec. 1847 (sk).

22 *County of Sligo, Valuation, Union of Dromore West* (Dublin, 1857), p. 92.

23 Edward Smyth to Stewart & Kincaid, 14 Apr., 5 Oct., 11 Oct. and 13 Oct. 1848 (sk).

24 These oyster beds are depicted on sheet 19 of the Ordnance Survey map of County Sligo, as revised in 1886.

25 Communication from the present Alexander Crichton, 16 Mar. 1999.

26 John Holliday to Kincaid, 17 July 1848 (sk). A stake net is T-shaped, moored by stakes, with a central pocket – the base of the 'T' – designed to trap fish which are drawn from the top of the 'T' to its base by the flow of a river or by an incoming tide.

27 Raymond Browne (ed.), *Cill Bhride: A History of Kilbride Parish, County Roscommon*, forthcoming.

28 A letter from Alex Crichton to Stewart & Kincaid, 18 Oct. 1847, refers to a house in Dorset Street, Dublin, as Chris Taaffe's 'retreat'. He is listed there in *The Post Office Directory for 1847* (Dublin, 1846/7), p. 304. A letter from his father, Patt Taaffe to Stewart & Kincaid, 29 July 1845, seeking a lease for land on the Roscommon estates of D. H. Ferrall, was written from Kingstown, County Dublin. He was the person listed in 1814 as Patrick Taafe, Foxborough, near Elphin, County Roscommon: see Ambrose Leet, *Directory to Noted Places in Ireland*, 2nd edn (Dublin, 1814), p. 189. Patrick Taaffe is listed as immediate lessor of land at Foxborough in 1857: see *Valuation . . . Union of Strokestown* (Dublin, 1857), p. 94. A letter from Wynne Peyton to Stewart & Kincaid, 19 Dec. 1846, pertains to 'rent of Decklin'. This land, near Carrick-on-Shannon, was the property of D. H. Ferrall.

29 William Sandys to Alexander Crichton, 9 Feb. 1849 (sk).

30 Browne, *Cill Bhride*, and *Valuation, Union of Roscommon*, p. 80.

31 Pettigrew and Oulton, *The Dublin Almanac . . . 1845*, p. 267, lists Wynne Peyton in residence at Carrick-on-Shannon.

32 *Union of Carrick-on-Shannon, Valuation . . . County of Roscommon* (Dublin, 1858), p. 29.

33 Alex Crichton to Kincaid, 18 Oct. 1847 (sk).

34 Browne, *Cill Bhride*.

35 *Valuation, Union of Roscommon*, p. 79.

36 Ibid., pp. 79–80.

37 These numbers have been drawn from Browne, *Cill Bhride*.

38 For detailed comparisons, see ibid.

39 In a letter of 26 January 1997, the Rev. Browne saved me from error by informing me that 'Mahon did not have any programme of assisted emigration in Doorty or in any part of Kilbride Parish. The list of 18 townlands in which he did carry out such programmes are to be found in the *Freeman's Journal*, 29 Apr. 1848.' In the same letter, Rev. Browne added that 'everybody in Doorty was severely interrogated immediately after the shooting, and threatened with eviction unless they gave information. I would think it was as a result of the shooting of Major Mahon in Doorty that the evictions took place'. But see note 10 above.

40 Such complexity was rare on estates managed by Stewart & Kincaid. But in the mid-1840s there were numerous layers of middlemen on some estates not managed by Stewart & Kincaid. See, for example, R. B. MacCarthy, *The Trinity College Estates 1800–1923* (Dundalk, 1992), pp. 10, 101, 103, 230.

41 In 1857 Thomas Narry was listed on 30 acres of Clooncullaan in *Valuation, Union of Strokestown*.

42 Board of Works to Alexander Crichton, 9 Sept. 1848 (s k), and to Stewart & Kincaid, n.d. Sept., 1848 (s k); Alex Crichton to Stewart & Kincaid, 24 Oct. 1848 (s k).

43 A convenient summary of the Land Acts can be found in D. J. Hickey and J. E. Doherty, *A Dictionary of Irish History 1800–1980* (Dublin, 1987), pp. 286–90.

44 As the Stewart & Kincaid correspondence reveals, many Irish landlords were already deep in debt in the years just before the famine. But the famine greatly increased the financial plight of landlords as a group. Many of them were forced to sell out under the Encumbered Estates Acts of 1848 and 1849. These were introduced in order, it was hoped, to encourage transfer of estates from impoverished landlords to persons of capital. As summarised by Christine Kinealy, in *This Great Calamity* (Dublin, 1994), p. 275: 'Within a few years of these Acts being passed, approximately five million acres of land – a quarter of Ireland – had changed hands. But 'the expectation regarding the investment of British capital into Ireland never materialised'. And as indicated by Cecil Woodham-Smith, *The Great Hunger* (London, 1962), p. 409, the Act of 1849 was drastic because 'under its provisions an estate could be compulsorily sold on the petition of a creditor or of the landlord himself'. But although 'properties were sold for bargain prices . . . no legislation protected the tenant . . . and the new landlords proved very hard masters'.

45 *Return of Owners of Land in Ireland* (Dublin, 1876), pp. 315, 320.

46 Personal communication from Andrew Lyall, 26 Mar. 1999.

47 Details here have been drawn from Pine (ed.), *Landed Gentry*, pp. 189, 190.

48 John C. McTernan, *Here's to Their Memory* (Dublin and Cork, 1977), pp. 274, 275.

FIVE: THE MYSTERIOUS DANIEL HENRY FERRALL OF ROSCOMMON

1 John Stewart to James Robert Stewart, 6 Mar. 1848, Stewart & Kincaid Papers in possession of the author. Subsequent references to the archive in this chapter will be given either in the text or in notes as (s k). Also, written communication to this author from William Gacquin of County Roscommon. Some earlier research on Ferrall has been published by William Gacquin, *Roscommon before the Famine: The Parishes of Kiltoom and Cam, 1749–1845* (Dublin, 1996).

2 Isaac Weld, *Statistical Survey of the County of Roscommon* (Dublin, 1832), pp. 647–53.

3 At the time of his death in 1823 Beechwood was the property of D. H. Ferrall's uncle, John Ferrall. Nevertheless, Ambrose Leet, *Directory to the Noted Places in Ireland*, 2nd edn (Dublin,

1814), p. 64, lists 'Daniel Ferrall' as resident at Beechwood. It seems that he was the D. H. Ferrall of this chapter.

4   A letter from Daniel Ferrall to Stewart & Kincaid, 3 Jan. 1848 (sk), indicates Edward's address as 102 Lower Gardiner St, Dublin, where he was a solicitor (Pettigrew and Oulton, *The Dublin Almanac . . . 1848*, p. 733).

5   William Gacquin, 'Mrs Julia Conmee (*c.*1786–1860), Benefactress of C. B. S. Roscommon', *Rosc Chomáin* (Roscommon, 1997), pp. 9–11, and a communication from Gacquin, Dec. 1997. See also S. F. O'Cianain, *The Davys Family Records* (Longford, 1931), pp. 11–13.

6   It seems that Terrence Ferrall also had a brother named Richard, and that this Richard was partner in the Dublin banking firm of Dillon and Ferrall which suspended payment in 1754, when the partners absconded. An archive on that firm acquired by the author in 2001 indicates that it had business links with Roscommon and northeast Galway. See also Charles Collins, *The Law and Practice of Banking in Ireland* (Dublin, 1880), p. 72; L. M. Cullen, 'Landlords, bankers and merchants: the early Irish banking world, 1700–1820', in Antoin Murphy (ed.), *Economists and the Irish Economy from the Eighteenth Century to the Present Day* (Dublin, 1984), p. 41; Malcolm Dillon, *The History and Development of Banking in Ireland* (Dublin, 1889), pp. 21–2.

7   J. R. Stewart to Kincaid, 28 June 1841 (sk).

8   See B. M. Walker (ed.), *Parliamentary Election Results in Ireland, 1801–1922* (Dublin, 1978), pp. 68–73. I thank Hazel Ryan and William Gacquin of County Roscommon for further details.

9   I thank William Gacquin for sending a copy of this listing to me.

10   James Nolan to Stewart & Kincaid, 14 June 1843 (sk).

11   Ferrall to Kincaid, 15 Aug. 1843 (sk).

12   Susan Stuart to Stewart & Kincaid, 27 Apr. 1846 and 5 Oct. 1846 (sk).

13   Isabella Soden to Kincaid, n. d., 1848 (sk).

14   Ferrall to Stewart & Kincaid, 30 Nov. 1846 (sk).

15   Ferrall to Stewart & Kincaid, 12 Jan. 1847 and 22 Feb. 1848 (sk).

16   W. A. Maguire, *The Downshire Estates in Ireland 1801–1845* (Oxford, 1972), pp. 96–103.

17   Ferrall to Kincaid, 28 Feb. 1841 (sk). This letter suggests that at least one of the loans was from the Taaffes, mentioned in chapters 4 and 6.

18   No R. Newcomen is listed by Pettigrew and Oulton for 1843. The letter states the address of the sender as 72 Great Britain St. However, Pettigrew and Oulton indicate that this address was that of John Lawrence, linen draper: see their *Dublin Almanac 1843*, p. 503. The same observation applies to the Pettigrew and Oulton volume for 1844, p. 505.

19   Ferrall to Kincaid, 5 July 1844 (sk).

20   Ferrall to Kincaid, 1 July 1844 (sk).

21   Ferrall to Stewart, 11 and 16 July 1844 (sk).

22   Pettigrew and Oulton, *Dublin Almanac 1845*, p. 582, lists Tabuteau as a wine merchant at 124 Abbey Street Upper.

23   Ferrall to Stewart & Kincaid, 3 Nov. 1848 (sk).

24   Raymond Browne (ed.), *Cill Bhride: A History of Kilbride Parish, County Roscommon*, forthcoming.

25   Robert James Scally, *The End of Hidden Ireland* (Oxford, 1995), pp. 206–15.

26   Ferrall to Stewart & Kincaid, 16 Oct. 1847 (sk).

27   Ferrall to Stewart & Kincaid, 14 Sept. 1847 (sk).

28   Copy in Ferrall to Stewart & Kincaid, 30 Nov. 1847 (sk).

29 Ferrall to Stewart & Kincaid, 29 June 1848 (s k).

30 Communication from William Gacquin, Dec. 1997.

31 *Return of Owners of Land in Ireland* (Dublin, 1876), p. 316.

SIX: FERRALL'S ROSCOMMON ESTATES

1 *Valuation . . . Union of Athlone . . . County of Roscommon* (Dublin, 1858).

2 *Valuation . . . Union of Roscommon in the Counties of Roscommon and Galway* (Dublin, 1857).

3 *Valuation . . . Union of Strokestown . . . County of Roscommon* (Dublin, 1857). As the Rev. Raymond Browne has indicated to me, the Union of Strokestown was not formed until 1850. The reader is reminded (from the Introduction, p. 4) that when reference is made to Poor Law Unions, the classification adopted is that of the *Valuations* of the 1850s.

4 *Union of Carrick-on-Shannon, Valuation . . . County of Roscommon* (Dublin, 1858).

5 *Valuation . . . Union of Boyle . . . County of Roscommon* (Dublin, 1858).

6 *Valuation . . . Union of Castlerea . . . Counties of Roscommon and Mayo* (Dublin, 1857).

7 James Nolan to J. R. Stewart, 5 Jan. 1843, Stewart & Kincaid Papers in possession of the author. Subsequent references to the archive in this chapter will be given either in the text or in notes as (s k).

8 Nolan to Kincaid, 5 Oct. 1841 (s k); Nolan to Stewart & Kincaid, n.d., Nov. 1841 (s k).

9 Nolan to Stewart & Kincaid, 14 July 1842 (s k).

10 Robert Scally, *The End of Hidden Ireland* (Oxford, 1995).

11 Nolan to Stewart & Kincaid, 23 Oct. 1842 (s k).

12 Nolan to Stewart & Kincaid, n. d., Nov. 1842 (s k).

13 Nolan to Stewart & Kincaid, 6 Feb. 1842 (s k).

14 I thank the Rev. Jim Casey of Clover Hill, John Fallon of Strokestown and Marian Harlow of Mullymux (all in County Roscommon) for helping me to identify the district which Stewart & Kincaid called 'Islands'. Marian Harlow is surely correct in suggesting that it was part of the townland of Caul, near Ballyfeeny. Notes from O'Donovan's Ordnance Survey Name Books, sent to me by Marian Harlow, state that 'in the bog of Caul is a cultivated isolated spot called the Islands'.

15 Con McGuire of Ballyfeeny is a descendent of this John McGuire. He has informed me that some of the McGuire family emigrated to Baltimore in the nineteenth century. I thank him for showing me the house on his lands where the rents were paid.

16 Nolan to Stewart & Kincaid, 7 Mar. 1841 (SK).

17 W. A. Maguire, *The Downshire Estates in Ireland 1801–1845* (Oxford, 1972), p. 43; R. B. MacCarthy, *The Trinity College Estates 1800–1923* (Dundalk, 1992), p. 32.

18 Ballyroe (County Roscommon) is not listed in the *General Alphabetical Index to the Townlands and Towns, Parishes and Baronies of Ireland* (Dublin, 1861); nor is it listed in the Griffith *Valuations*. It was close to Aghacurreen.

19 Nolan to Stewart & Kincaid, n. d., 1843 (s k).

20 Leonard Mac Nally, *The Justice of the Peace for Ireland*, 3rd edn, vol. 11 (Dublin, 1820), p. 11.

21 Nolan to Stewart & Kincaid, n. d., Oct. 1843 (s k).

22 Patrick Hanley, PP of Oran. Maxwell met him while staying at Runnamede: in his letter of 30 Sept. 1845 to Stewart, Maxwell wrote that he had experienced 'two days at Beechwood rather

dull but the two at Runnamede made up for them dancing till 3 in the morning . . . and his reverence father Hanley going to convert me' (s κ).

23 Patt Kelly to Stewart & Kincaid, 25 Apr. 1846 (s κ)

24 Nolan to Stewart & Kincaid, 24 Feb. 1842 (s κ).

25 Alexander Stewart to Ferrall, 26 June 1848 (s κ); J. C. Walker to Stewart & Kincaid, 20 July 1848 (s κ); W.W. Woods to Stewart & Kincaid, 21 July 1848 (s κ).

26 Scally, *Hidden Ireland*, p. 84. See also Liam Coyle, *A Parish History of Kilglass, Rusky and Slatta* (Boyle, 1994), pp. 27–32.

27 Nolan to Stewart & Kincaid, 16 Nov. 1846 (s κ).

28 Letty Missett to Stewart & Kincaid, 25 Apr. 1846 (s κ).

29 Golrich's communication, dated 5 Nov., was not through the post office; thus it is assumed that it was delivered in person.

30 A plaque in the graveyard at Ardcarn indicates that 110 persons were buried therein during the first 50 days of 1847.

31 Nolan to Kincaid, 16 Nov. 1846 (s κ).

32 Pettigrew and Oulton, *Dublin Almanac 1846*, p. 260. On King's problems, see Nolan to Stewart & Kincaid, 22 Dec. 1845, 30 Mar., 10 May and 20 May 1846 (s κ).

33 George Knox to Stewart & Kincaid, 13 June and 10 Oct. 1846 (s κ); Nolan to Stewart & Kincaid, 22 Apr. 1848 (s κ).

34 This place was otherwise known as Ballinvally: see *County of Sligo, Valuation . . . Union of Tobercurry* (Dublin, 1857), p. 1.

35 James S. Donnelly, Jr., *The Land and the People of Nineteenth-Century Cork* (London and Boston, 1975), p. 80.

36 There are up to five other townlands of this name in County Roscommon: see *Index to the Townlands*, p. 61.

37 Ferrall to Stewart & Kincaid, 30 Nov. 1847 (s κ).

38 Ferrall to Stewart & Kincaid, 18 Dec. 1847 (s κ).

39 Ferrall to Stewart & Kincaid, 4 June 1849 (s κ).

40 John Sharkey to Stewart & Kincaid, 5 Nov. 1848 (s κ).

41 Sharkey to Stewart & Kincaid, 8 Dec. 1848 (s κ).

42 Sharkey to Stewart & Kincaid, 13 Nov. 1848 (s κ).

43 Ferrall to Stewart & Kincaid, 30 Oct. 1848 (s κ).

44 Donnelly, *Nineteenth-Century Cork*, pp. 116–17, observes that some Cork proprietors had a similar aim, but he adds that little seems to have come of those resolves.

45 See the references in Edward Sheridan to Stewart & Kincaid, 6 Apr. 1848 (s κ).

46 Stewart to Kincaid, 16 Jan. 1846 (s κ); Nolan to Stewart & Kincaid, 20 Mar. 1846 (s κ).

47 Pettigrew and Oulton, *Dublin Almanac 1848*, p. 294.

48 Ferrall to Stewart & Kincaid, 2 Dec. 1847 (s κ).

49 John Sharkey to Stewart & Kincaid, 25 Feb. 1848 (s κ).

50 A letter from Ferrall, 10 May 1841, asked Sharkey to 'come up to Beechwood on Sunday . . . early and return home after Mass' (s κ). My thanks to Albert Siggins of County Roscommon for sending me a photocopy of this letter, which suggests that Ferrall had Mass celebrated in his home.

SEVEN: WINGFIELD'S SLIGO ESTATE

1   Bernard Burke, *Peerage and Baronetage of the British Empire* (London, 1864), p. 904.

2   The classifications used are those of the *Valuations* of the 1850s and of the *General Alphabetical Index to the Townlands and Towns, Parishes and Baronies of Ireland* (Dublin, 1861).

3   Details which immediately follow are drawn from *Report of the Case of Little and Clark against Wingfield and Others . . . 1857* (Dublin, 1857). What was under consideration was the right to fish on the Moy from Belleek Castle to the point of Scurmore. I thank Kevin McKenna of County Dublin for giving me a copy of the *Report* and Ivan Gawley of Carrowcardin near Scurmore for showing me around former Wingfield properties and for giving me the benefit of his knowledge on local history.

4   Quoted in Herbert Clifford to Stewart & Kincaid, 13 May 1846, Stewart & Kincaid Papers in possession of the author. Subsequent references to the archive in this chapter will be given either in the text or in notes as (s K). The reference to Loochoo is to the townland of Lough – in Irish called Locha – near Dingle. I thank Monsignor Pádraig Ó Fiannachta, PP of Dingle, for information on this point. Clifford worked actively with the Rev.Charles Gayer, mentioned in the introduction to this book.

5   Samuel Lewis, *Topographical Dictionary of Ireland* (London, 1837), p. 294.

6   John Hamilton to Stewart & Kincaid, 20 Apr. 1846 (s K).

7   The forge is now a ruin. The former schoolhouse is now again a residence.

8   John Stewart to Stewart & Kincaid, 24 June 1848 (s K).

9   *The Parliamentary Gazetteer of Ireland*, vol. C (Dublin, London and Edinburgh, 1845), p. 358.

10 There is a tombstone in Killanley churchyard to James Burrow, died Nov. 1850, aged 60. Nearby is a tombstone to the Rev. James Burrow, died Aug. 1819.

11 *Report . . . Little and Clark*, p. 69.

12 I. Slater, *National Commercial Directory of Ireland* (Manchester and London, 1846), section on Connaught, p. 105.

13 William Holliday to Stewart & Kincaid, 22 Feb. 1845 (s K); William Ormsby to Stewart & Kincaid, 13 Mar. and 14 Aug. 1845 (s K).

14 Edward Wingfield to Stewart & Kincaid, n. d., Dec. 1845 (s K).

15 Wingfield to Stewart & Kincaid, n. d., Dec. 1845 (s K).

16 John Garrett to Wingfield, 7 Feb. 1846 (s K).

17 Wingfield to Stewart & Kincaid, 25 Feb. 1846 (s K).

18 According to Ivan Gawley, Fry (who had a family of ten) ended his days in the workhouse in Sligo town.

19 In 1837 Lewis, *Topographical Dictionary*, p. 292, listed this Howley as resident at Seaville (now named Seaview).

20 Wingfield to Stewart & Kincaid, n. d., Mar. 1846 (s K).

21 Edward Smyth to Stewart & Kincaid, 11 May 1848 (s K).

22 Wingfield to Stewart & Kincaid, n. d., Mar. 1846 (s K).

23 Wingfield to an undetermined agent (probably J. R. Stewart), 4 Feb. 1846. The reference appears to be to John Dunbar: see *County of Sligo, Valuation . . . Union of Dromore West* (Dublin, 1857), pp. 34, 35. Dunbar was again a victim in July 1848, when John Stewart reported that 'last week there was a lamb of John Dunbar's stolen'.

24 Today there are two bridges, one over the Moy, the other over the Einagh.

25 Wingfield to Stewart & Kincaid, n. d., Dec. 1845 (s к).

26 It seems that the road in question is that which today cuts through the townland from near Toorlestraun into Cloongoonagh, where a bridge over the Einagh was subsequently erected.

27 On Howley and Grose, see Slater, *Commercial Directory*, section on Connaught, p. 104.

28 *Counties of Mayo and Sligo, Valuation . . . Union of Ballina* (Dublin, 1856), p. 150.

29 Pettigrew and Oulton, *The Dublin Almanac . . . 1846*, p. 261.

30 Holliday to Stewart & Kincaid, 22 Dec. 1846 (s к).

31 Located on the road from Ballina to Scurmore, the quay is 1.5 miles from the first (from the seaward side) bridge over the Moy at Ballina. Some of the remains of the channel excavated by Nimmo can be seen from the slipway at the quay, several hundreds of yards away, looking in the direction of Ballina, and on the opposite side of the river. Another section of the excavations can be seen by looking across the Moy from where the Brusna enters the Moy at Bunree.

32 For example, the following inconsistencies can be found in Wingfield's evidence in *Report . . . Little and Clark*, pp. 46–8: 'When did you build at Scurramore? About three or four years ago'; 'Did you ever live at Moyview? I did . . . prior to my going to Scurramore some six or seven years ago'; 'It is not quite twenty years since I left Moyview'.

33 Oliver MacDonagh, 'Irish emigration to the United States of America and the British Colonies during the Famine', ch. 6 in R. Dudley Edwards and T. Desmond Williams (eds), *The Great Famine* (New York, 1957), note 17; John McTernan, *Memory Harbour, The Port of Sligo* (Sligo, 1992), pt 2, pp. 26, 34.

34 J. C. Walker to Stewart & Kincaid, 20 Apr. and 11 May 1848 (s к).

35 J. C. Walker to Stewart & Kincaid, 16 May 1848 (s к); John Stewart to Stewart & Kincaid, 16 May, 27 July and 3 Sept. 1848 (s к).

36 Wingfield to Stewart & Kincaid, 16 Feb. 1848 (s к).

37 Smyth to Stewart & Kincaid, 11 May 1848 (s к).

38 In 1856 James Higgins held the entire 117 acres of the Wingfield townland of Lessard More: see *Valuation, Union of Ballina*, p. 134.

39 John Stewart to Stewart & Kincaid, 16 and 25 May 1848 (s к); Smyth to Stewart & Kincaid, 19 May 1848 (s к).

40 Wingfield to Stewart & Kincaid, n. d. late Mar. 1848, 5 and 25 June 1848, 23 Oct. 1848 (s к).

41 *Valuation, Union of Dromore West*, pp. 38–40.

42 Wingfield presumably meant the dispensary at Dooneen, close to Killanley.

43 Slater, *Commercial Directory*, section on Connaught, p. 104, indicates that she was the wife of Joseph Joyner, bank manager in Ballina.

EIGHT: THE ROSCOMMON ESTATES OF THE MARQUESS OF WESTMEATH

1 See *Valuation . . . Union of Castlerea* (Dublin, 1857); *Valuation . . . Union of Strokestown* (Dublin, 1857); *Union of Carrick on Shannon, Valuation . . . County of Roscommon* (Dublin, 1858). Note that in each of these publications Fulke S. Greville (husband of Nugent's daughter Rosa) is listed as immediate lessor of those lands.

2 Stewart Maxwell to Stewart & Kincaid, 20 May 1845. Stewart & Kincaid Papers in possession of the author. Subsequent references to the archive in this chapter will be given either in the text or in notes as (s к).

3   Kincaid to Stewart, 26 Nov. 1843 (sk). The lodge overlooked the Shannon, and faced Annaduff Church of Ireland on the opposite side of the river, in Leitrim. The site of the lodge is now owned by Tom Flanagan, who has indicated to me that the lodge was destroyed by accidental fire *c.*1920.

4   Lawrence Stone, *Broken Lives* (Oxford, 1993), p. 286. The details which immediately follow have been drawn from ch. 12 of that book.

5   Daniel Hanly to Stewart & Kincaid, 3 Nov. 1843 (sk); Michael Beirne to Stewart & Kincaid, 28 Jan. 1844 (sk); Thady Conniff to Stewart & Kincaid, 15 Mar. 1844 (sk); Peter Keenan to Stewart & Kincaid, 23 Mar. 1844 (sk).

6   Michael Johnston to Stewart & Kincaid, 11 Aug. 1845 and 29 Oct. 1846 (sk); Michael Dowd to Stewart & Kincaid, 12 Aug. 1845 (sk).

7   Peter Donnelly was still on the Kilglass estate in 1848: see Stewart & Kincaid's account book, *Receiving Rental of The Marquis of Westmeath Estate in the County of Roscommon for the half year ending May 1848,* n.d.

8   The *Receiving Rental* book suggests that O'Brien was no longer on the Kilglass estate in 1848.

9   Bridget McDonnell and Anne Dalton to Stewart & Kincaid, 16 June 1844 (sk); Loughlon Hoare to Stewart & Kincaid, 17 June 1844 (sk); John Crawford to Stewart & Kincaid, 25 June 1844 (sk). The *Receiving Rental* book indicates that Anne Dalton had recently surrendered her holding by May 1848.

10   The *Receiving Rental* book contains an entry 'Andrew Finn by Catherine'. Andrew may have died by May 1848. If that was the case, Catherine was probably his widow.

11   There were several Acts of Parliament prohibiting burning of land without the landlord's permission. A manual of 1842 which discussed advantages and disadvantages of burning land was generally opposed to it. See *The Farmer's Guide*, 2nd edn (Dublin, 1842), pp. 28–9. Nugent severely disapproved of the practice. See his testimony of October 1844 in *Evidence taken before Her Majesty's Commissioners of Inquiry into the State of the Law and Practice in respect to the Occupation of Land in Ireland*, pt III (Dublin, 1845), pp. 744–8.

12   Patrick Huroughoe to Kincaid, 20 Sept. 1844 (sk). The *Rental* book suggests that Huroughoe was no longer on the estate in 1848.

13   It seems (from the *Receiving Rental* book) that John Clancy was no longer on the estate in 1848.

14   Godfrey Hogg of Strokestown. See Pettigrew and Oulton, *The Dublin Almanac . . . 1845*, p. 268.

15   Francis Waldron, Drumsna, a magistrate. See Pettigrew and Oulton, *Dublin Almanac 1845*, p. 268.

16   Waldron to Stewart & Kincaid, n. d., 1845 (sk).

17   Thomas Blakeney to John Cusack, 15 July 1846 (sk). See also Pettigrew and Oulton, *Dublin Almanac 1846*, p. 623.

18   Messrs McCausland & Fetherstone, solicitors, to Stewart & Kincaid, 13 June 1845 (sk); Dowd to Stewart & Kincaid, 19 Dec. 1845 (sk).

19   Stewart Maxwell to Stewart & Kincaid, 20 May 1845 (sk).

20   The *Receiving Rental* book for May 1848 indicates that McGrevy had recently surrendered his holding.

21   Johnston to Stewart & Kincaid, 29 Oct. 1846 (sk).

22   Johnston to Kincaid, 2 Jan. 1846 (sk). The *Receiving Rental* book indicates that McDonell was no longer on the estate in 1848.

23 Dowd to Stewart & Kincaid, 31 Aug. 1846 (s k). The *Receiving Rental* book indicates that Henry Cline was still on the estate in May 1848 – almost three years in arrears of rent – but Frank McNon was no longer there.

24 *Union of Carrick on Shannon, Valuation, County of Roscommon.*

25 This inference from the Stewart & Kincaid correspondence is substantiated by Kincaid's evidence in 'Report from the Select Committee of the House of Lords on Colonization from Ireland; together with Minutes of Evidence; Session 1847', *British Parliamentary Papers, Emigration 4* (Shannon, 1968).

26 John Shannon to Stewart & Kincaid, 22 Feb. 1848 (s k).

27 Roderick Hanley to Stewart & Kincaid, 14 Mar. 1846 (s k).

28 See, for example, Mary Daly, *The Famine in Ireland* (Dundalk, 1986), pp. 73–87; Cecil Woodham-Smith, *The Great Hunger* (London, 1962), ch. 4.

29 Thomas Barton to Stewart & Kincaid, 19 July 1846 (s k).

30 J. R. Stewart to Kincaid, 12 Oct. 1848 (s k); Board of Works to the Marquess of Westmeath, 20 Nov. 1848 (s k); Board of Works to Stewart & Kincaid, n. d., Dec. 1848 (s k).

31 William Wilson to Crawford, 17 Mar. 1848, and to Stewart & Kincaid, 18 Sept. 1848 (s k).

32 George Nugent to Stewart & Kincaid, n. d., 1848 (s k).

33 *Receiving Rental*, n.d.

34 *The Parliamentary Gazetteer of Ireland*, vol. K–M (London, 1845), p. 548.

35 John Moran and Michael Flyn to Stewart & Kincaid, 20 Dec. 1843 (s k); Mathew Burns to Stewart & Kincaid, 23 Mar. 1845 (s k).

36 John Kirkpatrick to Stewart & Kincaid, 18 Dec. 1843 (s k). See also Kirkpatrick to Stewart & Kincaid, 29 Dec. 1843 (s k).

37 According to *The Farmer's Guide* of 1842, p. 82, 'no plant contributes more to fertility' than the turnip.

38 Patt Naghtin to Stewart & Kincaid, 6 June 1844 (s k); Stewart Maxwell to J .R. Stewart, 10 Oct. 1845 (s k).

39 Thomas Keaveny to Stewart & Kincaid, n. d., Oct. 1846 (s k).

40 Board of Works to Stewart & Kincaid, 13 Nov. 1848 (s k).

41 *Receiving Rental*, n.d.

NINE: THE STRATFORD LANDS IN CLARE

1 Bernard Burke, *Peerage and Baronetage of the British Empire* (London, 1864), p. 904.

2 *Union of Ennistimon, Valuation* (Dublin, 1855).

3 George Green, 'Account . . . May Rents 1751 of Robertstown', 24 Feb. 1752; 'George Evans's Account . . . Gale due out of Lord Powerscourts Estate in . . . Clare the 1st day of May 1761', and the same, 'the first day of November 1761', Stewart & Kincaid Papers in possession of the author. Subsequent references to the archive in this chapter will be given either in the text or in notes as (s k).

4 Documents in the Stewart & Kincaid archive indicate, *c.*1790, that Henry Stewart may have had some role in collection/distribution of rents from the Clare estate. See, for example, James O'Donnell 'Rental of Lord Powerscourts Estate in the County of Clare for half year Ending the first of Novr. 1787' and James O'Donnell to Lord Powerscourt, 24 Apr. 1791 (s k).

5   Arthur Vincent to Stewart & Kincaid, 8 Sept. 1843. *The Tithe Applotment Book, Parish of Kilshanny*, lists James Considine on 110 acres in Smithstown *c.*1830. I thank Mary Ronan of Lisdoonvarna for sending me details from this document.

6   Hugh Weir, *Historical Genealogical Architectural notes on some Houses in Clare* (Whitegate, County Clare, 1986), p. 280. Although Leet lists three residences named 'Wingfield', he does not indicate any of that name in Clare. See Ambrose Leet, *Directory to the . . . Noted Places in Ireland*, 2nd edn (Dublin, 1814), p. 390.

7   O'Donnell, 'Rental of Lord Powerscourt's Estate . . . in Clare . . . Ending the first of Novr. 1787'; John Blackwell to Stratford, 15 Jan. 1841, and to Stewart & Kincaid, 28 Oct. 1845.

8   See sheet 8 of the 1842 ordnance survey map of County Clare.

9   R. Purcell to Stewart & Kincaid, 20 Mar. 1843 (SK); M. Kelly to Stewart & Kincaid, 13 June 1843 (SK); Blackwell to Stewart & Kincaid, 23 Aug. 1846 (SK).

10   James Blackwell to Stewart & Kincaid, 29 Mar. 1844 (SK).

11   This is indicated in a letter from John Blackwell to Stewart & Kincaid, 28 Oct. 1845 (SK).

12   Thomas Blackwell to Stewart & Kincaid, 3 July 1844 (SK); John Blackwell to Stewart & Kincaid, 7 Apr. 1845, 25 July 1845 and 26 Apr. 1846 (SK).

13   On 10 Jan. 1846 James Spellissy asked Stewart & Kincaid to 'get' a place at Templemoyle for his son aged 17, who would have been about 53 in 1882 (SK). In 1999 I obtained, from a New York philatelic dealer, two letters sent from Clare to Denis Spellissy, an attorney on Broadway. Dated 1882, one of them asked the favour of assisting sons of James Thynes of Tooreen to secure employment in New York. The other, from Ennis in 1883, sought a loan from Denis Spellissy to pay the sender's passage to America.

14   Details here have been drawn from oral communications by the following helpful people: Michael Fitzgerald of Smithstown; Robert Crosbie and his wife Suzanne Linnane of Tooreen; Jimmy Leahy of Ballyalla; Jack Flanagan of Dough, Lahinch. Famine-era depopulation seems to have enabled our John Blackwell to extend his holdings. *The Tithe Applotment Book, Parish of Kilshanny* records that *c.*1830, a person named John Blackwell held only 4 acres of first quality land in Smithstown and 44 acres of mainly inferior land in Tooreen.

15   John Blackwell to Stewart & Kincaid, 28 June 1842 (SK).

16   John Blackwell to Stewart & Kincaid, 17 Aug. 1842 (SK).

17   John Blackwell to Stewart & Kincaid, 26 Aug. 1842 (SK).

18   Perse Stamer to Stewart & Kincaid, 19 Dec. 1843 (SK).

19   To Stewart & Kincaid from: Michael Moloney, 30 Jan. 1843; Blackwell, 27 Nov. 1843; James Spellissy, 16 Sept. 1844 (SK).

20   James Spellissy to Stewart & Kincaid, 3 May 1842 (SK); Memorandum signed by Spellissy, 21 June 1843 (SK).

21   Blackwell to Kincaid, 2 July 1845 (SK).

22   Blackwell to Vincent, 10 Sept. 1841 (SK).

23   Details here have been drawn from Blackwell to Stewart & Kincaid, 26 Feb., 16 Mar. and 3 Apr. 1843 (SK). *Union of Ennistimon, Valuation*, p. 122, lists Michael Considine as tenant on 78 acres in Gortnaboul in 1855.

24   Blackwell to Kincaid, 2 Nov. 1843 (SK).

25   For more general discussions of the famine in Clare, which complement that here, see the following publications by Ciarán Ó Murchadha: 'The onset of famine: County Clare, 1845–1846', *The Other Clare* 19 (1995), pp. 46–52; 'Sable wings over the land: County Clare

1846–1847', *The Other Clare* 20 (1996), pp. 25–32; *Sable Wings over the Land: Ennis, County Clare and its Wider Community during the Great Famine* (Ennis, 1998).

26 Blackwell to Stewart & Kincaid, 3 Apr. 1846 (sĸ).

27 Until I spoke to Michael Slattery of Ballygoonaun, I was unable to determine the whereabouts of the place described in the Stewart & Kincaid correspondence as 'Carronnebohel'. As he indicated to me, *The Tithe Applotment Book, Parish of Kilfenora*, 1827, pp. 41, 42, implies that it was the townland of Boghil.

28 Blackwell to Stewart & Kincaid, 5 Aug. 1846 (sĸ).

29 Blackwell to Stewart & Kincaid, 6 and 12 Oct. 1846 (sĸ).

30 Blackwell to Stewart Maxwell, 10 June 1846 (sĸ).

31 See note 13 above. On 26 Sept. 1848 James Spellissy wrote to Stewart & Kincaid indicating his intention to dispose of his interest in his farm (sĸ).

32 Board of Works to Stratford, 29 June 1848 (sĸ).

33 *Reports and Returns Relating to Evictions in the Kilrush Union*, Parliamentary Paper (London, 1849). For a modern survey, see Ignatius Murphy, *A People Starved: Life and Death in West Clare, 1845–1851* (Blackrock, County Dublin, 1996).

TEN: STRATFORD'S LIMERICK ESTATE

1 *County of Limerick, Barony of Shanid comprising a portion of The Unions of Glin, Newcastle & Rathkeale, Primary Valuation* (Dublin, 1852). Note that this does not list Stratford as immediate lessor of every townland which he owned in the barony in the 1840s. For comprehensive investigation of the district, see Thomas J. Culhane, *The Barony of Shanid* (n. p., 2003).

2 Letter from James O'Donnell, addressee not indicated, 6 Dec. 1799, Stewart & Kincaid Papers in possession of the author. Subsequent references to the archive in this chapter will be given either in the text or in notes as (sĸ). Ambrose Leet, *Directory to the . . . Noted Places in Ireland*, 2nd edn (Dublin, 1814), p. 113; Stewart & Kincaid to Richard Dickson *c.* 29 May 1841, Pakenham archive, Tullynally Castle, Castlepollard, County Westmeath, PAK m/33.

3 A letter from Richard Dickson to Stewart & Kincaid, 11 June 1841 (sĸ), indicates that his late brother's annual rent, paid to Stewart & Kincaid, was about £655.

4 Richard Dickson to Stewart & Kincaid, 8 June 1841 (SK). As explained by O'Rourke, 'a driver or bailiff' was 'a man employed by Irish landlords to warn tenants of rent day, serve notices on them, watch their movements, see how they manage their farms, play the detective in a general way. . . . They are called drivers by the people because one of their duties is to drive tenants' cattle off their lands, that they may be sold for the rent'. See John O'Rourke, *The History of the Great Irish Famine of 1847*, 3rd edn (Dublin, 1902), p. 263.

5 J. R. Stewart to Kincaid, 28 June 1841 (SK).

6 Arthur Vincent to Stewart & Kincaid, 12 Oct. 1843 (sĸ).

7 Vincent to Stewart & Kincaid, 29 Aug. 1843.

8 Mortimer Collins to J. R. Stewart, 27 Apr. 1843.

9 Edward Wingfield to Stewart & Kincaid, 12 July 1848 (sĸ); David Whitty to Stewart & Kincaid, 13 Aug. 1848 (sĸ).

10 John Wingfield Stratford to Stewart & Kincaid, n. d., 1848 (sĸ).

11   After obtaining judgment in ejectment, the plaintiff had to enforce it by issuing a writ of Habere (Latin 'to have'), addressed to the county sheriff. The sheriff had to make a Return, confirming what he had done. If the writ was not enforced within a certain period, no Return was made and, for legal validity, the Habere had to be renewed. I thank Andrew Lyall of the Faculty of Law at UCD for these details.

12   Vincent to Stewart & Kincaid, n. d., Dec. 1841 (s k).

13   Vincent to Stewart & Kincaid, n.d., Dec. 1841 (s k).

14   Widow Leahy to Stratford, and Bridget Ryan to Stratford, both n. d., Feb. 1842 (s k). See also John Enright to Edward Wingfield, n. d., Dec. 1841 (s k).

15   Vincent to Stewart & Kincaid, n. d., Dec. 1841 (s k).

16   *County of Limerick, Barony of Shanid, Valuation*, p. 89.

17   Martin Carroll to Kincaid, 10 Jan. 1842 (s k).

18   Early in 1842 Stewart & Kincaid wrote to Stratford requesting his permission to hire an agriculturalist to oversee improvements on his properties. See Stewart & Kincaid to Stratford, 21 Feb. 1842, Pakenham archive, PAK M/33.

19   Vincent to Stewart & Kincaid, 25 Apr. and 22 June 1842 (s k); John Stewart to Stewart & Kincaid, 7 June 1842 (s k).

20   Vincent to Stewart & Kincaid, 4 June 1842, 15 and 31 July 1843 (s k); John Stewart to Stewart & Kincaid, 7 June 1842 and 7 June 1843 (s k)

21   John Stewart to Stewart & Kincaid, 15 Oct. and 2 Nov. 1844 (s k).

22   Vincent to Stewart & Kincaid, 19 Apr. 1842 (s k).

23   Ibid.

24   On 17 Jan. 1845 Joseph Bridgeman mentioned to Stewart & Kincaid that he had spent three years studying agriculture. He was a student at an agricultural college in 1846. On 16 April of that year Vincent wrote to Stewart & Kincaid: 'I send £2–10 from Patrick Bridgeman for board and tuition due . . . for his son' (s k). The *Valuation* of 1852 indicates that Patrick Bridgeman then held 53 statute acres at Robertstown. Today a Peter Bridgeman farms there. Recall from chapter 7 that in 1848 a Peter Bridgeman came from the Robertstown estate to Wingfield's Coolrecuill in Sligo in order to supervise improvements. He was probably related to Joseph.

25   Vincent to Stewart & Kincaid, 4 Apr. 1842 (s k).

26   J. R. Stewart to Kincaid, n. d., Apr. 1843 (s k).

27   See, for example, John Blackwell to Stewart & Kincaid, 15 June 1842 (s k); Vincent to Stewart & Kincaid, 2 Oct 1846 (s k). Both letters refer to wage rates of 8*d.* per day.

28   W. H. Hall was listed by I. Slater, *National Commercial Directory of Ireland* (London and Manchester, 1846), section on Munster, p. 265, as house, land and insurance agent in Limerick City.

29   Vincent to Stewart & Kincaid, 13 Dec. 1846 (s k).

30   John Stewart to Stewart & Kincaid, 28 Feb. 1846 (s k).

31   Vincent to Stewart & Kincaid, 7 May 1846 (s k).

32   Vincent to Stewart & Kincaid, 13 Dec. 1846 (s k).

33   Stratford to Stewart & Kincaid, n. d., Oct. 1848 (s k).

34   Cornelius O'Shea to Kincaid, 18 Jan. 1842 (s k).

35   O'Shea to J. R. Stewart, n.d., 1843.

36   *County of Limerick, Barony of Shanid, Valuation*, p. 89.

37   Vincent to Stewart & Kincaid, 22 Jan. 1842 (s k).

ELEVEN: ON TWO ESTATES IN SOUTH LIMERICK

1   *County of Limerick, Barony of Coshma . . . Primary Valuation* (Dublin, 1851), pp. 69, 70.

2   Mainchin Seoighe, *The Story of Kilmallock* (Kilmallock, 1987), p. 326.

3   *County of Limerick, Barony of Connello Upper . . . Primary Valuation* (Dublin, 1852), pp. 9, 21, 24, 25, 93, 94.

4   Thomas Stewart to Joseph Kincaid, June 1841, Stewart & Kincaid Papers in possession of the author. Subsequent references to the archive in this chapter will be given either in the text or in notes as (SK). I thank Liam Irwin of the University of Limerick for some of the details which immediately follow. See Edward Walford, *The County Families of the United Kingdom* (London, 1860), p. 610.

5   *Thom's Irish Almanac and Official Directory . . . 1848*, p. 931.

6   Walford, *County Families*, p. 610. See also Walford, *The County Families of the United Kingdom*, new edn (London, 1893), pp. 959, 960.

7   The *Valuation* of 1852 lists Robert A. Warren as immediate lessor of most of Ballinruane. It also lists the representatives of Sergeant Warren as immediate lessors of Kilmihil and Gorteen West in the Ballinruane district. In 1876 Robert A. Warren was listed as owner of over 1,500 acres in County Limerick. See *Return of Owners of Land . . . in Ireland* (Dublin, 1876), p. 154.

8   *Thom's Directory 1849*, p. 1042.

9   See Robert Warren at 39 Rutland Square to Stewart & Kincaid, 7 Mar. 1843 and 17 Jan. 1847.

10   Walford, *County Families* (1860), p. 670. *Thom's Directory 1848*, p. 931, lists Graves Warren, solicitor, at 40 Rutland Square. This Graves was probably another son of Stewart & Kincaid's solicitor, Robert, at 39 Rutland Square. Hence, from the detail on Robert Warren (the solicitor) in Walford, 1860, Graves was probably a grandson of Barbera, daughter of Joseph Swan. The same listing in Walford indicates that in 1846 the eldest son of Robert the solicitor, also named Robert, married Anne Waddy. *The Post Office Annual Directory for 1845* (Dublin, 1844 or 1845), p. 475, lists Joseph Swan Waddy as a solicitor. It was indicated in chapter 1 above that in the early nineteenth century a barrister named Graves Swan had been partner with Henry Stewart (also a barrister) in the firm which evolved into that of J. R. Stewart and Joseph Kincaid in the 1840s. These details highlight very strong family links within the legal professions.

11   Christopher Reidy to Stewart & Kincaid, 17 Mar. 1844; Simon Brown to Stewart & Kincaid, 20 Mar. and 3 May 1844. Multiple layers of middlemen were rare on estates managed by Stewart & Kincaid; however, several layers of them were common on other estates. See James S. Donnelly, Jr, *The Land and the People of Nineteenth-Century Cork* (London and Boston, 1975), p. 9, and R. B. MacCarthy, *The Trinity College Estates 1800–1923* (Dundalk, 1992), ch. 5.

12   John Ryan to Kincaid, 30 Mar. 1844 (SK).

13   Donnovan informed Gertrude Fitzgerald: 'Such of the tenants as are going out of possession I would take their lands, and become one tenant for the entire'.

14   John Murnane to Stewart & Kincaid, 7 Apr. 1844 (SK); Martin and James Touhy and Jeremiah O'Keefe to Stewart & Kincaid, 28 Sept. 1844 (SK); Maurice Foley to Stewart & Kincaid, 12 Feb. 1845 (SK).

15   Murnane to Stewart & Kincaid, 26 Mar. and 7 Aug. 1845 (SK); John Russell to Stewart & Kincaid, 2 Apr. 1845 (SK).

16   I. Slater, *National Commercial Directory of Ireland . . . to which are added Classified Directories of Important English Towns* (Manchester and London, 1846), section on Liverpool.

17   The person who made the arrest was William Maloney: see Maloney to Stewart & Kincaid, 29 July 1845, in which he sought his fees.

18   Stewart Maxwell to Kincaid, 18 and 19 July 1845 (sk); William Maloney to Stewart & Kincaid, 29 July 1845 (sk); W. C. Bennett to Stewart & Kincaid, 10 Oct. 1845 (sk).

19   Patrick Donnovan to Stewart & Kincaid, 3 Jan. 1845 (sk); Maurice Foley to Stewart & Kincaid, 29 July 1845 (sk); James Donnovan to Stewart & Kincaid, 14 June 1845 (sk); Murnane to Stewart & Kincaid, 23 June, 25 July, 20 Sept., 18 Oct. and 4 Nov. 1845 (sk); Bank of Ireland, Cork, to Stewart & Kincaid, 7 Jan. and 26 July 1845 (sk).

20   Bank of Ireland, Cork, to Stewart & Kincaid, 9 Jan. 1845 (sk).

21   Murnane to Stewart & Kincaid, 23 June 1845 (sk); Bank of Ireland, Cork to Stewart & Kincaid, 26 July 1845 (sk).

22   The widow Ambrose might not have died late in 1845. A letter of Oct. 1846, to Stewart & Kincaid from Catherine Ambrose of Thomastown, enclosed a bank order for £9 odd 'in lieu of a half years rent deducting 9s 6d abatement which your Honour promised to allow me and which was allowed to the rest of the tennantry heretofore' (sk).

23   Bank of Ireland, Cork, to Stewart & Kincaid, 16 Jan. and 29 July 1846 (sk)

24   John Stewart to Stewart & Kincaid, 13 Feb. 1846 (sk).

25   David Nagle to Gertrude Fitzgerald, 29 Apr. 1846 (sk).

26   John Stewart to Stewart & Kincaid, 13 and 27 July 1846 (sk); Arthur Vincent to Stewart & Kincaid, 27 July 1846 (sk).

27   John Stewart to Stewart & Kincaid, 10 Aug. and 11 Nov. 1846 (sk).

28   This statement seems to be an exaggeration. The Poor Law Relief Act of 1838 provided for appointment of Protestant chaplains to the workhouses (see p. 2 above).

29   Donnelly, *Nineteenth-Century Cork*, p. 90, refers to an attack on Cloyne for food in 1846.

30   A letter from Gertrude Fitzgerald to J. R. Stewart, 17 Mar. 1848 (sk), refers to Mr Penrose Fitzgerald. For some details on the Penrose Fitzgeralds of the Whitegate district see Pat Fitzgerald, *Down Paths of Gold* (Midleton, County Cork, 1993), ch. 9, for which reference I thank Anne Ahern of Whitegate.

31   Writing of Whitegate, Lewis referred to 'a female and infants' school, maintained by Mrs Blakeney Fitzgerald, by whom the school-houses were erected'. See Samuel Lewis, A *Topographical Dictionary of Ireland*, vol. 2 (London, 1837), p. 714.

32   John and James [O'?] Keeffe had surrendered their holdings by 23 March, when William Mahony wrote to Stewart & Kincaid offering to rent their land on Mount Blakeney townland. However, the land of James Keeffe (who received at least £20 from Stewart & Kincaid following its surrender) was assigned to a person named Bennett. The Keeffes probably went to America during the summer of 1848. See Edmond Bourke to Stewart & Kincaid, 8 Apr. and 1 May 1848 (sk).

33   Board of Works to Stewart & Kincaid, 7 Oct. and 27 Nov. 1848 (sk); Board of Works to Mrs Fitzgerald, 7 Dec. 1848 (sk); J. R. Stewart to Kincaid, 15 Dec. 1848 (sk).

34   The reference here is presumably to the lands of Patrick Maloney who, in May 1848, agreed to quit the estate, for which he obtained compensation. See Edmond Bourke to Stewart & Kincaid, 1 May 1848 (sk).

35   *County of Limerick, Barony of Coshma, Valuation*, pp. 69, 70.

36   Henry Harte to Stewart & Kincaid, 10 July 1845 and 14 Mar. 1846; George Gubbins to Vincent, 3 Nov. 1846.

37 John Stewart to Stewart & Kincaid, 25 Jan. 1845 (sk).

38 Vincent to Stewart & Kincaid, 17 Mar. 1846 (sk); John Stewart to Stewart & Kincaid, 21 Mar. 1846 (sk).

39 This was how John Stewart names the river in his letter to Stewart & Kincaid dated 9 July 1846 (sk). I thank Liam Irwin of Mary Immaculate College, Limerick, for informing me that the correct name of the river is Finglasha.

40 Vincent to Stewart & Kincaid, 27 July 1846 (sk).

41 John Stewart to Stewart & Kincaid, 10 Aug. 1846 (sk).

42 J. R. Stewart to Kincaid, 15 Dec. 1848 (sk).

43 William N. Willis to Stewart & Kincaid, 18 June 1846 (sk).

44 Vincent to Stewart & Kincaid, 7 and 18 Nov. 1846 (sk).

45 Vincent to Stewart & Kincaid, 26 Dec. 1846 (sk).

46 *County of Limerick, Barony of Connello Upper, Valuation.*

47 Richard Holmes to Sergeant Warren, 7 June 1847 (sk); John Gaffney to Sergeant Warren, 23 June 1847 (sk).

48 Vincent to Stewart & Kincaid, 24 Nov. 1846 (sk).

49 Vincent to Stewart & Kincaid, 26 Dec. 1846 (sk).

50 Michael Fitzgerald probably stayed in Ireland. On 14 Sept. 1848 Sankey wrote to Stewart & Kincaid: 'Michl. Fitzgerald is an invalid and unfit to go to America. He wants £20 the amount formerly offered to him in case he remained at home' (sk).

51 The tenants were named Barrett and Blake: see Sankey to Stewart & Kincaid, 24 Mar. 1848 (sk).

52 Sankey to Stewart & Kincaid, 14 June and 14 Sept. 1848 (sk).

53 *County of Limerick, Barony of Connello Upper, Valuation*, pp. 9, 21, 24, 25, 93, 94.

TWELVE: THE FRANKFORT ESTATES IN KILKENNY AND CARLOW

1 Bernard Burke, *A Genealogical and Heraldic Dictionary of the Peerage and Baronetage* (London, 1892), pp. 559, 560.

2 *Return of Owners of Land . . . in Ireland* (Dublin, 1876), pp. 4, 37, 218.

3 William Nolan, *Fassadinin: Land, Settlement and Society in Southeast Ireland 1600–1850* (Dublin, 1979), p. 168.

4 A letter of early 1842 indicated that rents that had been recently received from Frankfort properties were as follows: Cavan, £489; Carlow, £910; Dublin, £514. The letter does not mention the Kilkenny estates. See letterbook copy of Stewart & Kincaid to Frankfort, 15 Feb. 1842, in Pakenham archive, Tullynally Castle, Castlepollard, County Westmeath, PAK m/33. Frankfort was not listed as owning any land in Dublin in 1876. See note 2 above.

5 Jeremiah Scully to Stewart & Kincaid, 3 Apr. 1846, and John Leehy to Stewart & Kincaid, 6 June 1846, Stewart & Kincaid Papers in possession of the author. Subsequent references to the archive in this chapter will be given either in the text or in notes as (sk).

6 *County of Kilkenny, Barony of Fassadinin, Unions of Castlecomer, Kilkenny and Urlingford, Valuation* (Dublin, 1850), pp. 80–2.

7 Nolan, *Fassadinin*, p. 167.

8 H. Devereaux to Stewart & Kincaid, 10 Oct. 1843 (SK).

9   Tom Lyng, *Castlecomer Connections* (Castlecomer, 1984), pp. 333, 336, 337; Nolan, *Fassadinin*, p. 186.

10   Norman McMillan and Martin Nevin, 'Tyndall of Leighlin: Carlow's genius', *Carloviana*, no. 27 (1978–9), pp. 22–7; and 'Tyndall of Leighlin', ch. 2 in H. W. Brock, N. D. McMillan and R. C. Mollan, *John Tyndall: Essays on a Natural Philosopher* (Dublin, 1981). McMillan and Nevin indicate that the scientist was born in Leighlinbridge, County Carlow – a few miles from Coolcullen. For a general survey, see A. S. Eve and C. H. Creasey, *Life and Work of John Tyndall* (London, 1945).

11   Communication of Richard Agar who resides beside the church.

12   That Matthew Brennan was slashed to death was told to me, independently, by John Agar, and by Martin Brennan of Muckalee, according to whom the murder was committed in a field near Mothel church.

13   I. Slater, *National Commercial Directory of Ireland* (Manchester and London, 1846), section on Leinster, p. 25.

14   *County of Kilkenny, Fassadinin, Valuation*, p. 81.

15   Matthew Sankey to Stewart & Kincaid, 27 Nov. 1848 (sk); William Sherriff to Sankey, 18 Mar. 1848 (sk).

16   William Cathro to Kincaid, 29 Jan. 1845 (sk); Major Diamond to Kincaid, 29 Jan. and 8 Mar. 1845 (sk).

17   Diamond to Stewart & Kincaid, 28 Apr. and 14 Aug. 1845 (sk).

18   Diamond to Stewart & Kincaid, 9 Apr. 1845 (sk).

19   Diamond to Stewart & Kincaid, 12 May and 14 Aug. 1845 (sk).

20   See the accounts in Diamond to Stewart & Kincaid, 12 Jan. 1846 (sk).

21   William Cathro to Stewart & Kincaid, 4 July 1846 (sk); Sarah Cathro to Stewart & Kincaid, 2 Nov. 1846 (sk).

22   Richard Graves to Stewart & Kincaid, n. d., 1846 (sk).

23   Sherriff to Stewart & Kincaid, 19 Feb. 1846 (sk).

24   Thomas Butler to Board of Works, 1 Sept. 1848 (sk); Sankey to Stewart & Kincaid, 2 and 9 Sept. 1848 (sk).

25   *County of Kilkenny, Fassadinin, Valuation*, pp. 80–2.

26   Diamond to Stewart & Kincaid, 15 Dec. 1845 (sk).

27   J. R. Stewart to Joseph Kincaid, 29 Jan. 1849 (sk).

28   *Unions of Kilkenny and Callan, Valuation* (Dublin, 1849), pp. 47–8; John Maher to Kincaid, 13 May 1845 (sk).

29   Robert Shearman to Stewart & Kincaid, 23 Feb. 1848 (sk).

30   Robert Shearman to Stewart & Kincaid, 17 Feb. 1848 (sk).

31   *County of Carlow, Primary Valuation* (Dublin, 1852), p. 292.

32   Thomas Kinsella to Stewart & Kincaid, 11 Nov. 1845 and 29 May 1846 (sk); John Coughlan to Stewart & Kincaid, 15 Oct. 1841 (sk); Sylvester Coughlan to Stewart & Kincaid, 30 Nov. 1841 (sk); John and Sylvester Coughlan to Stewart & Kincaid, 9 Jan. 1845 (sk).

33   Sylvester Coughlan to Stewart & Kincaid, 12 Nov. and 30 Nov. 1841; 23 June, 27 July, 29 July, 29 Nov. and 26 Dec. 1842 (sk); John Coughlan to Stewart & Kincaid, 9 Feb. 1843 (sk).

34   James Brennan to Kincaid, 30 Nov. 1843, 4 Dec. 1843, 15 Apr. 1844 and 2 Jan. 1845 (sk).

35   I thank Mary and Seamus Hogan of Rathrush House, Rathoe, County Carlow, for sending me a photocopy of this newspaper account.

36 The reference to 'a part of the mansion house of Rathrush' indicates that some of the Coughlans occupied part of the structure in which the Rev. William Kinsella, PP, resided: see the later observations on him.

37 John and Sylvester Coughlan to Stewart & Kincaid, 9 Jan. 1845 (SK).

38 Brennan to Stewart & Kincaid, 15 Jan. 1845 (SK).

39 Brennan to Stewart & Kincaid, 15 Jan. 1845 (SK), which contains (a copy of?) the petition to Hutton.

40 Ibid.

41 *County of Carlow, Primary Valuation*, p. 292.

42 Mary Hogan (born Kinsella), whom I thank for details.

43 William Kinsella to Stewart & Kincaid, 19 Sept. 1842.

44 Charles Grogan, vicar of Dunleckny, brother of Sir Edward Grogan, MP for Dublin City, 1841–65. See B. M. Walker (ed.), *Parliamentary Election Results for Ireland, 1801–1922* (Dublin, 1978), p. 418.

45 Slater's *Commercial Directory* lists only one person named Tyndall in the Leighlinbridge district: John Tyndall of Leighlinbridge, listed under 'boot and shoe makers'. He was the father of John Tyndall, FRS. Slater lists only one person named Tyndall in Carlow town – William Tyndall, a carpenter.

46 See Desmond Norton, 'Viscount Frankfort, Sir Charles Burton and County Carlow in the 1840s: Part II', *Carloviana*, no. 47 (Dec. 1999), pp. 2–6 and 15.

47 *County of Carlow, Primary Valuation*, pp. 32–3; *County of Kilkenny, Barony of Gowran, Unions of Kilkenny and New Ross* (Dublin, 1850), p. 47.

48 Letterbook copy of Stewart & Kincaid to Walker & Grant, 18 June 1842, in Pakenham archive, PAK M/33.

49 Edward Walford, *The County Families of the United Kingdom* (London, 1860), p. 91, and Edward Walford, *The County Families of the United Kingdom* (London, 1893), p. 150. In 1999 I acquired an accumulation of postal covers dated from the 1840s to the 1890s and addressed to Burton family members. They indicate that if Sir Charles Burton did go to India, he did not stay there for long.

50 Jimmy O'Toole, *The Carlow Gentry* (Carlow, 1993), p. 75.

51 James Dwyer, Michael Dyer and William Kelly to Stewart & Kincaid, 13 Feb. 1846 (SK).

52 James Burtchaele to Stewart & Kincaid, 13 Jan. 1846 (SK); David Burtchaele to Stewart & Kincaid, 19 Jan. 1846 (SK).

THIRTEEN: PROPERTIES OF PONSONBY,
PAKENHAM AND ST LAWRENCE

1 Law Walker to Stewart & Kincaid, 19 Mar. 1841, Stewart & Kincaid Papers in possession of the author. Subsequent references to the archive in this chapter will be given either in the text or in notes as (SK). Letterbook copy of Stewart & Kincaid to Michael Grogan, 3 April 1841, in Pakenham archive, Tullynally Castle, Castlepollard, County Westmeath, PAK M/33.

2 Quoted in *The Parliamentary Gazetteer of Ireland*, vol. VII (Dublin, London and Edinburgh, 1845), p. 71.

3 Law Walker to Stewart & Kincaid, 22 Dec. 1842 (SK).

4   Law Walker to Stewart & Kincaid, 29 Apr. 1841 (sk).

5   Law Walker to Stewart & Kincaid, 22 Dec. 1842 (sk).

6   Walker Grant & Co to Stewart & Kincaid, 9 Apr. 1844 (sk).

7   Ibid.

8   In a recent book on King's (Offaly) County history, there is confusion on the identities of different members of the Ponsonby family: see William Nolan and Timothy P. O'Neill (eds), *Offaly: History & Society* (Dublin, 1998). The Ponsonby to whom Gráinne Breen refers at p. 661 of that book was Frederick, while the local agent mentioned at the top of p. 685 represented Captain William-Brabazon Ponsonby. Chapter 20 of the book confuses three distinct Ponsonbys and regards them as the same person. First, there was John, the second Lord Ponsonby of Imokilly who died in 1855. Second, there was John's brother Frederick, who died in 1849. Third, there was the Captain Ponsonby of the present chapter. He was the only son of Richard Ponsonby, the Lord Bishop of Derry who died in 1853. This Richard was another of John's brothers. The Ponsonby to whom reference is made on p. 726 (note 130) of Nolan and O'Neill was not the owner of the Philipstown estate; nor was he the then 'Lord Ponsonby' of Imokilly or the Bishop of Derry. Contrast the references to Ponsonbys in chapters 19 and 20 of Nolan and O'Neill with those in Bernard Burke, *Peerage and Baronetage of the British Empire* (London, 1864), p. 896, and in the present chapter.

9   Timothy P. O'Neill has already quoted this passage. However, he has made three minor errors in the context at hand. First, Maxwell's letter was manually dated 6 January (not July) 1842. It bears a Philipstown (now Daingean) postmark of that date and a Dublin postmark of 7 January. Second, Maxwell's first name was Stewart (not 'P.'). Third, he was not 'Ponsonby's local agent in Daingean'; rather, he was employed – apparently as third in authority – at Stewart & Kincaid's office in Dublin. See Tim P. O'Neill, 'Famine evictions', in Carla King (ed.), *Famine, Land and Culture in Ireland* (Dublin, 2000), pp. 29–70.

10 Michael Grogan to Stewart & Kincaid, 18 Mar., 25 Mar. and 14 Apr. 1842 (sk).

11 I. Slater, *National Commercial Directory of Ireland* (Manchester and London, 1846), section on Leinster, p. 83.

12 Law Walker to Stewart & Kincaid, 23 Apr. and 12 Sept. 1845 (sk).

13 Slater, *Directory*, section on Leinster, p. 77.

14 Pettigrew and Oulton, *The Dublin Almanac . . . 1846*, p. 760, and the same for 1848, p. 770.

15 *King's County and County Westmeath . . . Valuation . . . Union of Tullamore* (Dublin, 1854), p. 24.

16 Walker Grant & Co to Stewart & Kincaid, 23 Feb. 1848 (sk).

17 Walker Grant & Co to Stewart & Kincaid, 5 Aug. 1844 and 13 Nov. 1845 (sk).

18 Law Walker to Stewart & Kincaid, 11 Aug. 1848 (sk).

19 An inference to the contrary might be drawn from O'Neill's observation that 'Lord Ponsonby paid £350 for emigrants' passage to the United States of America and to Australia': see Nolan and O'Neill, *Offaly*, p. 726, note 130, as well as note 8 above.

20 Gráinne Breen, 'Landlordism in King's County in the mid-nineteenth century', ch. 19 in Nolan and O'Neill (eds), *Offaly*, p. 661.

21 Michael Scully to Stewart & Kincaid, 11 Dec. 1846 (sk).

22 T. Dyer to Stewart & Kincaid, 23 May 1843 (sk).

23 *Valuation, Union of Tullamore*, pp. 14–26.

24 See 'Estimate of John McEvoy and William Dyer', 22 Apr. 1842 (sk); F. B. Woodward to Stewart & Kincaid, 20 May 1842 and 22 Nov. 1844 (sk); Walter Thorpe to Stewart & Kincaid, 19 Apr. 1845 (sk); Eustace Thorpe to Stewart & Kincaid, 13 Mar. 1846 (sk).

25 F. B. Woodward to Stewart & Kincaid, 27 April 1843 (SK).

26 William Little to the Lord Bishop of Derry, 2 May 1842 (SK); John Glover to Stewart & Kincaid, 22 May 1842 (SK); Joseph Grogan to Stewart & Kincaid, 31 May, 4 and 6 July 1843 (SK); William Little to Stewart & Kincaid, 11 May 1846 (SK).

27 Edward Murray to Stewart & Kincaid, 16 June and 3 Aug. 1842 (SK); William McOwen to Stewart & Kincaid, 23 Jan. 1843 (SK); Joseph Grogan to Stewart & Kincaid, 29 May and 29 Aug. 1843 (SK).

28 A similar practice was adopted elsewhere. Kinealy has noted that 'three unions – Antrim, Belfast and Newtownards – did not avail themselves of the provisions of the Temporary Relief Act' of Feb. 1847 for outdoor relief. As at Philipstown, it was provided privately, independent of the Poor Law authorities. See Christine Kinealy, *This Great Calamity* (Dublin, 1994), p. 152.

29 Timothy P. O'Neill in Nolan and O'Neill (eds), *Offaly*, pp. 713–14.

30 *Return of Owners of Land . . . in Ireland* (Dublin, 1876), pp. 54, 84.

31 William Gibson to Stewart & Kincaid, 2 Dec. 1841 (SK).

32 *Counties of Meath and Westmeath, Valuation . . . Union of Castletowndelvin* (Dublin, 1854), p. 78.

33 Pakenham archive, PAK U/1/5/1.

34 Listed by Slater, *Directory*, section on Leinster, p. 66, as resident of Sligo Road, Longford town.

35 J. E. Penser to Stewart & Kincaid, 29 Apr. 1846 (SK).

36 Daniel O'Donnell to Stewart & Kincaid, 13 Apr. 1846 (SK).

37 *Union of Longford, Valuation . . . County of Longford* (Dublin, 1854).

38 J. R. Stewart to Joseph Kincaid, n. d., Sept. 1846 (SK).

39 George West to Stewart & Kincaid, 19 Oct. 1841 (SK).

40 Thomas Moore published his satirical *Memoirs of Captain Rock* in 1824. The Rockites were one of a proliferation of early nineteenth-century rural protest movements.

41 William Pakenham to Stewart & Kincaid, 29 Aug. 1844 (SK).

42 Catherine Curran to Stewart & Kincaid, n. d, Aug. 1846 (SK).

43 John Slevin to Stewart & Kincaid, 11 Apr. and 1 Dec. 1848 (SK).

44 *County of Westmeath, Valuation . . . Union of Mullingar* (Dublin, 1854), p. 161.

45 John Boyan to Stewart & Kincaid, 18 Feb. 1846 (SK)

46 J. E. Penser to Stewart & Kincaid, 29 Apr. 1846 (SK).

47 Board of Works to Stewart & Kincaid, 2 and 18 Feb., 6 Apr. and 13 July 1848 (SK).

48 Pakenham archive, PAK U/1/5/1.

49 *Counties of Longford and Westmeath, Valuation . . . Union of Ballymahon* (Dublin, 1854), p. 86.

50 Peter Farrell to Stewart & Kincaid, 9 Feb. 1846 (SK).

51 *Owners of Land in Ireland*, pp. 14, 69, indicates that in the mid-1870s the Earl of Howth owned 7,377 acres in County Dublin and 2,062 acres in Meath.

52 Messrs Roy Blount & Co to Stewart & Kincaid, 19 Jan. 1844 (SK).

53 *Valuation . . . Barony of Balrothery East . . . County of Dublin* (Dublin, 1852), p. 58.

54 Messrs Roy Blount & Co. to Stewart & Kincaid, 19 Jan. 1844 (SK).

55 Joseph Hunt to Kincaid, 9 Jan. 1846 (SK); Earl of Howth to Kincaid, 19 July 1848 (SK).

56 Richard Booth to Stewart & Kincaid, 7 Nov. 1842 (SK).

57 H. Carty to Kincaid, 3 Mar. 1843 (SK).

58 Probably Thomas Farrell, lessor of houses at Normanstown. See *Union of Kells, Valuation . . . Counties of Meath and Cavan* (Dublin, 1854), p. 91.

59   Stewart to Kincaid, n. d., Oct. 1848 (sk).

60   Samuel Garnett to Stewart & Kincaid, 12 Dec. 1846 (sk); William Reid to Stewart & Kincaid, 15 Dec. 1846 (sk).

61   Peter Keegan to Stewart & Kincaid, 15 Aug. 1846 (sk).

62   Board of Works to Stewart & Kincaid, 25 Jan. 22 July and 14 Aug. 1848 (sk).

63   Earl of Howth to Kincaid, n. d., 1848 (sk).

64   *County of Dublin, Barony of Coolock, North Dublin and Balrothery Union* (Dublin, 1848), p. 12.

65   Earl of Howth to Kincaid, n. d., July 1848 (sk).

66   Charles Frizell is listed at Stapolin House, Baldoyle, in *Thom's Irish Almanac and Official Directory . . . for 1849* (compiled late in 1848), but he is not listed in the corresponding volumes for 1850 or 1851.

FOURTEEN: THE SHERLOCK AND BATTY ESTATES

1   Kenneth Bourne, *Palmerston, The Early Years 1784–1841* (London, 1982), p. 191.

2   Gordon Winter, *Secrets of the Royals* (New York, 1989, and London, 1990), p. 24.

3   According to Winter, *Secrets*, pp. 24–5, 'the cause of death was not disclosed to the public. But one basically honest historian couldn't resist stating . . . that a half-finished letter, found in Lord P's study, "showed that he had died in harness"'.

4   *County of Kildare, Valuation . . . Union of Naas* (Dublin, 1853), p. 157, lists the representatives of William Sherlock as immediate lessors of these lands.

5   Further details on these and subsequent matters pertaining to the Sherlocks, as well as further source material for what immediately follows, can be found in Desmond Norton, 'On the Sherlocks of Sherlockstown, Jane Coleman and County Kildare in the 1840s', *Journal of the County Kildare Archaeological Society*, xix: 11 (2002–3), pp. 289–99, and in the references cited there.

6   Francis Walker to Stewart & Kincaid, 28 Dec. 1842, Stewart & Kincaid Papers in possession of the author. Subsequent references to the archive in this chapter will be given either in the text or in notes as (sk).

7   Dr Walsh to Stewart & Kincaid, 7 and 21 Jan. 1842 (sk); Pierce Doyle to Stewart & Kincaid, 25 Mar. 1842 (sk).

8   Messrs Anderson and Adams to Stewart & Kincaid, 24 Nov. 1841 (sk).

9   Kinahan, Sons & Smyth, wine merchants in Dublin.

10   B. Murta to Stewart & Kincaid, 29 May 1843 (sk).

11   I thank Heinz Eggert, manager of the farm at Sherlockstown, for allowing me to inspect those lands.

12   Messrs Terry, Seymour & Webb, solicitors in Dublin to Stewart & Kincaid, 3 May 1845.

13   C. Sherlock (William R. Sherlock's sister) to Kincaid, n. d., June 1843 (sk).

14   For details on the Mc Leod case see Richard Morris, *Encyclopaedia of American History* (New York, 1976), p. 216.

15   Enclosure dated 13 Mar. 1841 in J. Lawrie at the War Office to Matilda Sherlock, 20 July 1841 (sk).

16   H. Keenan to Stewart & Kincaid, 27 Nov. 1846 (sk).

17   Pettigrew and Oulton, *The Dublin Almanac . . . 1845*, p. 722, and that for 1846, p. 735.

18 Some of the details in this paragraph have been drawn from Edward Walford, *The County Families of the United Kingdom* (London, 1893), p. 920.

19 *Return of Owners of Land . . . in Ireland* (Dublin, 1876), p. 33.

20 *Wilson's Dublin Directory . . . 1816*, p. 35.

21 Dan O'Leary of Sherlockstown, 'Sherlockstown' typescript, n. d. I thank Mr O'Leary for giving me a copy of this document. I also thank him for giving me a copy of his typescript entitled 'The Sherlocks of Kildare', n. d., which, by clarifying family relationships among the Sherlocks, saved me from error.

22 The Sherlockstown estate was in the Barony of North Naas. The impact of the famine in that district may have been less severe than elsewhere in Kildare. See *Lest We Forget Kildare and the Great Famine*, Kildare County Council, n. d. (1996), p. 11.

23 Edward Walford, *The County Families of the United Kingdom* (London, 1860), p. 38.

24 Pettigrew and Oulton, *Dublin Almanac 1846*, p. 270. A modern house is today on the site of the Batty residence.

25 *Counties of Meath and Westmeath, Valuation, Union of Castletowndelvin* (Dublin, 1854), pp. 2–11.

26 Stewart & Kincaid paid a jointure to Louisa Batty (Fitzherbert's mother) who resided at Portarlington, Queen's County. Kincaid's son William was at boarding school there. In 1846 Louisa Batty wrote to Kincaid: 'Your son William often dines with me' (s k).

27 Walford, *Families* (1860), p. 38. No person named Kincaid or Kincaide is listed in Dublin directories of the first two decades of the nineteenth century. It seems that Joseph Kincaid of Stewart & Kincaid came from County Armagh. No person named 'Kincaid' was listed by Leet in 1814. However, a 'John Kincaide' was listed at Newtownhamilton, County Armagh: see Ambrose Leet, *Directory to . . . Noted Places in Ireland*, 2nd edn (Dublin, 1814), p. 383. No other 'Kincaide' was listed by Leet. It seems that 'John Kincaide', MD, was the same person as John Kincaid, who was presumably Joseph's father.

28 Walford, *Families* (1860), p. 38.

29 Edward Walford, *The County Families of the United Kingdom* (London, 1893), p. 62.

30 Mary McNally to Stewart & Kincaid, n. d., 1848 (s k).

31 Pettigrew and Oulton, *Dublin Almanac 1848*, p. 574, lists a Mrs Ruxton at Merrion Square in Dublin City.

32 A letter from Fitzherbert Batty to Stewart & Kincaid, 5 August 1844 (s k), lists rent receipts from various tenants, including 'widow Caffrey'.

33 *Owners of Land in Ireland* (Dublin, 1876), p. 82.

34 Pettigrew and Oulton, *Dublin Almanac 1846*, p. 204.

35 Seamus MacPhilib, 'Ius primae noctis and the sexual image of Irish landlords in folk tradition and in contemporary accounts', *Béaloideas* 56 (1988), pp. 97–140. I thank Cormac Ó Gráda for indicating this reference to me.

36 MacPhilib, 'Ius primae noctis', p. 100.

37 Ibid., pp. 116, 120.

38 Ibid., p. 135.

39 An account of the alleged sexual behaviour of the third Earl of Leitrim (William Clemence) has been provided by James Keegan, a Catholic priest from Co Leitrim who emigrated to the USA. *Redpath's Weekly* was published in New York, and Keegan wrote for it under the name 'Pastheen Fionn'. In the issue dated 8 December 1883 he wrote as follows: 'One of the motives for the eviction of the Catholics [by Clemence] was in order for the people of other religions, or of

no religion, who had fair wives and daughters and were not chary of their virtue, to be in convenient distance of the [Clemence] castle. I have never been able to make out a single case of a Catholic girl being ruined by Lord Leitrim in the county of Leitrim. To their credit be it spoken, there were Protestants – notably one man – who gave up his house and farm sooner than sacrifice his daughter to the hoary reprobate. . . . It is not universally true . . . that his Lordship's "servant girls" were all sent off to England and America and elsewhere. No; his lordship made exceptions; he married some of them to his Orange tenants, and when the happy men afterwards resented further familiarities and refused to live with such vile women, his lordship evicted them'. It therefore seems that in Keegan's opinion Clemence specialised in having sex with Protestant females. We have no means of verifying Keegan's account. I thank my former colleague James Heslin for giving me a copy of the Keegan article cited above.

40 MacPhilib, 'Ius primae noctis', pp. 126–8.

FIFTEEN: CONCLUSIONS

1   The following are among the relatively recent works on the famine: Joel Mokyr, *Why Ireland Starved* (London, 1985); Mary Daly, *The Famine in Ireland* (Dundalk, 1986); Cormac Ó Gráda, *The Great Irish Famine* (Basingstoke and London, 1989); Christine Kinealy, *This Great Calamity* (Dublin, 1994); Cathal Póirtéir (ed.), *The Great Irish Famine* (Cork and Dublin, 1995); Peter Gray, *Famine, Land and Politics* (Dublin and Portland 1999); Cormac Ó Gráda, *Black '47 and Beyond* (Princeton, 1999).

2   Patrick Lynch and John Vaizey, *Guinness's Brewery in the Irish Economy 1759–1876* (Cambridge, 1960).

3   Lynch and Vaizey, *Guinness's Brewery*, p. 10.

4   E. D. Steele, *Irish Land and British Politics* (Cambridge, 1974), p. 6.

5   Lynch and Vaizey, *Guinness's Brewery*, pp. 12, 13, 25–27.

6   Pettigrew and Oulton, *The Dublin Almanac . . . 1845*, pp. 49–61.

7   It was not always the case that labour on public works was paid punctually. See John O'Rourke, *The History of the Great Irish Famine of 1847*, 3rd edn (Dublin, 1902), ch. 9.

8   Lynch and Vaizey, *Guinness's Brewery*, p. 165.

9   Cecil Woodham-Smith, *The Great Hunger* (London, 1962), pp. 202, 293. Another researcher reports that the potato blight 'did not affect Tory [Island]', see T. G. Wilson, *The Irish Lighthouse Service* (Dublin, 1968), p. 75

10   Ó Gráda, *Black '47* (Princeton, 1999), ch. 5, especially pp. 166, 169 and 172.

11   Ibid., p. 169.

12   The following were found useful: Leonard Mac Nally, *The Justice of the Peace for Ireland*, 4 vols (3rd edn, Dublin, 1820); Hamilton Smythe, *The Law of Landlord and Tenant in Ireland* (Dublin, 1842); John Furlong, *The Law of Landlord and Tenant as Administered in Ireland*, 2 vols (Dublin, 1845). A useful modern explanation of the law pertaining to ejectment in the 1840s can be found in Tim P. O'Neill, 'Famine evictions', in Carla King (ed.), *Famine, Land and Culture in Ireland* (Dublin, 2000), pp. 29–70.

13   O'Neill, 'Famine evictions'.

14   *House of Commons Parliamentary Papers, 1849*, tables providing 'Returns from the Courts . . . in Ireland, of the Number of Ejectments brought in those Courts' in 1846, 1847 and 1848, vol. XLIX,

pp. 236–41; *House of Commons Parliamentary Papers, 1881*, 'Return . . . of Cases of Evictions [in Ireland] which have come to the Knowledge of the Constabulary in each of the years from 1849 to 1880 inclusive', vol. LXXVII, p. 727.

15   According to O'Neill in 'Famine evictions', p. 29, in 1843 '250 families were evicted by Lord Lorton'.

16   *Evidence taken before Her Majesty's Commissioners of Inquiry into the State of the Law and Practice in respect to the Occupation of Land in Ireland*, pt I (Dublin 1845), p. 33.

17   O'Neill, 'Famine evictions', pp. 30, 31. The works to which he refers there are as follows: W. E. Vaughan, *Landlords and Tenants in mid-Victorian Ireland* (Oxford, 1994), p. 28; J. S. Donnelly, 'Mass eviction and the great famine' in Póirtéir (ed.), *Famine*, pp. 155–73; Daly, *Famine*, pp. 109–11; Kinealy, *Calamity*, 218.

18   *House of Commons Parliamentary Papers, 1849*, tables providing 'Returns from the Courts . . . in Ireland , vol. XLIX, pp. 236–41.

19   *House of Commons Parliamentary Papers, 1881*, 'Return . . . of Cases of Evictions, vol. LXXVII, p. 727.

20   O'Neill, 'Famine evictions', p. 31.

21   John Lynch to Joseph Kincaid,, 18 Dec. 1846, Stewart & Kincaid Papers in possession of the author.

22   In regard to nineteenth-century Irish emigrants to New York City see Luc Sante, *Low Life* (New York, 1992); also Ó Gráda, *Black '47*, pp. 114–21, and more recently, Gerard J. Lyne, *The Lansdowne Estate under the Agency of William Steuart Trench 1849–72* (Dublin, 2001), ch. 4.

23   Oliver MacDonagh, 'Irish emigration to the United States of America and the British colonies during the famine', ch. 6 in R. Dudley Edwards and T. Desmond Williams (eds), *The Great Famine* (New York, 1957), p. 474, note 17.

24   MacDonagh, in Edward and Williams, *Famine*, pp. 335, 475.

25   Kinealy, *Calamity*, p. 304.

26   Ó Gráda, *Black '47*, p. 115. In reference to the famine era, another researcher has more recently written that 'only about 6 to 8 per cent of emigrants in this period left Ireland . . . as the result of assistance from governments, religious and charitable organizations, or landlords': see Tyler Anbinder, 'Lord Palmerston and the Irish famine emigration', *Historical Journal* 44: 2 (2001), pp. 441–69.

27   David Fitzpatrick 'Emigration, 1801–70', ch. 27 in W. E. Vaughan (ed.), *A New History of Ireland*, vol. v (Oxford, 1989), p. 592. Neither Fitzpatrick, nor any of the earlier researchers cited, mention the landlord-assisted emigration from the huge Shirley estate in Monaghan during the famine years: see Patrick J. Duffy, 'Assisted emigration from the Shirley Estate 1843–54', *Clogher Record* XIV: 2 (1992), pp. 7–62.

28   See Fitzpatrick in Vaughan, ed., *Landlords*, pp. 593, 615 and 622, and the same author's *Irish Emigration, 1801–1921* (Dundalk, 1984), p. 20.

29   It might be argued that former landlords would have been better off because they would have been freed from the necessity of paying local property taxes. However, this liability would have been transferred to the buyers, and would have been reflected in lower prices which potential buyers were willing to pay.

30   The reasoning here can be clarified by referring to almost any basic economics textbook: see, for example, Desmond Norton, *Economics for an Open Economy: Ireland* (Dublin, 1994), pp. 58–64. Applying the reasoning to unregulated markets (as is done in many of such textbooks), the

problem can be seen as follows: in the developed world, the demand for food is price-inelastic: for example, a 10 per cent reduction in the price of food does not cause the quantity of food demanded to rise by as much as 10 per cent; total sales receipts equal price times quantity sold; thus, an increase in the supply of food due to better harvests, which causes any given proportionate reduction in the price of food, generates a smaller proportionate increase in the quantity of food sold; it therefore causes a reduction in total sales receipts; hence, in the absence of government intervention, if farmers as a group have better harvests, they end up worse off; of course, if one farmer has a better harvest whilst others do not (which implies effectively no reduction in price) then that farmer is better off. This kind of reasoning is applicable to the market for land in Ireland at the time of the famine. If one landlord had sold land whilst others did not, then that landlord would have been better able to assist the tenantry. But if many actual and potential sellers of land had increased the amount of land for sale, then total receipts from sale would have fallen, and as a group the financial position of the sellers would have deteriorated; therefore they would have been in a weaker position to take care not only of themselves, but also of others, such as their tenantry.

31 This observation applies not only to estates managed by Stewart & Kincaid, but to very many of those in Ireland generally. See Andrés Eiríksson and Cormac Ó Gráda, 'Irish landlords and the Great Irish Famine' (Working Paper 13, Department of Economics, UCD, June 1996).

32 This is probably because no correspondence archive on estates in Ireland, as broad in its coverage as that of Stewart & Kincaid for the 1840s, exists among official repositories for the same period. See Andrés Eiríksson and Cormac Ó Gráda, *Estate Records of the Irish Famine: A Second Guide to Famine Archives, 1840–1855* (Irish Famine Network, Dublin, 1995).

33 W. A. Maguire, *The Downshire Estates in Ireland 1801–1845* (Oxford, 1972).

34 Ibid., p. v.

35 Ibid., p. 183.

36 R. B. MacCarthy, *The Trinity College Estates 1800–1923* (Dundalk, 1992).

37 Ibid., p. 89.

38 Ibid., p. 22.

39 Quoted by Lyne, *Lansdowne Estates*, p. 39.

40 Ibid., p. 75.

Select Bibliography

PRIMARY SOURCES

MANUSCRIPTS

HARTLEY LIBRARY, UNIVERSITY OF SOUTHAMPTON
Broadlands (Palmerston) Papers
    Correspondence with Stewart & Kincaid land agents and related documents.

TULLYNALLY CASTLE, CASTLEPOLLARD, COUNTY WESTMEATH
Pakenham Archive:
    Correspondence with Stewart & Kincaid land agents and related documents.

IN POSSESSION OF THE AUTHOR
Stewart & Kincaid Papers:
    Stewart & Kincaid land agents' correspondence with landlords, tenants and others.
    Stewart & Kincaid's account book, *Receiving Rental of The Marquis of Westmeath Estate in the County of Roscommon for the half year ending May 1848*, n.d.
    George Green, 'Account . . . May Rents 1751 of Robertstown', 24 Feb. 1752; 'George Evans's Account . . . Gale due out of Lord Powerscourts Estate in . . . Clare the 1st day of May 1761', and the same, 'the first day of November 1761'.
    James O'Donnell, 'Rental of Lord Powerscourts Estate in the County of Clare for half year Ending the first of Novr. 1787'.

SLIGO COUNTY LIBRARY
Account book, *Rental of the Estates of the Right Hon. Visc. Palmerston in the County of Sligo for one years Rent/Arrears to May 1860*, document no. 558.

DIRECTORIES AND CONTEMPORARY PUBLICATIONS

Burke, Bernard, *A Genealogical and Heraldic Dictionary of the Peerage and Baronetage* (London, 1892).
Burke, Bernard, *Peerage and Baronetage of the British Empire* (London, 1864).
Clapperton, John, *Instructions for the Small Farmers of Ireland, on Croping and Culture of their Farms* (Dublin, 1847).
Farmer's Guide, The, 2nd edn (Dublin, 1842).
Fraser, James, *Hand Book for Travellers in Ireland*, 4th edn (Dublin, 1854), p. 449.
Furlong, John, *The Law of Landlord and Tenant as Administered in Ireland*, 2 vols (Dublin, 1845).

Gayer, Charles, *Persecution of Protestants* (Dublin, 1845).

General Alphabetical Index to the Townlands and Towns, Parishes and Baronies of Ireland (Dublin, 1861).

Leet, Ambrose, *Directory to the Noted Places in Ireland*, 2nd edn (Dublin, 1814).

Lewis, Samuel, *A Topographical Dictionary of Ireland*, vol. 2 (London, 1837).

Mac Nally, Leonard, *The Justice of the Peace for Ireland*, 4 vols (3rd edn, Dublin, 1820).

Nicholls, George, *A History of the Irish Poor Law* (London, 1856).

Parliamentary Gazetteer of Ireland, vols A, C, D–G, K–M, VII (Dublin, London and Edinburgh, 1845).

Pettigrew and Oulton, *The Dublin Almanac . . . 1845*, published annually in Dublin in the 1830s and 1840s.

Pigot, J. & Co., *City of Dublin and Hibernian Provincial Directory and Directory of London* (London and Manchester, 1824).

The Post Office Annual Directory for 1845 (Dublin, 1844 or 1845).

The Post Office Directory for 1847 (Dublin, 1846 or 1847),

Return of Owners of Land in Ireland (Dublin, 1876).

Slater, I., *National Commercial Directory of Ireland . . . to which are added Classified Directories of Important English Towns* (Manchester and London, 1846).

Smythe, Hamilton, *The Law of Landlord and Tenant in Ireland* (Dublin, 1842).

Stewart, James Watson, *Gentleman's and Citizen's Almanack*, published annually in Dublin.

Thom's Irish Almanac and Official Directory, published annually in Dublin, 1844 onwards.

Thompson, D. P., *Brief Account of . . . Change in Religious Opinion . . . in Dingle* (London, 1846).

Transactions of the Central Relief Committee of the Society of Friends during the Famine in Ireland (Dublin, 1852).

Walford, Edward, *The County Families of the United Kingdom* (London, 1860).

Walford, Edward, *The County Families of the United Kingdom* (London, 1893).

Weld, Isaac, *Statistical Survey of the County of Roscommon* (Dublin, 1832).

Wilson's Dublin Directory . . . 1788.

Wilson's Dublin Directory . . . 1816.

GOVERNMENT AND OFFICIAL PUBLICATIONS

Census of Ireland 1851, part I, vol. IV (Dublin 1852).

Evidence taken before Her Majesty's Commissioners of Inquiry into the State of the Law and Practice in respect to the Occupation of Land in Ireland, pt I (Dublin, 1845).

House of Commons Parliamentary Papers, 1849, tables providing 'Returns from the Courts . . . in Ireland, of the Number of Ejectments brought in those Courts' in 1846, 1847 and 1848, vol. XLIX, pp. 236–41.

House of Commons Parliamentary Papers, 1881, 'Return . . . of Cases of Evictions [in Ireland] which have come to the Knowledge of the Constabulary in each of the years from 1849 to 1880 inclusive', vol. LXXVII, p. 727.

Poor Inquiry (Ireland), Reports from Commissioners (London, 1836), appendix E.

Report of the Case of Little and Clark against Wingfield and Others . . . 1857 (Dublin, 1857).

'Report from the Select Committee of the House of Lords on Colonization from Ireland; together with Minutes of Evidence; Session 1847', *British Parliamentary Papers, Emigration 4* (Shannon, 1968).

Reports and Returns Relating to Evictions in the Kilrush Union, Parliamentary Paper (London, 1849).

Sixth Report of the Commissioners of the Irish Fisheries; for the Season of 1824, in *House of Commons Parliamentary Papers 1825*, vol. 15; *First Report of the Commissioners of Inquiry into the State of the Irish Fisheries, with Minutes of Evidence* (Dublin, 1836).

LAND VALUATIONS

County of Carlow, Primary Valuation (Dublin, 1852).

County of Dublin, Barony of Coolock, North Dublin and Balrothery Union (Dublin, 1848).

County of Kildare, Valuation . . . Union of Naas (Dublin, 1853).

County of Kilkenny, Barony of Fassadinin, Unions of Castlecomer, Kilkenny and Urlingford, Valuation (Dublin, 1850), pp. 80–2.

County of Kilkenny, Barony of Gowran, Unions of Kilkenny and New Ross (Dublin, 1850).

County of Limerick, Barony of Connello Upper . . . Primary Valuation (Dublin, 1852).

County of Limerick, Barony of Coshma . . . Primary Valuation (Dublin, 1851).

County of Limerick, Barony of Shanid comprising a portion of The Unions of Glin, Newcastle & Rathkeale, Primary Valuation (Dublin, 1852).

Counties of Longford and Westmeath, Valuation . . . Union of Ballymahon (Dublin, 1854),

Counties of Mayo and Sligo, Valuation . . . Union of Ballina (Dublin, 1856).

Counties of Meath and Westmeath, Valuation, Union of Castletowndelvin (Dublin, 1854).

County of Sligo, Valuation . . . Union of Boyle (Dublin, 1858).

County of Sligo, Valuation . . . Union of Dromore West (Dublin, 1857).

County of Sligo, Valuation . . . Union of Tobercurry (Dublin, 1857).

King's County and County Westmeath . . . Valuation . . . Union of Tullamore (Dublin, 1854)

Union of Carrick-on-Shannon, Valuation . . . County of Roscommon (Dublin, 1858).

Union of Ennistimon, Valuation (Dublin, 1855).

Union of Kells, Valuation . . . Counties of Meath and Cavan (Dublin, 1854).

Unions of Kilkenny and Callan, Valuation (Dublin, 1849).

Union of Longford, Valuation . . ., County of Longford (Dublin, 1854).

Valuation . . . Barony of Balrothery East . . . County of Dublin (Dublin, 1852).

Valuation of the Several Tenements in the Union of Sligo (Dublin, 1858).

Valuation . . . Union of Athlone . . . County of Roscommon (Dublin, 1858).

Valuation . . . Union of Castlerea . . . Counties of Roscommon and Mayo (Dublin, 1857).

Valuation . . . Union of Roscommon in the Counties of Roscommon and Galway (Dublin, 1857).

Valuation . . . Union of Strokestown . . . County of Roscommon (Dublin, 1857).

SECONDARY SOURCES

BOOKS AND ARTICLES

Anbinder, Tyler, 'Lord Palmerston and the Irish famine emigration', *Historical Journal* 44: 2 (2001), pp. 441–69.

Bell, Herbert, *Lord Palmerston*, vol. 1 (London, 1966).

Bourne, Kenneth, *Palmerston, The Early Years 1784–1841* (London, 1982).

Bowen, Desmond, *Superism: Myth or Reality* (Cork, 1970).

Breen, Gráinne, 'Landlordism in King's County in the mid-nineteenth century', in William Nolan and Timothy P. O'Neill (eds), *Offaly: History & Society* (Dublin, 1998), pp. 627–80.

Browne, Raymond (ed.), *Cill Bhride: A History of Kilbride Parish, County Roscommon* (forthcoming).

Brunicardi, Niall, *John Anderson, Entrepreneur* (Fermoy, 1987).

Butler, Beatrice, 'John and Edward Lees, Secretaries of the Irish Post Office, 1774–1831', *Dublin Historical Record* III (1952–4), pp. 138–50.

Collins, Charles, *The Law and Practice of Banking in Ireland* (Dublin, 1880).

Coyle, Liam, *A Parish History of Kilglass, Rusky and Slatta* (Boyle, 1994).

Culhane, Thomas J., *The Barony of Shanid* (n. p., 2003).

Cullen, L. M., 'Landlords, bankers and merchants: the early Irish banking world, 1700–1820', in Antoin Murphy (ed.), *Economists and the Irish Economy from the Eighteenth Century to the Present Day* (Dublin, 1984), pp. 25–44.

Daly, Mary E., *The Famine in Ireland* (Dundalk, 1986).

Dillon, Malcolm, *The History and Development of Banking in Ireland* (Dublin, 1889).

Dixon, F. E., *Irish Postal Rates before 1840* (Munich, 1986).

Donnelly, James S. Jr, *The Land and the People of Nineteenth-Century Cork* (London and Boston, 1975).

Dudley Edwards, R. and T. Desmond Williams (eds), *The Great Famine* (New York, 1957).

Duffy, P. J., 'Management problems on a large estate in mid-nineteenth century Ireland: William Steuart Trench's Report on the Shirley Estate in 1843', *Clogher Record* XVI: 1 (1997), pp. 101–22.

Duffy, Patrick J., 'Assisted emigration from the Shirley Estate 1843–54', *Clogher Record* XIV: 2 (1992), pp. 7–62.

Eiríksson, Andrés and Cormac Ó Gráda, *Estate Records of the Irish Famine: A Second Guide to Famine Archives, 1840–1855* (Dublin, 1995).

Eiríksson, Andrés and Cormac Ó Gráda, 'Irish landlords and the Great Irish Famine' (Working Paper 13, Department of Economics, UCD, June 1996).

Eve, A. S. and C. H. Creasey, *Life and Work of John Tyndall* (London, 1945).

Feldman, David and William Kane, *Handbook of Irish Postal History to 1840* (Dublin, 1975).

Fitzpatrick, David, 'Emigration, 1801–70', ch. 27 in W. E. Vaughan (ed.), *A New History of Ireland*, vol. v (Oxford, 1989), pp. 562–622.

Fitzpatrick, David, *Irish Emigration, 1801–1921* (Dundalk, 1984).

Gacquin, William, 'Mrs Julia Conmee (*c.*1786–1860), Benefactress of C. B. S. Roscommon', *Rosc Chomáin* (Roscommon, 1997), pp. 9–11.

Gacquin, William, *Roscommon before the Famine: The Parishes of Kiltoom and Cam, 1749–1845* (Dublin, 1996).

Gilbert, J. T. *History of the City of Dublin*, vol. 11 (Dublin, 1859).

Goodbody, Rob, 'Obelisk Park', *Blackrock Society*, vol. 7 (1999), pp. 24–33.

Goodbody, Rob, *A Suitable Channel, Quaker Relief in the Great Famine* (Bray, County Wicklow, 1995).

Gouch, G. P. (ed.), *The Later Correspondence of Lord John Russell 1840–1878*, vol. 1 (London, 1925).

Gray, Peter, *Famine, Land and Politics* (Dublin and Portland 1999).

Haden, Christopher and Catherine O'Malley, *The Demesne of Old Rathmines* (Dublin, 1998).

Hickey, D. J. and J. E. Doherty, *A Dictionary of Irish History 1800–1980* (Dublin, 1987)

Hough, Richard, *Edwina Countess Mountbatten of Burma* (London, 1985).

James, Dermot, *John Hamilton of Donegal, 1800–1884* (Dublin, 1998).

Johnson, J. Stafford, 'The Dublin Penny Post, 1773–1840', *Dublin Historical Record* iv: 3 (Mar.–May 1942), pp. 81–95.

Kelly, Patricia, 'Sisters of Mercy in Sligo during the Great Famine', in Raymond Browne (ed.), *The Destitution Survey, Reflections on the Famine in the Diocese of Elphin* (Boyle, 1997), pp. 86–95.

Kerr, Donal, *'A Nation of Beggars'? Priests, People and Politics in Famine Ireland, 1846–1852* (Oxford, 1994).

Kerr, Donal, *The Catholic Church and the Famine* (Blackrock, County Dublin, 1996).

Kildare County Council, *Lest we Forget Kildare and the Great Famine* (Naas, 1996)

Kinealy, Christine, *This Great Calamity* (Dublin, 1994).

Lynch, Patrick and John Vaizey, *Guinness's Brewery in the Irish Economy 1759–1876* (Cambridge, 1960).

Lyne, Gerard J., *The Lansdowne Estate in Kerry under the Agency of W. S. Trench 1847–72* (Dublin, 2001),

Lyng, Tom, *Castlecomer Connections* (Castlecomer, 1984).

MacCarthy, R. B., *The Trinity College Estates 1800–1923* (Dundalk, 1992).

MacDonagh, Oliver, 'Irish emigration to the United States of America and the British Colonies during the Famine', in R. Dudley Edwards and T. Desmond Williams (eds), *The Great Famine* (New York, 1957), pp. 319–88.

MacPhilib, Seamus, 'Ius primae noctis and the sexual image of Irish landlords in folk tradition and in contemporary accounts', *Béaloideas* 56 (1988), pp. 97–140.

Maguire, W. A., *The Downshire Estates in Ireland 1801–1845* (Oxford, 1972).

McGowan, Joe, *In the Shadow of Benbulben* (n. p., 1993).

McMillan, Norman and Martin Nevin, 'Tyndall of Leighlin: Carlow's genius', *Carloviana*, no. 27 (1978–9), pp. 22–7.

McMillan, Norman and Martin Nevin, 'Tyndall of Leighlin', in H. W. Brock, N. D. McMillan and R. C. Mollan (eds), *John Tyndall: Essays on a Natural Philosopher* (Dublin, 1981), pp. 15–48.

McTernan, John C., *Here's to Their Memory* (Dublin and Cork, 1977).

McTernan, John, *Memory Harbour, The Port of Sligo* (Sligo, 1992), pt 2.

McTernan, John C., *Sligo Long Ago* (Sligo, 1998).

Mokyr, Joel, *Why Ireland Starved* (London, 1985).

Morris, Richard, *Encyclopaedia of American History* (New York, 1976).

Murphy, Ignatius, *A People Starved: Life and Death in West Clare, 1845–1851* (Blackrock, County Dublin, 1996).

Murphy, William, *Prodigal Father: The Life of John Butler Yeats (1839–1922)* (Ithaca, 1978).

Nolan, William, *Fassadinin: Land, Settlement and Society in Southeast Ireland 1600–1850* (Dublin, 1979).

Nolan, William and Timothy P. O'Neill (eds), *Offaly: History & Society* (Dublin, 1998).

Norton, Desmond, *Economics for an Open Economy: Ireland* (Dublin, 1994).

Norton, Desmond, 'Viscount Frankfort, Sir Charles Burton and County Carlow in the 1840s: Part II', *Carloviana*, no. 47 (Dec. 1999), pp. 2–6 and 15.

Norton, Desmond, 'On the Sherlocks of Sherlockstown, Jane Coleman and County Kildare in the 1840s', *Journal of the County Kildare Archaeological Society*, XIX: 11 (2002–3), pp. 289–99.

Norton, Desmond, 'Lord Palmerston and the Irish famine emigration: a rejoinder', *Historical Journal* 46: 1 (2003), pp. 155–65.

Norton, Desmond, 'Where was Major Denis Mahon shot?', *County Roscommon Historical and Archaeological Society Journal* 9 (2003), pp. 54–8.

Norton, Desmond, 'On Lord Palmerston's Irish estates in the 1840s', *English Historical Review* CXIX: 484 (Nov. 2004), pp. 1254–74.

Norton, Desmond, 'On landlord-assisted emigration from some Irish estates in the 1840s', *Agricultural History Review* 53: 1 (2005), pp. 24–40.

Norton, Desmond, 'Irish postal history circa 1660 to circa 1860', *Genealogical Society of Ireland Journal* 6: 1 (Spring 2005), pp. 20–38.

Ó Gráda, Cormac, 'The investment behaviour of Irish landlords 1850–75: some preliminary findings', *Agricultural History Review* 23 (1975), pp. 139–55.

Ó Gráda, Cormac, *The Great Irish Famine* (Basingstoke and London, 1989).

Ó Gráda, Cormac, *Black '47 and Beyond* (Princeton, 1999).

Ó Murchadha, Ciarán, 'The onset of famine: County Clare, 1845–1846', *The Other Clare* 19 (1995), pp. 46–52.

Ó Murchadha, Ciarán, 'Sable wings over the land: County Clare 1846–1847', *The Other Clare* 20 (1996), pp. 25–32.

Ó Murchadha, Ciarán, *Sable Wings over the Land: Ennis, County Clare and its Wider Community during the Great Famine* (Ennis, 1998).

O'Cianain, S. F., *The Davys Family Records* (Longford, 1931).

O'Neill, Tim P., 'Famine evictions', in Carla King (ed.), *Famine, Land and Culture in Ireland* (Dublin, 2000), pp. 29–70.

O'Rorke, T., *History of Sligo* (Dublin, n. d.), vol. I & II.

O'Rourke, John, *The History of the Great Irish Famine of 1847*, 3rd edn (Dublin, 1902).

O'Toole, Jimmy, *The Carlow Gentry* (Carlow, 1993).

Pine, L. G. (ed.), *Burke's Landed Gentry of Ireland*, 4th edn (London, 1958).

Póirtéir, Cathal (ed.), *The Great Irish Famine* (Cork and Dublin, 1995).

Pomfret, John E., *The Struggle for Land in Ireland 1800–1923* (Princeton, 1930).

Proudfoot, Lindsay J., *Urban Patronage and Social Authority* (Washington, DC, 1995).

Sante, Luc, *Low Life* (New York, 1992).

Scally, Robert, *The End of Hidden Ireland* (Oxford, 1995).
Seoighe, Mainchín, *The Story of Kilmallock* (Kilmallock, 1987).
Steele, E. D., *Irish Land and British Politics* (Cambridge, 1974).
Stone, Lawrence, *Broken Lives* (Oxford, 1993).
Swords, Liam, *In Their Own Words, The Famine in North Connacht, 1845–49* (Blackrock, County Dublin, 1999).
Vaughan, W. E., *Landlords and Tenants in Mid-Victorian Ireland* (Oxford, 1994).
Walker, B. M. (ed.), *Parliamentary Election Results for Ireland, 1801–1922* (Dublin, 1978).
Weir, Hugh, *Historical Genealogical Architectural Notes on Some Houses in Clare* (Whitegate, County Clare, 1986).
Winter, Gordon, *Secrets of the Royals* (New York, 1989, and London, 1990).
Wilson, T. G., *The Irish Lighthouse Service* (Dublin, 1968)
Woodham-Smith, Cecil, *The Great Hunger* (London, 1962).

UNPUBLISHED PAPER

Norton, Desmond, 'On the Sligo estates of three proprietors in the 1840s', presented to Group for the Study of Irish Historical Settlement, Annual Conference, Sligo, 6–8 May 2005.

Index